ENCYCLOPEDIA OF
EDUCATIONAL
Reform AND *Dissent*

Editorial Board

ENCYCLOPEDIA OF
EDUCATIONAL
Reform AND *Dissent*

EDITORS

Thomas C. Hunt
University of Dayton

James C. Carper
University of South Carolina

Thomas J. Lasley
University of Dayton

C. Daniel Raisch
University of Dayton

volume

Los Angeles | London | New Delhi
Singapore | Washington DC

For information:

SAGE Publications, Inc.
2455 Teller Road
Thousand Oaks, California 91320
E-mail: order@sagepub.com

SAGE Publications Ltd.
1 Oliver's Yard
55 City Road
London EC1Y 1SP
United Kingdom

SAGE Publications India Pvt. Ltd.
B 1/I 1 Mohan Cooperative Industrial Area
Mathura Road, New Delhi 110 044
India

SAGE Publications Asia-Pacific Pte. Ltd.
33 Pekin Street #02-01
Far East Square
Singapore 048763

Printed in the United States of America

Library of Congress Cataloging-in-Publication Data

Encyclopedia of educational reform and dissent / Thomas C. Hunt ... [et al.], editors.
   p. cm.
Includes bibliographical references and index.
ISBN 978-1-4129-5664-2 (cloth)

   1. Educational change—United States—Encyclopedias. 2. Critical pedagogy—United States—Encyclopedias.
I. Hunt, Thomas C., 1930–

LB2805.E528 2010
371.200973—dc22   2009026080

This book is printed on acid-free paper.

10 11 12 13 14 10 9 8 7 6 5 4 3 2 1

Publisher:	Rolf A. Janke
Acquisitions Editor:	Jim Brace-Thompson
Editorial Assistant:	Michele Thompson
Reference Systems Manager:	Leticia M. Gutierrez
Reference Systems Coordinator:	Laura Notton
Production Editor:	Kate Schroeder
Copy Editors:	Kristin Bergstad, Colleen B. Brennan
Typesetter:	C&M Digitals (P) Ltd.
Proofreader:	Penelope Sippel
Indexer:	Julie Grayson
Cover Designer:	Bryan Fishman
Marketing Manager:	Amberlyn Erzinger

Contents

List of Entries

KINDERGARTEN

Kindergarten (from the German: *kinder,* children; *garten,* garden) refers to an educational experience that takes place the year prior to first grade. Designed to ease the transition between the home and more formal schooling, kindergarten was originally developed as a play-based program that supported social, emotional, language, cognitive, and physical development. While not compulsory in all states, the vast majority of American children are required to attend kindergarten. Kindergarten was invented amid controversy in Germany in 1837 by Friedrich Froebel, who believed that children should be able to grow as freely as flowers in a garden. His philosophy of education recognized, for the first time, that young children learn and view the world differently from older children and adults. Froebel's views, considered radical at the time, are the basis of early childhood practice today. Kindergarten continues to be true to its controversial roots, with strong and often opposing views about the purpose of kindergarten, the definition of readiness, and the value of half-day versus full-day programs. This entry provides a historical context and addresses the issues that drive the discourse surrounding kindergarten today.

Historical Perspectives

Froebel's "child's garden" was intended for children between the ages of 3 and 7 and focused on development through play, music, movement, interaction with the outdoors, and opportunities to engage in independent and creative activities. Froebel felt that the best setting for children was a place where they could explore their own interests, and believed that children learned through active exploration with materials and interaction with others. These views of children and learning were considered radical at the time.

Froebel's kindergarten was brought to the United States in 1857 by Margarethe Schurz, who opened the first Froebelian program, in Wisconsin, and by Elizabeth Palmer Peabody, who opened a kindergarten in Boston in 1861. Between 1890 and 1910, America's interest in kindergarten grew and continued to be based on the belief that early formal academic instruction was detrimental to the development of young children. Over the next several decades new kindergartens were established in urban areas impacted by poverty. Most kindergartens were privately funded until the 1920s, when they began to be more commonly included in public schools.

Froebel's philosophy continued to drive kindergarten practice until the 1970s, when the educational value of early childhood programs began to be recognized. In reaction to the Soviet Union's successful 1957 launch of *Sputnik*, the first artificial satellite, American education policymakers became more aware of the emerging research on cognitive growth in infants and young children and began to focus on intervention programs such as Head Start. With more mothers working outside of the home, the attention to quality in early childhood programming was growing in importance. All of these factors contributed to a greater focus on the academic dimensions of child development. As a result, kindergarten experienced a shift from a play-based curriculum to one that focused on the formal teaching of discrete skills, which was strongly reinforced during the assessment movement of the 1990s. As a result, kindergarten classrooms became more like first-grade classrooms.

The Role of Kindergarten in Education Reform

The Purpose of Kindergarten

The purpose of kindergarten continues to be the subject of debate among early childhood educators, policymakers, and the public. Many advocate, often passionately, for a traditional model of kindergarten where young children learn through play, with an emphasis on educating the "whole" child. Others believe in a kindergarten where formal structured lessons with academic content take place. This philosophical tug-of-war often forces educators to find a balance between their concern for the child's overall development and the push for the child to acquire reading and math skills at an earlier age. They often find themselves at odds with the Code of Ethical Conduct of the National Association for the Education of Young Children, which states that educators should appreciate childhood as a unique and valuable period in the human life cycle. Those who advocate for the developmentally appropriate kindergarten are often criticized for underestimating young children and their ability to learn a wide variety of skills and concepts. Others, who advocate for a formal kindergarten, are criticized for overlooking the developmental needs of young children and narrowing the curriculum, overlooking the power of the young child's natural curiosity and passion for learning.

Definition of Readiness

In contrast to the common practice of kindergarten readiness screening that currently exists as the ritual entrance to formal education, there is no commonly agreed-upon definition of kindergarten readiness, which means that there is no common standard of measurement. Kindergarten readiness can refer to the maturation process determined by an illusive biological clock or to the acquisition of experiences that serve as the foundation for academic skill development. Because there is no common definition of kindergarten readiness, preschool teachers are often preparing children to meet standards that vary greatly from district to district, from school to school, and even from teacher to teacher.

District policies related to kindergarten readiness vary greatly but do appear to have common characteristics when sorted by socioeconomic status. In middle and upper socioeconomic areas, the school culture more commonly supports delayed entry to kindergarten, a trend that has been identified as unacceptable by the National Association for the Education of Young Children. Delayed entry is thought by many middle- and upper-class parents and educators to allow young children to mature so that they can better handle the demands of kindergarten. Arbitrary dates are often set and then pushed back as parents strive to have the oldest and most mature child in the kindergarten class. Many schools contribute to this practice by administering readiness evaluations that measure criteria that have no basis in research. Advocates of developmentally appropriate kindergarten claim that the practice of delayed entry has allowed many kindergarten teachers to focus on the child as lacking versus on their own classroom practice, which should be ready for all children regardless of developmental level. In contrast, districts serving families with lower incomes do not typically engage in delayed entry practices. The goal of these districts is to encourage children to enter kindergarten when their date of birth permits, and, in many cases, early intervention programs have been developed for children who are too young for kindergarten. Efforts to provide rich experiences to young children prior to kindergarten are essential because children who start behind tend not to catch up.

The federal No Child Left Behind Act (NCLB) has attempted to address this trend by requiring all school districts receiving Title I funds to meet state "adequate yearly progress" (AYP) goals for their total student population. This means that all children must have access to a comprehensive and challenging academic curriculum. To this end, most states have adopted early learning content standards in order to identify what young children need to know and be able to do upon entrance to kindergarten. These new standards tend to be developmentally appropriate while also providing young children with rich learning experiences. Early learning content standards provide parents and educators with a more defined concept of readiness, one that can be used to engage and empower children and families.

Full- Versus Part-Day Kindergarten

The diverse needs of American society have led to another area for debate related to kindergarten. After decades of part-day kindergarten, there is a movement toward full-day programs. Full-day advocates argue that the additional time allows more opportunity to address educational needs while offering a broader range of experiences and more in-depth study of the curriculum. The longer day also benefits the growing number of working parents who may need a longer school day. However, not all educators, researchers, and parents favor full-day kindergarten. Detractors argue that young children who attend full-day kindergarten are at risk of stress and fatigue due to the long day. This may have been true at one time, but apparently kindergarteners are evolving, as research suggests that children attending full-day kindergarten demonstrate less frustration and fatigue than children in half-day programs.

Shauna Meyers Adams

See also Blow, Susan E.; Developmentally Appropriate Practice; National Association for the Education of Young Children; No Child Left Behind Act (NCLB); Peabody, Elizabeth Palmer

Further Readings

Brosterman, N., & Togashi, K., (1997). *Inventing kindergarten.* New York: Harry N. Abrams.

Froebel, F. (1826). *Die Menschenerziehung* [The education of man]. Keilhau/Leipzig: Wienbrach.

Lee, V. E., Burkam, D. T., Ready, D. D., Honigman, J., & Meisels, S. J. (2006). Full-day versus half-day kindergarten: In which program do children learn more? *American Journal of Education, 112*(2), 163–208.

Manning, J. P. (2005). Rediscovering Froebel: A call to re-examine his life and gifts. *Early Childhood Education Journal, 32*(6), 371–376.

National Association of Early Childhood Specialists in State Departments of Education. (2000). *Still unacceptable trends in kindergarten entry and placement: A position statement.* Retrieved September 18, 2008, from http://www.naeyc.org/about/positions/pdf/Psunacc.pdf

NICHD Early Child Care Research Network. (2007). Age of entry to kindergarten and children's academic achievement and socioemotional development. *Early Education and Development, 18*(2), 337–368.

Pianta, R. C., Cox, M. J., & Snow, K. L. (2007). *School readiness and the transition to kindergarten in the era of accountability.* Baltimore: Paul H. Brookes.

KING, MARTIN LUTHER, JR. (1929–1968)

Americans of a certain age remember where they were on April 4, 1968, when they heard the news of the assassination of the Reverend Martin Luther King, Jr., in Memphis, Tennessee. Since the organization of the Montgomery Bus Boycott in 1955–1956, King had become a household name in America. The extremes of emotion that King evoked in America derived from the fact that for over a dozen years prior to his murder, he had been a major force in America's fight against racism, discrimination, and injustice. By the time of his death, King's activities had forced landmark legislation in the areas of civil rights, educational opportunity, voting rights, and fair housing. As King himself stated, his goal was "to save the soul of America." In this struggle for America's salvation, King endured vilification, public ignominy, and incarceration, and ultimately gave his life.

A descendant of a long line of preachers, King was born on January 15, 1929, in Atlanta, Georgia, to the Reverend Martin Luther King, Sr., and Alberta Williams King. King Sr. was a preacher at the Dexter Baptist Church in Atlanta. King Jr. grew up surrounded by love at home and his community. Given the power of positive influences in his formative years, King was able to lean more toward optimism regarding human nature. His subsequent education and religious development reinforced those views. King attended Morehouse College in Atlanta, from which he graduated with a B.A. in 1948. After Morehouse, King attended Crozer Theological Seminary in Chester, Pennsylvania, and received a Bachelor of Divinity degree in 1951; and later went on to Boston University where he received, in 1954, a doctorate in philosophy. At Crozer and at Boston University, King studied the works of major Western thinkers, including Reinhold Niebuhr, Plato, and Emmanuel Kant. He also became acquainted with the tactics and techniques of Mahatma Gandhi—skills of social reform, which would be pivotal to his career as a social activist and reformer.

Following his education in Boston, King returned to Alabama in 1954, where he was hired as a pastor at the Dexter Avenue Baptist Church in Montgomery. The culture of segregation was deeply entrenched in Montgomery. Events in this city quickly forced King's life to move in a new direction. In December 1955, Rosa Parks, a member of the local chapter of the National Association for the Advancement of Colored People (NAACP), was arrested and charged with a violation of the city's segregation ordinance. Parks had refused to give up her seat on the bus to a White man and a major crisis ensued. In response, African Americans in the city established a new civil rights organization, the Montgomery Improvement Association (MIA), and made King its leader. King and others utilized the MIA on two fronts: They organized the Montgomery Bus-Boycott and simultaneously filed a lawsuit against bus segregation in the city. Such actions represented a direct challenge to Montgomery's long-standing racist tradition of segregation. Almost a year after the lawsuit, the U.S. Supreme Court ruled that bus segregation in Alabama was unconstitutional, and with that the boycott ended. King and his tactic of nonviolent direct action had scored a major victory. In *Stride Toward Freedom: The Montgomery Story,* King recalled the rationale and effectiveness of this method as one of the most powerful weapons accessible to exploited people in their quest for social justice. Montgomery proved to be merely the beginning. In later years, King's tactics involved marches, sit-ins, kneel-ins, and much more. His actions put him at the center stage of social reform in the 1960s, in the crosshairs of America's powerful segregationists.

Between Montgomery and the passage of the Voting Rights Act in 1965, King's strategy was nonviolence, and protesting using the weapon of love. In a 1963 speech, "The Ethical Demands for Integration," King stressed the importance of desegregation, racial equality, justice, and an end to all forms of discrimination and poverty. With this, he said, the nation would accomplish his vision of a beloved community. His civil rights organization, the Southern Christian Leadership Conference (SCLC), created in 1957, was designed to serve as the engine room for his policies. King's methods desegregated buses, lunch counters, and other public areas.

Yet by 1965, it was clear that the reality of his beloved society remained an illusion. Despite the passage of legislations to end segregation legally, the Chicago Campaign of 1965 revealed that King's efforts had barely scratched the surface. Many years of segregation had created a permanent Black underclass, and the ghetto conditions had grown unbearable. King demonstrated with followers, marched with hundreds of thousands on Washington, D.C., organized the Poor People's Campaign, sought alliances with world leaders, challenged America's involvement in the Vietnam War, and called for the radical redistribution of economic wealth. He dedicated his life to calling attention to the lives of the poor and the oppressed.

Toward the end of his life, King had grown impatient with the slow pace of change. In a 1967 speech, "Where Do We Go From Here," he declared that Blacks must be dissatisfied with inferior schools, poor housing, police brutality, ghetto conditions, and racism. A year before his assassination, in "America's Chief Moral Dilemma," King wondered about America's overall commitment to racial equality and justice. Shortly before he died, he stated that "yes it is true . . . America is a racist country." King's pessimism stemmed from the growing recognition that the civil rights movement of the '50s and '60s had largely engaged only the surface of much deeper problems. The roots of racism were much deeper. Yet, he remained hopeful that good would eventually triumph over evil.

In a world oppressed and gripped by abject poverty King's message of hope and humanity resonated and transcended America's national boundaries. That he was a leading voice of the 20th century is attested through his numerous honorary degrees and awards. In 1964, he was awarded the Nobel Peace Prize. From all corners of the globe people named children, schools, buildings, and streets after him. Many decorated their living rooms with his picture on the wall beside those of important family members. His published books and speeches became must-reads.

The man who was killed on April 4, 1968, in Memphis was the voice of many generations, an icon, and a spokesman for the wretched of the earth. King represented the best of traditions in service, sacrifice, courage, and dedication. His vision of a beloved society remains an elusive dream for America, but the lessons of his life are everlasting. He taught us that each one must strive to be "the brother's [sister's] keeper." His views of America's promise are still timely, and still to be redeemed.

Julius A. Amin

See also Civil Right Act of 1964; Desegregation/Integration; Diversity; Inclusion; National Association for the Advancement of Colored People (NAACP); Racism

Further Readings

Carson, C. (Ed.). (1998). *The autobiography of Martin Luther King, Jr.* New York: Warner Books.

Dyson, M. (2000). *I may not get there with you: The true Martin Luther King, Jr.* New York: The Free Press.

Garrow, D. (1988). *Bearing the cross: Martin Luther King, Jr., and The Southern Christian Leadership Conference.* New York: Vintage Books.

King, M. L. K., Jr. (1958). *Stride toward freedom: The Montgomery story.* New York: Harper & Row.

Oates, S. (1982). *Let the trumpet sound: A life of Martin Luther King, Jr.* New York: HarperCollins.

Washington, J. (Ed.). (1991). *The essential writings and speeches of Martin Luther King, Jr.* New York: HarperCollins.

KNOWLEDGE IS POWER PROGRAM (KIPP)

Founded in 1994 by two teachers (Mike Feinberg and Dave Levin), KIPP represents one of the most significant and high-profile efforts at comprehensive school reform in the United States. The KIPP schools did not begin as a comprehensive school reform movement, but over time they impacted the way both traditional and nontraditional educators approached schooling in urban contexts. The KIPP schools were launched in Houston, Texas, originally as a fifth-grade program for public school students, but they have gradually migrated into 19 states and currently enroll more than 19,000 students.

Mike Feinberg created the KIPP Academy Middle School in 1995. At that same time, Levin created the KIPP Academy in the South Bronx (New York City). These two schools fostered a framework for rethinking what might be possible in terms of education for urban students. The high drop-out rates and the academic achievement gap problems that plague urban environments have been largely immune to a wide variety of educational innovations. Feinberg and Levin created a structure that they believed would allow them to tap the potential of young people who came from high risk and high poverty environments.

The KIPP schools are grounded on five operating principles. First, each KIPP school defines and creates a set of measurable high expectations for both student achievement and student conduct. The KIPP schools make "no excuses" for the students' behavior based on the types of home environments from which the students may come. The teachers and school leaders attempt to create a strong school culture where students understand that in order to achieve their full potential they need to behave in ways that allow them to tap the academic and social excellence that they possess. The schools rely heavily on a range of rewards and consequences to reinforce student progress toward the high expectations that have been defined.

Second, KIPP schools are schools of choice. Students are not forced or required to attend KIPP academies, because the schools typically represent a choice option within large urban school districts. Those attending the KIPP schools make a commitment to the KIPP approach and make an equal commitment to others in the school environment to put forth the time and effort needed in order to experience success.

Third, the use of time is critical to the success of the KIPP schools. They are based on an expanded school day, week, and year. As a consequence, students have more time to acquire the knowledge and skills they need in order to meet the high expectations that have been defined. The expanded time at school is one of the most distinctive features of the KIPP academies. Quite simply, teachers and students are at school for longer time than is evidenced in traditional K–12 settings, and the expanded school day and school year represents one of the most distinctive reform elements of the KIPP approach.

Fourth, leadership is localized rather than centralized within the KIPP structure. Specifically, KIPP principals have more control over their budgets and personnel than is evidenced in traditional school environments. As a result they can make decisions at the program and personnel level that they believe are in the best interests of the young people and the schools' environment. KIPP focuses heavily on identifying high-quality school leaders because they vest those leaders with significant autonomy and authority.

Finally, KIPP schools place great emphasis on results and especially student achievement on both standardized tests and other assessment for learning measures. The KIPP schools expect their students to do well academically and socially, and they create environments where the students can perform to their potential on all the different assessment measures that are required at the state and local level.

For years, educators have struggled with the question of whether and how urban students can really be successful. The statistics on the failure of urban schools to meet the needs of high-poverty students suggests that there were few, if any, program structures that can really be successful.

KIPP illustrated a way in which educators, especially those who represent more conservative ideological perspectives, could define positive structures for meeting the needs of young people in urban environments. Because of the success of KIPP, neoconservative policymakers began to call on more urban school leaders to consider the KIPP option and, even if they chose not to pursue that vehicle for change, they still argued that approaches such as an extended school day and school year represented reforms that were essential to both urban student success and to closing the academic achievement gap.

In essence, KIPP is both a real approach to the education of urban young people and a symbolic representation of what is possible with students in high poverty environments. Both the real and the symbolic have influenced the way in which reformers have begun to think about urban school practices. That is, more and more urban school leaders are talking about creating KIPP-type schools (or actually creating KIPP charter schools) or they are trying to find ways to extend and expand the school year to better meet the needs of the wide variety of young people who populate urban school classrooms.

Thomas J. Lasley II

See also Charter Schools; Finn, Chester E., Jr.; Neoconservatives; No Child Left Behind Act (NCLB); Teach For America

Further Readings

Hess, F. M. (2005). *With the best of intentions: How philanthropy is reshaping K–12 education.* Cambridge, MA: Harvard Education Press.

Hoffman, N., Vargas, J., Venezia, A., & Miller, M. S. (2007). *Minding the gap: Why integrating high school with college makes sense and how to do it.* Cambridge, MA: Harvard Education Press.

Kuykendall, C. (2004). *From rage to hope: Strategies for reclaiming Black and Hispanic students.* Bloomington, IN: Solution Tree.

KOPP, WENDY

See Teach For America (TFA)

KOZOL, JONATHAN (1936–)

Jonathan Kozol is recognized as one of America's most high-profile and influential advocates for public education. He is one of the primary educational thinkers who put the nation's public schools on the national public and policy agenda. Advocates of his ideas would describe him as someone who fights tirelessly for the rights and needs of children and especially for those who come from high-poverty environments.

His books, which have been read widely by both educators and noneducators, set the agenda for social change in America's urban centers. His book *Death at an Early Age,* which was published in 1967, has sold over 2 million copies. In this book Kozol describes his first year of teaching in the Boston Public Schools and the unique way in which he began to understand the world of high-poverty students and also to think about new ways of teaching content to them so that they could realize their personal potential. In 1986 he published *Illiterate America* and made public the debate about adult illiteracy, another issue of considerable importance to those who evidence strong social justice concerns.

In 1985, Kozol spent a year working in a homeless shelter, and his book, *Rachel and Her Children,* gave voice to the people living in desperate poverty and to the tragic death of an 8-month-old child. His more recent books have included *Savage Inequalities, Amazing Grace,* and most recently, *Ordinary Resurrections.* All of these books deal with children in high-poverty environments and the unique problems they face, as well as the way in which policies at the local, state, and federal level often mitigate the potential for those in urban environments to receive a quality education.

Kozol questions why, in a nation of such economic abundance, so many children go without a decent education. What are the true costs of childhood poverty, and why does the American educational and political system seem incapable of addressing the problems of poverty? Kozol has spent his career fighting for the rights of young people who often cannot fight for themselves or who are without adult advocates who can help them realize their full potential.

Kozol is an accomplished writer and speaker. His public presentations are searing accounts of the tragedy of childhood poverty and substandard education. They also develop in audiences a deeper understanding of, and provide an arsenal of practical solutions for, the ways in which the educational establishment can more effectively address the rights and needs of children.

Jonathan Kozol (born September 5, 1936, in Boston, Massachusetts) graduated from Noble and Greenough School in 1954, and Harvard University summa cum laude in 1958, with a degree in English Literature. He was awarded a Rhodes Scholarship to Magdalen College, Oxford. He did not, however, complete his Rhodes appointment, deciding instead to go to Paris to write a novel, where he spent 4 years writing his only published work of fiction, *The Fume of Poppies.* While in Europe, and during this time of personal searching, he befriended a number of exceptional individuals, including the writer William Styron. It was upon his return to the United States that Kozol began to tutor children in Roxbury, Massachusetts, and soon became a teacher in the Boston Public Schools. He was fired for teaching a Langston Hughes poem, an "event" that he describes in *Death at an Early Age,* and then became deeply involved in the civil rights movement. After being fired, he was offered a job to teach in the Newton Public Schools, which was the school district that he had attended as a child. He taught there for several years before becoming more deeply involved in social justice work; he also began to dedicate more time to writing the books that have subsequently established his prominent place in American education.

Kozol has since held two Guggenheim Fellowships, has twice been a fellow of the Rockefeller Foundation, and has also received fellowships from the Field and the Ford foundations.

He is currently on the Editorial Board of *Greater Good Magazine,* published by the Greater Good Science Center of the University of California, Berkeley. Kozol's contributions include the interpretation of scientific research into the roots of compassion, altruism, and peaceful human relationships.

Kozol is truly a reformer who has influenced the thinking of teachers and the policies of educational leaders. His convictions about the importance of social justice continue to be evident in the dialogue across the college campuses of the United States and within the policy think tanks that support and critique current PreK–12 practices.

Janet E. Kearney

See also Brown v. Board of Education; Desegregation/Integration; Racism

Further Readings

Kozol, J. (1995). *Amazing grace: The lives of children and the conscience of a nation.* New York: Crown.

Kozol, J. (2000). *Ordinary resurrections: Children in the years of hope.* New York: Crown.

Kozol, J. (2005). *The shame of the nation: The restoration of apartheid schooling in America.* New York: Crown.

LABORATORY SCHOOLS

In 1896 John Dewey opened the doors of his Laboratory School to 16 children and 2 teachers. Professor Dewey was the newly appointed head of the departments of philosophy, psychology, and pedagogy at the University of Chicago. With $1,000 appropriated by the university, he was creating a laboratory for his department of pedagogy.

Laboratory schools were emerging across the United States at that time. They were, by definition, attached to a college or university, either public or private. But the points of connection varied. Some, like at the University of Chicago, were attached to an academic unit in the general and liberal arts, and dedicated to preparation of supervisors and professors of pedagogy. Others, most notably Teachers College at Columbia University, were originally dedicated to preparing school administrators and teacher educators. More generally, and to keep pace with increasing demands for preparation of teachers and a steady rise in states' credentialing requirements, the mission of the laboratory schools grew to include teacher preparation for entry-level teaching positions.

The University of Chicago Laboratory Schools are perhaps the most widely known, even today, in part because Dewey was a prolific author. His books and essays provide vivid examples of his pedagogy and the general framework that came to be known as the Lab School Method. His intent was to provide a site for demonstration and scientific experimentation. It was not the kind of science

practiced in, for instance, a chemistry lab. Rather, it was about applying the scientific habits of the mind in the social interactions among children and their teacher. For instance, teachers at the lab school were positioned to raise questions in and through and about their own teaching, and then adopt a scientific method for confirming or disconfirming their general knowledge and assumptions about children. Thinking was the process of intellectual inquiry and, therefore, the lab school method of teaching. For Dewey, intelligence did not reside in a person; it was prompted among persons in action around a common and shared interest. Rather than adopting curriculum as a given and fixed body of knowledge to be taught, the teachers and children, together, were to work out a number of possibilities that could soon enough become the curriculum. This was, in fact, learning at its best. There was no drill. Learning was a creative act of shared questioning and problem solving. Knowledge that resides in theory could not be separated from its practice; each could be worked out only with the other. Similarly, practice without inquiry could not sustain either. In concert, each could nourish the other. Separated, each would reduce to mindless procedure.

In laboratory schools, parents of the children at the school were a first audience for Professor Dewey's lectures, two of which were later published as essays—*The School and Society* and *The Child and the Curriculum*; both are still available. His essays emphasize the social world of the child, including family, community, occupations, economy, history, and daily life, as providing real and material resources for curriculum that are intrinsically interesting to children. The school was to be at the center of life in the larger community. In a reciprocal direction, home and community life, including cooking, weaving, and manual arts as well as adult occupations, were to be brought from the outside in to become central features of life in school. There was no place in a lab school for memorizing the rules of grammar or doing the rote exercises that were typical fare in other schools of the day. Dewey was framing a pedagogy that placed him at a leading edge of the progressive movement in education.

The progressive education movement was part of a larger set of reforms in the United States known as the Progressive era (1890s–1920s). These times were marked by tremendous population growth. Westward expansion was full of hope, bringing 10 new states into the United States along with large waves of European immigrants to populate them. There was corruption in the cities, crowded conditions and poor housing, and rampant exploitation of children and women in sweatshop factories. The Progressives sought political, social, and education reforms that gave rise to antitrust laws, child labor laws, and minimum wage laws for women, as well as compulsory schooling and expansion of high schools and construction of playgrounds for children, among other initiatives. There was hope for a better future. Four amendments were added to the U.S. Constitution: (1) women's right to vote, (2) the prohibition of alcohol, (3) income tax, and (4) the direct election of senators.

The number of laboratory schools in the United States increased steadily during the Progressive era and up through the 1940s. But their doors began to close in the 1950s, and a steady decline continued through the mid-1980s. The demand for teachers in the baby boom generation that followed World War II was far greater than the lab schools could accommodate. In addition, as public school curricula became increasingly standardized, a credibility gap emerged. Community or laboratory schools were becoming a thing of the past. Preparation for teaching in a lab school was increasingly called into question on the basis of its adequacy as preparation for "real" teaching. At the same time, supporters of the laboratory school concept continued to ask, "What is real teaching if it does not connect with children and their lives? What is real teaching if it fails to nurture hope, creativity, and innovation?" Today, the International Association of Laboratory and University Affiliated Schools (NALS) counts more than 100 laboratory schools worldwide—resilient survivors of the Progressive era.

Renee A. Middleton and Ginger Weade

See also Alternative Schools; Differentiated Instruction; Early College High Schools; Latin Grammar Schools; National Association of Independent Schools; School Size

Further Readings

Goodlad, J. (1999). Whither schools of education. *Journal of Teacher Education, 50*(5), 325–338.

International Association of Laboratory & University Affiliated Schools: http://ncate.edinboro.edu/nals/nalshome.htm

Putney, L., & Green, J. (in press). The relationship between teacher-based action research and curriculum inquiry. In P. Peterson, E. Baker, & B. McGaw (Eds.), *International encyclopedia of education*. Amsterdam: Elsevier Science.

Rogers, J., & Oakes, J. (2005). John Dewey speaks to Brown: Research, democratic social movement strategies, and the struggle for education on equal terms. *Teachers College Record, 107*(9), 2178–2203.

Stengel, B. (2001). Making use of the method of intelligence. *Educational Theory, 51*(1), 109.

Tanner, L. (1997). *Dewey's laboratory school: Lessons for today*. New York: Teachers College Press.

LANCASTER SYSTEM

At the turn of the 19th century, the Industrial Revolution was well under way in America. Urban industrialization attracted millions of workers to the cities, bringing growing social concerns over poverty and crime. Given these worries, urban schools were ripe for reform, and one of the first systems for school organization was imported from England: the Lancaster system, also known as the monitorial system. Under the Lancaster system, a single teacher managed the education of hundreds of children, using older students as monitors to oversee lessons. The system was heralded as "creating a new era in education," with its efforts around efficiency, discipline, motivation, and scriptural education for the masses. Although the origin of the Lancaster system has been disputed, Joseph Lancaster has received principal credit for promoting the innovative method that was widely implemented in the early 1800s but fell from public favor with the advent of the common school movement.

Joseph Lancaster and the Lancaster System

Joseph Lancaster, an English Quaker, was born in 1778, the son of a shopkeeper in Southwark, England. In his youth, Lancaster believed he had religious visions directing him to become a missionary and teacher to children in the West Indies. As a teenager, Lancaster aspired to travel to Jamaica to educate its poor Black children; however, he was unable to afford the trip and, instead, joined the Society of School Friends. Dedicated to serving the poor, in 1798 he opened a school in London. Lancaster's school quickly became popular and thus overcrowded; he admitted the poorest students for free and found it difficult to manage the finances. Consequently, Lancaster devised a system of dividing students into homogeneous classes based on subject proficiency and monitored by older students. The monitors were responsible for supervising the class, teaching lessons, judging recitations, and ensuring discipline. The system was described as an all-day spelling bee, where students competed in content mastery. A teacher was responsible for training the monitors, teaching specific skills to large numbers of students, and handling administrative tasks. Standardized procedures were uniformly followed, enabling a single person to "teach" hundreds of students efficiently and cost effectively. The system also created a form of hierarchical apprenticeship: One could move from student to monitor to assistant teacher to principal teacher. Thus, the system provided an educational career path, producing lifelong, loyal employees, and serving as a precursor to normal schools.

Lancaster's system also fostered discipline by requiring constant activity and competition, set in place by rules and routines around emulation. As a Quaker, Lancaster was opposed to physical force to discipline students, using instead a reward system to encourage positive performance and behavior. Students received awards for individual

achievement and were promoted in specific subjects based on performance. Lancaster believed this motivated students to compete, which led to ambition and learning—certainly attractive alternatives to corporal punishment.

Additionally, Lancaster developed a nondenominational approach to religious instruction called "scriptural education." Instruction occurred without doctrine, and interpretation was up to the individual. This approach found strong support and served as an early form of nonsectarian public education in America.

In 1803 Lancaster published his first pamphlet, *Improvements in Education*, outlining the system's instructional methods. The publication was met with immediate acclaim, drawing the attention and patronage of English noblemen. By 1805 the Lancaster system reached the desk of Thomas Eddy, a Philadelphia-born Quaker living in New York. Eddy distributed copies of Lancaster's publications to the Free School Society in New York City, a philanthropic group interested in addressing poverty and crime through education. In 1805, New York adopted Lancaster's system in its schools, and the system continued to spread throughout the country.

The Appeal of the Lancaster System in America

The Lancaster system advocated constant activity, immediate reinforcement, and moral education through the operation of a single teacher. As a result, students could receive a basic education supported by a small financial investment. The system received eager backing from the nation's wealthy, who understood the need to educate children to encourage moral and industrious values. The Lancaster system was well suited to the demands of the Industrial Revolution and the overcrowded conditions and low budgets of urban schools. The system's supporters were particularly enthusiastic about its prospects for order and discipline. The highly structured routines of drill and recitation, the regimented activity and continuous surveillance represented a factory-like, militaristic approach to mass education, promising to teach poor children desirable habits and a respect for authority.

Along with its emphasis on efficiency and discipline, advocates of the Lancaster system also thought it to be pedagogically sound. The competitive achievement of the students was based on meritocracy, desire, and rewards—what proponents believed were the proper motivations for learning. The system was considered the best method to influence an industrious mind, manner, and character.

The Lancaster system also had a utilitarian and moral mission: It required temperance, which was viewed as a remedy for urban problems. School officials testified that students' manners were improved and crime was reduced in the neighborhoods of Lancaster schools. Thus, the promulgated values of discipline and scriptural education were considered beneficial to both student and society.

Lastly, the Lancaster system was presented as an effective method for educating not only urban children but also Native Americans. As enthusiasm for the Lancaster system spread in urban centers, government officials used the system to gain public acceptance and funding for Native American education. Although the Native American schools were presumed to use the Lancaster system, the system's role was secondary to the primary emphasis on manual training.

Criticism and Decline of the Lancaster System

Although the Lancaster system's popularity continued throughout the first half of the 19th century, the system had a relatively short life span. When Joseph Lancaster arrived in the United States in 1818, he was greeted with great acclaim. In spite of the system's economic efficiency and factory-like routine of educating the masses, critics saw the system as devoid of true learning. In fact, there was little evidence for the exaggerated claims of achievement. The system was deemed mechanical, unimaginative, rigid, and superficial, with an overemphasis on memorization. Additionally, the system was portrayed as class-based, interested in order and discipline rather than educational advancement. And as the common school movement developed, educational reformers and the public rejected a system designed for the masses. Moreover, as Pestalozzi's ideas around nurturing students' development through the teacher–student relationships were lauded, the Lancaster system seemed even more outdated. Nonetheless, for a time, this reform caught the spirit of a technological age and played

an important role in the development of the American education system.

Sylvia L. M. Martinez

See also Common School Movement; Moral Education; Native American Education; Normal Schools; Pestalozzianism; Society of Friends Schools

Further Readings

Hogan, D. (1989). The market revolution and disciplinary power: Joseph Lancaster and the psychology of the early classroom system. *History of Education Quarterly, 29,* 381–417.

Kaestle, C. F. (1973). *Joseph Lancaster and the monitorial school movement: A documentary history.* New York: Teachers College Press.

Rayman, R. (1981). Joseph Lancaster's monitorial system of instruction and American Indian education, 1815–1838. *History of Education Quarterly, 21,* 395–409.

LATIN GRAMMAR SCHOOLS

Latin grammar schools were the first college preparatory schools in colonial America. Arising from a long-established English educational tradition, the American grammar school represented an adaptation of that tradition to the conditions of the new world rather than a movement of either pure reform or dissent. In order to adapt, the schools developed unique structures that differed from the British model and that established a pattern of local government responsibility for the maintenance of community schools that remains the distinctive characteristic of American education to this day. In this case, then, adaptation rather than deliberate action led to educational reform.

In England, the Latin grammar school was the usual preparation for young men who wished to matriculate at Oxford or at Cambridge, which was the more popular British university for Puritans. A high proportion of the Puritans who emigrated to Massachusetts during the 1630s were Cambridge College graduates, and they viewed classical learning as an essential prerequisite for proper civic as well as religious leadership. In addition, the literacy of the general population was of the greatest import to Massachusetts Puritans, who in 1642 passed a law requiring literacy. In 1647, the Old Deluder Satan Law was passed, which mandated that towns of 50 families engage a schoolmaster to teach reading and writing, while towns with 100 families were required to maintain a grammar school.

Some grammar schools predated the 1647 statute. Harvard College opened its doors in 1636, and the grammar schools were to be the preparatory schools for the new college. Boston hired Philemon Pormont to serve as master in 1635, teaching boys in his home. In 1636, schools were founded in Ipswich and Charlestown, and by 1645 there were schools in Cambridge, Dorchester, Watertown, Roxbury, Salem, and Newbury. Historians estimate that by 1700 about 27 grammar schools were in operation in Massachusetts. In 1650, Connecticut passed a law similar to the Massachusetts statute, but by 1700 only the four county seats at New Haven, Fairfield, Hartford, and New London were required to maintain a school.

Communities sponsored and supported grammar schools in several ways. Boston supported its grammar school through taxation as well as by revenue generated by the rental of land on a harbor island. Hadley, Massachusetts, and New Haven, Connecticut, were endowed by former Connecticut governor Edward Hopkins, while the Roxbury School, founded by John Eliot, was governed by an independent board, and as such it was free from the political control of the town and relied on subscriptions, endowments, and the rental of lands for revenue. Despite their relative independence, these schools were not private schools in the modern sense; they were independent in terms of governance and the generation of revenue, but their charge was the same as the schools maintained primarily by taxation in that they were *the* grammar school of the community. The fact that the responsibility for the maintenance of the grammar school rested with the town set the New England grammar school apart from its British predecessor, where the church generally controlled the school. Towns that did not maintain a school could be fined, with the money from the fine divided among the towns bordering the town that broke the law.

Although grammar schools had diverse forms of maintenance, their curriculum was essentially the same. Boys generally started in a grammar school between the ages of 7 and 9. To be admitted to a grammar school a boy needed to be able to read English, which he could have learned at home, or at a petty or dame school, usually in the home of a woman who offered instruction in reading. Once in the grammar school, the boy would study between 4 and 7 years of Latin, beginning with rote phonetic pronunciation and continuing through classical and Renaissance texts in literature and history. A boy would be expected to be able to read, write, and speak Latin by the time he finished his course of study. Greek was introduced during the boy's last 2 or 3 years in the grammar school, and it was rare for a boy to leave the Latin school with the same facility in Greek that he possessed in Latin. School met for 6 days a week, with religious topics being discussed on Wednesday afternoons and Saturday mornings.

In the 17th century it was not uncommon for a boy to be admitted to Harvard who could speak Latin and read Greek but was unable to add a column of figures. Curricular change was slow in the grammar schools, and was usually driven by the needs of Harvard rather than by the needs of the grammar school or the community. By the 18th century, most grammar schools offered arithmetic as well as courses in navigation, through which a boy would learn some geometry and science, as well as some geography and other topics that would serve him well in a commercial center like Boston, Portsmouth, or Newport.

Grammar schools also accepted boys who came not for the classics but to learn to write English. Latin scholars were often a minority of the pupils in a school, as there were not always large numbers of boys headed for college. Towns frequently found it difficult to support two masters, so the grammar schools would also serve as writing schools. Boston was a notable exception to this, in that by 1720 the city could boast two Latin schools and three writing schools.

Masters tended to be young men recently graduated from Harvard. While there were men like Ezekiel Cheever, who taught for 70 years and who authored the *Accidence*, the most popular introductory Latin text of the 17th and 18th centuries, for most masters teaching was a temporary position. Pay was low, and a Harvard man had better options than teaching Latin to 9-year-olds in a frontier New England town. The master was

responsible not only for teaching the Latin scholars, but the writers as well. Boston was once again
an exception. The masters in each of the town's
two Latin schools had assistant teachers, called
ushers, who often worked with the younger boys.

After the American Revolution, many grammar
schools lost their curricular independence and
were forced to drop their emphasis on the classics
in favor of more "useful" subjects that prepared
young men for secular vocations. Also, the rise of
Unitarianism changed the religious atmosphere of
New England, and the rise of the academies presented the grammar schools with high-quality
competition. No longer was the grammar school
the only route to the colleges. By the 1830s, most
of the grammar schools had vanished. Those that
survived eventually became independent day
schools like the Hopkins School in New Haven or
the Roxbury Latin School. Boston Latin, the oldest
of the grammar schools, continues to serve the city
of Boston as a public examination school.

John J. White

See also Academies; Old Deluder Satan Law

Further Readings

Cremin, L. A. (1970). *American education: The colonial
    experience, 1607–1783.* New York: Harper & Row.
Holmes, P. (1935). *A tercentenary history of the Boston
    Public Latin School, 1635–1935.* Cambridge, MA:
    Harvard University Press.
Jarvis, F. (1995). *Schola illustris: The Roxbury Latin
    School, 1645–1995.* Boston: Godine.
Middlekauff, R. (1963). *Ancients and axioms: Secondary
    education in eighteenth-century New England.* New
    Haven, CT: Yale University Press.
Morison, S. E. (1956). *The intellectual life of colonial
    New England.* Ithaca, NY: Cornell University Press.

LAU V. NICHOLS

Generally considered to be the most consequential
U.S. Supreme Court decision regarding language,
Lau v. Nichols (1974) helped to establish a new
civil rights principle of particular import to
English-language learners: *to provide an equal
educational opportunity, it may be necessary to
accommodate different needs.* The case, credited
with spurring modern bilingual education policy
and leading to significant reforms in the education
of English-language learners, captures the critical
role of grass-roots dissent in the transformation of
state and national education policy. This entry
highlights the context of the case, provides an
overview of the decision, and considers current
evaluations of the legacy of Lau.

Background

Until the *Lau* decision, the majority of students
with minimal English skills, labeled as Limited
English Proficient (LEP), learned in classrooms
where English was the only language of instruction.
The San Francisco Unified School District (SFUSD),
like many other school districts across the United
States in the 1960s and 1970s, offered supplemental English-language classes to children on a limited
basis. The increasing number of language-minority
students in California public schools, in part a
result of 1965 immigration reform, expanded the
scope and severity of this problem with each passing year. In San Francisco, the supplemental language provisions for the approximately 2,800
children from Chinese-speaking families were
restricted to 1,000 students, leaving 1,800 pupils
without any extra instruction. Chinese parents
attempted to address these inadequate services with
administrators from the San Francisco school
board, but their efforts were met with resistance;
requests for bilingual education were denied.

In 1970, Kinney Lau and a dozen Chinese-
speaking children filed a class-action lawsuit
against the San Francisco Unified School District
on behalf of the thousands of Chinese-speaking
students who received no specialized English assistance. The plaintiffs charged that the San Francisco
schools had violated their Fourteenth Amendment
rights to an equal educational opportunity. The
defendant argued that schools were not responsible
for students who lacked requisite English-language
skills. Furthermore, the district maintained, in
using English as the medium of instruction for all
students within the system, it was treating every
student equally, not discriminating against the
Chinese-speaking pupils. The Federal District
Court and the Court of Appeals rejected the students' claim and found the SFUSD not responsible

for providing special language services to language-minority students. The problem, according to the district court, rested with the children: "[e]very student brings to the starting line of his educational career different advantages and disadvantages caused in part by social, economic and cultural background, created and continued completely apart from any contribution by the school system." The case advanced to the U.S. Supreme Court and was argued in December 1973.

The Decision

In a unanimous 1974 decision, the Supreme Court reversed the decision of the lower court and ruled in favor of the plaintiffs. The Court found that the San Francisco school system in failing to provide bilingual language instruction, or any other adequate instructional procedures, to the 1,800 Chinese-speaking students had violated Title VI of the Civil Rights Act of 1964, which prohibits discrimination on the basis of national origin, color, and race in institutions receiving federal financial assistance. The Court's decision rested specifically on the 1970 regulations issued by the Office for Civil Rights requiring affirmative efforts to provide special training for non–English-speaking pupils as a condition for receiving federal aid. In this case, language discrimination was an expression of national-origin discrimination. The Court further highlighted the SFUSD's failure to fulfill the education codes and policies of the state of California, which called for a student's mastery of English and allowed for bilingual instruction. The Supreme Court found the SFUSD's violations and curricular inadequacies denied students "a meaningful opportunity to participate in the public educational program." In delivering the opinion of the Court, Judge William O. Douglas reasoned, "there is no equality of treatment merely by providing students with the same facilities, textbooks, teachers, and curriculum, for students who do not understand English are effectively foreclosed from any meaningful education."

While the Supreme Court helped to redefine equal education as access to comprehensible instruction, the judges did not specify a remedy or particular approach to language learning in the initial ruling. Instead, the Court looked both to school districts to make the necessary accommodations

and to the Office of Civil Rights to enforce Title VI's protections. Specific recommendations, the so-called Lau Remedies, were issued in 1975 by the U.S. Department of Health, Education and Welfare and the U.S. Department of Education to help all school districts comply with the Supreme Court decision. The remedies recommended bilingual education for LEP elementary-school students, transitional bilingual education in districts where bilingual education was limited, and English-as-a-second-language (ESL) classes for middle- and secondary-school students.

Assessment of the *Lau* Decision

The *Lau* decision launched a new era of bilingual education in U.S. schools. The Lau remedies led to sustained reforms in the education of English-language learners, including the development of transitional bilingual education, ESL, two-way immersion, and maintenance bilingual education. Yet, on the 35th anniversary of the Lau decision, language policy researchers continue to find persistent conditions of inequality for LEP students in public schools. Educators call for further reform in the education system in at least two areas. First, the placement or tracking of LEP students into English-language classes (e.g., English as a Second Language) has largely resulted in remedial instruction and has potentially contributed to the high drop-out rate among Spanish-speaking students. Second, the weak recruitment and training of a qualified bilingual teaching force needs immediate attention. Despite these enduring problems, the Lau decision along with the Bilingual Education Act (1968) fundamentally transformed expectations and policies for the education of language-minority students in the United States.

Kara D. Brown

See also Bilingual Education; Civil Rights Act of 1964; English as a Second Language (ESL); Equal Education Opportunity; Immigration and Education Reform

Further Readings

ARC Associates. (Ed.). (1996). *Revisiting the Lau decision: 20 years after* (Symposium Proceedings November 3–4, 1994). Oakland, CA: Author.

Gandara, P., Moran, R., & Garcia, E. (2004). Legacy of Brown: Lau and language policy in the United States. *Review of Research in Education, 28*, 27–46.

Malakoff, M., & Hakuta, K. (1990). History of language minority education in the United States. In A. Padilla, H. Fairchild, & C. Valadez (Eds.), *Bilingual education: Issues and strategies* (pp. 27–43). Newbury Park, CA: Corwin.

McPherson, S. S. (2000). Lau v. Nichols: *Bilingual education in public schools.* Berkeley Heights, NJ: Enslow Publishers.

Moran, R. F. (2005). Undone by law: The uncertain legacy of *Lau v. Nichols. Berkeley La Raza Law Journal, 16*, 1–10.

LEAGUE OF SMALL DEMOCRATIC SCHOOLS

In 2004, John Goodlad and colleagues from the Institute for Educational Inquiry (IEI), a 501(c)(3) organization founded in 1992, created the League of Small Democratic Schools (LSDS) with a grant donation from the Arthur Vining Davis Foundations. In August 2007, the League of Small Democratic Schools was renamed the League of Democratic Schools (LODS).

The purpose of the LODS is to promote professional development that emphasizes the growth of students as individuals who are successful members of a democratic society and to help preserve schools that successfully advance the Agenda for Education in a Democracy. The Agenda for Education in a Democracy is mission-driven and research-based, consisting of a four-part mission, a set of strategies, and conditions required for implementing the strategies. The four components of the mission include enculturation of youth into a social and political democracy, introducing the young to human conversation, practicing pedagogical nurturing, and ensuring responsible stewardship. The Agenda is primarily implemented by the Institute for Educational Inquiry, the Center for Educational Renewal at the University of Washington, and the National Network for Educational Renewal (NNER).

Schools initially selected for participation in the LODS were chosen because of their commitment to preparing students to be productive members of a democratic society and their possession of the following five characteristics: (1) democratic purpose, (2) student achievement, (3) ongoing professional development, (4) approaches to learning, and (5) personalization. According to the Institute for Educational Inquiry (IEI), schools possessing democratic purpose believe that developing the knowledge, skills, and attitudes students require for successful participation in social and political democracy is the primary purpose of schooling. Schools evidencing student achievement demonstrate that students are and can be successful both academically and socially. For ongoing professional development, the IEI maintains that all members of the school community should engage in continuous learning. Schools with this characteristic use a variety of approaches, including engaging students with parents and other adults within the community. Finally, the characteristic of personalization is exemplified by schools through the deliberate personalization of relationships among students, teachers, parents, and administrators.

LODS initially consisted of 12 charter schools organized into geographic clusters. The clusters were organized to encourage both cross-age activity and the transfer of professional knowledge. Schools were (and are) required to identify a partner agency that in many cases is a member of the NNER. However, there is no direct requirement for partner agencies to possess an NNER membership.

Activities of the LODS are classified in two ways: professional growth and development, and protection and preservation. Professional growth and development are supported by the LODS through capacity building, provision of assistive materials, mutual assistance, supportive relationships, research, community engagement, and leadership development. Protection and preservation are supported by the LODS through local support, recognition, providing support in communications with the media, technical assistance in obtaining external funding, and providing access to expert help.

The IEI provides support to participating schools through funding the participation of school leaders in an annual leadership session, funding to support regional coordinators, technical support visits by IEI staff members/regional coordinators to schools in each cluster, cross-site visits, books and other materials, newsletter sharing information about work in the League, and membership recognition.

The IEI lists the following benefits for participating schools: capacity building related to the school's vision, core values, and renewal; facilitated sharing of strategies and ideas; professional development to expand knowledge and strengthen connections between classroom practice and the Agenda; research and inquiry conducted and shared on successful practices; leadership development that expands knowledge/skills for effective leadership; collaboration in getting grants; provision of materials and expert help; communication and collaboration to strengthen local support; visitation sites and networking with national networks associated with the IEI; providing a forum for support and sustainability; and national recognition. Colleges also receive benefits for participating as partner agencies.

Reformers continue to search for ways to foster the democratic values and principles that have been essential to the growth of the United States. LODS is another example of how reform-minded educators create opportunities to foster and enhance American democracy.

Barbara J. Mallory

See also Dewey, John; Jefferson, Thomas; Moral Development; Moral Education

Further Readings

Institute for Educational Inquiry. (2008). *Agenda for education in a democracy*. Retrieved October 22, 2008, from http://www.ieiseattle.org/AED.htm

Institute for Educational Inquiry. (2008). *Brief description of the League of Democratic Schools*. Retrieved October 22, 2008, from http://www.ieiseattle.org/Brief_Description_LODS_Jan2008.pdf

Lloyd, D. (2007, November). Announcement LSDS/LODS name change. *LODS Newsletter, 4*(1). Retrieved October 22, 2008, from http://www.ieiseattle.org/LODSnewsletters.htm

LEARNING PACKAGES

Learning packages, also known variously as experiential learning packages, individualized learning packages, or learning activity packages, developed largely during the mid- to late 1960s and the early 1970s in response to several factors. First, an increase in available media technologies such as Xeroxing, microfilm, microfiche, film strips, and audio cassettes enabled a much wider range of instructional techniques than was previously possible. In addition, this was an era that was still firmly entrenched in the tenets of behavioral learning theory. While behavioral learning theory is often erroneously interpreted as being dehumanizing, in fact the theory lends itself well to the idea of individualized instruction and self-paced learning. Finally, the 1960s and 1970s were a time of renewed interest in empowerment of the individual and breaking out of the structured mind-set of the establishment. During this era, experiments with team teaching, open-concept classrooms, flexible scheduling, nongrading, and various other alternative educational techniques and structures were widespread.

Although much longer in coming than the structural and organizational changes described above, eventually the curriculum began to be examined more critically and it became evident that traditional instructional methods and materials were not amenable to meeting the needs of individual learners; education was still largely teacher centered, based on whole-class instruction, and geared toward a conceptual norm that might or might not in fact exist among the students within a given classroom. Instead, a movement began that sought to empower individual students to take more responsibility for both the pacing and the methods of their own learning, and encouraged the teacher to act more as facilitator of learning than the primary source of learning. Overall, the goal of the movement to incorporate learning packages as a primary learning technique was to enable teachers to deal more effectively with the unique combinations of skills, knowledge, interests, motivation, preferences, aptitudes, and learning rates of individual students as well as to allow students greater freedom in their own learning process, thus ensuring a more enriching and meaningful educational experience.

Definition of Learning Packages

While it may be somewhat difficult to identify exactly what constitutes a learning package, there are common components and requirements that distinguish them from other instructional materials. A learning package is a cohesive, integrated set of instructional materials aimed at developing learner proficiency in one or more learning topics. With some variation, most learning packages include (a) concepts, (b) behaviorally stated instructional objectives, (c) multidimensional instructional materials, (d) diversified learning activities to accomplish the learning objectives, (e) preevaluation, (f) self-evaluation, (g) postevaluation, and (i) in-depth experiences (often referred to as Quest). Learning packages could be teacher developed or commercially available products intended for continuous improvement and could also include remedial learning packages. Furthermore, the importance of multidimensional instructional materials and diversified learning experiences cannot be overstated; the concept of individualized instruction is based on the idea that not all students will learn in the same way. Therefore, it is critical to provide instruction using multiple modalities and using activities that students can choose or skip, depending on their interest and skill or knowledge level.

Some concerns obviously emerged out of the trend to utilize learning packages as the primary, if not sole, instructional method. First, there was concern that students would become easily bored with the individualized instruction or perhaps lack the motivation that was assumed to underlie self-instruction. In addition, there were concerns about the logistics and practicality of a single teacher overseeing the individual learning of a classroom of 30 or more students. In response to these concerns, educational researchers and leaders suggested that a high degree of efficiency would be needed to utilize individualized learning packages effectively without spending inordinate amounts of time in planning and preparation or in record-keeping activities such as monitoring pre- and posttest results and materials checkout. In addition, it was suggested by educational experts that students would develop independence and self-reliance as they assumed more responsibility for their own learning. However, it was also cautioned that the use of learning packages should not preclude students working with other students; students at similar levels could work together in learning teams or informal learning groups while more advanced students could tutor struggling students. It was also suggested that whole-class instruction not be abandoned entirely. While lock-step instruction involving the whole class was

considered an ineffective method for achieving true student learning, it was still considered valuable as an occasional instructional technique that would satisfy the social and emotional needs for security and togetherness. Meanwhile, the individual attention the student would receive as she or he planned, implemented, and evaluated his or her own learning program with the teacher was considered invaluable quality time otherwise lacking in the traditional classroom environment.

Current Uses of Learning Packages

Most of the literature and research available on learning packages was published during the 1970s and the early 1980s. It appears there has been little investigation since that time, at least in the K–12 environment. This is most likely due to the panic induced by the 1983 report, *A Nation at Risk,* that decried the American system of public education as wasteful, ineffective, and the leading cause for the perceived economic downfall of the United States. Evidence of falling rates of achievement among American students and unfavorable comparisons between scholastic achievements in the United States and in other developed nations appeared to support the back-to-basics agenda that would emphasize improved basic literacy as well as improvement in mathematics and science achievement. Experimental nontraditional instructional methods fell out of favor as schools by and large returned to the traditional model of self-contained classrooms headed by a single, highly qualified teacher.

This is not to say, however, that learning packages have fallen out of use entirely. In fact, as the use of personal computers and multimedia interfaces has expanded, learning packages have become a viable and efficient model for professional development, vocational training, higher education, and even lifelong learning. A search of the Internet yields many companies that specialize in learning packages that take learners through a variety of topics at a variety of levels, including foreign language, computer skills, statistics, as well as a variety of vocational and professional skill sets. Furthermore, learning packages have not entirely disappeared from the K–12 setting, although these packages are most likely now utilized as supplemental or remedial more than a core instructional technique. Additionally, many commercially pre-pared learning packages are developed for K–12 learners but marketed to parents who wish to supplement the instruction their children receive in schools or for the purpose of homeschooling rather than marketing the packages to schools. With bur-geoning technology and innovative ways of com-munication being developed everyday, public education may soon revisit the potential of indi-vidualized learning via learning packages.

Eileen S. Johnson

See also Ability Grouping; Alternative Assessment; Constructivism; Differentiated Instruction; Experiential Learning; Inquiry-Based Learning; Mastery Learning; Project Learning; Time on Task

Further Readings

Casey, B. R. (1976). A study comparing learning activity packages and traditional instruction in selected units of general business. Unpublished doctoral dissertation, Georgia State University. *Dissertation Abstracts International, 38,* 699.

Farley, A., & Moore, D. M. (1975). Utilizing self-instruction or learning packages: Teacher and student implications. *Educational Technology, 15*(8), 9–13.

Kapfer, P. G., & Ovard, G. F. (1971). *Preparing and using individualized learning packages for ungraded, continuous progress in education.* Englewood Cliffs, NJ: Educational Technology Publications.

Meehan, M. L. (1981). *Learning activity packages: A guidebook of definitions, components, organization, criteria, and aids for their development.* Charleston, WV: Appalachia Educational Lab. (ERIC Document Reproduction Service No. ED 221490)

Murray, N. J. M. (1976). Competency-based learning packages—A case study. *Training and Development Journal, 30*(9), 3–7.

Thiagarajan, S. (1980). *Experiential learning packages.* Englewood Cliffs, NJ: Educational Technology Publications.

LEMON V. KURTZMAN

The First Amendment to the U.S. Constitution states "Congress shall make no law respecting an establishment of religion, or prohibiting the free exercise thereof. . . ." *Lemon v. Kurtzman* is a landmark decision by the U.S. Supreme Court that struck down laws in Pennsylvania and Rhode Island that included provisions that allowed pub-lic funding to be paid to parochial schools. The Court held that such laws were a violation of the Establishment Clause of the First Amendment. The Court heard arguments on the case on March 3, 1971, and issued its decision on June 28, 1971. In delivering the opinion for the Court, Chief Justice Warren Burger provided a three-point test that has been used to determine the constitutional-ity of a law with regard to separation of church and state. First, the law must have a nonreligious pur-pose. Second, the law must not advance or inhibit religion or religious practice. Third, the law cannot involve excessive government entanglement with religion or religious practices. These three points have come to be known as the Lemon Test. If any law violated any of the three points of the Lemon Test, it was deemed to be unconstitutional.

The case involved the Pennsylvania 1968 Nonpublic Elementary and Secondary Education Act. The Pennsylvania Act included provisions that allowed the Pennsylvania Superintendent of Public Instruction to reimburse nonpublic schools for costs related to textbooks, instructional materials, and teacher salaries. An examination of this practice revealed that most of the schools receiving these funds were Catholic schools being administered by the Archdiocese of the Roman Catholic Church. This decision also upheld a similar case in Rhode Island where the First Circuit Court of Appeals had ruled that the Rhode Island Salary Supplement Act was unconstitutional. The Rhode Island Act pro-vided state funds to offset 15% of the salaries for nonpublic elementary schools. The Rhode Island law also heavily favored mostly Catholic schools. While the Act stated that the funds could be used only for teachers who taught courses that were offered in the public schools using only materials used in the public schools and could not teach any religion courses, the First Circuit found that the only teachers benefiting from the law were 250 teachers in the Catholic school system.

The Court found that the laws were unconstitu-tional and upheld the decisions of the appellate court. Regarding the Rhode Island case, Chief Justice Burger wrote that the extensive religious character of these religious schools gave rise to entangling church–state relationships of the kind the Lemon Test sought to avoid. His writing regarding the Pennsylvania case stated the Pennsylvania Act, moreover, had the further defect of providing state financial aid directly to a religious school. The issues argued in both of these cases provided the framework for the Lemon Test.

The evolution of the issue of separation of church and state has its roots in the Establishment Clause of the First Amendment. The term was first used by Baptist theologian Roger Williams, the founder of the colony of Rhode Island, when he first wrote regarding a wall of separation between the church and the wilderness of the world. This was in response to his personal experiences of being persecuted for his religious beliefs and practices. The phrase gained its current prominence when it was used by Thomas Jefferson in a letter to a group of Connecticut Baptist leaders who had written to him with concerns regarding the emerging dominance of the Congregationalist Church. Jefferson reaffirmed believing that "religion is a matter which lies solely between man and his god," that man owes account to none other for his faith or his worship, and that the legitimate powers of government reach to actions only, and not opinions. Jefferson considered as critical that act that declared that the people's legislature "should make no law respecting the establishment of religion, or barring the free exercise thereof, thus building a wall of separation between church and state." The Lemon Test seeks to maintain this separation.

In recent years the use of the Lemon Test has been modified. Justice Sandra Day O'Connor advocated a shift in the second point of the Lemon Test to determine whether a law constitutes an endorsement or condemnation of religion and religious activity. More conservative justices tend to be critical of the Lemon Test. In recent years, a clear pattern of using the Lemon Test as a guide in deciding First Amendment cases has not been established.

Douglas M. DeWitt

See also School Finance; Separation of Church and State; Vouchers

Further Readings

Alley, R. S. (1999). *The constitution & religion: Leading Supreme Court cases on church and state.* New York: Prometheus.

Kowalski, K. M. (2005). Lemon v. Kurtzman *and the separation of church and state debate: Debating Supreme Court decisions.* Berkeley Heights, NJ: Enslow.

LESBIAN, GAY, BISEXUAL, AND TRANSGENDER (LGBT) ISSUES

The lesbian, gay, bisexual, and transgendered population (LGBT) is no longer completely invisible and uncomfortably denied in a traditionally heterosexist-dominant culture. Despite this change, discrimination, hostility, harassment, and even violence toward LGBT individuals persists. Only within the past 30 years have LGBT individuals been identified as a unique population deserving attention from educational researchers and policymakers. Estimates of their proportion in the population range from 1% to 10%. Although a clearly defined group, LGBT individuals remain quite diverse—coming from all races, ethnicities, socioeconomic levels, geographic regions, religions, and family constellations.

Background

Homosexuality has existed throughout human history and is acknowledged and sometimes celebrated in many cultures. In U.S. culture, however, it has been common for gay and lesbian individuals to have been labeled deviant, ostracized, and largely forced to keep themselves hidden. Change began relatively recently. In 1973, the American Psychiatric Association removed homosexuality from its list of mental illnesses. The American Psychological Association followed suit in 1975.

Science has no definitive answer as to the sources or causes of one's sexual orientation. Multiple and complex causal factors no doubt exist. Children usually identify themselves as a girl or a boy during their second or third year. Awareness of sexual attraction in any form to others begins during prepubescent years—around age 10 or 11. However, some gay and lesbian persons report feelings toward same-gender persons at much earlier ages. "Coming out," announcing oneself as gay, lesbian, bisexual, or transgendered to others, is a decision that usually comes much later, depending on life circumstances, including a support system and feeling secure.

LGBT Development

Sexual identity is not a clear-cut category for any one individual. A myriad of factors are at play in how someone's sexual identity is formed, including both genetic and environmental dynamics. Both sexual identity (how one sees oneself) and sexual orientation (to whom one is sexually attracted) are more appropriately considered as places along a continuum rather than a male–female dichotomy.

Some scholars have theorized that young people progress through several developmental stages in declaring their LGBT identity. Arthur Lipkin synthesized a number of development models promulgated by several other scholars. He suggests that, first, young LGBT preadolescents have mostly nonsexual feelings. Second, they may feel ambivalent about gender attraction. If they feel attracted to same-gender individuals, they may reason that those are merely "good friends." Such children may possibly become confused and withdrawn when their feelings do not clearly fit in the relationships they see in the world around them. During a third phase, they may begin to realize attraction toward only same-gendered persons. They may also feel isolated because no adult LGBT relationship models exist for them. They also may see and hear the denigration and the ridicule to which LGBT persons are subjected. During the fourth stage, they accept their identity and are open only with other LGBT peers. They socially explore the LGBT community and test how they would fit into this culture. Only carefully and hesitantly would they disclose their feelings to non-LGBT individuals. Lipkin labels the next phase "pride," a point of "coming out," a stage in which the individual incorporates feelings for same-gender partners into his or her total identity. The final stage is one in which sexual orientation becomes a part of "who I am," but not the most compelling part of one's identity.

While theses stages are not always directly ordered in this way, Arthur Lipkin maintains that they are not reversible. Once a stage has been achieved, it cannot be taken away. Some LGBT individuals navigate through all stages to live in the final phase; some do not. One might spend one's life at any one point along the developmental continuum.

Life Experiences of LGBT Youth

The developmental model presented here is absent of all the complexity of actual human experience. The life experiences of young LGBT adolescents as they traverse this path are not simple, linear, or this bounded and clear-cut. What we know of adolescents is their strong motivation to conform to their peers in our heterosexualized and highly homophobic culture. Young LGBT persons usually constitute an invisible population due to the strong rejection to "who they are" by those in their environment. LGBT students have higher rates of problematic interpersonal relationships. They have more experiences of school failure, largely due to being distracted, being withdrawn, being isolated. They decide to drop out of school more frequently than do non-LGBT students. Most devastatingly, they experience the highest rates of completed suicides among adolescents.

LGBT Within the Cultural Context

U.S. culture is historically anti-LGBT, a popular prejudice against homosexuality perhaps originating from dominant religious traditions that condemn homosexual behaviors. The LGBT population is subjected to the overwhelming popularity of antigay messages that are highly more likely to be found than are positive, healthy LGBT images in most widely disseminated media outlets. Unfortunately for LGBT youth, LGBT adults around them are frequently "closeted" and fear the negative repercussions of revealing themselves to a probably hostile culture. Even family members have been known to turn against their LGBT children when they reveal themselves.

Same-sex marriage has been an increasing part of public discourse since 2004. Increased acceptance of these unions may begin to erase the stereotypes that keep young people closeted; however, such unions remain controversial. In 2004, Massachusetts began to permit same-sex marriage and Connecticut followed suit in 2008. Several states have banned same-sex marriage.

LGBT Issues in Schools

Public schools are, among other things, composites of their surrounding cultures. The assumption in the culture, and, therefore, in the school, is that heterosexuality is the norm. Pressure may be felt by LGBT students to pretend they are heterosexual or to hope that they will outgrow or be able to deny their feelings. When LBGT people are denigrated with impunity in the culture, that pattern transfers to the schools. Many powerful role models and people with strong influences on children's lives in schools are likely to have homophobic attitudes because such attitudes are common, acceptable, and usually unquestioned. Stereotypes about LGBT individuals, homophobic humor, religious bigotry against a homosexual lifestyle, antigay sentiments, and derogatory language that often goes unpunished—faggot, dyke, and "you're so gay"—are likely to face LGBT students.

The public school curriculum has rarely included exploration of LGBT issues. Many educators may not feel comfortable addressing this curriculum. And, in cases where LGBT issues are addressed, the perspective may not be positive or healthy. On the other hand, many educators prefer not to address LGBT issues because they believe such a curriculum may have the effect of advocating a lifestyle they reject.

Numerous studies, including two of national scope, concluded that large numbers of public school students experience sexual harassment and that harassment using derogatory LGBT references has grown between the 1990s and early 2000. Students who are (or are perceived to be) lesbian or gay are similarly ostracized. Harassment of LBGT students is not always met with reprimand, even when the harassment includes physical punishment. LBGT students have suffered harassment also from those responsible for protecting them—teachers, administrators, and other educational professionals. According to recorded interviews in some LGBT lawsuits against schools, educational professionals may respond to harassment by blaming the LGBT student for not keeping his or her sexual identity hidden. Non-LGBT students are not well served either, according to some educators, when they are allowed to harass LGBT students with impunity, allowing them to believe harassing behaviors are acceptable.

In addition to public schools, colleges and universities have been sites of sexual harassment of LGBT students. Verbal abuse has been reported by the majority of lesbian and gay undergraduate students according to some studies, while physical abuse has been reported by far fewer. Both non-LGBT students and LGBT students have reported frequent anti-LGBT behaviors on their campuses.

Many dissenters have made public the injustices suffered by LGBT individuals. Bringing the truth of LGBT experiences to light has reinforced the obligations of educational professionals to protect these students and staff members. Jamie Nabozny and Derek Henkle are just two of the increasing numbers of young people who have revealed the suffering they experienced at the hands of both peers and professionals. Both filed lawsuits, Nabozny in Wisconsin and Henkle in Nevada. Both young men were awarded substantial monetary damages from school systems that failed to protect them from physical, mental, and emotional abuse. Increasingly, public school personnel have begun to acknowledge that LGBT students' experiences of harassment and abuse in educational settings can no longer be denied.

Carolyn S. Ridenour

See also Diversity; Equal Education Opportunity; Equity; School Climate; School Social Services; Sex Education

Further Readings

Arons, M. (2005). *Uncloseting the abused: A historical survey of American lesbian, gay, bisexual, and transgendered middle and secondary students' struggle for protection.* Unpublished doctoral dissertation, University of Dayton, Dayton, Ohio.

Campos, D. (2003). *Diverse sexuality and schools: A reference handbook.* Santa Barbara, CA: ABC-CLIO.

Olive, J. (2008). *Life histories of lesbian, gay, bisexual, and queer postsecondary students who chose to persist: Education against the tide.* Unpublished doctoral dissertation, University of Dayton, Dayton, Ohio.

LIBERTARIANISM

Libertarianism occupies a unique space in politics and economics. Whereas liberalism is based on the utilitarian premise of the greatest good for the greatest number, with the caveat that what constitutes "good" is not an absolute conception but good based on the preferences of the members of a given society, conservatism is based on the idealist premise of an absolute and true "good" that must be upheld regardless of whether the individual or members of a given society desire that good. Libertarianism is considered to be a form of liberalism, but it is based on the premise that each person has the right to life, liberty, and property; these constitute natural human rights that preexist any form of government. In other words, an individual has the right to live life in any way he or she chooses as long as the chosen way of life does not impinge on the rights of others. Accordingly, all human relationships and interactions should be voluntary and only those actions involving the use of force or that restrict or infringe upon the rights of others should be forbidden by law. Furthermore, according to the libertarian perspective, governments should be in place merely to protect the rights of individuals, and should also adhere to the principles of natural human rights and avoidance of force. In terms of PreK–12 education and reform, however, the issue is not so clear and there is much current debate among libertarians as to the role of government-sponsored vouchers for school choice and the future of public education itself.

History of Libertarianism

While it may seem that libertarianism is a relatively recent development, born out of frustration with both left- and right-wing political agendas, it is in fact a pragmatic philosophy that has existed in various forms for thousands of years. To the extent that libertarianism, at its very core, is concerned with the juxtaposition of power and freedom, some consider the Chinese philosopher and author of the *Tao Te Ching,* Lao-tzu, who lived during the 6th century BCE, to be the original libertarian. Lao-tzu proposed a theory of spontaneous order and harmony arising out of competition, and advised rulers to avoid interfering with the private lives of individuals.

Despite regarding Lao-tzu as the original libertarian, libertarianism is considered to be a largely Western philosophy emerging from Greek and Judeo-Christian conceptions of individual freedom, natural law, pluralism, religious tolerance, and a resistance to absolutism. The main impetus behind the liberal movements in the Netherlands during the 17th century and in England, Scotland, Germany, and France a century later was the growing idea and evidence of spontaneous harmony and order arising from limited government and free economic exchange. Indeed, America in the 18th century was dominated by liberal ideas, and the entire foundation of the U.S. system of government and economics was originally based on libertarian principles. Toward the end of the 19th century, however, classical liberalism began to wane and ultimately gave way to increased collectivism and state power.

It seems paradoxical that liberalism, which had spurred revolutions and enlightenments across the western hemisphere, encouraged unprecedented improvements in standards of living, and resulted in staggering intellectual, economic, and creative developments, ultimately seemed to fade. Socialism, however, was a rapidly evolving theory that attracted many younger intellectuals who had entered the world amid rapid improvements in wealth, technology, and living standards; one theory is that, rather than in spite of—but because of—this, society became complacent, taking for granted the relative economic prosperity and individual liberties available to them. It is not difficult to recognize, however, that not *all* members of society benefited from this prosperity or enjoyed the liberties associated with the liberal era. Socialism in general and Marxist ideology in particular seemed to promise, if not increased prosperity, increased *equity* in standard of living and access to social institutions such as education and health care. But this new social order came at the expense of the libertarian ideal of individual rights. Instead, the greatest good for the greatest number took over liberal thinking, yet was confounded by the conservative views of "good"; the individual became secondary, forced to sacrifice individual interests to that of the collective, and "good" became defined by those in power in terms of an absolute good (equity in standard of living, glorification of the worker, and elevation of the collective) regardless of whether the members of that society deemed it a worthy good. At the same time, antisocialist sentiment and the devastation caused by war in the middle of the 20th century led to greater and greater increases in the power and control resting with governments across the western hemisphere. In the United States, in particular, there have been unprecedented increases in government regulation of education and business, as well as increased interference in what libertarians consider basic individual rights.

Modern Libertarianism

With the decline of socialism in the latter part of the 20th century, and increasing dissatisfaction with both liberal and conservative policies, libertarianism experienced something of a reawakening in modern society as political schisms and economic instability become increasingly prevalent. Many libertarians now argue that modern liberalism is more reminiscent of socialism than its original position with regard to the individual and society; modern liberalism, sometimes referred to as social democracy, accepts the necessity of civil society and the open market but still advocates government and policy that subsumes individual decision making in favor of the benefit to overall society. On the other hand, modern conservatism increasingly appears to advocate for political intervention for the purpose of bringing about a particular social order.

Modern libertarians point out that many government programs designed to reduce or eradicate social problems such as crime, poverty, illiteracy, and lack of access to education and health care have been largely ineffective and, in some cases, have actually appeared to exacerbate the very problems they were intended to address. Modern libertarians also point out that excessive governmental regulation has led to heavy taxation and increased unnecessary costs that are absorbed by individuals in society. Government regulation, for example, of foods, medicines, and health care practitioners, according to modern libertarians, has caused unprecedented interference with an individual's rights to make decisions about his or her own health and well-being and has resulted in costs for health care spiraling out of control. Modern libertarianism takes a strong stance on several issues, including advocating for minimal government and refusal to participate in alliances, treaties, world organizations, government contribution to foreign aid, and opening of free trade in

order to stabilize economic inputs and outputs as well as to increase the likelihood of peace among nations. The modern libertarian movement is, at its heart, a call to return to severely restricted government and a return to civil society in which the highest ideal is for individuals to retain their natural rights as well as their responsibility for the consequences of the decisions that are made. This is seen particularly well in the libertarian view of public education.

Libertarianism and Education

The basic premise of the libertarian view of public education is simple: It is ineffective and costly. Libertarians point to the escalating costs of education and the concomitant (albeit arguable) decline in academic performance among American students and maintain that as long as education is regulated and controlled by the government, improvement will be impossible. Instead, modern libertarianism advocates for a free-market economy of schools—that is, free choice of schooling: Schooling should be entirely free of government interference, both federal and state. According to the theory, if individuals are not required to support public schools through taxes, those same monies are then available to individuals to subsidize whatever type of schooling they would choose. And, according to the theory, even those families without means to fund the education of their children will benefit from the *voluntary* support of others in the form of funded scholarships and assistance. Furthermore, as there is no agreed-upon function or purpose of schooling, one could theoretically choose for one's own children the type of school they would attend: strictly academic, emphasis on performance arts or social activism, or religiously based. Each family and community, according to this view, has the right to determine both the structure of the schools and content of the school curriculum as well to assume the responsibility for ensuring appropriate funding and running of the educational institution. Government, including federal, state, and local, should have no role in regulating schools or educators. The idea behind this premise harkens back to the very foundation of libertarianism. The rights and responsibilities of individuals stand paramount; given freedom from coercion and force from the government, various forms of education and schooling will coexist and prosper, and improvements in education will arise spontaneously out of free-market competition and freedom of purpose.

How, then, is the shift away from government-controlled schooling to take place? Somewhat ironically, there is a strong libertarian parallel to the current conservative movement toward school vouchers, in which parents are given partial or complete funding to send their child to a school of their choice, public or private. Some libertarians indeed see school vouchers as one way—if not the only way—of eventually achieving complete separation of government and schools and argue that a voucher system of education would liberate schools and families from bureaucratic and political control of schools. Other libertarians, however, are adamant that school voucher programs are still administered by government bureaucracy and with a sometimes thinly veiled political agenda to elevate religious-based schooling. Furthermore, these libertarians argue that those who advocate for school vouchers have arrived at the "solution" before defining the problem. Accordingly, a tax-based voucher system, rather than eliminating government involvement in schools, will simply serve to make government-run schools more effective, and may ultimately ensnare those already dependent and marginalized in a system that is opaque and difficult to navigate. Economist Milton Friedman, considered to be the originator of the school voucher movement, espoused vouchers as a way to reduce inequalities and natural inefficiencies of government-run schools but did not view vouchers as a means of achieving the ultimate goal—elimination of government compulsion, provision, and funding of education. Ivan Illich went even farther, in proposing a complete deinstitutionalization of schooling and, thus, society. He proposed that a more effective model of education would be that of learning webs in which individuals transform every living moment into learning, sharing, and caring. At issue may be the very definition of education and what it means to be an educated individual; the libertarian argument for school vouchers ultimately rests on the assumption that education equals mind-control, and there exists, therefore, a need to wrest such control from the government in order to place control back into the hands of civilians. Ultimately, one must weigh

these arguments and consider the question of the extent to which government represents an entity entirely divorced from its constituent citizenry.

Libertarian Organizations

Many libertarian organizations support the goal of separation of government and schools. Among these organizations are:

Alliance for the Separation of School & State. This organization is dedicated to the belief that parents, and not the state, should be in charge of their children's education.

CATO Institute. A nonprofit public policy research foundation founded in 1977, committed to increasing public policies based on the principles of limited government, free markets, individual liberty, and peace.

Foundation for Economic Education. The mission of this organization, founded in 1946, is to study and advance "first principles" of freedom: the sanctity of private property, individual property, the rule of law, the free market, and the moral superiority of individual choice and responsibility over coercion.

Fraser Institute. This organization measures and studies the impact of competitive markets and government interventions, including education, on individuals and society.

The Heartland Institute. This organization publishes *School Reform News,* a national outreach publication of the school reform movement; *Heartland Policy Studies,* peer-reviewed original research on education topics; and *Research & Commentaries,* a collection of best available research on the education reform debate.

Reason Foundation. Founded in 1968, this organization's mission is to advance a free society by developing, applying, and promoting libertarian principles and by producing public policy research on a variety of issues, including school reform.

School Choice Special Interest Group of the American Education Research Association. This group offers a nonpartisan, multidisciplinary community engaged in scholarly analyses of all forms of school choice, including charter schools, magnet schools, open enrollment, and vouchers.

Eileen S. Johnson

See also Alliance for the Separation of School & State; Exodus Mandate Project; Friedman, Milton; Illich, Ivan; Rushdoony, Rousas; School Choice; Tax Credits; Vouchers

Further Readings

Bast, J. L., Harmer, D., & Dewey, D. (1997). Vouchers and educational freedom: A debate. *Policy Analysis, 269,* 2–39.

Boaz, D. (1997). *Libertarianism—A primer.* New York: The Free Press.

Browne, H. (1995). *Why government doesn't work.* New York: St. Martin's.

Gaynlin, W., & Jennings, B. (1996). *The perversion of autonomy: The proper use of coercion and constraint in a liberal society.* New York: The Free Press.

Illich, I. (1971). *Deschooling society.* New York: Harper & Row.

Mele, A. R. (2006). *Free will and luck.* New York: Oxford University Press.

Narveson, J. (2001). *The libertarian idea.* Toronto, Ontario, Canada: Broadview Press.

Sciabarra, C. M. (2000). *Total freedom: Toward a dialectical libertarianism.* University Park: University of Pennsylvania Press.

Sprading, C. T. (1972). *Liberty and the great libertarians.* New York: Arno Press.

LICENSURE AND CERTIFICATION

In order to be qualified to teach, all public school teachers need a license or certificate. Teacher licensure or certification is a program of required college coursework mandated by a state. Since each state is responsible for the requirements to teach in that state, licenses or certificates are actually issued by the state with verification from the college or university where the candidate completed the licensure program. The license or certificate gives a person the legal right to be a teacher in the state that has issued the credential.

Generally, the state-mandated certification program at a college or university includes completion of general education courses; professional education courses, including some field experiences, which may also be called internships or clinical experiences; and successful completion of state testing requirements. Most licensure programs include the basics of learning, development, curriculum, and teaching. An example of a state testing requirement is the PRAXIS II tests that include the principles of learning and teaching at specific grade levels and the subject-area assessment tests. While there is some consistency between tests required by the states for licenses or certificates, passing scores differ from state to state, leading to a question of what determines a highly qualified teacher based on these tests.

State licensing systems have come under criticism, however, for setting requirements that do not address demanding standards. There are Web sites that can be visited to find the requirements for each state; most of these include a disclaimer warning that states are continually making changes to their requirements, so each state's department of education Web site needs to be researched for updated information.

Each state establishes its own requirements to teach in that state; thus, earning a teaching license in one state does not automatically qualify that person to teach in another state. A teacher with credentials in one state who moves to another state must meet the new state's requirements. Many states have licensing reciprocity with other states, but requirements differ, so a person moving to another state is often provided a temporary license until appropriate coursework is taken to qualify for the new license.

While many teacher licensing programs are part of an undergraduate degree program, there are also master's degree programs and postbaccalaureate programs for prospective teachers who already hold a bachelor's degree but want to earn the teaching license in a graduate program.

Variation in Licenses and Certificates

Not all states issue the same types of licenses or certificates. Some states issue elementary and high school certificates. Elementary certificates are usually issued for Grades 1–8, and all subject areas can be taught; while high school certificates are usually issued for a specific subject area and for Grades 7–12. Other states issue early childhood licenses generally to teach all subject areas for age 3 through Grade 3; middle school licenses, which are subject specific for Grades 4–9; and adolescence to young adult licenses, which are subject specific for Grades 7–12. There are also licenses issued in areas such as multi-age groups, including physical education, foreign language, intervention specialist or special education, music, and visual arts. While states try to issue the most comparable license or certificate when a license from another state is being transferred, grade bands are not always the same from one state to another. Teachers with an elementary certificate for Grades 1–8, for instance, moving to a state with early childhood, middle, and adolescence to young adult licenses will often be issued an early childhood license for age 3 to Grade 3 even though they have not been trained to teach the very young students. Teachers with a middle school license for Grades 4–9 moving to a state with certificates might be issued the elementary certificate for Grades 1–8.

To meet the need for teachers in critical teaching areas, some states have issued emergency teaching certificates. Teachers teaching under emergency teaching certificates are often hired in schools with high minority or low socioeconomic populations. A study of California schools showed that schools with high minority populations had a higher number of teachers teaching under emergency or temporary licenses or certificates. Consequently, those students considered to be in greatest need of the best, most qualified, and experienced teachers were being taught by teachers without standard credentials.

Some prospective teachers begin working in schools under a substitute teaching license or certificate. For substitute teaching licenses, requirements differ from one state to another, but most states require a college degree, and some states also require a passing score on a competency test.

The alternative license is a way to try to alleviate teacher shortage and at the same time train qualified teachers. However, alternative license programs vary in their characteristics and requirements, and have a wide diversity of participants. It is difficult to generalize about these programs. Teacher development in these programs is a function of the school that hires the alternative licensed

persons, resulting in little consistency in this aspect of the programs.

Teachers hired under emergency or alternative licenses are often thought to be underprepared, to have difficulty with classroom management skills, and to have little chance of improving student learning. Underprepared teachers are sometimes accused of blaming their students, rather than their own teaching inadequacies, for poor student performance.

The term often used by states for the initial teaching license is *provisional license,* which usually means that there are requirements to fulfill under the provisional license in order to advance to the professional license. For example, in Ohio, the PRAXIS III assessment must be passed during the first or second year of teaching in order to advance to the professional license.

The requirement to complete a license or certification program still leaves unresolved the question whether teaching is a profession or a semiprofession. By definition a profession includes performance standards for admission and also standards to be followed after admission, while a semiprofession is not as specialized and is not based on specific knowledge and skills. Educators have worked conscientiously to achieve the status of being professionals. Some states require a master's degree or equivalent coursework within a period of time after a teaching license has been earned. Teachers are given professional development opportunities, encouraged to attend professional conferences, and encouraged to take additional courses. However, not everyone views teachers as having the same social status as doctors, lawyers, or college professors. It has been noted that states do not allow doctors and lawyers to be certified when they have not met professional standards, yet states have issued emergency or alternative licenses for teaching.

Historical Overview

Historically, teachers were hired not necessarily because of their content knowledge, experience, or training but rather for such reasons as their being considered worthy or righteous; willing to work for little pay; having agreed to live with a neighborhood family; or being perceived as firm disciplinarians. Some elementary teachers never attended secondary school. Often teaching was seen as temporary work before advancing to a permanent career. At the turn of the 20th century the National Teachers Organization, now known as the National Education Association (NEA), was formed and standards for teachers began to be established. Normal schools were being initiated to provide teacher training. Teachers who had attended normal school or teacher institutes began to be hired because of their training. At the same time, many private colleges and universities began developing teacher education programs, and normal schools were becoming state teachers' colleges. It was not until the 1950s and 1960s that teachers were required to have bachelor's degrees in education, and states began requiring a national teacher exam as a condition for completing the requirements of the teaching license. Teacher training began to change in the 1980s to make teaching more professional and for preparation programs to be more consistent. Higher standards were recommended and some universities even adopted a 5-year teacher preparation program.

In the 1990s, an advanced certification program was established to acknowledge outstanding and experienced teachers. The National Board for Professional Teaching Standards (NBPTS) offers the national board-certification for teachers holding a bachelor's degree, a standard teaching certificate or license, and having at least 3 years of teaching experience. The requirements for a teacher to become nationally board certified include passing a written assessment, evaluation of teaching knowledge, and compiling a portfolio showing classroom performance. All 50 states acknowledge national board certifications, and some states offer additional incentives for teachers to earn this certification.

Today's jobs require workers to have greater skills than were required 20 years ago. Currently, high school dropouts have little chance of finding high-paying jobs. Enhancing the education of children in underperforming schools that traditionally did not provide students with adequate materials, upper-level courses, or qualified teachers, through the employment of highly qualified teachers, was seen as the way to provide the knowledge and skills for future jobs. This solution included increasing not only the quality of teachers, but also the number of qualified teachers in schools having

difficulty recruiting teachers, which would then raise the level of student achievement in these schools. In 2002, the No Child Left Behind Act (NCLB) was enacted by the federal government to ensure that qualified teachers are in our classrooms or to verify that teachers, especially in Grades 7–12, have the content knowledge to teach their specific subjects. The highly qualified teachers provision in the act was an important part of the NCLB. It is felt that teacher quality is the most important influence on student learning and only highly qualified teachers guarantee student learning. To be highly qualified, teachers of math, science, social studies, the arts, reading, and languages must have experience under a standard teaching license and have exhibited content knowledge by either having majored in their subject area in college, having passed a qualifying test, or by meeting guidelines set by the state.

The disparity between high-poverty schools and wealthier schools hiring highly qualified teachers continues to be a concern. In the 2006–2007 school year at the secondary level in high-poverty schools, there were fewer core courses, especially in subject-specific courses, taught by highly qualified teachers. Only one state, North Dakota, met that year's deadline to have 100% of its teachers highly qualified in its core-subject classes.

While the No Child Left Behind Act has been seen to be innovative, it should be noted that in 1938 the National Education Association published information regarding the disparity between teachers hired in rural schools and those hired in nonrural areas. The publication included information that the teachers in rural areas received lower pay, were younger, had little or no teaching experience, and had less training than their nonrural counterparts. The 1945 solution, similar to the one in effect today, led to a teacher shortage in rural areas.

States now require background checks of persons applying for teaching licenses to ensure applicants meet ethical and moral standards. While there are shortfalls with background checks, they are used to determine who should or should not be issued a teaching license. Background checks are then often required periodically after an individual has been issued a certificate or license. There are a variety of types and severity of criminal convictions, making the decision of issuing licenses based on a background check difficult. Even when persons with criminal convictions are issued a license, the school district has the discretion not to hire someone with an arrest record.

Conclusion

While it is agreed that all schools should be hiring qualified teachers, there is no agreement on the best way to prepare these teachers for a teaching license or certificate. However, there is consensus that persons earning a teaching license should have a strong knowledge of their subject area, effective professional education courses, and intensive student teaching or clinical experiences.

Mary Lou Andrews

See also Accreditation; Alternative Licensure; National Board for Professional Teaching Standards (NBPTS); National Council for Accreditation of Teacher Education (NCATE); National Education Association (NEA); No Child Left Behind Act (NCLB); Professional Development; State Departments of Education; Test of Teaching Knowledge (TTK)

Further Readings

All Education Schools. (2009). *Teacher certification & licensure information*. Retrieved May 1, 2009, from http://www.alleducationschools.com/faqs/certification

Amrein-Beardsley, A. (2007). Recruiting expert teachers into hard-to-staff schools. *Education Digest, 7*(4), 40–44.

Clement, F., Clement, M., & Outlaw, M. (2007). Then and now: Developing highly qualified teachers. *Delta Kappa Gamma Bulletin, 73*(4), 26–39.

Darling-Hammond, L. (2008). Real federal leadership. *Independent School, 68*(1), 22–32.

Darling-Hammond, L., & Baratz-Snowden, J. (Eds.). (2007). A good teacher in every classroom: Preparing the highly qualified teachers our children deserve. *Educational Horizons, 85*, 111–132.

Fields, C. (2005). Background checks. *Change, 37*(4), 6–7.

Honawar, V. (2008, June 11). Teachers achieving "highly qualified" status on the rise. *Education Week*, pp. 14–15.

Humphrey, D. C., & Wechsler, M. E. (2007). Insights into alternative certification: Initial findings from a national study. *Teachers College Record, 109*, 483–530.

Murdock, G. F. (2003). Polishing the apple. *Delta Kappa Gamma Bulletin, 69*(2), 20–24.

National Board for Professional Teaching Standards. (2009). *Standards by certificate*. Retrieved April 30, 2009, from http://www.nbpts.org/the-standards/standards-by-cert

U.S. Department of Education. (2009). *State information*. Retrieved May 3, 2009, from http://www.ed.gov/about/contacts/state/index.html?src=gu

LIFE ADJUSTMENT EDUCATION

The progressive reform impulse that gained momentum at the turn of the 20th century signaled a fundamental shift in educational thought and practice in the modern era. Educational progressivism, as this movement came to be known by scholars, was an integral part of the broader progressive project and shared its interest in the democratic reconstruction of American society. With a philosophical commitment to democracy, community, and the whole child on the one hand, and an administrative embrace of efficiency, expertise, and differentiation on the other, the progressive education movement gave rise to a spate of innovative—and often conflicting—pedagogical and curricular reforms that spanned the 20th century.

Among the most notable, and deeply contested, curricular innovations to grow out of progressivism's commitment to the education of democratic citizens was the life adjustment movement. Proponents of the life adjustment movement expanded upon the progressive ideals first articulated in the National Education Association's 1918 *Cardinal Principles of Secondary Education* that forged an explicit connection between the public functions of the school and the private lives of students. Borrowing from the administrative and pedagogical progressive lexicon, the *Cardinal Principles* advocated that the school should test and track students at the same time that it should tend to their physical and emotional well-being. With "health," "citizenship," "ethical character," and "worthy home membership" as defining objectives for secondary education, the NEA's *Cardinal Principles*—and the life adjustment educators who drew inspiration from them—championed a functional curriculum that eschewed traditional academic disciplines as it aimed to prepare students for healthy and productive citizenship in modern American life.

While the life adjustment project drew upon progressive antecedents like the *Cardinal Principles*, as a standalone movement, it gained its first expression in the post–World War II era. Like their Progressive era counterparts, life adjustment educators charged that the modern curriculum focused its attention at two ends of the educational spectrum: a classical, college-preparatory program on the one hand and a broad vocationalism on the other. In so doing, life adjustment educators insisted that the public school failed to meet the needs of *all* American youth. In order to develop a more comprehensive and inclusive curriculum, Charles Prosser, a proponent of life adjustment education and leading vocational educator who helped craft the 1917 Smith-Hughes Vocational Education Act, convened a committee of educators in 1945 under the auspices of the U.S. Office of Education. The findings of the committee, later dubbed the "Prosser Resolution," stipulated that in order to prepare students adequately for democratic living, schools must extend their reach beyond the 20% of youth going to college, and the 20% headed for the vocations. The other 60% of modern American youth, Prosser noted, required a curriculum geared toward the development of sociability, personality, and industrious habits of mind. Using the concept of "adjustment" as an idiom of reform, life adjustment educators sought to meet the private and personal needs of students while socializing them into public life.

John H. Studebaker, the U.S. Commissioner of Education, convened the first national life adjustment conference in 1947 to revise and implement the findings of the Prosser Resolution. Drawing representatives from leading educational organizations and advocacy groups across the country, the meeting established a National Commission on Life Adjustment Education for Youth and propelled a bulwark of state commissions to integrate life adjustment education into the curriculum of public schools. Carried out under course names such as "life skills," "basic living," and "family life education," and with remarkably uneven results, the life adjustment curriculum addressed a capacious range of issues from marriage to child rearing, from safety education to leisure studies, and from personal maladjustment to personal finance.

While the life adjustment courses and programs differed in kind, they were united by the fundamental belief that the school curriculum should center on the ever-changing social needs of students living in a democracy, and prepare all young Americans for meaningful employment, fulfilling marriages, and model citizenship.

Conventional wisdom among life adjustment educators held that if the schools could help make better spouses, better parents, and better financial planners, then in the end they could help make better citizens. Yet precisely what constituted good citizenship in the cold war era—and the role the school should play in cultivating it—was up for debate. According to the most vocal critics of life adjustment education, the cold war would be waged and won in the hearts, and more importantly in the minds, of American citizens. Therefore, the future of American democracy depended on a return to a more traditional approach to public instruction rooted in the core academic disciplines.

Critics of Life Adjustment Education

In the hands of life adjustment educators, critics charged, the public school became an anti-American, anti-democratic, and thoroughly anti-intellectual institution. The public school's shift toward an overtly functional curriculum, life adjustment's penchant for child-centered classroom instruction, and the alleged liberal political orientation of progressive education cut against the grain of the conservative turn in America during the 1950s. Set against the backdrop of Joseph McCarthy's communist witch hunt, critics insisted that the educational establishment's devotion to feel-good progressive techniques and inattention to the rigors of physics, mathematics, and "disciplined scientific schooling" were a threat to national security and the spread of democracy in the cold war world.

But it was the anti-intellectual orientation of life adjustment pedagogy that fueled the most rancorous debate. University of Illinois historian Arthur Bestor led the charge against the anti-intellectualism of life adjustment education. In his mid-century jeremiad *Educational Wastelands* (1953), Bestor charged that the movement's emphasis on life management skills constituted a "retreat from learning": It diluted intellectual rigor in the classroom and marginalized the place of traditional core subjects in the modern American curriculum. Mortimer Smith's *And Madly Teach* (1949) and Hyman Rickover's *Education and Freedom* (1959) echoed Bestor's critique in arguing that the most persistent problem with the public schools was an intellectual one: The postwar resurrection of educational progressivism in the form of life adjustment education was an assault on academic excellence and American superiority in the cold war era. *Life* magazine offered a similar assessment of the postwar "Crisis in Education" and issued an urgent call to close the "carnival" that had become the American public school. Along with other educational luminaries such as Robert Maynard Hutchins and James Bryant Conant, critics of the life adjustment movement maintained that it was impossible to be a fully educated person in the absence of exposure to traditional liberal studies, and thus challenged citizens to think anew about the direction of American public education.

Amidst the storm of controversy surrounding the life adjustment curriculum, the Progressive Education Association, which served as the principal administrative organ of the progressive education movement, closed its doors in 1955. But it was not until 2 years later when the Soviet Union successfully launched the first artificial satellite, *Sputnik I,* that the rejection of life adjustment pedagogy and the embrace of traditional academic studies in the liberal arts, mathematics, foreign language, and the hard sciences gained widespread support. Indeed, the Soviet Union's success in penetrating the "final frontier" before the United States seemed to further highlight the institutional failures of the nation's system of public schooling and expose the intellectual shortcomings of a pedagogical movement that held up "adjustment" as the overarching goal of American public education.

Catherine Loss

See also Cardinal Principles Report; Conant, James Bryant; Council for Basic Education; Dewey, John; National Defense Education Act (NDEA); Progressive Education; Progressive Education Association (PEA); Rickover, Hyman; Vocational Education

Further Readings

Angus, D., & Mirel, J. (1999). *The failed promise of the American high school, 1890–1995.* New York: Teachers College Press.

Bestor, A. (1953). *Educational wastelands: The retreat from learning in our public schools.* Urbana: University of Illinois Press.

Cremin, L. (1961). *The transformation of the school: Progressivism in American education.* New York: Knopf.

Hofstadter, R. (1963). *Anti-intellectualism in American life.* New York: Vintage.

Kliebard, H. M. (1995). *The struggle for the American curriculum, 1893–1958.* New York: Routledge.

Ravitch, D. (1983). *The troubled crusade: American education, 1945–1980.* New York: Basic Books.

Rickover, H. G. (1959). *Education and freedom.* New York: E. P. Dutton.

Smith, M. B. (1949). *And madly teach: A layman looks at public school education.* Chicago: Regnery.

Zilversmit, A. (1993). *Changing schools: Progressive education theory and practice, 1930–1960.* Chicago: University of Chicago Press.

LOCAL CONTROL

The American colonies were established by settlers from Europe who sought religious freedom that had been denied to them in their homelands. When the first colonial towns were created, local schools became mandatory under the Old Deluder Satan Law of 1647, which required that children attend school so that they could learn to read the Bible. At first, the governance of schools was a function of the town governments. As towns grew in size, however, a separate system for operating and overseeing the local schools was needed, therefore a separate branch of the town government was created for the sole purpose of managing the schools. Beginning in Massachusetts, local committees were elected to act as governing bodies for the local schools, and this concept spread to the other colonies. *Local control* became the term used to describe the governance of a local school system by a committee (later called a school board) elected by the community to make decisions for the schools. These were decisions regarding issues such as finances, hiring of personnel, curriculum and instructional materials, school buildings and facilities, and others directly affecting the schools. This type of school governance did not have the backing or support of the state or federal governments to govern local schools. Local control has been a school reform issue for many years, but has recently come to the forefront as topics such as school funding inequities, accountability, low test scores, and criticisms of teacher and school quality have become popular with the media and political candidates.

While the U.S. Constitution itself does not contain any reference to providing an educational system for its citizens, it does delegate to the states all those powers not specifically stated within it. One of these important powers, provided under the Tenth Amendment, includes the authority of the states to establish and govern the public schools within their borders. But, because no state can efficiently monitor the daily operations of all of its schools, and because this type of governance would not be consistent with a democratic society, this authority is given to locally elected school boards or boards of education. Local school boards, as political subdivisions of the states, serve the purpose of governing public school districts. Local control involves the decision-making authority of these boards for the schools within their own districts about local instructional, personnel, and operational issues. Some of these issues include hiring, discipline, and termination of staff; attendance, grading, and curriculum; selection of instructional materials; developing the school district's yearly calendar; establishing bus routes; extracurricular activities; fund-raising; and the like. The majority of states have a central department of education that through their legislatures, formulates laws, policies, and regulations affecting education and the operation of schools within the state. All public schools must follow the policies and regulations of the state when creating their own local policies. Examples of the policies and regulations that a state department of education may create include criteria for teacher and administrator certification, graduation requirements for high school students, school finance and district budget procedures, creation of personnel policies, curriculum for all grade levels, standardized testing of students at designated grade levels, school building codes, length of the school year, division of the state into school districts, and others. The local school board makes its decisions about local issues within the framework of these regulations, and sets policies that must be consistent with state laws.

School Boards and Their Powers

Local school boards have been referred to as "arms of the state," as board members are in reality officials of the state because the authority to create a board comes from the state legislature. Acting as unified boards or committees, school boards exercise executive, legislative, and judicial powers for the local schools under their authority. These correspond to the three branches of the state and federal governments. School boards use their *executive* authority, for example, any time they enter into a contract with administrators, teachers, staff, or other personnel in the district for the purpose of employment. As part of the notion of local control, hiring personnel for school districts is done at the local level. Other examples of this contract relationship include agreements with contractors, electricians, plumbers, waste disposal companies, food service and bus transportation providers, technology installation and maintenance, and so on, for agreed-upon work or services to be performed in the schools. This also includes the construction of new buildings. School boards exercise their *legislative* powers when they develop and approve rules and policies pertaining to the schools in their districts. An example of this is a board's adoption of an attendance policy for students. As stated before, any policies created by a local board of education must comply with the regulations and policies of the state legislature or state department of education, as well as with federal laws, particularly in the area of antidiscrimination. Finally, school boards have limited *judicial* powers, which are used mainly when they conduct hearings based on policies they have created. Examples include hearings held for student expulsions and grievances filed by employees.

Accountability and the Redistribution of Control

Over the past two decades, serious concerns about the quality of public schools overall and about student achievement have arisen from federal and state policymakers, as well as from parents and community members at the local level. Along with the passage of the federal No Child Left Behind legislation in 2001 came increased levels of accountability for schools and, in particular, for classroom teachers and school administrators. Under this law, all children in all public schools must have their learning needs met, or the whole school can suffer serious consequences. These may include: offering parents the choice to send their children to a higher-performing school, replacing teachers and principals, or takeover by the state department of education. In the case of the latter, the local school board's decision-making authority is suspended until the schools in the district begin to show significant improvement. If this happens, local control ceases to exist while the district is under state control.

Many believe that local control has been eroding over the past 20 years, mainly due to school districts depending more heavily on their state legislatures and departments of education to formulate policies for areas like teacher certification, curriculum, and assessment. No Child Left Behind has put increasing pressure on school districts to hire only highly qualified teachers and to develop more challenging curriculum in all areas to improve student achievement, as measured by annual standardized tests. Many of these new accountability requirements have presented a financial burden to school districts, especially those located in poor and rural areas. As a result of this financial challenge, many school districts and their boards have turned to the states for help, which has resulted in less decision-making power at the local level.

The dependence of local boards on state policy making has led to the states having a greater voice in how districts can spend their money. In most districts, state subsidies make up well over half of the revenue needed to balance the budget and operate the district. The rest comes from the districts' ability to raise money by collecting local taxes, such as property taxes, per capita (per person) taxes, and wage taxes. Many districts struggle with this local effort to fund their schools, resulting in more dependence on the state.

Those who favor less local control and a greater degree of state-level control seem to believe that centralization would make school district management more efficient in many areas, particularly in setting standards for instruction by setting common educational targets. With all of the criticism of public schools in the past 20 years, citizens have tended to blame local boards of education, school administrators, and classroom teachers for students' lower achievement levels, and have demanded

improvement. Observing that this cooperation would not come from the local level, special interest groups like parents of children with special needs, along with lobbyists, have influenced state legislatures and departments of education to take a closer look at what happens in the schools.

If public schools were to relinquish the majority of their local control to the states, the other major area of concern is funding. States could distribute funds in ways that would ensure that they were dedicated to areas with the greatest need, for example, highly populated inner-city schools, sparsely populated rural areas, and those districts with high numbers of poor or special needs students. This would serve to distribute state subsidies more evenly so that wealthier districts would not receive more money than poorer ones. This inequity in school funding has raised great concerns, because school districts with greater resources have historically been able to offer more alternatives to their students in the form of better teachers, instructional materials, technology, and other means of support. Proponents of greater state control of the public schools view this as a way to reform a system they believe to be "broken."

Those who favor stronger local control cite the centralization of school district management at the state level to be a less effective means of resolving the issues of improved student achievement and equitable funding. They point out that at the local level it is easier to meet the needs of individual students, rather than to combine all students in the state into one large homogeneous group. Local control gives the local community a greater voice in decisions that directly affect the schools in their neighborhoods. Parents and other community members have the freedom to elect school board members who share their vision for quality education, and to remove those who do not. With increased local control, teachers and administrators can be held to a higher standard of accountability, because they would answer to the local community instead of to several layers of state bureaucracy. Also, local boards could hire highly qualified teachers who understand the needs of local students. Other issues, such as setting salary scales, offering merit pay, putting caps on class sizes, and spending district funds as needed would be in the hands of the local board. Proponents of stronger local control believe that school boards could be more creative about fund-raising efforts to support the district as state subsidies continue to dwindle.

Conclusion

To summarize, local control is the term used to describe the decision-making authority of elected school boards to manage the public schools in a school district. These decisions involve the exercising of executive, legislative, and limited judicial powers over the personnel, policies, and programs of education in the schools. This authority is shared to some degree with the state and federal governments in areas such as school funding, teacher quality, curriculum, assessment, and student achievement. The role of the federal government was expanded by the passing of the No Child Left Behind Act in 2001, and the states continue to increase their roles in making decisions and developing policies for local schools as individual districts become more dependent on them. There are proponents of increased local control by boards and less control by state officials, who contend that locally elected boards should be making the decisions for their local schools. Those who favor more state control of public schools believe that a more centralized system, controlled by the state, is a more efficient and effective way to govern public schools. The local control of public schools is an important school reform issue and is of critical importance in American culture today.

Mary Harris-John

See also Boards of Education; Community Control; District Schools; Site-Based Management; State Departments of Education

Further Readings

Alsbury, T. L. (2008). *The future of school board governance: Relevancy and revelation.* Blue Ridge Summit, PA: Rowman & Littlefield.

Cook, G. (2006, January). Squeeze play. *American School Board Journal*, pp. 12–16.

First, P. F., & Walberg, H. J. (Eds.). (1992). *School boards: Changing local control.* Berkeley, CA: McCutchan.

Imber, M. (2004, October). Equity in school funding. *American School Board Journal*, pp. 50–52.

Jacobson, L. (2008). States eye looser rein on districts. *Education Week, 27,* 1.

Kirst, M. (1988). Who should control our schools? *NEA Today,* 6(6), 74–79.

National School Boards Association. (2006, March). Local control is slipping away. *American School Board Journal*, pp. 12–13.

Yglesias, M. (2008, March). *Against local control.* Retrieved May 21, 2008, from http://matthewyglesias .theatlantic.com/archives/2008/03/against_local_ control.php

LOOPING

See Age Grading

LOWELL PLAN

The Lowell Plan was an innovative but practical program that allowed Catholic children to attend public schools that were amenable to the religious values of the Catholic Church.

The establishment and survival of parish schools in Massachusetts was in serious question in the decades before the Civil War. The intense poverty of the immigrant Catholic population and the low priority given to the establishment of parish schools by the priests and bishops of the diocese combined to limit the number of parish schools in the state.

The majority of parish pastors were well aware that Catholic parents could ill afford to send their children to any school, let alone pay for the establishment of parish schools. In many Catholic households, children were needed as wage earners to contribute to the welfare of their families. Keeping the family together was their first priority and that meant that everybody worked. Parish pastors understood the plight of their flocks and asked for nothing more than the establishment and support of the Church.

Yet in spite of the poor response to the call for parish schools, there was some Catholic educational activity in Massachusetts during these years. Throughout the 1830s and 1840s, the Diocese of Boston counted only a handful of Catholic schools in the state, and these institutions provided instruction for only a few hundred of the 12,000 to 17,000 Catholic children in the diocese during those years.

The one Catholic educational venture that did achieve a measure of success was the Catholic Sunday school. By 1845, Boston Catholic Sunday schools were enrolling more than 4,000 children per year and these schools continued to grow throughout the decade and into the 1850s. It must be said, however, that Sunday school was a short-term measure and parish schools in Massachusetts were virtually nonexistent in the years before the Civil War.

In this climate of inactivity there emerged in Lowell, Massachusetts, an educational reform experiment that was to have important implications for the history of Catholic education throughout the United States. In an effort to "consider the expediency of establishing a separate school for the benefit of the Irish population," the Lowell Town Meeting of 1831 appropriated $50 for the support of the local Catholic school. At the time, most Massachusetts schools were affiliated with religious denominations and the grant to the Catholic school seemed the most logical way of providing for the education of Lowell's small but growing Irish population. The relationship worked well and, by 1835, Catholic education in Lowell was being supported with public funds.

The terms of the agreement between the town school committee and the parish pastors were straightforward. The committee reserved the right to examine and appoint all teachers working in parish schools; to prescribe and regulate the "textbooks, exercises and studies" used in the schools; and to examine, inspect, and supervise the school on the same basis as other town schools. The parish pastors insisted that qualified Catholics be appointed as teachers in their schools and that the textbooks contain no statements offensive to Catholics or the Catholic Church. The committee and the pastors mutually agreed that parish school buildings were to be provided and maintained by the parishes and that teachers were to be paid by the school committee.

The plan worked well throughout the 1830s and 1840s, and enrollments increased from a few hundred in 1835 to more than 3,800 a decade later. As late as 1850, Barnabas Sears, secretary of the Massachusetts Board of Education, wrote that

he had no schools equal in quality to the Catholic schools of Lowell.

But the "Lowell Plan," as it was later called, quickly ended in 1852 when one Catholic parish, unable to find qualified lay Catholic teachers, invited the Sisters of Notre Dame to staff the school. Catholics claimed that the school staffed by the sisters was just as worthy of support as the other Catholic schools, but the Lowell school committee objected to the nuns and this experiment in cooperation ended in acrimony and bitterness.

Even though educational cooperation ended in Lowell in 1852, the idea was too powerful and appealing to die. One small community in Massachusetts had solved the problem of public funding of parochial education and the plan worked well for almost 20 years. Other communities in other states also would try the Lowell Plan with varying degrees of success in the later decades of the 19th century.

Timothy Walch

See also Catholic Schools; Faribault-Stillwater Plan; Hughes, John; Ireland, John; Poughkeepsie Plan

Further Readings

Dolan, J. C. (1985). *The American Catholic experience.* New York: Doubleday.

Mitchell, B. C. (1983). Educating Irish immigrants in antebellum Lowell. *Historical Journal of Massachusetts, 11,* 94–103.

Walch, T. (2003). *Parish school: American Catholic parochial education from colonial times to the present* Washington, DC: National Catholic Educational Association.

LUTHERAN SCHOOLS

Lutheran education in the United States has reflected the diversity of theological belief and ethnic background of the Lutheran church itself. In spite of such differences, however, the history of Lutheran schools has been unified by three elements. First, Lutheran educators have persistently found themselves in the role of obdurate educational dissenters from both Protestant and secular educational establishments. Also, Lutheran educators of various ethnic backgrounds have attempted to instill a reverence for Lutheran doctrine in each new generation. Finally, Lutherans of all ethnicities have sought to boost their students' sense of ethnic identity and pride. From the colonial period through the late 19th century, this emphasis on ethnic distinctiveness often served as the primary raison d'être for Lutheran schools. In more recent years, the emphasis on ethnic tradition has often given way to a more emphatically religious education.

Since the colonial period, Lutheran schools have reflected the different ethnicities and theological commitments of their religious affiliations. The mostly German immigrants who founded what eventually became the Lutheran Church–Missouri Synod founded a vibrant network of elementary, secondary, and tertiary schools. This reflected their founders' admonition that every new American congregation must also found a school. Scandinavian Lutherans more often supported a public-school education for their children, complemented by religious and ethnic summer schools. In the 19th century, each synod usually supported its own colleges and seminaries, each teaching the distinctive theology and language of its immigrant founders.

Well into the 20th century, a wide spectrum of Lutheran synods supported networks of schools at every level. Each synod's school network reflected the differing interests and history of its founders. The large Evangelical Lutheran Church in America (ELCA), for instance, tended to run mostly preschools for its congregants, many of whom supported public elementary and secondary education for their children. By the end of the 20th century, the ELCA operated 1,200 preschools, 128 elementary schools, and 2 high schools. The smaller Lutheran Church–Missouri Synod (LCMS), on the other hand, energetically continued its tradition of independent elementary and secondary schools. In the 1990s, the LCMS ran 999 preschools, 998 elementary schools, and 64 high schools nationwide.

These schools had long combined theological goals with ethnic considerations. The powerful Lutherans in colonial Pennsylvania, for instance, led by prominent leaders such as Henry Melchior Muhlenberg, used their schools as a locus from which to fight against Americanization and Anglicization efforts. Non-Lutheran educational leaders such as Benjamin Franklin sought to force schools to teach exclusively in English in order to bring German colonists into a single, British-dominated colonial culture. German resistance often centered on the symbol of their German-language Lutheran schools, which they successfully defended against Franklin's efforts.

By the early national period, German American Lutherans in Pennsylvania had achieved enough political clout that their educational leaders called for public funding of German-language Lutheran schools. When speaking to Anglo-American audiences, Lutheran promoters cannily downplayed the importance of both German language and Lutheran theology in Lutheran education. They knew many Anglo-Americans agreed with Franklin's vision of a united Anglicized America. Among German American audiences, they emphasized the benefits such public-funded schools would have for maintaining ethnic distinctiveness, rather than theological purity. As did later Lutheran educators, they recognized that many German Americans valued their German linguistic and cultural heritage much more than traditional Lutheran religious doctrine.

Other Lutheran ethnic groups favored less-confrontational educational strategies in the 18th and early 19th centuries. Swedish and other Scandinavian Lutherans tended to embrace Americanization and English-language acquisition eagerly. Many became earnest supporters of public English-language elementary and secondary schools. Yet even most Scandinavian Lutherans supported educational opportunities to inculcate their American-born children with the language, culture, and religion of their birth countries. Well into the 20th century, Scandinavian American Lutherans often sent their children to rigorous summer academies, where the children were trained in the ethnic, linguistic, and religious traditions of the ancestral lands.

Until the end of the 19th century, German American Lutheran leaders continued to balance a desire for theological purity with their constituencies' interest in German-language education. Wisconsin's Bennett Law and Illinois's Edwards Law forced Lutheran educators to ally with their most ardent theological foes in order to maintain their ethnically distinct schools. In Wisconsin, the 1889 Bennett law mandated both schooling within residential districts and English-language instruction. German American Lutherans tactically abandoned their theological antipathy for the Catholic Church to fight against this Americanization drive. Together, Wisconsin Lutherans and Catholics, both largely German American at the time, succeeded in having the law repealed in 1891. As had the drive for public funding of Lutheran schools in 18th-century Pennsylvania, the fight against the Bennett law had the political effect of turning Lutheran schools into a potent political symbol of German cultural pride. Many Wisconsinites of German extraction rallied to the defense of such schools, even as many of them had grown less attached to the finer points of Lutheran theology.

By the late 20th century, in contrast, the relationship between ethnic tradition and religious instruction had largely reversed itself. The ferocious persecution of German-language speakers and educators during World War I contributed to an ethnic mainstreaming of Lutheran schools. By the 1960s, Lutheran education leaders maintained that their schools existed primarily for theological reasons. They argued that parents wanted a religious option for their children as public schools became perceived as purely secular institutions.

Lutheran schools, much like other public and private schools, also changed in other significant ways. One of the thorniest issues for the theologically conservative Lutheran Church–Missouri Synod was the issue of female administrators. As had other schools, during the 20th century Lutheran schools had seen an increase in teaching opportunities for women. Since the LCMS prohibited women from serving in a ministerial role above men, many female school administrators felt caught in an awkward position. They could not take an active pastoral role among adults, even though their administrative duties required pastoral leadership of their colleagues.

In addition, with a growing number of non-Lutheran students, the later 20th century had seen a change in attitude among many Lutherans toward the role of their school system. The system had long served as a tool to maintain the theological and ethnically distinctive traditions of Lutherans. With a growing number of non-Lutheran students, Lutheran educational philosophy has had to change as well. Instead of their schools being separate havens for Lutheran children, many Lutheran educators have come to see their schools as primarily

a missionary opportunity: a chance to get their religious message to children who would not have been exposed to it in any other way.

Lutheran educators have consistently promoted their schools as sanctuaries for their congregations against hostile trends in the wider American culture. In the 18th and 19th centuries, leaders usually emphasized their schools' ability to provide ethnic havens in an Americanizing culture. In the later 20th century, Lutherans promoted their schools as Christian bulwarks in a hostile secular society.

Adam Laats

See also Americanization; Bennett Law; Bilingual Education; Franklin, Benjamin; Separation of Church and State

Further Readings

Blanck, D. (2006). *The creation of an ethnic identity: Being Swedish-American in the Augustana Synod, 1860–1917.* Carbondale: Southern Illinois University Press.
Coburn, C. K. (1992). *Life at four corners: Religion, gender, and education in a German-Lutheran Community, 1868–1945.* Lawrence: University Press of Kansas.
Pardoe, E. L. (2001). Poor children and enlightened citizens: Lutheran education in America, 1748–1800. *Pennsylvania History, 68,* 162–201.

LYON, MARY (1797–1849)

Mary Lyon was born in Buckland, Massachusetts. At the age of 4, she began walking a great distance to attend the nearest school. Her love of learning was the driving force in her early life, and, later, this passion would lead to her efforts to transform the course of women's education in America as the founder of the Mount Holyoke Female Seminary (since 1887, Mount Holyoke College).

Lyon's reputation as an outstanding student helped her to obtain her first teaching job in a one-room schoolhouse at the age of 17. As a teacher, she was paid 75 cents a week, along with meals and a place to live. Teaching inspired her to further

her own education, a goal not generally accomplished by a woman of limited wealth in the 1800s. Supporting herself at a young age by teaching, she took college courses at Sanderson Academy, Amherst Academy, and Byfield Female Seminary in Massachusetts. She would travel hundreds of miles by stagecoach over dirt roads to attend these higher education schools when she was not teaching in the one-room schoolhouse. Thus, despite the lack of money, a busy teaching schedule, and the colleges being great distances away, Lyon was determined to continue her learning. In this pursuit of an education, she stated that she "gained knowledge by the handfuls."

After several years as a teacher, Lyon became an assistant principal at Ipswich Female Seminary. Seminaries like Ipswich were higher education institutions for young women, but they did not provide the same courses as the men's institutions. For example, these female seminaries taught subjects such as needlework, music, and drawing, instead of the math and science courses found at the men's colleges. From Lyon's perspective, these seminaries were like finishing schools, and she felt women deserved the same opportunity to learn math and science as did men.

Mary Lyon believed that women's education was extremely important. Inspired by her own struggles to attain a college education, she endeavored to create academic opportunities for women and to open doors for them to become teachers, missionaries, and productive citizens throughout the nation and world. Her ultimate goal was to establish a higher education institution for women. This goal led her in 1834 to undertake the raising of funds for a school. For the next 3 years she crusaded tirelessly in her fund-raising efforts even though the United States was in an economic depression. She persisted with her efforts, writing papers and advertising about the plan for a women's college that offered higher education programs. Throughout this time, Lyon faced ridicule from those who felt her ambitious undertaking was "wasted" on women. Her enthusiasm, drive, and endless spirit eventually helped her to secure the financial support for her dream.

In 1837, Lyon returned to Massachusetts and founded Mount Holyoke Female Seminary in

South Hadley. The institution was an immediate success, with many more students desiring to attend than the school could accommodate. She served as the first president (referred to as "principal") of Mount Holyoke, and continued in that capacity for the next 12 years.

Her energy and vision for this college were major reasons for the school's early success. She set Mount Holyoke apart from other female institutions with the student requirement of seven courses in the science and mathematic areas. This requirement was similar to the men's schools at that time, but new for the women's institutions. As a higher education institution, Mount Holyoke provided the model for numerous women's colleges that were later founded in the 19th century, such as Wellesley College, Smith College, and Mills College.

Lyon also incorporated a new teaching methodology in the study of science—that being laboratory experiments performed by the students. In addition to being the school's leader, she wanted to teach freshman-level chemistry, in order that the incoming students would receive a solid science foundation.

Mary Lyon was an educator ahead of her time. Her innovative pedagogical advancements made Mount Holyoke Female Seminary a very progressive school. Her interest in the sciences and high expectations for women made her a pioneer in women's education in America. Mount Holyoke was the first higher education institution to offer women the same kind of educational program as was offered to men. Her impact on education was felt across the United States and the world as Mount Holyoke's graduates took Lyon's philosophy of education and ideals into the high schools and colleges as teachers.

After working tirelessly to build Mount Holyoke, and then leading it for 12 years, Mary Lyon began to suffer from severe headaches and exhaustion in her later years. She was 52 years old when she died in an apartment at the seminary. She is buried on the grounds of the college, and today her gravesite remains a landmark on the campus.

Robert H. Thiede

See also Academies; Willard, Emma Hart

Further Readings

Banning, E. I. (1965). *Mary Lyon of Putnam's Hill: A biography*. New York: Vanguard Press.

Gilchrist, B. B. (1910). *The life of Mary Lyon*. Boston & New York: Houghton Mifflin.

Green, E. A. (1979). *Mary Lyon and Mount Holyoke*. Hanover, NH: University of New England Press.

James, E. T. (Ed.). (1971). *Notable American women, 1607–1950: A biographical dictionary*. Cambridge, MA: Harvard University Press.

Magnet Schools

Magnet schools were first developed in the 1960s as a means to achieve a measure of racial integration through voluntary enrollment of pupils from noncontiguous residential areas on the basis of the distinctive theme or program offered by the school. In some large northern cities like New York and Chicago where comprehensive desegregation through mandatory assignments seemed politically or practically impossible, the promotion of magnet schools served as a token effort toward integration. In suburban communities with small but residentially concentrated minority populations, magnet schools were a means of reversing "White flight" from impacted schools.

Although the results were seldom adequate to meet court orders requiring comprehensive desegregation, magnet schools often provided evidence to parents and the wider public that Black and White (and, less commonly, Hispanic and Asian) pupils could be educated together without racial conflict or loss of educational quality. On the contrary, the quality of education was often higher in magnet schools, either because of additional resources provided to attract White parents to a school located in a predominantly Black or racially mixed neighborhood, or because the effort on the part of staff to develop and implement attractive themes produced many of the characteristics of effective schools.

A variation of magnet schools was "magnet programs," which took at least two different forms.

The first, employed in Chicago and many other cities, was a racially integrated program housed within, but separate from, a predominantly minority school. Such a program, typically for academically talented pupils, would enroll its minority participants from the local attendance zone while drawing White pupils from other areas. Although the motivation behind the creation and placement of such programs was often to give a misleading impression that the overall population of the school was racially integrated, they did serve to put a superior program within reach of some minority pupils who would otherwise have lacked such an opportunity.

The other type of magnet program brought together White and minority students, and sometimes urban and suburban students, for part-time educational experiences, often in connection with cultural institutions. Typically such programs would provide 8 or 10 sessions over the course of a year, providing some opportunity for learning and for socializing in integrated groups, without affecting the regular school assignments of the participants. When the cultural or other experiences were designed well, they gave diverse pupils an opportunity to get to know one another and to learn together without the pressures of the school setting.

Different strategies were employed to make magnet schools attractive to parents living in areas of a different racial character than those in which the schools were located. In some cases, significant additional resources were put into schools in predominantly minority neighborhoods in an effort to attract White pupils, a strategy most dramatically (and unsuccessfully) used in Kansas City, Missouri. In other cases, the emphasis was on specialized career-oriented programs at the secondary and even the intermediate level. Yet other magnet schools (typically at the elementary level) adopted a theme or pedagogical strategy that was considered attractive to target groups of parents, whether it was a Montessori-type curriculum, or the use of the arts to teach all subjects, or a "two-way bilingual" program with children learning each other's languages.

In Massachusetts, where the state invested more than $100 million during the late 1970s and the 1980s to promote voluntary school desegregation, a policy decision was made not to fund the operation of magnet schools more generously than that of other schools, but instead to pay for summer and after-school teacher planning time for any urban school that sought to develop a distinctive educational profile as a means of attracting pupils and maintaining an integrated student population. Surveys identified themes with strong appeal to both White and minority parents, and school staff were invited to select one of those themes and implement it consistently, in order to respond to an identified sector of the demand for schooling. This proved a hard sell in some cases, so accustomed were teachers and principals to providing a "lowest-common-denominator" program designed more to avoid displeasing any group of parents than to please any.

A problem that emerged with magnet schools was their tendency to create a two-tiered school system, as they attracted teachers with clear ideas about how to teach and parents who were looking for such teachers and schools for their children. In Cambridge and a dozen other Massachusetts cities during the 1980s, magnet schools were made universal under so-called controlled choice plans. These eliminated all individual school attendance districts and established parent information centers through which parents were counseled, indicated their choices, and received school assignments that respected those choices so far as possible. The intention was to force every school to compete for pupils through developing a clear educational profile responsive to the concerns of parents. Although this happened to some extent, the high morale and focus characteristic of most magnet schools could

not easily be spread to every school and every teacher within bureaucratic school systems, and it became clear that more radical reform was needed that would permit the supply of schooling to respond more flexibly to parental demand. That reform was the charter school.

In the long run, the most significant impact of magnet schools may have been acceptance of the idea that public schools could be deliberately different; this was a reversal of the effort since the 1840s to make public schools more similar through various forms of standardization of curriculum, procedures, and resources. Magnet schools, by being deliberately different, demonstrated that public education can legitimately be provided in a variety of ways. Emerging as an educational strategy in the 1960s and 1970s when alternative schools were attracting considerable attention in the United States and Canada as an expression of the counterculture, magnet schools were an opportunity for some to bring fresh thinking into the mainstream of public education.

Differences among public schools had (correctly) been seen as the cause of unequal educational opportunity between, for example, schools attended by Black and White pupils, or schools in metropolitan and rural areas. The development of magnet schools as precisely a strategy to promote educational equity, and their notable success in providing good education in urban contexts, changed the perception of what school distinctiveness could mean. This prepared the way for the adoption of legislation authorizing charter schools, beginning in the early 1990s, and to the more recent openness to a whole range of new ways of providing and organizing education. What magnet schools failed to accomplish, however, was a significant reduction of the racial isolation of American schools.

Charles L. Glenn

See also Charter Schools; Desegregation/Integration; School Choice; School Climate

Further Readings

Glenn, C. L. (1991). Controlled choice in Massachusetts public schools. *The Public Interest, 103,* 88–105.

Metz, M. H. (2003). *Different by design: The context and character of three magnet schools.* New York: Teachers College Press.

Rossell, C. H. (1992). *The carrot or the stick for school desegregation policy: Magnet schools or forced busing.* Philadelphia: Temple University Press.

Smrekar, C., & Goldring, E. B. (1999). *School choice in urban America: Magnet schools and the pursuit of equity.* New York: Teachers College Press.

MAINSTREAMING

The concept of "mainstreaming" was developed in the mid-1980s as an initial attempt to provide access to general education. Mainstreaming can be defined as the process of transferring students who are being served in separate special education classrooms into general education classrooms, on the basis of two criteria. Criteria for mainstreaming individuals with disabilities were (1) academic achievement at or near grade level requiring little accommodation or support and (2) behavior that was manageable with minimal supports. The concept of mainstreaming created an educational reform movement referred to as the Regular Education Initiative of the mid-1980s. This reform led in turn to the inclusion movement of the mid-1990s. This entry discusses the history and development of mainstreaming, the movement from mainstreaming to inclusive practices, the difference between mainstreaming and inclusion, and issues related to the field of education maintaining a mainstreaming mind-set.

History of Mainstreaming

The Education for All Handicapped Children Act of 1975, later reauthorized as the Individuals with Disabilities Education Act (IDEA), was the seminal law giving students with disabilities access to public school. Prior to the passage of IDEA, students with disabilities were not guaranteed access to public education. State policies could deny access. IDEA created the first inclusive education movement for individuals with disabilities by allowing those individuals access to public school campuses. Although the law mandated that students be educated in the least restrictive environment, in practice many students with disabilities were limited to primarily physical access to the public school campus and facilities. Segregated classes for students

with disabilities were the primary means of service at that time in the public school setting.

In 1986, Madeleine Will, former assistant secretary of education, introduced the Regular Education Initiative. Will proposed that a separate system to educate students with primarily mild to moderate disabilities out of the "mainstream" of general education was limiting the educational achievements and experiences of those students. By constructing special education programs for students with disabilities that were distinct from general education programs, students with disabilities were excluded from participation in general education. Lack of efficacy data supporting greater academic gains by students with disabilities in separate programs supported this movement. The Regular Education Initiative was a call for reform of both special education and general education systems. The Regular Education Initiative was launched as an educational movement to have general education teachers assume more responsibility for the education of students with disabilities. The Regular Education Initiative proposed that general education and special education teachers cooperate to return students with disabilities to the mainstream of general education. It supported a merger between the educational systems of special education and general education.

From Mainstreaming to Inclusion

Historically, mainstreaming primarily focused on returning students with mild to moderate disabilities back to general education classrooms. The opportunity to go to general education for all or part of the day was perceived as an "earned" privilege. As mentioned previously, two criteria were considered before selecting a student for the opportunity of mainstreaming: (1) The student's levels of progress needed to be at or near peers and (2) the student's behavior must not be disruptive to the general education class. These readiness criteria meant that students with mild disabilities were most often the only students selected for the mainstream. This left students with significant disabilities no opportunities for accessing the general curriculum. Because of that lack of opportunity to ever be included, the concept of inclusion in education was born. Parents of students with significant disabilities led the movement for inclusive educational practices for students with any level of disability. The practice of mainstreaming did not adequately apply to individuals with significant disabilities and did not convey permanent membership in general education to students with mild to moderate disabilities. It is for this reason that the terms *mainstreaming* and *inclusion* mean two different things.

Differences Between Mainstreaming and Inclusion

The concept of inclusive education grew out of the concept of mainstreaming. Both concepts have at their foundation the idea of providing access to general education for students with disabilities. This similarity has confounded many in the field of education. Some educators see the terms *mainstreaming* and *inclusion* as interchangeable. Other educators view them as completely different concepts. Whereas conceptually the terms may represent similar ideas, in practice they seem to have clear differences.

As stated earlier, mainstreaming is viewed most frequently as an earned privilege. REI advanced the idea that if students could progress in the general education curriculum, they should be allowed to participate. Selected students that were able to perform at an academic level at or near their peers and were able to self-manage or require little teacher management of behavior were allowed to "go out" into general education classrooms. Students who had strengths in academic areas such as math, science, social studies, or English/language arts might be eligible for mainstreaming in those areas. Students who needed to address social goals might be eligible to participate in special areas like art, physical education, or music. If students fell too far behind their peers or their behavior caused classroom disruptions, they were returned to the special education classroom. Because privileges that are earned can also be lost, students who were placed into the mainstream might be placed there temporarily. In addition, students' real membership remained with the special education setting. The special education teacher maintained the primary responsibility of planning, adapting, delivering, and evaluating most of students' instruction.

Inclusion is a very different practice. In inclusive settings, there are no eligibility criteria. The general education teacher has primary responsibility for the students with disabilities in his or her classroom. Students with disabilities are members of the general education classroom in the same way as are students without disabilities. Students with disabilities would not be removed from the general education classroom for failure to make progress. Instead, additional supports or instructional methods would be applied to accommodate the student's needs within that setting. If changes in behavior occur, students would not be removed unless they posed a threat to themselves or to other students or in the event that the behavior caused consistent disruption to the academic progress of others. Instead of removal, assessments, such as a functional behavior assessment, would be performed to determine additional supports necessary to continue a student's participation in the general education classroom. Mainstreaming is primarily centered on altering the student to fit the environment. Inclusive practices are centered on altering the environment to fit the student's needs.

In addition to a student's supports and services being delivered in the general education environment, inclusive settings include an expectation of student participation and progress. In each general education setting, specific learning outcomes for student achievement are identified. The student's inclusion in a general education setting is for meaningful activities that promote academic and social growth. There is an expectation of reciprocity: The student gains something from the general education setting and also contributes something to the general education setting. This expectation of reciprocal engagement is another defining difference between inclusion and mainstreaming.

Working in a Mainstreaming World and Calling It Inclusion

Because professionals may use mainstreaming and inclusion interchangeably in practice, some confusion may exist in implementation. Current works on inclusive practices report that schools often include students with disabilities (a) intermittently rather than consistently in general education classrooms, (b) without establishing or maintaining appropriate supports or services, and (c) without clear learning priorities identified for the general education setting. Schools report that students may not be ready for inclusive settings. This supports the remaining influence of the readiness model embedded in mainstreaming. When students are intermittently included or are returned to special education teachers because they are having a bad day or do not want to complete their work, the influence of mainstreaming is seen again in temporary membership. On the surface, discussion regarding differences between mainstreaming and inclusion may seem to be arguments of word choice. The differences between the two, however, are evident in practice. It is for this reason that discussion of the practice of mainstreaming and inclusion is likely to continue.

K. Alisa Lowrey

See also Federal Educational Reform; Inclusion; Individualized Education Program; Individuals with Disabilities Education Act (IDEA); Special Needs Education

Further Readings

Lewis, R. B., & Doorlang, D. H. (2003). *Teaching special students in general education classrooms* (6th ed.). Upper Saddle River, NJ: Merrill Prentice Hall.

Lipskey, D. K., & Gartner, A. (1997). *Inclusion and school reform: Transforming America's classrooms.* Baltimore: Brookes.

Salend, S. J. (2005). *Creating inclusive classrooms: Effective and reflective practices for all students* (5th ed.). Upper Saddle River, NJ: Merrill Prentice Hall.

Will, M. (1986). Educating children with learning problems: A shared responsibility. *Exceptional Children, 52,* 411–415.

MANAGEMENT BY OBJECTIVES

First promoted as a concept by Peter Drucker in his 1954 book *The Practice of Management*, management by objectives is the process undertaken within an organization to create consensus around an organization's objectives and goals. Through this process, management and employees agree to the content of their work and understand what their respective roles and goals for this work are within the organization. This process underpins the foundational assumptions within the world of schools

through the constructs of accountability, backward design, data-driven decision making, evidence-based assessment, learning organizations, laws such as the No Child Left Behind (NCLB) reform, school improvement plans, and the standards movement. This entry reviews how objectives are created; explains how this process of management by objectives translates into the world of education; and identifies some of the challenges, unique to educational institutions, when employing this process.

The objectives, or *learning outcomes* as they are referred to in education, are set either in a collaborative fashion between management and staff or are set by management and then communicated to staff. Within either process—be it collaborative or top-down, for the objectives to be meaningful they must be "SMART." Smart goals were first popularized through Drucker's aforementioned work and transported to education through the work of Robert Eaker and Richard and Rebecca DuFour. Smart objectives must adhere to the following criteria: S = specific, M = measurable, A = achievable, R = relevant, and T = time specific. In recent iterations of these SMART principles, most notably developed in 2002 by Eaker and the DuFours in their response to the NCLB accountability measures, many educational institutions have adopted the notion of "SMARTER" objectives, with the E = extendable (to acknowledge the need for continuous improvement in the face of a changing reality) and R = recorded (to acknowledge the need for documentation of progress and accountability).

Any organization, whether in business or in education, constructs its management by objectives process through a three-step procedure. In 1975 C. P. Heaton, editor of *Management by Objectives in Higher Education: Theory, Cases and Implementation* described this method as one that involves (1) having the institution's constituents define its central purpose and goals, (2) requiring all personnel to mutually determine and agree upon their responsibility in achieving these goals, and (3) necessitating each individual to establish his or her own performance criteria. Peter Senge, in his 1990 book *The Fifth Discipline: The Art and Practice of the Learning Organization*, stresses that if the objectives are to be meaningful, there is a critical need for this process to be one that is collaborative and reflective of the culture of the school and its constituents.

In particular, Senge stresses that in order for these objectives to truly facilitate school improvement for all learners, the objectives must be created in a fashion that acknowledges the realities of what educators hope schools to accomplish. In order for schools to be true learning communities, the creation of such objectives or standards must foster the following attributes: (a) the creation of norms of continuous critical inquiry, (b) the promotion of norms of continuous improvement, (c) the facilitation of a widely shared vision for what all children can achieve, and (d) the empowering of all constituents to act in a manner that requires all to be involved in the decision-making process.

In their 2005 book, Grant Wiggins and Jay McTighe have developed a structure for creating these central objectives for an educational institution through a process called "understanding by design." Within this procedure for creating objectives, the following steps are undertaken. First, the objective or outcome is established. This demands that there is consensus on what needs to be learned. Then, from this outcome, educators decide how to measure the attainment of said outcome. Finally, the process for teaching this outcome is aligned with the assessment. This ensures that what is being taught aligns with the assessment, which in turn, aligns with the desired student outcome that drives the attainment of the objective in the first place. It is considered "backward" because the educator starts with the end in mind—the objective—and works backward from there to create meaningful assessments and learning opportunities for goal attainment for all students.

In today's schools, the process of creating objectives and the documentation of the progress made toward these objectives can be found in the school improvement plan. The school improvement plan codifies the school's envisioned improvement design and publicizes these objectives, and subsequent outcomes, to the consumers (taxpayers) at large. The school improvement plan details the process and objectives that all students will experience and eventually master, the accountability instruments that will measure progress toward these objectives, and finally, development or remediation measures that will be used if these objectives are not met. These aforementioned accountability measures have led to the practice of high-stakes accountability measures that are reported through the NCLB federal reporting requirements. However, unlike

the world of business where achievement, or the lack thereof, of objectives is tied to individual monetary bonuses or demotions, within the world of education, rewards and punishments are tied to positive school recognition or school failure status. Unlike any other educational reform measure of its time, NCLB, with its publicized adequate yearly progress–monitoring scores, brings a level of sanctions to school personnel, and sometimes to individual children, heretofore not known within the world of schools.

Management by objectives relies on the assumption that educational institutions are rational, orderly systems where cause and effect can be specifically linked to one another. Specifically, management by objectives assumes that if an educator defines the objectives and then plans a course of action for obtaining these objectives, the data will articulate the successes and failures of the implementation of the said plan. However, many critics of this "rational-systems" approach to education (e.g., Michael Fullan and Senge) speak to the "messiness" and "culturally constructed nature" of educational organizations that exist within a volatile external environment rendering a simple cause–effect relationship between school objectives and outcomes to be an inadequate portrayal of the complex human processes that constitute an educational system. In other words, education is often a messy, nonrational, and nonsequential process making the cause–effect relationship between objectives and outcomes difficult to attribute to a single process or system. Furthermore, critics of management by objectives as a process for establishing and measuring fidelity of student achievement outcomes note that such a process renders educational outcomes as static points on a mastery scale lacking a depth of comprehensiveness as to what it truly means to learn and be educated.

Marla Susman Israel

See also Accountability Era; Evidence-Based Education (EBE); High-Stakes Testing; No Child Left Behind Act (NCLB); Performance-Based Assessment; Standards Movement

Further Readings

Drucker, P. F. (1954). *The practice of management.* New York: Harper & Brothers.

Eaker, R., DuFour, R. P., & DuFour, R. B. (2002). *Getting started: Reculturing schools to become professional learning communities*. Bloomington, IN: National Education Service.

Fullan, M. (2001). *Leading in a culture of change*. San Francisco: Jossey-Bass.

Heaton, C. P. (Ed.). (1975). *Management by objectives in higher education*. Durham, NC: National Laboratory for Higher Education.

Senge, P. (2000). *Schools that learn: A fifth discipline fieldbook for educators, parents and everyone who cares about education*. New York: Warner.

Wiggins, G., & McTighe, J. (2005). *Understanding by design* (2nd ed.). Alexandria, VA: Association for Supervision and Curriculum Development.

MANN, HORACE (1796–1859)

Among the dozens of men and women who promoted the "common school" as the most important solution to the problems facing American society in the decades before the Civil War, Horace Mann was then and remains the best known. He was not an educator but a lawyer and politician and, above all, a superb publicist for the idea that education, rightly organized, could have an almost magical effect on individuals and on society.

Born in Franklin, Massachusetts, Mann was educated haphazardly and then at Brown University and as a lawyer at Litchfield Law School. While serving in the state legislature he became active in various social reforms of the period. With the establishment of the state board of education in 1837, Mann was appointed its secretary, a position which he occupied until 1848, when he replaced John Quincy Adams in Congress. From 1853 to his death, he served as first president of Antioch College in Ohio. His appointment as secretary of the board of education was a tribute to his political skills rather than to any previous leadership in education, but Mann quickly made himself an eloquent spokesman for currently discussed ideas, derived ultimately from the Swiss educator Johann Pestalozzi and reinforced by the vogue for phrenology, about how to give schooling a more powerful effect.

Though his new position had little authority over local school districts, they were required to submit statistical reports in order to receive state funding, and Mann made powerful use of this information in his *Annual Reports,* which were read far beyond Massachusetts and indeed beyond the United States. Through these and through his *Common School Journal,* Mann made himself the most influential spokesman for the emerging program of the common public school. Typically, when a group of New England businessmen settled in New Orleans wanted to establish a public school system, they turned to Mann to recommend one of his allies to become its superintendent.

The problem that Mann identified was not a lack of schooling—Massachusetts had long been one of the best-schooled areas in the world—but lack of system and coordination in a state with hundreds of local communities, each in complete control of its school or schools.

In an address Mann delivered in 1837, he discussed the concern of having nearly 3,000 schools, all teaching the fundamentals of education and at the same time all being self-governed and independent of any coordinated oversight. He advocated for a state governance structure, such as a state superintendent of schools, which would provide support and evaluation of the local schools. He set out, within his limited authority, to make himself that superintending power, with a concern for all the details of pedagogy and of organization, in each of which he was able to find great moral significance.

One of his immediate concerns was the great diversity of schoolbooks in use, which he argued would cause cynicism about the very possibility of truth. Although he would always deny any desire to impose his own Whig and Unitarian views, in fact Mann had a strong tendency to doubt the sincerity of any who differed with him. By creating a library of schoolbooks approved by the board (effectively, by Mann himself) and recommended to local school committees, he sought to ensure that only ideas he thought worthy would be presented in schools. One of the controversies that bedeviled his administration arose when he refused to approve the schoolbooks of the American Sunday School Union for school use, because they conflicted with his own Unitarian beliefs.

In his *First Annual Report* (1837), Mann stressed what would become a central theme: Through the community school, a common friendship should be produced between the students and the local vicinity. It is here, in the local community, that the common bonds of friendship should unite the children and community so as to take advantage of the stability that the neighborhood provides yet prepares the children for their future lives. It was on the basis of this role of the common school in breaking down social barriers that Mann was fiercely opposed to private schools with a religious character; he accused them of teaching children the practice of arguing passionately for their cause. On the other hand, he conceded that parents with strong concerns about education were justified in continuing to make use of private schools until the common schools were of equivalent quality.

What seems most striking today about Mann is his almost unlimited confidence in what the common school could accomplish. In his *Tenth Annual Report* (1847), Mann assured the public that the establishment of the free public schools was the boldest policy ever promulgated and one almost unique to New England. In his *Twelfth Annual Report* (1849), summing up his labors for the previous dozen years, he promised that the common school would become the most successful of all the forces in the world. Under the common school's influence, all people would seek a loftier status, be better prepared for the future, and be better able to achieve the tasks and withstand the burdens of life. Social class distinctions would fade away. He assured the reader that this was not mere speculation; the moral effects of the common school would be as predictable as a scientific experiment. But this experiment of free schooling had by no means yet been tried. Mann continued, stating that schooling had in no way yet been brought to bear with a fraction of its impending power, in the preparation of students, and, through them, upon the dispositions of people.

To achieve such schooling, however, it was essential to have better-prepared teachers. He wrote eloquently in his *Fourth Annual Report* (1840) about the intellectual and moral qualifications of an effective teacher, and he was able to obtain private and public funding to establish the first public "normal schools" in the United States to train teachers.

The influence of Mann's eloquent reports was felt far beyond Massachusetts. They were read and cited in European debates on education policy, and Diego Sarmiento, later, president of Argentina, was a great admirer and would-be imitator of Mann's work. On the other hand, he attracted considerable opposition, including an effort by Democrats in the state legislature in 1840, which almost succeeded in abolishing the Massachusetts Board of Education and thus his position, as well as the normal schools he had created. The legislative committee, matching Mann's own hyperbole, warned that surrendering control of education to the government would destroy the usefulness of the common schools and would be fatal to religious liberty and political freedom. Mann insisted that what he called "the pure religion of heaven" was at the core of his program for the common school, which was the surest means of preparing loyal citizens.

Charles L. Glenn

See also Alliance for the Separation of School & State; Common School Movement; Community Control; Cubberley, Ellwood; Normal Schools; Old Deluder Satan Law; Pestalozzianism; Religion and the Curriculum; State Departments of Education

Further Readings

Cremin, L. (Ed.). (1957). *The republic and the school: Horace Mann on the education of free men.* New York: Teachers College Press.
Cremin, L. (1980). *American education: The national experience, 1783–1876.* New York: Harper & Row.
Culver, R. B. (1929). *Horace Mann and religion in the Massachusetts public schools.* New Haven, CT: Yale University Press.
Glenn, C. L. (1988). *The myth of the common school.* Amherst: University of Massachusetts Press.
Messerli, J. (1972). *Horace Mann: A biography.* New York: Knopf.

MANUAL TRAINING

Manual training garnered great appeal in America's public schools from 1870 to 1900. Although attempts at manual training in schools stretch back to Antebellum America, it was not until the need arose for a skilled workforce in the industrial economy that there was widespread support for such an educational reform. Nevertheless, the economic impact of manual training was secondary to reformers who were most concerned with the social breakdown of values surrounding family and work. Proponents argued that manual training made education relevant and practical, a way to educate the mind through the hand while developing a moral character for work. Accordingly, manual training offered a pedagogical reform that promised to enlarge the intellectual and moral enterprise of schools and prepare youth with habits of industriousness.

The Promise of Manual Training

The introduction of manual training in America occurred at the 1876 Philadelphia Centennial Exhibition where the Moscow Imperial Training School showcased its model of engendering hand–eye coordination through instruction in basic tool techniques. The goal was not to produce goods but to teach skills that could be transferred to myriad trades such as woodworking and metalworking. Manual training was first implemented by engineering faculty at Massachusetts Institute of Technology to improve the preparation of future engineers by focusing on practical skills in carpentry and mechanics; it became popularized for use in the public schools through advocates within the National Education Association.

As an intellectual enterprise, proponents argued, manual training merited a place in education because it promised to enhance and diversify the existing curriculum. It emphasized the practical aspect of hand–eye coordination and taught students observation, judgment, accuracy, and dexterity through learning by doing. Additionally, it was a moral enterprise aimed at preserving the traditional values of dignity and respect for honest labor. Manual training promised to familiarize students with the drills of factory life but also to teach habits of industriousness, like punctuality and obedience. Hence, manual training ensured moral and social stability, which was appealing to tradition-minded educators and the public alike. As proponents laid their focus on the educational value of the reform, the economic value of training a future workforce was also heralded. As students received instruction in manual skills, the principles learned were to be transferable to later occupations. Although the emphasis was on training the mind, an ambiguous line was drawn between practical skill building and preparation for a trade.

The pedagogical justification for manual training was based on active learning. Kindergarten innovations around learning by doing, object teaching through the use of tangible items rather than abstractions, and laboratory learning focused on participation and experimentation laid the pedagogical groundwork. Proponents argued that learning by doing augmented the traditional passive learning of textbooks and recitations. Thus, manual training represented a rearrangement of the curriculum that focused equally on mental and hand training, where younger children would focus on skill acquisition with chisels, hammers, and needles, and older students would focus on workshop and domestic trades.

Support for Manual Training

As manual training was introduced, several competing rationales supported its progress. The ideas of enriching the common school curriculum, instilling respect for the dignity of work and family, and bringing industry into the classroom became issues of tension among supporters and critics. Nonetheless, educators could not afford to fall behind in educational innovation and progressive thought, so manual training expanded greatly even though the justification for the reform was widely debated. One of the biggest debates was around its curricular purpose: Was it to expand or shrink occupational opportunities? This question was answered in the varied practices of manual training and in the rationale for its use.

One of the trademark schools in manual training was Calvin Woodward's Manual Training School for boys in St. Louis. Woodward sought to meet the demand of the industrial age by melding common school education and manual training. He believed learning the practical use of tools would increase educational interest, provide intellectual and moral education, and restore the significance and dignity of physical labor.

While educators and philanthropists were quick to note the intellectual role of manual training in education, the need for moral rehabilitation and renewal was often asserted to justify its use for the immigrant working class, African Americans, Mexican Americans, and Native Americans. These groups were seen as well-suited for manual training, in accordance with popular mainstream beliefs about their economic and psychological differences. While manual training was embraced for these groups before the Civil War, in the age of industrialization it was primarily seen as a logical socializing agent for correcting defects in character. By and large, boys were trained in masonry, carpentry, farming, and blacksmithing, whereas girls were trained in sewing and cooking. The emphasis for girls' training was predicated on preparing them for domestic duties and promoting household tranquility.

As manual training spread, educators found implementation of this reform extremely costly, as new tools, equipment, and spaces were required. The success of developing a program depended on contributions from outside the school, which manual training found in industry and among philanthropists who aimed at making schools useful to society. Business owners saw schools as the perfect training ground for industrial skills and attitudes, whereas philanthropists tended to downplay the vocational implications of manual training, touting family and home benefits.

Move to Vocational Education

Critics of manual training attacked the reform not only as a waste of time and money but also as a diversion from the intellectual studies of common school education. One of the strongest critics of manual training was William Torrey Harris, an advocate of humanities education, who assailed manual training as overly focused on preparing students for passé trades that had no vocational or intellectual value. He charged manual training as a superficial reform that undermined and detracted from the intellectual and moral purpose of education. Others deemed manual training an educational frill that served to limit students' futures to physical and domestic labor, rather than broaden opportunities as proponents had argued. Furthermore, schools were criticized for allowing special interest groups to use schools as a means of correcting industrial and social ills. Yet, as the criticisms mounted against manual training, interest in vocational education for specific industrial trades increased. At the turn of the century, manual training moved from complementing the existing curriculum and pursuing moral ends to laying the groundwork for vocationalizing the American

education system—the idea that every subject must hold an occupational utility to meet the needs of the economy.

Sylvia L. M. Martinez

See also Common School Movement; Harris, William Torrey; Moral Development; Philanthropy in Education; Progressive Education; Vocational Education

Further Readings

Kantor, H. A. (1998). *Learning to earn: School, work, and vocational reform in California, 1880–1930*. Madison: University of Wisconsin Press.

Kliebard, H. M. (1999). *Schooled to work: Vocationalism and the American curriculum, 1876–1946*. New York: Teachers College Press.

Lazerson, M. (1971). *Origins of the urban school: Public education in Massachusetts, 1870–1915*. Cambridge, MA: Harvard University Press.

Love, S. G. (1887). *Industrial education: A guide to manual training*. New York: Kellog.

MARSHALL, THURGOOD (1908–1993)

Thurgood Marshall was a civil rights lawyer and later U.S. Supreme Court associate justice. He was known for his high success rate in cases he argued before the U.S. Supreme Court, most notably *Brown v. Board of Education of Topeka*, which declared school segregation unconstitutional. The first African American to serve on the Supreme Court, Marshall compiled a liberal record that included support for abortion rights, affirmative action, court-ordered school desegregation, and opposition to the death penalty.

Marshall was born in Baltimore in 1908. He graduated from the historically Black Lincoln University in Pennsylvania but was discouraged from applying to the University of Maryland Law School because of his race. He attended Howard University Law School, where he studied with the new dean, Charles Hamilton Houston. It was Houston's contention that the key to civil rights for African Americans lay in the development of a cadre of well-trained African American lawyers who could methodically assault segregation and discrimination as enshrined in the 1896 *Plessy v. Ferguson* decision, which was used as the basis of legalized segregation in virtually all areas of public life by means of a doctrine of "separate but equal" facilities, opportunities, and access.

In 1934, the National Association for the Advancement of Colored People (NAACP) hired Houston as its special counsel. Upon graduating from law school that year, Marshall joined with Houston in what would be Marshall's first civil rights case, *Murray v. Pearson,* in which the same University of Maryland Law School that had not admitted Marshall was ordered by a state court to admit a Black student. Houston and Marshall won, but the state chose not to appeal the case, which meant that the effects of the decision would not go beyond the state of Maryland.

In 1936, when Marshall joined the NAACP as assistant special counsel, education became the prime target as he and Houston sought cases that could be used to overturn Jim Crow laws. They began to file suits as part of their new Public Education Initiative, a strategic plan that sought equal pay for White and Black teachers with similar qualifications, equality of buildings and equipment, equal per capita funding and expenditure for Blacks and Whites, and equality in graduate and professional training.

In 1945, no southern state university offered the Ph.D. degree for African Americans. There were 37 engineering schools for Whites and none for Blacks, and 2 law schools and 2 medical schools for Blacks, whereas there were 29 White-only law schools and 20 public medical schools that only trained Whites. Therefore, as the NAACP determined its legal strategy, graduate and professional schools were targeted because there was little chance that states could claim that separate but equal schools existed. The hope was that the prohibitive cost of creating new Jim Crow schools would force southern states into integrating their graduate schools. Marshall successfully argued for the integration of the law schools at the Universities of Oklahoma and Texas before the U.S. Supreme Court in *Sipuel v. University of Oklahoma* (1948) and *Sweatt v. Painter* (1950), respectively. Also, Marshall, whose mother had been a schoolteacher, filed successful suits over unequal teacher salaries in virtually every southern state between 1936 and 1944.

There was a greater impatience with Jim Crow and an increased willingness to challenge segregation among African Americans after World War II. African Americans who had risked all fighting for their country were justifiably dissatisfied with the segregation they found upon returning home. As the military, professional baseball, and other areas of American public life began to be integrated, the NAACP policy of litigating cases to force states into creating schools that were separate but equal in terms of quality was being called into question. In September 1947, Marshall began a direct assault on segregated public schools rather than continuing the attempt to break the states by forcing them to strictly enforce the doctrine of separate but equal as enshrined in *Plessy.*

Five cases were put together for the Supreme Court in 1952 that were intended to challenge segregation in public schools, one of which was *Brown v. Board of Education of Topeka.* Using the research of social psychologist Dr. Kenneth Clark, Marshall argued that segregation not only violated the Fourteenth Amendment but that it also had the debilitating effect of causing stigmatic psychological injury to African American children. In the unanimous decision handed down on May 17, 1954, Chief Justice Earl Warren incorporated the psychological argument into the decision. *Plessy v. Ferguson* was reversed, segregated schools were declared unconstitutional, and the next year the court ordered that all schools be integrated "with all deliberate speed."

Brown was met with massive resistance in the South and led to violence and the formation of White Citizens' Council to prevent integration. African Americans responded with the nonviolent resistance movement that began with Rosa Parks and the Montgomery bus boycott. In November 1956, Marshall won the case of *Browder v. Gale* in which the Supreme Court upheld a lower court ruling that declared segregated buses unconstitutional.

In September 1957, Arkansas Governor Orville Faubus attempted to halt a city plan to integrate Little Rock's Central High School by ordering 300 National Guardsmen to prevent Black students from entering the school. Eventually, President Dwight D. Eisenhower had to send regular army troops into the city to protect the Black students. In September 1958, the Supreme Court declared *Brown* to be "the law of the land" in *Cooper v.*

Aaron, which Marshall argued on behalf of the parents of Little Rock's Black students.

In 1961, President John Kennedy named Marshall to the U.S. Court of Appeals for the Second Circuit. In 1965, President Lyndon Johnson named Marshall solicitor general; from this position he was able to see the *Brown* mandate broadened, and he successfully defended the constitutionality of Johnson's 1964 Civil Rights Act and the 1965 Voting Rights Act.

In 1967, Johnson nominated Marshall for the U.S. Supreme Court. More than a decade after *Brown,* there still was little desegregation in the South, and the Court abandoned the vague notion of "deliberate speed." In *Green v. County School Board, New Kent County, Virginia* and *Alexander v. Holmes County, Mississippi,* the Court ordered immediate desegregation. In *Swann v. Mecklenburg, N.C. Board of Education,* the Court ruled unanimously that federal court judges had broad powers to order busing to integrate schools. Busing became an integral part of desegregation efforts throughout the nation in the 1970s. In *Milliken v. Bradley,* however, Marshall wrote an emotional dissent. In a 5–3 decision the Supreme Court reversed a lower court ruling that the largely White Detroit suburbs should be integrated with the predominantly Black Detroit city schools.

In several affirmative action cases involving education, Marshall consistently held the position that the Constitution had never been color blind, and that set asides and other attempts at racial remediation should be viewed as efforts to include rather than to exclude. In *Regents of the University of California v. Bakke,* the divided high Court upheld a lower court ruling that the practice of reserving 16 seats for economically or educationally disadvantaged students was unconstitutional, but the Court also said that race could be taken into account in setting admission policy. After *Bakke,* the Court validated 7 of 10 cases involving race-conscious affirmative action plans.

With his health in decline and a growing conservative majority on the bench, Marshall found himself writing more and more dissents as the years went on, including *Wygant v. Jackson Board of Education,* in which the majority decision said that despite the fact that most of the Black teachers in the district were the last hired because of relatively recent affirmative action hiring initiatives, the school district could not use race as a factor in determining layoffs.

Seriously ill, Marshall retired from the Court in 1991. He died in 1993 at age 84 in Bethesda, Maryland.

John J. White

See also Affirmative Action; *Brown v. Board of Education*; De Facto Segregation; De Jure Segregation; Desegregation/Integration; *Milliken v. Bradley*; Race- and Ethnic-Based Schooling; Racism

Further Readings

Ball, H. (1996). *A defiant life: Thurgood Marshall and the persistence of racism in America.* New York: Crown.

Bland, R. W. (2001). *Justice Thurgood Marshall, crusader for liberalism: His judicial biography.* Bethesda, MD: Academica.

Williams, J. (1998). *Thurgood Marshall: American revolutionary.* New York: Random House.

MASLOW, ABRAHAM (1908–1970)

Abraham H. Maslow founded a humanistic movement in psychology in the late 1950s that placed significant value on individuality, creativity, and personal freedom as essential factors contributing to mental health and general well-being. Along with his colleagues Rollo May and Carl Rogers, Maslow created the Association of Humanistic Psychology, whose members shared an appreciation of the worth and dignity of all persons. This humanistic movement was referred to as the "third wave" in psychology because its theoretical constructs varied so greatly from Freudian psychoanalysis and Skinnerian behaviorism, which were the two dominant trends in psychology during the 1950s. Today the influence of humanistic psychology extends far beyond the discipline of psychology itself and informs many areas of mainstream culture, including education.

Although Maslow acknowledged his admiration of Freudian psychoanalysis, his own view of human nature varied greatly from Sigmund Freud's. Maslow thought Freud's theory was unnecessarily pessimistic with respect to our human potential for decency and kindness. He disagreed strongly with

Freud's contention that we are essentially selfish beings, with little real regard for others. Freud's view of human nature portrayed human potential as a fight to keep our baser instincts in check. Maslow, by contrast, believed that we are capable of becoming fully human through a process of self-actualization. Maslow conceded that we do not always show our most fully human side; indeed, we often act without dignity and respect toward our fellow brothers and sisters. But Maslow believed that such reactions were due to extenuating circumstances such as stress, pain, and the lack of basic physical needs such as food and shelter. Beneath those needs lay a core of decent and good human values, which could be brought to the surface when our basic needs were met.

Maslow's commitment to the full development of human potential was centrally concerned with the psychological constructs of self-actualization and self-esteem. Unlike the psychoanalysts and behaviorists who both rejected the notion of free will, Maslow placed strong value on an understanding of human life as both spiritual and intuitive. He studied the lives of persons he believed best exemplified the fullest account of human potential, such as Albert Einstein, Jane Addams, Eleanor Roosevelt, and Frederick Douglass. This methodology represented a significant shift away from Freud, who had studied mentally ill and neurotic people to formulate his theory of human nature, and B. F. Skinner, who had conducted most of his studies regarding human psychology with laboratory mice. Both Freud and Skinner had observed very little difference between the motivation of humans and animals, despite their respectively varied conclusions regarding the prognosis for optimal human development. By contrast, Maslow's studies signaled a humanistic approach to developmental psychology that regarded humans and animals as vastly different with respect to motivation theory.

Maslow's most renowned work in motivational theory is his development of a hierarchy of needs and information that culminated in the most fully human construct of self-actualization. Maslow's hierarchy plays a significant role in teachings in management and educational leadership. At the lowest rung of his hierarchy were the most basic physiological needs such as food, water, sex, and sleep; these needs were not distinctly human insofar as they were shared with all living creatures. Beyond the basic physiological needs were safety needs such as the need to feel secure and protected from danger, and the need to have structure and order in one's daily interactions with the community.

The third rung of Maslow's hierarchy was the need for love and a sense of belongingness; the lack of satisfaction at this level of need would inevitably result in isolation and alienation of one's self from both family and society. The need for love and belongingness could be fulfilled by a combination of close friends, strong identification with group affiliations, intimate relationships, and a supportive family. However, Maslow believed that the lack of fulfillment at this level of the hierarchy was best evidenced by major social problems he identified as contributing to the countercultural movement in the 1960s.

The fourth rung of Maslow's hierarchy was the need for esteem, which has been closely aligned with Erik Erikson's need for generativity and the desire to engage in creative and useful activities Lack of fulfillment at this level would negatively impact one's self-concept as a responsible citizen and a productive member of society. Each of these four categories of needs was essential in order to achieve the highest level of human development, which Maslow called *self-actualization*. The characteristics of the self-actualized person are myriad, and include a resistance to acculturation, an acceptance of self and others, and a need for privacy.

In addition to his substantial work in motivation theory, Maslow conducted the first American studies on human sexuality, several years before Alfred Kinsey. He interviewed women whom he labeled as high dominance or low dominance with respect to their sexual preferences. He defined high dominance as the possession of strong levels of aggression and self-confidence, and he found that high-dominance women were mostly attracted to men who were highly masculine and self-assured. Low-dominance women were defined as strongly maternalistic and nurturing, and were attracted to men whom they described as kind and gentle and possessing a strong love for family values. The influence of Abraham Maslow's body of work continues to be of tremendous value for humanistic psychologists today as well as in management and education teachings.

Monalisa Mullins

See also Behaviorism; Moral Development; Social Efficiency; Social Reconstructionism

Further Readings

Bridges, W. (2004). *Transitions: Making sense of life's changes*. New York: De Capo Press.

DeCarvalho, R. (1991). *The founders of humanistic psychology*. New York: Praeger.

Maslow, A. H. (1954). *Motivation and personality*. New York: Harper & Bros.

Maslow, A. H. (1968). *Toward a psychology of being*. New York: Wiley.

MASTERY LEARNING

Mastery learning is a nontraditional instructional approach that can be traced to Benjamin Bloom's learning for mastery model. Mastery learning, was first introduced in American schools in the 1920s, with the work of Carleton Washburn. The plan grew for a few years; nevertheless, without the aid of technology to maintain the concept, expansion among developers and implementers progressively weakened. Mastery learning was revitalized in the form of programmed teaching and learning in the late 1950s in an effort to offer students instructional resources that would permit them to pro-gress at their own speed in addition to receiving continuous feedback on their specific level of mastery. The 1960s saw a resurgence with Bloom's learning for mastery ideas, which suggested that, given sufficient time and appropriate instruction, nearly all students could learn.

Bloom is considered the major theorist and supporter of the mastery learning approach. Bloom's instructional strategy, learning for mastery, was later shortened to mastery learning. He was interested in the effectiveness of individualized instruction and one-to-one tutoring as instructional approaches. Bloom built on the ideas of John B. Carroll, who revived the concept in the early 1960s and who posited that student aptitude is a reflection of individual learning rate. Bloom believed that, by recognizing relevant individual differences among students and then adjusting instruction to meet their individual needs, achievement gaps between different groups of students could be closed and eventually disappear.

During the 1970s and 1980s many research studies on mastery learning were published; however, the research has declined since the 1980s. More recently, mastery learning has resurfaced in the context of computer-based learning and e-learning. It has also been linked to research and interest in outcome-based education.

A second model of mastery learning was developed by Fred Simmons Keller and is known as the personalized system of instruction. This model includes written materials for self-instruction as the major teaching activity, self-paced learning, demonstration of mastery before proceeding to new units, and instruction to address areas where mastery is not evident.

The approach is built on the premise that all students should succeed in learning new concepts and skills and that everyone can learn given the right circumstances.

Mastery learning requires a student to reach a level of predetermined mastery on instructional concepts and skills before progressing to the next instructional unit. While individual students may require differing amounts of time to master or learn content, all students are expected to achieve the same level of mastery through ordered steps. One fundamental principle of mastery learning is that 90% of students can learn what is normally taught in schools at an A level when given enough time to demonstrate mastery of objectives and appropriate instruction.

A mastery learning classroom is characterized by a variety of group instructional activities, frequent and specific feedback, diagnostic and formative assessments, and frequent correction of students' mistakes and misconceptions. Student success is measured through criterion-referenced tests to assess students' mastery of the identified concepts and skills. Student learning is largely dependent on the provision of adequate time and quality instruction provided by the teacher so all students can achieve the same level of learning. Teachers who use mastery learning provide frequent and specific corrective feedback to students, often through formative assessments.

Mastery learning requires the educator to identify major objectives and then divide the content into smaller learning units with identified objectives, expectations, and assessments. Learning materials and instructional strategies are identified.

Before instruction begins, a diagnostic assessment is given and results are used to guide decisions about instruction. Students work through each unit in an organized fashion, either independently or in groups. Bloom proposed at least two formative assessments should be administered during each instructional unit to determine what each student has or has not learned. Each instructional unit typically requires 1 to 2 weeks. The assessment for each student informs reteaching and continuing instruction. No student is permitted to proceed to new material until mastery of basic prerequisite material is demonstrated, typically at 80%. Students who do not achieve mastery receive remediation and additional individualized instruction through tutoring, peer monitoring, small group work, or individualized assignments with a variety of resources, including learning manipulatives, videos, textbooks, or guided practice activities. Students are expected to invest additional time until mastery is demonstrated on a second formative assessment. Only grades of A or B are considered acceptable levels of mastery. Those students who demonstrate mastery on the first formative assessment are expected to continue learning concepts through enrichment or extension activities. Students often choose an activity, game, or individual project based on interest or options provided by the teacher to pursue until the entire class can progress together.

Mastery learning is often implemented with students who struggle with basic skills and those considered slow learners. Proponents of mastery learning argue that if students have mastered the fundamental concepts and skills, less time should be required for mastery of more advanced materials. Additional studies suggest that mastery learning supports students' motivation, attitudes, and interest in learning.

Mastery learning does not focus on content, but on the process whereby content is presented. One challenge that must be addressed with mastery learning is the issue of time. Mastery learning is built on the concept that, with additional time, all students can master the content; however, most schools only allow students and educators a finite amount of time for instruction. Additionally, the structure and organization of many schools do not lend themselves to the mastery learning model. Mastery learning requires teachers to be competent in task analysis and instructional design. It also demands strong classroom management since all students will not progress at the same pace. The requirement of varied materials for reteaching, individual pacing, and alternate forms of assessments for each unit have been identified as obstacles to implementation of mastery learning. Critics have also questioned whether mastery learning promotes learning through memorization and basic comprehension rather than supporting higher levels of learning.

Beth Nason Quick

See also Assessment; Competency-Based Education; Cooperative Learning; Student Assessment and School Accountability; Testing-Students

Further Readings

Block, J. (1971). *Mastery learning: Theory and practice.* New York: Holt, Rinehart & Winston.

Bloom, B. (1968). Learning for mastery: Instruction and curriculum. *Evaluation Comment, 1*(2), 1–12.

Keller, F. S. (1968). "Good-bye teacher . . ." *Journal of Applied Behavior Analysis, 1,* 79–89.

Kulik, C., Kulik, J., & Bangert-Downs, R. (1990). Effectiveness of mastery learning programs: A meta-analysis. *Review of Educational Research, 60*(2), 265–306.

Slavin, R. E. (1987). Mastery learning reconsidered. *Review of Educational Research, 57*(2), 175–214.

McGUFFEY READERS

With over 122 million copies sold since 1838, the McGuffey Readers taught more Americans to read than any other textbook. Initial publication coincided with a unique period in U.S. history as the West was settled, newly arrived immigrants assimilated, and the common school movement gained momentum. At this time, the nation was at a critical point of forming a distinct identity. These phenomena created a demand for textbooks that would not only meet the practical need for curriculum in developing schools but also extend prevailing American values both to children new to the frontier and those new to the nation. In the emerging textbook industry, McGuffey Readers reformed the content of America's textbooks and how that content was presented to students.

William H. McGuffey was born in Pennsylvania in 1800 before his family moved to Ohio during his infancy. A prodigious child, he was issued a teaching certificate at 14 years of age and served as an itinerant teacher. He graduated from Washington College with a degree in ancient languages in 1826, was ordained as a Presbyterian minister 3 years later, and wrote his readers while teaching at Miami University in Oxford, Ohio. He continued to contribute to revisions of the readers while he was president of Cincinnati College and later when he returned to Miami University as president. However, in 1845 when he left Ohio to serve as professor of philosophy at the University of Virginia, his input into further editions ceased. The most popular edition was published in 1879, 6 years after his death. Although remembered primarily for his series of readers, McGuffey was also a popular professor and an outspoken advocate for the common school movement in Ohio and Virginia.

Origins and Early Editions

The success of the McGuffey Readers could be credited as much to the astute business tactics of Cincinnati publisher Winthrop B. Smith as to the authors and compilers themselves. Smith observed the dominance New England publishers held over the growing textbook industry and determined the need for a graded series of readers marketed to the burgeoning West and to the South. He first sought the assistance of Harriet Beecher Stowe, who declined his offer but recommended her friend William Holmes McGuffey. A professor and Presbyterian preacher, McGuffey had already begun work on such a project. Smith contracted him to compile a primer, four readers, and a speller. His compensation would be 10% of the profits not to exceed $1,000. Though a great sum at the time, it was not representative of the vast proceeds publishers brought in and hardly compensated McGuffey for the impact his work had on the nation.

The first and second readers were published in 1836 with the third and fourth following within the year. McGuffey had compiled and written the material to be age appropriate. To establish which material best suited particular ages, he experimented with his own children and those in the community, teaching them in his home as well as outdoors, seated on logs. Incorporating the element of competition, he reserved the largest end of the log for students who recited their lessons most accurately. He documented the effect of the content on various age groups and made necessary adjustments before submitting the final work. Typical in many ways of other graded readers of the time, the primer began with the alphabet and phonetically taught single-syllable words. Not as successful as the series that followed it, the primer was pulled from publication shortly after it was introduced. The content of the first reader moved on to more difficult words and introduced simple sentences. The second reader progressed to multi-syllabic words, and the stories grew more complex as the book progressed. Comparable to the level of junior high school material, the third and fourth readers taught thinking skills and included selections from authors such as Irving, Byron, Jefferson, and Shakespeare. Two particular characteristics made McGuffey's work distinct from other readers of the day. First, it included more illustrations than was common for schoolbooks at the time. Second, it was a complete language arts curriculum integrating spelling, speech, comprehension, and word studies.

A Question of Copyright

Though it was common for readers to include selections from various authors, the McGuffey Readers initially drew criticism from Samuel Worcester, a Boston author, for "over-imitation" of material. Citing 10 identical pieces in both his and McGuffey's readers, Worcester filed suit against McGuffey and his publishers for violation of copyright laws. Whether it was a legitimate case or not, the conflict reflected the intense rivalry between New England and Cincinnati publishers over the growing market for schoolbooks. Nevertheless, after only 2 years in print, the McGuffey Readers underwent a redaction, ridding them of any selection that could be considered an infringement of copyright. The plaintiffs agreed to settle out of court for $2,000. The looming lawsuit brought about the first and most sweeping of many revisions to come.

Content and Moral Tone

In the 1840s, William H. McGuffey's younger brother Alexander added a Rhetorical Guide, which was later developed into the fifth and 6th readers. Literary selections in these volumes included portions of the Bible and the works of Longfellow, Dickens, Addison, and many others. In addition to the variety of literature, these higher-level readers incorporated elocutionary exercises and lessons on such broad topics as farming, science, history, and biography. The instruction in elocution was deemed necessary because of the increasing number of immigrants learning the English language. These final books of the series have been credited for determining America's taste for literature and for exemplifying themes foundational to the American experience.

Although a forerunner to the 20th-century basal reader, the McGuffey Readers were distinctly different. Their selections were much shorter, were intended for oral rather than silent reading, and were more culturally and morally monolithic. Unlike modern basals conceived and produced by publishers, 19th-century readers like McGuffey's were largely written and compiled by a single author—normally a clergyman or schoolmaster. Although they were not as stern in moralizing as *The New England Primer* had been, the McGuffey Readers clearly taught a Calvinistic ethic that both reflected the moral tone of the time and wove it into the fabric of American society. *The New England Primer* included a greater degree of religious content and emphasized eternal damnation in hell as punishment for wrongdoing, whereas the McGuffey Readers focused on practical consequences children might experience here on earth for lacking in kindness or productivity. Like the modern basals, McGuffey's stories resonated with what children found interesting, such as fables about animals and play.

Other than the first revision in 1838, which was conducted to avoid copyright infringement, all other revisions of *McGuffey's Eclectic Readers* were completed to make the books more visually and conceptually appealing to a changing society. The flourishing magazine industry of the 1870s, with its improvements in pictorial images, influenced an overhaul in the quality of the readers' illustrations. Religious content was gradually diminished over time, but the high moral tone was retained.

Critical Response

Among critics of the McGuffey Readers was Horace Mann. While he agreed with McGuffey in promoting the spread of free public schools throughout the nation, Mann vociferously argued that much of the content in the McGuffey Readers was inappropriate for children's textbooks. Other critics have pointed out omissions. For instance, though moralistic about many issues, including cruelty to animals, they did not address the injustice of slavery as the textbooks of New England had. Also absent are mentions of Jefferson, Lincoln, Twain, and such events as the California Gold Rush and the Oregon Trail. Only cursory mention is made of the Civil War. Political critics indicate that these oversights reflect the pro–Whig Party leaning of the compilers and an effort not to offend consumers in the South. Other concerns have existed over anti-Semitic references, identification of Native Americans as "savages," and the limitation of women to domestic roles.

Three books ubiquitous in 19th- and early 20th-century schools and homes, particularly in the West and South, were the Bible, Webster's dictionary, and the McGuffey Readers. Along with Webster's *Blue Back Speller*, the McGuffey Readers helped to standardize English language usage in the United States. They not only reflected the moral values of the 19th century but also shaped them. Since the first publication in 1836, they continue to be in print and to sell tens of thousands of copies each year. They are mainly popular in the homeschool movement, but are also implemented in a few school systems.

Samuel James Smith

See also Calvinist Schools; Common School Movement; Homeschooling and the Home School Legal Defense Association; Mann, Horace; *New England Primer, The*

Further Readings

Lindberg, S. W. (1976). *The annotated McGuffey: Selections from the* McGuffey Eclectic Readers, *1836–1920*. New York: Van Nostrand Reinhold.

Sullivan, D. P. (1994). *William Holmes McGuffey: Schoolmaster to the nation*. Rutherford, NJ: Fairleigh Dickinson University Press.

Venezky, R. L. (1990). The American reading script and its nineteenth-century origins. *Book Research Quarterly, 6*, 16–29.

Westerhoff J. H., III., (1978). *McGuffey and his Readers: Piety, morality and education in nineteenth century America*. Nashville, TN: Abingdon.

MERCER, CHARLES F. (1778–1858)

Charles Fenton Mercer, a contemporary of Thomas Jefferson, is a relatively unknown educational reformer in Virginia.

Mercer was involved in many civic activities, as a member of the Virginia House of Delegates and later as a member of the U.S. House of Representatives. He opposed the slave trade and unsuccessfully sought its abolition. He favored the resettlement of free Blacks in Africa, which eventually led to the creation of Liberia. He championed the extension of suffrage to all free men of property and was an advocate of the federal role in internal improvements such as the Chesapeake and Ohio Canal which would have connected the Potomac with the Alleghany, Ohio, and Monongahela rivers. He was an ardent patriot, serving as a military officer for several periods, including a stint in the War of 1812.

It is Mercer's role as an educational reformer that is relevant here. The Virginia General Assembly had created the Literary Fund in 1810, by which funds obtained from various kinds of penalties were to be used for the schooling of White children from indigent families. These funds were augmented by a contribution to Virginia from the federal government for Virginia's role in the War of 1812, a happening in which Mercer played a leading role.

Mercer was not content with such a limited role of the state in public education. Accordingly, on February 24, 1816, he proposed a resolution to the General Assembly, which was agreed to by both houses of the legislature, and which called for the president and directors of the Literary Fund to prepare a report for the next session of the legislature on a system of public education in the state that would include primary schools (for every White child) through other schools, including the University of Virginia. The report, issued on December 8, 1816, called for a system of public schools throughout the state, beginning with a primary school in each township; intermediate schools, called academies, for boys of high ability; and the establishment of the University of Virginia. All levels of institutions were to be supported by the Literary Fund. The report noted that the Literary Fund's income would need to be substantially increased for such a level of expenditures to be financially possible. The order of execution recommended was the primary schools first, followed by the academies, with the University of Virginia last. No money was to be taken from the treasury for any postprimary schooling until every primary school throughout the state was provided for.

Following the publication of the report, Mercer introduced legislation into the General Assembly that followed the report's recommendations. The bill passed the House but failed in the Senate by a tie vote. The bill was defeated, first, because of the opposition of the well-to-do who feared a tax on their property in order to meet the financial obligations incurred by the plan. Second, some, including Thomas Jefferson, thought that there would not be enough resources to support the university, as it was to be established only after primary and intermediate schools had been established. In fact, Jefferson, who was not present at the time, wrote a letter to his floor "lieutenant," Joseph C. Cabell, in which he specifically raised that objection. Jefferson also was opposed to the centralized government called for in Mercer's bill, preferring that primary schools be supported at the local, not the state, level. As it turned out, the University of Virginia, Jefferson's first priority, was established and the erection of primary schools throughout the state was "postponed." In 1817 Mercer was elected to the U.S. House of Representatives and no further action was taken on his bill.

Mercer continued his espousal of popular education while a member of the House. In 1826, for instance, he delivered a discourse on it at the commencement exercises at Princeton University. The main theme of this address was that the nation's happiness and well-being are only possible with the diffusion of virtue and knowledge that the public schools alone can dispense. Primary schools, within the reach of every citizen, were indispensable in this process. The combination of funds (such as the Literary Fund) with taxation would be able to bring a complete system of public education within the reach of every citizen.

Mercer resigned from Congress in 1839 and moved to Florida where he worked as a cashier in a bank. It has been reported that this move was due to his despair at the continued existence of what he thought was the barbaric practice of slavery and the popular opposition to him in Virginia for his position on this practice.

Mercer died in 1858. He stands as a statesman and educator, relatively unknown among the reformers of education in the Antebellum South.

Thomas C. Hunt

See also Dabney, Robert L.; Jefferson; Thomas; Mann, Horace; Ruffner, William Henry

Further Readings

Buck, J. L. B. (1952). *The development of public schools in Virginia, 1607–1952*. Richmond, VA: State Board of Education.

Heatwole, C. (1916). *A history of education in Virginia*. New York: Macmillan.

Maddox, W. (1918). *The free school idea in Virginia before the Civil War*. New York: Teachers College.

Mercer, C. F. (1826). *A discourse on popular education*. Princeton, NJ: Princeton University Press.

MERIAM, LEWIS (1883–1972)

Lewis Meriam was a statistician and editor of many studies on public administration, including *The Problem of Indian Administration* (1928), better known as the Meriam Report, which prompted reforms in the education of Native Americans. After graduating from Harvard in 1906, Meriam joined the Census Bureau and enrolled in George Washington University Law School, where he completed his studies in 1909. In 1916, he joined the Institute for Government Research, now known as the Brookings Institution.

In the aftermath of severe federal cuts to Indian services in the early 1920s, Secretary of Interior Herbert Work requested from Meriam in June 1926 a survey of the "economic and social condition of the American Indians." Meriam assembled a staff of nine experts who traveled to Indian reservations, schools, and hospitals over 7 months. The final report, published in February 1928, made several important recommendations for reform of administration, personnel training, and salaries, as well as improved recordkeeping, health facilities, economic opportunities, legal protections, and a reexamination of the role of women and missionaries in American Indian policy. The most important recommendations, however, were directed at Indian schools.

The educational section was written primarily by progressive educator W. Carson Ryan, Jr., and the Reverend Henry Roe Cloud, a Winnebago and graduate of Yale who led the American Indian Institute in Wichita, Kansas. Referring to the entire reform effort as an "educational problem," the Meriam Report advocated a "fundamental change in the point of view" away from a strict separation of Indian children from their homes in order to "civilize" them, toward "upbringing in the natural setting of home and family life." The report also advocated better understanding of Indian culture, language, and traditions with the belief that limited cultural pluralism would hasten "their absorption into the general citizenship of the Nation" and "make the Indian cease to be a special case in a comparatively short time."

The Meriam Report recommended six fundamental changes to Indian education. First, the individual and unique characteristics of tribal cultures required curricular reform. The report strongly criticized the Tentative Course of Study for United States Indian Schools (1915) for being rigid, uniform, and outdated, and called for more community surveys to learn about unique tribal needs. Curriculum for Indian students should teach the "duties of citizenship" through "directed experiences," including the necessity of paying taxes to support public education.

Second, the Meriam Report recommended improved training for administrators, teachers, and school staff. The report noted that many Indian schools were employing teachers who could not meet established state standards and that many teachers in Indian schools were not trained in modern pedagogical methods. Administrators and dormitory "matrons" were found to be underprepared, and compensation was found to be lower than "any ordinary standard" in Indian schools.

The third recommendation emphasized better attention to the students' home lives in order to improve attendance. While avoiding discussion of the use of police power to forcibly enroll children in boarding schools, the report called for a "school social worker" type of attendance officer and better coordination between school and home.

The fourth recommendation was investment in school facilities. The report argued that funds spent to improve existing buildings could have been better spent on new structures, and it criticized the use of outdated military barracks for schools. Also criticized was the dumping of surplus military and government equipment on Indian schools.

The fifth change was an end to the policy of sending elementary students to boarding schools, and the expansion of day schools on reservations. Emphasizing the importance of home and school connections, the report criticized the separation of children from their families and reinforced the belief that Indian homes were essential social institutions "from which it is generally undesirable to uproot children."

Finally, the report recommended implementation of full-day study. Under earlier curricular and institutional models, Indian students at times tilled fields, worked as domestics, or produced crafts as part of their vocational training. The Meriam Report recommended that schools end "child labor" and refocus practical training on fields that would prepare students for available jobs.

Several important reforms were initiated because of the Meriam Report. W. Carson Ryan became director of Indian education in 1930 and attempted to implement the six recommendations. Progressive educational ideas were integrated into some aspects of the curriculum, including recognition of the "environmental experiences" of children as a foundation for learning.

Though his report had a sustained impact on Indian education policy, Meriam devoted the remainder of his career to studying government administration at the Brookings Institution, particularly health policy, public employee retirement, social security, and the overall structure of the federal government. Meriam also served as the mayor of Kensington, Maryland, from 1958 to 1960. He died on October 30, 1972.

Christopher J. Frey

See also Federal Educational Reform; Progressive Education

Further Readings

Brookings Institution, & Meriam, L. (1928). *The problem of Indian administration. Report of a survey made at the request of Honorable Hubert Work, Secretary of the Interior, and submitted to him, February 21, 1928.* Washington, DC: Brookings Institution.

Reyhner, J., & Eder, J. (2004). *American Indian education: A history.* Norman: University of Oklahoma Press.

MERIT PAY

Merit pay for teachers is a perennial issue in public education. It is introduced every 20 or 30 years as a solution to what ails the schools. This is despite the fact that researchers have repeatedly demonstrated that merit pay programs do not provide effective incentives for teachers. Examples of failed merit pay programs have been carefully documented in Great Britain during the 1880s and in the United States in the 1920s, 1960s, and 1980s. Yet despite these specific examples of the failure of merit pay to provide effective incentive for teachers, the issue of merit pay continues to be proposed by reformers. In the 2008 presidential campaign, for example, each of the four main presidential contenders, Senator Hillary Rodham Clinton, Senator Barack Obama, Governor Mike Huckabee, and Senator John McCain, expressed support for one or another form of merit pay and of implementing merit pay as a means of reforming teacher education.

This ongoing interest in merit pay as a means of educational reform can be explained as part of an attempt to apply business principles to education. It is something that seems to be common sense. The logic of these programs is simple. In much the same way that a good sales person is rewarded for selling more, teachers should be rewarded for producing academic achievement in students. Higher levels of achievement should bring higher levels of compensation. President Ronald Reagan articulated the model during the last national call for merit pay in a speech at Seton Hall University in May 1983, when he declared, "Teachers should be paid and promoted on the basis of their merit and competence. Hard-earned tax dollars should encourage the best. They have no business rewarding incompetence and mediocrity."

Yet evidence from the research literature clearly suggests that individual-level merit pay is an inappropriate method of providing incentives for teachers. Rewards and incentives that function well for people in business settings do not necessarily work effectively for teachers.

In research conducted for the National Institute of Education on the implementation of two state-funded merit pay programs for teachers in Florida, during the mid-1980s by Provenzo, Cohn, Kottkamp, McCloskey, and Proller (the Florida Meritorious Teacher Program and the Quality Instruction Incentives Program), it was found that rather than financial rewards and incentives, the primary motivators for teachers in their work involved helping them reach students and make meaning for them. In a survey of 40% of the public school teachers in Miami-Dade County that yielded a 64% response rate (N = 2,718), only 14.2% reported that "the salary I earn in my profession" was the motivating factor for teaching. This was nearly identical to the 14.3% response rate received by Dan Lortie in 1964 when he asked the same question of teachers in Miami-Dade County as part of the research for his book *1964 Schoolteacher*. What seemed to be the primary extrinsic reward for teachers was not salary, but reaching out and making a difference in the lives of students. Lortie found that this desire took the greatest precedence for the overwhelming majority of teachers. In his 1964 research in Miami-Dade County, Lortie found, for example, that 86.2% reported that the most satisfying aspect of their work involved the times "I have reached my students and I knew they had learned." Kottkamp reports that when this question was asked of a nearly identical group of teachers 20 years later, the figure was 86.7%.

What these figures clearly suggest is that teachers are not primarily motivated by salary. Instead, they are intrinsically motivated by the satisfaction

they receive from making a difference in the lives of the students with whom they work. These findings have significant implications for our understanding of teachers and merit pay. What is clearly suggested is that teachers are less motivated by financial rewards than are people in business. Making money to live may be necessary, but it is not a prime motivator for entering the teaching profession.

In the case of Florida and its merit pay programs in the early 1980s, the business group, Associated Industries of Florida, under the leadership of its president and chief lobbyist Bob Shebel, argued successfully with the Florida State Legislature for restructuring the salaries of Florida teachers using a merit pay model (i.e., a device for adjusting salaries on the basis of measured performance). According to Shebel, under the extant Florida pay system excellent teachers received the same percentage pay raise as incompetent teachers. He believed that was wrong and that teachers could be motivated by an increase in their salaries. Shebel's commonsense assumption, and analogy with business models, was completely false in light of the research. This misconception continues today and explains the ongoing interest in merit pay, despite the fact that it has not worked in the past and is not likely to work in the future unless teachers change significantly in terms of the reasons that they are motivated in their work.

Merit pay also fails as a reform, as reported by Lewis, because the measurement of teacher effectiveness can be highly problematic. Although it can be reasonably argued that teachers who demonstrate substantial subject-matter knowledge and mastery of pedagogical techniques deserve greater salaries and rewards than less-competent and less-skilled teachers, accurate evaluation does not necessarily take place, as peer and principal evaluation often involves bias, nepotism, and favoritism, making accurate assessments of teacher efficacy highly problematic.

Merit pay, particularly if assessments of teacher quality are inaccurate or incomplete, will lead to teachers becoming less motivated in their work. Merit pay can work only if there is a significant improvement in the assessment of teachers. In this context, student achievement as the measure of teacher success is often pointed to as the best means of assessing teacher effectiveness. This seemingly simple solution does not work, however, because teachers who have high-achieving students are obviously at an advantage if teacher efficacy is simply based on the student achievement scores. Are gain scores of low-achieving students equivalent to those of high-achieving students? Should teachers be rewarded the same for students whose likelihood to make high scores is less than that of other students? What is a significant level of accomplishment (i.e., one deserving merit pay) for teachers working with radically different student populations? Should the measures be the same for a teacher working with gifted or economically privileged children versus children of poverty or children with special physical and intellectual needs?

Other issues contribute to the failure of merit pay as an educational reform. Many communities are not willing to commit enough money to reward teachers sufficiently to change how they conduct their work. In business, merit pay systems, in the form of commissions and bonuses, often make up a significant portion of a worker's salary—sometimes significantly more than the base salary received. This is never the case in teacher merit systems where salary increases are rarely more than 5% to 8% of the teacher's total salary.

In conclusion, merit pay is a highly problematic instrument of educational change and reform. Its assumptions and models, drawn from business, clearly do not match the realities of teachers' work and the primary forces that motivate them. Unless better systems of teacher assessment and efficacy are developed, it is not likely that merit pay will succeed as a means of school improvement.

Eugene F. Provenzo, Jr.

See also Business and Educational Reform; Differentiated Staffing; Licensure and Certification; No Child Left Behind Act (NCLB); Performance Contracting; Teacher Evaluation

Further Readings

Kottkamp, R. B., Provenzo, E. F., Jr., & Cohn, M. (1986). Stability and change in a profession: Two decades of teacher attitudes, 1964–1984. *Phi Delta Kappan, 67*(8), 559–567.

Moore-Johnson, S. (1984). Merit pay for teachers: A poor prescription for reform. *Harvard Educational Review, 54,* 175–185.

Provenzo, E. F., Jr., & McCloskey, G. N. (1996). *Schoolteachers and schooling: Ethoses in conflict.* Norwood, NJ: Ablex.

Provenzo, E. F., Jr., McCloskey, G. N., Cohn, M. M., Kottkamp, R. B., & Proller, N. (1987). *A comparison of individual and school level approaches to merit pay: A case study of the Dade County Public Schools.* Washington, DC: Office of Educational Research and Improvement. (ERIC Document Reproduction Service No. ED292751)

Solomon, L. C. (2004). What's fair about performance pay? *Phi Delta Kappan, 85*(5), 407–408.

MEYER V. NEBRASKA

The state of Nebraska passed legislation in 1919 that made it a misdemeanor to teach any subject in any language other than English to a student who had not passed the eighth grade. A teacher in a parochial school was tried and convicted, in 1920, of unlawfully teaching reading classes in German to eighth-grade students.

The Nebraska Supreme Court later upheld the teacher's conviction, on the grounds that the statute was a valid exercise of police powers and did not violate the Fourteenth Amendment of the U.S. Constitution. Interestingly, the Nebraska Supreme Court had held in a previous case that "the so-called ancient or dead languages," such as Latin, Greek, and Hebrew, were not within the spirit or purpose of the legislation and therefore could be taught to students in the lower grades, but German, French, Spanish, Italian, and other "alien speech are within the ban."

The case was brought before the U.S. Supreme Court; Justice James McReynolds wrote the opinion for the Court, whose decision in 1923 (*Meyer v. State of Nebraska*) reversed that of the Nebraska Supreme Court. The Court stated that the Nebraska statute violated the liberty rights of the teacher under the Fourteenth Amendment:

> While this court had not attempted to define with exactness the liberty thus guaranteed, the term had received much consideration and some of the included things had been definitely stated. Without doubt, it denoted not merely freedom from bodily restraint but also the right of the individual to

contract, to engage in any of the common occupations of life, to acquire useful knowledge, to marry, establish a home and bring up children, to worship God according to the dictates of his own conscience, and generally to enjoy those privileges long recognized at common law as essential to the orderly pursuit of happiness by free men.

The Court stated that the liberty rights of an individual may not be interfered with "under the guise of protecting the public interest." The mere knowledge of German or other modern languages cannot possibly be viewed as harmful. In a majority of cases, the knowledge of a foreign language enhanced education.

Although numerous people over the years have cited *Meyer* as giving parents the right to control their child's education, this case did not specifically rule in that manner. The passage that is frequently cited by parents who protest against the public school curriculum states, "Corresponding to the right of control [of education and acquisition of knowledge], it is the natural duty of the parent to give his children education suitable to their station in life."

The Court made clear that schools, and not the parents, control the curriculum when it stated,

The power of the state to compel attendance at some schools and to make reasonable regulations for all schools, including a requirement that they shall give instructions in English, is not questioned. Nor has challenge been made of the state's power to prescribe a curriculum for institutions which it supports. Those matters are not within the present controversy. Our concern is with the prohibition approved by the Supreme Court (in *Adams v. Tanner*, 244 U.S. 590 37 S. Ct. 662).

The Adams case

pointed out that mere abuse incident to an occupation ordinarily useful is not enough to justify its abolition, although regulation may be entirely proper. No emergency has arisen which renders knowledge by a child of some language other than English so clearly harmful as to justify its inhibition with the consequent infringement of rights long freely enjoyed. (*Brown v. Hot, Sexy and Safer Productions, Inc.* 68 F.3d 525 at 533 1st Cir. 1995, explaining *Meyer*.)

Michael David Alexander

See also Curriculum Controversies; *Pierce v. Society of Sisters*

Further Readings

Alexander, K., & Alexander, M. D. (2009). *American public school law* (7th ed.). Belmont, CA: Wadsworth.
Brown v. Hot, Sexy & Safer Productions, 68 F.3d 525 C.A. 1 (1995).
Fields v. Palmdale School District, 427 F.3d 1197 C.A. 9 (2005).
Pierce v. Society of Sisters of the Holy Names of Jesus and Mary, 268 U.S. 510, 5 S. Ct. 571 (1925).
Prince v. Massachusetts, 321 U.S. 158, 64 S. Ct. 43 (1944).

MIDDLE SCHOOL

The rise of schools dedicated to serving the needs of young adolescents began in the early 20th century with the development of the junior high school. As the number of years of compulsory education increased in the United States, the junior high school served as a bridge between elementary school and high school. By the 1960s, however, those who studied young adolescents and their schools recognized that the junior high school was not adequately meeting the developmental needs of the students who populated them. With growing awareness and research regarding the needs of young adolescents, in an effort to reform the junior high school model, the National Middle School Association was founded in 1973. The Association codified the reform effort by providing a vision, resources, and support for those concerned with the education and development of young adolescent students. The effort to transform junior high schools into developmentally responsive middle schools for young adolescents was a comprehensive school reform effort that impacted all aspects of the school. This entry describes the underlying principles and organizational structures of the middle school as well as criticism of the middle school reform movement.

Foundations for Middle Schools

Middle school principles are based on the distinctive nature of early adolescence. Early adolescence, defined as the approximate ages of 10 to 15, is marked by rapid growth and development. In fact, it is said that the rate of change in early adolescence is exceeded only by the rate of change in infancy. During this time, the young adolescent experiences rapid but uneven physical, social, emotional, and cognitive growth. Physically, the young adolescent experiences the beginning stages of puberty. Physical growth in height and weight are accompanied by the development of secondary sexual characteristics. With this physical growth, the young adolescent's focus on the self becomes predominant.

In addition to physical growth, the young adolescent in modern cultures experiences social and emotional changes. During this time the influence of the family begins to fade and the influence of the peer group increases. Young adolescents rely on peers to set the standards for dress, appearance, preferences, and actions. Because growth is uneven for an individual and across individuals, the focus on the self and heightened comparison to peers can cause emotional distress. Emotions can range across the spectrum from very negative to very positive feelings. Although this is true at all ages, the newness of unfamiliar feelings, the rapidity of change, and the struggle for self-regulation can make the young adolescent seem highly emotional.

Finally, early adolescence marks a shift in cognitive development. Young adolescents straddle what psychologist Jean Piaget called the *concrete operational* and *formal operational* stages. This means that they are only beginning to think in abstract terms. Instruction for young adolescents, then, must focus on providing concrete examples and experiences while at the same time challenging students to think abstractly about concepts.

Because the shifts in physical, social, emotional, and cognitive development are fluid and uneven, young adolescents require a school that provides a flexible environment to accommodate their ever-changing needs. Large, subject-centered, inflexible junior high schools seemed unable to address students' changing needs. While the founders of the National Middle School Association began the work of reforming junior high schools in the 1960s and 1970s, the focus on the deficits of the U.S. educational system of the 1980s, sparked by *A Nation at Risk,* accelerated their work. In 1989, the Task Force on Education of Young Adolescents

of the Carnegie Council on Adolescent Development published its influential report, *Turning Points: Preparing American Youth for the 21st Century.* This report drew attention to the great risks that young adolescents face as they progress from elementary to high school. It chastised the educational reform movement for its lack of attention to young adolescents and implicated large, impersonal, academically weak junior high schools with putting students at risk for alienation, school failure, drug and alcohol abuse, and dropping out. The *Turning Points* report supported many of the practices that the National Middle School Association recommended for middle schools. Since that time, the research on young adolescents and middle schools has helped to refine the principles and practices of effective middle schools.

Characteristics of Effective Middle Schools

Effective middle schools respond to the developmental needs of the young adolescent while maintaining an emphasis on academic rigor and achievement. Although the sign on the front of the building may claim a school to be a middle school, it is what goes on inside the school that determines if it is implementing the middle school model. The implementation of the model varies considerably from one school to the next. Several features, however, define the middle school model. One of the most visible characteristics of a middle school is the development of small communities of learning. Whereas the junior high school is often criticized for being too large and impersonal, with students interacting with as many as eight or nine different teachers and a hundred classmates over the course of a day, the middle school strives to establish an environment where each student is known well.

Two features of a middle school that promote small learning communities are the use of interdisciplinary teaming and the establishment of advisory programs. Rather than organizing the school by academic departments as in the junior high school, the interdisciplinary team is the organizing feature of a middle school. The team generally consists of a small group of teachers who take primary responsibility for instruction in the core academic content areas (i.e., language arts, mathematics, science, and social studies) of a small group of students. The team is usually housed in a common area of the school and has flexibility in scheduling the students' day. This model contrasts with the junior high model in which students travel across the school from one academic department to another at 45- to 50-minute intervals for instruction, encountering several teachers for a short time each day. In the team-based middle school, students interact with a small group of teachers who get to know them well. In addition, the team structure allows students to form a consistent peer group, thus alleviating the alienation that can occur in large junior high schools. Another essential part of creating a community for learning is the development of an advisory program that matches an adult with a small group of students. The purpose of an advisory program is to aid in the development of close, trusting relationships between students and adults to foster engagement, self-esteem, and a sense of belonging.

The interdisciplinary team model promotes a third feature of the middle school, the use of a relevant, challenging, integrative, and exploratory curriculum. Whereas the junior high school curriculum centers on distinct academic disciplines, the middle school curriculum focuses on promoting connections among disciplines. Although no specific curriculum is endorsed, the ideal middle school curriculum engages learners in solving relevant problems that require them to draw from knowledge and skills in multiple disciplines. Academic subjects are not abandoned but are taught in the context of integrated units of study that address problems of personal or global concern.

Another important characteristic of the middle school model is the use of heterogeneous grouping practices. With heterogeneous grouping, students are not assigned to classes according to their ability level but are assigned to classes of mixed ability. Grouping by ability is common practice in the subject-centered junior high model. With ability grouping, or tracking, however, students are seldom able to move out of the low-ability tracks as the achievement gap between the low-ability and high-ability tracked students tends to widen over time. In its place, the middle school model recommends that students be grouped in flexible, heterogeneous classrooms where cooperative grouping, multi-age grouping, and cross-age tutoring are used to arrange students for instruction. In addition, the middle school model emphasizes that multiple teaching, grouping, and learning strategies be employed by teachers in efforts to provide instruction to meet the diverse needs of students in the diverse classroom.

Other characteristics of middle schools include empowering teachers and administrators by developing site-based decision-making teams, specifically preparing teachers for middle school service, and involving families and communities as partners in educating young adolescents. In addition, middle schools promote the development of exploratory programs that allow students to engage in a variety of academic, vocational, and recreational subjects that might involve exploration of career options, community service, and personal enrichment. In summary, middle schools are specifically designed to focus on academic rigor and excellence in a context that promotes equity and honors the well-being, safety, and development of young adolescent students.

Criticism of Middle Schools

In recent years, middle schools have come under attack for their presumed priority on psychosocial development at the expense of academic rigor. The release of the Third International Mathematics and Science Study (TIMSS) in 1996 highlighted the deficiencies in mathematics and science achievement at the middle school level. Whereas U.S. fourth graders scored above the international average in mathematics and in science, by eighth grade U.S. students' performance had fallen below the international average in mathematics. Further, in the TIMSS Repeat (TIMSS-R) that was conducted in 1999 as a follow-up to the 1995 study, the mathematics and science performance of the United States relative to the group of nations that participated in both the 1995 and the 1999 studies decreased. This means that the fourth-grade cohort from the 1995 study performed lower as eighth graders in 1999, relative to the international average of the participating nations. As a result of this poor showing, William H. Schmidt, U.S. research coordinator for TIMSS, claimed that the American middle grades curriculum is an intellectual wasteland.

In addition to receiving criticism for lack of academic rigor, middle schools have been blamed for their inability to handle disciplinary problems. Cities such as Baltimore, Cincinnati, Cleveland,

and Pittsburgh have dismantled middle school programs due to widespread disciplinary problems and poor achievement.

Critics disagree whether the problems facing middle schools stem from a faulty model or from incomplete implementation of the middle school design. Although structural changes have been made to many schools serving young adolescents, in their 2000 report, *Turning Points 2000: Educating Adolescents in the 21st Century,* Anthony Jackson and Gayle Davis claim that curriculum, instruction, and assessment in middle schools have not changed substantially from the junior high school model that the middle school movement aimed to reform.

Mary Kay Kelly

See also Junior High School; *Nation at Risk, A*; Trends in International Mathematics and Science Study (TIMSS)

Further Readings

Carnegie Council on Adolescent Development. (1989). *Turning points: Preparing American youth for the 21st century.* Washington, DC: Author.

Erb, T. O. (Ed.). (2005). *This we believe in action: Implementing successful middle level schools.* Westerville, OH: National Middle School Association.

Jackson, A. W., & Davis G. A. (with Abeel, M., & Bordonaro, A.). (2000). *Turning points 2000: Educating adolescents in the 21st century.* New York: Teachers College Press.

National Middle School Association. (2003). *This we believe: Successful schools for young adolescents.* Westerville, OH: Author.

Yecke, C. P. (2005). *Mayhem in the middle: How middle schools have failed America and how to make them work.* Washington, DC: Thomas B. Fordham Institute.

MILLIKEN V. BRADLEY

A federal district court ruled in 1971 that the city of Detroit was racially segregated because of official policies and state actions. To establish a unitary nonracial school system, the court ordered the Detroit school board to submit a Detroit-only desegregation plan and also a plan that covered 3 counties and 85 surrounding school districts. The court determined that a metropolitan plan was appropriate since a Detroit-only plan was inadequate to accomplish desegregation; therefore the desegregation remedy would go beyond the district's limits of Detroit. A panel was appointed by the court to produce a plan that would place 53 of the 85 suburban school districts into a desegregation plan with Detroit. The U.S. Court of Appeals of the Sixth District upheld the district court's desegregation remedy plan of having interdistrict busing and combining the 53 districts plus Detroit into one system. The Court of Appeals ruled in 1972 that this was an appropriate remedial plan within the equity powers of the federal district court.

The case was appealed to the Supreme Court. The Court agreed to hear the case

to determine whether a federal court may impose a multidistrict, areawide remedy to a single-district de jure segregation problem absent any finding that the other included school districts have failed to operate unitary school systems within their districts, absent any claim or finding that the boundary lines of any affected school districts were established with the purpose of fostering racial segregation in public schools, absent any finding that the included districts committed acts which effected segregation within the other districts, and absent a meaningful opportunity for the included neighboring school districts to present evidence or be heard on the propriety of a multidistrict remedy or on the question of constitutional violations by those neighboring districts.

Chief Justice Warren E. Burger, writing for the majority, ruled that it was improper to impose a multidistrict remedy unless there was evidence that the adjoining districts had not operated unitary school systems and had committed acts of segregation. If it could be established that the 53 districts were involved in racial segregation or some constitutional violation, then a multidistrict desegregation plan may be appropriate.

The 5–4 decision was delivered by a sharply divided Court. Justice Potter Stewart noted this when he filed his concurring opinion. He stated, "I think it appropriate, in view of some of the extravagant language of the dissenting opinion, to state briefly my understanding of what it is the Court decided today." He went on to say that it violated common sense to include school districts that were not in the original desegregation lawsuit against Detroit that had not engaged in unconstitutional discrimination. Justice Stewart did say that an interdistrict remedy could be proper or even necessary if the factual situation showed purposeful racial discrimination by all parties.

Michael David Alexander

See also *Brown v. Board of Education*; De Facto Segregation; De Jure Segregation; Desegregation/ Integration; Marshall, Thurgood; *Swann v. Charlotte- Mecklenburg*

Further Readings

Alexander, K., & Alexander, M. D. (2009). *American public school law* (7th ed.). Belmont, CA: Wadsworth.

Brown v. Board of Education of Topeka, 347 U.S. 483, 74 S. Ct. 686 (1954).

Freeman v. Pitts, 503 U.S. 467, 112 S. Ct. 1430 (1992).

Milliken v. Bradley, 418 U.S. 717, 94 S. Ct. 3112 (1974).

Missouri v. Jenkins (Jenkins II), 515 U.S. 70, 115 S. Ct. 2038 (1995).

Swann v. Charlotte-Mecklenburg Board of Education, 402 U.S. 1, 91 S. Ct. 1267 (1971).

MINIMUM COMPETENCIES

At its core, the educational process serves as the means by which individuals develop themselves intellectually, emotionally, psychologically, philosophically, and artistically. It is widely agreed that there should be a minimum level of competency expected on a wide range of subject matter as a base to build on; minimum competencies are the expectations of achievement for each student at specified levels of learning.

In keeping with the requirement for students and staff to meet the minimum competencies in a wide array of contextual settings, it is important to maintain a focus on opportunities to maximize learning. Ideally, the development of minimum competencies through competency-based reform will help ensure that all children will receive an equivalent level of education. All students must meet the minimum requirements regardless of differences in teachers,

economics, disabilities, or school or community factors. Minimum competencies allow for consistency and continuity of learning. Through the utilization of minimum competencies, school officials are more effectively able to measure a student's progress in the fundamental areas of reading, writing, arithmetic, and language, as well as an individual's capacity to learn.

The late Mortimer Adler maintained from the 1970s until his death in 2001 that the curriculum should be standardized for all. Teachers and curriculum directors are better able to plan a school's or a district's curriculum for students who are assumed to follow it from start to finish, kindergarten through graduation. A set of consistent standards also allows for greater accountability of those who have received the public trust. Through the use of minimum competencies, one could reason that teachers would have a better grasp of expectations and assessment. The determination of minimum competencies defines the expectations of all students.

Throughout history, learning has taken place with or without formal schooling. However, compulsory education has increased the learning opportunities for individuals. One could argue that without compulsory education laws (and more recently the No Child Left Behind legislation), and without defined minimum competencies, U.S. society would be of lesser educational quality. There should be a minimum level of competency expected on a wide range of subject matter as a base of knowledge upon which to build. However, a regimented standardized curriculum, depending on how it is designed and implemented, could pose concerns.

Concerns: Considering Minimum Competencies

Some observers have expressed concern that the minimum competency, when achieved, also becomes the maximum expectation and maximum achievement of staff and students alike. This view is not the designed purpose of minimum competency achievement; however, the spirit of the minimum competency achievement could result in a practice of watered-down goals that all can achieve, thus rendering standards of achievement less meaningful.

Another concern that may accompany minimum competency achievement is that of grade inflation. It lies in the fear educators have of being called to defend their judgment. The way to escape this judgment is to give such high ratings that no recipient would be foolish enough to challenge them. Instead we must determine minimum competencies that are based on reasonable knowledge and sensible judgment.

If the concern is to exceed the minimum competency, the challenge is to assist students in achieving levels that exceed the minimum competency requirements. Focusing upon the minimum competencies as essential, the delivery of instruction becomes a prime consideration for teachers. Differentiated instruction should accompany minimum competencies so that each child has not only the opportunity to successfully address the minimum but the opportunity to do so with varied abilities and experiences.

Finally, a common concern, beyond the expected concrete subject matter of math, science, language arts, and social studies, is that elements of the arts need to be considered as minimum competencies. As educators strive to address the individual strengths of each student and to address areas of interest, educators need to keep in mind that assessment may be equated with importance. Therefore, exploration into the arts may be of benefit to students, but the arts may not be introduced if minimum competencies are not established and assessed during the course of formal schooling.

Consistency in Curriculum

Although the establishment of minimum competencies may create an image of inflexibility, an image of strict adherence to programmed minimum competencies, and a one-size-fits-all mentality, educational professionals widely agree the proper usage of standards requires adaptations and accommodations for inherent differences in learning styles among students. A consistent curriculum, one that can be monitored to reflect current educational needs, creates educated persons and innovative leaders. Standards add rigor to the curriculum and focus on what students need for today and for the future.

History has shown that children of color and economically disadvantaged children are not always treated equitably with other students in the educational system. Contemporary society has embraced the principle that all students should be afforded similar opportunities to learn and compete with everyone. Thus, to ensure a fair assessment for all students regardless or race, ethnicity, or socioeconomic status, it is necessary to have a curriculum that is standard for all children.

The No Child Left Behind Act (NCLB) of 2001 has forced many districts to evaluate curriculum and align it with the state standards. Many districts now enforce the teaching of the standards for all students, with a focus on students with limited English proficiency, economically disadvantaged students, ethnic minorities, and special-needs children. The NCLB legislation holds districts accountable for educating all students using a set of standards for various grade levels. To conclude, there must be a standardized curriculum to meet the needs of all children.

Having high expectations for every child and allowing each child to have access to a rigorous curriculum is widely understood as the only way to level the playing field for the children who attend school with the odds stacked against them because of their socioeconomic status. Minimum competencies will be developed and utilized not only to assess the current state of academic affairs, but also to serve as a springboard as students pursue interests and matriculate through the varied programs of education and processes of instructional delivery. Minimum competencies and a standardized curriculum are seen as providing the necessary framework for learning to be assessed, analyzed, and then customized to meet individual needs. If reliable and valid assessments cannot occur in an environment that lacks control and accountability, minimum competencies provide a common foundation of learning.

Richard Carl Baringer

See also Alternative Assessment; Comprehensive School Reform; Curriculum Controversies; Effective Schools Movement; Paideia Proposal; Standards Movement; Value-Added Education

Further Readings

Cech, S. (2008). Engineering a blueprint for success. *Education Digest, 73*(5), 39–42.

Gallagher, J. J. (1979). Minimum competency: The setting of educational standards. *Educational Evaluation and Policy Analysis*, *1*(1), 62–67.

Levy, H. M. (2008). Meeting the needs of all students through differentiated instruction: Helping every child reach and exceed standards. *Clearing House*, *81*(4), 161–164.

Ruggieri, C. A. (2008). Finding success in a standardized world: An interview with Alfie Kohn. *Ohio Journal of English Language Arts*, *48*(1), 12–16.

Wolfe, F. (2008). Scholars urge NAEP expansion to test broader skills, dropouts. *Education Daily*, *41*(65), 4.

Minorities in Educational Leadership

Throughout the history of the United States, minorities and especially those within the African American and Hispanic communities have struggled to achieve equal footing in terms of educational opportunities with their majority counterparts. The literacy rates of these groups over the past 2 centuries illustrate the magnitude of the problem. Before the Civil War, approximately 95% of all Blacks were illiterate mainly because they were refused access to educational opportunities. Approximately 50 years later (1910), that rate had dropped dramatically, with only 30% evidencing illiteracy. Reforms occurring throughout the 1800s and continuing through the 20th century enabled persons of color to have some of the same educational opportunities as those from the majority culture.

In the segregated schools of the South, minority school administrators were commonplace. With desegregation, a concomitant decrease occurred in the number of Black school leaders. States such as North Carolina, Alabama, and Mississippi evidenced dramatic changes (i.e., decreases) in the number of Black school leaders. Without any type of affirmative action and given the highly racially political nature of hiring practices immediately following the 1954 *Brown v. Board of Education* decision and occurring along with the desegregation of schools, the number of Black school administrators decreased. This circumstance began to change in the 1970s when Blacks and Hispanics, in particular, began to evidence an increase in terms of their representation in administrative roles.

The *Brown* decision and other federal mandates influenced not only the way in which students of color could attend school (i.e., which schools they could attend) but also the teachers who would teach them and the type of school leaders who would be responsible for administering their schools. Prior to the 20th century, racial segregation limited those opportunities and influenced who would provide classroom and school leadership. Persons of color were limited by what types of opportunities were available and what options they could exercise. In the post-*Brown* era, Blacks in particular struggled initially to be appropriately represented in school leadership positions, but as affirmative action and civil rights legislation emerged, the opportunities for school leadership expanded.

Schools serving minority student populations struggled to be recognized for their excellence even though there were examples of exceptionally high-performing African American schools. Thomas Sowell documents the performance of four public high schools (three White schools and one Black school) in Washington, D.C., during the late 1800s and poignantly describes how strong the achievement scores on standardized tests were for the students in the segregated Black school. Sowell notes that the school (originally M Street School and renamed in 1916 as Dunbar High School) "repeatedly equaled or exceeded national norms on standardized tests." The challenge confronting educational reformers has been to find ways to replicate what researchers now know can be a reality in all urban settings: Schools can help students of color achieve their full intellectual potential.

One of the ways of making that possible is by creating schools that have teacher and administrator leadership that is reflective of the student culture being served. One of the salient findings of the work of researchers such as Gloria Ladson-Billings has been ensuring that the teacher population serving students of color has a deep appreciation of the learners in the classroom. Part of that deep appreciation means that the teacher possesses cultural and racial understandings that often are only possible if one is from the culture or racial group being served. Schools and school districts have translated this understanding into policies and practices focused on trying to ensure that a representative portion of their teacher population and school administration are persons of color.

Clearly education is a significant element in the way in which any group of individuals is able to participate in a democratic society. Persons of color in the United States, and especially Blacks and Hispanics, were intentionally excluded from the educational process for a significant part of U.S. history. Racial policies and prejudicial practices that were in place mitigated the educational options available to students of color. Those practices also limited leadership opportunities for Blacks and Hispanics.

As we enter the 21st century and as it becomes more evident that persons of color will eventually represent the majority culture in the United States, the types of leadership opportunities are beginning to expand and the way in which minorities are assuming responsibility for reforming educational institutions are beginning to be enhanced. Some of the changes have been the result of federal policies, but others have been because of the specific practices of Black school reformers who clearly understood that students of color could learn just as well as others. The issue in terms of learning was not racial or ethnic background but educational opportunity and the leadership in place to make that opportunity a reality. For example, Marva Collins and others began to communicate in pointed ways the fact that Black students could learn to read, write, and compute just as well as their White counterparts. Collins's message was not accepted by everyone (likely because of her heavy emphasis on "back to basics"), but it clearly began to influence the way educators in urban settings thought about the academic potential of Black students.

The 21st-century schools in the United States are beginning to experience an influx of next-generation minority leaders. These are individuals who understand the culture of the young people they are serving and who are willing to invest themselves heavily in making schools successful. Schools such as Rice High School in Harlem, which serves an urban minority student population and has a strong African American principal, illustrate the way in which the leadership of persons of color is becoming even more significant as we move toward a multicultural and multiracial society.

Thomas J. Lasley II

See also Afrocentric Schools; Black High School Study; Busing; Cristo Rey Schools; Holt, John; Kozol, Jonathan

Further Readings

Ladson-Billings, G. (2001). *Crossing over to Canaan*. San Francisco: Jossey-Bass.
McCloskey, P. (2008). *The street stops here*. Berkeley: University of California Press.
Sowell, T. (2005). *Black rednecks and White liberals*. San Francisco: Encounter Books.

MODERN RED SCHOOLHOUSE

The Modern Red SchoolHouse (MRSH), a nonprofit organization based in Nashville, Tennessee, began as part of a larger reform effort in the United States to design and create schools for the 21st century—where all students could achieve world-class academic standards. Development of the MRSH design began in 1992 when the New American Schools Development Corporation awarded the Hudson Institute a contract to design and pilot a comprehensive blueprint for 21st-century schools. Practitioners from six school districts in Arizona, Indiana, New York, and North Carolina collaborated with Hudson Institute researchers to develop a design for schools that would enable all, rather than some, students to master high academic standards.

The original design rested on the fundamental premise that realizing high academic standards for all students required school and classroom practices that allow students different paths (in time and instructional experiences) to reach the same goals. Although simple in concept, this premise represented a stark contrast to the ways in which public schooling evolved in the United States in the 20th century—when a student's opportunities to learn differed depending on his or her presumed ability and the interest of a given student. Even with these presumed differences, the pedagogy and time to learn was the same for all students. MRSH relied upon research in sociology and psychology showing (a) that intelligence is heavily influenced by a learner's effort and opportunity to learn, rather than simply inherited; and (b) that instructional methods that make effective links to students' prior experiences and learning are essential to learning.

Specific Design Elements

The designers sought to structure a school environment that enables students to spend more or less time in learning a given concept and encourages teachers to adapt or integrate a variety of instructional strategies to meet the needs of students. Whereas those factors vary, all students are expected to reach the same high academic standards.

Although the designers assumed ungraded classrooms, accountability for both the student and school were built into the assessment systems. All students would have Individual Education Compacts (IECs) collaboratively developed by parents, teachers, and the student. As students grew older, they would take increasing responsibility for creating and presenting the plans in the IECs. Reports to parents on student progress were to be framed in terms of current student mastery of the MRSH standards. Ongoing assessments were embedded into the daily life of schools and were unique to each school. Remediation should occur when students struggled with a concept—with extra time or varying approaches to instruction—not in remediation courses offered in the summer or following year. All MRSH schools shared in the use of Capstone Units, which provided a culminating assessment of proficiency in a number of subjects over a subset of standards within those subjects. Capstones were interdisciplinary, focusing on such things as inventions, construction, or tall tales at the primary level, where a student might complete as many as 12 Capstone Units. As students demonstrated proficiency in all the standards for one subject, they were ready to complete a subject exam at the primary, intermediate, or secondary level. MRSH academic standards and subject exams existed for English, mathematics, history, geography, and science. Teachers at each school developed (or adapted from other MRSH schools) instructional units that prepared students for the Capstones—aligning with MRSH academic standards. Over time, the bank of instructional units developed at all MRSH sites would support teachers in providing multiple paths to the same outcome, that is, MRSH standards.

High school completion could be realized in less or more than 12 years. Students could be at different levels in different subjects. Schools were seen as accountable for ensuring that most students reached proficiency within 4 years for primary and similarly for intermediate and secondary levels. That goal was balanced by also holding schools accountable for the proportion of students that were successful the first time they took a relevant subject exam.

Technology was an essential component for realizing both the vision of the development of instructional units as well as allowing different IECs for each student. MRSH also envisioned that the subject exams could be taken online anytime during the year when students were ready. MRSH also viewed technology as an essential vehicle to improve communication within the school as well as with parents.

Community and parent partnerships would vary in the specifics but would consistently focus on activities that support student learning. Partnerships could assist teachers in establishing links between disciplinary knowledge and concrete problems in industry and communities or provide students with additional opportunities to advance their understanding or mastery of standards outside the regular school day.

Leadership and action teams were an integral component of the design and were intended to develop and sustain the capacity of schools to improve the quality of their work and adapt to changing circumstances in their district and state. Action teams were established in the six core areas of the design: (1) standards and assessment, (2) instruction, (3) parent and community partnerships, (4) school organization, (5) technology, and (6) professional development. The chair of each action team also served on the leadership team to minimize the difficulty in sustaining communication across teams, ensure coordination of activities, and provide the principal with diverse perspectives on a given problem. Action teams served a number of other functions: They established ties across grade levels or departments that became sources of innovation; expertise in areas such as technology became more evenly distributed throughout the organization, and teachers' professional lives became more rewarding.

Piloting

Seven schools in Indiana and New York—four elementary, two middle, and one high school— were involved in the piloting phase of the work between 1993 and 1995. Three of the schools served primarily economically disadvantaged students—two of which enrolled almost entirely minority students; three served predominantly working-class families; and one served students largely from college-educated parents. Summer workshops provided opportunities for teachers to collaborate in developing instructional units with their colleagues with the guidance of nationally recognized experts in various subjects. Specialists in the six core areas of the design supported the work of the action teams throughout the school year. Leadership coaches worked with school administrators and the leadership teams. MRSH supplied four to five computers and several printers for each classroom in schools where they were lacking.

Schools were expected to vary in their staffing, length of school day or year, and community and parent support to reflect the needs of their student population. Frequently, those adjustments required no additional funding but only shifts in practice. School bus schedules were altered to allow those students in need of assistance to be the last group of students taken home. Maintenance engineers altered their schedule to increase security at the building. High school biology teachers collaborated with special education teachers to provide different instructional activities in classes that included students previously excluded from biology courses because of their presumed limited ability to master the concepts. A community partnership was formed with neighborhood social service and medical organizations to address parent educational needs. Parents volunteered to help in creating learning centers in young student classrooms; others helped teachers prepare the materials they needed for instruction. Students initially screened new software and videos for their likely appeal to their classmates. Classics professors recruited their students to help teachers with their work on ancient civilizations. Architects volunteered their time to help teachers with a Capstone Unit that involved experiments with weight-bearing structures. Principals had teachers conduct initial interviews with new teacher candidates. Some additional funding was required to provide teachers with additional time for creating and reviewing instructional units.

Even though the assessment system was piloted at all sites, continuous access to subject exams was not realized in the 2 years allotted for piloting. Piloting the interdisciplinary Capstone Units proved to be most challenging at the middle school level, where coordination across classes remained a problem. Implementation of the IEC and proficiency reports to parents occurred only at the elementary grades.

After 2 years, student achievement results were promising, but not unequivocal. Faculty participation was almost universal at the elementary and middle schools. Although a majority of faculty at the high schools participated in the pilot, it was not universal.

Going to Scale

In 1998, an infusion of federal funding allowed schools serving primarily economically disadvantaged students to adopt a comprehensive school-reform design. More than 100 schools adopted the MRSH design between 1998 and 2003; these were typically urban elementary or middle schools with the vast majority of their students from economically disadvantaged circumstances (80% on average). Like the students they served, schools had different needs when they adopted the MRSH design—not only in terms of leadership and organization but also in terms of technology, instruction, and community and family partnerships. Universally, though, the MRSH assessment system was replaced by that of the relevant state or district, and the expectations for acquiring technology were adapted to meet funding and architectural limitations at the schools.

MRSH advisors worked within the scope of autonomy accorded schools and helped principals identify some meaningful methods to address school needs. Within those constraints, coaches encouraged astute management of a district's policies (as in staffing) or by direct requests for a specific change in practice (such as bus schedules) to address school needs. The reauthorization of the Elementary and Secondary Education Act in 2002 (also known as the No Child Left Behind Act) narrowed the curriculum focus at most adopting sites to reading and mathematics but vastly improved the ability to target student needs with more timely access to student performance data.

Even as the type of school served changed and district and state policies were altered, the leadership team remained a robust component of the school improvement process. Consistent with research on all types of organizations, participation in the decision-making process at MRSH sites generated a greater commitment to changing practices. While parent partnerships were nourished during the scale-up phase, community partnerships were almost entirely absent. As the number of middle schools adopting the program increased, MRSH adapted its design to provide more direct attention to school culture and climate issues.

The MRSH Institute's essential contribution to school reform strategies was the process used by teachers to align standards and instruction—a process of beginning with the end in mind. That, along with the strategy for developing a system of school leadership, has been adopted by districts without other elements of the design. The wisdom of adapting the design to fit the emerging circumstances and opportunities in the early 21st century is debatable.

Sally Kilgore

See also Comprehensive School Reform; No Child Left Behind Act (NCLB); Standards Movement

Further Readings

Borman, G., Hewes, G., Overman, L., & Brown, S. (2003). Comprehensive school reform and achievement: A meta-analysis. *Review of Educational Research, 73,* 125–230.

Bransford, J., Brown, A., & Cocking, R. (Eds.). (2000). *How people learn.* Washington, DC: National Academy Press.

Champagne, D., & McQuade, F. (2002). *How to make a better school.* Needham Heights, MA: Allyn & Bacon.

Kilgore, S. (1997). *Designing schools for the 21st century: Essential elements of a Modern Red SchoolHouse.* Nashville, TN: Modern Red SchoolHouse Institute.

Kilgore, S. (2002). *Guiding principles of the Modern Red SchoolHouse design: Research-based solutions for 21st century schools.* Nashville, TN: Modern Red SchoolHouse Institute.

Newmann, F., Smith, B., Allensworth, E., & Bryk, A. (2001). Instructional program coherence: What it is and why it should guide school improvement policy. *Educational Evaluation and Policy Analysis, 23,* 297–321.

Wiggins, G., & McTighe, J. (1998). *Understanding by design.* Alexandria, VA: Association for Supervision and Curriculum Development.

MODULAR SCHEDULING

Modular scheduling is an innovation that emerged in the late 1960s. Implemented mainly in high schools, modular scheduling provides flexibility in the scheduling of instruction. Modules (mods) are usually 20 minutes long as compared to the normal class period of 45 to 55 minutes. The school day permits the use of a number of mods per day. Twenty-one mods per class per week is typical.

Classes are scheduled in different modular configurations. For instance, classes can be scheduled for one mod, two mods, three mods, or more. On different days, the same class can meet for different numbers of mods. For example, on Monday, Wednesday, and Friday, a class can meet for two mods. On Tuesday and Thursday, the same class can meet for three mods.

The schedule is designed to provide flexibility in instruction and to meet student and course content needs. All students may not attend the same classes. A greater number of students may attend the class when it is a large group activity and may then meet in separate classes for small-group activities. Classes are scheduled in different modular configurations to permit large, medium, and small group meetings as well as unstructured time. Generally, large groups of students are scheduled together for a lecture or special presentation. A medium size class could be scheduled for a more traditional discussion, question, and answer lesson, whereas a small group may be scheduled for in-depth discussion and analysis.

The number of mods per class is based on the instructional goals and subject. Science classes, language classes, and advanced classes could meet for three mods. Laboratory experiences could be scheduled for three or more mods. Classes would meet from a range of 20 minutes (one mod) to 100 minutes (five mods).

The student benefits of modular scheduling include opportunities for students to take more classes and more electives. Modular scheduling permits flexibility in matching instruction to learning styles. Students have greater freedom of movement through unstructured time. The freedom of modular scheduling is considered helpful in preparing students for college. Students have more time to schedule special activities, sports, and club activities. Students have time to meet individually with teachers during the school day. For students who are not free to stay after school because of jobs or transportation issues, this is an advantage. Students have more opportunity to socialize because of the flexible schedule.

Teacher benefits of modular scheduling include more time for collaboration, more time for individual conferences, greater teacher autonomy, more opportunity to diversify instruction, more time for instructional planning, the impetus to try different instructional approaches, and a greater sense of professionalism. Experience has shown, given the changes in teachers' and students' paradigm, or way of doing business, that schools that move to a modular schedule are better served if the change is done so in a planned and systematic process.

Observers of flexible modular scheduling, such as Shannon Murray, suggest that relationships between students and teachers are more positive, student interest in learning increases, discipline concerns decrease, and the school atmosphere becomes more relaxed and friendly in this system. Flexible modular scheduling continues to be evident in schools 40 years after its inception. Examples include Wisconsin's Wausau High School and San Francisco's Lowell High School.

Modular scheduling is also used and described as a system of scheduling that is responsive to different instructional goals and students' differing learning styles. The NCLB legislation and the 1996 *Breaking Ranks* report released by the National Association of Secondary School Principals are examples of initiatives that suggest the need for flexible scheduling for both students and teachers.

Modular scheduling is often touted as a solution to overcrowded facilities. Because all classes do not need to meet daily, this frees classroom space for other classes or activities. However, there are some pitfalls, especially when there are a number of 20-minute modules open. A single module generally has little usefulness.

Since the late 1960s, the change from "hand" scheduling to computer scheduling of classes has made modular scheduling more feasible. Modular scheduling, when completed by hand, takes an inordinate amount of time and is often not accurate. To implement modular scheduling, a number of changes may be necessary. Modular scheduling requires different space sizes due to the large, medium, and small class size formats. Instructional objectives need to be matched to the variable time frames. Curricular and instructional adjustments may be necessary and new methods of instruction may be required. Teachers' strengths and interests need to be matched to the course offerings and the change in schedule and professional development training should be provided for faculty and administrators.

Administrative leadership is critical to the success of modular scheduling. Communication among teachers, students, parents, and community members is essential for the success of modular scheduling. School leaders should be well-versed spokes-persons for the change in practice and should clearly understand and be able to communicate the strengths and challenges of modular scheduling.

Marilyn L. Grady

See also Ability Grouping; Block Scheduling; Class Size; Co-Curricular Activities; Differentiated Instruction; School Size; Secondary Curricular Reform; Site-Based Management; Year-Round Schools

Further Readings

Beggs, D. W., III, & Buffie, E. G. (1965). *Independent study: Bold new venture*. Bloomington: Indiana University Press.

Dodd, A. W. (1973). Modular scheduling: A personal view. *The English Teacher, 62*(2), 272–274.

Dunlop, R. S. (1968). Toward improved professional practice under flexible-modular scheduling. *Journal of Teacher Education, 19*(2), 159–168.

Murray, S. (2008). Flex mod scheduling redux. *Principal Leadership, 8*(7), 42–46.

Trump, J. L. (1959). *Images of the future*. Washington, DC: National Association of Secondary School Principals, National Education Association.

MONTESSORI, MARIA (1870–1952)

Maria Montessori was a physician, professor, school administrator, educator, philosopher, advocate for women's rights and a champion for children, especially those with physical and intellectual disabilities. She is best known for developing what is known as the Montessori method of education, which emphasizes self-directed activities and self-correcting materials for children in a sensory-rich environment. Montessori was born in Chiaravalle, in the province of Ancona, Italy, on August 31, 1870, the only child of Alessandro Montessori and Renilde Stoppani. Her father was a government accountant and was transferred to Rome, where Maria attended public elementary school. At the time, the schools were described as dirty, crowded, and dreary, and the education system antiquated and in dire need of reform. Montessori eventually initiated reforms in education based on the premise that all children can learn and become self-motivated, lifelong learners. She advocated for children's rights and helped reform the educational environment from dreary and austere to pleasant and attractive. She is considered one of the pioneers and champions of educating young children and those with disabilities.

Before her involvement in education, Montessori had other career goals. After elementary school she attended a technical school with the intention of becoming an engineer. She graduated with honors but then decided she wanted to become a doctor. This was unheard of for women at this time in Italy, and at first she was not admitted to the University of Rome medical school. She persisted in her desire to attend the medical school and was finally admitted as the first female medical student. Those years at medical school presented constant obstacles for her to overcome, and she was described as a diligent student and received prestigious scholarships and recognition for her hard work. During her last 2 years, she studied pediatrics and she worked at the Children's Hospital while also attending the psychiatric clinic. In 1896 she was the first woman to graduate from the University of Rome medical school. After graduation she worked as an assistant at the hospital attached to the university and eventually opened her own practice.

At the time Montessori graduated from medical school, she was chosen as a delegate to represent Italy at an international women's congress in Berlin on the condition of women and the need for social and political reforms. She was endeared as a role model and an advocate for women. After returning to Rome from the women's congress, Montessori was appointed surgical assistant at the psychiatric hospital; this position stimulated her interest in children's emotional problems.

She studied the work of Jean-Marc-Gaspard Itard, physician and pioneer of education of the deaf and mentally handicapped, and his pupil Edouard Seguin, and wrote articles on their work for Italian newspapers and magazines. By 1898 she was considered an authority on educating retarded children and was asked to give lectures throughout Europe. Afterward she was asked to codirect (with Guiseppe Montesano) a new lab school to train teachers in educating mentally disabled children. The school was considered a success, especially when after a couple of years 8 of the 22 children at the school passed the public school exams along with "normal" children.

Although Montessori and Montesano had a child together, they never married. In 1901, Montesano married another woman and Montessori made a career change by becoming a professor at the University of Rome. A few years later she took another career turn when in 1907 she agreed to head a government school for pre-school-age children in a poor neighborhood in Rome. The Casa dei Bambini, as the school was called, is considered one of the first models of day care. Montessori based the program on the methods she had devised for working with the mentally disabled children, using materials designed to appeal to the senses. The school was regarded as a success, and other similar schools soon opened all over Italy. She developed a primer of her teaching philosophies and methods that became known as the Montessori method of education.

After Montessori's mother died in 1912, she brought her son Mario to live with her. Mario was born in 1898 and had been living with her mother while Montessori traveled. In 1913, she made her first visit to the United States and was asked to establish and teach at a newly formed Montessori Institute. She did not accept the position and returned to Italy. The following year World War I broke out, and Montessori moved to Spain where she lived until 1936 and oversaw the establishment of Montessori schools. After the end of World War I, Mussolini invited her back to Italy and she went, but she refused to have her teachers take an oath of loyalty to fascism. Mussolini closed the Montessori schools and Montessori returned to Spain. When the Spanish Civil War broke out, she moved to Amsterdam, which became the headquarters of the Montessori movement and the home of the Association Montessori Internationale. She continued to travel and lecture and in 1939 was invited to India. There she and her son, who had become her manager, established India's Montessori movement. After World War II, they returned to the Netherlands and she continued traveling, giving lectures, and providing training courses.

The postwar Italian government invited Montessori back in 1947 to help reorganize the Montessori schools. She lectured again at the University of Rome, where she had graduated and worked. She continued to travel and returned to India and then back to the Netherlands, where she died in 1952.

Montessori and her method were not without controversy, and many believe that she became rigid and isolated herself and her following from further development and related ideas. She was, however, a remarkable woman, who accomplished a great deal in her lifetime. She worked to further women's rights and social reform and to promote children's healthy development, especially children with disabilities, and developed an innovative approach to children's education that is used today in schools throughout the world. Montessori was nominated for the Nobel Peace Prize three times.

Her impact on educational reform in the United States began when she visited in the early 1900s. Several American Montessori schools were opened, but their popularity declined in the 1930s when American schools' focus turned to adult authority and control. Popularity of the Montessori method grew again in the United States in the 1950s, and today there are more Montessori schools in the United States than in any other country. Her work has greatly influenced the development of early childhood education and special education programs.

Christine Ann Christle

See also Montessori Schools; Women in Educational Leadership

Further Readings

Kramer, R. (1976). *Maria Montessori: A biography.* Chicago: University of Chicago Press.

Lillard, A. S. (2005). *Montessori: The science behind the genius.* Oxford, UK: Oxford University Press.
Standing, E. M. (1998). *Maria Montessori: Her life and work.* New York: Plume.

MONTESSORI SCHOOLS

Montessori schools use an educational method characterized by self-directed activities and self-correcting materials, as developed in Europe during the early 1900s by Italian physician and educator Maria Montessori (1870–1952). Montessori had studied the work of Jean-Marc-Gaspard Itard and Edouard Seguin; she first worked with children who were mentally disabled, observing that they responded well to sensory-rich environments and succeeded in learning when engaged in purposeful activities. Montessori used materials designed to appeal to the senses, created learning games and activities, and developed strategies for teachers to guide children in learning rather than lecture them from a book. She published a primer and handbook on her teaching methods and philosophies in 1914 that became known as the Montessori method of education. After working with children who were mentally disabled, Montessori adapted her methods for preschool-age children and then further adapted her approach for elementary and secondary students. Her method emphasizes self-direction by the student and clinical observation by the teacher.

Although Montessori schools had wide popularity throughout Europe during the early 20th century, they did not catch on in the United States until the 1950s. During the social reforms of the 1950s and 1960s many educators adopted her developmental and child-centered approach to early childhood education as well as her belief that all children could learn regardless of economic status or disability. Today there are Montessori schools all over the world; however, the United States boasts more than any other country with estimates of over 8,000. Montessori schools are part of both private and public school systems and the Montessori influence is evident particularly in early childhood education and early childhood special education.

The name Montessori is not legally protected and can be used by anyone; hence there are many Montessori organizations. The two major organizations that have been sanctioned by Maria Montessori and her son Mario are the Association Montessori Internationale (AMI, with a U.S. branch office called AMI-USA) and the American Montessori Society. The tenets of the Montessori philosophy are self-motivation and autoeducation. The main purpose of a Montessori school is to help the child develop an excellent foundation for creative learning by providing a carefully planned, stimulating environment. The specific goals for children who attend Montessori schools are developing the following: a positive attitude toward school, self-confidence, a habit of concentration, a sense of curiosity, habits of initiative and persistence, inner security, and a sense of order.

There are three basic elements of the Montessori approach to education: (1) the structured environment, (2) the Montessori curriculum, and (3) the Montessori teacher. The structured environment is known as a prepared environment, and teachers arrange and maintain the physical classroom and materials based on six principles. The first principle is freedom of movement and choice. Children are free to move around the room instead of staying at desks, and they choose the order in which to work in the various areas. Second, there is a particular structure and order in how learning materials are arranged and the sequence in which they are to be used. The classroom consists of work centers arranged according to subject areas included in the curriculum. Once a student chooses an area and materials, the teacher guides the student in learning the knowledge and skills in that area. Third, the atmosphere should be attractive, warm, and inviting for the children. There should be the right amount of educational materials without cluttering the environment. Fourth, the learning materials should provide active learning experiences, encouraging students to engage in many types of activities using all five senses to develop their observational skills. Fifth, students are grouped in mixed ages and abilities in 3- to 6-year age spans. Student interaction, peer teaching, problem solving, and socialization are encouraged, and students are challenged according to their ability levels. Sixth, activities and materials should reflect the natural environment and the real world as opposed to fantasy. Montessori classrooms are stocked with living plants and small animals.

The Montessori curriculum consists of six areas of learning, with specified outcomes for knowledge and skills. The first area is practical life, and the goal is for students to learn how to care for themselves, each other, and the environment. In this area they learn skills from how to dress themselves to community service activities. The second area is sensorial, and includes colors, shapes, and various manipulative objects. The sensorial area falls over into the third area, mathematics, which is based on the children's understanding that math goes from concrete to abstract. The fourth area is language and literacy in which an integrated approach is used, combining phonetics with whole language. Culture (geography, history, natural and experimental sciences) is the fifth area. Students study different areas of the world and are introduced to the world's great diversity of people. Science is a hands-on activity and includes biology, botany, zoology, and physical science. The focus is to teach students to be scientists by being objective and organized, by observing and experimenting, and by recording results. The creative arts (the sixth area) rounds out the curriculum (arts and crafts, music and movement, drama). Montessori schools promote the creative arts to help children develop control of their fine and gross motor movement and to develop ways to express themselves.

The Montessori teacher is seen as an observer of, and facilitator for, student learning and development rather than an instructor. The teacher observes the students to determine their individual developmental needs and then prepares the environment and materials to meet those needs. Once students make their own free choices as to which materials they wish to interact with, the teacher guides them in the acquisition of the knowledge and skills within the curriculum. Standards for Montessori teacher training vary widely by state and country. Traditional Montessori teacher training is a full year of graduate work for each of the three age levels and child developmental stages: (1) birth to 3 years, (2) 3 years to 6 years, and (3) 6 years to 12 years. Montessori middle and high school teachers ideally take all three training courses plus graduate work in an academic area or areas.

Other aspects of Montessori schools include the expanded schedule and lack of grades in assessment. The Montessori schedule includes 3-hour work periods for students under age 6. Older students may schedule study groups with each other and the teacher. The Montessori method discourages the traditional measurements of achievement, such as tests and grades. Instead, assessment is based on student-developed portfolios and teachers' observational data. Teachers help students to make improvements to reach the specified knowledge and skills in each of the curricular areas.

Some critics of Montessori schools have complained about the freedom students are given in the choice of what to study. Others have registered concern that certain students will not master all areas of the curriculum if they remain uninterested in them and thus do not have to study them. Montessori schools also have been criticized for not assigning homework, not giving tests, and not giving grades. Some Montessori schools today provide grades, especially at the secondary level, because grades are an important consideration for college entry requirements. Another criticism that is sometimes voiced is the rigid Montessori requirement regarding classroom materials. Some schools do not have the funds to provide the high-quality, natural materials that are sanctioned by the Montessori associations and instead use cheaper materials.

Montessori schools and the Montessori movement have had a significant impact on educational reform. For example, the open classroom, manipulative learning materials, teaching games and toys, individualized education, and programmed instruction have been adapted from Montessori's theories. Montessori schools particularly have influenced reforms in early childhood education and special education.

Christine Ann Christle

See also Early Childhood Education; Montessori, Maria

Further Readings

Montessori, M. (1912). *The Montessori method*. New York: Cosimo.

Montessori, M. (1914). *Dr. Montessori's own handbook*. New York: Stokes.

Orem, R. C. (1974). *Montessori: Her method and the movement*. New York: Putnam.

MORAL DEVELOPMENT

Moral education has always been central to the educational process. Since the time of the Greek philosophers those responsible for educating young children have been concerned either directly or indirectly with moral questions. What has changed is the way in which educators have approached moral issues in the classroom and in the curriculum. The questions and issues are complex and form the basis of reformers' efforts to change the way in which schools confront the moral dimensions of education in a postmodern world. The challenges educators confront today have clear grounding in what has occurred over the past 200 years, as schooling moved increasingly toward a public good.

The Roots of Moral Development

Moral development finds root in the philosophy of Immanuel Kant (1724–1804). Kant's conception of morality was based on duty and performance regardless of circumstance or consequence. Morality depended upon the distinction between actions directed by hypothetical imperatives and actions directed by categorical imperatives. To Kant, hypothetical imperatives predicated on the just reward principle were the antithesis of moral behavior. Only categorical imperatives represented a higher order of morality, a universal law.

Kant constructed a dichotomy of morality, contrasting heteronomous morality with autonomous morality. Heteronomous morality depended upon external authority such as God or obedience to the state. Autonomous morality was a personal choice, a free will, where actions were based on individual conscience. Moral actions, as conceived by Kant, were both altruistic and formalist in concept. A formalist perceived moral development to occur in stages of universal categorical imperatives (moral rules) that guided social action. An altruist perceived moral development to be based solely in self-sacrifice and the desire to help others, a tenet of prosocial behavior.

The 20th-century developmental psychologist Jean Piaget based his theories of moral development on the prosocial behavior of children during play. Piaget's theory of moral development displayed the Kantian influence of formalism. Piaget observed children's application of rules as they played. He interviewed young children to determine their reactions to acts such as stealing and lying. Piaget found that young children's moral reasoning could rarely go beyond the formalist concept of a forbidden act. Piaget concluded that within this heteronomous stage of moral reasoning, a child made moral decisions based on duties, rules, and obedience to authority. Additionally, Piaget found that a young child's moral reasoning was egocentric and founded on a form of moral realism. Moral realism, a form of hypothetical imperative, would, for example, value the letter of the law above the purpose. Young children were more concerned about the outcome of the action than the underlying intent. Powerless, young children adhered to principles of immanent justice, expecting punishment to be the natural result of wrongdoing. Piaget determined that as children matured, moral reasoning became autonomous. Older children's level of moral awareness commonly assigned importance to the intention of the act and concepts of mutual respect and cooperation. This shift from egocentric morality to perspective taking was a significant stage in Piaget's theory of moral development.

Kantian formalism also served as a guideline for the academic moral philosophy of Lawrence Kohlberg. Concepts of heteronomous and autonomous morality were reflected in the stages of moral development proposed by Kohlberg. Styles of moral reasoning within the Kohlberg theory of moral development were universal and predictable and based on issues of moral and political justice. The six stages of moral thought consisted of three levels with two stages in each set. As the individual developed ability to reason morally he or she progressed through stages moving from morality based on hypothetical imperatives to morality based on categorical imperatives.

The first stage of Kohlberg's theory of moral development is the *preconventional level,* a stage during which rules are followed without discernment. Stage 1 decisions are based on external authority and the avoidance of unpleasant consequences, heteronomous morality. Stage 2 morality is hedonistic, in which the morality of action becomes self-serving. At the *conventional level* of morality, the individual conforms to social norms. Stage 3 decisions are morally based on hypothetical imperatives, situations in which the individual seeks rewards for conforming. Stage 4 moral choices, still within the realms of heteronomous morality, depend on the individual's desire to

maintain the social order by following the rules. *Postconventional level* changes the basis of morality from hypothetical imperatives to categorical imperatives. The moral reasoning in this stage of development depends on discernment or individual conscience and therefore becomes a form of autonomous morality. Stage 5 moral choices fully embrace the concepts of autonomous formalist reasoning. In Stage 6 moral reasoning advances to categorical imperatives, as critical decisions involving universality of justice, natural rights, and democratic principles are made. Kohlberg was said to equate this stage with the foundations of the American legal system.

The Debate About Moral Development

In the early 1980s Carol Gilligan disputed Kohlberg's formalist approach to moral development. Gilligan proposed that Kohlberg's theories were predicated on gender, as his participant pool was all male. She ascertained that Kohlberg's mature moral reasoning should incorporate the ethic of care as equivalent to justice reasoning. Her theories are considered to be a rejection of Kantian formalism and are interpreted as altruistic, focused on the welfare of others.

Nancy Eisenberg extended Kohlberg's line of research and took exception with Gilligan's altruistic concepts. Eisenberg's study concluded that altruism, as a form of advanced reasoning, led to prosocial choices that prioritized the needs of others. In many ways Eisenberg confirmed Kohlberg. All nonaltruistic responses were categorized as hedonistic, and prosocial choices followed stages similar to those established by Kohlberg's Stages 5 and 6. In essence, Eisenberg's determination that refusals to act altruistically were representative of moral immaturity was disputed. Yet her conception of altruistic acts as manifested by self-sacrifice was of true value to the conception of prosocial behavior as a measure of moral development.

Elliot Turiel shared the formalist assumptions of Kohlberg that moral development was based on moral rules that were both categorical and obligatory. Larry Nucci and Turiel expanded this notion to include how children differentiated between their social domains and moral domains. The research into moral domains was based on the premise that moral rules are separate from conventional rules,

rules that are circumstantial, and both are separate from prudential rules, personal rules considered outside the realm of morality. Nucci and Turiel concluded that, contrary to Kohlberg's theory, preschoolers adhered to forms of moral conventions and social rules. Moral development occurred through a maturation process that fine-tuned the distinction in the child's mind between the three types of rules.

Applying Moral Development in the Classroom

The application of moral development to education draws primarily from the developmental theories of Piaget, Gilligan, Nucci, and Kohlberg. Piaget concluded that moral development was fostered in the schools by the opportunity for children to problem solve and use elements of personal discovery to determine their personal perspective on moral decisions. Gilligan emphasized an educational curriculum that developed empathy. Nucci recommended a domain-appropriate, teacher-led, value-laden education. Kohlberg took issue with character education, a concept that determined moral development on a list of commonly accepted virtues. He advocated for student participation in a community discussion that established a moral consensus based on actual problems and issues faced within the school community. Kohlberg proposed the concept of "Just Community" schools, in which teachers played a leadership role in moving students to the next level of moral reasoning. Kohlberg's Just Community schools were miniature models of John Dewey's ideal democracy and fostered the development of amorally autonomous individuals.

Critics of moral development theory believe that Kohlberg did not consider the moral orientation of Eastern philosophy, based on the principles of Buddhism, Hinduism, or Confucianism, when he developed his principles of universality, or moral domains. Kohlberg and Power proposed moral developmental Stage 7: a stage of moral development where religious speculation about the nature of existence, transcendence, the role of the saint, or the mystique surrounding the Dalai Lama might exist. In the end, Kohlberg acknowledged that morality might lie beyond rational comprehension. There still exists an ongoing disagreement over the multicultural, universal application of the moral structure behind the developmental stages; disagreement on the use of stages rather than levels; and the ongoing debate about the relationship between moral decisions and moral actions.

Victoria Zascavage

See also Character Education; Developmentally Appropriate Practice; Moral Education; Piaget, Jean

Further Readings

Eisenberg, N., Miller, P. A., Shell, R., McNalley, S., & Shea, C. (1991). Pro-social development in adolescence: A longitudinal study. *Developmental Psychology, 27,* 849–857.

Gilligan, C. (1982). *In a different voice: Psychological theory and women's development.* Cambridge, MA: Harvard University Press.

Kant, I. (1991). *The metaphysics of morals* (M. Gregor, Trans.). Cambridge, UK: Cambridge University Press. (Original work published 1797)

Kohlberg, L., & Power, C. (1981). Moral development, religious thinking, and the question of a seventh stage. In L. Kohlberg (Ed.), *Essays on moral development. Vol. 1: The philosophy of moral development* (pp. 311–372). San Francisco: Harper & Row.

Nucci, L. (2001). *Education in the moral domain.* Cambridge, UK: Cambridge University Press.

Nucci, L. P., & Turiel, E. (1978). Social interactions and the development of social concepts in children. *Child Development, 49,* 400–407.

Piaget, J. (1932).*The moral judgment of the child.* New York: The Free Press.

MORAL EDUCATION

Moral education is not so much a subject in American education as a vibrant and contentious debate with deep historical roots. Moral education, broadly construed, refers to the effort by educators to inculcate specific values such as honesty and integrity in young students. The idea is that public schools not only should be responsible for teaching core academic content such as reading and arithmetic but also should help children develop into thoughtful and ethically responsible human beings. For many educators, therefore, moral education is a critical component of civic education and a necessary component of training for citizenship.

Scholars and many American citizens believe that moral education requires a meticulous pedagogy that draws on psychology and philosophy to help students develop traits, such as empathy and critical thinking, which are essential to the functioning of democracy in a complex global society. At the same time, many Americans and some scholars believe that moral education should be explicitly religious so that moral education as it is taught in schools will draw upon natural law, religion, or both, and not merely human experience. Thus, any attempt to help large numbers of citizens develop certain forms of "morality" inevitably raises the question of exactly what defines moral thought and action in the first place. Given the cultural diversity of the United States, educators, community members, clergy, and citizens all struggle to clarify the meaning of morality and ensure that their version is taught—or at least not contradicted—in the nation's public schools. Moral education is, therefore, one of the most controversial and durable subjects of educational reform in the United States and one that habitually provokes an angry backlash from dissenters. This entry offers a broad definition of moral education and analyzes the historical trajectory of moral education as an ongoing reform process in American public schools.

Moral Education Defined

American models of moral education have been informed by leading theorists in psychology, philosophy, and religion. Proponents of moral education in American public schools believe that existing pedagogy fails to account for the vital need to train young children in the complicated and ambiguous subject of ethics. Although certain models of moral education are rooted in particular normative or faith communities, such as Jewish, Muslim, Mennonite, Protestant, or Catholic, many academics and educators are motivated to support moral education as a secular component of public schooling that promises to enrich the lives of all citizens in a pluralistic nation.

Psychologist Jean Piaget's groundbreaking studies of the moral lives of children connected the development of moral thinking to lived experience. Later scholars built on and expanded Piaget's work; these scholars include Lawrence Kolhberg, who mapped out six distinct stages of moral development. Kolhberg believed that children progressed through these stages as part of their cognitive development and that each stage represented a fundamental shift in the social-moral perspective of the individual. Because he also believed that moral growth occurred through lived experience, Kolhberg proposed that teachers create opportunities for children to take moral action designed to help them advance through the various stages of moral growth. He located these moral stages in the realm of human cognition and therefore outside of the realm of culture. The work of psychologists like Kohlberg seemed to offer a moral education pedagogy that was immune to charges of cultural relativity. By the mid-1960s, reformers crafted Kohlberg's theories into a promising curriculum called "values clarification." This new curriculum was intentionally nonprescriptive. Instead of instructing students in the specifics of moral thoughts and deeds, the goal was to help students identify those values that were important to them. This was especially valuable, according to proponents, because values clarification would remain flexible in the face of changing or contradictory values that were only natural given the complications of modernity.

Later studies revealed, however, that Kohlberg's moral stages did not always function the way they were supposed to, and this prompted new versions of moral education. Elliot Turiel found that some realms of morality were in fact influenced by cultural norms such as what constituted harm, welfare, and fairness. Feminist scholars, including Carol Gilligan and Nel Noddings, proposed that Kohlberg had failed to understand the gendered nuances of morality, for example, the feminine disposition for "caring." These scholars suggested that teachers should pay careful attention to the different cognitive and social ways that men versus women, and boys versus girls, may experience morality and moral development. Today, a diverse range of scholars employ theoretical models from the social sciences and humanities relating to human cognition and the essence of morality to design practical models of moral education in American schools.

Historical Trajectory of Moral Education

Public support for moral education has proven difficult to sustain. Any attempt to institute moral education in practice tends to call into question not only the meaning of morality but more specific questions about who is instituting these programs and why. Historically, moral education has been complicated by the tendency of White, Protestant, middle-class Americans to target the poor and racial minorities as the individuals in need of extra moral guidance. Two good examples include the nativist backlash against immigrants from eastern and southern Europe in the 1920s that prompted the first round of "character education," and the more recent push for "moral clarity" in American schools that insisted children be trained exclusively in western European traditions. In these situations, otherwise moderate and local debates about the content and nature of American public education flared into national culture wars in which various sides disagreed about the definition of morality and the role of public institutions in promoting ethical behavior in the nation's youth. Emerging at moments of national crisis, moral education is often a proxy for anxieties about American identity, nationhood, and cultural authority. A historical perspective on moral education therefore sheds light on how and why this subject engenders such controversy today.

According to historian Edward McClellan, moral education was once a primary purpose of American public schools, but it disappeared from the curriculum as modernity made new demands for highly skilled workers in the late 19th century. Technical skill, efficiency, and social competence became desirable traits of educated citizens, while the development of personal morality was relegated to the private sphere of church and home. As moral education was pushed out of the curriculum in the early 20th century, critics maintained that schools should promote traditional values drawn from older, well-established texts in order to safeguard morality in an age of uncertainty. These educators looked to the past for answers they believed served as foundations to American democracy and developed a curriculum called "character education" to promote what they claimed were traditional Protestant values, such as honesty,

cleanliness, punctuality, and hard work. Proponents of character education believed that these traits were lacking in a majority of American citizens, an insult that was not lost on either students or their parents. Character education was most notable for its strict codes of conduct, or list of traits that students were expected to memorize and enact. In contrast, during the same era, progressive educators believed that a modern democracy required an entirely new approach to the challenge of moral education. They denigrated character education and its static moral codes, instead encouraging a more flexible and critical approach to morality in the classroom. Meanwhile, other Americans remained suspicious of both versions of moral education and asserted that public schooling must include direct instruction in religious texts and mandates—a particularly vexing proposition given the nation's heterogeneous population and government control of schooling.

Often two or even three of these different approaches to moral education coexisted in American schools at a given time, sometimes even within a particular school. The progressive vision for moral education, expanded as character education, declined in the late 1920s. By the 1930s, progressive educators wanted to train students to be flexible and critical in their approach to morality. They believed relativity was the best way to deal with rapid change, such as the social, political, and economic transformations erupting around them. In this new social order, many educators believed that moral codes could not be memorized, because the complexity of modern life meant that what might be moral in one situation could be terribly immoral in another.

This new understanding of moral relativity seemed to offer a scientifically grounded approach to the troubling question of how to train millions of citizens, a large number of whom were immigrants or the children of immigrants, in the ethical habits of an "educated" democratic citizen. Reversing the emphasis of early moral educators who focused on personal conduct, later progressives designed moral education to confront larger social issues such as social-class inequality and tolerance with the goal of fostering a more humane society. To guide their new pedagogy, progressives turned not to old and established texts but to new methods of scientific inquiry and democratic decision making informed by the emerging social sciences. Like character educators, Progressives valued group learning, but they intended group activities to promote discussion and decision making, not peer pressure and conformity as in the past. Moral education in this vein was integrated into the curriculum at all levels and not taught as a separate course. The newly defined field of "social studies" proved to be a particularly rich site for considering complex issues of social justice and individual responsibility. Whereas these programs attempted to foster critical thinking, later critics charged they left the individual child subject to the whims of his or her young and morally underdeveloped peers.

The rise of the cold war in the late 1940s dampened efforts to discuss controversial issues like social justice or economic inequality in American classrooms. In the 1980s, however, multicultural education emerged as a powerful new curriculum that promised to train students in social justice, critical thinking, and empathy for minorities. Although not often designated as a form of moral education, the curriculum's emphasis on cultivating "transformative knowledge" tends to overlap with educators' intent on shaping individual and social morality in the classroom.

In the early 21st century, political demands for additional moral instruction in American public schools are often intertwined with fears about social ills such as teenage pregnancy, high dropout rates, disciplinary problems, or drug and alcohol use. The ascendancy of multiculturalism in American schools since the 1990s means that educators have become more cautious about "imposing" certain strands of morality onto others, and recently some scholars have reasserted that western European heritage is the "true" cultural heritage of the United States. In the wake of the terrorist attacks of September 11, 2001, conservative pundit and former secretary of the U.S. Department of Education William J. Bennett attacked American schools for promoting postmodernism and multiculturalism in American schools, an act he claimed complicated the "righteous anger" he insisted Americans should feel for Islamic terrorists. Bennett discounted efforts to teach about Islam or American foreign policy, asserting that these relativistic interpretations undermined what he imagined to be a clearer moral vision of good versus evil. Bennett's vocal demands for moral education in America

and his concurrent attack on multiculturalism reverberated across the country as teachers, activists, and intellectuals weighed in on the best way to teach American students about Islam and terrorism in an ethically responsible way.

In the late 20th century, the concept of "character education" made a comeback in both academia and popular culture. Sponsored alternatively by corporations, evangelical Protestants, public school administrators, or academics, there is now a dizzying array of programs available in the 21st century that all claim to be programs of moral education. Some organizations continue to offer simple lists of moral objectives for students in each grade, but others, especially those associated with universities, attempt to bridge the divide between scholarly theories of child psychology and philosophy and the specific needs of local communities. These partnerships between academics and public schools help foster a pedagogical approach to moral education that is fully grounded in social science theory and empirical studies while also taking into account the cultural and religious diversity of local communities.

The impressive range of programs operated under the rubric of character education today tends to create confusion and uncertainty about moral education. Many academics remain suspicious of the ways that corporations and business leaders in America support programs of moral education as a philanthropic endeavor. David Purpel, for example, contends that public schools are unable to institute substantial moral education because of the dominant influence of capitalism and meritocracy on American culture. He argues schools are controlled by political leaders and business interests that value obedience, docility, conformity, and individualism. These leaders therefore require state-sponsored educational institutions to instill these values. Scholars like Purpel suggest that American public schools *intentionally* restrict effective moral education because it would expose capitalism as a particularly unjust political economy. Others, however, remain more optimistic that an intellectually rigorous moral education is already in place in many schools. J. Mark Halstead and Mark A. Pike, for example, conceive of moral education as directly related to citizenship education, or the promotion of civic training. They view moral education as a key component of citizenship training that enables people from different beliefs and backgrounds to live together peacefully despite differing allegiances, opinions, and tastes. Moral education thus provides students with the fundamental values and critical thinking skills all children need to live and work together, and more importantly, to forge constructive alliances across cultural, national, and ideological boundaries.

Zoë Burkholder

See also Americanization; Character Education; Civic Education; Moral Development; Multicultural Education; Peace Education; Piaget, Jean; School Choice; Secular Humanism; Values Clarification

Further Readings

Bennett, W. J. (2003). *Why we fight: Moral clarity and the war on terrorism.* New York: Doubleday.

Fraser, J. W. (1999). *Between church and state: Religion and public education in a multicultural America.* New York: St. Martin's Press.

Gilligan, C. (1993). *In a different voice: Psychological theory and women's development.* Cambridge, MA: Harvard University Press.

Halstead, J. M., & Pike, M. A. (2006). *Citizenship and moral education: Values in action.* London: Routledge.

Hunter, J. D. (2001). *The death of character: On the moral education of America's children.* New York: Basic Books.

McClellan, B. E. (1999). *Moral education in America: Schools and the shaping of character from colonial times to the present.* New York: Teachers College Press.

Noddings, N. (2003). *Caring: A feminine approach to ethics and moral education* (2nd ed.). Berkeley: University of California Press.

Purpel, D. E. (2003). The decontextualization of moral education. *American Journal of Education, 110,* 89–95.

Reimer, J., Paolitto, D. P., & Hersch, R. H. (1990). *Promoting moral growth: From Piaget to Kohlberg* (2nd ed.). Prospect Heights, IL: Waveland Press.

Reuben, J. A. (1997). Beyond politics: Community civics and the redefinition of citizenship in the Progressive era. *History of Education Quarterly, 37,* 399–420.

Salili, F., & Hoosain, R. (Eds.). (2006). *Religion in multicultural education.* Greenwich, CT: Information Age Publishing.

Zimmerman, J. (2005). *Whose America? Culture wars in American schools.* Cambridge, MA: Harvard University Press.

MOSES, ROBERT

See Algebra Project

MULTICULTURAL EDUCATION

Multicultural education began in the United States in response to the civil rights movement during the 1960s and is defined by reformers as the ability of all students—regardless of gender, socioeconomic class, ethnic, racial, or cultural qualities—to be able to learn in school, free of prejudice and discrimination. The reform movement of the 1960s had an influence within the school system as African Americans became adamant that school curricula reflect their particular and unique points of view, history, and culture. Other ethnic groups then began insisting that their forms of cultural expression be recognized and represented in schools. After World War II, citizens immigrating to Westernized countries were often referred to as "newcomers" or "immigrants," and expectations were that these individuals would assimilate into their "new" cultures. A focus on multiculturalism emerged when the attitudinal shift toward a cultural mosaic or pluralistic society, as opposed to assimilation into American culture, occurred.

Although *multicultural education* is the most common term used to describe a pluralistic education, it has also been referred to as intercultural education (especially in Europe). Other program names associated with multicultural education include multi-ethnic, multiracial, and antiracist education. Schooling that incorporates multicultural ideals within its curricula comprises a variety of courses and programs. Thus, multicultural education cannot be classified as one definable course of instruction. Courses have been developed in relation to educational justice, equality, women, ethnic and language minorities, citizens having lower incomes, and persons with disabilities. Thus, the scope of this field is broad, having an emphasis on democratic attitudes and values and teaching students the knowledge and attitudes necessary to thrive in a complex and culturally diverse world.

Multicultural education strives to reduce prejudicial attitudes and discrimination toward oppressed groups, support equal opportunity, foster social justice for all, and share the distribution of power equitably among all citizens regardless of cultural affiliation. A thorough and complete education cannot be based on the canons of one culture: This is one of the main ideals that teachers, school administrators, and counselors keep in mind when designing curriculum, engaging in school reform, and encouraging student action, all of which guide students toward a multicultural education. Another aim of multiculturalism is to have students learn about other cultures for the purpose of understanding their own culture in different cultural contexts. Thus, multicultural education is developed for all learners, not only for those who are ethnically diverse or marginalized. Importance within the multicultural curriculum is placed on appreciating, recognizing, and empowering diverse cultural, racial, ethnic, and language groups, thus creating in schools a cultural mosaic or ethnic pluralism. Within a democratic and multicultural society, justice, compassion, dignity, and equality for all must be strongly promoted.

Leadership in Multicultural Education

Often referred to as "the father of multicultural education," James Albert Banks is a renowned scholar and researcher having a deep commitment to social justice and multicultural education. He is the founding director of the Center for Multicultural Education at the University of Washington in Seattle.

Growing up as an African American in Arkansas during the time of racial segregation, Banks was an avid reader and book lover, who was not permitted to use the local public library because it was for Whites only. This educational and social limitation did not hinder Banks from becoming an exemplary scholar, his work spanning over 4 decades in the discipline of multicultural education, a rich and dynamic arena within the educational field. Banks left Arkansas to complete his bachelor's degree with honors in elementary education and social science at Chicago State University. From there he obtained his master's degree and Ph.D. (1969) from Michigan State University.

James Banks's contribution to emergent multicultural issues within education has spawned debates as to the best or most appropriate methodologies for teaching and incorporating multicultural education into public and state schools, colleges, and universities. Possibly the most significant dispute occurring within the multicultural arena took place in the late 1980s and early 1990s, which witnessed dissent over what constituted the curriculum canon. Widely circulated nonscholarly published books defended the Western traditional curriculum while attacking the multiculturalists who proposed the induction of ethnic group content and subject matter on women into educational curriculum. Two organizations that opposed multicultural education are the National Association of Scholars and the Madison Center. Conversely, the organization known as Teachers for a Democratic Culture was encouraged by the focus on multicultural education and wanted to see it included in college and university curricula. The National Association for Multicultural Education supported diversity and multiculturalism for teacher education as well as for elementary and high schools.

To accomplish the goals he outlined in his writings for a multicultural education, Banks investigated how theory and research could enhance programs in schools to improve race relations. Banks proposed a schema for multicultural education that has several different layers designed to reduce prejudice and racism through school reformation. The first layer, content integration, focuses on the extent to which educators incorporate multicultural texts, concepts, and theories into the curriculum. The second layer, knowledge construction process, asks educators to question relevant culturally implicit assumptions within the curriculum. With this new knowledge, students also learn about personal cultural assumptions, stereotypes, and biases, which can have a negative effect on racial and ethnic relations. Reformers concerned about multiculturalism view the more inclusive curriculum as essential to ensuring a quality education for all students.

Reform-minded multiculturalists also argue for equity pedagogy, whereby teachers revamp their teaching strategies in order to assist ethnically diverse students and both genders to succeed academically. Thus, the goal is to see that all students have an equal opportunity to academically and socially succeed. The development of a positive racial mind-set is key to another layer known as prejudice reduction. And yet another dimension or layer, empowering school culture and social structure, places emphasis on empowerment and involves the entire structure and culture of the school.

Although multicultural literacy and social justice strive to reduce prejudiced and discriminatory attitudes while developing skills and awareness for living in a culturally diverse society, the outcome can never be fully attained; educational equality is identified by multicultural reformers as a goal that needs to be shaped and refined. This goal is important because emerging demographic information suggests that one in every three citizens of the United States is a person of color. It is projected that non-Hispanic Whites will decrease as cultures are more intertwined than ever, with global migration and international economic ties. By 2020, it is expected that almost half of the country's youth will be students of color. Even those who reject the assertions of reformers concerned with multicultural issues are forced to confront the reality of significant changing demographics in the United States. Those demographic changes are necessarily changing the landscape of the PreK–12 educational curriculum.

Grace Beatrice Hopcraft

See also English as a Second Language (ESL); Immigration and Education Reform; National Association for the Advancement of Colored People (NAACP)

Further Readings

Banks, J. (2001). *Cultural diversity and education: Foundations, curriculum, and teaching* (4th ed.). Boston: Allyn & Bacon.

Banks, J. (2008). An introduction to multicultural education (8th ed.). Boston: Allyn & Bacon.

Banks, J. (Ed.). (2009). *The Routledge international companion to multicultural education.* New York: Routledge.

Banks, J., & Banks, C. (Eds.). (2004). *Handbook of research on multicultural education* (2nd ed.). San Francisco: Jossey-Bass.

Banks, J., & Banks, C. (2004). *Multicultural education: Issues and perspectives* (5th ed.). Hoboken, NJ: Wiley.

Grant, C., & Chapman, T. (Eds.). (2008). *History of multicultural education.* New York: Routledge.

Irvine, J. (2003). *Educating teachers for diversity: Seeing with a cultural eye.* New York: Teachers College Press.

Takaki, R. (2008). *A different mirror: A history of multicultural America.* New York: Back Bay.

MULTIPLE INTELLIGENCES

Multiple intelligences (MI) is a theory of psychology and education first proposed by Harvard psychologist Howard Gardner in his 1983 book, *Frames of Mind.* At its core is the proposition that individuals have the potential to develop a combination of seven separate intelligences, or spheres of intelligence, and the suggestion that the measuring of an individual student's overall cognitive capacity should not be focused on a single measurement or attempt to quantify intelligence. Rather, because a diversity of separate "intelligences" can be measured in an individual and each person manifests varying levels of each one, a unique cognitive profile is a better representative of individual strengths and weaknesses than those measures that are normally emphasized in educational curricula.

MI is not meant to be a relativistic theory of education. The theory as applied should not be used to justify a student's failure in one area by claiming that his or her intelligence should instead be measured based on that area in which he or she performs best. Rather, applications of the theory account for successes and failures of the student in an array of cognitive capacities, and the student's overall cognitive profile merely distinguishes between them.

It is important to note that Gardner claims that every person possesses all intelligences to some degree. In the field of education, the application of MI is toward integrating all intelligences into the means of instruction employed by teachers. That is, the task of the educator becomes one of addressing different learning styles among students, accounting for differing strengths and weaknesses, and teaching to each of the different intelligences in the classroom. Adherents of MI assert that nurturing intelligences in which the student is already strong and developing those in which he or she is weak is the best way to facilitate a healthy integration of all the intelligences and represent most accurately each student's success and failure.

In order for a cognitive capacity to qualify for description as an independent "intelligence" (rather than as a subskill or a combination of other kinds of intelligence), it must meet eight specific criteria. First, it must be possible to thoroughly symbolize that capacity using a specific notation that conveys its essential meaning. Second, neurological evidence must exist that some area of the brain is specialized to control that particular capacity. This is often proven through case studies of individuals who have suffered brain damage and have lost that specific capacity while retaining others. Third, case studies must exist that show that some subgroups of people (such as child prodigies or autistic savants) exhibit an elevated mastery over a given intelligence. Fourth, the intelligence must have some evolutionary relevance through history and across cultures. Fifth, the capacity must have a unique developmental history for each individual, reflecting each person's different level of mastery over it. Sixth, the intelligence must be measurable in psychometric studies that are reflective of differing levels of mastery across intelligences. Seventh, the intelligence must have some definite set of core operations that are indicative of its use. Lastly, the proposed intelligence must be already plausible based on existing means of measuring intelligence.

Gardner's original theoretical model included seven separate intelligences: linguistic, musical, logical-mathematical, spatial, bodily-kinesthetic, interpersonal, and intrapersonal. In 1999, Gardner added the naturalistic dimension of intelligence to his theory, and he continues to investigate whether or not there is an "existential" intelligence. Each of the eight intelligences is further grouped according to their relationship to the learning environment based on whether they are language-related, person-related, or object-related.

The linguistic and musical intelligences can be said to be language-related. These two intelligences engage both auditory and oral functions, both of which Gardner is certain are central to the development of verbal and rhythmic skill. He has even gone so far as to hypothesize that, at some prehistorical point in human development, music and language may have arisen from the same early attempts at communication and self-expression.

Verbal-linguistic intelligence, manifested both orally and in writing, is the ability to use words and language effectively. Poets, writers, lawyers, homilists, politicians, and salespeople all typically have exceptional ability in linguistic intelligence. Specifically, Gardner identifies four distinct aspects of this intelligence that are important in everyday use: (1) the rhetorical aspect of language, used to persuade others; (2) the explanatory capacity of language; (3) the ability to use language to explain language; and (4) the mnemonic potential for language to be used in recalling information. Those who possess a high degree of verbal-linguistic intelligence have an ability to manipulate sentential syntax and structure, easily acquire foreign languages, and typically make use of a large vocabulary.

Musical intelligence includes the ability to perceive and express variations in rhythm, pitch, and melody; the ability to compose and perform music; and the capacity to appreciate music and to distinguish subtleties in its form. It is similar to linguistic intelligence in its structure and origin, and employs many of the same auditory and oral resources. Musical intelligence has ties to areas of the brain that control other intelligences as well, such as is found in the performer who has a keen bodily-kinesthetic intelligence or the composer who is adept at applying logical-mathematical intelligence toward the manipulation of ratio, patterns, and scales of music.

Person-related intelligences include both interpersonal and intrapersonal cognitive capacities. They include both an individual student's self-awareness and his or her ability to discover and relate to his or her community at all levels, inclusive of peers, superiors, and subordinates.

Intrapersonal intelligence is identified with self-knowledge, self-understanding, and the ability to discern one's strengths and weaknesses as a means of guiding one's actions. Those high in intrapersonal intelligence are often especially reflective, socially independent, and prudent.

Interpersonal intelligence is manifested in the ability to understand, perceive, and appreciate the feelings and moods of others. Those with high interpersonal intelligence are able to get along well with others, work cooperatively, communicate effectively, empathize with others, and motivate others to do certain things. According to Gardner, the ability to see things as others see them contributes to one's ability to persuade or influence others. This may give the leader, for example, an uncanny advantage in addressing the concerns of the opposition. Interpersonal intelligence may be found in a compassionate, selfless, altruistic person, who senses the needs of others and moves to meet them immediately. Conversely, a more self-centered person with high interpersonal intelligence might use the same ability to discern the fear of the community in an effort to control the group for sinister purposes.

The four object-related intelligences—logical-mathematical, bodily-kinesthetic, naturalistic, and spatial—are stimulated and engaged by concrete objects and experiences one encounters in the environment. These objects include physical features of the environment such as plants and animals, concrete things, and abstractions or numbers that are used to organize the environment.

Logical-mathematical intelligence is highly valued in our culture. Those who exhibit high degrees of this intelligence are able to easily perceive patterns, follow series of commands, solve mathematical calculations, generate categories and classifications, and apply these skills to everyday use.

Bodily-kinesthetic intelligence is manifested in physical development, athletic ability, manual dexterity, and understanding of physical wellness. It includes the ability to perform certain valuable functions, such as those of the surgeon or mechanic, as well as the ability to express ideas and feelings as artisans and performers.

Spatial intelligence, according to Gardner, is manifested in at least three ways: (1) the ability to perceive things accurately, (2) the ability to represent one's ideas in a two- or three-dimensional form, and (3) the ability to maneuver an object through space by imagining it rotated or by seeing it from various perspectives. Those high in spatial intelligence are highly visual learners who think best in images, pictures, and mental illustrations. Though spatial intelligence may be highly visual, its visual component refers more directly to one's ability to create mental representations of reality.

Naturalistic intelligence is the most recent addition to Gardner's theoretical model and is not as widely accepted as the other seven. It includes the ability to recognize plants, animals, and other parts of the natural environment, as well as to see patterns and organizational structures found in nature. Thus, it has strong ties to the logical-mathematical dimension of intelligence and is sometimes seen as merely a subset of logical-mathematical abilities. Most notably, research remains inconclusive as to whether the naturalistic intelligence fulfills the criteria of being able to be isolated in neurophysiology.

Generally speaking, school curricula nationwide have traditionally placed a greater emphasis on some of the intelligences discussed here more than others. Through lectures, written assignments, reading, and textbooks, schools have long emphasized linguistic intelligence as a means of both pedagogy and evaluation. Logical-mathematical ability is a prerequisite for advanced work or study in scientific fields, and aptitude in this area has long been a key component of evaluating general intelligence. Interpersonal intelligence is naturally acquired in the learning environment through the process of normal socialization. Musical and spatial intelligences, on the other hand, are less likely to be emphasized in school curricula and are often seen as supplemental to more traditional areas of pedagogy, usually in the form of music lessons and art classes. Intrapersonal intelligence has been traditionally absent from school curricula altogether. Bodily-kinesthetic intelligence falls somewhere in-between. While sports, physical development, and manual activity have long been present in school environments, they have only recently become emphasized in educational curricula. Though it is still often left at the gymnasium door, bodily-kinesthetic development is ever more important to our increasingly health-conscious society.

Whereas MI was first advanced as an alternative view of how an understanding of intelligence might be applied toward school curricula, the theory has been adopted by a large number of educators over the past 2 decades. A number of schools now employ MI-guided programs, and many individual teachers incorporate some or all of the theory into their methodology. The most famous MI-driven school in the United States is the New City School in St. Louis, Missouri, which implemented an MI-focused curriculum in 1988.

Ronald J. Nuzzi

See also Intelligence Testing

Further Readings

Armstrong, T. (2000). *Multiple intelligences in the classroom* (2nd ed.). Alexandria, VA: Association for Supervision & Curriculum Development.
Gardner, H. (1983). *Frames of mind: The theory of multiple intelligences.* New York: Basic Books.
Gardner, H. (1993). *Multiple intelligences: The theory in practice.* New York: Basic Books.
Gardner, H. (1999). *Intelligence reframed: Multiple intelligences for the 21st century.* New York: Basic Books.

Nuzzi, R. J. (1999). *Gifts of the spirit: Multiple intelligences in religious education.* Washington, DC: National Catholic Educational Association.

MUSIC EDUCATION

Music education in the schools during the past 5 decades has witnessed a continuous transformation in curriculum content, scheduling, its function in academia, as well as course offerings. Several key events have played a role in this transformation.

Many public educators viewed school curriculum in the 1950s as imbalanced—particularly lacking education in the arts. According to Ole Sand, the American Association of School Administrators responded in 1959 with a statement specifying that a well-balanced school curriculum will include the arts alongside other academic subjects such as history, mathematics, and science, emphasizing the value that general education teaches students to "appreciate, understand, create, and criticize with discrimination those products of the mind, the voice, the hand, and the body which give dignity to the person and exalt the spirit of man." The National Education Association through its Project on Instruction document also supported the inclusion of arts in the school curriculum.

The Elementary and Secondary Education Act of 1965 (Public Law 89-10) provided support specifically for music education in Title I, permitting low-income–area school districts to receive funding to hire music teachers and purchase instruments and equipment. This was extremely significant, as participation in school music programs in the 1960s grew considerably nationwide.

Several national meetings occurred in the 1960s to address issues and concerns in music education. The Yale Seminar (1963) was a federally funded project to explore the problems facing music education and to find potential solutions. The current curriculum did not appear to produce musically literate students and active participatory adults. Music curriculum in Grades K–12 needed to be examined. Results of the Yale Seminar were highly critical of the quality of instructional materials used in music classrooms. The Juilliard Repertory Project (1964) was then created to locate music of the highest quality for instruction in K–12 music classrooms. In 1967 another historic meeting took place, this time in Massachusetts, with representation from the field of music education as well as from sociology, philosophy, history, psychology, labor, and the media. The Tanglewood Symposium sought to identify the role of music education. Outcomes included the call for music as a core curricular subject in the school curriculum and for music education to be taught comprehensively, specifically including music of various cultures. Curricular revisions followed.

Michael L. Mark and Charles L. Gary noted a concern for accountability in the schools rose in the 1970s from noticeably declining results in SAT scores. A return to the "basics" prompted cuts in music programs throughout the country. Music Educators National Conference (MENC) responded with efforts toward music education advocacy through publications, advertisements, and conferences. In 1988 MENC was a part of a national ad hoc coalition monitoring policy that affected the arts. The Goals 2000 Act included arts education as a core subject due to this coalition. Advocacy efforts also led to an MENC publication on the National Commission on Music Education report (whose members included notable actors and musicians) titled *Growing Up Complete: The Imperative for Music Education.* This publication played a key role in future decisions to include the arts in the core curriculum.

One of the most significant projects for arts education initiated by the government was the establishment of the national standards of arts education. MENC published these standards in 1994 and they continue to be utilized as the primary resource in arts education curricula. These standards emphasize what every child should know and be able to do in the arts, K–12. Although the National Standards for the Arts are not required by all school districts, many states have adapted them into their own state academic content standards for the arts.

Affecting lifelong learning beyond the K–12 curriculum, the New Horizons music education movement was established in 1991 by Roy Ernst of the Eastman School of Music, for adults 55 years and older. Today there are over 150 bands, choirs, and orchestras created for adults who are learning to play an instrument or sing for the first time, or who want to rekindle musical skills from their high school musical experiences. Several of these organizations are associated with universities with music education programs, allowing future music educators to assist in educating adult learners. The New Horizons Music programs have reinforced and expanded a goal of all music educators—that of lifelong learning and participation in music making.

A monumental meeting took place in 1999 to review the status of music education and to lay the groundwork for the future—Vision 2020: The Housewright Symposium of the Future of Music Education. Sponsored by MENC and Florida State University, this symposium called together music educators and representatives from the music industry and community. A culmination of agreements and invited papers were published by MENC as a result of the symposium. The Housewright Declaration gave affirmation to the Tanglewood Symposium of 1967 and also recognized concerns produced over the previous 4 decades, which included inadequate instruction time, shortage of music teachers, and vast technological advances. The declaration emphasized that professional and accrediting organizations, universities, and PreK–12 schools must encourage and implement policy, curricular, and pedagogical innovations, which will engage all children as musicians.

In January 2002, the No Child Left Behind Act (NCLB) declared that the arts (to include music, visual arts, drama, and dance in most states' definition) are core academic subjects in America's educational system. In Section 5551–Assistance for Arts Education, the NCLB states its goals:

1. To support systemic education reform by strengthening arts education as an integral part of the elementary school and secondary school curriculum

2. To help ensure that all students meet challenging state academic content standards and challenging state student academic achievement standards in the arts

3. To support the national effort to enable all students to demonstrate competence in the arts.

Although funding assistance for these initiatives was to be made available for such capacities as research, planning model-based arts education programs, development of arts education assessments, curriculum development, and professional development programs, it appears that insufficient funding has been devoted to the arts.

The NCLB impetus during this past decade has been to emphasize basic skills (particularly reading and math) and high-stakes testing versus learning in an environment that educates the whole person. School administrators have been forced to devote more time to core subjects that are tested, often leaving music and the other arts with less instruction time. However, music education leaders continue to advocate the significance of a comprehensive education to include the abilities to appreciate, create, and produce musical works of art. In today's global society, music educators have the means to reinforce students' understanding of our own culture and those around us, and to help develop students who will be able to think critically and creatively, and appreciate the meaning of music.

The avenues through which we produce, consume, enjoy, express, and understand music have changed considerably over the past 5 decades. Computer technology has transformed the nature of musical products, processes, and delivery systems, opening new creative possibilities. We now have 24/7 access to music from throughout the world. Research in the fields of sociology, psychology, and neuroscience has provided educators with new information about how music is learned. The disciplines of musicology and ethnomusicology have provided and expanded the range of music worthy of study. In response to these decades of change, an international group of distinguished music educators, performers, researchers, and scholars from a variety of fields assembled in 2007 to examine these issues. Tanglewood II: A Symposium on Charting the Future was a symposium conducted in the same spirit of the groundbreaking Tanglewood Symposium of 1967. The Tanglewood II Symposium examined the challenges that these transformations pose to the practice and instruction of music and called for radical change.

Including music education in the schools to enhance all students' education PreK–12 is widely considered a priority in overall curricular reform. In an effort to reinforce and augment other academic subjects, many music educators have adapted their curriculum to integrate the teaching of music with other academic subjects, such as reading, science, and mathematics. This practice is a direct result of the National Standards for the Arts, which state that students should be able to "understand relationships between music, the other arts, and disciplines outside the arts." Currently, the traditional music education curriculum offered after elementary school involves only those students who participate in bands, choirs, or orchestras. To meet the National Standards in Music Education, high schools in particular need to offer more courses that would appeal to and be accessible to students who do not choose to participate in the traditional music offerings.

Music education in PreK–12 has changed with societal events, in response to governmental policies, and most often has taken a back seat in the curriculum. However, as is widely recognized and understood, music education can be one of the most positive influences in a child's education. And yet, the curricular imbalance recognized in the 1950s continues 5 decades later. Advocacy, not only by music educators but also by school, community, and governmental leaders, is vital if music is to be consistently treated as a core academic subject.

Linda A. Hartley

Further Readings

American Association of School Administrators. (1959). *Official report for the year 1958; including a record of the annual meeting and work conference on "Education and the Creative Arts."* Washington, DC: Author.

Consortium of National Arts Education Associations. (1994*). National Standards of Arts Education: What every young American should know and be able to do in the arts.* Reston, VA: Music Educators National Conference.

Madsen, C. (Ed.). (2000). *Vision 2020: The Housewright Symposium on the future of music education.* Reston, VA: Music Educators National Conference.

Mark, M., & Gary, C. L. (2007). *A history of American music education* (3rd ed.). Lanham, MD: Rowman & Littlefield.

Sand, O. (1963). Current trends in curriculum planning. *Music Educators Journal, 50,* 42–96.

Tanglewood II: A symposium on charting the future. (2007). Retrieved July 28, 2009, from http://www.bu.edu/tanglewoodtwo/declaration/declaration.html

U.S. Department of Education. (2002). Pub. L. No. 107-110, Elementary and Secondary Education, Subpart 15–Arts in Education, Sec. 5551: Assistance for Arts Education. Retrieved July 28, 2009, from http://www.ed.gov/policy/elsec/leg/esea02/pg80.html

National Assessment of Educational Progress (NAEP)

The National Assessment of Educational Progress (NAEP) is the ongoing, national assessment of students' academic performance in the United States of America. It is administered annually by the National Center for Education Statistics of the U.S. Department of Education, under the policy direction of the National Assessment Governing Board. This program was formally created by the U.S. Congress in 1969 as a mandate to continuously monitor the knowledge, skills, and performance of the nation's children and youth. The NAEP measures how well students are meeting today's educational standards; it shows patterns of student achievement over time in core content areas, such as mathematics, reading, science, and writing, since 1969; it provides objective data of student performance for comparing states to each other and to the nation; it serves as a primary indicator of the impact of national and state educational reform efforts; it is a trustworthy information source about the condition of education in the United States for the general public, the U.S. Congress, and the U.S. Department of Education; and it provides student performance results used by professional associations and organizations, major newspapers, and journals.

As the nation's report card, NAEP measures and reports on a regular basis what America's 4th, 8th, and 12th graders know and can demonstrate. It is the only measure of student achievement in the United States by which one can compare the performance of students in one state with the performance of students in other states and across the nation. It provides objective data about students' performance at national, regional, and, as of 1990, state levels in mathematics, reading, writing, science, U.S. history, civics, geography, economics, and the arts; other assessments are pending.

NAEP was initially begun with a grant from the Carnegie Corporation to establish the Exploratory Committee for the Assessment of Progress in Education. The first national assessments were approved by the U.S. Congress and conducted in 1969. Voluntary assessments for the states began in 1990 on a trial basis, and in 2002, 2003, and 2005, selected urban districts participated in the assessments on a trial basis.

The Commissioner for Education Statistics, which heads the National Center for Education Statistics within the U.S. Department of Education, is responsible by law for carrying out the NAEP program. The U.S. Congress created the 26-member National Assessment Governing Board in 1988; this board, appointed by the Secretary of Education, but independent of the department, sets policy for NAEP and is responsible for developing the framework and test specifications that serve as the blueprint for the individual assessments. This board is a bipartisan group whose members include governors, state legislators, local and state school officials, educators, business representatives, and members of the general public. Contractors assist in carrying out NAEP operations.

Since 1988, the National Assessment Governing Board has selected the subjects assessed by NAEP. Specifically, the board oversees creation of the frameworks that underlie the assessments and the specifications that guide the development of the assessment instruments. The framework for each subject is determined through a collaborative development process that involves teachers, curriculum specialists, subject-matter specialists, school administrators, parents, and members of the general public.

NAEP has two major goals: (1) to compare student achievement in states and other jurisdictions and (2) to track changes in achievement of 4th-, 8th-, and 12th-grade students over time in mathematics, reading, writing, science, and selected content areas.

According to its own publications and Web site, NAEP is the only nationally representative and continuing assessment of what U.S. students know and can do in various subject areas. Because NAEP assessments are administered uniformly using the same sets of test booklets across the nation, the results serve as a common measurement for all states and selected urban districts.

NAEP provides results on subject-matter achievement, instructional experiences, and school environment for populations of students and select groups within those populations. NAEP does not provide scores for individual students or schools, although state NAEPs can report results by particular urban school districts. NAEP results are based on representative samples of students at Grades 4, 8, and 12 for main assessments, or samples of students at ages 9, 13, or 17 years for the long-term trend assessments. NAEP results are widely reported by the national and local media.

Subject-matter achievement is reported in two ways—scale scores and achievement levels—so that student performance can be more easily understood. NAEP scale score results provide a numeric summary of what students know and can do in a particular subject and are presented for groups and subgroups. Achievement levels categorize student achievement as *basic, proficient,* and *advanced,* using ranges of performance established for each grade. A fourth category, *below basic,* is also reported for this scale. Achievement levels are used to report results in terms of a set of standards for what students should know and be able to do.

NAEP samples are provided for the state assessments and for the national sample. The NAEP sample in each state is designed to be representative of the students in that state. At the state level, results are currently reported for public school students only and are broken down by several demographic groupings of students. When NAEP is conducted at the state level on selected tests—mathematics, reading, science, writing—results are also reported for the nation. The national NAEP sample is then composed of all the state samples of public school students as well as a national sample of non–public school students. States have a choice whether or not to participate in the NAEP program, but in nonparticipating states a certain number of students are selected to complete the national-level sample.

Beginning with the 2003 assessments, under the provisions of No Child Left Behind Act of 2001, NAEP national and state assessments have been conducted in mathematics and reading at least once every 2 years at Grades 4 and 8. These assessments are conducted in the same year and initial results are released 6 months after test administration. Other NAEP assessments are conducted at the national level for Grade 12, as well as Grades 4 and 8.

Current federal law specifies that NAEP is voluntary for every student, school, school district, and state. However, federal law requires all states that receive Title I funds to participate in NAEP mathematics and reading assessments at Grades 4 and 8. Moreover, school districts that receive Title I funds and are selected for the NAEP sample are also required to participate in NAEP mathematics and reading assessments at Grades 4 and 8. Other NAEP assessments are voluntary.

In addition, federal law mandates complete privacy for all test-takers and their families. Under the National Assessment of Educational Progress Authorization Act, the commissioner of the National Center for Education Statistics is charged with ensuring that NAEP tests do not question test-takers about personal or family beliefs or make information publicly available about a test-taker's personal identity.

Because NAEP findings have an impact on the public's understanding of student academic achievement, certain precautions are taken to ensure the reliability of these findings. In current legislation, as in previous legislative mandates, Congress has called for an ongoing evaluation of the assessment (process and findings) as a whole. In response to these legislative mandates, the National Center for Education Statistics has established various panels of technical experts to study NAEP, and panels are formed periodically by the National Center for Education Statistics or by external organizations, such as the National Academy of Sciences, to conduct requested evaluations.

NAEP's Web site features assessment information, publications, and analytic tools. It includes specially designed sections for teachers, parents, students, principals, state and local administrators, policymakers, researchers, and the media; quick, one-stop access to free informative NAEP publications and assessment data; national and state report cards on student performance in core content areas; state-of-the-art assessment methodology and frameworks; sample test questions, student responses, and scoring guides for assessment programs for schools, school districts, or states; an online tutorial for learning to score extended student responses to sample test questions; summary data tables and selective student performance results from past assessments; calendars of current NAEP events, training, and professional development activities; and technical assistance and online discussions with leading assessment or subject-matter experts.

Thomas A. Kessinger

See also Accountability Era; Assessment; National Center for Education Statistics (NCES); No Child Left Behind Act (NCLB); Performance-Based Assessment; Standardized Tests; Standards Movement; Testing Students

Further Readings

Jones, L. V., & Olkin, I. (Eds.). (2004). *The nation's report card: Evolution and perspectives.* Bloomington, IN: Phi Delta Kappa Educational Foundation.

National Assessment of Educational Progress (NAEP): http://nces.ed.gov/nationsreportcard

National Center for Education Statistics. (2004). *The nation's report card: An overview of NAEP* (NCES 2004–552). Washington, DC: Author.

National Center for Education Statistics. (2005). *The nation's report card: An introduction to the National Assessment of Educational Progress (NAEP)* (NCES 2005–454). Washington, DC: Author.

National Center for Education Statistics. (2008, March). *Digest of educational statistics (2007)* (NCES 2008–022). Washington, DC: Author.

NATIONAL ASSOCIATION FOR THE ADVANCEMENT OF COLORED PEOPLE (NAACP)

The National Association for the Advancement of Colored People (NAACP) is the oldest existing civil rights organization in the United States of America. The NAACP is currently headquartered in Baltimore, Maryland, and has a membership of approximately 400,000. The organization's current president and chief executive officer is Benjamin Todd Jealous. Founded in 1909, the NAACP's mission "is to ensure the political, educational, social and economic equality of rights of all persons and to eliminate racial hatred and racial discrimination." From inception to the present, the organization's tactics have included litigation, protests, nonviolent direct action, demonstrations, boycotts, collaboration, and voter registration campaigns. An understanding of the origins, activities, and functions of the NAACP must be placed within the broader context of the contours of America's racial history.

Historical Background

At the turn of the 20th century, America was a deeply racist nation. A Jim Crow system, developed in the American South, had spread to the rest of the country. Everywhere laws were written to segregate, humiliate, disenfranchise, and debase Black people. Increasingly, the *Plessy v. Ferguson* court decision in 1896 was interpreted broadly to include every facet of American political, economic, and social life. In schools, churches, and newspapers, Blacks were not only depicted as ugly, subhuman, shiftless, and barbaric but also as rapists—labels that seemed to justify White-on-Black violence. By 1900, the number of lynchings had risen to the point where it was calculated that a Black person was being lynched every other day.

Between 1900 and 1908, the nation was rocked by an intense wave of race riots. Atlanta, Waco, Brownsville, and New York are just a few examples. The Springfield (Illinois) Riot of 1908 proved a tipping point. Springfield, Abraham Lincoln's hometown, erupted in chaos on August 14, when White mobs stormed into the Black community burning, looting, and striking terror in the neighborhood. The casualties were typical of the times: Two Blacks were lynched, six were killed, and more than 2,000 fled the city. Stunned by the riot and the chronic pattern of abuse that it represented, a number of progressive-minded individuals were moved to act. Oswald Garrison Villard of the *New York Evening Post,* and William English Walling, a reporter, called for an end to the racial violence that infused American racism. In an article titled "The Race Riot in the North," Walling lashed out at mainstream society for failing to condemn the racial violence. Walling and Villard were soon joined by Mary White Ovington, Charles Edward Russell, Henry Moskowitz, Bishop Alexander Walters, Florence Kelly, Lillian Wald, Ida B. Wells, and W. E. B. Du Bois. On February 12, 1909, Lincoln's birthday, the group issued "The Call" for "A Lincoln Emancipation Conference to Discuss Means for Securing Political and Civil Equality for the Negro."

Founding and Early Years

It was here that the NAACP began. Calling itself the National Negro Committee, the group deliberated on its strategy to end racism and its attendant violence. At their second conference in 1910, the group renamed the organization the National Association for the Advancement of Colored People (NAACP). It was at this time that the group affirmed the structure of the new organization. The administration of the NAACP was composed of Moorefield Storey as president, Walling as chairman of the executive committee, Frances Blascoer as executive secretary, John Milholland as treasurer, Villard as assistant treasurer; and Du Bois as director of publicity and research. Du Bois edited *The Crisis,* the monthly magazine of the NAACP. For an organization whose focus was to correct the wrongs committed against Blacks, it was disheartening to African American observers that Du Bois was the only Black person

on the administrative board at the time of inception. It was not until 1920 that the organization hired its first African American executive secretary, James Weldon Johnson. Early critics pounced on this. Marcus Garvey ridiculed the organization as "The National Association for the Advancement of Certain People." The headquarters of the new organization was in New York, and within a few months the first branch office opened in Chicago. Despite the work and effort, membership grew slowly. In 1913, the organization had 1,100 members, with a few branches located in a few northern states.

The new organization vowed to bring an end to lynching. Lynching struck terror into the Black community. Whether committed by organized groups such as the Ku Klux Klan or by mobs or by individuals, it constituted terror. With the Eighth Amendment of the U.S. Constitution on its side, the NAACP went to work. Its publications exposed in graphic detail the culture of lynching. In 1912, it published *Notes on Lynching in America.* The organization began to challenge candidates for Congress on their views of Blacks and discrimination. Progress was slow, and the lynching continued. The lynching of Jesse Washington, Anthony Crawford, and Mary Turner was particularly disturbing, more especially as they occurred at the time when America was in Europe in a war "to make the world safe for democracy." Simultaneously, the number of race riots mounted. They were in cities all over the country: Tulsa, Oklahoma; Washington, D.C.; Longview, Texas; Omaha, Nebraska; and Chicago, Illinois. In fact, during the summer of 1919 more than 20 race riots took place; this prompted James Weldon Johnson, the future executive secretary of the organization, to label it "Red Summer."

Legislative and Legal Advances

The NAACP was undeterred. In 1919, it organized an antilynching conference in New York's Carnegie Hall, and published another pamphlet, *Thirty Years of Lynching in the United States, 1889–1919.* Beyond exposing lynching in America, the NAACP also continued to pursue its aggressive legislative and legal strategy. In 1918 the organization worked with St. Louis Republican Congressman Leonidas Dyer to introduce a House bill designed to end lynching. The Dyer bill languished in Congress and was finally defeated in the Senate 4 years later. Despite this setback, the organization was able to convince the courts to support its position that defendants have rights that must be protected. In the *Moore v. Dempsey* decision of 1926, the high court affirmed the NAACP's position that defendants cannot be denied rights such as the right to question witnesses against them, the right to trial by jury, and the right to protection against self-incrimination.

Following the Court's decision in the *Powell v. Alabama* case in 1932, numerous appeals were filed based on the foundation already established by the NACCP to provide more rights to defendants. All of this enhanced the NAACP's stature. Of course, the most successful venture of this organization in the 1930s was its effort to desegregate education. In 1935, Charles Hamilton Houston became chief counsel of the NAACP Legal Defense Fund. A World War I veteran and a graduate of Harvard Law School, Houston argued that discrimination in education was symbolic of discrimination in the larger society. He brought his former student, Thurgood Marshall, to his camp. Houston had seen a weakness in the application of the "separate but equal" doctrine, because what was practiced was separate but unequal. Both Houston and Marshall agreed that the way to attack segregation was to make it so expensive that the states would be forced to abandon it. Together they presented and received approval of their strategy from the board of directors of the NAACP. Lawsuits filed by them successfully equalized teachers' pay, integrated professional and graduate programs, and began an overall challenge to *Plessy v. Ferguson*. By 1950, the organization had already set the stage for the final assault on segregation, with a series of victories in *Missouri ex rel. Gaines v. Canada* (1938), *Smith v. Allwright* (1944), *Morgan v. Virginia* (1946), *Sipuel v. Oklahoma State Board of Regents* (1948), *Henderson v. United States* (1948), *McLaurin v. Oklahoma* (1950), and *Sweatt v. Painter* (1950). On May 17, the Supreme Court issued its unanimous *Brown v. Board of Education of Topeka* decision, striking down segregation in public education.

With maturity came a broadening of goals. After the Great Depression, the NAACP initiated grassroots efforts to improve the political and economic conditions of African Americans, supporting protest activities and campaigns such as "Don't Buy Where You Can't Work." Those efforts coincided with a new relation between the White House and the Black community. Not only did President Franklin D. Roosevelt appoint Blacks such as William Hastie and Mary McLeod Bethune to significant positions, but Harold Ickes, a former member of the NAACP, was a key member of Roosevelt's cabinet. It was, in part, through the relentless efforts of the NAACP that African Americans abandoned Lincoln's party in the 1930s. Increasingly disenchanted with the Republican Party, African Americans began to shift overwhelmingly to the Democratic Party in the 1936 presidential election, a shift that has remained to the present day.

As World War II approached, Walter White, then executive secretary of the organization, teamed up with labor organizer A. Philip Randolph. They submitted to Roosevelt a series of demands designed to end discrimination and challenged Roosevelt to act or face a march on Washington. The year was 1941, and America was already working in Europe to stem the tide of Nazism. Threatened by the possibility of a march on Washington, Roosevelt issued Executive Order 8802, which banned discrimination by any company that did business with the government. Roosevelt's order became the cornerstone of the modern civil rights movement and was a milestone for the NAACP. There were high hopes, and NAACP membership increased. In 1940, the organization had 335 branches and 50,000 members, and by 1946 that had jumped to 1,073 branches and 500,000 members.

The Postwar Era and the Battle Against Segregation

In the postwar era, the NAACP continued with its all-out offensive to end segregation. Capitalizing on the wartime ideology of Roosevelt's four freedoms and a new focus on human rights, the organization called on President Harry Truman to act decisively on civil rights. Given the cold war and American propaganda as the last best hope for all, the organization challenged the Truman administration to implement its own pronouncements. There was no turning back. The stakes were exceedingly high. Black troops had fought to guarantee human rights in Europe, and African Americans were no longer prepared to return to the prewar status. The NAACP called for more demonstrations. In 1948, Truman used executive order to desegregate the armed forces, and the NAACP rightly celebrated.

After *Brown*, the pace of events quickened. When on December 1, 1955, Rosa Parks, a member of the Montgomery chapter of the NAACP, refused to give up her seat on the bus, the wheels of the civil rights movement were put in high gear. At every stage from the Montgomery Bus Boycott, through the Freedom Rides, sit-in activities, March on Washington, Voters' Participation Campaign, to the March on Selma and other protest activities of the 1960s, the NAACP was ever present. The NAACP collaborated with the Southern Christian Leadership Conference, Student Non-Violent Coordinating Committee, and the Congress of Racial Equality. Its leadership worked closely with the Rev. Martin Luther King, Jr., Stokeley Carmichael, James Farmer, Ella Baker, Fannie Lou Hamer, Robert Moses, and many more. All worked together to produce the monumental civil rights gains of the 1960s and 1970s.

The 1980s and Beyond

The 1980s and beyond offered new challenges for the NAACP. The administrations of Ronald Reagan, George H. W. Bush, and George W. Bush made attempts to reverse the civil rights gains of the previous decades. Not only did they attempt to fill the courts with extremely conservative judges, they worked to undermine programs such as affirmative action. As expected, the NAACP protested, went to court, and led marches. It continued to organize voter registration drives. Among other things, the NAACP campaign contributed to the defeat of conservative judge Robert Bork's confirmation to the Supreme Court.

For all this, the NAACP has had to deal with significant internal problems. Fund-raising has always been a challenge for the organization. In the early 1990s, leaders rose and fell in rapid succession. In 1995, the organization forced out Rev. Benjamin Chavis as president, and his successor, William Gibson, was also dumped. As a nonprofit organization dependent on donations, instances of

financial impropriety and mismanagement were detrimental to the overall functioning of the organization. Stability at the top was restored when Kweisi Mfume was named the organization's president in 1996.

Another recurring weakness of the NAACP has been its inability to engage itself in the foreign policy debates of the time. Even though the NAACP had been involved in pressing the government to intervene in countries such as Ethiopia during the hostile invasion of that nation in the 1930s and also organized a series of anti-Apartheid rallies, the organization has sought, not always successfully, to be involved in some of the most urgent crises in Africa. During the past 20 years, Africa has been the scene of numerous critical and moral crises, including those in Rwanda, Darfur, Sierra Leone, Congo Republic, and Liberia, and yet, critics point out, little initiative or response has emanated from the NAACP. It is widely felt that the organization has a responsibility to mount pressure on the U.S. government to pursue and promote more humane policies in African nations. Some of the founders of the organization were also leading members of the Pan-Africanist movement.

Today, as the NAACP celebrates its 100th anniversary, its president, Benjamin Jealous, warns of impending challenges. The organization must always be on the lookout, as racism remains a powerful force on the American landscape. After 100 years in existence, the NAACP can point to some significant achievements. Race relations in America are fundamentally different from what they were 100 years ago. Legally, America is desegregated. Politically, African Americans serve on school boards and are elected regularly to city, state, and national governments. In 2009, Barack Obama took the oath of office as president. It was a high point, and by electing Obama, Americans chose the "content of his character" over the "color of his skin."

Yet, despite vigorous efforts the NAACP has not realized its objective of guaranteeing full equality for African Americans. Over 4 decades ago the National Advisory Commission on Civil Disorders wrote in its report that America was moving "towards two societies, one black, one white—separate and unequal," and that conclusion remains as relevant today as when first written. America is still a nation in which the legacy of slavery and its institutions is deeply entrenched in the cultural landscape. Presently the African American community leads in every category on the misery index, chronically subject to high rates of unemployment, school dropout, police brutality, and incarceration, as well as debilitated school systems with acute shortages of educational resources and a raft of enormous challenges. More than half a century after the *Brown v. Board of Education* decision, a large proportion of young Blacks still attend de facto segregated schools. The promise of the civil rights movement is not fully redeemed, and for the NAACP, much remains to be done.

Julius A. Amin

See also Affirmative Action; Afrocentric Schools; Black Alliance for Educational Options; *Brown v. Board of Education*; Busing; Desegregation/Integration; Minorities in Educational Leadership; Race- and Ethnic-Based Schooling

Further Readings

Janken, K. R. (2003). *White: The biography of Walter White, Mr. NAACP.* New York: New Press.

Jonas, G. (2005). *Freedom's sword: The NAACP and the struggle against racism in America, 1909–1969.* New York: Routledge.

Kellogg, C. F. (1967). *NAACP: A history of the National Association for the Advancement of Colored People.* Baltimore: Johns Hopkins University Press.

Kluger, R. (1975). *Simple justice: The history of* Brown v. Board of Education *and Black America's struggle for equality.* New York: Knopf.

Lewis, D. L. (1994). *W. E. B. Du Bois: A biography of race, 1868–1919.* New York: Henry Holt.

Lewis, D. L. (2000). *W. E. B. Du Bois: The fight for equality and the American century, 1919–1963.* New York: Henry Holt.

McNeil, G. R. (1983). *Ground work: Charles Hamilton Houston and the struggle for civil rights.* Philadelphia: University of Pennsylvania Press.

NAACP & *The Crisis.* (2009). *NAACP: Celebrating a century: 100 years in pictures.* Layton, UT: Gibbs Smith.

Nieman, D. (1991). *Promises to keep: African-Americans and the constitutional order, 1776 to the present.* New York: Oxford University Press.

Sitkoff, H. (2008). *The struggle for Black equality.* New York: Hill & Wang.

Zangrando, R. (1980). *The NAACP crusade against lynching.* Philadelphia: Temple University Press.

National Association for the Education of Young Children

The National Association for the Education of Young Children (NAEYC) is an organization that supports children from birth through age 8, their families, and professionals who work in the field of early care and education. NAEYC is a critical force in educational reform as it serves to advocate for the profession of early care and education, provides political oversight for the early childhood agenda, develops policy and standards, defines and promotes quality in early childhood programs and teacher preparation, and provides opportunities for professional development. One goal of NAEYC is to reform the current educational structure in order to improve the quality of early care and education for the children, families, and professionals who impact or are impacted by current practice. To provide a more extensive description of NAEYC, this entry includes a historical overview and a summary of the impact that the organization is making on the field of early care and education through its current initiatives.

Historical Overview

NAEYC grew out of the National Association for Nursery Education (NANE), which was formed after a multidisciplinary group gathered to discuss concerns about the quality of programs for young children that were being established in the 1920s. Patty Smith Hill is credited with bringing together this small group, which included Arnold Gesell, Lois Meek (Stolz), and Abigail Eliot, among others. During this gathering, the group discussed the need for a new association and, in 1926, planned a public conference to address issues related to the nursery school movement. The initial conference led to the formation of the NANE in 1929.

NANE members were true to their mission through the Great Depression of the 1930s and World War II of the 1940s and were instrumental in the development of the Works Progress Administration nursery schools and child care programs. By the 1950s, NANE had dramatically increased its membership to more than 5,000 by inviting existing state, local, and regional organizations for nursery education to become affiliate organizations. This emphasis on unifying early childhood professionals at the grassroots level continues today as NAEYC consists of more than 300 affiliate organizations.

With the start of the federal Head Start program in 1964, it became apparent that programs for young children went beyond the nursery school. In an effort to be far reaching, NANE adopted a new name, the National Association for the Education of Young Children. The early childhood community of the 1970s responded well to the new name as was demonstrated by a period of rapid growth with membership reaching 50,000 by the middle of the decade.

A growing number of women working outside the home led to an increased focus on child care and preschool programs and eventually to the development of a quality accreditation system for early childhood programs in the 1980s. Also in the 1980s and 1990s, a new focus on educational reform emerged with the release of *A Nation at Risk: The Imperative for Educational Reform* in 1983 and the subsequent 1994 legislation, *Goals 2000: Educate America Act,* which declared, "All children in America will start school ready to learn" as its first goal. This enhanced emphasis on the experiences that young children have prior to starting school led to a series of NAEYC position statements, including *Developmentally Appropriate Practice in Early Childhood Programs* (1986, 1997, 2008), which, in its third revision, continues to serve as the guide to research-based practices for the field. Currently, NAEYC has nearly 100,000 members and hosts an annual conference that is among the largest educational meetings in the United States.

Current Initiatives That Impact the Field

NAEYC continues to lead the field of early care and education as an international presence that sets a research and policy agenda designed to improve early childhood program quality and advocate for children, families, and professionals. NAEYC collaborates with other organizations to develop position statements that respond to current challenges in the field. Research and quality practice is communicated not only through position statements but also through a variety of publications, including the journals *Young Children, Teaching Young Children,* and *Early Childhood Research Quarterly.* The National Institute for Early Childhood Professional Development also serves as a vehicle for improving the quality of teacher preparation and ongoing professional development for teachers of young children by providing a forum to learn from researchers about new developments in the field.

NAEYC continues to grow as an organization, responding to the needs of a changing society. To involve more members in this work, interest forums were created on issues that advance the field and address a critical need. These forums create a network for members who share common research and policy interests. NAEYC has secured external funding for special projects including the Supporting Teachers, Strengthening Families project to prevent child abuse and promote social development. This project helps teachers communicate with families about difficult issues.

As an international organization, NAEYC established Global Alliance, which brings together early childhood professionals from around the world in order to make an impact on the lives of children and families. Whether global or nationally focused, NAEYC continues to take a lead to improve professional practice, to support early childhood programs, and to organize groups and individuals through political advocacy.

Improving Professional Practice

NAEYC developed the first version of its position statement, *Developmentally Appropriate Practice in Early Childhood Programs: Serving Children Birth Through Age 8,* in 1986, with revisions following in 1997 and 2008. This document provides preferred practice in early childhood programs. This unifying document allows a wide variety of early childhood program models to share a common metric for quality. The document is based on research and serves as a springboard for a series of position statements and evaluation tools that have informed professional preparation programs for the past 2 decades.

One document that has been instrumental in aligning professional preparation programs with the research base is *Preparing Early Childhood Professionals: Standards for Programs*. This document identifies and describes the standards for associate degree, initial, and advanced programs in early childhood teacher preparation. All accredited teacher preparation programs must align with these standards and must also provide evidence of student performance.

Supporting Early Childhood Programs

NAEYC has identified the need to support early childhood programs in an effort to improve quality. To that end, NAEYC established a national voluntary accreditation system based on 10 program standards for center- and school-based early childhood programs. Early childhood professionals developed the 10 program standards after an exhaustive review of the research. The accreditation process was validated and evaluators go through rigorous training, after which interrater reliability is established.

Accreditation begins with a self-study process during which programs compare their practice with the NAEYC program standards and make adjustments. The program applies for candidacy once it determines that the NAEYC program standards can be met. Candidacy materials are evaluated, and if the evidence warrants it, a site visit by an NAEYC assessor is scheduled. During the site visit, assessors evaluate the 10 standards, which are grouped into the following topic areas: (1) relationships, (2) curriculum, (3) teaching, (4) assessment of child progress, (5) health, (6) teachers, (7) families, (8) community relationships, (9) physical environment, and (10) leadership and management.

In addition to defining quality in early childhood programs, NAEYC provides resources and training that support programs through the accreditation process. An NAEYC publication, *NAEYC Early Childhood Program Standards and Accreditation Criteria: The Mark of Quality in Early Childhood Education,* guides programs through the accreditation process and several supporting documents are available through the NAEYC Web site. Technical assistance is also available during NAEYC workshops and conference sessions.

Organizing Groups and Individuals Through Political Advocacy

NAEYC serves as a national leader and resource for those in the field who seek to use the political process to advocate for young children and families. At a time when early childhood has a national audience, NAEYC is instrumental in writing policy and has allocated resources and personnel to track the progress of legislation at both the national and state levels. Early childhood stakeholders who advocate for young children have access to the following tools available through the NAEYC Web site.

Toolbox for Advocates

NAEYC has developed a Toolbox for Advocates, which is designed to promote effective advocacy and includes the following informational resources:

- Do's and Don'ts in an Election Year Guide
- Raising Your Voice for Children: An Advocacy Training
- Guide to Nonpartisan Voter Registration and G.O.T.V. Drives
- State-by-State Voter Registration Information
- Steps in Making a Bill Into a Law
- Appropriation and Budget Terms
- Questions and Answers on New Federal Programs and Grants

Children's Champions Action Center

The Children's Champions Action Center provides those seeking to use the political system as a forum for advocacy with a series of easy access links. This Web-based support system organizes political advocacy resources in one easy-to-navigate Web site that includes links to state and national legislators as well as the following:

- *Action Alerts.* NAEYC provides members and nonmembers with an opportunity to become part of an e-mail list that sends out regular updates and calls for action on important issues.
- *Issues and Legislation.* Each day that Congress is in session, NAEYC provides a schedule for the House, Senate, and committee hearings. Early childhood stakeholders can use this tool to follow the progress of bills related to the field.

- *Elections and Candidates.* NAEYC prepares an election guide for national and state-level elections. Biographies for each candidate, as well as his or her stance on the issues, are provided. Statewide issues are also described in detail.
- *Communicating with the Media.* NAEYC provides resources for early childhood leaders and advocates who need to communicate with the media effectively. Links are provided to national media organizations, local newspapers, and television and radio stations. NAEYC strives to facilitate communication about early childhood issues by providing sites where a message can be constructed and sent simultaneously to national and local media outlets.

Shauna Meyers Adams

See also Accreditation; Early Childhood Education; Head Start; Infant Schools; Kindergarten; Montessori Schools; Piaget, Jean; Vygotsky, Lev; Waldorf Schools

Further Readings

Bredekamp, S., & Copple, C. (Eds.). (1997). *Developmentally appropriate practice in early childhood programs.* Washington, DC: National Association for the Education of Young Children.

Hyson, M. (2003). *Preparing early childhood professionals: Standards for programs.* Washington, DC: National Association for the Education of Young Children.

Kagan, S. L., Kauerz, K., & Tarrant, K. (2008). *The early care and education teaching workforce at the fulcrum.* New York: Teachers College Press.

National Association for the Education of Young Children (NAEYC): http://www.naeyc.org

National Association for the Education of Young Children (NAEYC). (2005, April). *Code of ethical conduct and statement of commitment.* Washington, DC: Author. Retrieved July 30, 2009, from http://208.118.177.216/about/positions/pdf/PSETH05.pdf

National Association for the Education of Young Children (NAEYC). (2005). *NAEYC early childhood program standards and accreditation criteria: The mark of quality in early childhood education.* Washington, DC: Author.

National Association for the Education of Young Children. (2008). *Developmentally appropriate practice in early childhood programs serving children from birth through age 8* [Position statement]. Washington, DC: Author.

National Association for the Education of Young Children (NAEYC) & National Association of Early Childhood Specialists in State Departments of Education (NAECS/SDE). (2002, November). *Early learning standards: Creating the conditions for success* [Joint position statement]. Retrieved July 30, 2009, from http://208.118.177.216/about/positions/pdf/position_statement.pdf

National Association for the Education of Young Children (NAEYC) & National Association of Early Childhood Specialists in State Departments of Education (NAECS/SDE). (2003). *Early childhood curriculum, assessment, and program evaluation: Building an effective, accountable system in programs for children birth through age 8* [Joint position statement]. Retrieved July 30, 2009, from http://208.118.177.216/about/positions/pdf/pscape.pdf

NATIONAL ASSOCIATION OF ELEMENTARY SCHOOL PRINCIPALS (NAESP)

This entry presents a brief history of the National Association of Elementary School Principals (NAESP), with emphasis on the role NAESP has played in national educational reform.

A group of more than 50 principals convened in 1921 to promote the profession and share ideas and formed what became the NAESP. At its inception it was part of the National Education Association. However, in the early 1970s, with the onset of collective bargaining in schools, laws emerged in many states that would not allow administrators to be within the same bargaining unit as the teachers they supervised. As a result, though individuals could remain members of the National Education Association, the majority of the membership determined it was in their best interest for NAESP to become a separate organization. Early on, many schools had what was referred to as a principal teacher with less than 25% of schools in 1946 having full-time administrators, but by 1980, the average was more than one administrator per school. By 2008, NAESP had approximately 30,000 members interested in issues important to PreK–8 principals. Its mission supports and advocates for educational leaders, especially elementary and middle-level principals committed to the education of all children.

NAESP has two concepts central to its fundamental beliefs that were conceived during the researching and writing of *Standards for Quality Elementary Schools: Kindergarten Through Eighth Grade.* The first concept is that the most crucial years in a student's life are the early ones. This concept has been supported by research, and as a result, the federal government has enacted programs such as Head Start to assist younger children. The second belief has to do with the key role of the principal in the quality of a school, which has also been supported in the literature. This belief is shared with the National Association of Secondary School Principals and has led to a strong focus on ensuring that elementary school principals have the training necessary to lead elementary schools. In 1986, NAESP addressed principal preparation programs with a publication titled *Proficiencies for Principals* (now in its third edition). It combines research data with best practices to be used as a workbook for growth and acquisition of new skills, which can lead to improving leadership in schools. The intended audience is both principals and university faculty.

Most importantly, as NAESP headed into a new century, it acknowledged the increased role of community stakeholders and the benefits of strategic planning as necessary components for principal success. NAESP specifically addressed the future attributes preferred for principals in their publication *Principals for 21st Century Schools.* This effort involved a strong collaboration with university professors through NAESP's Organization of Professors of Elementary School Administrators, which they formed in 1985. NAESP forecasted a substantial demographic shift in schools at the turn of the century in the following areas: student population changes caused by increased immigration, poverty among children, and the changing family structure. Another issue addressed was the potential for a large principal turnover, which was estimated to be 60% within 12 years of its publication. The organization wanted to be sure it had a voice in the desired characteristics of the principalship and potential future policy initiatives.

Collaboration with similar national organizations has long been emphasized and recently has gained momentum. NAESP has a long history of collaboration with other interest groups in educational reform, among them the American Association of School Administrators, the National Association of Secondary School Principals, and both teachers associations the American Federation of Teachers, and the National Education Association. One result of this collaboration came in 1999 with the publication of *An Educator's Guide to Schoolwide Reform,* in which quantitative research was used to rate the effectiveness of 24 reform programs used in schools. Its appraisal found that few schoolwide reforms had the data necessary to verify their value to student achievement, indicating to schools that systematic evaluation must be given a higher priority. NAESP sent a strong message that research is crucial to the development of future reform, especially research supported, at least in part, by the federal government. Although the No Child Left Behind Act emphasized best practice being informed by research, there has not been federal funding at adequate levels. NAESP also believes that others, such as private industry, should support this effort.

There must be follow-up studies and critiques done to determine a program's success and failure. The NAESP did not expect that one approach would prove to be equally effective in all settings but that research could provide a variety of possible approaches from which principals and communities could choose the most suitable approach for their particular students and setting. NAESP, along with the other organizations and individuals, renewed a commitment to coordinate its advocacy efforts at the national level for these improvements.

One aspect that stands out when NAESP is examined is that it is very much an organization oriented toward the future and builds on the past in preparing to celebrate its 100-year anniversary in 2021. To mark this milestone, and to attempt to align reform with the changing educational environment, a policy discussion VISION 2021, is taking place. VISION 2021 is a partnership with the Institute for Alternative Futures, whose mission is to support principals, strategies, structures, and relationships necessary for sustained improvement of schools.

In fulfilling this mission, VISION 2021 will concentrate on five relevant issues when developing an advocacy strategy. First, it seeks to find equity in the funding of public education. Second, it is focused on educating students to be connected to the world through their exposure to issues of peace, the environment, and the economy. Third, NAESP understands the rapid rate of growth in technology and believes principals need to stay current with innovation and become what they term the *chief learning officers* of a building. Fourth, VISION 2021 calls for more support of early childhood centers. Lastly, cultural diversity is addressed, with the understanding that the ethnic makeup of public schools in America is rapidly broadening. It believes that principals are crucial models for cooperation, justice, and understanding. It is the hope of NAESP that principals will facilitate a learning structure that embraces diversity, while unifying the instruction, and create a new generation of individuals sensitive to diversity.

As a part of ongoing dialogue about VISION 2021, NAESP is accepting suggestions from state affiliates, nonmembers, NAESP staff, national leaders in educational theory, and various stakeholder groups during a series of conferences, Webcasts, podcasts, and blogs. They also have tool kits for principals and facilitators to incorporate the five relevant issues into everyday school practices.

The National Association of Elementary School Principals advocates for elementary and middle school principals by speaking out and promoting reform of educational policy at the national and state levels with the purpose to improve education for all children. It supports numerous programs such as the National Distinguished Principals Program, which honors principals, and the No Child Left Behind–Blue Ribbon Schools Program, which honors schools for excellence and proven innovation.

A. William Place and Tracey R. Smith

See also American Association of School Administrators (AASA); National Association of Secondary School Principals (NASSP); National Council of Professors of Educational Administration (NCPEA); National Education Association (NEA)

Further Readings

American Institutes for Research. (1999). *An educator's guide to schoolwide reform.* Arlington, VA: Educational Research Service.

National Association of Elementary School Principals. (1984). *Standards for quality elementary schools, kindergarten through eighth grade.* Alexandria, VA: Author.
National Association of Elementary School Principals. (1988). *Effective teachers: Effective evaluation in America's elementary and middle schools.* Alexandria, VA: Author.
National Association of Elementary School Principals. (1990). *Principals for 21st century schools.* Alexandria, VA: Author.
National Association of Elementary School Principals. (1997). *Proficiencies for principals* (3rd ed.). Alexandria, VA: Author.
National Association of Elementary School Principals. (n.d.). *Vision 2021.* Retrieved September 10, 2008, from http://www.vision2021.org

NATIONAL ASSOCIATION OF INDEPENDENT SCHOOLS

Founded in 1963, the National Association of Independent Schools (NAIS) is a nonprofit organization that represents 1,300 member schools and regional associations in the United States as well as affiliates abroad. It promotes, among other things, ongoing efforts among its members to reform educational practice. NAIS is guided by a board of directors or trustees, who make decisions about the course of the organization and further represent the advancement of independence in education from any governmental or religious control.

The schools NAIS represent are independent in several ways. First, in relation to any government or religious control, they receive no funding from state or federal taxes or from any religious organizations. Second, the curriculum and instructional content for each school is determined by individual teachers, or teams of teachers and administrators, and reflects content that is independent of state or national standards, therefore reflecting each school's unique mission and vision. Third, the member schools can choose the characteristics that define their community, such as having coeducational or single-sex student bodies; attendance that includes day school–only or boarding-only settings, or a combination thereof; whether or not they wish to have a unified campus or several campuses for elementary, middle, and upper school levels; or whether or not to have a religious or nonsectarian orientation. Fourth, the schools are independently governed by a group of parents, community leaders, and others invested in the school's future, known as trustees or directors. This board directs the future of the school and is usually responsible, along with the heads of school, for raising money for the school's endowment, regulating tuition and fees, and managing annual funding and all other associated fiduciary obligations and responsibilities entrusted to them. In addition, the board of trustees is considered the guardian of the school's mission and is responsible for ensuring that it remains relevant and pertinent to the school community it serves.

Mission and Values

The NAIS mission is to represent and support schools that are independent, innovative, and college preparatory in nature. NAIS members consider themselves the national voice for these member schools and their affiliated regional associations, changing focus as an institution when new issues become apparent from the schools or associations themselves, or as dictated by social concerns and issues at large. The mission also entails keeping NAIS at the center of all efforts to promote independent education in the media on behalf of all member schools.

NAIS exists to promote freedom from government or church control, to promote and sustain intellectual freedom and expression, and ultimately to preserve the self-determination of its member schools in mission and program. NAIS contributes leadership and service for member schools and associations toward the goal of becoming effective learning environments that reflect financial sustainability, as well as programmatic and environmental excellence and independence. NAIS standards are high, and embrace creativity, performance, and integrity, while fostering a global network meant to support the independence, from any outside control, of each of its member schools.

The vision of NAIS is to ensure that member school graduates have the requisite skills to make sound moral and intellectual choices for themselves, their communities, and the world. At the same time, NAIS seeks to help create environments in member schools that encourage the adaptation of these skills to an ever-changing world and the values of a complex future marketplace defined by globalization.

NAIS has made a firm commitment to diversity. It provides leadership, training, and access to all programs for all people, regardless of race, religion, creed, color, sexual orientation, age, physical challenge, nation of origin, gender, or any other characteristic, thus reflecting the spirit of the laws promoting civil rights and liberties for all persons.

Principles of Good Practice

NAIS has developed principles of good practice for member schools as evidence of commitment to supporting high standards of education quality and ethical behavior for its membership. Each set of principles is drafted by an NAIS committee of practitioners, submitted to the NAIS board of directors for approval, and then disseminated to member schools. By articulating expectations in these principles of good practice, member schools can refer to already established goals when working toward fulfilling their missions, developing strategic plans, and earning their status as fully accredited members of NAIS. The principles of good practice cover topics such as admission, athletics, board of trustees, early childhood educators, educating for global citizenship, equity and justice, heads of schools, hiring process, independent school trustees, parents working with schools/schools working with parents, secondary school educators, and technology use.

To become a member school, candidates must carry out a self-study and submit to a review process conducted by NAIS review teams within a prescribed period of time. The independent school community must demonstrate effectiveness in meeting NAIS principles of good practice through provided examples. This self-study process may take months to complete, and schools must adhere to a timeline established by NAIS. When a school's self-study has been completed, the national review team created by NAIS is sent to the member school to complete the review. Schools have time to use the evaluation of the NAIS review team in ameliorating any problems indicated in the evaluation. These reviews are intimately tied to whether or not a given school receives its approval for accreditation within the organization.

Training

NAIS annual conferences have a variety of focuses, from instructional creative strategy and outcomes to major world issues, such as environmental concerns. Furthermore, the organization also provides training for leadership and governance for faculty, administrators, students, and the board of trustees. NAIS also organizes two annual conferences addressing the principles of diversity: the People of Color Conference and the Student Diversity Leadership Conference for students and advising faculty members. In addition, summer diversity institutes are offered and study trips to other countries are available.

NAIS provides training in financial aid for students, as well as acquisition and development of sustained endowed funds to perpetuate the future of independent education in the United States and worldwide. NAIS is the national and international clearinghouse for the marketing and exposition of the philosophy of independent education.

Since 1963, NAIS has encouraged its member schools to constantly reform themselves in order to enhance their ability to achieve their own intellectual and spiritual destinies. This is accomplished by advocating separation from legislative bodies or institutions such as churches and state and federal governments.

Martha Gallagher Michael

See also Academic Freedom; Professional Development; Single-Sex Schools; Society of Friends Schools

Further Readings

Burnett, J. G., & Diemer, M. V. (1996). *Take it or leave it: Questions and answers on federal assistance for independent schools.* Washington, DC: National Association of Independent Schools.

Grace, C. O. (2001). *Marketing independent schools in the twenty-first century.* Washington, DC: National Association of Independent Schools.

Sizer, T. R. (1985). *Horace's compromise: The dilemma of the American high school.* Washington, DC: National Association of Independent Schools.

NATIONAL ASSOCIATION OF SECONDARY SCHOOL PRINCIPALS (NASSP)

The National Association of Secondary School Principals (NASSP) was founded in 1917 and became a department of the National Education Association in 1927. In the early 1970s when state collective bargaining laws became prevalent, NASSP split off from the National Education Association and became an independent organization. The mission of NASSP is to promote excellence in middle level and high school leadership. NASSP membership consists of more than 30,000 principals, approximately 51% of its overall membership; assistant principals, approximately 31%; and other educational leaders, such as teachers, counselors, professors, or other site level administrators, approximately 18% of the membership. It is the primary organization for school administrators in buildings with students above the sixth-grade level, which includes high schools, junior high schools, and middle schools. The importance of these leaders is widely recognized as vital if there is to be any real change or reform in America's schools. Research supports the direct impact good teaching has on student learning, and it is the leaders who have an indirect impact because the leaders attract, support, and retain teachers.

Although active in the national policy debates concerning educational reform, NASSP is nonpartisan and does not endorse, support, advocate for, or encourage people to vote for any political candidate or party. It has a tax status of a 501(c)(3) organization. The NASSP Web site has a principal's blog that informs members about current legislation, responds to high impact pieces of legislation, including the No Child Left Behind Act and the Individuals with Disabilities Education Act. When a pending piece of legislation has relevance to schools, it encourages NASSP members to contact federal legislators. It works with both Republicans and Democrats to inform and advise national political leaders about the issues affecting school buildings and the students within those schools. As a representative of the leaders of those buildings NASSP provides a unique perspective. The NASSP has often collaborated with other organizations that are related to its mission. A few of the more common partnerships have been with the National Association of Elementary Principals (NAESP) and the American Association of School Administrators, which serves superintendents. NAESP parallels NASSP and has similar goals except NAESP represents leaders in schools for younger students. NASSP often works to find common ground with the teachers associations or others with whom they may have differences, so that they can work together to achieve positive results.

NASSP was one of 10 organizations that collaborated in creating the National Policy Board for Educational Administration to set national standards for the preparation of principals and other administrators. In addition to NASSP, the collaboration included superintendents (American Association of School Administrators), elementary school principals (National Association of Elementary Principals), and university professors and administrators (National Council of Professors of Educational Administration and University Council for Educational Administration). There was some controversy among university professors about this, but the National Policy Board for Educational Administration is now an established organization that periodically reviews and revises the national standards for the preparation of school administrators.

The executive director of NASSP is Gerald N. Tirozzi. Tirozzi acquired this crucial role in March 1999, contributing his more than 45-year tenure as a leader in reform to the common effort and vision of promoting high academic standards for all schools, reforming instructional practices, and further advancing NASSP as an important player in the national dialogue of high school and middle school reform. Tirozzi has also increased the focus of NASSP on assistant principals, with the knowledge that at the secondary level the majority of principals start their administrative careers as assistant principals.

NASSP has been involved in a number of reform efforts in addition to the National Policy Board for Educational Administration. State affiliates are active in working with the national organization to support principals in educational reform. Many of the state affiliates have annual meetings and numerous specialized meetings that deal with specific topics of concern (e.g., accountability measures, innovative reforms or legal updates). NASSP has several publications to inform and assist administrators, including *A Legal Memorandum*, which is published quarterly, and two *Principal Leadership* magazines, one at the middle school level and one at the high school level, which are published monthly from September through May. NASSP also holds an annual meeting, which moves around the country. Demonstrating the emphasis NASSP places on change and reform, the theme for the 2009 convention in San Diego, California, was "For we dare not stand idly by."

Additionally, NASSP is the parent organization for the National Honor Society, the National Junior Honor Society, and the program of the National Association of Student Councils. These organizations may seem tangential to the principalship, but they are a result of and evidence of the student centeredness of principals and NASSP. NASSP has also been a leader in the development of assessment centers that have been used in the selection and professional development of principals. Perhaps most notable among NASSP's reform efforts is the publication of *Breaking Ranks: Changing an American Institution* in 1996, *Breaking Ranks II* in 2004, and *Breaking Ranks in the Middle: Strategies for Leading Middle Level Reform* in 2006. NASSP personnel have involved many practicing principals as well as university professor groups, such as the Education Alliance at Brown University, in the development of these documents.

In these documents, NASSP has taken the position that almost all schools need to change and reform. Even if the vast majority of students within a school are performing at or above state and national benchmarks, there is usually a portion of the student population within each school that needs to be better served, and even the students performing at acceptable levels could be performing at higher levels if the school knew the strengths and weaknesses of each individual student and adjusted the instruction appropriately. These efforts again emphasize the student-centered nature of NASSP, add the newer national trend of being data driven and involve a balancing of the whole child while addressing the pressures of accountability. There are efforts to connect what happens in the classroom with the needs of students entering a global economy. Making connections that work for all students is central to these efforts, in that one of the three core areas of *Breaking Ranks II* and *Breaking Ranks in the*

Middle is personalizing the school environment. The second core area deals with the data-driven concept and the accountability movement because it is curriculum, instruction, and assessment which, when tied together, are at the heart of improving student learning. The third area is collaborative leadership and professional learning communities, which are at the heart of implementing any change. Change cannot happen unless the human personnel involved understand, accept, and are committed to making the reforms work. These publications and the dialogue that has come forth from them have provided a wealth of actual examples of principals leading meaningful 21st-century reforms that are, in some buildings, benefiting all students.

A. William Place

See also American Association of School Administrators (AASA); Association for Supervision and Curriculum Development; National Association of Elementary School Principals (NAESP); National Council of Professors of Educational Administration (NCPEA); Women in Educational Leadership

Further Readings

National Association of Secondary School Principals. (1996). *Breaking ranks: Changing an American institution*. Reston, VA: Author.

National Association of Secondary School Principals. (2004). *Breaking ranks II: Strategies for leading high school reform*. Reston, VA: Author.

National Association of Secondary School Principals. (2006). *Breaking ranks in the middle: Strategies for leading middle level reform*. Reston, VA: Author.

National Association of Secondary School Principals (n.d.). *Executive director Gerald N. Tirozzi*. Retrieved July 24, 2008, from http://www.principals.org/s_nassp/sec.asp?CID=833&DID=52717

NATIONAL BOARD FOR PROFESSIONAL TEACHING STANDARDS (NBPTS)

In 1985 the president of the American Federation of Teachers, Albert Shanker, recommended that a national teaching standards and evaluation board be established. The following year, the Carnegie Forum on Education and the Economy created a task force on teaching as a profession. The task force produced a report in 1986 titled *A Nation Prepared: Teachers for the 21st Century*. The report called for the creation of the National Board for Professional Teaching Standards (NBPTS), which would define what teachers should know about content and teaching and what teachers should be able to do in a classroom. The recommendation called for assessments that would be rigorous evaluations of teacher content and pedagogical knowledge. The Carnegie Corporation of New York provided the funds and former North Carolina governor, James B. Hunt, Jr., served as the first chairman of the newly formed NBPTS in 1987. Hunt called for the involvement of teachers who were practicing professionals to be on the board and for them to take an active role in all phases of the program. Teachers continue to be fully involved in writing the NBPTS standards, composing the assessments, and evaluating the candidates' work.

Mission and Core Propositions

The mission of the NBPTS is to advance the quality of student learning by recognizing excellence in teaching practice, identifying and maintaining rigorous sets of standards for teachers that define what teachers should know and be able to do in the classroom. The ideal elements of an accomplished teacher, as envisioned by the National Board, were identified in the 1989 NBPTS document *What Teachers Should Know and Be Able to Do*. It remains the cornerstone of the organization and NBPTS certification. Five core propositions for accomplished teaching were identified in the 1989 document.

Proposition 1

Teachers are committed to students and learning. Underscoring this element is the belief that all students can learn. It is the responsibility of the teacher to make the curriculum and content accessible to all students. Knowing each student and appreciating the differences in each student intellectually, culturally, and in their family situations helps accomplished teachers create learning situations that enable students to engage in the learning process. Developing the student as a whole person and responsible citizen are elements that accomplished teachers include in their practice.

Proposition 2

Teachers know the subjects they teach and how to teach those subjects to students. The basis of this proposition is the background knowledge of the teacher. That knowledge should be at the conceptual level of the content. Teachers has a solid grasp of how the content that they teach was developed and how to use that content in real-world situations. From their past teaching experiences and developed skills, they know where students have incomplete understanding and they are aware of typical content misconceptions. The goal of teachers is to instruct using multiple strategies and methods to ensure that all students will have a deep understanding of the content.

Proposition 3

Teachers are responsible for managing and monitoring student learning. They move fluidly from one instructional strategy to another in a manner that engages students while keeping them motivated to learn. They organize their instruction to meet content standards. Their presentation of the content engages students to learn in an active, disciplined environment. Throughout the teaching process, teachers know how to assess students individually and collectively, using multiple and varied methods. Teachers can communicate student progress effectively to parents.

Proposition 4

Teachers think systematically about their practice and learn from their experiences. Teachers model active learning by researching and creating new ways to engage students in their content areas. Keeping up with changing teaching strategies, methods, and issues involving their profession are prime goals for accomplished teachers. On a regular basis, teachers reflect upon their practice to make improvements in their teaching.

Proposition 5

Teachers are members of learning communities. Teachers are collaborators who work effectively with colleagues, parents, and the community. They are educational leaders who build partnerships within their schools, districts, and with community businesses to improve student learning. They contribute to their schools by implementing their research on curriculum and professional development. Teachers help their schools meet state and local standards by reviewing the allocation of resources and making constructive observations to improve student learning.

Assessment Process

The assessment process has two components: a performance-based element that demonstrates the professional judgments made by teachers on a daily basis; and a written examination that identifies the content mastery. The candidates create a portfolio according to NBPTS guidelines of typical assignments and assessments that the teachers create for students. Student work samples from these assignments and assessments must be included. Videotaping the candidates' actual teaching in multiple teaching situations is required. Finally, the portfolio must have a personal, comprehensive examination of the teaching practices that teachers use. The final element of the assessment is the rigorous testing focused on the content taught by the candidates. Teachers voluntarily participate in this review of their practice and are identified as accomplished teachers when their work is judged as meeting the NBPTS defined standards.

The NBPTS identifies and continually increases the number of areas of certification. As of 2008, there were 25 areas of certification. The certification areas are listed by content and student developmental level. The content areas include art, career and technical education, English as a new language, English language arts, exceptional needs specialist, generalist, health education, library media, literacy, reading, language arts, mathematics, music, physical education, school counseling, science, social studies–history, and world languages other than English. The student developmental levels are early childhood (3–8 years old), middle childhood (7–12 years old), early adolescence (11–15 years old), and adolescence to young adult (14–18+ years old). Not all content areas offer all developmental levels as certification domains.

Each content area has a set of standards that must be met in the creation of the candidate's portfolio and are assessed in the rigorous written examination. The content standards reflect the five core propositions, but have elements that are specific to the content area. The standards provide opportunities for teachers to demonstrate actions that represent their professional judgment within specific content areas and developmental levels. The areas covered in the standards include the teachers' commitment to students; student learning; and issues of equity, diversity, and fairness in teaching, assessing, and interacting with students in classrooms. Content knowledge is a key element in the standards for each area. Knowledge of how students within a developmental level learn and identification of appropriate teaching practices are included in the standards. Pedagogical concerns are identified, and candidates are required to write about the learning environment, assessment, and process standards. Professional growth is the final area noted in each set of standards. Candidates are required to identify their involvement with families and the local community. This element recognizes the work done by teachers outside of the classroom. They list how they have contributed to the growth of their professional community and reflect upon their practice and growth within their careers. Evidence of pedagogical practices is included in the candidates' portfolio. Content knowledge mastery is identified when candidates takes the examination within their content and developmental level.

The NBPTS content-specific standards committees are composed of 8 to 12 members who are primarily classroom teachers. Additionally, there can be content specialists, professional development specialists, or university educators on the committees. The committee members represent multiple professional perspectives that define accomplished teaching. The committees are charged with creating, reviewing, and updating standards that define accomplished teaching.

The NBPTS supports research into the effectiveness of certified teachers. There have been more than 150 examinations of the effectiveness of NBPTS board certification. Over 75% of the results of the studies identified the teaching of NBPTS-certified teachers as statistically significant when examining student learning and achievement, teacher performance, and student engagement. Studies listed on the research Web page of the NBPTS by W. Sanders of the Statistical Analysis System Institute and W. McCloskey and J. Stronge, of the University of North Carolina, Greensboro, and the College of William and Mary found which students' rate of academic progress

were not significantly higher than students of teachers who were not NBPTS certified. On June 11, 2008, a study by the National Research Council found that students of NBPTS-certified teachers made bigger gains on standardized tests than did students of teachers who were not NBPTS certified. The NBPTS continues to sponsor research aimed at improving the standards and process of national teacher certification.

Janet M. Herrelko

Further Readings

Carnegie Forum on Education and the Economy's Task Force on Teaching as a Profession. (1986, May 15). *A nation prepared: Teachers for the 21st century.* New York: Carnegie Foundation.

National Board for Professional Teaching Standards: http://nbpts.org

National Board for Professional Teaching Standards. (2002, August). *What teachers should know and be able to do.* Retrieved June 6, 2008, from http://www.nbpts.org/UserFiles/File/what_teachers.pdf

NATIONAL CENTER FOR EDUCATION STATISTICS (NCES)

Part of the U.S. Department of Education, the National Center for Education Statistics (NCES) is a federal statistical agency, charged with the responsibility of collecting and disseminating high-quality, reliable, valid, useful, and unbiased statistical information about the condition of education in the United States and other countries. These data are used by both proponents of educational reform and defenders of the status quo just as statistics on unemployment and economic growth are used to argue both for and against economic policies. This entry reviews the history of NCES and major factors that affect its work.

History and Mission

The mission of NCES dates back to 1867, when Congress created a Department of Education to collect statistics on the condition and progress of education in the states and territories. NCES, however, came into being, as a distinct federal agency, in January 1965 when the Office of Education was reorganized (preceding passage of the Elementary and Secondary Education Act of 1965, which greatly expanded the federal role in education). The creation of NCES was in large part a response to growing concerns in the early 1960s about the objectivity and reliability of federal statistics.

Until the 1970s, NCES continued to do the same statistical work that had been done at the Office of Education. This consisted mostly of compiling and tabulating, on calculators, administrative data collected from states, districts, and schools, based on occasional surveys sent out to all known schools or institutions of higher education. These summary data were then published in national reports on U.S. public and private elementary and secondary schools and institutions of higher education. Such data were generally meager (e.g., largely limited to total enrollment counts, numbers of teachers, basic revenues and expenditures, number of degrees conferred) and suffered from the poor administrative record keeping of some states, districts, and schools as well as from incomplete and missing survey responses.

To improve the quality of available national data, NCES entered the business of data production in the 1970s. In 1971, NCES first took over responsibility for the National Assessment of Educational Progress, which directly assesses achievement of a nationally representative sample of students and collects background information about them, their teachers, and their schools. In 1972, NCES launched the first of a series of longitudinal studies with the National Longitudinal Study of the 1970s (NLS-72), which surveyed a nationally representative sample of high school seniors in 1972, collecting detailed information about their background and school experiences, and surveyed them again five times between 1973 and 1986 to see what their further education and job experiences were. National Assessment of Educational Progress and NLS-72 transformed NCES from an agency primarily dedicated to tabulating received data into a true statistical agency, facing issues of sample designs, response rates, imputation methods, standard errors, inferences, valid statistical comparisons, and computer programming. At the same time, the data from these studies gave educational reformers the means to

make more compelling claims about student achievement in the nation at large, such as the authors of *A Nation at Risk* famously did by selectively using National Assessment of Educational Progress data to argue that U.S. students' knowledge was in decline.

Also beginning in the 1970s, NCES began to expand the amount and type of information it asked states, school districts, and schools to report. The NCES budget and staff, however, were not up to all of the new demands placed upon them. As a result, a series of embarrassing missteps befell some of NCES's programs, the most notable being in 1983 when the Office of Management and Budget halted the NCES Vocational Education Data System (started in 1978), because it was "unreliable and subject to serious misinterpretation." Criticism of NCES, including charges of lack of timeliness and lack of quality control, grew steadily in the early 1980s—especially of NCES's lack of center-wide statistical standards.

In 1984, the Office of Educational Research and Improvement Assistant Secretary Donald Senese asked the National Academy of Science to undertake a thorough analysis of the center. In 1986, the National Academy of Science issued a scathing report. Finding the center's problems so serious, the report concluded that "serious consideration should be given to . . . abolishing the center and finding other means to obtain and disseminate education data."

In response to the National Academy of Science report, Emerson Elliot, then head of NCES, convinced Congress to remake NCES as an independent commission and to provide significantly more funding. Elliot became the first NCES commissioner, Congress tripled its budget between 1987 and 1991, and Elliot led a complete overhaul of NCES. NCES staff size and statistical expertise increased. NCES adopted its first written statistical standards in 1987. NCES replaced its Elementary and Secondary General Information System (which compiled state and school district data from the 1960s until 1986) with the Common Core of Data, the first annual Public School Universe Survey, which remains the source for standardized student enrollment counts in all elementary and secondary public schools, by grade, sex, race/ethnicity, and free or reduced-price school lunch eligibility; it also serves as the frame for drawing all public school and student samples. At the same time, NCES replaced its Higher Education General Information Survey with the Integrated Postsecondary Education Data System. It launched and planned several new data series, including the School and Staffing Survey, a cross-sectional sample survey of school teachers, principals, and other school staff; the National Household Education Survey, a national household sample survey about children's and adults' educational experience; and the Educational Longitudinal Study of 1988 (ELS), a longitudinal study following students in the eighth grade in 1988 for 12 years to record their education and careers.

In 1988, Congress mandated an annual statistical report on the status and progress of education in the country. The NCES annual report *The Condition of Education* fulfilled this mandate and developed a host of indicators with data from an array of new NCES surveys.

In the mid-1990s, led by Commissioner Pat Forgione, NCES began to participate in what has become the Trends in International Mathematics and Science Study and planned an ambitious national longitudinal education study of children born in 2001, from birth through kindergarten with its Early Childhood Longitudinal Study. Also in 2001, NCES launched its first longitudinal study of children from kindergarten through fifth grade. The results of the Early Childhood Longitudinal Study provide the first national data for advocates of PreK, school-readiness programs, and other early education policies.

In 1999, NCES lost its commissioner, and the Senate did not confirm a new commissioner until 2003, when Mark Schneider became commissioner until 2008. In the interim, NCES had three acting commissioners and one pocket appointee, and during that time, the course and energy of the NCES foundered. The center's focus shifted from developing new surveys and measurements to institutionalizing its existing ones and rigorously applying its statistical standards.

Besides the vicissitudes of leadership, NCES efforts to fulfill its mission have been and continue to be constrained and shaped by (a) the challenge of being nonpartisan and objective in Washington, D.C., where choosing topics for surveys and analysis is itself political; (b) the inherent institutional conflict between getting out information quickly and ensuring statistical information is of the highest quality; (c) the center's institutional independence, support, and professionalism; and (d) the U.S. federalist system of government and the special interests of nongovernmental organizations.

Given the U.S. federalist system of government and the traditional U.S. ideological commitment to state and local control over public education, NCES has no authority to compel states or school districts to report information or, if they do, to require them to use standardized definitions. NCES relies solely on voluntary participation, which can be compromised by local budgetary constraints, reluctance to reveal unflattering information, or just indifference. Thus, NCES data collection involves statistical work as well as negotiation with data providers. For example, the Common Core of Data's standardized data did not exist when the Common Core of Data began operation. In the late 1980s, state departments of education neither collected these basic data consistently nor were uniformly keen to adopt national data reporting standards. Such standardized data are largely the product of NCES's negotiating and cajoling of state departments of education throughout the 1990s.

NCES's dependence on the good will of local districts and state education departments means that nongovernmental organizations that have influence in these areas (e.g., National Governors Association, National Education Association, National Association of State Boards of Education, and National Association of Elementary School Principals) must be accommodated when they disagree with NCES data collection practices or categories, lest they encourage their members to withhold data. Given these realities, one of the pivotal moments in the history of NCES was a decision by a nongovernmental organization. In 1984, the Council of Chief State School Officers agreed to sanction the collection by NCES of state educational data that would allow detailed and potentially unflattering comparisons of state school systems, something that they had blocked for years previously. This opened the door to the (initially voluntary) expanded state samples for the National Assessment of Educational Progress that became the state-by-state "main" National Assessment of Education Progress comparisons mandated under the No Child Left Behind Act of 2001.

From 1965 until 1974, NCES was an organizational unit within the Office of Education, reporting to the commissioner of education. In 1974, Congress wrote NCES into legislation, making it a statutory entity reporting to the assistant secretary of education. In 1980, when the Office of Education became the U.S. Department of Education, NCES became part of the Office of Educational Research and Improvement, under the direction of the Office's assistant secretary. In 1986, Congress authorized NCES as a separate agency, to be run by a commissioner of education statistics, a 4-year presidential appointee. At this time, NCES gained the authority to independently review and approve its reports for release; however, this was not a statutory mandate. After Congress created the Institute of Education Sciences in 2002, NCES lost this authority and was placed under the direction of the director of the Institute of Education Sciences, who attempted to restrict the work of NCES (to data collection only) by curtailing NCES's practice of publishing reports that explained or analyzed the data it collected.

Stephen J. Provasnik

See also National Assessment of Educational Progress (NAEP); Trends in International Mathematics and Science Study (TIMSS); U.S. Department of Education

Further Readings

National Research Council. (1986). *Creating a center for education statistics: A time for action* (D. B. Levine, Ed.). Washington, DC: National Academy Press.
National Research Council. (1992). *Research and educational reform: Roles for the office of educational research and improvement* (R. C. Atkinson & G. B. Jackson, Eds.). Washington, DC: National Academy Press.
Weiss, J. A., & Gruber, J. E. (1987). The managed irrelevance of federal education statistics. In W. Alonso & P. Starr (Eds.), *The politics of numbers* (pp. 363–391). New York: Russell Sage Foundation.

NATIONAL COMMISSION ON TEACHING AND AMERICA'S FUTURE (NCTAF)

Starting with its first report in 1996, the National Commission on Teaching and America's Future

(NCTAF) has worked to ensure that teacher quality be understood as a key policy issue crucial for successful education reform in the United States. Led at its inception by North Carolina governor Jim Hunt and Stanford professor Linda Darling-Hammond, who served as the Commission's executive director, NCTAF published *What Matters Most: Teaching for America's Future* and called for widespread changes in how K–12 teachers are recruited, prepared, and retained. The report's recommendations inspired creation of state partnerships, facilitated new alliances among nonprofits, and led to efforts at state and federal levels to rethink policies and practices about teachers and teaching quality.

The Commission included elected officials (two governors, one member of Congress, and state legislators), college presidents, teachers and school administrators, union leaders from the American Federation of Teachers and the National Education Association, university faculty, business leaders, and philanthropists. Almost 15 years after *What Matters Most* appeared in print, the Commission's five core recommendations still resonate with education reformers and with members of the public worried about schooling and the outcomes of schooling.

1. Get serious about standards, for both students and teachers.

2. Reinvent teacher preparation and professional development.

3. Fix teacher recruitment and put qualified teachers in every classroom.

4. Encourage and reward teacher knowledge and skill.

5. Create schools that are organized for student and teacher success.

In one way or another, the nation still grapples with the challenges behind each of these recommendations. Their importance has been cast into bolder relief because accountability for student outcomes has become a central force in American public education. While NCTAF did not address accountability for student and teacher outcomes in its first publication, the Commission's subsequent work has sought to link improved student, teacher, and system performance to NCTAF's values and policies.

Today, NCTAF membership also includes prominent figures from public life; it is cochaired by former U.S. secretary of education Richard Riley and by Ted Sanders, former president of the Education Commission of the States, as well as accomplished leaders from the public sector, business, education, and higher education.

Thomas Carroll has served as NCTAF president since 2001, and he leads a Commission staff that has state, national, and other policy expertise. NCTAF continues to produce work that helps to define or redefine the core issues surrounding successful schooling and learning in the United States.

Through its 2003 report, *No Dream Denied: A Pledge to America's Children,* NCTAF reconfirmed its commitment to the five core recommendations from *What Matters Most,* and it gave major emphasis to organizing "every school for teaching and learning success." To that end, the Commission took steps to raise the national visibility of teacher retention. The Commission was particularly concerned with teacher turnover and the multiple reasons for teachers deciding not to continue professional practice. The real problem was not teacher supply but rather the fact that too many schools were hiring unprepared or underqualified individuals to provide classroom instruction. The inability of schools to create strong professional cultures engendered conditions for high teacher turnover.

Three themes emerged as significant grounding for the Commission's work: high teacher turnover, the need to build professional learning communities, and improved teacher preparation and hiring strategies. These themes run through all of NCTAF's work after *No Dream Denied* was released to the public in 2003. Just as NCTAF's earlier work brought teacher quality to the center of education policy considerations, its focus on the corrosive influence of high teacher turnover rates on school improvement efforts and on pupil learning outcomes changed the conversation in policy and media circles. By documenting the huge numbers of teachers moving in and out of schools each year (through analysis of the federal Schools and Staffing Survey), the Commission made a powerful case for taking sustained action against the causes of turnover.

As a result, there is increased attention now on solutions to the teacher persistence problem through induction and mentoring programs for new teachers, clinically based preparation programs to prepare new teachers for real-world schools, and experiments with incentive or "bonus" pay for talented men and women to enter and stay in teaching, and to teach in challenging school settings.

Building on *No Dream Denied* through a series of conferences and research projects, NCTAF published a pilot study on the cost of teacher turnover in five school districts. This project was one of the first efforts to measure teacher turnover at the school level with actual district data (rather than survey responses or extrapolations from small data sets). *The Cost of Teacher Turnover in Five Districts* (2007) also pioneered calculation of the financial costs of teacher turnover, using personnel and business records from the five districts. Most previous work in this area had built cost estimates on assumptions adapted from other fields about district- and school-level costs.

More recently, NCTAF has written about the impact on the teacher workforce—and on schools—of impending retirements by large numbers of baby-boomer teachers. *Learning Teams: Creating What's Next* (2009) predicted that because more than half of the public school teachers in 18 states and in the District of Columbia are more than 50 years old, schools in these states will face a teacher workforce crisis in the next few years. Calling for flexible pension systems, improved compensation policies, and expansion of multimember "learning teams" in schools, NCTAF argued that these structural changes are essential to the welfare of schools and students.

This latest NCTAF effort to move policy and practice in education notes the importance of the impending demographic crisis—specifically, that crisis can serve as an impetus for change in the next generation of American schools. Over the past century far too many teachers have stood alone in the classroom, isolated from professional peers. The emerging challenges create opportunities for reinventing schools in ways that would permit teachers to ensure that the students have the competitive edge they need to function effectively in a globalized society.

NCTAF goes on to argue that conventional recruit-and-replace strategies will fail because far too few schools have the capacity to identify the teachers needed for the challenges evident in U.S. classrooms and even fewer schools evidence an ability to institutionalize the strengths that teachers manifest in a way that is transferable between classrooms and across schools.

As part of its ongoing work to stimulate action about the issues raised in its reports, the Commission conducted regional forums on teacher quality topics across the country. Covered by Public Broadcasting Service television stations in Boston, Nashville, Albuquerque, and Bloomington (Indiana), this work is one outgrowth of the Commission's partnership with the MetLife Foundation. Local schools were featured on these broadcasts as the Commission and its partners sought to build broad public understanding of newer ways to organize schooling and learning.

Other recent NCTAF initiatives include a reinvigorated state partnership network, supported in part by funding from the Knowledge Works Foundation. From its beginning in 1996, NCTAF understood the importance of state partners because many key policies and practices affecting teacher quality are state responsibilities. Other key funding for the Commission has come from the National Science Foundation, the Joyce and Spencer Foundations, Ford, the Carnegie Corporation of New York, the Fund for the Improvement of Postsecondary Education, and the Rockefeller Foundation.

Edward Crowe

See also Education Commission of the States (ECS); National Council for Accreditation of Teacher Education (NCATE); National Council on Teacher Quality (NCTQ); Teacher Education Accreditation Council (TEAC)

Further Readings

Darling-Hammond, L. (Ed.). (2000). *Studies of excellence in teachers.* Washington, DC: National Commission on Teaching and America's Future.

National Commission on Teaching and America's Future. (1996). *What matters most: Teaching for America's future.* New York: Author.

National Commission on Teaching and America's Future. (1997). *Doing what matters most: Investing in quality teaching.* New York: Author.

NATIONAL COUNCIL FOR ACCREDITATION OF TEACHER EDUCATION (NCATE)

In 1954, the National Council for Accreditation of Teacher Education (NCATE) was formed with a charge to develop a consensus concerning what new teachers should know and be able to do. Five groups were instrumental in the creation of NCATE: (1) the American Association of Colleges for Teacher Education, (2) the National Association of State Directors of Teacher Education and Certification, (3) the National Education Association, (4) the Council of Chief State School Officers, and (5) the National School Boards Association. When NCATE was founded as an independent accrediting body, it replaced the American Association of Colleges for Teacher Education as the agency responsible for accreditation in teacher education.

By contemporary definition, accreditation informs the public that the accredited college or university operates at a high level of educational quality and integrity. NCATE accreditation is the process by which a professional education unit is recognized by the profession as meeting national standards for the content and operation of the unit. During its tenure, NCATE has been at the center of controversy and criticism, support and praise, and perpetual change for its role in education reform (especially as related to teacher education), teacher quality assurance, and accountability within the teaching profession.

The concern for teacher quality is a phenomenon that reaches back more than a century. In the mid-1800s, teachers were chosen by community or spiritual leaders based on a candidate's moral character. Toward the end of the 19th century, it was common to see communities administer examinations that continued to address character but also encompassed subject-matter knowledge and child development. These initial certification systems were fraught with challenges, including political favoritism of appointed teachers and minimal educational standards. To counter, state departments of education were formed during the early 20th century to centralize control over the field by introducing state licensure requirements. The Progressive education movement further called attention to defining what constitutes appropriate teacher preparation. Between 1927 and 1948 the examination of teacher education practice was performed by the American Association of Teachers Colleges. One educational leader noted that this agency, though criticized for certifying a very small number of teachers, did help disseminate good practice and improved teacher education in the member institutions. In 1948, the American Association of Colleges for Teacher Education was formed and partnered with other professional education agencies to develop programs for coping with the growing shortage of teachers and to improve teacher education and raise professional standards. By 1954, the American Association of Colleges for Teacher Education changed its mission to research and service and became the parent organization of NCATE.

As NCATE evolved between 1954 and 2000, it faced controversy and criticism on a number of key issues, including the fundamental purposes of accreditation and the application of standards and processes for accreditation. In response to these criticisms and mounting calls for reform, most notably through the National Commission on Excellence in Education's report (*A Nation at Risk*), NCATE undertook a comprehensive review of its standards. Prior to 1987, NCATE framed its standards, according to the former head of NCATE (Arthur Wise), similar to other professional accrediting agencies at the time (i.e., in terms of inputs, on the presumption that these would lead to the desired knowledge and skills of teacher candidates). In 1987, it reframed its standards in terms of curriculum guidelines on the presumption that these would lead to enhanced teacher quality; it is a premise of the standards movement that in well-functioning schools, teacher hiring and professional development, curriculum, and instructional methods are all aligned to enhance student achievement.

In the early 1990s, NCATE required all of its specialty associations to revise existing standards to be based on performance. In the 1995 version of its standards, NCATE began the move toward performance accreditation by placing greater emphasis on the competence of candidates. NCATE required institutions to use multiple measures of performance to demonstrate candidate ability.

In 2001, NCATE formally reframed its standards to directly express its consensus concerning the needed knowledge, skills, dispositions, and abilities through expectations for the graduates of its institutions. This reframing led to performance-based accreditation, a system in which institutions must provide evidence of competent teacher candidate performance. By 2004, NCATE member organizations coordinated with the Educational Testing Service to ensure that licensing assessments were aligned with the profession's standards in the various subject-matter areas and developmental levels. NCATE standards also became congruent with the Interstate New Teacher Assessment and Support Consortium standards as well as the National Board of Professional Teaching Standards for advanced certification. Additionally, NCATE aligned teacher preparation standards with national standards for PreK–12 students. The NCATE system expects performance measures to include the candidate's impact on student learning. The focus on performance and student learning changed the type of evidence institutions must collect, aggregate, and analyze in order to demonstrate the effectiveness of their preparation programs. A change of this magnitude required significant modifications in program structures, staffing, data collection, and data analysis; these changes were required of NCATE and its accredited institutions.

Along with the continual evolution of standards, NCATE also responded to the request by institutions and states to integrate professional and state standards for new teachers. Until the late 1980s, NCATE and the respective states did not collaborate in the review of teacher preparation programs. Each had separate systems with little or no overlap. In 1989, NCATE implemented the state partnership program which aimed to eliminate duplication in an institution's preparation for state program approval and professional accreditation. Joint review of schools, colleges, and departments of education was a central feature of partnership agreements. In 2008, NCATE had 50 state partnerships, including agreements with the District of Columbia and Puerto Rico. All public teacher education institutions are NCATE accredited in 17 states; a majority of the teacher education institutions are NCATE accredited in 28 states.

The alignment of NCATE and the states has not been appreciated by all institutions, especially those who sought greater autonomy and quality control for the conformance to standards. In 2003, the secretary of education of the United States formally recognized the Teacher Education Accreditation Council as an accreditor of teacher education programs in the United States. The Teacher Education Accreditation Council is grounded on the premise that every institution should be able to set its own educational standards for teacher candidates and be held accountable on these terms.

NCATE currently accredits approximately 650 schools, colleges, and departments of education with nearly 100 more seeking NCATE accreditation. NCATE is a coalition of 33 member organizations of teachers, teacher educators, content specialists, and local and state policymakers. Accreditation, once granted, is continuous as long as the institution fulfills its responsibilities under NCATE's continuing accreditation process. Continuing accreditation status is granted after an institution has been accredited. Continuing accreditation requires institutions to file annual reports and host an on-site board of examiners team every 5 years. Official NCATE policy is to have a visit every 7 years. However, a few states use a 5-year visit cycle based on previous NCATE policy.

NCATE today is a nonprofit 501(c)(3) organization funded through dues from its 33 member organizations, fees from NCATE-accredited institutions, and foundation grants. NCATE is the largest alliance of professional education and public organizations in the nation devoted to quality teaching and one of the longest-standing national coalitions of stakeholders in the education community.

Ginger L. Zierdt

See also Accreditation; American Association of Colleges for Teacher Education; National Board for Professional Teaching Standards (NBPTS); Standards Movement; Teacher Education Accreditation Council (TEAC)

Further Readings

Bowers, H. (1959). The NCATE: Suicide or salvation. *Journal of Teacher Education, 10*(1), 112–116.

Hermanowicz, H. (1978). The present status and future of NCATE. *Journal of Teacher Education, 29*(1), 33–37.

Murray, F. (2005). On building a unified system of accreditation in teacher education. *Journal of Teacher Education, 56*(4), 307–317.

National Council for Accreditation of Teacher Education (NCATE): http://www.ncate.org

Russell, J. (1950). The accrediting of institutions of higher education. *Journal of Teacher Education, 1*(2), 83–94.

Tamir, E., & Wilson, S. (2005). Who should guard the gates? Evidentiary and professional warrants for claiming jurisdiction. *Journal of Teacher Education, 56*(4), 332–342.

Wise, A. (2005). Establishing teaching as a profession: The essential role of professional accreditation. *Journal of Teacher Education, 56*(4), 318–331.

Wise, A., & Leibbrand, J. (2001). Standards in the new millennium: Where we are, where we're headed. *Journal of Teacher Education, 52*(3), 244–255.

NATIONAL COUNCIL FOR HISTORY EDUCATION

The National Council for History Education (NCHE) is a not-for-profit corporation based in College Park, Maryland, dedicated to the promotion of the study of history in schools and in society. NCHE is motivated by the belief that current issues are best understood in their historical context and that historical study is the precondition for intelligent political judgment, the implications of which call for a fundamental reordering of the American curriculum from grade school to graduate school.

The position of history in the K–12 curriculum has been debated at least since the 1890s, when the National Education Association's Committee of Ten met and issued a report urging the reform of the general school curriculum. The Committee of Ten recommended that all students should study history for all 4 years of high school. The Progressive era and the rise to social and academic ascendancy of the social sciences led to the incorporation of the "social studies" into America's school curricula, comprising history, geography, civics, economics, anthropology, and sociology. In the 1960s and into the 1970s, social studies teachers were encouraged to employ issues-based instruction that reflected the social tumult of that era, and academic depth was often sacrificed to relevance. Some even wondered whether there was a place for historical study in the K–12 curriculum.

Several elements converged in the 1980s that helped to create the NCHE. First, the National

Assessment for Educational Progress and the National Endowment for the Humanities funded a research study by Diane Ravitch of Columbia University and Chester Finn, Jr., in which 8,000 eighth graders were surveyed regarding their knowledge of U.S. history. Their research, published in *What Do 17 Year Olds Know: A Report of the First National Assessment of History and Literature* (1987) determined that there was insufficient instruction in history in America's schools. They recommended at least 10 years of historical study, with at least 4 years between Grades 7 and 12.

The next year, two teachers, Elaine Wrisley Reed and Joseph P. Ribar, were encouraged by Ravitch to seek funding from the Lynde and Harry Bradley Foundation to examine the state of history education in schools. They solicited Paul Gagnon of the University of Massachusetts, Boston, to serve as principal investigator for the grant.

Gagnon and Ravitch contacted eminent historians across the nation, and the result was the Bradley Commission on History in Schools, a group of 17 scholars and teachers, chaired by Kenneth T. Jackson of Columbia University. Several past presidents of the Organization of American Historians and the American Historical Association served on the Commission, which issued its report, titled *Building a History Curriculum: Guidelines for Teaching History in Schools,* in 1988. The report expressed concern over inadequacies in both the quantity and the quality of history instruction and set forth a consensus of perspectives on history education and "ways of historical thinking" intended to transcend specific facts and content knowledge. To nurture what it called the "habits of mind" needed to develop historical understanding, the Commission established a set of vital themes and narratives designed to serve as the foundation for three sets of topics of study: U.S. history, Western civilization, and world history. It also recommended that the history requirement from kindergarten through Grade 12 be expanded greatly, with virtually all of the geographic, economic, and civics content taught as "social studies" being subsumed into history and taught historically. The next year, Gagnon edited *Historical Literacy: The Case for History in American Education* (1989), a collection of essays

that expanded upon the Commission's earlier work and which reflected the spirit that animated the Bradley Commission.

To keep the work of the Commission alive, a monthly newsletter was printed; conferences, workshops, and symposia were held; and meetings were held with curriculum review committees around the country. As the Bradley Commission was not intended to be a permanent organization, in 1990 Jackson, Gagnon, and 180 historians and educators created the National Council for History Education to carry on the work begun by the Bradley Commission. Theodore Rabb of Princeton was named chair, and Elaine Wrisley Reed, the Pennsylvania elementary school teacher whose questions about history instruction first led to the Bradley Commission was named executive director, a position she held until her retirement in 2007.

NCHE immediately set to work assisting districts in curriculum revision and working with states to revise or create history standards and frameworks. NCHE task forces worked on the National Association of Education Progress test for U.S. history and reviewed and critiqued drafts of the controversial national standards for history that were developed at the National Center for History in Schools at the University of California, Los Angeles. Professional development conferences were held in school districts, which included the innovative "colloquium" model, whereby academic historians, K–12 teachers, and education specialists collaborate as peers. These colloquia reflect the essential NCHE principle that history education is a combination of research, content, and methods combined in the skillful hands of the classroom teacher. NCHE also began to send out *History Matters!*, a monthly newsletter with updates on NCHE activities and initiatives as well as concrete ideas for lesson plans and instruction.

The preparation of history teachers has become a major concern of NCHE. The Bradley Commission recommended that middle and secondary history or social studies teachers should have at least an undergraduate minor, if not a major, in history. In 2004, NCHE developed and issued its long-range plan, which stated that by 2010, NCHE would become a national leader in pre-service history teacher education and in professional development. In December 2006, the NCHE board of trustees adopted a statement on teacher qualifications, which called for deep and advanced undergraduate history instruction ("preferably the equivalent of a college major in History") in courses that develop historical understanding through the study of historiography, historical writing, and historical research. NCHE urged schools of education to provide pre-service teachers with teaching methods classes taught by historians rather than by educationists and with clinical experiences guided by highly qualified licensed history teachers.

NCHE also works to protect and expand the position of history in the curriculum as the No Child Left Behind statutes, with their premium on mathematics and science, have led to a narrowing of the curriculum. Although NCHE did not issue a position paper on the No Child Left Behind legislation, it actively lobbies to protect and expand the role of history and the need for proper teacher preparation in history. NCHE has recommended that mandatory testing in history become part of the No Child Left Behind legislation and that its performance in history should be included in measuring a school's adequate yearly progress.

John J. White

See also Committee of Ten; National Endowment for the Humanities; No Child Left Behind Act (NCLB); Social Studies, New; Teacher Education

Further Readings

Bradley Commission. (1988). *Building a history curriculum: Guidelines for teaching history in schools.* Washington, DC: Educational Excellence Network.

Evans, R. W. (2004). *The social studies wars: What should we teach the children?* New York: Teachers College Press.

Gagnon, P. (Ed.). (1988). *Historical literacy: The case for history in American education.* New York: Macmillan.

Ravitch, D., & Finn, C., Jr. (1987). *What do our seventeen year olds know? A report of the first national assessment of history and literature.* New York: Harper & Row.

Symcox, L. (2002). *Whose history? The struggle for national standards in American classrooms.* New York: Teachers College Press.

NATIONAL COUNCIL FOR THE SOCIAL STUDIES

The National Council for the Social Studies (NCSS) is the largest organization in the United States dedicated to social studies education. The organization's core purpose, as articulated in the NCSS strategic plan, is "to lead the community of social studies professionals in promoting a knowledgeable and engaged citizenry." Since its modest beginnings as a department within the National Education Association (NEA) in 1921, NCSS has grown to be one of the largest education associations with a membership that spans the globe and affiliate organizations in every region of the United States. Over the years, NCSS has provided leadership for the social studies community by providing forums for the discussion and dissemination of ideas; by building a professional network of social studies educators; by articulating positions on key issues affecting social studies education and advocating for social studies reform; by bringing rigor and coherence to the social studies curriculum; and by enhancing the status of the profession.

Since its founding, NCSS has suffered a definitional crisis. While many founding members of the organization viewed social studies as a unified field, others saw social studies as a set of separate, but closely related, disciplines which at the time included history, geography, civics, economics, and some content from the humanities and the natural sciences. This entry will trace the birth and growth of NCSS as an agent of progressive curricular reform in the United States, and it will highlight critical points in the ongoing debates within the organization.

The Founding of NCSS

By the turn of the 20th century, the position of history in the school curriculum had come under scrutiny. In 1892, the NEA Committee of Ten appointed a subcommittee on history, civil government, and political economy to look closely at the secondary school curriculum related to these three academic areas. The subcommittee concluded that history instruction in elementary and secondary schools was inadequate and largely textbook driven. Furthermore, it recommended that content related to civil government should be integrated with the American history curriculum, and that these subjects should be taught in the last year of elementary school and the last year of high school. In 1899, the American History Association Committee of Seven concurred with most of the NEA Committee of Ten recommendations, but it also advocated for historical inquiry and critical thinking in schools, and it explicitly opposed rote memorization as a pedagogical strategy.

The work of the Committee of Ten and the Committee of Seven marked the first concerted efforts to reform the history curriculum in the United States. Critics charged that the history curriculum was too narrow and unable to prepare students for the complex social issues of the 20th century. Progressive historians of the period, including James Harvey Robinson and Charles A. Beard, called for a "new" history that would help students to understand problems of the present through the study of the past.

In 1916, the NEA convened the Committee on Social Science, which was renamed the Committee on Social Studies by its chairman, Thomas Jesse Jones. The committee recommended three courses at the core of the secondary social studies curriculum—history, geography, and civics—with a new civics-oriented course in the 12th grade called Problems of Democracy—Social, Economic, and Political. The creation of the Problems of Democracy course was a curricular compromise between traditionalists, who favored a discipline-focused social studies with history at the center, and progressive reformers, who favored an integrated social studies that would help students understand and solve societal problems.

Although the Problems of Democracy course never took hold, the curricular debate between progressives and traditionalists that led to its creation continued. On March 3, 1921, at a meeting of the NEA in Atlantic City, New Jersey, a group of progressive, reform-minded professors and graduate students led by Harold and Earle Rugg founded NCSS as a way to support and advance the idea of a unified "social studies." At first, the membership of NCSS consisted primarily of college and university faculty, but the organization quickly grew to include teachers and other school-based personnel. Externally, NCSS maintained relationships with other professional associations, including NEA, American History Association, and the Progressive Education Association.

Development of NCSS

The 1930s and 1940s marked a period in which wartime education, patriotic citizenship, and international understanding were pillars of the social studies curriculum. NCSS produced and disseminated instructional materials and supported an integrated curriculum with social issues at the core. Critics of social studies, such as the conservative historian Allan Nevins and his associate Hugh Russell Fraser, thought the curriculum was weak, and they saw NCSS as an organization closely allied with radicals and extremists at Columbia University's Teachers College.

NCSS positioned itself to influence the shape of the social studies curriculum during the postwar years. Throughout the United States, social studies offerings expanded and intensified in elementary and junior high schools. By the 1950s, NCSS boasted a national membership of more than 5,000, and the annual conferences drew in excess of 1,000 participants. During the 1950s, the organization worked to close the membership gap between college and university members and social studies supervisors, who tended to dominate the organization, and the classroom teachers it sought to assist and influence.

NCSS addressed many of the leading issues of the day, including the collapse of colonial empires, the cold war, civil rights issues, McCarthyism, and the war in Vietnam. NCSS promoted peace education and education for international understanding during the postwar years, but by 1948 the organization cautiously took an anticommunist stance. In 1953, NCSS adopted the Freedom to Learn and Freedom to Teach resolution, and the organization later formed the NCSS Academic Freedom Committee. Whereas NCSS walked a fine line with regard to academic freedom and its anticommunist position, the organization held a consistently firm stand with regards to civil rights.

NCSS vigorously appealed for heightened funding for social studies between 1957 and 1968. The federal National Defense Education Act did not include funding for social studies when it was first passed in 1958 or when it was reauthorized in 1961. NCSS was instrumental in gaining federal funding for history, geography, and civics materials and teacher preparation in 1964.

NCSS and the New Social Studies

During the 1960s, the U.S. Office of Education and the National Science Foundation funded numerous New Social Studies projects that emphasized the structure of the social science disciplines and supported inquiry-oriented pedagogy. The most visible and controversial of these was *Man: A Course of Study,* a federally funded curriculum project for middle school students developed at Harvard University that focused on anthropological perspectives. By the late 1960s, the New Social Studies gave way to a "Newer" Social Studies that tended to embrace the meliorist stream of progressivism. The NCSS flagship journal *Social Education* began to portray students as social activists rather than social scientists, and the 1971 *NCSS Curriculum Guidelines* explicitly called for an issues-centered approach to social studies.

The late 1970s and early 1980s witnessed a conservative restoration in the curriculum, as some educators and politicians sought a movement back to basics. During this period, many Newer Social Studies programs came under harsh attack, and NCSS supported its members in numerous academic freedom cases. Ultimately, though, the conservative movement had a profound impact on NCSS, as evidenced by the 1980 position statement *Essentials of Social Studies,* which reflected a more traditional focus on the academic disciplines of history, geography, and civics.

The Standards Movement

In the early 1990s, NCSS lobbied unsuccessfully to have social studies added to the five academic disciplines identified in America 2000 legislation. History and geography were already among the five, and these fields received funding for the development of instructional materials and academic standards. NCSS responded to the revival of history and criticism of social studies by creating their own set of standards. In 1994, NCSS published a comprehensive set of national curriculum standards for social studies, using the following 10 themes as an organizing framework:

1. Culture
2. Time, Continuity, and Change
3. People, Places, and Environments
4. Individual Development and Identity
5. Individuals, Groups, and Institutions
6. Power, Authority, and Governance
7. Production, Distribution, and Consumption
8. Science, Technology, and Society
9. Global Connections
10. Civic Ideals and Practices

The new standards revived the ongoing debate between progressive and traditionalist camps within the field. Social educators with progressive and social reconstructionist leanings criticized the standards for being too discipline centered and lacking in issues and problems-oriented elements.

NCSS in the 21st Century

Social studies is an enduring legacy of the progressive curricular reform movement of the early 20th century. At the dawn of the 21st century, NCSS continues to be an agent of progressive educational reform. Today, NCSS serves more than 25,000 members from all 50 states and nearly 70 countries. Through its publications and conferences, NCSS disseminates research findings, highlights best practices in social studies education, and facilitates debate about the definition, nature, and purposes of social studies among practitioners and scholars.

David C. Virtue

See also Committee of Ten; Progressive Education; Progressive Education Association (PEA); Social Reconstructionism; Social Studies, New

Further Readings

Evans, R. B. (2004). *The social studies wars: What should we teach the children?* New York: Teachers College Press.

Gagnon, P., & the Bradley Commission on History in Schools. (Eds.). (1989). *Historical literacy: The case for history in American education.* New York: Macmillan.

Jenness, D. (1990). *Making sense of social studies.* New York: Macmillan.

Mehlinger, H. D., & Davis, O. L. (Eds.). (1981). *The social studies: Eightieth yearbook of the National Society for the Study of Education.* Chicago: University of Chicago Press.

Nash, G. B., Crabtree, C., & Dunn, R. E. (1997). *History on trial: Culture wars and the teaching of the past.* New York: Knopf.

Saxe, D. W. (1991). *Social studies in schools: A history of the early years.* Albany: State University of New York Press.

NATIONAL COUNCIL OF LA RAZA (NCLR)

Hispanic participation in education reform has been limited in the past to debates over access to educational opportunity, bilingual education, and other areas that can define a traditional civil rights agenda. The National Council of La Raza (NCLR), the largest national Hispanic civil rights and advocacy organization in the United States, believes it cannot achieve the outcomes it seeks in Hispanic education through this strategy alone. Thus, although NCLR continues to pursue a civil rights agenda in education reform, it has added an excellence agenda that includes controversial policy and program strategies such as the No Child Left Behind Act (NCLB) and charter school development.

Founded in 1968, NCLR is a private, nonprofit, nonpartisan, tax-exempt organization headquartered in Washington, D.C. Through its network of nearly 300 affiliated community-based organizations, NCLR reaches millions of Hispanics each year in 41 states, Puerto Rico, and the District of Columbia. To achieve its mission, NCLR conducts applied research, policy analysis, and advocacy. In addition, it provides capacity-building assistance to its affiliates working at the state and local levels to support individuals and families. Throughout its history, NCLR has identified education as a priority issue. Since its inception, NCLR has advocated for legislation, including the Bilingual Education Act, to increase access to educational opportunities for Latina/o students. Over the past decade, as noted previously, NCLR has added an

excellence agenda to augment its traditional civil rights agenda. This process began in 1997 with the establishment of the NCLR Task Force on Education, which was composed of distinguished education scholars and practitioners. Through the task force's work, NCLR adopted an official position in support of standards-based reform and charter schools.

Standards-based reform rests on several assumptions. First, high standards will motivate students to improve their performance if they are challenged by rigorous academic courses. Second, this type of reform calls for the use of assessments to measure improvement and make important decisions about students. Third, standards-based reform leads to school system accountability. NCLR believes that this educational theory can improve schooling for Latinas/os.

Standards-based reform represents a major shift in how the public schools intend to educate Latina/o students. It has the potential to expose Latina/o students to rigorous curricula. This is where NCLR's excellence and civil rights agendas connect. Specifically, NCLR believes that providing Latinas/os with more rigorous coursework increases the likelihood that they will graduate from high school prepared for college and the workplace. As such, this approach creates access to educational and life opportunities based on the presence of excellent schools. The No Child Left Behind Act encompasses standards-based reform.

NCLR has embraced NCLB as a civil rights law. Simply put, NCLB holds the entire public school system accountable for ensuring that all students, including Latina/o and English language learner students, receive a quality education. Prior to the enactment of NCLB in 2002, the low achievement and attainment rates of Latina/o students were of little concern to the broader education community. Now that schools, districts, and states are held accountable for improving Latina/o education, the question is not should a community educate Hispanic children, but how can educators increase their achievement and graduation rates. NCLB has clearly been a game changer for organizations such as NCLR, who are committed to improving educational opportunities for economically disadvantaged and minority children.

In addition to its policy work, NCLR has worked to provide Latina/o children with quality education services through a network of charter schools. In 2001, as a direct response to the poor educational outcomes of Latina/o students and to the growing involvement of NCLR affiliates in offering educational services and programs to students in their communities, NCLR launched an ambitious initiative to support the development of 50 charter schools throughout the country. These 50 new schools form part of a larger network of existing NCLR-affiliated charter and alternative schools, with a total of 100 schools. The NCLR Charter School Development Initiative is designed to significantly increase educational opportunities and high school graduation rates for Latinas/os.

At the end of 2005, NCLR met its ambitious goal of assisting community-based organizations in opening 50 new charter schools throughout the United States. Together these schools form a network of small, community-based, charter, and alternative schools that embrace the low-income, Latina/o, and English language learner students who often have distinct learning needs and seldom receive the services they need from traditional public schools. This network includes a diverse mix of start-up charter schools, conversion charter schools, and alternative schools serving students from preschool to Grade 12 from different backgrounds. All schools have a majority Latina/o population and a high percentage of English language learners, and many serve adjudicated youth and former dropouts.

NCLR's role as a Hispanic civil rights organization requires it to consider all appropriate strategies to improve the public schools for all children. That is why the organization continues to support NCLB and charter schools even though the approaches are considered controversial. NCLR believes that over the past 5 years, NCLB and charter schools have improved the academic prospects of Latinas/os, unlike policies and programs have in the previous 5 decades.

Raul González and Delia Pompa

See also Bilingual Education; Charter Schools; Federal Educational Reform; Hispanic/Latino Education; No Child Left Behind Act (NCLB); Standards Movement

Further Readings

González, R. (2002). *The No Child Left Behind Act: Implications for local educators and advocates for Latino students, families, and communities* (Issue Brief No. 8). Washington, DC: National Council of La Raza. (ERIC Document Reproduction Service No. ED471049)

Lazarín, M. (2006). *Improving assessment and accountability for English language learners in the No Child Left Behind Act* (Issue Brief No. 16). Washington, DC: National Council of La Raza. Retrieved March 1, 2009, from http://www.nclr.org/files/37365_file_IB16_InclusionEnglang_FNL2.pdf

National Council of La Raza. (1998). *Latino education: Status and prospects: State of Hispanic America 1998.* Washington, DC: Author.

National Council of Professors of Educational Administration (NCPEA)

This entry presents a brief overview of the role of NCPEA in reform and educational dissent. The national dialogue about educational administration and leadership has, for more than 60 years, been influenced by NCPEA. Although under attack, educational administration remains an important academic field, with thousands of students with specialized education in the field filling administrative positions as they open in U.S. schools. The first NCPEA meeting was in 1947, hosted by Walter Cocking, dean of the College of Education at the University of Georgia, and International Business Machines. By some accounts this places the beginning of NCPEA around the time of the beginning of educational administration as a profession. NCPEA has worked closely with the practitioner groups such as the American Association of School Administrators (AASA) since the beginning. A NCPEA–AASA advisory committee started in the mid-1970s and a "Conference Within a Convention" began in 1989. J. R. Hoyle and D. M. Estes posit that this partnership has helped balance research with practice.

Early on, much like the field of educational administration, NCPEA tended to believe and act as if the way to reform was through the various social sciences. However, professors came from a variety of perspectives and used a variety of methods, and this variety expanded in the 1980s to include critics of traditional social sciences. One group of critics, known as critical theorists, believe that the process and theories used to study education may further legitimize the inequities that exist. Critical theorists led the way for more recent scholars seeking to expand educational administration toward social justice. These critics are prominent in the literature. An examination of recent articles and conference presentations shows an increasing number of scholars attempting to deal with social justice. Critics (such as postmodernists or poststructuralists) are part of the collegial dialogue at NCPEA. Yet there is still strong federal emphasis on quantitative data and traditional approaches, and these elements remain part of the dialogue.

The nature of NCPEA has changed since 1947 when an assembly of more than 70 male educational administration leaders (mostly professors) gathered. Lesley H. Browder discusses the exchange of ideas, especially those grouped together as visions, such as what he refers to as traditional (in search of truth) and the postmodern to liberated education from the "regime of truth."

NCPEA has become more diverse in terms of gender, race, and so forth, making the organization richer and a better reflection of the present world. This demographic change is viewed as positive, but other aspects of change raise some concern. Browder described the first 3 decades of NCPEA as a "nonorganization," which was less pretentious, not as formal, and definitely not a "gladiatorial arena type of professional organization, where professors go to advance their careers, their reputation, and their egos in the arena of impeccably correct scholarship." Browder asserts this valuing of the relationship over prestige represents the essence of the NCPEA professoriate. NCPEA has supported a climate in which an idea foreign to one gets a reasonable hearing.

A decade ago national administrator certification guidelines were developed by the National Policy Board for Educational Administration. An additional change to NCPEA came in 1988 when the organization voted to join the National Policy Board for Educational Administration and hire an executive director in addition to opening a national

headquarters. This change coincided with other changes in the organizational culture of NCPEA (e.g., the addition of more awards and the lessening of a family atmosphere). Traditionally many professors would bring their whole family to the summer conference (often held on a college campus with professors and families staying in the dorms), but in the mid-1990s the conference shifted to hotels with conference facilities and attendance of family members started to decrease. The question became whether NCPEA could be a national player and be more scholarly, with the attachment of prestige to some selected scholars or works, and still maintain the supportive collegial atmosphere. Browder states that the NCPEA elected to do both, betting that NCPEA could convert itself, deal with contradictory vision and desires, and hold on to its core mission in the process.

University Council for Educational Administration (UCEA) is another national organization in which some professors of educational administration have been involved, but UCEA has limited itself to research institutions that grant doctoral degrees. On the other hand NCPEA is open to all individual professors of educational administration from any institution. There have been a number of past presidents and members of NCPEA who teach at institutions that belong to UCEA, but the majority of professors of educational administration work at universities that are either not eligible or choose not to apply to UCEA. The inclusiveness of NCPEA has allowed the organization to grow and be a voice for all professors of educational administration.

By 2005 NCPEA had grown and was two and a half times what is was in 1995. During this growth NCPEA was involved in the de facto national standards that had arrived. NCPEA has a history of examining the professoriate, even before Arthur Levine's 2005 attack on university preparation programs, and NCPEA is a place where professors examine the preparation programs that they are leading. John R. Hoyle and Dwain Estes noted the need for NCPEA members to lead the reformation of school administrators so that administrators view themselves as transformative agents with abilities of teamwork and empowerment.

For over a dozen years, NCPEA has published an annual yearbook that expands the national dialogue on reform and dissent. In addition,

NCPEA Education Leadership Review is a national refereed journal published two times a year. NCPEA's 2005 annual meeting, held in Washington, D.C., was a national summit on the preparation of school leaders. Another example of NCPEA's bold willingness to lead reform and debate is that NCPEA signed the Cape Town Open Education Declaration. The goal of the declaration was to advance efforts to promote open resources, technology, and best teaching practices in education.

One forum for discussion about the knowledge base and its accessibility to practitioners is the Joint Research Taskforce on Educational Leadership Preparation, sponsored by the UCEA; American Education Research Association/Administration, Organization, and Leadership (AERA, Division A); AERA Teaching in Educational Administration Special Interest Group; and NCPEA. Robert Beach identified two areas needed for advancing the knowledge base. The first is to clearly articulate the knowledge base. The second involved a lack of information about how to provide resources for administrators facing difficult situations. A criticism of educational administration research has been that practitioners have not been involved. NCPEA is working with both national principal associations to solicit more contributions from practitioners. This effort is an attempt to seek input from practitioners, such as members of the principals associations, to develop what Beach referred to as a desk reference to be part of what could be an important addition to the knowledge base. The innovative Connections (a place to share and view education materials) conveys the dynamic nature of the knowledge base in a medium free of charge worldwide, while maintaining original author license.

The beginning of the 21st century for NCPEA was a time for even more emphasis on improving administrator preparation programs through expanding and strengthening relations with some of the 10 organizations that collaborated in the National Policy Board for Educational Administration. The National Policy Board for Educational Administration included NCPEA as well as the superintendents (American Association of School Administrators), the secondary principals (National Association of Secondary School Principals), the elementary principals (National

Association of Elementary School Principals), and UCEA.

A. William Place

See also American Association of School Administrators (AASA); National Association of Elementary School Principals (NAESP); National Association of Secondary School Principals (NASSP)

Further Readings

Beach, R. (2005). Living legend lecture: Educational leadership: Knowing the way, showing the way, going the way. In C. Fulmer & F. L. Dembrowski (Eds.), *The thirteenth yearbook of the National Council of Professors of Educational Administration, National summit on school leadership: Crediting the past, challenging the present, and changing the future* (pp. 19–22). New York: Rowman & Littlefield.

Browder, L. H. (1995). The struggle for recognition and the NCPEA professoriate: Challenges and promises. In P. Bredeson & J. Schribner (Eds.), *The third yearbook of the National Council of Professors of Educational Administration, The professoriate: Challenges and promises* (pp. 19–29). Lancaster, PA: Technomic.

Hoyle, J. R., & Estes, D. M. (1993). An optimistic voice for educational administration and NCPEA. In J. R. Hoyle & D. M. Estes (Eds.), *The first yearbook of the National Council of Professors of Educational Administration, NCPEA: In a new voice* (pp. 362–373). Lancaster, PA: Technomic.

National Council of Teachers of English

The National Council of Teachers of English (NCTE) was founded in 1911, by a group of educators from Chicago Teachers College. This group of 54 recognized a need for reform in the curriculum and instruction of English language education. In 1919, NCTE membership had grown from the original 54 and was recognized as a national organization. Membership was divided into three divisions: elementary, secondary, and postsecondary with voting rights granted to all but student and affiliate members. In 1947, a group of NCTE members interested in advancing reading instruction formed the International

Council for the Improvement of Reading Instruction, later named International Reading Association (IRA). Then in 1948, the Conference on College Composition and Communication was formed to address the needs of composition and communication teachers at the college level.

NCTE's current membership is more than 60,000 members, representing elementary, middle, and secondary schools; college and university faculty; teacher educators; local and state agency English specialists; and other related fields. Membership is open to individuals interested in advancing English language arts education within the United States and other countries.

Today, there are four divisions for membership: elementary, middle, secondary, and college. These divisions give members the opportunity to interact with colleagues who have similar issues, concerns, and professional growth needs. There are a variety of interest groups for members focusing on specific interests concerning teaching English language arts. For example, conferences such as the Conference on College Composition and Communication serve major interest groups interested in college writing and rhetoric and whole language, teacher educators in higher education, K–12 supervisors, and so forth. Assemblies are informal special interest groups that meet during the NCTE conventions. Commissions monitor and report on trends and issues pertaining to the teaching of language, composition, literature, reading, media, and curriculum. Committees and task forces investigate issues and topics of current concern such as urban education, testing and evaluation, censorship, technology, teacher preparation, and certification and licensure. The various interest groups develop studies and generate research from the specific topics and issues that can influence the teaching of English and language arts.

NCTE's reform mission is to promote the development of literacy through the use of language to construct personal and public worlds and to achieve full participation in society, through the learning and teaching of English and the related arts and sciences of language. This mission was developed for the strategic plan of August 1990. The mission of NCTE, from its inception in 1911, has always been to improve the teaching and learning of English and the English language arts. One way this is accomplished is through a variety of professional growth opportunities for its members.

NCTE's seven core values are writing, literature, integrated language arts, diversity, knowledgeable, caring teachers, advocacy, and public education. Writing is seen as the central tool for learning, thinking, and communication. NCTE takes the responsibility of assisting educators in understanding the value of writing across the curriculum and how to use it in evaluation and assessment. Literature is viewed as a means to awaken and extend the imagination as well as acquaint students with multiple perspectives. NCTE's role is to assist teachers in learning new literature and instructional strategies at all levels, kindergarten to university. The integrated language arts demonstrate the uniqueness of the role of literacy that includes reading, writing, speaking, listening, viewing, and media study. NCTE's view is to assist teachers in integrating the expanded role of literacy in the curriculum for students in the 21st century. The purpose of the diversity core statement is to help everyone develop and respect all voices. NCTE presents opportunities for members to hear from individuals from diverse backgrounds and to study diverse works and research. NCTE's stance is that every classroom has a teacher who is knowledgeable and caring. Through NCTE's professional development activities, teachers have the opportunity to collaborate with others in the profession. The role of teacher as advocate can be viewed as having the ability to individually or collectively influence educational policy. NCTE gives educators opportunities to be informed decision makers through various means (journals, conventions, newsletters, committees, etc.). The final core statement supports inclusive, public education where teachers are given the opportunity to teach and students to learn.

NCTE and IRA published jointly the *Standards for the English Language Arts*. The vision that guided this joint venture was the belief that all students have the opportunities and resources to develop the language skills needed to pursue life's goals and to participate as informed productive members of society. From this vision emerged the English and language arts content standards. There are seven content standards with multiple descriptors based on student performance. The following content standards represent the joint effort of

NCTE and IRA. Students are to read a wide range of print and nonprint texts and literature from many periods and genres. Students are to apply a wide range of strategies to comprehend, interpret, evaluate, and appreciate texts. Students are to adjust spoken, written, and visual language to communicate effectively. Students are to use a wide range of strategies for writing that are appropriate for various audiences. Students apply knowledge of language structure and convention to create, critique, and discuss text. Students conduct research. Students use technology and information resources. Students develop respect for diversity. English language learners make use of their first language to assist in developing competency across the curriculum. Students use language to accomplish their own purposes.

NCTE publishes books, journals, magazines, and e-newsletters that are available for members and interested parties. NCTE offers 12 journals and periodicals that cover all grade levels. The journal *Language Arts* is for elementary and middle school teachers and teacher educators. Its primary focus is on language arts learning and teaching from prekindergarten to eighth grade. *Voices for the Middle* deals with issues relevant to middle school educators and considers input from middle school students on book reviews of adolescent literature. *English Journal* focuses on ideas for junior high, middle, and senior high schools. Each issue examines topics such as theory and research to classroom practice. *Research in the Teaching of English* focuses on research concerning language teaching and learning at all levels. *English Education* is published by the Conference on English Education with a focus on teacher preparation. *Talking Points* is published by the Whole Language Umbrella, a conference of NCTE that focuses on promoting literacy research and the use of whole language instruction.

Other publications include *School Talk*, a newsletter aimed at bridging the theory to the practice of teaching. Topics center on issues that teachers are facing in the classroom. Two other periodicals are *Classroom Notes Plus*, which focuses on innovative teaching strategies contributed by middle and high school teachers, and *English Leadership Quarterly*, published by the Conference on English Leadership. The focus of this quarterly is improving English instruction. The magazine *The Council*

Chronicle contains articles dealing with trends and issues in teaching English language arts. The e-newsletter *INBOX* is a weekly source for news, views, and ideas.

NCTE states that its purpose is to improve teaching and learning of English and language arts at all levels of education. This is evidenced through its core values, the development of content standards collaboratively with IRA, its professional development opportunities, its conventions, and publications. NCTE views its mission as being an advocate for teachers and students and developing public policy that influences the teaching of English language arts.

Connie L. Bowman

See also Critical Literacy; International Reading Association; Reading First; Reading Recovery; Reading Reform; Standards Movement; Testing Students

Further Readings

Applebee, A. (1974). *Tradition and reform in the teaching of English: A history.* Urbana, IL: National Council of Teachers of English.

Hook, J. N. (1979). *A long way together: A personal view of NCTE's first sixty-seven years.* Urbana, IL: National Council of Teachers of English.

International Reading Association and National Council of Teachers of English. (1996). *Standards for the English language arts.* Urbana, IL: Author.

Monseau, V., & Gerlach, J. (1991). *Missing chapters: Ten pioneering women in NCTE and English education.* Urbana, IL: National Council of Teachers of English.

National Council of Teachers of English: http://www.ncte.org

Steiner, J., & Delfino, C. (1998). From the secondary section: Secondary reading: Whose issue is it? *The English Journal, 87*(2), 11–13.

NATIONAL COUNCIL OF TEACHERS OF MATHEMATICS

Since its inception, the National Council of Teachers of Mathematics (NCTM) has had a significant influence on mathematics teaching and learning as well as national policy. The organization's history has been intertwined with different educational reform movements and influenced every major school mathematics initiative in the past 100 years. Today NCTM is headquartered in Reston, Virginia; includes a professional staff under the supervision of the executive director; and is governed by its elected officers and board. Throughout its history, NCTM has issued key publications and supported reform initiatives that have distinguished the group and influenced mathematics education.

History

Founded in 1920 and currently comprising more than 100,000 individual members as well as over 2,230 affiliate organizations, NCTM ranks as arguably the largest, most influential professional organization of teachers in the world. The organization's current mission is to serve as a public voice for mathematics education and provide the vision, leadership, and professional development needed to support teachers. Through its publications and conferences, NCTM has evolved as an influential force on the teaching and learning of school mathematics in the United States and Canada.

The NCTM emerged from the Association of Teachers of Mathematics in the Middle States and Maryland. This latter group published its first *Bulletin* in July 1904, and then in September 1908 published the first issue of the journal *Mathematics Teacher*. The *Mathematics Teacher* became the official journal of NCTM at the organization's founding on February 24, 1920, at a meeting of the National Education Association in Cleveland, Ohio. Since its founding, NCTM has been governed by elected officers beginning with a president, vice president, secretary-treasurer, and board members to the current structure of president-elect, president, past-president, board of directors, and an executive director.

The genesis of NCTM resulted from a perceived attack on school mathematics in the early 20th century by advocates seeking to reorganize secondary education around social efficiency goals related to vocational education. School mathematics in the 19th century served the practical needs of primary education and the interests of those fortunate enough to pursue secondary education. Mathematical education was promoted primarily as an academic endeavor and as a means of preparing young men for education at the collegiate level. The 1893 Committee of Ten report had firmly established the study of mathematics at the school level. The Vocational Education Act of 1917 and research on the transfer of abstract learning to practical applications represented a perceived threat to teachers of mathematics and to mathematicians who feared the potential of degrading mathematical study from formal learning to practical skill development. NCTM was founded so that future curricula and reforms could be derived from the wisdom of teachers of mathematics rather than from general educational reformers.

The early work of NCTM related to the establishment of commissions and recommendations related to the methods and materials for teaching mathematics as well as for the curriculum structure of school mathematics. Often these commissions worked jointly with the Mathematics Association of America, a professional organization of mathematicians. Increasing high school enrollments in the first half of the 20th century led to a need for curriculum that addressed a population beyond the college-bound students. New school structures, such as the junior high school, and the critical role of mathematics in school learning were key issues during this period.

At the end of World War II, NCTM began to address a perceived lack of rigor in the school mathematics curriculum. The NCTM Commission on Post-War Plans was among the first to propose goals assuring mathematical literacy for all citizens and curriculum improvements. NCTM leadership in collaboration with the American Mathematical Society and the Mathematics Association of America supported innovative school improvement efforts such as the University of Illinois Committee on School Mathematics and the School Mathematics Study Group, the latter of which was closely identified with what became known as the "new math" movement. "New math," to some, carries a pejorative connotation suggesting overly rigorous abstract concepts and mathematical structures. A reaction to the newness of this mathematics reform effort led to a back-to-basics era in the early 1970s.

Publications and Professional Development

NCTM gave new attention to elementary education as highlighted by the launching of its journal the *Arithmetic Teacher* in 1954. During the mid-1950s interest in a journal devoted to mathematics education research developed. A monograph titled *Research in Mathematics Education* was published in 1967, and this was followed by the publication of the first issue of the *Journal for Research in Mathematics Education,* then the NCTM's third journal, in January 1970. The journal *Mathematics Teaching in Middle School* was launched in April 1994, simultaneous with the renaming of the *Arithmetic Teacher* to *Teaching Children Mathematics.* This inception of a new journal, focusing on mathematics in Grades 5 through 9, allowed NCTM to revise the implied notion that one learns only "arithmetic" in the early grades and mathematics in upper grades. Thus the *Arithmetic Teacher* title was abolished with a statement that mathematics, not just arithmetic, is studied by learners at all levels. *On-Math, the Online Journal of School Mathematics,* was initiated in fall 2002 as NCTM's first electronic journal addressing school mathematics from prekindergarten to Grade 12.

In 1980, NCTM published *An Agenda for Action: Recommendations for School Mathematics of the 1980s.* This 29-page booklet enumerated and explained eight recommendations that proposed problem solving as the focus of school mathematics and offered suggestions related to teaching, learning, technology, and professionalism. The agenda was endorsed by several other professional organizations, including the National Council of Supervisors of Mathematics, and served as a guide for NCTM publications and initiatives throughout the 1980s.

The *Curriculum and Evaluation Standards for School Mathematics* was released in 1989, a bellwether for what was to become the "standards movement" across all school subjects. NCTM's work toward national standards as a nongovernment organization embodied a grassroots effort that was widely praised and emulated across diverse constituencies in education and politics. Complemented by the *Professional Teaching Standards* (1991) and the *Assessment Standards for School Mathematics* (1995), the Standards projects served as a touchstone for mathematics education reform for a decade. *Principles and Standards for School Mathematics* (2000) was developed as a planned refinement of the original

curriculum standards and played a similar role in the decade that followed. Not only have these standards had an impact on national policy, but nearly every state has used NCTM's work to guide state and local adopted policies and curriculum materials related to mathematics. As was the case in other reform eras, the strong influence of the standards influenced a backlash period, particularly in California. Similar to the reading controversy between proponents of whole language and phonics, "math wars" began as critics pointed to an erosion of basic skills and computational fluency as broader goals related to problem solving and conceptual understanding were emphasized. In 2006, NCTM published *Curriculum Focal Points* designed to clarify key content areas with grade levels. This document was also viewed by some as a means of achieving an armistice in the math wars by balancing emphases related to skills and understanding.

Besides publications, NCTM realizes its mission by offering professional development through conferences and other venues. Annually since 1920, NCTM has organized meetings for members that have drawn as many as 20,000 attendees. Regional meetings organized in collaboration with state and local affiliates have ranged from three to six per year and take place in geographically diverse locations, thus reaching thousands of teachers. These meetings are marked by a program of sessions and workshops that include speeches and hands-on experiences enabling attendees to learn from leaders in mathematics education and their peers.

Within teacher education, NCTM since the 1960s has participated with the National Education Association to guide the preparation and professional development of pre-service and in-service teachers. In 1978 NCTM partnered with the National Council for the Accreditation of Teacher Education, which adopted NCTM's standards for teacher education programs in 1993. NCTM administers the program report reviews of some 700 teacher preparation programs seeking national accreditation.

Edwin M. Dickey

See also Algebra Project; Committee of Ten; Curriculum Controversies; Secondary Curricular Reform; Standards Movement

Further Readings

Donoghue, E. (2003). Emergence of a profession: Mathematics education in the United States, 1890–1920. In G. M. A. Stanic & J. Kilpatrick (Eds.), *A history of school mathematics* (pp. 159–194). Reston, VA: National Council of Teachers of Mathematics.

Fey, J. T., & Graeber, A. O. (2003). From new math to the *Agenda for Action*. In G. M. A. Stanic & J. Kilpatrick (Eds.), *A history of school mathematics* (pp. 521–558). Reston, VA: National Council of Teachers of Mathematics.

Gates, J. D. (2003). Perspective on the recent history of the National Council of Teachers of Mathematics. In G. M. A. Stanic & J. Kilpatrick (Eds.), *A history of school mathematics* (pp. 737–752). Reston, VA: National Council of Teachers of Mathematics.

McLeod, D. B. (2003). From consensus to controversy: The story of the NCTM standards. In G. M. A. Stanic & J. Kilpatrick (Eds.), *A history of school mathematics* (pp. 753–818). Reston, VA: National Council of Teachers of Mathematics.

National Council of Teachers of Mathematics. (2000). *Principles and standards for school mathematics.* Reston, VA: Author.

NATIONAL COUNCIL ON TEACHER QUALITY (NCTQ)

The National Council on Teacher Quality (NCTQ) is a nonpartisan research and advocacy group committed to restructuring the teaching profession, led by its vision that every child deserves effective teachers. By working to improve federal, state, and local teacher policies, as well as lend greater transparency to the institutions that influence teacher quality, NCTQ seeks to increase public knowledge and build a mandate for change and reform.

Based in Washington, D.C., NCTQ was founded in 2000 to provide an alternative national voice to existing teacher organizations and build the case for a comprehensive reform agenda that would challenge the current structure and regulation of the profession. For the first 2 years, NCTQ focused on the development of the American Board for Certification of Teacher Excellence, an alternative pathway into the teaching profession. NCTQ's current president, Kate Walsh, arrived in February 2003, seeking to broaden and depoliticize the policy agenda of the organization. In fall 2003, NCTQ reconstituted its board of directors and ceased its formal relationship with the American Board for Certification of Teacher Excellence.

The work of NCTQ concentrates on three institutions: states, teachers' unions (along with, but to a lesser degree, school districts), and teacher preparation programs. It produces regular work aligning with these three focus areas.

On an annual basis, NCTQ publishes the 52-volume report, the *State Teacher Policy Yearbook*. That report examines what is arguably the single most powerful authority over the teaching profession: state government (both legislatures and school boards). NCTQ's report on the teacher quality–related policies in the 50 states and the District of Columbia is of unprecedented breadth, and it constitutes an original contribution to the field of education policy. All of NCTQ's work on state policy is available online, presented in an easily accessible format.

In the area of school districts and teachers' unions, NCTQ is breaking new ground by offering the public unprecedented access to the content of collective bargaining agreements and school board policies from across the nation. NCTQ has developed an innovative database—TR³ (Teacher Rules, Roles, and Rights)—facilitating comparisons between policies from 100 districts from all 50 states. The database allows users to compare over 300 distinct provisions in the collective bargaining agreements, covering a wide range of contractual topics, such as salary and differential pay, professional development, leave benefits, employment termination procedures, class size, and many more. NCTQ is the first to create a national, publicly accessible Web site that contains both the full text of the agreements and a database that permits easy search on key terms and an in-depth analysis and comparison. The organization plans to maintain and further develop this database—to add features to it and extend the breadth of material it contains.

Aside from maintaining this extensive database, NCTQ is currently working with selected districts and cities to provide a customized analysis of their teachers' contracts. The end goal of each analysis is to identify the strengths and weaknesses of the contract and make concrete recommendations for improvement.

The third area of focus for NCTQ is the nation's approximately 1,200 schools of education. In May 2006, NCTQ launched a series of studies to examine how well education schools prepare teachers to deliver instruction in different subject areas. The first study, *What Education Schools Aren't Teaching About Reading—and What Elementary Teachers Aren't Learning*, examined teacher preparation in reading instruction in 72 randomly selected education schools across the nation. The end result was not only a review of teacher preparation in effective reading instruction but also a set of practical recommendations to states, the federal government, textbook publishers, and education schools on how to tackle the problems that plague this crucial area of teacher training.

In June 2008, NCTQ followed up on this report with a similar study on the state of preparation of elementary teachers in mathematics, titled *No Common Denominator*. The study examined 77 education programs in 49 states and the District of Columbia, and having revealed that this area of teacher preparation, too, is in dire need of improvement, the report makes recommendations to educators and policymakers on how to effect the changes needed. Currently, NCTQ is developing a third study in this line of work that will examine prospective teachers' preparation in the crucial area of student teaching.

In all of its current as well as planned work, NCTQ upholds its vision that every child deserves effective teachers and that only rigorous, evidence-based, and pragmatic reform can ensure that this goal is ultimately met. NCTQ is a major voice associated with the reform of both how teachers are prepared and how education is delivered in the United States. NCTQ maintains a Web site and publishes a monthly newsletter, *Teacher Quality Bulletin*, to help keep reformers abreast with important developments. The Web site averages 26,000 visits per month and *Teacher Quality Bulletin* has a circulation of 4,400.

Kate Walsh

See also American Diploma Project; Finn, Chester E., Jr.; Ravitch, Diane; Teach For America (TFA)

Further Readings

Cross, R. W., Rebarber, T., & Torres, J. (2004). *Creating the systems: The guide to state standards, test, and accountability policies.* Washington, DC: Thomas B. Fordham Foundation.

Finn, C. E., Jr., Kanstoroom, M., & Petrilli, M. J. (1999). *The quest for better teachers: Grading the states.* Washington, DC: Thomas B. Fordham Foundation.

National Council on Teacher Quality: http://www.nctq.org

National Council on Teacher Quality. (2009). *2008 state teacher quality yearbook: What states can do to retain effective teachers.* Retrieved July 30, 2009, from http://www.nctq.org/stpy

NATIONAL DEFENSE EDUCATION ACT (NDEA)

The National Defense Education Act (NDEA), enacted on September 2, 1958, stands as a major act of reform. It marked the beginning of large-scale involvement of the federal government in education, pairing what was billed as "good education" with the national interest.

In the wake of World War II the major movement in the nation's schools was the life adjustment movement, headed by the vocational educator Charles Prosser. This movement, claiming to represent true "democracy" in education, was roundly criticized by academicians as "soft." Adherents of the National Science Foundation and others held education professors and schools of education as mainly responsible for what they believed was the low-achieving status of American students, particularly in mathematics, science, and modern foreign languages.

The criticism of American education, especially its public schools, increased immensely with the launching of *Sputnik*, the world's first artificial satellite, by the Soviet Union in October 1957. President Dwight D. Eisenhower, in his Message to Congress on January 27, 1958, called for matching educational programs with national defense and recommended the federal government play an important part in this activity. Warning of the Soviet threat, Eisenhower called for the nation to beat the Soviet Union in the military competition, which included directing schooling toward that end. The NDEA was the result of the enlarged federal role in education.

The purpose of the NDEA was to improve and strengthen all levels of the school system and to encourage students to continue their education beyond high school. Specific provisions included scholarships and loans to students in higher education, with loans to students preparing to be teachers and to those who showed promise in the curricular areas of mathematics, science, engineering, and modern foreign languages; grants to states for programs in mathematics, science, and modern foreign languages in public schools; the establishment of centers to expand and improve the teaching of languages; help to graduate students, including fellowships for doctoral students to prepare them to be professors at institutions of higher learning; assistance for the improvement of guidance, counseling, and testing programs; provisions for research and experimentation in the use of television, radio, motion pictures, and related media for educational purposes; and the improvement of statistical services at the state level.

Educators were called to the bar to do their part in meeting the challenge posed by Soviet totalitarianism in service, industry, government, military strength, and international relations. Supporters of the legislation pointed to precedents, such as the federal aid to land grant higher education institutions in the 1862 Morrill Act in 1862 and vocational education, embodied in the Smith-Hughes Act in 1917, during World War I. The NDEA differed from Smith-Hughes, however, in that professors of education, who had lost credibility by their espousal of, and involvement in, life adjustment education, played at best a minor role in the structure and operation of the NDEA. Advocates of the NDEA contended that they were not interfering with the fundamental principle that states and local communities were responsible for the conduct of American schooling and institutions of higher education in the operation of higher education. Opponents maintained, however, that categorical aid such as was proposed by the NDEA would shape educational policy and would place the federal government in charge. This was not, in their view, as NDEA supporters averred, a constructive policy on the part of the federal government. Other critics, such as the National Education Association and the Council of Chief State School Officers objected to what they felt was the narrow focus of the NDEA on science and technology plus the Act's reliance on the National Science Foundation university-oriented community for direction as opposed to the broader approach of the education-oriented U.S. Department of Education.

Overall, the NDEA reflects political support for an academic curriculum and an attempt to garner public support of same. It placed education in a role of supporting and assisting national policy. *Sputnik* galvanized political leaders into action. Books such as *What Ivan Knows That Johnny Doesn't* (1961) contributed to the national climate. The NDEA established a precedent and led to programs on behalf of gifted and talented students (especially those in mathematics and science and related subjects) in the early 1960s, to programs such as ability grouping and to challenges to the very existence of the comprehensive high school.

The NDEA was amended in 1964. The words "which have led to an insufficient proportion of our population educated in science, mathematics, and modern language and trained in technology" were deleted as was the reference to giving preference in student loans to those preparing to teach and those with superior capacity in mathematics, science, engineering, or foreign language. Subjects eligible for aid now included "science, mathematics, history, civics, geography, modern foreign language, English or reading in public elementary or secondary schools." One new feature was instituted for those who were teaching, or preparing to teach, "disadvantaged youth."

The NDEA stands as a testament to coupling national educational policy with national needs. It represents an involvement (some would say, an intrusion) of the federal government in the conduct of schooling at all levels in the nation.

Thomas C. Hunt

See also Ability Grouping; Conant, James Bryant; Federal Educational Reform; National Science Foundation; *Nation at Risk, A*; Presidents and Educational Reform; Rickover, Hyman; Trends in International Mathematics and Science Study (TIMSS)

Further Readings

Bremner, R. (Ed.). (1974). [Discussion of the National Defense Education Act of 1958]. *Children and youth in America: A documentary history* (pp. 1791–1793, 1922–1924). Cambridge, MA: Harvard University Press.

Krug, E. (1966). *Salient dates in American education, 1635–1964.* New York: Harper & Row.

National Defense Education Act of 1958, Pub. L. No. 85-864, 72 Stat. 1580, 20 U.S.C. 401 *et seq.*

NATIONAL EDUCATION ASSOCIATION (NEA)

Founded in 1857, the National Education Association (NEA) functioned for the rest of the 19th century as an annual platform for the school reform plans of the leaders of America's developing public school movement. The NEA was, in the main, a rhetorical outlet for these leaders and their plans until the early 20th century. In the first 2 decades of that century, women pushed for a voice in the NEA. This push was answered by an internal reorganization after World War I in which NEA moved its headquarters to Washington, D.C.; adopted an annual Representative Assembly as its legislative body, with members chosen by election from state and local affiliates of NEA; and determined to become a force for education in national affairs. The place of women in the NEA was not a signal feature of this reorganization, but women were recognized in various ways after its adoption, including the alternation of the presidency of the association, by tradition, between a man and a woman each year. This structure, and tradition, remained in place until the late 1960s when the forces that were animating the union movement of teachers in large cities, mainly through the American Federation of Teachers, found traction within the NEA. By 1972, the NEA had again reorganized and become an organization that advocated collective bargaining for teachers. It waged and won bargaining campaigns, more often in small and medium-sized cities than in the large cities that were still dominated by the American Federation of Teachers. A few years later, an internal reorganization allowed the NEA president to serve more than one term and, thereby, made the organization more member dominated and less influenced by staff leadership. In the late 20th century, the NEA moved from the position of bitter rival of the American Federation of Teachers to form a partnership in which the two organizations represented teachers collectively in an effort to buttress the position of public schools in the United States, during a time when they endured a variety of attacks from the political and religious right. While the alliance has not been fully realized through a merger of the two groups, they cooperate on a wide variety of issues and are fully aware of each other's platforms and priorities.

The unionization of the NEA was never completed, because many states, particularly those in the South and the West, never adopted collective bargaining for teachers. This left sometimes strong NEA affiliates in those states with the traditional activities of lobbying the state or local legislature for teacher benefits and school improvements tied to those benefits. The contemporary NEA proudly wears the label of teachers' union at the same time that, in many settings, it is a leader in the movement to represent an occupation without a formal process by which to conduct that representation.

The roster of NEA leadership reads like a who's who of American education. Nineteenth-century NEA leaders were the same people who were leading the movement for American public schooling. Luminaries such as William T. Harris and Charles W. Eliot led both the NEA and movements for school reform such as Eliot's Committee of Ten on Secondary Education. This committee, which operated in the 1890s, addressed the secondary school curriculum and attempted to grapple with curricular change while also attempting to retain some continuity in the curriculum.

Twentieth-century NEA leaders were less luminous than Harris and Eliot, but more in line with the professionalization that was taking place within the American educational enterprise. They tended to gain office through holding leadership positions in the administrations of the public schools and, less so, in the nation's colleges and universities. Holders of these positions, however, were lesser known publicly than were their 19th-century counterparts, as education became one competitor for attention and support rather than a "cause" to be advocated zealously for quasi-moral and patriotic purposes. NEA considered itself to be the instigator and the leader of the constant school "reform" movement by which public schools became larger and more important to the American educational enterprise. As the 20th century developed, however, NEA and the public schools often became the target of reformers and their efforts, including pedagogical progressives in the early and middle decades of the century, romantic critics and militant teachers in the 1960s, and market-oriented advocates of charters and vouchers later in the century. As the NEA became a union after 1972, it began to be pummeled as an obstacle to reform by voucher advocates, whose major target was actually the public schools, and by standards-oriented reformers who saw the teacher group as a major obstacle to the reinstallation of educational standards and intellectual values in the nation's schools.

The major "reform" for which NEA pushed, almost from the beginning of its existence, was federal financial aid to the nation's public schools. The pursuit of federal aid was taken to a new level with the move of NEA headquarters to Washington, D.C., after World War I, and federal aid was a constant goal of the NEA and its federal lobbying through the 20th century. Whereas targeted, or categorical, federal aid for things like vocational education was passed by Congress beginning in the early 1900s and again in the 1930s and 1940s, NEA pursued nontargeted, or general, federal aid—that is, money that went to state and local school systems that they would allot to whatever program or policy was in greatest need. Landmark federal aid to education measures were passed by Congress in the mid-20th century, including the National Defense Education Act in 1958 and the Elementary and Secondary Education Act in 1965. Although neither of these measures was true general federal aid, they both increased the categories under which aid was distributed and the amount of money available to public schools. In addition to federal aid, NEA sought cabinet status for the federal education agency. This objective was partially reached during the cabinet reorganization by President Dwight D. Eisenhower early in his first term when the Office of Education went to the new Department of Health, Education and Welfare. It was fully realized in 1979 when President Jimmy Carter sparked the creation of the Department of Education, thereby granting full cabinet status to the educational enterprise and fulfilling a commitment he made to the NEA, in return for its full political support in the 1976 presidential election.

Within the larger NEA and the story of its various organizational iterations, much of the historical development of American education and its several reforms can be found and illustrated. The

nation's encounter with race in schooling was especially well illustrated by race relations within the NEA and its affiliates, before, during, and after the historic *Brown v. Board of Education* Supreme Court decision of 1954. Prior to *Brown*, the NEA was a largely White organization that had racially segregated state and local affiliates in the South and in some of the border states. The NEA itself entered into a relationship with the all-Black American Teachers Association in the late 1920s and continued that hesitant, but constant, relationship until the 1950s. After *Brown*, the NEA undertook a desegregation of its segregated state affiliates in the South and elsewhere, a process that was not completely finished until the early 1970s. Thus, the NEA was a microcosm of the racial forces and a target of racial reformers at the same time that the public schools were undergoing the trauma of desegregation in the 1960s and 1970s. The NEA, however, unlike the public schools, emerged as one of the most integrated entities in the nation, a result unhappily not matched within the public schools. Visible minority leadership emerged in the NEA, through the presidencies of Elizabeth Koontz, Mary Hatwood Futrell, and Reg Weaver, all African Americans and articulate spokespersons of the cause of teachers, both Black and White.

The position of the late–20th- and early–21st-century NEA on issues such as standards-based reform of schools is worthy of attention. Beginning shortly after publication in 1983 of the famous pamphlet decrying a decline in the standards of American schools, *A Nation at Risk,* the NEA embraced a variety of reform initiatives and thrusts to combat the image of the NEA and teachers as obstacles to standard-based and other reforms of the public schools. Under Futrell, Keith Geiger, and Bob Chase especially, the NEA worked hard to portray itself as a friend of school reform, not an opponent. In the mid-1990s, Chase discussed in a variety of forums the parameters of a new unionism that he embraced, intending to make teachers and their organizations the advocates of school change and not the label of opponents of change that critics used to characterize the NEA and its members.

For Chase, and others in the NEA before, during, and after his presidency, a new unionism was characterized by an NEA focused on school achievement and school improvement, in achievement and in a variety of other areas. Concern with teaching and learning was a visible part of the new unionism and the segments of the NEA that embraced it. Somewhat ironically, concern with teaching and learning had been a long-time priority of the pre-union NEA of the 19th century and much of the 20th century. Subject-matter groups in areas such as mathematics (National Council of Teachers of Mathematics), social studies (National Council for the Social Studies), and science (National Science Teachers Association) all originated as departments of NEA in the 20th century and pursued the intellectual interests of teachers in their respective subjects as assiduously as the parent organization tried to pursue occupational interests. The American Educational Research Association also began as a department of the NEA and has evolved into a large and powerful representative of the importance of educational research in the advocacy of school reforms of various kinds. Other contemporary educational bodies such as the National Council for Accreditation of Teacher Education and the American Association of Colleges for Teacher Education also were originated as departments under the large umbrella in the NEA which preceded the teacher union that developed after 1970.

Even after unionization, the NEA never completely dropped its focus on teaching and learning. It kept a division devoted to instructional development and tried to focus the effort of that division on school improvement at the same time that it zealously pursued collective bargaining rights and representation for teachers. It continued the work of its Research Division, founded in 1922, providing and publicizing data relating to teachers' salaries and benefits as well as school finance policies at the same time that it undertook to use that data directly in its organizing activities.

In terms of school reform, one of the most important activities of the NEA is also among the least well known. The NEA created the National Foundation for the Improvement of Education (NFIE) in the early 1970s, at the same time that the association unionized. This change allowed the NEA to continue its long-standing pursuit of teaching and learning reform while it underwent a severe internal restructuring. The NFIE, after a decade or so of relative inactivity, became a major player in the world of educational reform in the mid-1980s, fueled by a commitment of one dollar per year per NEA member, undertaken by the NEA Representative Assembly in response to a challenge from then NEA president Futrell. This financial commitment was continued subsequently by the NEA and made permanent by action of the Representative Assembly in 2002. With this financial base, NFIE undertook an expansion of internal grants to teachers who proposed various programs to improve their instruction or alter their curriculum to make it more attractive to students. Shortly after 2000, the NFIE undertook the Closing the Gap initiative through which it sought to address the achievement gap between poor and minority students and their more affluent peers. Closing the Gap now funds major efforts in Milwaukee, Wisconsin, Chattanooga, Tennessee, and Seattle, Washington, as well as other initiatives in southeast Ohio and Connecticut. All of the NFIE grant programs (only a few of which have been mentioned here) were undertaken to bring the NEA and its members into the forefront of the movement for reform of the nation's classrooms. Although the work has been underpublicized, it clearly shows an association interested in school improvement as well as the welfare of its members.

Wayne J. Urban

See also American Federation of Teachers (AFT); National Board for Professional Teaching Standards (NBPTS); Teacher Education; Teacher Evaluation; Testing Students

Further Readings

Urban, W. J. (1998). *More than the facts: The research division of the National Education Association, 1922–1997.* Lanham, MD: University Press of America.

Urban, W. J. (2000). *Gender, race, and the National Education Association: Professionalism and its limitations.* New York: Routledge.

West, A. (1980). *The National Education Association: The power base for education.* New York: The Free Press.

NATIONAL ENDOWMENT FOR THE ARTS

What is art? Should government provide public dollars to support the arts? Do the arts support or subvert family values and morals in the United States? These are among the basic questions and issues that have surrounded the creation and ongoing federal support of the National Endowment for the Arts (NEA) since its inception as an independent agency of the federal government on September 29, 1965. The agency's own Web site says that it is the nation's largest annual funder of the arts and that it brings great art to all 50 states, which includes rural areas, inner cities, and even military bases.

What Is Art?

"Art" includes all of the visual arts (drawing, painting, sculpture, film, etc.). It also embraces all forms of music including vocal and instrumental, from composition to performance. It includes all types of theater from on-stage performance to the technical side of set design and lighting. In addition, it entails creative writing, from poetry and fiction to journalism. The arts are diverse but also inclusive, as they may involve a blend of many elements and approaches.

From its inception, the NEA has been dedicated to strengthening the artistic life of the United States. It seeks to foster America's creativity and investment in its cultural heritage. It does this by supporting artistic excellence, forging partnerships, building more livable communities, promoting lifelong arts education, and improving access to the arts for all citizens. By focusing on these elements, the agency has worked to strengthen America's democracy.

In its first 35 years, the NEA awarded more than 110,000 grants to arts organizations and artists in all 50 states and the 6 U.S. jurisdictions. The number of state or jurisdictional organizations grew from 5 to 56. Local arts agencies grew in number from 400 to 4,000. Nonprofit theaters increased from 56 to 340. Similar increases in the number of symphony orchestras, opera companies, and dance companies have been the result.

Arts Education

Many of the "arts" grants included a significant element for adding to arts education in the local schools. Musicians performed and explained their music to pupils. Artists-in-residence programs at schools grew rapidly since the 1965 NEA founding. Writers worked with students to motivate and teach them to become more effective writers. Acting and performing on stage were a part of what was shared with the K–12 schools. PreK–12 arts education has received a major boost since the NEA's founding.

The noted sculptor Magdalena Abakanowicz claimed that art does not solve problems "but makes us aware of their existence." The George Lucas Education Foundation's 2008 report begins with this significant summary in its first paragraph: "Years of research show that it's [the arts] closely linked to almost everything that we as a nation say we want for our children and demand from our schools: academic achievement, social and emotional development, civic engagement, and equitable opportunity."

More specifically, involvement in the arts is associated with gains in math, reading, cognitive ability, critical thinking, and verbal skill. Arts learning can also improve motivation, concentration, confidence, and teamwork. Some contend that strong arts programming in schools helps close an academic achievement gap that has too often left many a child behind when less affluent families were unable to provide the lessons, trips to museums, attendance at concerts, and so forth, for their children.

Dissent

Those who tend to take a more conservative view of life and of education have raised many questions over the decades about the arts and their role in life and schools. Emphasis on the "three R's" has sometimes moved the arts almost out of the school curriculum. The most recent example has been the math and reading emphasis of the No Child Left Behind Act of 2001. To give more time to those two subjects, many schools have cut back on the time allotted for music and art.

Funding for the NEA has also reflected the philosophical values of the major parties. For example, the 1994 appropriation for NEA under a Congress and president of the same party was $170,228,000. By the year 2000, with a different party controlling both branches of Congress, the appropriation fell to $97,627,600. In 2009, the party leadership of both Congress and the presidency had again changed and the appropriation became $155 million and was supplemented by a stimulus allocation of $50 million.

Objections by those focusing on "family values" issues have been raised about the quality and nature of artistic expression with such comments as "public dollars should not pay for pornography!" But the work of the NEA has continued even when its budget has been cut and public objections made to specific grants and programs.

NEA at Work

Three recent research reports from the NEA illustrate its ongoing efforts in the field. The first, *Artists in the Workforce: 1990–2005*, looked at the recent work and employment patterns of artists. The second, *To Read or Not to Read: A Question of National Consequence*, was a comprehensive analysis of reading patterns of children, teenagers, and adults in the United States. And, a third, *2002 Survey of Public Participation in the Arts*, examined adult activity and attendance as well as the percentage of adults visiting art museums and reading literature.

It is clear that the NEA has had a well-defined mission that has included work with U.S. schools. Keeping the arts as a key and significant part of U.S. culture remains a sharp focus of its work.

James K. Uphoff

See also Co-Curricular Activities; Comprehensive High Schools; Culturally Relevant Teaching; Curriculum Controversies; Elementary Curricular Reform; Experiential Learning; Extracurricular Activities; Gifted Education; National Endowment for the Humanities; Secondary Curricular Reform

Further Readings

National Endowment for the Arts: http://arts.endow.gov

National Endowment for the Arts. (2000). *NEA 1965–2000: A brief chronology of federal support for the arts.* Retrieved April 30, 2009, from http://www.arts .gov/pub/NEAChronweb.pdf

Smith, F. (2009, February). Why arts education is crucial, and who's doing it best. *Edutopia.* Retrieved May 1, 2009, from http://www.edutopia.org/arts-music-curriculum-child-development

National Endowment for the Humanities

The National Endowment for the Humanities (NEH) was created in 1965 when Congress passed the National Foundations for the Arts and Humanities Act. The NEH was designed to be an independent agency that encouraged a greater emphasis on the knowledge of the humanities. The Act provided a working definition of humanities:

> The term *humanities* includes, but is not limited to, the study of the following: language, both modern and classical; linguistics; literature; history; jurisprudence; philosophy; archaeology; comparative religion; ethics; the history, criticism and theory of the arts; those aspects of social sciences which have humanistic content and employ humanistic methods; and the study and application of the humanities to the human environment with particular attention to reflecting our diverse heritage, traditions, and history and to the relevance of the humanities to the current conditions of national life.

The development of these areas is encouraged by the NEH through a series of grants that are awarded annually. Funding for these grants is provided for in the federal budget.

NEH grants are generally awarded in the areas of education, public programs, research, and creating public access to cultural resources. Grant funding usually goes to institutions of higher education, libraries, museums, and public radio and television studios. Individuals may also receive NEH grant funding.

The chairperson of the NEH has ultimate responsibility for administering the organization. The NEH chair is appointed by the president of the United States to a 4-year term. The chairperson must also be confirmed by the Senate. Additionally, the NEH has a 26-member advisory board whose members are also appointed and confirmed to 4-year terms. The board serves as an advisory to the chairperson.

History

In the early 19th century, Congress began enacting a set of long-range reforms designed to support and enhance the arts and humanities in the United States. The first step was the creation of the Library of Congress in 1800. This was followed in 1836 with the acceptance of a bequest by Englishman James Smithson valued at $508,318.46. These funds were the seed money for the development of the Smithsonian Institute in Washington, D.C. The acceptance of the Smithson estate was not without controversy and dissent. Leading the opposition were the U.S. senators from South Carolina John C. Calhoun and William Campbell Preston. Both senators questioned the constitutionality of Congress's acceptance of the funds. Calhoun cited the need for individual states to be involved in the decision and Preston was a vocal opponent until he was persuaded to assist in the creation of the Smithsonian Institute as part of a move to establish a national university.

Further developments were made in the 20th century under New Deal provisions in the Works Progress Administration, which offered support for advancing the arts and humanities by funding the activities of a variety of writers, musicians, artists, and thespians. In 1954 Health, Education, and Welfare Undersecretary Nelson Rockefeller led a movement to establish a national arts council. Although the effort failed to gain approval, it nevertheless created a serious dialogue concerning a national foundation for the arts and humanities at the national level. In the early 1960s, President John F. Kennedy made the arts and humanities a national priority. In 1964 a blue ribbon commission, that included Phi Delta Kappa, the Council of Graduate Schools, and the American Council of Learned Societies, issued a report that called for the creation of a national foundation for the humanities. These efforts peaked in 1965 when Congress passed legislation creating the National Endowment for the Arts and the National Endowment for the Humanities. The funding for both was initially modest ($2.9 million for the National Endowment for the Arts and $5.9 million for the NEH), but the creation of the endowments was seen as a major milestone in advancing the arts and humanities. This amount has grown over the years. For fiscal year 2009, the NEH requested funding in the amount of $144,355,000 million.

Between 1971 and 1979, congressional reform in support of the humanities continued. A series of state-based councils were formed to operate in conjunction with the NEH. Each state council is an independent nonprofit grant-making organization that enhances the goals and mission of the NEH. By 1979 a state council was established in each of the 50 states. The state councils for the humanities each have a board of directors consisting of gubernatorial appointees, scholars from the humanities fields, and members of the general public. The state councils have come to be known for their innovation in the advancement of the humanities at the local and regional levels. The state councils were responsible for initiating programs that supported and advocated for the humanities, including a variety of local library programs, family reading programs, lecture series, oral histories, book festivals, and cultural tourism activities. The state councils have also generated significant partnerships with institutions of higher education with humanities faculty members becoming involved in a variety of projects and programs. The work of the state councils has increased public awareness and support for the humanities across the United States.

From the beginning, the NEH acted as a grant-making organization offering competitive grants to educational and cultural organizations in the core humanities disciplines as defined by congressional mandate. The NEH is the greatest funding source for the humanities in the United States. The NEH established funding categories that have changed periodically over time to adjust for societal changes and national priorities. Grant applications are reviewed by a rotating panel of outside reviewers consisting of professionals and experts in the various fields of funding. Recommendations are made to the National Council on the Humanities. The chair of the NEH makes the final decision on funding awards.

Although the NEH over the years has, as a rule, remained outside the scope of partisan politics, there have been periods of controversy and dissent. During the Reagan administration, both the National Endowment of the Arts and NEH were targeted for elimination. William Bennett and Lynne Cheney, former chairpersons of the NEH, testified before Congress that the NEH had become too politicized and they advocated for the elimination of both agencies. Although the NEH budget experienced major cuts, the agency survived due to bipartisan support for its general mission. Strong support remained for both the NEH and the state humanities councils.

The NEH weathered the political storm and saw an increase in funding in the beginning of the 21st century. Recent nominations for NEH chair, which have included staunch advocates for the humanities, signal willingness by both Democratic and Republican administrations to lend strong support to the NEH and the state humanities councils. Additionally, after dramatic budget cuts during the 1990s (up to 40% in some years), the NEH budget has been steadily increasing.

Programs

Over the years, the NEH has initiated a variety of programs that serve to advance the humanities and humanities education in American society. No other agency funds humanities-related programs and projects at the level of the NEH. In addition to its grant-making function, the NEH sponsors a series of summer undergraduate internships, provides funding for public radio and television programming, and financially supports the state humanities councils.

According to the NEH, their grants program supports programs and projects that (a) support instruction and learning in the humanities in schools and colleges across the country, (b) make research and innovative scholarship possible, (c) make available opportunities for lifelong education, (d) maintain and afford access to cultural and educational resources, and (e) build up the institutional foundation of the humanities.

Among the more innovative of the NEH-funded programs were the Ken Burns Emmy-winning documentary *The Civil War*, viewed by more than 38 million people; the "Treasure of Tutankhamen" exhibit, viewed by more than 1.5 million people; the U.S. Newspaper Project, with a goal of converting more than 63 million pages of early newspapers to microfilm; and 15 Pulitzer Prize–winning books written by such authors as James M. McPherson, Bernard Bailyn, Louis Menand, and Joan D. Hedrick.

Historically, the NEH has funded such projects as the publication of the complete works of John Dewey; the publication of the papers of Booker T. Washington; the publication of the first comprehensive edition of the papers of George Washington;

a collaboration with the National Science Foundation to develop the Science, Technology, and Human Values Program; the launching of the Bay Area Writing Project that evolved into the National Writing Project; Summer Seminars for Secondary School Teachers; Stanley Karnow's 13-part documentary *Vietnam: A Television History*; and the We the People initiative.

Douglas M. DeWitt

See also National Council for History Education; National Council for the Social Studies; National Council of Teachers of English; National Endowment for the Arts

Further Readings

Commission on the Humanities. (1964). *Report*. New York: American Council of Learned Societies, Council of Graduate Schools in the United States, & United Chapters of Phi Beta Kappa.

Miller, S. (1984). *Excellence and equity: The National Endowment for the Humanities*. Lexington: University Press of Kentucky.

National Foundation on the Arts and Humanities Act of 1965, Pub. L. No. 89-209.

NATIONAL GOVERNORS ASSOCIATION

This entry describes the education reform initiatives undertaken by the National Governors Association (NGA). Education has long been a top priority of governors, and in recent decades, states have led the way in improving the quality of education in the United States. The NGA advocates for governors on national education reform issues and, through its Center for Best Practices (NGA Center), supports them in their efforts to implement policies to improve schools and boost student achievement.

Following publication of the 1983 report *A Nation at Risk*, governors took the lead on education reform. In 1985–1986, NGA chair, Governor Lamar Alexander of Tennessee, focused his chair's initiative on improving education. As part of the initiative, NGA issued *Time for Results: The*

Governors' 1991 Report on Education (1986), which recommended actions states needed to take over a 5-year period to address critical areas in education, such as teaching, school readiness, and accountability for results.

NGA partnered with President George H. W. Bush in convening the historic Charlottesville Education Summit in September 1989, which brought the president together with governors to work toward a consensus on the direction of education reform. Following the summit, the White House and NGA issued a joint communiqué calling for setting national education goals and annual progress reports. The next year the president and NGA announced six goals to be accomplished by the year 2000 addressing school readiness, high school graduation rates, the assessment of student progress, science and math excellence, adult literacy, and drugs and violence.

Concerned about U.S. international competitiveness, NGA and business leaders held a second National Education Summit in 1996, which led to the formation of Achieve, Inc., a partnership between governors and business leaders that provides expertise and support to states in their efforts to establish rigorous standards and accountability in education.

Subsequently, NGA and Achieve, Inc., in partnership with the Business Roundtable, the James B. Hunt Institute, and the Education Commission of the States, held National Education Summits in 1999, 2001, and 2005. These summits included educators and addressed a variety of issues, from raising standards and achievement in schools to improving teacher quality to providing supports for struggling students.

The 2005 National Education Summit on High Schools was convened as part of Virginia governor Mark Warner's NGA chair's initiative, *Redesigning the American High School.* During the summit, Warner and NGA released a five-point state action agenda aimed at restoring value to the high school diploma through improved teacher quality, clear identification of goals and measurement of progress, and increased accountability for high schools. At this summit many states committed to join the American Diploma Project Network and raise high school graduation standards to match requirements for success in college and the workplace.

Also in 2005, the nation's governors made a commitment to a more accurate and consistent measure for calculating state high school graduation rates. Governors of all 50 states signed the NGA Graduation Counts Compact to implement a common formula for calculating their state's high school graduation rate. A 2008 report by the NGA Center showed states are on track to publicly report their high school graduation rates using the formula by 2012.

Through its *Innovation America* initiative in 2007, NGA called upon states to improve the curriculum and teaching of STEM disciplines— science, technology, engineering, and math. Later that year NGA awarded grants to five states to establish STEM education centers to improve instruction and learning in STEM fields.

In September 2008, the NGA Center undertook a joint effort with the Council of Chief State School Officers and Achieve, Inc., to give states a roadmap for benchmarking their K–12 education systems to those of top-performing nations. Recommendations for helping states implement international benchmarking are contained in the report *Benchmarking for Success: Ensuring U.S. Students Receive a World-Class Education.*

And in June 2009, the NGA Center announced that 49 states and territories had signed on to the Common Core State Standards Initiative. Through this initiative, the NGA Center and the Council of Chief State School Officers, in partnership with Achieve, Inc., ACT, and the College Board, will coordinate a state-led process to develop a common core of state standards in English language arts and mathematics for Grades K–12. These standards, which states may adopt voluntarily, will be research- and evidence-based, internationally benchmarked, aligned with college and work expectations, and will include rigorous content and skills.

Bob Taft

See also Accountability Era; Achieve, Inc.; American Diploma Project; Early Childhood Education; No Child Left Behind Act (NCLB); Student Assessment and School Accountability

Further Readings

American Diploma Project. (2004). *Ready or not: Creating a high school diploma that counts.* Retrieved

July 30, 2009, from http://www.achieve.org/files/ADPreport_7.pdf

Conklin, K. D., Curran, B. K., & Gandal, M. (2005, February 21). *An action agenda for improving America's high schools.* Achieve, Inc., & National Governors Association. Retrieved July 30, 2009, from http://www.nga.org/Files/pdf/0502ACTION AGENDA.pdf

Finn, C. (2008). *Troublemaker, a personal history of school reform since* Sputnik. Princeton, NJ: Princeton University Press.

National Governors Association. (2009, February 24). *Policy position ECW-02. Education reform.* Retrieved August 2, 2009, from http://www.nga.org/portal/site/nga/menuitem.8358ec82f5b198d18a278110501010a0/?vgnextoid=20ca9e2f1b091010VgnVCM1000001a01010aRCRD

Swanson, C., & Barlage, J. (2006). *Influence, a study of the factors shaping education policy.* Bethesda, MD: Editorial Projects in Education Research Center.

Vinovskis, M. (1999). *The road to Charlottesville—The 1989 Education Summit.* Washington, DC: National Education Goals Panel.

National Network for Educational Renewal (NNER)

The National Network for Educational Renewal (NNER) grew out of the work of the internationally recognized educator John Goodlad and the Center for Educational Renewal, which Goodlad and his colleagues established at the University of Washington in 1985. The underlying argument of both the NNER and the Center for Educational Renewal is based on Goodlad's 1985 book *A Place Called School,* which begins with the statement that "American schools are in trouble" and ends with a call for re-envisioning the purpose of American education.

American schools, the NNER contends, must focus not on job preparation and economic advancement but instead on preparing individuals to be thoughtful and informed participants in our democratic society. In naming the organization, Goodlad and his colleagues deliberately chose the term *renewal* over *reform,* believing that the latter suggests a finite beginning and ending, whereas *renewal* reflects the ongoing nature of educators' work.

The Center for Educational Renewal provided the research component in this reexamination of American schooling, and the National Network for Educational Renewal laid the groundwork for implementation by inviting institutions of higher education and their PreK–12 school partners to join the NNER in furthering the four primary goals of the organization's Agenda for Education in a Democracy: (1) providing young people with the knowledge, skills, and dispositions to effectively participate in a social and political democracy; (2) providing all students with access to knowledge that will allow them to effectively participate in the democratic process; (3) encouraging educators to engage in nurturing pedagogy in their classrooms; and (4) promoting stewardship of the schools by all members of the community.

Lying at the heart of the NNER agenda is the concept of "simultaneous renewal," the belief that schools and schooling will not improve without the combined efforts of both the PreK–12 schools and the colleges and universities that prepare educators for those schools. Thus, institutions of higher education expressing interest in joining the NNER must demonstrate that they have established viable partnerships with local PreK–12 schools and that those partnerships have taken meaningful steps toward implementing the four primary goals delineated in the Agenda for Education in a Democracy. In addition, the NNER also posits that the college/university faculty engaged in the work of the NNER must include faculty not only from colleges of education but also from colleges of arts and sciences, because it is the "tripartite" work of PreK–12, education, and arts and sciences faculty that shares in the responsibility of preparing future educators and renewing America's schools.

In focusing on the preparation of future educators, the NNER identified 20 conditions that must be in place for simultaneous renewal to occur. These 20 "postulates" set a high standard for institutions of higher education and their partner schools, including a call for teacher preparation programs to be recognized "as a major responsibility to society and be adequately supported and promoted and vigorously advanced by the institution's top leadership" and given "parity with other professional education programs, full legitimacy and institutional commitment, and rewards for faculty geared to the nature of the field." In addressing both the significance of real-world classroom experiences and the quality and quantity of teacher candidates, the postulates further note that "programs for the education of educators must assure for each candidate the availability of a wide array of laboratory settings for simulation, observation, hands-on experiences, and exemplary schools for internships and residencies," and "they must admit no more students to their programs than can be assured these quality experiences."

The organization began with a small number of member institutions in the mid-1980s but by 2008 had grown to 25 settings in 20 states and 1 Canadian province. Most "settings" consist of one institution of higher education in partnership with one PreK–12 school or school district. Some settings, however, involve multiple institutions of higher education in partnership with multiple schools and school districts; thus, more than 40 institutions of higher education are in fact affiliated with the national organization. These colleges and universities are located in the states of California, Colorado, Connecticut, Georgia, Hawaii, Illinois, Maine, Minnesota, Missouri, Nebraska, New Jersey, New Mexico, New York, Ohio, South Carolina, Texas, Utah, Washington, West Virginia, and Wyoming, and the Canadian province of Manitoba.

The organization holds an annual conference, which rotates from setting to setting, but it also provides other opportunities for discussions throughout the year. For example, in collaboration with the Institute for Educational Inquiry (a related organization created by Goodlad and his associates in 1992), the NNER has provided Leadership Associates Training for its member institutions as a way of stimulating conversation and understanding of the Agenda for Education in a Democracy. In recent years it also has reached out to school districts, which may or may not be directly affiliated with an NNER institution, by offering the Leaders for Teacher-Preparing Schools program for school administrators. It also has invited members of the broader community, including journalists as well as local and state policymakers, to participate in NNER-sponsored discussions of the purpose of education, and it has collaborated with the League of Small Democratic Schools in that group's efforts to advance the goals it shares with the NNER.

The NNER, in combination with the Institute for Educational Inquiry, has published numerous reflections on its work, including occasional papers, a "reflection on practice" article series, and multiple books written or cowritten by Goodlad and other educators involved in the work of the NNER. Its Agenda for Education in a Democracy series, released in 1999, includes four volumes (*Leadership for Educational Renewal, Centers of Pedagogy, Effective Professional Development Schools,* and *The Professional Teacher*), which best summarize the work of the organization.

Bruce E. Field

See also Goodlad, John; Professional Development Schools; Schools of Education; Teacher Education

Further Readings

Clark, R. (1999). *Effective professional development schools.* San Francisco: Jossey-Bass.
Goodlad, J. (1984). *A place called school: Prospects for the future.* New York: McGraw-Hill.
Goodlad, J., Mantle-Bromley, C., & Goodlad, S. (2004). *Education for everyone: Agenda for education in a democracy.* San Francisco: Jossey-Bass.
Norlander-Case, A., Reagan, T., & Case, C. (1999). *The professional teacher: The preparation and nurturance of the reflective practitioner.* San Francisco: Jossey-Bass.
Patterson, R., Michelli, N., & Pacheco, A. (1999). *Centers of pedagogy.* San Francisco: Jossey-Bass.
Smith, W., & Fenstermacher, G. (1999). *Leadership for educational renewal.* San Francisco: Jossey-Bass.

NATIONAL ORGANIZATION FOR WOMEN (NOW)

The founding of the National Organization for Women (NOW) can be directly linked to Title VII of the 1964 Civil Rights Act. The Equal Employment Opportunity Commission (EEOC) was the enforcement tool for the Civil Rights Act. A small group of women gathered in a Washington, D.C., hotel room in June 1966 to discuss the refusal of EEOC to include a ban on sex discrimination in employment ads—ads labeled "Help

Wanted–Male" and "Help Wanted–Female." As an outgrowth of this discussion, 4 months later the women established NOW as an organization devoted to equal rights for women, which included gender equity in education.

Betty Friedan was a member of that small group in the hotel room. Her social critique, *The Feminine Mystique* (1963), became a bestseller as it raised questions among millions of women across the country about the primary aspiration toward which women were then being socialized, that is, the content suburban "housewife." Pauli Murray was also in that 1966 meeting. A law professor at Yale University and a member of the President's Commission on the Status of Women in 1966, she strongly opposed the refusal of EEOC to ban sex-based employment ads. Long a reformer for women's rights, Murray had been the only woman in the Howard University Law School graduation class of 1944 and received the first doctorate in juridical science awarded by Yale University to an African American.

In October 1966 other women and men joined Friedan and Murray, approximately 300 in all, to become charter members of NOW at a meeting in Washington, D.C. Friedan was NOW's first president, Aileen Hernandez and Richard Graham became the first vice presidents, and Caroline Davis became secretary-treasurer. Hernandez and Graham had been commissioners with the EEOC (appointed by President Lyndon Johnson). Each had opposed the EEOC's refusal to enforce Title VII in addressing sex-based employment discrimination as forthrightly as it addressed discrimination on other grounds. Hernandez was the only woman on the five-member EEOC, and Graham was a man dedicated to women's rights.

NOW adopted a statement of purpose at the 1966 gathering, which was "to take action to bring women into full participation in the mainstream of American society now, exercising all the privileges and responsibilities thereof in truly equal partnership with men." Education and schooling were focal areas of NOW, along with equal employment opportunity (its reason for the first gathering), legal rights, women in poverty, the family, public images of women, and religion.

During its first decade, NOW not only grew nationally but also operated at the grassroots level. In local communities across the country, informal groups of women met and talked. These local consciousness-raising groups were known widely as "CR groups." In these conversations, held almost always in one of the women's homes, women talked about their lived experiences. Collectively, they began to reflect on those individual experiences through a common lens—what they shared as women. A dramatic shift occurred as women learned to trust other women and create a sense of "sisterhood," a word increasingly used as a metaphor among NOW members. Relative to men, women in the 1950s and 1960s had little power. They were dependent on men for their power base, and, to some, for their very identity—through marriage or family status. As a result, many women had been socialized from childhood not to trust other women. The sisterhood emerging from CR groups reversed that conditioning for many women; no one could deny that from these groups a political movement had emerged. This emerging consciousness coincided with the 1960s civil rights movement to end discrimination against people of color. Many women who had become activists in the civil rights movement declared themselves feminists. Their advocacy for full rights for African Americans grew into a similar and strong advocacy for all oppressed groups, especially women.

NOW challenged traditional societal roles played by women and men. It promoted the idea that women must be full partners with men not only in all areas of public life but also in family life as well. It portrayed its purpose as an "action" organization, one that would attempt to break down sex-based stereotypes, especially in schools and educational policies. It publicized the status of women in the 1960s as over 50% of the U.S. population but only a tiny fraction of the lawyers, doctors, and chief executive officers and the largest proportion of teachers, librarians, and nurses. At its charter meeting, NOW declared that 46% of women worked outside the home but over three-fourths were in routine clerical, sales, factory, or household and hospital cleaning jobs.

NOW refused tokenism and promoted equal educational opportunities for boys and girls. Arguably, the most important achievement during the aftermath of Title IX was the Women's Educational Equity Act (WEEA), passed in 1974. This legislation funded the WEEA Equity Resource Center, which housed the development and dissemination of educational materials that challenged stereotypes of masculinity and femininity. This national center was a structural outgrowth of Title IX, a place that promoted the gender-fair education that Title IX mandated.

The center provided technical assistance to those who received WEEA grants, provided training for educators, and disseminated materials to schools and educators. The original focus of the center was on the education of girls and women, and that grew over time to become a focus on gender, including boys and men. The statistical trends of girls' and women's academic achievement have increased over the past 4 decades (according to a U.S. Department of Education 2000 study, *Trends in Educational Equity of Girls and Women*), attesting to the success of Title IX and WEEA. Some policymakers and some political activists have argued against the need for continued WEEA funding.

NOW was a chief proponent of WEEA and educational equity. NOW's founding members challenged traditional stereotypes fostered in schools, curricula, and textbooks. NOW publicly objected to women being portrayed primarily as "housewives" in school texts and, at the same time, called for recognition of the economic value of domestic housework and child care work. It called for an end to images that denigrated women in published educational materials and mass media.

NOW was active at local levels across the country in the late 1960s and through the 1980s and beyond. They boycotted community libraries to express rejection of what they saw as sexist books that narrowly depicted aspirations for girls and boys. NOW activists marched in front of the offices of local newspapers protesting the editorial practice of including women's names in newspaper accounts only when their marital status was included. No such requirement was made of men. They demanded that newspapers cover accomplishments of local schoolgirls' sports as much as local schoolboys' sports. They attended school board meetings to address sex-role stereotyping in curricular materials. They held public forums on the treatment of women as sex objects in corporate advertising campaigns. They organized letter-writing campaigns demanding elected officials address the illegal differential salaries paid women and men for the same or similar jobs. They sponsored workshops on women's physical and mental

health at local churches or YWCAs. They challenged beauty pageants as public spectacles that objectified women. They sought out and supported candidates for elective office who would promote women's rights.

At the national level, NOW almost immediately succeeded in its first priority when the EEOC held hearings on sex discrimination in job advertisements in 1967. Other issues became publicized. NOW pressured colleges and universities to establish women's studies programs. It also pressured Congress for federal child care legislation. In 1970, 50,000 women marched in New York City as a part of a national Women's Strike for Equality Day on the 50th anniversary of the Nineteenth Amendment, which gave women the right to vote. This was only one of many demonstrations.

In that same year, primarily due to NOW pressure, the U.S. House of Representatives passed the Equal Rights Amendment to the U.S. Constitution (ERA), which stated, "Equality of rights under the law shall not be denied or abridged by the United States or by any state on account of sex." In a 1977 protest demonstration, NOW demanded that President Jimmy Carter take strong action to achieve the amendment's ratification. In July 1978, more than 100,000 people marched on Washington, D.C., to demand that Congress extend the time for ratification. Both the House of Representatives and the Senate agreed to extend the time until 1982. That year came and went with no more than 35 of the 38 needed states ratifying the amendment. Despite yearly reintroduction into the legislative agenda, the ERA has never been ratified.

As women's and men's lives changed over time, NOW worked for changes in other areas such as equal treatment of women in the military, women's reproductive rights, and equal rights of lesbians and gays in all aspects of life. NOW has routinely joined with other groups to reject any narrowing of the scope of Title IX, a 1972 law prohibiting sex discrimination in education. NOW has operated on both sides of party politics, opposing President Ronald Reagan's anti-abortion decisions in the 1980s and opposing President Bill Clinton's leadership of welfare reform in the 1990s.

Carolyn S. Ridenour

See also Equal Education Opportunity; Feminist Perspectives; Title IX

Further Readings

Friedan, B. (1963). *The feminine mystique*. New York: Norton.

National Organization for Women. (n.d.). *The founding of NOW: Setting the stage*. Retrieved March 10, 2009, from http://www.now.org/history/the_founding.html?printable

National Organization for Women. (n.d.) *The National Organization for Women's 1966 statement of purpose*. Retrieved August 2, 2009, from http://www.now.org/organization/bylaws.html#ArticleII

NATIONAL SCHOOL BOARDS ASSOCIATION

Starting with the Massachusetts Law of 1642, the American colonies began a commitment to public education created and funded by the public and governed at the local level. This became the common pattern for public education following the War of Independence, with local boards of education being elected to oversee the public schools of the community. But as the nation and states grew in size and diversity, the state and federal governments began to assume more and more control and power over the local school districts.

Beginning in the late 1800s, school districts within states joined together and formed state school board associations so as to exert a greater voice within their respective states. By 1940 these state associations recognized that a collective voice was needed at the national level and created the National School Boards Association (NSBA), designed to be the national voice of thousands of local boards of education through their state associations. The goal from the outset has been to help this democratic system of local governance be a highly effective system for enabling the nation's children to succeed in life.

Each state association is a constituent member of NSBA, electing two local school board members to serve as official NSBA delegates (total 150). This body adopts all policies by at least a two-thirds vote and all annual resolutions by a simple majority vote minimum. The policies become the organization's legislative platform until specifically revised. The super majority for policies ensures that there exists widespread support for any proposed position statement. Individual local school districts can choose to become a national affiliate member for many services, but they will not have direct vote status.

NSBA also works together with a number of other education-related national organizations to seek common agreements on issues and then to advocate for those positions together, speaking with a unified voice. This effort includes teacher unions, administrative and leadership groups, the PTO and PTA (Parent Teacher Organization and Parent Teacher Association), and curriculum-related organizations so as to bring together those who, at times, have disagreed with each other in the past.

The NSBA Federal Relations Network has nearly 1,000 local board members acting as legislative lobbyists. *The School Board News*, a newsletter, and the *American School Board Journal*, a monthly magazine, serve as major communication tools of NSBA. In addition, its e-mail newsletter, *Legal Clips*, provides weekly updates of court cases and decisions that are impacting public schools in the nation.

NSBA's legal services regularly file amicus briefs on behalf of local districts when the case has a potential significant impact on all public schools. For example in *MAL v. Kinsland*, 543 F.3d 841 (6th Cir. 2008), a Sixth Circuit panel unanimously held that the legal standard for evaluating a mere time, manner, and place regulation of student speech is not the very high one of whether the regulation is necessary to avoid a material and substantial disruption of school operations, but a more lenient one of whether the regulation fulfills the First Amendment requirements. The majority opinion closely tracked the arguments in NSBA's amicus brief, at one point using a nearly verbatim passage.

Legislatively, NSBA has argued strongly against unfunded mandates as found in the Individuals with Disabilities Education Act and the No Child Left Behind Act, which together required local expenditures of billions of local dollars in order to meet the rules of the laws. It has fought to preserve the role and place of locally elected boards of education and against politically motivated attempts by some city mayors to take over control of their city's local schools.

Other major legislative priorities of NSBA have included efforts to improve teacher quality, a much stronger emphasis on early childhood education, and opposition to school vouchers and charter schools when either or both would take vitally needed funds away from the largely underfunded public schools. Such issues as the E-rate impact the growth of technology in the public schools, which the NSBA sees as a vital element in the United States' remaining globally competitive. Finally, NSBA has affirmed the importance of good school nutrition and appropriate physical education to combat the growing problem of obesity among the nation's youth.

Because the U.S. system of grassroots democracy is tied to its system of locally elected boards of education, the NSBA has been especially cognizant of the attempts by some groups to undermine this system. For example, election laws that have the effect of reducing the power of minority voters have been a special focus of NSBA over the years.

Another major priority of the organization has been to help local board members become better informed and thus able to make better decisions. When controversy surfaces on a national topic, NSBA has provided speakers and/or published articles by those on all sides of the issue. It has also advised districts how to become more effective in communications with their own public, so as to build confidence in the local board and its openness to differing views.

James K. Uphoff

See also American Association of School Administrators (AASA); Boards of Education; Community Control; Council of the Great City Schools; District Schools; Local Control; State Departments of Education; U.S. Department of Education

Further Readings

American School Board Journal: http://www.asbj.com

Bauman, P. (1996). *Governing education: Public sector reform or privatization.* Boston: Allyn & Bacon.

Carver, J. (1990). *Boards that make a difference.* San Francisco: Jossey-Bass.

Howell, W. (Ed.). (2005). *Besieged: School boards and the future of education politics.* Washington, DC: Brookings Institution.

National School Boards Association: http://www.nsba.org

NATIONAL SCIENCE FOUNDATION

Headquartered in Arlington, Virginia, the National Science Foundation (NSF) is supported by the U.S. federal government to advance knowledge in the fields of science, technology, engineering, and mathematics (STEM); foster innovation among scientists, engineers, and educators; and develop society's scientific knowledge through the dissemination of scientific information. As a means of advancing this mission, NSF has actively promoted and supported educational reforms in K–12 science and mathematics instruction. NSF is divided into seven directorates to support its mission: Biological Sciences, Computer and Information Science and Engineering, Engineering, Geosciences, Mathematics and Physical Sciences, Social Behavioral and Economic Sciences, and Education and Human Resources. A 24-member National Science Board sets general policy, and a director and associate director oversee the daily operations, budgets, program development, and administration of the foundation. These individuals are appointed by the president of the United States and confirmed by the U.S. Senate.

To support its core mission, NSF funds research programs that strengthen science and engineering education programs from PreK through graduate school, awards graduate fellowships in the sciences and engineering fields, sponsors basic research and education in STEM fields, and fosters the use of technology and the development of other scientific methods for research and STEM education. The NSF is the only federal agency dedicated entirely to the support of research and education in all scientific and engineering disciplines other than the medical sciences, which are supported by the National Institutes of Health.

History

NSF was established in 1950 by an act of Congress as an independent federal agency charged with ensuring the United States maintained a leadership position in scientific discovery and technology. Its ongoing mission as stated in the legislation is "to promote the progress of science; to advance the national health, prosperity, and welfare; to secure the national defense; and for other purposes."

Following the launch of *Sputnik* by the Soviet Union in 1957, the increased international focus on competitiveness in science and technology led to active political debate in the United States. The discussions led President Dwight D. Eisenhower to direct the NSF to concentrate its efforts on the dissemination of scientific information and endeavors in science and technology. To support these efforts, Congress dramatically increased federal funding for the Foundation, more than doubling the total appropriation and tripling funding designated for educational programs.

During the 1960s and early 1970s, NSF developed educational initiatives under the supposition that American schools were falling behind those of other nations in their ability to produce high-quality professionals in science, technology, and engineering. Educational curriculum development and implementation efforts attempted to reformulate traditional subject-oriented science curricula to adopt a more discipline-centered approach that exposed students to the basic ideas of each distinct discipline. A major trend of these efforts was to cut back the amount of curricular emphasis on basic factual information in favor of a focus on connections to more abstract scientific theories that experts believed were necessary for performing science in a professional capacity. This approach included reducing the role of "everyday science," in which science education highlights the scientific principles involved in common devices and phenomena, and increasing emphasis on the development of scientific inquiry skills applied within discipline-specific courses and the articulation of theories and arguments that formed the basis of scientific conclusions.

Examples of curricula developed through such NSF support include the Physical Science Study Committee textbook and laboratory guide, three textbooks by the Biological Sciences Curriculum Study, and the Chemical Bond Approach and CHEM Study curricula developed by the American Chemical Society at the high school level. Additional basic content was introduced at the elementary school level through Science—A Process Approach, Elementary Science Study, and Science Curriculum Improvement Study. Another notable example of this approach was the new math curriculum, which rejected the teaching of standard algorithms to allow students to quickly perform arithmetic.

Instead, it required students to learn formal set theory, work with functions, and perform computations in number systems other than base 10.

These programs were highly popular among university academics, but they diverged from the mainstream public's notions of what math and science education should look like. Many critics charged that the materials were inappropriate for various reasons. Some argued that the curricula were not appropriate for students who were not already interested in and motivated by science because they were too challenging or required the mastery of skills that were not applicable outside a scientific laboratory. Others suggested that the lack of local input failed to prevent the inclusion of material that parents deemed inappropriate for their children on moral or religious grounds, for example, macroevolution and sexual reproduction. Consequently, public support for NSF's efforts began to erode, and students' interest in pursuing science and engineering majors in college showed a noticeable decrease during the period of the reform effort.

An additional challenge for NSF arose in the 1970s as social conservatives reacted negatively to a widely disseminated fifth-grade anthropology curriculum developed with NSF support called *Man: A Course of Study* (MACOS). The course presented a study of life that began with simple life cycles in lower animals and progressed through discussions of topics with greater depth and sophistication until it culminated with the examination of human life cycles within specific cultures. Although the course was revolutionary in its use of Jerome Bruner's spiral curriculum design and its emphasis on processes of inquiry, such as asking fundamental questions and formulating evidence-based answers, it raised great controversy because it encouraged students to question mainstream cultural beliefs and standards of morality, including topics like infanticide and euthanasia. Critics argued that, among other problematic issues, it advocated cultural and moral relativism, which infringed on parents' discretion to address issues of morality with their children according to their own beliefs.

By the mid-1970s, the MACOS controversy, lackluster performance of NSF's educational initiatives (due in part to insufficient training of teachers to implement the new curricula), and increasing emphasis on aspects of education other than science led to major reductions in NSF's curriculum reform efforts. During the early 1980s, funding for science education decreased significantly, and NSF ceased to play a major role in education.

In the late 1980s, however, a major effort to return the focus of the nation back to science education arose, and the educational mission of NSF was renewed as fears arose of a critical labor shortage for technical and scientific fields. In response, the federal government increased its funding for NSF significantly, and the resulting programs were designed to sharply increase the number of U.S. students receiving doctorates in those fields. The renewed strategic plan for that time period included goals such as raising the standards of student performance in science, technology, and engineering education; developing new curricula to aid teachers in meeting high standards of achievement; raising qualifications of K–12 teachers; and increasing the number of graduate students in science, technology, and engineering fields. By the late 1990s, approximately 20% of NSF's budget was allocated to fund programs focusing on science education and specifically human resource development.

In response to this renewed effort by the NSF, critics cited similar patterns to the 1960s in which American schools were being compared to their international counterparts and deemed unsatisfactory in terms of curriculum efforts to engage the interest of young students in the science, technology, and engineering fields. Some critics have pointed out that a parallel situation has developed and the nation will again see that curriculum efforts entirely focused on discipline-specific efforts will fail.

Today, with a current annual budget of approximately $6 billion, NSF issues approximately 10,000 short-term grants to an average of 200,000 educators, students, scientists, and engineers all over the world. These awards account for nearly 20% of all federally supported research conducted at American institutions of higher education. The NSF makes certain all supported projects are fully integrated with education to ensure future scientists and engineers are trained by today's innovative leaders in those fields.

Current Structure and Programs

The Directorate for Education and Human Resources consists of four divisions that each provide funding specifically targeted at different facets of the STEM education pipeline: (1) the Division of Research on Learning in Formal and Informal Settings, (2) the Division of Undergraduate Education, (3) the Division of Graduate Education, and (4) the Division of Human Resource Development.

Division of Research on Learning in Formal and Informal Settings

The Division of Research on Learning in Formal and Informal Settings funds two major categories of programs. The first sponsors basic research on variables that influence science learning in a variety of educational settings, including motivation, cognitive development, and technology use. The second sponsors curriculum development efforts that are intended to improve achievement or engagement in STEM-related topics in schools or informal learning settings such as museums.

Division of Undergraduate Education

The Division of Undergraduate Education funds three types of programs to support STEM education at the undergraduate level. The first type sponsors basic research on factors that influence academic success for students pursuing bachelor's degrees in STEM. The second type supports efforts to improve and reinvigorate undergraduate curricula and degree programs to improve student success. The third type of support is provided directly to undergraduate students in the form of scholarships designed to support academically talented students in need of financial support.

Division of Graduate Education

The Division of Graduate Education funds fewer programs than other divisions but offers a greater proportion to directly supporting STEM graduate students. NSF Graduate Research Fellowships are prestigious awards granted to between 900 and 1,600 students per year that support 3 years of graduate tuition and additional funding to enrich students' research programs. GK–12 Fellowships offer individual graduate student support with an emphasis on integrating research training with teaching experiences in K–12 classrooms to foster enhanced communication and teaching skills. In contrast, the Integrative Graduate Education and Research Traineeship program provides funds to universities to develop innovative models of graduate training that entail cross-disciplinary and interdisciplinary research efforts to prepare graduates for careers in a shifting scientific landscape.

Division of Human Resource Development

The Division of Human Resource Development supports activities that are designed primarily to broaden participation in STEM disciplines. A variety of programs seek to increase the recruitment and retention of underrepresented groups, including women, people with disabilities, and ethnic minorities through research grants, scholarships, and the establishment of centers of excellence in research.

Conclusion

During its history, NSF's role in educational reform has varied widely. Its early advocacy and support of curricular change and its current support of educational research and development projects have enabled STEM and educational researchers to directly impact the practices of teachers in K–12 classrooms. In deference to its history and political demands for demonstrations of effectiveness, current policies require extensive evaluation of funded projects and strongly encourage collaborative partnerships between researchers and K–12 teachers to maximize the likelihood of projects' success in schools serving a highly diverse student population.

David F. Feldon and Melissa Hurst

See also Bruner, Jerome S.; Federal Educational Reform; National Defense Education Act (NDEA)

Further Readings

Block, E. (1990). Education and human resources at the National Science Foundation. *Perspective, 24,* 839–840.

DeBoer, G. (1991). *A history of ideas in science education: Implications for practice.* New York: Teachers College Press.

Hoff, D. J. (1999). The race to space rocketed NSF into classrooms. *Education Week, 18*(36), 34–35.

Katzenmeyer, C., & Lawrenz, F. (2006). A history of education evaluation at NSF. *New Directions for Evaluation, 109,* 7–18.

National Science Foundation. (2003, September 30). *National Science Foundation strategic plan: FY 2003–2008.* Retrieved October 6, 2008, from http:// www.nsf.gov/pubs/2004/nsf04201/FY2003-2008.pdf

National Science Foundation. (2007, October 30). *National action plan for addressing the critical needs of the U.S. science, technology, engineering, and mathematics education system* (NSB 07-114). Arlington, VA: Author. Retrieved October 6, 2008, from http://www.nsf.gov/nsb/documents/2007/ stem_action.pdf

NATIONAL SCIENCE TEACHERS ASSOCIATION

The National Science Teachers Association (NSTA) describes itself as "the largest organization in the world promoting excellence and innovation in science teaching and learning for all." Located in Arlington, Virginia, NSTA was founded in 1944 and has more than 59,000 members. Membership is made up of a diverse group of individuals interested in science education. These individuals come from the ranks of pre-service science teachers, science teachers (elementary to college level), school administrators, science curriculum specialists, scientists, and representatives from business and industry.

Mission and Vision

The vision of NSTA is to be the leader in science education, and its mission is "to promote excellence and innovation in science teaching and learning for all." It depicts itself as the keeper of the conversation on science education in the United States. The association also states that the national scale of its work is unmatched in the science education community

The core work of the NSTA is focused on delivering professional development and resources that enhance the quality of classroom instruction to reflect research-based policy and practice. This work is carried out in connection with its membership, which is divided among state and province chapters, student chapters in colleges and universities, and associated groups across the United States and Canada.

Governance

A board of directors oversees the NSTA's work to be the "leader in science education." The NSTA board actively seeks input from NSTA members on critical issues in science education through its two elected advisory groups. One such group, the National Congress on Science Education, meets annually to discuss critical issues related to the science education community. Issues discussed include teaching science to students of poverty; 21st-century skills; and science, technology, engineering, and mathematics critical to America's prosperity.

Support to the Science Education Community

The NSTA recognizes that the goal of improving the quality of all science teachers does not occur in isolation and needs support from the larger educational community. Therefore, the NSTA works with school administrators at the campus and district levels, university science teacher preparation programs, college professors, government agencies, private corporations, researchers, government officials, students, and parents. Such coordination builds the capacity of the overall system to improve science education.

Support to Universities and School Districts

Within the education community, NSTA works to strengthen university science teacher preparation programs, school district science programs, and the professional development of all science teachers and administrators.

University science teacher preparation programs are supported by the NSTA in several ways. A document, *Standards for Science Teachers Preparation*, was produced in 1998 and revised in 2003 to provide guidance to science teacher preparation programs. Universities undergoing accreditation through the National Conference for Accreditation in Teacher Education may request

special NSTA program recognition based on these standards.

The NSTA offers support to schools at the district level through an initiative titled Science Program Improvement Review. The review program is designed to assess a school's complete science program across all grade levels and provide written recommendations for improvement.

The NSTA also advocates for science educators through an office of legislative affairs and public relations and works with the U.S. Congress on specific legislation and issues that impact science education. The NSTA publishes numerous position papers on critical issues related to science education, including its lead paper, *Beyond 2000— Teachers of Science Speak Out,* on how all students learn science and the implications to the science education community.

Core Work–Support for Science Teachers

The NSTA supports excellence in science teaching by offering an extensive array of professional development opportunities, publications, teaching resources, and networking initiatives for science teachers from elementary to college level.

Publications

The NSTA publishes member journals, an association newspaper, electronic newsletters, and books that are of importance to science educators. Four peer-reviewed journals are offered for educators of all levels: *Science and Children, Science Scope, Science Teacher,* and the *Journal of College Science Teaching.* A member newspaper, *NSTA Reports,* is published nine times a year. Three electronic newsletters are offered: *NSTA Express* (weekly science news), *Science Class* (monthly theme-based content in three levels—elementary, middle, and high school) and *Scientific Principals* (monthly). *Scientific Principals,* launched in 2007, is the newest newsletter initiative designed for elementary administrators.

Conferences

The association offers one national NSTA Conference on Science Education and three regional conferences on an annual basis. In addition to the national conference, the NSTA offers numerous professional development institutes (workshops and classes) connected to the national conference and research dissemination conferences. More than 25,000 educators annually participate in the conferences.

Web-Based Professional Development Opportunities

Multiple Web-based professional development opportunities are available to teachers on the NSTA Web site. Participation opportunities include live online classes, Web seminars, e-mentoring for new teachers, and online discussion forums.

The major online learning initiative offered by NSTA is the Learning Center, an e-professional development portal, which offers science teachers on-demand access to professional development. Science teachers may individualize learning opportunities and resources to match the needed grade level, subject area, and state standard. Teachers are able to build an electronic portfolio that illustrates professional growth over time. Such learning supports the association's goal of continuous improvement in the quality of all science teachers, resulting in learning for all.

Michelle H. Abrego

See also National Council for Accreditation of Teacher Education (NCATE); National Science Foundation; Trends in International Mathematics and Science Study (TIMSS); U.S. Department of Education

Further Readings

American Association for the Advancement of Science. (1989). *Science for all Americans.* Washington, DC: Author.

National Science Teachers Association. (2003). *Beyond 2000—Teachers of science speak out. An NSTA lead paper on how all students learn science and the implications to the science education community* Arlington, VA: Author. Retrieved August 4, 2009, from http://www.nsta.org/pdfs/positionstatement_beyond2000.pdf

National Science Teachers Association. (2003). *Standards for science teacher preparation.* Arlington, VA: Author. Retrieved September 29, 2008, from http://www.nsta.org/pdfs/NSTAstandards2003.pdf

National Science Teachers Association. (2005). *Strategy 2005 goals.* Arlington, VA: Author. Retrieved September 29, 2008, from http://www.nsta.org/pdfs/Strategy2005.pdf

NATIONAL SOCIETY FOR THE PROMOTION OF INDUSTRIAL EDUCATION

Organized in 1906, the National Society for the Promotion of Industrial Education (NSPIE) was formed by business leaders and educators to initiate reform by bringing public attention to the importance of and need for industrial education and to promote the establishment of institutions for industrial training. The organization was the leading group to advance the concept of vocational education and to successfully lobby the U.S. government to federally fund state vocational education programs in secondary schools across the nation. The organization has grown in membership and, after merging with another organization, is now called the Association for Career and Technical Education.

James Haney, director of the New York Public Schools Manual Training Program, and Charles Richards of Teachers College at Columbia University organized the first formal meeting on June 9, 1906, in New York City to discuss formation of NSPIE. The 13 men in attendance were of the opinion that there was a "deep and widespread interest" in industrial education throughout the country, and they set a political agenda "to unite the many forces making toward industrial education the country over." The early NSPIE organizers realized that the United States trailed a European effort to formalize training programs that would give their citizens an advantage in responding to the advances taking place in the industrial world. Undoubtedly, new concepts and approaches were needed to meet the increasing demands of manufacturing. During the first meeting, a subcommittee was formed to continue discussions throughout the summer, and on November 16, 1906, an organizational meeting was held in Cooper Union, New York, and was attended by approximately 250 businesspersons and educators. During that meeting, a constitution was approved and officers and a board of managers were elected, including Henry S. Pritchett as president. According to its constitution, the purpose of the organization was (a) to bring to public attention the importance of industrial education as a factor in the industrial development of the United States, (b) to provide opportunities for the study and discussion of the various phases of the development of industrial education, (c) to make available the results of experiences in the field in the United States and abroad, and (d) to promote the establishment of institutions for industrial training. The NSPIE held its first convention on January 23–25, 1908. During that convention it was decided that securing federal funding for vocational education would be another primary objective of the organization. They also set for themselves the task of convincing the public of the need for public education to provide preparation for industrial occupations. By November 1908, the NSPIE had formal state branches active in 29 states and membership had reached nearly 900.

Between 1908 and 1911, the leaders of NSPIE decided to enlist the support of the National Association of Manufacturers and the American Federation of Labor, powerful organizations that had visions of "functional" school systems, to assist them in working toward federal funding for public secondary vocational education. In 1912, Senator Carroll Page of Vermont and Congressman William Wilson of Pennsylvania agreed to cosponsor a bill in close collaboration with Charles Prossner, the executive secretary of NSPIE and a powerful and effective lobbyist. Their initial efforts led to the shaping of Bill S-3, also known as the Page–Wilson bill, which would provide federal aid to industrial, agricultural, and home economics education in secondary schools. Also that same year, Senator Hoke Smith of Georgia and Congressman A. F. Lever of South Carolina introduced the agriculture extension bill, which had much the same intent as the Page–Wilson bill but without the provision for secondary schools. Congress was politically deadlocked on the bills, with a Democratic House refusing to vote favorably on the Page–Wilson bill and a Republican Senate reusing to vote for the Smith–Lever bill. The deadlock was finally broken by a "gentlemen's agreement" in which Senator Smith agreed that if

the Smith–Lever bill were adopted, he would offer a resolution to create a commission to study the unsolved problem of the Page–Wilson bill. In January 1914, the Smith–Lever Act was adopted.

On January 20, 1914, Congress approved a joint resolution authorizing President Woodrow Wilson to appoint a commission to study national aid to vocational education. The Commission on National Aid to Vocational Education was organized on April 2, 1914. Several members of the Commission were members of NSPIE, including Prossner. The Commission prepared a questionnaire that was sent to representatives of various departments of the federal government, representatives of national organizations, and private individuals, and within several months of its existence the Commission released a two-volume report of testimony from participants of the study. Subsequently, a presentation of the study's findings was given before the Commission on National Aid to Vocational Education representing the points of view of more than 12 million persons. Respondents overwhelmingly supported the goals that were reflected in the vision of NSPIE. The Commission found that public sentiment showed the need for vocational education; that an urgent social and educational need existed; and that national grants were necessary because the problem was too large to be worked out on a local basis. The Commission recommended that grants be given for stimulating vocational education; for training teachers; for partial payment of salaries of teachers, supervisors, and directors; and for the support of a federal board for making studies and investigations useful in vocational schools. Aided schools would be publicly supported and controlled, and vocational education would be offered in secondary schools. In consideration of the total findings and recommendations, a proposal for legislation, including a draft of a bill for vocational education, was made part of the final report. On December 7, 1915, Senator Hoke Smith and Congressman Dudley Hughes introduced Senate Bill 703 (Smith-Hughes bill) to Congress. This bill copied the Commission's bill verbatim, with some necessary changes, and provided for federal funding in the amount of $1.7 million for the 1917–1918 academic year for vocational education. It also created the Federal Board for Vocational Education to administer the provisions of the new law and to work on program planning and resolution of disputes. The bill was signed by President Wilson on February 23, 1917, and the NSPIE is credited with being the dominant factor in its development and passing.

In 1918 the NSPIE changed its name to the National Society for Vocational Education and in 1925, it merged with the Vocational Education Association of the Middle West to become the American Vocational Association. Organized in 1914, the Vocational Education Association of the Middle West was formed to study problems relating to vocational education and to bring the results of the study to public attention for the purpose of fostering types of education that would meet the vocational needs of youth and the reasonable demands of industry for efficient workers while preserving those elements of general education necessary for good citizenship in a democracy. During the next few years, federal funding for the Smith-Hughes Act increased until it reached $7.2 million for 1925–1926. At that time, the Federal Board for Vocational Education began to look at the differences in the ways states were utilizing funds to carry out their state vocational programs. The two organizations decided to merge after recognizing that their union would give them greater power on Capitol Hill and in dealing with the Federal Board as they governed vocational education. By 1926, enrollment in vocational education programs of agriculture, home economics, and trade and industrial education had grown to almost 900,000. In 1929, Congress passed the George–Reed Act, authorizing an increase of $1 million annually from 1930 to 1934 to expand vocational education in agriculture and home economics.

In December 1998, the American Vocational Association changed its name to the Association for Career and Technical Education, and the organization began to work toward program improvement and an emphasis on excellence in career and technical education to meet a changing societal need. Today, there are 12 divisions in the Association for Career and Technical Education: (1) Administration, (2) Adult Workforce Development, (3) Agricultural Education, (4) Business Education, (5) Family and Consumer Sciences Education, (6) Guidance, (7) Health Occupations Education, (8) Marketing Education, (9) New and Related Services, (10) Special Needs, (11) Technology Education, and (12) Trade and Industrial Education.

M. Yvette Turner

See also Business and Educational Reform; Curriculum Controversies; Vocational Education

Further Readings

Association for Career and Technical Education. (2002). *75th anniversary: Celebrating 75 years of success.* Alexandria, VA: Author.

Barlow, M. L. (1967). *History of industrial education in the United States.* Peoria, IL: Charles A. Bennett.

Craig, L. R. (1996). *The ASTD training and development handbook: A guide to human resource development.* New York: McGraw-Hill.

Smith, N. B. (1999). A tribute to the visionaries, prime movers and pioneers of vocational education, 1892 to 1917. *Journal of Vocational and Technical Education, 16*(1), 67–76.

Thompson, J. D. (1921). Personnel research agencies: A guide to organized research in employment management, industrial relations training, and working conditions. *Bulletin of the United States Bureau of Statistics,* No. 299. Washington, DC: U.S. Department of Labor.

NATION AT RISK, A

More than 25 years ago a blue-ribbon commission issued a report on the state of public education in America. The report, titled *A Nation at Risk,* which was extremely critical of the nation's education system, ignited considerable controversy. It addressed a national crisis in education using stark and forceful language. Moreover, the report proposed a solution that required an urgent commitment to educational quality among teachers, administrators, parents, students, and the general public. It is among the most widely read and debated educational reform treatises in American history.

Background

In August 1981, President Ronald Reagan asked Secretary of Education T. H. Bell to create a

National Commission on Excellence in Education to examine the quality of education in the United States. In 1983, the Commission issued its report titled *A Nation at Risk: The Imperative for Educational Reform*. The purpose of the report was to define the problems afflicting the American educational system and to provide solutions to these problems. In a ceremony at the White House, President Ronald Reagan accepted the results of the nearly 2 years of work of the Commission.

The Commission's Charge

The Commission was charged with the following tasks: (a) Assess the quality of teaching and learning in America's public and private schools, and college and universities, (b) compare American schools and colleges with those of other advanced nations, (c) study the relationship between college admissions requirements and student achievement in high school, (d) identify educational programs that result in notable student success in college, (e) assess the degree to which major social and educational changes in the last quarter of a century have affected student achievement, and (f) define problems that must be faced and overcome if American education is to achieve excellence. The Commission directed most of its attention to education in high schools, although the Commission also assessed elementary schools, vocational and technical programs, and higher education. In its work, the Commission analyzed five primary sources of information:

1. Papers commissioned from experts that addressed a variety of educational issues

2. Testimony of students, teachers, administrators, parents, scholars, and other stakeholders at eight meetings of the entire Commission, six public hearings, two panel discussions, a symposium, and a series of meetings organized by regional offices of the U.S. Department of Education

3. Existing papers that analyzed the problems in education

4. Letters from concerned citizens, teachers, and administrators

5. Descriptions of exemplary programs and promising practices in education

The Findings

According to the report, which was issued on April 26, 1983, the nation was at risk because America's educational system was producing mediocre results and students were falling behind their foreign counterparts. In an often quoted statement, the commission wrote,

> Our nation is at risk. . . . The educational foundations of our country are presently being eroded by a rising tide of mediocrity that threatens our very future as a Nation and as a people. . . . If an unfriendly foreign power had attempted to impose on America the mediocre educational performance that exists today, we might well have viewed it as an act of war. We have, in effect, been committing an act of unthinking, unilateral educational disarmament.

The report listed a number of indicators of risk, including the following:

- International comparisons of student achievement showed that American students did not do well when compared with their peers in other industrialized nations.
- Approximately 23 million adults were functionally illiterate.
- Approximately 13% of all 17-year-old youth were functionally illiterate, and among minority youth this rate may have been as high as 40%.
- Average achievement of high school students on standardized tests was lower than it was in 1957 (when *Sputnik* was launched).
- The College Board's Scholastic Achievement Test (SAT) showed consistent declines in the previous 15 years.

The Commission noted that these declines were occurring despite the fact that the demand for highly skilled workers was rapidly increasing. The basic problem, according to the Commission, was that high school curricula had been so diluted and weakened that students who graduated from high school knew less than graduates who had graduated earlier in U.S. history and less than their counterparts in developed countries. Much of this problem was due to the wide variety of nonacademic curricula that was offered in high schools, which detracted the amount of time that students were learning important academic content. The report characterized the declining nature of education as an extremely serious problem that required immediate attention. The Commission also noted its confidence that educators, legislators, and the public could address the risk presented by public education by creating "a learning society" in which American education institutions would offer opportunities and choices for all persons to learn throughout their lives.

The Commission's Recommendations

The report stressed the urgent need to place education at the top of the nation's agenda. The Commission made 4 major recommendations and 32 implementing recommendations. The Commission called for higher standards in education in issuing the following recommendations:

1. State and local high school graduation requirements should be strengthened. The decline in academic standards was, in large part, due to the view espoused by the educational establishment that schools should solve personal and social problems that afflict society. To address these needs, the proponents of the high schools as multiservice agencies believed that high schools should offer curricula aimed at developing the child in areas other than traditional academic achievement. According to the Commission, this "curriculum smorgasbord," which included too many nonacademic courses, resulted in lower academic expectations and standards. To combat this trend, the Commission called for all high school students to take the following courses (called the new basics): 4 years of English, 3 years of mathematics, 3 years of science, 3 years of social studies, and ½ year of computer science. The commission also recommended 2 years of foreign language for students planning to go to college.

2. Schools, colleges, and universities should adopt more rigorous and measurable standards for academic performance and student conduct. Moreover, state and local education agencies need to have strategies to determine how much students are actually learning. The Commission further suggested that college and universities raise their requirements for admission.

3. Schools should devote significantly more time to learning the new basics. This would require more effective use of the school day or lengthening the school day or year. The Commission suggested that schools should last 7 hours per day for between 200 and 220 days a year.

4. Teacher preparation should be improved by strengthening teacher training. Moreover, teaching had to be made a more rewarding and respected profession. This could be accomplished by (a) requiring pre-service teachers to meet high educational standards, to demonstrate an aptitude for teaching, and to demonstrate competency in their academic disciplines; (b) increasing salaries for teachers, making them market-sensitive and performance-based, and developing evaluation systems on which to base salary, promotion, tenure, and retention decisions; (c) placing teachers on 11-month contracts to ensure time for curriculum and professional development; (d) creating career ladders for teachers that distinguish among beginning instructors, experienced teachers, and master teachers; (e) developing alternative methods to certify qualified persons as teachers to solve the problem of teacher shortages; (f) providing incentives, such as grants and loans, to attract outstanding students to the teaching profession; and (g) using master teachers to design teacher preparation programs and to supervise probationary teachers.

The Commission recognized the difficulties and obstacles to carrying out the reforms that they suggested; nevertheless, they expressed confidence that America could achieve these reforms. Moreover, educators and elected officials should be held responsible for providing the leadership required to achieve these reforms. The Commission also noted the importance of parents and students to achieving the Commission's educational goals.

The Controversy

The Commission's troubling list of findings and provocative language led to a firestorm of controversy. Proponents of the report lauded *A Nation at Risk* as the opening salvo in an attempt to save public education from sinking into irrelevance and mediocrity. They claimed that the Commission's report led to 2 decades of reform, eventually culminating in the No Child Left Behind Act.

Opponents of the report denounced *A Nation at Risk* as a politically motivated document that was based on inaccurate findings and misleading recommendations. Moreover, other opponents, even within the White House, denounced the report because they believed that the recommendations, which did not include any mention of issues such as vouchers and school choice, were banal suggestions that would not lead to meaningful improvements in education.

Education in America
20 Years After *A Nation at Risk*

In *A Nation at Risk,* the National Commission on Excellence in Education identified what it believed to be a rising tide of mediocrity in American education and noted that to improve the education of its youth, Americans had to thoroughly commit to quality education. In 2003 the Koret Task Force on K–12 Education, a team of educational experts brought together by the Hoover Institution, examined the progress that education had made in the 20 years following the publication of *A Nation at Risk.*

In its report, *Our Schools and Our Future: Are We Still at Risk?* the Koret Task Force wrote that the tide of mediocrity was still on the rise in American education. In fact, numerous measures of educational outcomes revealed very little improvement since the publication of the report. Moreover, only a few of the Commission's original recommendations had been adopted, and the call for excellence that *A Nation at Risk* had prescribed needed renewed commitment. Additionally, the Koret Task Force noted that to achieve meaningful structural changes in education, Americans needed to demand educational accountability, choice, and transparency.

According to the Task Force, the Commission that produced *A Nation at Risk* had also failed to address two major shortcomings of the American educational system. First, the Commission primarily addressed secondary education and had paid scant attention to K–8 education and the problem of children receiving an inadequate education in their early years, which led to failure in the later years. Second, the Commission had failed to confront the monopolistic nature of American education. Because it had not examined the issues of

power and control in education, it did not challenge the system's lack of meaningful accountability mechanisms and tangible incentives to improve. Additionally, the Koret Task Force noted that the Commission had underestimated the power of the nation's colleges of education, which too often imposed, on future teachers and administrators, ideas of how children were to be educated, despite the fact that too often there was no evidence of effectiveness of these theories.

The Task Force concluded that fundamental changes were needed in the following three areas: accountability, choice, and transparency. In the area of accountability, every state and local educational agency needed to adopt statewide academic standards, statewide assessments of student and school performance, and statewide systems of incentives tied to academic results. Choice meant that parental decisions rather than bureaucratic regulations should drive education. Thus, charter schools, voucher experiments, and incentives and rewards for excellent teachers and administrators should be encouraged. Finally, transparency meant that parents, teachers, and policymakers need to know exactly how schools and students are performing. Having rigorous indicators of student and school progress was essential for improvement. According to the Koret Task Force, accountability, choice, and transparency are essential if America education is to be reconstructed in ways that will help to achieve the results envisioned by the Commission in *A Nation at Risk.*

Conclusion

The message of *A Nation at Risk* was that curricular offerings in schools must be improved and that educators must be prepared properly in order to ensure that all students receive an excellent education. Although many question whether the report actually led to reforms in public education, there are few who question the political impact that the report had on American education. *A Nation at Risk* certainly captured the public's attention and initiated a dialogue about improving and reforming education that continues to this day. More than 25 years after its publication, *A Nation at Risk* continues to be an important part of the debate regarding education in America.

Mitchell L. Yell

See also Accountability Era; Achievement Gap; Federal Educational Reform; No Child Left Behind Act (NCLB); Standards Movement

Further Readings

National Commission on Excellence in Education. (1983, April). *A nation at risk: The imperative for educational reform.* Washington, DC: Education Publications Center. Retrieved July 28, 2009, from http://www.ed.gov/pubs/NatAtRisk/index.html

Peterson, P. E. (2003). *Our schools and our future: Are we still at risk?* Stanford, CA: Hoover Institution.

NATIVE AMERICAN EDUCATION

Since Europeans began colonizing what is now known as North and South America, there have been deep disagreements between colonists and their descendants and Native Americans about how and what Native American children should learn. In many pre-Columbian societies, education focused on survival skills, cultural maintenance, and technological adaptation. To a great degree, this style of education persisted among Native American societies until they came in close contact with European and American colonists. Though "schools" as institutions were rare before 1492, hieroglyphic writing among the Maya likely required intensive, formalized study. In the 16th century, Spanish Catholic priests trained Indian "notaries" to keep public records in indigenous languages across Mexico and Central America.

Before the American Revolution, Protestant missionaries founded schools for Native American children. In Massachusetts, John Eliot established several schools for "praying Indians." Along with Algonquin translators Nesuton and others, Eliot published a Massachusetts translation of the Old and New Testament, the first book printed in the colonies. Dartmouth and Harvard Colleges were both founded in part to Christianize Indian students. In areas subject to Spanish and French control, few schools were opened.

In 1819, the U.S. government authorized $10,000 per year for education under the Indian Civilization Act. The money was distributed to missionary groups to establish schools in order to introduce the "habits and arts of civilization." Teachers were also expected to promote government policy, including westward removal of native tribes. Many schools used Native language as a medium, and literacy in some Indian languages grew among tribes not subject to removal. Nearly half of the 147 Indian schools in existence in 1861 were administered by the Cherokee, Choctaw, Creek, and Chickasaw Nations in present-day Oklahoma, and funded by government annuity payments. The Cherokee national school system taught students in English and Cherokee, the latter using a syllabary created by Sequoyah in the 1820s.

Indian education policy changed abruptly after the Civil War. Though President Ulysses S. Grant's "peace policy" maintained the paternalistic outlook of earlier approaches, missionary control of Indian schools was formalized under the Board of Indian Commissioners. Aiming to eliminate corruption in the Indian Service, government leaders concentrated on efficient use of funds in Indian schools, which often led to underfunding. English-only policies were implemented, and Indian school curricula began focusing on industrial and vocational education. Seeking to "Americanize" Indian children, the government supported off-reservation boarding schools. Carlisle in Pennsylvania and Hampton in Virginia were among the best known of these schools. In these schools, reformers sometimes disagreed about the capacity of Indian students to become "civilized," but nearly all agreed on the necessity to "Americanize" the Indian students.

Resistance to boarding schools was often strong in Indian communities. The mortality rate at boarding schools was high, and Indian children were often removed from their homes and taken to school by force. When students did return home, they were often ignorant of tribal customs and languages and had to relearn practices or face ostracism. For those who remained in White communities, racism and discrimination reminded "civilized" Indians that they remained apart from both worlds. Within schools, students were often hungry, housed in dilapidated facilities, subjected to humiliation and punishment if they spoke their own language, and taught by underprepared teachers who relied on a regimented curriculum.

Reform of Indian education became a priority in the 1890s. Commissioner of Indian Affairs Thomas Morgan attempted to standardize Indian education after finding incompetent teachers, low enrollment, and poor conditions at many schools. In 1901, superintendent of Indian Schools Estelle Reel published the *Uniform Course of Study*, which concentrated on domestic and manual training and limited academic subjects. The U.S. government initiated federal support of public schools for Indian students in 1891, and by 1930 the majority of Indian students attended public schools.

The Meriam Report of 1928, a comprehensive review of Indian policy, instigated a series of reforms in Indian education, including curricular revisions, improved training for teachers and administrators, better attention to students' home lives, improved school facilities, fewer boarding schools, and the end of half-day work for students. In a few schools, Dewey-inspired reforms led to the publication of culturally informed textbooks and courses on Indian crafts. The Johnson O'Malley Act of 1934 formalized federal compensation to states for the costs of enrolling Indian children in public schools and, for a time, limited the educational role of the Bureau of Indian Affairs (BIA).

World War II priorities resulted in limited federal funding for Indian education, though other important changes occurred. Military deployments exposed many young Indians to life beyond the reservations and propelled changes to Indian education, including expanded school construction. On the Navajo reservation, for example, a 5-year plan to expand schools included Navajo-language textbooks and bilingual teacher-interpreters to ease the transition into school. At the same time, New Deal–era reforms came under pressure in the 1950s, with the Eisenhower administration favoring termination of the Indians' "communistic" tribal status. In 1952, approximately 40% of Indian students were enrolled in public schools, 30% in Bureau of Indian Affairs schools, and 8% in mission schools. The remaining 22% were not in school.

The 1960s were a decade of major reforms in Indian education. Early in the decade, the federal government focused on expanding access for Indian students, particularly on the Navajo reservation and Alaska, where most students attended boarding schools. School leaving continued to be a major concern, as did funding and overall institutional quality. The decade's most important reform, however, was in the expansion of community control of local schools.

The first community-controlled school funded by the federal government was the Rough Rock Demonstration School near Chinle, Arizona, on the Navajo Nation. Opened in 1966, the school became a model for community political control, bilingual/bicultural curriculum, and local participation. The school also functioned as an employment and cultural center for the area, which led to some criticism of the school's academic rigor. The establishment of Rough Rock and other community-controlled schools highlighted the poor state of Indian education, which was augmented by reports of abuse at the Chilocco Indian School and publication of the 1969 Kennedy Report on Indian Education. Repeating many of the findings and recommendations of the 1928 Meriam Report, the Kennedy Report harshly criticized the BIA and public schools for denigrating Indian students, devaluing their communities and culture, and perpetuating a cycle of poverty that contributed to academic failure for many Native American children.

During the late 1960s and 1970s, Indian activists protested for changes in Indian policy. Starting in November 1969, a group of Indians occupied Alcatraz for 18 months to publicize the failure of the U.S. government to honor the 1868 Laramie Treaty provisions that redundant federal properties would be returned to tribes. In 1973, tribal political tensions led to the takeover of the Wounded Knee church by some members of the American Indian Movement, to which the federal government responded with a blockade of the town with 15 armored personnel carriers and at least 130,000 rounds of ammunition. American Indian Movement activists also seized the BIA headquarters in Washington, D.C. This was also a period of literary renaissance, with works by Native American authors Vine Deloria, Jr., Leslie Silko, N. Scott Momaday, and others gaining wide readership.

Three important legal changes also occurred during this time. Congress passed the Bilingual Education Act in 1968, which led to expanded training for new BIA teachers in 1969 and other program developments in the early 1970s. The Indian Education Act of 1972 expanded community control of education funding on reservations, in urban areas, and for Indians in the eastern United States. Three years later, the Indian Self-Determination Act formally reversed the federal policy of termination of federal–tribal relations and expanded the community control through the contract system to include health and welfare.

The election of Ronald Reagan to the presidency stalled the expansion of programs for American Indian students, and many schools struggled to find resources and materials on local languages and history. A 1988 BIA report found that Indian children were enrolling in public schools at higher rates and that achievement was similar to that of other children in similar socioeconomic and sociocultural circumstances. The Native American Languages Act of 1990 reinforced the federal policy of self-determination and the right of Indian children to study in their tribal language. Broader changes in education policy were also being felt in Indian education. The Indian Nations at Risk Task Force of 1991 mirrored President George H. W. Bush's goals of "readiness," "achievement," and "restructuring" while reinforcing the need for culturally appropriate curricula, highly qualified Native teachers and Native language programs.

Many of the challenges identified in the myriad reports on Indian education remain today. While acknowledging the central role of Native languages, legislation such as the No Child Left Behind Act of 2001 requires Indian students to demonstrate proficiency only in English. Indian leaders have also fought against proposed "official English" laws, fearing that under such laws the Native languages could no longer be taught in public schools. Out of the reform movements of the 1960s and 1970s, American Indian educators have organized efforts to promote culturally appropriate schooling and favorable legislation through a variety of means, including the National Indian Education Association, regional and local groups, and outreach to national educational associations.

Christopher J. Frey

See also Bilingual Education; Federal Educational Reform; Meriam, Lewis

Further Readings

Restall, M. (1997). Heirs to the hieroglyphs: Indigenous writing in colonial Mesoamerica. *The Americas, 54,* 239–267.

Reyhner, J., & Eder, J. (2004). *American Indian education: A history.* Norman: University of Oklahoma Press.

Szasz, M. C. (1999). *Education and the American Indian: The road to self-determination since 1928.* Albuquerque: University of New Mexico Press.

NEILL, A. S. (1883–1973)

Alexander Sutherland Neill was a Scottish educator, author of 21 books, and founder of the well-known Summerhill School, the world's first progressive and democratic school. Neill's unconventional and radical beliefs about children were shaped by his early experience and his educational philosophy. His revolutionary teaching practices stimulated much controversy during his lifetime and have an impact on current-day education. The progressive and democratic school movement inspired by Neill's education philosophy and practice has found adherents around the world. Neill's child-centered democratic approach to schooling is still regarded as innovative and refreshing in a world where conventional education continues to become ever more controlled and standardized.

Early Life and Career

Neill, one of seven sons of a village schoolteacher, became a problem child for his poor achievement at strictly controlled schools. His teaching career started at age 15 when he worked as a pupil teacher for his father at Kingsmuir Village School. Later, he received a teaching certificate, went to Edinburgh University, and received an M.A. in 1912. Before World War I, he became the headmaster of the Gretna Green School in Scotland. He found conventional school practices extremely oppressive and futile, so he started to write and publish his discontent in his *Dominie* series (*dominie* means teacher in Scottish), *A Dominie's Log* (1915), *A Dominie Dismissed* (1917), *A Dominie in Doubt* (1920), and *A Dominie Abroad* (1923).

Influenced by progressive educator Homer Lane, psychoanalytical innovator Wilhelm Reich, and Freudian psychoanalysis, Neill rejected traditional ideas about how children should grow and learn.

He advocated a child-centered theory of education and practiced it in his Summerhill School, believing that all children are good, and if left alone without adults' interference and the coercion of traditional schools, they are capable of self-governing, motivating, and directing their own life and learning. He also promoted personal freedom and rights opposing the imposition of strict Victorian moral standards on children. To him, to be antisex was to be antilife; for this statement he was also highly criticized. He believed it was against the law to punish children physically and to force them to do things not by their own will, except out of consideration for others. He traced many adulthood psychological problems to childhood unhappiness, repression, and deprivation of freedom. Neill, however, had to convince the skeptical world of the value and practicality of his unconventional beliefs and teaching methods. They were absolutely revolutionary and dissenting in the 1920s and described as anarchic at that time.

In 1921, Neill chose Dresden, Germany, to found the *Neue Schule* ("New School"), an international school to experiment with his unconventional curriculum and methods. This predecessor of Summerhill School was forced to move several times in Europe because of political turmoil and opposition from local authorities. In 1923, the school was moved to a house called Summerhill in Lyme Regis, England, and thus acquired its name. In 1927, Neill moved Summerhill School to Leiston, Suffolk, in England, where Neill lived and worked for the rest of his life.

As a small, coeducational, self-governing boarding school, Summerhill School enrolls a variety of problem children rejected by traditional schools. Children are put in houses by age groups with house mothers. As Neill wanted to make the school fit the children instead of making the children fit the school, he renounced all discipline, all direction, all suggestions, all moral training, and all religious training. At Summerhill, children are given absolute freedom to choose what they want to do and what they want to learn. Neill offered private lessons to students who wished to study with him on self-selected topics. In this do-as-you-please school, class attendance and extracurricular activities are optional. Students hold weekly meetings, *Schulgemeinde,* to make and enforce rules agreed upon by the entire school community with

one vote from each student and teacher. Neill was described as making wonders with disturbed children with his extraordinary blend of gruff humor, intuition, and patience.

During the 1930s, Summerhill School became internationally known for its self-governing student-teacher body and its flexible curriculum. In Neill's words, the school stopped being an experiment and became a demonstration that proved freedom worked. The school operates on these tenets—democracy, equality, and freedom. Neill went on several lecture tours, and wrote more books, including *The Problem Child* (1927), *The Problem Parent* (1932), *That Dreadful School* (1937), and *The Problem Teacher* (1939). As Neill challenged the established educational practices and beliefs, many people felt threatened. As a result, he generated fierce debates about alternatives to conventional schooling and received frequent harsh and often inaccurate criticisms of his progressive philosophy. He was criticized as being naive, unrealistic, idealistic, and morally indifferent.

Legacy of A. S. Neill

In his lifetime, Neill challenged educational convention with total faith in children's ability to direct their own learning, advocacy for children's rights and freedom, refusal to conform to popular moral and academic standards, and emphasis on children's emotional happiness and character development. He created a school community in which children are free from adult authority and practice democratic values within the educational curriculum and education process itself.

By the 1960s, his radical humanistic approach to child rearing gradually gained popularity. It greatly influenced the dissenting alternative school and free school movements of the 1970s in the United States, West Germany, and Japan. By the 1970s, Neill's *Summerhill: A Radical Approach to Child-Rearing* (1960) had sold 2 million copies and was used in many American university courses. Modern American dissenting progressive educators, such as John Holt (1923–1985) and John Taylor Gatto (1935–), have adopted and updated Neill's democratic tenets of education to today's education in America. As a major proponent of homeschooling and father of the unschooling movement, Holt believed that traditional schooling with standard curricula and conventional grading methods are counterproductive to the education of children. Gatto, a radical critic of the compulsion-based schooling, asserts that standardized tests are useless indicators of proficiencies and wants children to be engaged in authentic learning and have choices in what they do.

As the best-known British progressive educator of the 20th century, Neill was recognized by the *Times* (London) *Educational Supplement* as one of the 12 people who had most influenced British schooling during the last millennium. His dissent from conventional schooling practices found a welcome audience among some educators in the United States as well.

Guofang Wan

See also Alternative Schools; Free School Movement; Goodman, Paul; Holt, John; Illich, Ivan; Kozol, Jonathan

Further Readings

Croall, J. (1983). *Neill of Summerhill: The permanent rebel*. New York: Pantheon.

Neill, A. S. (1927). *The problem child*. London: Herbert Jenkins.

Neill, A. S. (1932). *The problem parent*. London: Herbert Jenkins.

Neill, A. S. (1937). *That dreadful school*. London: Herbert Jenkins.

Neill, A. S. (1939). *The problem teacher*. London: Herbert Jenkins.

Neill, A. S. (1960). *Summerhill: A radical approach to child rearing*. New York: Hart.

Neill, A. S. (1972). *Neill! Neill! Orange peel!* New York: Hart.

Neill, A. S. (1975). *A dominie's log*. New York: Hart. (Original work published in 1915)

NEOCONSERVATIVES

Neoconservatives formed a new conservative political movement in reaction to the growing influence of liberalism in American life in the 1960s and 1970s. Most neoconservatives were former liberals themselves but drifted toward conservatism and away from the Left because they had come to believe that liberalism had failed to live up to its promises. Neoconservatism, or the "new" conservatism, initially focused on an increased aggressiveness in U.S. foreign policy to thwart threats to its position as an international superpower. One of the threats the neoconservatives wanted to confront related to educational policy and practice. As a consequence, they acted aggressively to foster reforms they perceived would make the United States both educationally and economically more competitive.

Today the movement continues to also play a major role in national policy development in areas such as poverty, welfare, and education. Protection of individual rights and responsibilities, equitable opportunities, and minimal governmental interference with free enterprise are the dominant positions supported by neoconservatives.

Educational Reform Influence

The neoconservative movement has been influential in recent educational reform. Based on a free market fundamentalism, neoconservatives seek educational privatization and commercialization by replacing K–12 public schools with corporate-owned and corporate-operated schools. They believe offering options through school choice will increase effectiveness and efficiency in the educational system. They also seek to create a competitive market in deregulating teacher training and certification by allowing private for-profit training enterprises to compete with higher education institutions. Applying a business model of competition and efficiency to learning, neoconservatives believe quality will be guaranteed, as the most effective models will rise to the top. Accountability, as demonstrated through the No Child Left Behind Act, along with national standards, testing, and curriculum, will help cement the lost traditions of competition and discipline in education and ensure success, according to the neoconservatives.

Early Development

Michael Harrington, a political activist, first popularized the term *neoconservative* in a 1973 *Dissent* article, in which he applied the label to liberals of the time who had moved toward the political Right in addressing welfare issues.

Contemporary neoconservatives came into the limelight in the 1970s, but their impetus began earlier. A number of prominent neoconservatives emerged from the Jewish academic-intellectual world disillusioned with the direction of 1960s liberalism. The radical anti-Americanism espoused by some figures associated with the anti–Vietnam War movement deeply offended those later who became known as neoconservatives.

One political theorist who influenced the articulation of the neoconservative philosophy is Irving Kristol, considered the "godfather" of American neoconservatism. Kristol was the managing editor (1947–1952) of *Commentary* magazine, often referred to as the "neocon bible." He was the first to formulate the movement's aspirations. In the 1970s, as liberal Democrats took political advantage of the Watergate scandal that brought down the Nixon administration, two forces emerged to foil the American liberal point of view and traditional conservatism: neoconservatives and the religious New Right.

Early differences between neoconservatives and traditional conservatives, sometimes referred to as paleoconservatives or the Old Right, were their perspectives on the welfare state, civil rights, and communism. Traditional conservatives wanted to dismantle the welfare state. Neoconservatives' approach was not to dismantle the welfare state, but to stop its expansion. This was a major shift in conservative thinking. They also supported civil rights for minorities in America. Early on, traditional conservatives opposed any federal legislation forbidding racial discrimination, but eventually they supported it.

Both neoconservatives and traditional conservatives were against communism but from opposite viewpoints. Neoconservatives emphasized communism's external threats to the United States. They considered communism as an enemy of freedom and democracy. Traditional conservatives were more concerned with the internal subversive threats of communism. They believed communism's internal and external spread was a threat to American religious beliefs and values.

Early neoconservatives were the first to refute the liberal Left in their own language and apply social science methods to support their positions. Couching new arguments in the liberal Left's lexicon, neoconservatives used the law of unintended consequences to document the failure of the 1970s court-ordered school busing as an example. Traditional conservatives argued that the government's mandate of forced school busing disrupted local communities and uprooted neighborhood children. Neoconservatives documented that forced busing had failed to bring about the intended results of government intervention. With the use of data and analysis, they argued that racial harmony did not progress as anticipated, and student learning for all children did not increase due to busing.

Point of View

No single political position represents all present-day neoconservatives. Some consider neoconservative ways of thinking as a philosophical movement rather than a political position. However, most neoconservatives share in some common approaches in analyzing the social world. In general, neoconservatives believe in individual rights and responsibilities, minimal government intervention, and equality of opportunity; they reject simplistic solutions to America's social problems.

Neoconservatives support individual rights and condemn unequal treatment. However, they reject liberalism's strategies in remedying social inequities. Historically, neoconservatives have not supported affirmative action, governmental poverty programs, or income redistribution through tax incentives. For most neoconservatives, these liberal solutions perpetuate inequities rather than diminish them. They believe the government is obligated to protect individual rights and welfare without creating special consideration for just a few, because to do so creates an unfair playing field.

Neoconservatives also reject the liberal point of view that structural barriers to upward social mobility cause low aspirations and low achievement or dependence on social welfare payments. Rather, they believe individual behaviors cause poverty, and structural barriers are only secondary to these associated problems. They believe where poverty does exist, it is because of individual choices, and it is not the government's responsibility to provide everyone economic stability. According to neoconservatives, most legislative programs to remedy poverty only foster government dependency and discourage self-sufficiency.

Neoconservatives are critical of simplistic liberal solutions to social constraints. Socialistic endeavors to remove the poor's economic deprivation do not address the larger issues underlying these social challenges. Simply removing economic restraints does not guarantee an emergence of individual self-direction and upward mobility. Neoconservatives perceive American society as having social problems, which government intervention may or may not solve.

Neoconservatives prefer to reflect on fundamental principles when addressing issues and unintended results of social actions. They question the obvious solutions supported by liberal thought. For example, is money really the best solution to poverty? Does poverty cause crime? Is equality for all obtainable and desirable? Neoconservatives believe a welfare state of economic equality has value, but they question social and economic systems supported by liberals as the most efficient ones to implement without harming the individual rights of others.

Sharon C. Hoffman

See also Affirmative Action; Busing; Equity; War on Poverty

Further Readings

Buras, K. L., & Apple, M. W. (2008). Radical disenchantments: Neoconservatives and the disciplining of desire in an anti-utopian era. *Comparative Education, 44*(3), 291–304.

Kristol, I. (1995). *Neoconservatism: The autobiography of an idea.* New York: Ivan R. Dee.

Saltmann, K. (2005). *The Edison schools: Corporate schooling and the assault on public education.* New York: Routledge

Schneider, G. L. (Ed.). (2003). *Conservatism in America since 1930.* New York: New York University Press.

Steinfels, P. (1979). *The neoconservatives: The men who are changing America's politics.* New York: Simon & Schuster.

New Commission on the Skills of the American Workforce

The National Center on Education and the Economy is a nonprofit organization that sponsored the efforts of the New Commission on the Skills of the American Workforce (NCSAW). The purpose of the NCSAW was to analyze the current education and training systems in America and to generate processes and policies that would ensure that the United States continued to compete in a global market. To meet this demand the Commission conducted international industry and workforce development studies, generated several staff research papers, commissioned expert papers from the field, interviewed experts, and engaged in 13 international organization visits. This research and analysis led to the report titled *Tough Choices or Tough Times,* which was released on December 14, 2006. Reports such as these establish the foundation for many of the calls for reform that are evident within the policy-making community.

The first Commission on the Skills of the American Workforce generated a report titled *America's Choice: High Skills or Low Wages.* This initial report indicated that if America wanted to continue to compete on the international market, it would have to produce a highly educated workforce that would be able to compete with other countries to produce high-skilled labor. The low-skilled jobs were already being outsourced to other countries that could provide laborers at a lower cost. If the United States desired to continue to educate its workforce at the current low level to keep low-paying jobs at home, it cautioned that employees would need to change their expectations of their standard of living and work for lower wages and longer hours. The solution offered was to raise the bar in terms of the workforce's educational level to compete with other countries for high-skilled careers.

The New Commission's research revealed that over the past few decades, other countries have been producing a more educated workforce. These workers are more educated and more willing to work for lower wages. Thus, these countries are not only competing for the low-skilled, low-wage jobs but also for those high-skilled careers that require an education while still offering low wages. Technological advances have made it possible to communicate across the globe in literally seconds; this allows industries to outsource various jobs within an organization without losing production time.

The authors of *Tough Choices or Tough Times* espouse that the United States needs to produce a workforce that can think ahead creatively to produce those products and services that might not even be available or imaginable. The report lists a series of 10 steps to produce the necessary skilled workforce so the United States can remain competitive in the worldwide market. These 10 steps are not merely a call for a superficial revision of the current K–12 system, they are a strong message that the current system needs to be reformed and significantly changed to address the competing demands of a global market.

Step 1: Do the Right Thing the First Time. A series of state, national, and international board exams will be generated. The first of these exams might come at the end of 10th grade and can be taken again if it is not passed initially. The standards for these exams will be set by the countries that are successful in educating their students and consist of a "pass" benchmark that is no lower than the level needed to attend a community college. Individuals who meet specified benchmarks will be guaranteed attendance at a 2-year college or will stay in high school and take a second exam for the privilege of attending a 4-year college. Graduates of the 2-year programs can also take this second exam to move forward. The 2-year colleges will have articulation agreements with 4-year state colleges.

Step 2: Make Efficient Use of Resources. The monies saved from Step 1 will be allotted to (a) hiring highly skilled graduates as teachers, (b) constructing a PreK program for 3- and 4-year-olds, and (c) providing funds for disadvantaged students.

Step 3: Build a Top-Notch Teaching Force. To produce a creative, innovative workforce, the United States needs teachers who are highly skilled and are top-level graduates. To recruit these individuals, teachers will have to be paid wages competitive with business and industry. Teachers would be state employees.

Step 4: Create a Performance-Based Curriculum. For students to meet the demands of current and future business needs, individuals will need specialized skills (e.g., creativity, ability to work with others as a team, self-discipline, organization), and SCANS (Secretary's Commission on Achieving Necessary Skills, adopted by the Secretary of Labor in 1992). The educational system should rework the current standards, assessments, and curriculum to ensure that required skills are being taught and assessed for mastery.

Step 5: Construct Performance-Based School Systems. The management, organizational, and governance structures of schools have to change. School districts would write contracts with independent contractors to run the schools, collect performance data, and connect individuals with area social services. The schools would be self-governed public schools funded by the state. More money would be given to schools that serve challenged and economically disadvantaged students.

Step 6: Create PreK Opportunities. Funds will be committed to developing PreK opportunities for 3- and 4-year-olds. These early opportunities will provide a feeder of better-prepared students into kindergarten.

Step 7: Fund Support for Disadvantaged Students. Funding will be an incentive for schools to provide assistance to specific populations by perhaps extending the school day, offering tutoring, or providing screening and diagnosis services, among other programs. Incentives to schools and teachers will ensure that disadvantaged students will receive the best services possible.

Step 8: Provide Education Opportunities to the Current Workforce. The current workforce will be offered learning experiences at no cost to continue their education so they can meet the standards on the board exams that the 16-year-olds will take in 10th grade. Meeting these standards will ensure that these individuals have the opportunity to attend college.

Step 9: Create a Lifelong Learning Fund. The government would deposit $500 at birth and thereafter $100 per year up to the age of 16 into every citizen's educational account. Others can contribute to the account; however, the money can be used only for educational purposes.

Step 10: Create Regional Authorities. Legislation will be written to create regional authorities whose goals are to develop strategies and objectives to assist each region's educational and training systems in meeting labor market needs.

The NCSAW authors caution that these recommendations will not be easy to implement; however, if a new system is not built soon, the United States will lose its competitive edge. The recommendations outlined in *Tough Choices or Tough Times* were directed more toward the states and were not meant to be limiting or narrowly prescriptive. The authors encourage variations in specific state programs, but they also make clear the need for significant educational reform.

Qetler Jensrud

See also Education Commission of the States (ECS); No Child Left Behind Act (NCLB); School-to-Work

Further Readings

Commission on the Skills of the American Workforce. (1990). *America's choice: High skills or low wages.* Washington, DC: National Center on Education and the Economy.

National Center on Education and the Economy: http://www.ncee.org

National Commission on Excellence in Education. (1983). *A nation at risk.* Washington, DC: Author.

New Commission on the Skills of the American Workforce: http://www.skillscommission.org

New Commission on the Skills of the American Workforce. (2006). *Tough choices or tough times.* Washington, DC: National Center on Education and the Economy.

Secretary's Commission on Achieving Necessary Skills. (1991). *What work requires of schools: A SCANS report for America 2000: Executive summary.* Washington, DC: Author.

NEW ENGLAND PRIMER, THE

For more than 150 years *The New England Primer*, often called "the little Bible of New England," served as the principal textbook for millions of colonists and early Americans. First compiled and published circa 1688 by Benjamin

Harris, a British journalist who emigrated to Boston, it gained popularity not only in New England but also throughout colonial America and parts of Great Britain with estimates of copies sold from 6 to 8 million by 1830. Less than 100 pages in length, this early textbook proved significant in both reflecting the norms of Puritan culture and propagating those norms into early American thought. In *The New England Primer,* Harris provided a tool of reform that promoted literacy, proliferated compulsory education, and solidified a Calvinist ethic in colonial America.

The historical milieu in which the primer emerged contributed to its rise to prominence. In 1630 a group of Puritans settled the Massachusetts Bay area with the goal of developing a society based on biblical principles as embodied by the English Reformation. The doctrine of the priesthood of the believer motivated Puritans to teach reading to all citizens so that they could know and follow the Christian scriptures. As early as 1642, Massachusetts law required literacy instruction to all children, servants, and apprentices. The 1647 Old Deluder Satan Act—in order to ensure that "learning may not be buried in the grave of our forefathers"—required every township of 50 households to hire a teacher. Towns twice that size were mandated to set up schools that would prepare students for Harvard. With only the hornbook and Bible available in most schools, New England was ready for a textbook that would be affordable, portable, and compatible with the predominant worldview.

Borrowing principles from Comenius's *Orbis Pictus* and his own *Protestant Tutor*, Harris incorporated crude woodcut illustrations and religious content to teach reading skills and to encourage rote memorization of Calvinist doctrine. Graduated literacy instruction began with the alphabet, simple letter combinations, and syllables, increasing to complex sentences intended for rote memorization. Themes of sin, death, punishment, salvation, and respect for authority were displayed through alphabetic rhymed couplets, poems, prayers, and scriptures. The theme of punishment, for instance, was exhibited in the rhyming couplet for the letter *F:* "The idle fool/Is whipt at school." Such themes for a child's textbook may seem morbid in light of Jean-Jacques Rousseau's notions of childhood innocence, but they would not seem so to Puritan families who embraced the doctrine of infant corruption caused by the original sin of Adam.

The primer was reproduced by a variety of publishers, resulting in 450 editions by 1830. Adaptations were printed for various geographic regions and ethnic groups, such as the 1781 *Indian Primer* printed in both Mohawk and English languages. With each new edition came content changes, though the core elements of the pictured alphabet and catechism remained constant. The couplet for the letter *A* never changed—"In Adam's fall/We sinned all," but many of the others were modified to reflect evolving political or religious beliefs. For instance, independence from Britain saw the alteration of "Our king the good/No man of blood" to "The British king/Lost states thirteen" and later to "Queens and kings/Are gaudy things." One of the most blatant political alterations was made in 1776 when an image of King George III was simply relabeled with the name of John Hancock.

The influence of the Great Awakening brought about several changes to the primer. For example, the couplet for the letter *C* was amended from "The cat does play/And after slay" to "Christ crucify'd/For sinners dy'd." The Great Awakening's influence shifted the primer's emphasis from God's wrath to God's love and contributed to the addition of more prayers and hymns, such as Isaac Watts's "Cradle Hymn." As moral education became more secularized, the emphasis on punishment and sin softened. For example, in later versions, consuming fire as a punishment was replaced with the threat of having treats taken away. Literacy as a means to finding eternal salvation was replaced in one 1790 version as a path to financial security, and in an 1819 edition, the rhyme for *K* expressed the value of play—"Tis youth's delight/To fly their kite."

Various adaptations included the Lord's Prayer, Apostles' Creed, Ten Commandments, Westminster Shorter Catechism, John Cotton's *Milk for Babes,* and the common children's prayer "Now I Lay Me Down to Sleep." Also present in some editions was an account of John Rogers's martyrdom accompanied by a woodcut of his burning at the stake while his wife and children watched. The catechetical drill included some of the following questions: "What is the chief end of man?" "What is the first commandment?" "What is faith in Jesus Christ?"

Later, such secular questions were included as "Who saved America?" and "Who betrayed America?"

Though criticized for depicting children as depraved and for using God as a metaphor to manipulate submission to the political and religious authority of New England, the primer made a lasting impact on the moral landscape of America. Of the millions printed, fewer than 1,500 copies remain, the earliest having been published in 1727. This relatively low number of surviving texts indicates the constant use the primer received and the impact its principles had on the development of American values. The multiple editions of existing copies serve as a valuable record chronicling the changes in early American philosophy of education.

Samuel James Smith

See also Calvinist Schools; McGuffey Readers; Old Deluder Satan Law; Religion and the Curriculum

Further Readings

Cohen, D. A. (1976). The origin and development of *The New England Primer. Children's Literature, 5,* 52–57.

Crain, P. (2000). *The Story of A: The alphabetization of America from* The New England Primer *to* The Scarlet Letter. Stanford, CA: Stanford University Press.

Ford, P. L. (Ed.). (1899). *The New England Primer.* New York: Dodd, Mead.

Watters, D. H. (1985). "I spake as a child": Authority, metaphor and *The New-England Primer. Early American Literature, 20,* 193–213.

NO CHILD LEFT BEHIND ACT (NCLB)

The No Child Left Behind Act (NCLB) is a complex and controversial federal educational reform initiative that was signed into law in 2002. It was a reauthorization of the Elementary and Secondary Education Act of 1965. NCLB dramatically increased federal mandates and requirements on states and public school districts and schools. In fact, NCLB represented the most significant expansion in U.S. history of the federal government into education. At the same time, NCLB gave states a great deal of flexibility in determining how they will implement much of the law.

Much of the political impetus for the passage of NCLB was provided by the results of state and national assessments of student progress, particularly the National Assessment of Educational Progress, which had shown that student achievement in reading and math had remained stagnant over the previous 40 years despite massive infusions of federal money. These facts led legislators to argue that the federal educational funds should be spent in a more effective manner and should be tied to measures of accountability. Specifically, NCLB was a reaction to low academic achievement in general, and reading in particular, by America's students. For the first time, the federal government in NCLB began requiring states and school districts to use numerical data to provide evidence of improved student outcomes.

The primary purpose of NCLB was to ensure that students in public schools achieved important learning outcomes while being educated in safe classrooms by well-prepared teachers. To accomplish these goals, NCLB required that states develop challenging academic achievement standards and assess public school students annually on their progress toward meeting these standards. Specifically, public schools were required to ensure that all public school students would reach proficiency in reading, math, and science by the 2013–2014 school year. NCLB included three mandates to reach this ambitious goal: accountability, evidence-based instruction, and highly qualified teachers.

Accountability for Results

The law focused on increasing the academic performance of all public school students and improving the performance of low-performing schools by requiring that states establish their own standards of what students should know and be able to do in reading, math, and science. The statewide standards also enabled stakeholders (e.g., teachers, administrators, parents, and the general public) to understand and compare the performances of schools against the standards for proficiency set by the states. The law also required every state to develop or adopt an assessment, which was aligned to the state standards, to measure students' academic performance.

NCLB required that all public school students in Grades 3 through 8 (and once in high school) be tested on their state's assessment instrument. Furthermore, schools had to test at least 95% of their students, including at least 95% of students in each of the following subgroups: (a) low-income students, (b) students with disabilities, (c) students with limited English proficiency, and (d) students from racial and ethnic groups. The test scores of these subgroups would then be disaggregated and reported separately, in addition to being reported as part of the entire student body of a school.

States were also required to develop benchmarks that schools had to meet in reading, math, and eventually science. Students would take the assessments, and the states would score and report the results of the tests. State officials would then determine the levels of student achievement in all public schools within the state and compare the test results to the benchmark to determine if the school or school district was making adequate yearly progress (AYP) toward meeting the state standards. The AYP benchmarks represented proficiency targets that schools and school districts had to meet to ensure that all students would meet the 100% proficiency goals in reading, math, and science by the 2013–2014 school year. These targets progressively increased the percentage of students in a school who were required to show proficiency on the statewide assessment. If the target percentage of students in a school met the targets, then the school made AYP. If the target percentage of students in a school did not meet the target, the school did not make AYP. In such situations, the law mandated that corrective actions be taken.

NCLB also had specific requirements of schools that did not make AYP. If a school failed to make AYP, this information was to be published and disseminated to parents, teachers, and the community. The state also provided technical assistance to help the school. Schools that did not make AYP for 2 consecutive years were designated in need of improvement and had to offer the parents of students in the school the option of transferring to another public school within the district. If a school failed to make AYP for 3 consecutive years, the school would additionally offer supplementary services, such as private tutoring, to low-income students. If a school failed to meet AYP for 4 consecutive years, the school would take additional corrective actions, such as implementing a research-based curriculum or appointing an outside expert to advise school officials. If a school failed to meet AYP for 5 consecutive years, the school would need to take corrective actions that involved major restructuring of the school, such as replacing all or most of a school's staff or entering into a contract with an entity, such as a private management company, to operate the school.

Scientifically Based Instruction

Prior to the passage of NCLB, there had been a number of national efforts to ensure that teachers across the nation use instructional procedures that have been validated as effective by scientific research. For example, in 2002 both the National Research Council and the Coalition for Evidence-Based Policy issued reports stating that education will see progress only if educators built and used a knowledge base of educational practices that rigorous research has proven effective. The second major principle of NCLB, therefore, required that federal funds be expended to support *only* educational activities that were proven by scientifically based research to improve the achievement of students. This meant that there was reliable evidence that a program was effective.

Many legislators believed that schools had used programs and practices based on fads, fancy, and personal bias rather than evidence that these practices had a positive effect on student achievement. All too often, such practices had proven to be ineffective and, unfortunately, the victims of such ineffective practices were students. NCLB, therefore, emphasized using educational programs and practices that have been demonstrated to be effective by rigorous scientific research. Rod Paige, secretary of the U.S. Department of Education, noted that the intent of NCLB was to require that rigorous standards be applied to educational research and that research-based instruction be used in classroom settings. Furthermore, he asserted that states must pay attention to this research and ensure that teachers use evidence-supported methods in classrooms.

Highly Qualified Teachers

The third principle of NCLB required that all teachers in public schools be highly qualified in the core academic subjects that they taught (i.e., English, reading/language arts, mathematics, science, foreign languages, civics, government, economics, art, history, and geography). NCLB included three requirements that public school teachers had to meet to be considered highly qualified. Teachers had to (1) hold a minimum of a bachelor's degree, (2) have full state teacher certification or licensure, and (3) demonstrate subject matter competency in the core academic subjects in which they taught.

The Controversy

Despite being very bipartisan legislation and passing the House and Senate by large majorities, NCLB has been a controversial law. Critics of the law have focused on five primary areas of controversy. First, there was not enough federal money in the statute to pay to implement the federally funded mandates of NCLB. Thus, states have had to divert educational resources to meeting these mandates. Senator Edward Kennedy and Representative George Miller, both of whom played a large role in drafting the NCLB legislation in 2001, and Arne Duncan, President Obama's Secretary of Education, have called for increased federal funding of the law. Second, because states were allowed to set their own proficiency standards, some states set their standards so low that schools could achieve them too easily. Thus, their standards were essentially meaningless. Third, the accountability mechanism of the law, which called for annual testing and comparing a school's results to the proficiency standards set by states, was too blunt an instrument because schools either passed or did not pass, and no provision was made to differentiate struggling schools whose students were making good academic progress even though they still did not make AYP, and schools that were not making reasonable gains at any level. Fourth, some critics noted that once-a-year assessments were not adequate measures of student learning because they are summative evaluations, which do not provide the data necessary to allow teachers to alter their instruction in an effort to improve student achievement. Fifth, NCLB's emphasis on teacher credentials before they enter the classroom may not have been an adequate method to raise the quality of the teaching force and that a teacher's effectiveness in actually raising student achievement would be a more appropriate indicator.

In 2007, the Commission on No Child Left Behind, which was cochaired by former Health and Human Services Secretary Tommy Thompson and former Georgia Governor Roy Barnes, issued their report titled *Beyond No Child Left Behind: Fulfilling the Promise to Our Nation's Children.* The Commission found that NCLB had accomplished much by setting public education on a productive course and spurred some improvement through its emphasis on accountability. The Commission also noted, however, that many children were not achieving high standards in every state and that struggling schools were not improving as effectively or rapidly as hoped. The report addressed many of the concerns and controversy regarding NCLB and suggested remedies for these problems. The following are a few of the Commission's recommendations: (a) Allow states to include achievement growth in their AYP calculations, (b) allow states to adopt formative assessment systems as tools to improve instruction rather than merely relying on one statewide assessment at the end of the year for accountability purposes, (c) include the subject of science in AYP calculations, (d) develop a national model for content and performance standards, (e) develop a national model for statewide accountability tests based on the NAEP, (f) assess the quality of teachers based on their effectiveness in raising student achievement rather than just by qualifications for entering the classroom, and (g) require states to certify principals as highly effective principals by producing improvements in student achievement that are comparable to similarly situated high-achieving schools.

Conclusion

No Child Left Behind directly affected America's public education system by requiring that school districts be held accountable for making real improvements in student outcomes. The law accomplished this by (a) requiring that states use numerical data to provide evidence of student outcomes, (b) mandating that federal funds be spent only on reading and math programs that have been proven effective by scientifically based instruction, and (c) that all teachers in public schools be highly qualified.

Mitchell L. Yell

See also Elementary and Secondary Education Act; Evidence-Based Education (EBE); Federal Educational Reform; *Nation at Risk, A;* Scientifically Based Research

Further Readings

Commission on No Child Left Behind. (2007). *Beyond No Child Left Behind: Fulfilling the promise to our nation's children.* Washington, DC: Aspen Institute. Retrieved August 2, 2009, from http://www .aspeninstitute.org/policy-work/no-child-left-behind

U.S. Department of Education. (2002). *No Child Left Behind: A desktop reference.* Washington, DC: Education Publications Center. Retrieved August 2, 2009, from http://www.ed.gov/admins/lead/account/ nclbreference/reference.pdf

Yell, M. L., & Dragsow, E. (2005). *No Child Left Behind: A guide for professionals.* Upper Saddle River, NJ: Pearson/Merrill Education.

No Child Left Behind–School Partnerships

For years, researchers, policymakers, and educational administrators have acknowledged that there is a profound gap in educational outcomes among children of different races, backgrounds, and cultures, particularly between poor children from ethnic minority groups and children from the White middle class. Due to disparities among students' learning levels, race/ethnicity, and socioeconomic factors, as well as demographic changes in society, programs targeted for extended learning and school improvement must meet the needs of the whole student and include academic, physical, social, emotional, and mental health resources. The fact is that many students face problems that hinder their success in school. Moreover, many schools and districts work with limited resources and lack the infrastructure needed for school and student success. Responding to the need to provide alternate learning environments, Congress passed the No Child Left Behind Act (NCLB) in 2001. The NCLB raised the bar by issuing policy-based incentives that were created to force schools to reach proficiency on state-level mandated tests. Significantly, NCLB required that schools and districts draw upon the powers of parents and members of community agencies to provide supplemental educational services to schools. The proposed mandates must be met, regardless of the viewpoints of districts and schools.

NCLB requirements necessitate that school and district leaders have the knowledge and skills necessary to engage community partners in whole-school reform planning related to student achievement. Importantly, they must draw upon the resources and power of parents and the communities for students' alternative academic needs and work to involve partners in whole-school systemic improvement efforts. The requirement is that all students achieve proficiency, in math and reading by 2014. The aim is that all schools and districts meet adequate yearly progress (AYP). This means that schools and districts plan AYP goals and set specific targets for all students, including subgroups such as students with limited English proficiency, students with disabilities, students with different ethnic and racial backgrounds, and low-income students. To measure progress toward the goals, NCLB requires states to annually test students in Grades 3 through 8. The districts and schools that continue to fail to make AYP are subject to sanctions that include corrective actions and restructuring. Importantly, the districts and their schools have to target school improvement strategies that assist in planning and meeting goals. Parents and community organizations who demonstrate the ability to positively impact achievement, particularly for low-income and minority students, are then chosen to provide supplemental education services.

School accountability systems, improved instructional practices, and school community alliances are not isolated entities and must work collectively to bring about desired instructional improvement. The premise is that the partnerships work together to meet and enhance the instructional needs of educational programs in schools. Alternatively, many school districts, especially those in low-income and isolated rural areas, have children and families with inadequate health care. Some may not have access to adequate health care. Furthermore, many of those districts do not have school psychologists or social workers and need health care partnerships that provide case management services for families and children in need of

outside supports. These connections are important in the prevention of future problems and play important roles in the development of effective school–community partnerships.

In addressing some of these concerns, principals should understand the importance of good community relationships. This requires school leaders who are collaborative, are goal centered, have visionary leadership, and are able to engage community partners in a whole-school reform effort for school improvement. Importantly, they should make every effort to be communicators who have the ability to involve various stakeholders in a systemic effort of school improvement. Although the partnership effort should be designed to meet the needs of the entire school or district, individual student needs should be targeted in the plan. This should involve community stakeholders who represent parents, community and business organizations, higher education and university personnel, mental health and social agencies, law officials and legal representatives, and state department officials and policymakers. Such a collaborative union promises to provide an infrastructure that will represent a variety of human, financial, and technical supports that will address and benefit student performance and foster positive community relationships.

Parents, educators, policymakers, and youth-serving organizations have come to view after-school programs as a promising strategy to promote intentional learning. Significantly, schools receive external support services from relationships with families, businesses, community service personnel, health agencies, and higher education institutions. The results of those partnerships have assisted in enhancing student achievement by providing support and needed services for schools, teachers, educational leaders, and all concerned stakeholders. The school partnerships connect families, local community members, local business leaders, local and state agencies, and other organizations in the school improvement process.

Prior to NCLB, the partnerships were committed to whole-school planning of the school improvement effort, which included needs assessment, goal setting, and process planning. The focus was on strengthening the academic environment and assisting school leaders in improving the organization structures within the school by tapping community resources with academic supports. Professional development activities that related to district needs as well as parent and community responsibilities were provided and integrated in district and administrative policies. School administrators and leaders, district and teaching staff, as well as entire district and school personnel were equipped to participate in the school reform effort. Additionally, school-level objectives, plans for implementation, and evaluation criteria were created and disseminated to the public. The school team consisted of administration, faculty, staff, and state and local partners who were vested in the school improvement effort. Procedures for evaluating goals, objectives, and outcomes in relation to the school improvement process were articulated and evaluated for constant improvement. The current NCLB policy has forced community partners to add assessment criteria related to accountability sanctions to their planning efforts.

Community Resources

The rapid expansion of extended learning opportunities for schools to link with parents and communities has several advantages. First, in addressing their children's educational needs, parents are given choices and options for selecting organizations identified by school districts. Second, the fiscal incentives designed by NCLB entice and motivate competition among service providers. Lastly, parents and community organizations servicing the after-school and enrichment programs are chosen based on their ability to offer research-based plans and practices.

The major focus of school improvement is that schools and districts infuse their strategic planning efforts with goals and objectives that focus on positive academic outcomes. Schools alone do not have the infrastructure to build the social and developmental foundations needed for all students to achieve academically. However, they have been provided meaningful opportunities to partner with community stakeholders in order to provide challenging enrichment and educational services to meet the challenging needs of all students. Close collaboration with schools is considered critical to efficient service provision. Some of the community resources and services that may be of greatest value to schools in meeting student needs and positively influencing student achievement are discussed next.

Parents

Parent involvement is one of the most important elements for student success and is an essential component of the school improvement process. With regard to NCLB, school districts (local education agencies) must sign agreements with supplemental education providers to offer educational services to students in schools that do not meet the AYP standards. Providing information and engaging parents, especially parents from historically underrepresented groups, plays a key role in forging positive relationships with families. Significantly, NCLB stipulates that schools and districts prepare and report academic achievement results to parents to inform them of the progress of their schools. Districts are not required to arrange for the provision of supplemental educational services for a student unless the parent of the student has requested the service. However, the local education agencies must inform the parents of the availability of the services. Parents may also apply to become certified supplemental educational service providers.

Community-Based Organizations

For the most part, community-based organizations have a vested interest in the success of school districts in their community. These organizations usually have the willingness, concern, and ability to recognize and meet the needs of schools. Prominently, ground broken by NCLB offers the availability of multiple community organizations to provide supplemental educational services after the regular school day. However, these providers must be certified by the state education agency as qualified to enable students to achieve proficiency on state academic assessments. Examples of potential community partnerships include chambers of commerce, faith-based initiatives, government entities (e.g., the mayor's office), and community civic leaders. Local businesses such as banks, newspaper organizations, service clubs, and union and trade associations also are influential community resources, as are members of local ethnic and language minority groups.

Health and Social Services

Children's academic success depends on their maintaining mental and physical health. This group of service providers can assist schools in maintaining the health and well-being of children and their families. They may help schools by offering in-school agency services or by providing services to assist in matters such as prevention of substance abuse and child abuse. They may also provide individual and family counseling services to families.

Institutions of Higher Education

Colleges and universities are open to school partnerships, and many are already investing in K–12 education by assisting schools in school improvement efforts. These alliances enable institutions of higher education to increase their enrollment, keep abreast of current educational issues, and apply theories and research. Some of those endeavors include assisting in curriculum design, overseeing business management, designing professional development for teachers and administrators, providing strategic reform efforts, and sustaining learning environments. In addition, many colleges of education have professional development schools that combine the knowledge and skills of schools and universities to develop the instructional performance of teachers. Some colleges and universities utilize student interns in providing supplemental educational assistance to schools and districts.

Business and Industry

Businesses can be influential and powerful entities in partnership efforts. They are excellent resources for funding and providing instructional materials. Many businesses and industries also serve as valuable resources in policy and planning management, implementation, and outcome of the school improvement process. Most businesses have a vested interest in the schools in their community because they have a need for qualified personnel in prospective employees. Businesses may also provide internships and mentorship programs for students. Examples of these partnerships include utility companies, corporations, banks, insurance companies, real estate agencies, management firms, and credit unions.

Federal and State Government

All districts and schools can benefit from state and regional agencies in school improvement efforts. Sources may include regional education liaisons, educational research–based agencies, state and local legislators, state government agencies, and state departments of education. Many of these programs are funded by federal programs and grants. Federal and state programs also fund the cost of providing after-school tutoring or academic enrichment programs for school districts. The sources can be tapped for staff development and training as well as strategic planning support.

NCLB requires schools to develop community practices that deal with accountability, standards, and assessment and utilize community resources more effectively by requiring research-based plans and services. Student achievement and the provision of needed services for schools, teachers, educational leaders, and other stakeholders have been enhanced by the mandate. Additionally, parents provided with choices of supplemental educational services for their children give them a voice in decisions affecting their children's educational outcome. As a result, many failing schools and districts improve. Significantly, relationships formed with families, businesses, community service personnel, health agencies, colleges and universities, and other external support services are seen as vital to the achievement of successful student outcomes.

Brenda F. Graham

See also Accountability Era; Achievement Gap; Assessment; No Child Left Behind Act (NCLB)

Further Readings

Epstein, J. E. (1998). *Critical issue: Constructing school partnerships with families and communities.* North Central Regional Educational Laboratory. Retrieved August 2, 2009 from http://www.ncrel.org/sdrs/areas/issues/envrnmnt/famncomm/pa400.htm

Epstein, J. L. (2001). *School, family and community partnerships: Preparing educators and improving schools.* Boulder, CO: Westview Press.

Public Education Network. (2002). *Using NCLB to improve student achievement: An action guide for community and parent leaders.* Washington, DC: Author.

Public Education Network. (2007). *Open to the public: How communities, parents and students assess the impact of the No Child Left Behind Act, 2004–2007, The realities left behind.* Retrieved July 23, 2008, from http://www.publiceducation.org/nclb_main/2007_NCLB_National_Report.pdf

U.S. Department of Education. (2002). *No Child Left Behind: A desktop reference.* Washington, DC: Author. Retrieved July 1, 2008, from http://www.ed.gov/admins/lead/account/nclbreference/reference.doc

U.S. Department of Education. (2005). *No Child Left Behind: Supplemental educational services: Non-regulatory guidance.* Retrieved July 23, 2008, from http://www.ed.gov/policy/elsec/guid/suppsvcsguid.pdf

NORMAL SCHOOLS

Normal schools were American educational institutions that were, initially, focused on training teachers to work in the nation's common schools. The first U.S. normal school was founded in 1839 in Lexington, Massachusetts. The institutions quickly spread to neighboring states, then to the entire nation. The normal school movement was a necessary feature of 19th-century American life because of two phenomena. First, the proliferation of free public education—first across the North and then the South in the aftermath of the Civil War—meant that large numbers of teachers were needed to staff the schools of the emerging public school movement. Second, because American colleges and universities did not begin to accept teacher education as a legitimate academic function until the late 19th and early 20th centuries, there was a market demand for teacher training institutions. Not all teachers were, or were even required to be, trained at a normal school. Many teachers were simply hired without any formal training. In many midwestern states, for example, less than half of the teaching force had attended a normal school of any kind.

In addition to the teacher training function, many normal schools established "practice schools" to function in tandem with the normal school. Practice schools were regular tuition-based schools for school-age children. The normal school students often "practiced" teaching in these schools under the supervision of normal school faculty. Normal schools existed as publicly subsidized "state" institutions and as private and proprietary schools.

Aspiring teachers studying in the normal school were usually confronted with a 19th-century epistemology known as the "branches of knowledge." The normal school curriculum was divided between the common branches (e.g., reading, writing, basic arithmetic) and the higher branches (e.g., anthropology, chemistry, history). Through a process of lecture, drill, and recitation, normal school students were expected to demonstrate they had memorized relevant facts and could answer likely questions about the topic at hand.

After the American Civil War, many private and proprietary normal schools expanded their academic offerings to include an array of subjects, including pharmacy, medicine, law, telegraphy, and dentistry, among other subjects. Because of the lack of agreement over what constituted appropriate training in many professions, normal schools were able to offer degree or certificate programs to aspiring professionals in these fields. At their height, normal schools rivaled or surpassed regular colleges and universities in terms of student enrollment. For example, National Normal University in Lebanon, Ohio, enrolled over 2,000 students annually between 1885 and 1893, making it the largest school of any kind in Ohio and one of the largest in the country. Another normal school of national fame was New York's Oswego Normal School. Rising to prominence in the 1860s and presided over by Edward Sheldon, the Oswego Normal School was an early pioneer of Pestalozzian (i.e., object-based) teaching methods.

Normal schools went into decline in the early 20th century as a result of several factors, including increasing teacher education requirements, the increasing availability of public high schools (which limited the need for the "practice schools" associated with the normal schools), and the embrace of teacher education as an academic discipline by colleges and universities. Moreover, the training requirements for other professions were also becoming more standardized (e.g., organizations of physicians, pharmacists, and other professions were effectively raising the training requirements for practitioners in their respective fields).

In their demise, normal schools met one of two fates—closure or metamorphosis. The private and proprietary institutions, often depending on student tuition for operating money, were, by and large, closed. Many public normal schools, however, were able to survive and find new life as state teachers' colleges and, later, as state universities. Western Kentucky University and the University of Southern Mississippi are two examples of normal institutions that were able to transition to the status of a state university.

There is a paucity of book-length studies on the normal school movement. Significant treatments include Willard Elsbree's *The American Teacher* and Jurgen Herbst's *And Sadly Teach: Teacher Education and Professionalization in American Culture*. One notable exception to the lack of recent research on normal schools is Christine Ogren's *The American State Normal School: "An Instrument of Great Good."* Ogren's contribution is that she explains how state normal schools adapted to survive and how larger forces caused the weaker and less adaptable normal schools to become extinct. Research on the private normal schools is hindered by poor record-keeping. According to Ogren, there were many more private normal schools than public institutions, but through institutional events such as changes in ownership and administration, records were lost.

Nancy Beadie's edited *Chartered Schools: Two Hundred Years of Independent Academies in the United States, 1727–1925* contains insightful chapters devoted to the history of the American academy movement, forerunners to and contemporaries with normal schools. Another genre of book-length treatments are those published by state teachers organizations detailing the history of teacher education in various states. Among the best of these is Robert Potter's *A History of Teacher Education in Hawai'i*. Two article-length treatments pertaining to normal schools include David Diener's *The Intellectual Climate of the Late Nineteenth Century and the Fate of American Normal Schools* and Nathan Myers's *American Pestalozzianism Revisited: Alfred Holbrook and the Origins of Object-Based Pedagogy in 19th Century America*.

Nathan R. Myers

See also Academies; Herbartian Movement; Oswego Movement; Pestalozzianism; Schools of Education; Teacher Institutes

Further Readings

Beadie, N. (Ed.). (2002). *Chartered schools: Two hundred years of independent academies in the United States, 1727–1925*. New York: RoutledgeFalmer.

Diener, D. (2008). The intellectual climate of the late nineteenth century and the fate of American normal schools. *American Educational History Journal, 35*(1), 61–79.

Elsbree, W. S. (1939). *The American teacher: Evolution of a profession in a democracy*. New York: American Book Company.

Herbst, J. (1989). *And sadly teach: Teacher education and professionalization in American culture*. Madison: University of Wisconsin Press.

Kaestle, C. F. (1983). *Pillars of the republic: Common schools and American society, 1780-1860*. New York: Hill & Wang.

Myers, N. R. (2007). American Pestalozzianism revisited: Alfred Holbrook and the origins of object-based pedagogy in 19th century America. *American Educational History Journal, 34*(1), 85–96.

Ogren, C. A. (2005). *The American state normal school: "An instrument of great good."* New York: Palgrave Macmillan.

Potter, R. (1995). *A history of teacher education in Hawai'i*. Honolulu: Hawai'i Education Association.

NORTHWEST ORDINANCE

The Northwest Ordinance (1787) was an act of the U.S. Congress, which provided an outline for how the "Old Northwest" territory would achieve statehood. Prior to the 1787 Ordinance, the Land Ordinance of 1784 established that the area would be divided into states, and the Land Ordinance of 1785 provided that the territory, and future states, would be divided into townships. The Northwest Ordinance of 1787 superseded the 1784 Land Ordinance, while supplementing the Land Ordinance of 1785. In effect, the Northwest Ordinance sustained the previous federal policy of supporting public education in the form of land grants in the territories of the Old Northwest.

The Old Northwest was composed of the current U.S. states of Ohio, Indiana, Michigan, Illinois, and Wisconsin. Federal land in this area was sold to the privately held Ohio Company, led by Connecticut-resident Manasseh Cutler, on the condition that the land company would develop the area according to the guidelines set forth in the 1785 and 1787 ordinances. The Northwest Ordinance of 1787 established that once the population reached 60,000 inhabitants, the territory could draft a constitution and apply for statehood. This ordinance resembled portions of the U.S. Bill of Rights and guaranteed freedom of religion, habeas corpus, and trial by jury; prohibited slavery; and guaranteed Native American property rights.

The policy for the settlement of the Old Northwest, laid out in the Ordinance of 1785, was modeled on New England's Township form of government. Unlike the Land Ordinance of 1785, which specified that a one-square-mile section of each township be dedicated to the support and establishment of public schools, the 1787 Ordinance simply encouraged the establishment of schools. The absence of an actual mechanism for establishing and supporting public schools in the 1787 Northwest Ordinance was an apparent endorsement of the plan established by the Land Ordinance of 1785. Another educational precedent in the Land Ordinance of 1785 was the provision that two townships in each state be set aside for the establishment of universities. In the following years, all of the states of the Old Northwest accepted a state responsibility toward free, public education in their state constitutions and built public institutions of higher learning.

The mechanism by which this land was to be converted to support education was by land rentals. The practice of renting land to support education was an English practice, carried to the New England colonies. Recent scholarship has established that although the spirit of the Northwest Ordinance aimed to support free public schooling through land grants, often the grants did not translate into significant revenue for schools. Because there was an abundance of available land, the school lands often sat vacant, producing no financial support. Another shortcoming of the land-grant policy was that land was often sold immediately for pennies on the dollar or was leased on permanent leases, thus insulating the renters from paying market rates in future years. In *A History of American Education,* Joseph Watras argues that the money generated from the sale or

rental of these lands was often used for noneducational purposes, as a result of little to no oversight by the Continental Congress. As a result, abuses were present in the system and the land grants produced much less support for public schools than was originally thought.

Whereas the land-grant policy of the 1785 Land Ordinance (and its subsequent acceptance by the Northwest Ordinance of 1787) was perhaps flawed in execution, in intent the policy was arguably sound. The Northwest Ordinance was passed by the Congress which was still operating under the Articles of Confederation. In the period prior to the existence of the U.S. Constitution, the federal government was considerably weaker than the domestic and foreign power which would emerge in the 19th century. Under the Articles of Confederation, the U.S. Congress was funded at the leisure of the states. In the absence of significant revenue, one of the most valuable commodities the pre-constitutional federal government possessed was federal land. By establishing that schools would receive a portion of the Old Northwest territory, Congress, essentially, marked the first federal legislative provision for the education of American citizens.

More important than the commitment to land grants for schools, however, was the plan that the Northwest Ordinance set forth for populating the territory. The Northwest Ordinance of 1787 settled the question of whether the United States would grow as an empire, allowing the original 13 states to claim, settle, and govern distant western lands; or grow as a republic, allowing local populations of citizens to create and elect representative state governments. The civic stability afforded by the Northwest Ordinance's stance on republican government encouraged settlers to migrate west and become actively concerned about building the foundations for lasting communities, including schools. This was due to the fact that settlers were assured that they would be governed by their peers, locally. The commitment to eventual statehood had at least as much to do with the relative success of public schooling in the region as did the land grants targeted for schools.

In sum, the Northwest Ordinance of 1787 can be viewed as a document that accomplished two important purposes. First, it implicitly continued the township settlement policy laid out in the Land Ordinance of 1785, thereby continuing the federal practice of giving a portion of the land of each township in support of public education and two townships in each state to support universities. Second, the ordinance established a pathway to statehood for populations in the region and ensured that citizens would be governed locally, taking active concern in their communities and its schools.

Nathan R. Myers

See also District Schools; Federal Educational Reform; Local Control; Rural Education

Further Readings

Cremin, L. A. (1980). *American education: The national experience, 1783–1876.* New York: Harper Colophon.

Kaestle, C. F. (1983). *Pillars of the republic: Common schools and American society, 1780–1860.* New York: Hill & Wang.

Onuf, P. S. (1987). *Statehood and union: A history of the Northwest Ordinance.* Bloomington: Indiana University Press.

Urban, W. J., & Wagoner, J. L. (2000). *American education: A history* (2nd ed.). New York: McGraw-Hill.

Watras, J. (2008). *A history of American education.* New York: Pearson.

OFFICE OF ECONOMIC OPPORTUNITY (OEO)

The Office of Economic Opportunity (OEO) was created in 1964 to carry out the mandate of the Economic Opportunity Act. The OEO sponsored many of the most important social, economic, and educational initiatives to come out of President Lyndon B. Johnson's Great Society and War on Poverty. The OEO coordinated the Job Corps, Neighborhood Youth Corps, and other vocational training and study programs, as well as a "domestic Peace Corps" named Volunteers in Service to America (VISTA) and the community action program (CAP) that led to the early-childhood Head Start program. Arising out of an optimistic view of government's power to effect social change through education and access to opportunity, the War on Poverty, and the OEO in particular, represented a high water mark for the involvement of social and educational theorists in determining the social policy of the American government.

When President Johnson, a Democrat, created the OEO, he retained control of it by keeping it under the Executive Office of the President where he felt that it could avoid becoming part of the Washington bureaucracy. The first director of the OEO, Sargent Shriver, drafted much of the Economic Opportunity Act and had helped create the Peace Corps. Prior to entering the Kennedy administration, Shriver had worked with urban Catholic schools in Chicago and had served as president of the Chicago Board of Education.

Shriver saw to it that OEO programs were designed to maximize local community control, and reflected the influence of the late President Kennedy's Mobilization for Youth Program, which organized and coordinated educational and community efforts aimed at lowering juvenile delinquency.

Unlike welfare programs, the philosophy behind the OEO programs was to provide the poor with opportunities for advancement through education and training. The Job Corps, for example, was an attempt to provide urban and rural poor young adults, many of whom were high school dropouts, with vocational and technical education that would prepare them for quality jobs. "At-risk" youth from social environments where drug use and crime were rampant became the target for this "second chance" vocational education program. Job Corps was patterned on the Civilian Conservation Corps (CCC) of the 1930s, and Job Corps candidates were also often relocated from their hometowns to other cities to receive their training.

Unlike the CCC, the Job Corps relied on the private, for-profit sector to serve as partners in the training and employment effort. Large corporations like Xerox, Westinghouse, and Litton Industries were deeply involved with many Job Corps centers. Long before the notion of "privatization" of federal programs became popular, the Job Corps served as a government conduit to private businesses interested not only in government contracts but in participating in this great social experiment.

Volunteers in Service to America (VISTA) was a program that appealed to the altruism of many individual Americans who wished to serve disadvantaged populations. Like the Peace Corps, VISTA relied on individuals who agreed to leave their homes to volunteer among the poor for set periods of time. Qualified volunteers worked directly with neighborhood and community organizations to combat malnutrition, inadequate housing, poor education, and other conditions associated with poverty. Active in cities, VISTA also served the rural poor in Appalachia and migrant farm workers in Florida, California, Texas, and other agricultural states.

Programs created by the OEO operated under the principle of "maximum feasible participation." This concept was enshrined in the notion of the community action program (CAP), through which OEO funds were to be spent on the local level. Designed to bypass the Washington bureaucracy and put control of programs into the hands of local people who understood local needs, the theory was often misapplied in practice. This created difficulties with mayors like Richard Daley of Chicago and Sam Yorty of Los Angeles who saw the federal government attempting to establish local patronage systems beyond the control of existing political structures. The fact that many of the urban poor who were expected to operate these programs had no experience developing and implementing educational, training, and health services left these programs vulnerable to radical activists who had no voice in the urban political system. Many CAPs fell victim to racial demagogues who used the CAPs to further their own activist ends in what the essayist and novelist Tom Wolfe, in *Radical Chic & Mau-Mauing the Flak Catchers* (1970), referred to as "mau-mauing."

The most enduring agency to come out of the CAP is the Head Start program. As early as the fall of 1964, many local officials were angered at the way that the OEO appeared to be bypassing their patronage systems and urged their governors to use their vetoes over OEO programs coming into their municipalities. Also, southern politicians resented the way in which OEO programs appeared to be empowering Black activists. Shriver, who had budgeted $300 million in 1964 for CAPs, was faced with the prospect of a substantial surplus as local political officials blocked OEO programs. There was also a "sympathy gap" between working- and middle-class Whites

and the young urban Black adolescents that the Job Corps and other programs were designed to assist. Unlike the young men who were helped by the CCC in the 1930s, the popular perception among many Whites was that urban high school dropouts were not societal victims but were rather victims of their own poor choices. But in a nation in which one half of the 30 million U.S. poor were young children, Shriver realized that no one could argue that a 3- or 4-year-old child was not a victim of poverty. He believed that a comprehensive early childhood health and education program could provide OEO with a wedge that would break through the resistance of urban machines and southern racists.

In 1964 there was very little research literature on early childhood education and development. The Head Start planning committee of pediatricians and experts on child development, retardation, and education urged Shriver to run a small, pilot program, but both Shriver and President Johnson wanted to create a program that would have an immediate and popular impact, a first volley in the War on Poverty that would involve at least 100,000 young children. When Head Start was established, a formal tea was held in the White House Rose Garden and the First Lady, Lady Bird Johnson, was announced as the chairperson of the program. Within a few months there were over 1,000 centers open around the nation offering a 2-week summer program for 3- to 5-year-olds.

Head Start had a "health first" emphasis, creating preschool programs intended to give children comprehensive health, social, educational, and mental health services. This environmental and "whole child" perspective reflected the ideas of Benjamin Bloom, J. McVicker Hunt, and Cornell child psychologist Urie Bronfenbrenner. These theorists, in general, believed that children were deeply affected by social and cultural environmental factors, and that early childhood was a stage in life during which intervention could have a lasting impact. At the level of the local Head Start center, however, there was always tension between the expert opinions of educational psychologists, developmentalists, and pediatricians and the language of "empowerment," community activism, and mobilization characteristic of the people who actually ran the Head Start centers. It was not until the mid-1970s that any sort of national performance standards were created for Head Start programs.

Head Start showed an almost immediate positive impact on children who were given IQ tests. This success led to the passage of amendments to the Equal Opportunity Act in 1966 and 1967, which greatly strengthened Head Start. The success was short lived, however, when in 1969 the Westinghouse Learning Corporation released data demonstrating that gains in IQ in children involved in Head Start "faded out" within a couple of years. Alternating between periods of favor and disfavor, Head Start was transferred to the Department of Health, Education, and Welfare's new Office of Child Development in 1969.

With the election of Richard Nixon, a Republican, OEO's days were numbered. Shriver resigned in 1969, and by Nixon's second term he was no longer requesting funds for community action programs. Like Head Start, other successful agencies within the Office had been transferred to existing federal departments, and Nixon ordered his director of the OEO, Howard Philips, to dismantle the agency. A series of federal lawsuits resulted in a ruling that the president could not refuse to spend funds already appropriated by Congress. Nixon's successor, Gerald Ford, finally closed the Office in January 1975, after securing most of OEO's functions either within existing departments or in his newly created Community Services Administration, which was itself abolished by President Reagan in 1981.

John J. White

See also Early Childhood Education; Federal Educational Reform; Head Start; Job Corps; Local Control

Further Readings

Hacsi, T. (2002) *Children as pawns: The politics of educational reform.* Cambridge, MA: Harvard University Press.

Sealander, J. (2003). *The failed century of the child: Governing America's young in the twentieth century.* Cambridge, UK, and New York: Cambridge University Press.

Zigler, E., & Styfco, S. (1993). *Head Start and beyond: A national plan for extended childhood intervention.* New Haven, CT: Yale University Press.

OLD DELUDER SATAN LAW

Among the forces that influenced British colonial life in America were an increased momentum for political self-determination, religious expression, and social change; and a desire to educate colonial children according to the principles of English society. To achieve the desired outcomes of these forces would require the unwavering commitment of every resident, all government officers, all church elders, and every parent. The common means to sustain colonial laws, religious precepts, and cultural mores would be assigned to the local school and the appointed teacher. Such was the rationale for an early attempt at educational reform—Massachusetts' Old Deluder School Law of 1647. Some historians regard the Old Deluder Law as an early step toward the beginning of public education in America.

The colonial citizenry were intent on upholding the basic tenets of Protestantism and ensuring the local schools' capacity to reinforce colonial customs. In its different forms, the religious force focused on the belief that humans could achieve, and should achieve, a higher level of perfection and moral conscience. The school was expected to function in a lockstep manner with both conventional church teachings and common laws.

Church elders and local government officers shared the belief that with continued waves of new immigrants coming to the colonies, it was the mission of schools to concentrate on reading, writing, and religious training, so as to minimize negative influences. The representatives of government and church strategically merged their interests with the passage of the Old Deluder Law, promulgated to ensure that Satan would not interfere with a child's opportunity to learn about the Bible and colonial common law.

The 1647 law established four requirements: (1) every town within the colony was to create a school, or if a school was not established, the town had to make payment to another nearby town to provide an education for their school-age children; (2) each town with 50 families or more was expected to provide a teacher for the purpose of providing instruction in reading and writing as well as in Latin; (3) each town with 100 families or more was expected to provide both an elementary school and a secondary school; and (4) residents were required to provide support for these schools. Some scholars have argued that the law presaged public financing of schools; others have opined that the law marked the beginning of public schools. In fact, the Old Deluder Law required no more than the selection of a teacher and support for the school, which often involved a mixture of tax and private support.

Colonial citizens were not universally concerned that Satan would lead Christians astray and "work his evil on the uneducated youth." Indeed, many citizens did not attach a high level of importance to this law. These dissenters viewed the law in a more pragmatic way. In their view, if the town had a very small number of school-age students that was less than required by law, no effort was made to establish a local school. Some citizens were more steadfast in their rejection of the local school concept. Even if there were a sufficient number of students to require a local school, the citizens would accept a monetary fine rather than create a school. In such instances, citizens considered the monetary fine to be less burdensome than having to find a teacher. Some citizens went so far as to mislead government officers and church elders into believing they were in compliance when, in fact, the citizens were only pretending to comply. Citizens would tell the government and church leaders they had hired a teacher to provide instruction, while the town shared a teacher with another town to give the impression that the law was being followed. In reality, neither town actually had hired a teacher; instead, the citizens tried to create the perception that a full-time teacher had been hired and, as a result, each town maintained an active school. To deceive government officers and church elders even more, citizens would not hire a full-time teacher but would have school be in session only while the General Court was in session. When the Court was not in session, the citizens would not maintain a school.

Contrary to the expectations of government officers and church elders, many parents believed they themselves, and not the local colonial school, had the primary responsibility for their child's education. Given this belief, some parents decided their children would not attend public school; instead, they would continue to educate their children at home. In this way the family, not the

school, remained the primary source of religious and educational training. Basic skills were to be taught in the home. If these skills could not be provided at home, then it was the responsibility of the government leaders and the citizens to decide if a school was even necessary in the town.

Patrick Michael O'Donnell

See also Calvinist Schools; Compulsory Attendance; *New England Primer, The*

Further Readings

Good, H. G., & Teller, J. D. (1973). *History of American education.* New York: Collier-Macmillan.
Odden, A. R., & Picus, L. O. (2004). *School finance: A policy perspective* (3rd ed.). Boston: McGraw-Hill.
Van Scotter, R. D. (1991). *Public schooling in America.* Santa Barbara, CA: ABC-CLIO.

ONLINE TEACHING

See Web-Based Teaching

OPEN EDUCATION

Throughout the early 20th century, progressive educationists argued for more child-centered and educationally relevant experiences for young people. Progressive educationists were countering a system of education that was often teacher centered, didactic, and controlled. Schools were organized with teachers at the front of the classroom and the students' desks in rows. There was limited flexibility because in many cases the students' desks were actually nailed or bolted to the floor. Open education emerged in the 1960s as a wide variety of educational critics such as John Holt and Herbert Kohl began to argue for more humanistic goals and classroom structures that would permit more individualization and personalization.

Early Innovators

Some suggest that the beginning of the open education movement can be traced to 1967 when a parliamentary commission in Great Britain asserted the need for more child-centered educational practices, including open classroom structures. Also working at this time were psychologists such as Jean Piaget who argued for the importance of working through the interests of the child and structuring learning centers in the classroom.

John Bremer was one of the early architects of the open education concept. In *Open Education: A Beginning* (with Anne Bremer) and in *The School Without Walls* (with Michael Von Moschzisker), he provided descriptions of what it means to create an open classroom environment. He was the first director of the Parkway Program in Philadelphia, and he was one of the first persons to assert that the traditional American comprehensive high school had reached the limits of its functional and educational utility. Bremer wanted a new kind of school where education could be individualized and children's interests could be explored. His ideas gained popularity and were eventually copied in a number of major urban centers, including schools in Chicago and Los Angeles.

Structural Characteristics

Open education is also known by many as informal education. It typically is contrasted with traditional or formal educational models. Open education treated space and time as flexible and provided a wide range of activities to children. The child was the center of the educational process and the child had considerable power to shape and guide interactions with the teacher. Students select their own materials; teachers are guides in the instructional process and help by identifying student academic weaknesses or needs.

In the traditional classroom, by way of contrast, space is treated as fixed and time is highly routinized. The teacher identifies the topics and the content to be covered; students do not direct or shape the instructional process; they respond, instead, to the guidance and direction of the teacher. Much of the work is whole-group oriented, and in most cases all the students in the class are engaged in or doing the same kind of work.

In most cases, schools do not fit nicely into one of these two classroom structure models. Clearly there is an educational continuum, with some schools being prototypic of open education and others being very traditional and structured. In the middle of the continuum are wide ranges of classroom and school types where teacher direction varies and student-initiated educational activities are, at times, encouraged if not provided.

Public policy has generally favored those arguing for traditional structures, but during the late 1960s and early 1970s a variety of child-centered advocates began to attack the ways in which schools were organized to educate the child. One of the harshest critics of the "accepted" practices was Herbert Kohl. Kohl observed in *36 Children* (1967) that many of the troubled urban schools were really the result of teachers' inabilities to reach out to the children and to make the learning process meaningful. In essence, the structure of the schools, a structure that was highly teacher focused in nature, mitigated the interests of the students and enhanced the likelihood that schools and classrooms would become unmanageable. That is, students became disruptive because they were simply uninterested and bored by what they experienced.

Does Open Education Work?

Results of the empirical research on open education are mixed and much of the conceptual work is ideological. Those advocating for open structures believe that children learn best by pursuing their own interests and making their own choices. Allow the child the freedom to learn and the child will make a decision that is both personally satisfying and educationally gratifying. In fact, what far too many educators found through open environments was that it was difficult to manage the classroom; with few restrictions on what students needed to do and accomplish, the level of off-task student behavior frequently escalated. Interestingly, it appears that many young people rejected open classroom structures (and the learning expectations associated with them) just as much as they appeared to reject traditional practices. Some researchers even concluded that teachers embraced open education because of personal insecurity; they were simply afraid of imposing their will on the children because they were afraid that the children would reject the educational opportunities they were offering.

The parents who visited open classrooms often were frustrated by the lack of structure, with children playing games, teachers being called (in some instances) by their first names, and everyone somewhat unfocused in terms of what educational objectives were being achieved. Parents also questioned what constituted the curriculum: What educational goals were established and what materials would be used to help students with their learning? On one level, open environments were "natural places" where the child could explore personal interests. On another level they appeared to be an educational free-for-all, and the critics questioned whether the students were learning any of the skills necessary for subsequent success in adult life.

Some researchers attempted to collect achievement data to determine what types of structures (open or traditional) were most efficacious. Unfortunately, a lot of the data were collected before good psychometrics were available to assess the value added to the educational experiences provided by the teacher. Further, operational definitions for *open education* are largely absent, so the term is often used in reference to a wide range of educational practices. Though the findings from different studies have been mixed, in general the students who were in more formal classrooms showed higher levels of achievement. One of the largest studies ever conducted involved approximately 18 schools in North Carolina. The classrooms were assessed for their "degree of openness," and the degree of openness scores were then connected to the students' achievement, attendance, and even self-assessment. None of the findings indicated statistical significance, and the researchers concluded that openness appeared to be disconnected from student achievement, though it may be connected to enhanced student creativity and attendance.

Potential Misunderstandings

Open education and open space education are not conceptually or practically equivalent. Open education describes a way of thinking about and organizing the classroom. Open space education deals more with the actual structural attributes of the school. True, there are definite connections between the two educational concepts, but they are not mutually inclusive. That is, a teacher could be practicing open education in a very architecturally traditional classroom with four walls and a chalkboard at the front of the classroom. A teacher could also be practicing a very traditional teacher-centered instruction in an open space school. In essence, the school's architecture or design does not dictate whether the program would be described as either traditional–formal or open–informal.

A lot of educational reformers embraced open education because they saw in the approach an ability to create educational environments that draw on the natural interests of the child. They asserted, often without any real evidence, that children would not only evidence more positive attitudes about school but they would also feel better about themselves and perform better academically. Research does not support these types of assertions, especially regarding academic achievement. In fact, research would suggest that although children in open classrooms often have positive attitudes toward themselves and others, they evidence no enhanced self-esteem or academic performance. Some researchers did find that children from particular types of socioeconomic backgrounds benefited in terms of their self-concepts in open environments, but equally true is the fact that some researchers have found that students from high-poverty environments often benefit most significantly from highly teacher-structured approaches.

One of the most significant synthesis reports ever completed on the overall effects of different types of educational programs (traditional vs. open) was published by Jeanne Chall in *The Academic Achievement Challenge* (2000). Chall's conclusions favored more traditional teacher-centered approaches and were much less favorable toward open structures. Indeed, one of her most prominent recommendations was that teachers should place a greater emphasis on "directing" the instruction process. She argued against progressivist ideas, especially when the educational process involved high-poverty students.

Chall's only caveat was that it was possible that learners who are just acquiring skills need the most structure, and learners who have progressed developmentally and have more mature, sophisticated understandings may be able to benefit in environments that are less formal and more open.

The Significance of Open Education

Educators historically have always looked for pedagogical "silver bullets." They have also evidenced significant ideological biases, and they have allowed those biases to influence how they thought classrooms and schools should be structured. For some, open education represented a silver bullet. They believed in the concept even though they did not have empirical evidence to support its use with young people. It just seemed like an intuitively and educationally good idea, and no doubt with some exceptional teachers open education did prove to be a powerful way of engaging students. Clearly, teachers are the key dynamic in the classroom. They make a difference and they may even make more of a difference than the parent, but unless teachers have incredible management skills and unless they know how to guide the learning process in highly individualized environments, the effectiveness of open education, especially with young children and students who come from high-need environments, is highly questionable. More to the point, there simply is not research available to support the use of open education structures with students who are young or come from high-poverty families.

Some reformers still embrace the open education approach, but in the current No Child Left Behind policy environment they tend to be individuals who are not directly involved in the education of young people or they are involved through private niche schools. The stakes associated with assessing and ensuring the progress of the students are so high for most schools that teacher-centered models have begun to reemerge as the dominant model for instructional delivery. No doubt there will be another swing at some point toward some form of open education, but given the apparent permanence of academic standards and the emphasis on global competiveness it is questionable whether schools will ever return to the type of open structures that were popularized and espoused during the 1960s and 1970s.

The unanswered question is whether some academic outcomes are possible with open education that are simply not achievable through traditional structures. It seems clear that the preponderance of research supports the use of traditional structures if the focus is strictly on short-term academic achievement. Many of the advocates of open education argue that schools are about much more than academic achievement, and the burden is really on them to demonstrate what might be possible

through open education that simply is not feasible through traditional structures. It remains to be seen whether new technologies will make it possible for educators to achieve both academic and effective outcomes in open education settings that to this point have not been realizable. It also remains to be seen whether teacher education institutions can "skill" or educate teachers to structure open environments in ways that have academic integrity and ensure that students are able to meet the academic content standard expectations that are prescribed by both states and local school districts.

Part of that teacher "skilling" process may be fostered with the significant advantages made possible through computer technology. The open education movement occurred at a time when students relied almost exclusively on the teacher for guiding, directly or even indirectly, the learning process. With the emergence of computer technology, classrooms can become more student centric and students can direct more of their own learning.

The teacher-centered model treats time as fixed (students have a defined and similar amount of time to learn the content) and the amount of learning that occurs, as a consequence, is variable because not all the students are able to learn the material in that fixed amount of time. In open education environments, time varies (students' instruction is more individualized) and learning outcomes vary, though all students should achieve more because they are fully engaged and directing their own learning. In the 1970s, the open education idea was compromised because neither the technology nor the teacher expertise (at least in most cases) were available to make the goals of open education achievable. In the early 21st century, the technology is available to "reinvent" the open education concept. What is not known is how and whether teachers and the political systems that support teachers will encourage such reform.

Thomas J. Lasley II

See Also Free School Movement; Progressive Education

Further Readings

Chall, J. S. (2000). *The academic achievement challenge: What really works in the classroom?* New York: Guilford Press.

Kohl, H. A. (1967). *36 children*. New York: Plume.

Kohl, H. A. (1970). *The open classroom*. New York: Random House.

Postman, N., & Weingartner, C. (1973). *The school book: For people who want to know what all the hollering is about*. New York: Delacorte Press.

OPPORTUNITY TO LEARN

See Time on Task

OSWEGO MOVEMENT

Oswego, located on the shore of Lake Ontario in New York State, was the birthplace of a successful education reform movement during the second half of the 19th century. Its leader, Edward Austin Sheldon (1823–1897), was instrumental in bringing ideas of Swiss educator Johann Heinrich Pestalozzi (1746–1827) into American education through the development of the object method. Sheldon, with the assistance of British and continental educators, contributed significantly to formalizing teacher education. Upon completing their programs, teachers who had come to Oswego obtained administrative and teaching positions around the country and internationally, spreading the noted method. Today the movement associated with Oswego's method retains its historical importance, and the normal school started in 1861 has been transformed over the years into a branch of the state university that continues to be recognized as a progressive teacher education institution.

Sheldon, raised as a farm boy, disliked studying. In his autobiography, edited by daughter Mary Sheldon Barnes, he revealed that country school life was "one continuous holiday." He detested memorization, and books were valued only for interesting pictures. He enjoyed minding the social classroom scene, indicating that he had observed, besides the use of fool's caps and dunce-blocks as forms of punishment of misbehavior, the commonplace whippings with "the rod and ferrule" and actions that today would be considered mild forms of physical torture.

Sheldon's negative attitude toward education changed only when an enthusiastic teacher, Charles Huntington, inspired him at 17 to read and reflect. Sheldon decided to attend Hamilton College, where he studied classical languages and mathematics. Later, he dropped out and moved to Oswego to pursue a newly found interest in horticulture.

Despite his own lack of success in the new venture, Sheldon became concerned about the lives of the poor and illiterate in Oswego. With the help of supporters, in 1849 he founded a school for orphans, styling himself as a schoolmaster who "had never read any theories of school teaching, and certainly had none of [his] own at the outset." Sheldon brought this teaching background and later experience as school superintendent in the upstate New York city of Syracuse to the newly formed Oswego free public school system in 1853. To secure good teaching, he held meetings with teachers to provide "the necessary instruction in regard to organization, classification, instruction, and discipline." He scheduled classroom visits to discuss "principles of education and methods of teaching." Barnes states that Sheldon perfected the smooth running "machine" (school system) but found it wanting because the instructional methods lacked "vitality."

The habit of calling on good school systems took Sheldon to Toronto, Canada, where he set his eyes on a collection of educational materials developed at the London's Home and Colonial Training Institution. Paying with his own money, he acquired books for teachers and the desired collection of manipulatives—objects, pictures, charts of colors, reading charts—and made a decision to hire a British educator who could teach how to use them.

A well-paid Margaret E. M. Jones came to Oswego to train the first nine teachers at the newly opened Oswego Primary Teachers Training School in 1861. Impressed with the results, the next year Sheldon invited a group of fellow educators to observe the method of object teaching. Their favorable report helped draw students from other places to Oswego. Eagerly sought out by schools across the country and abroad, these new teachers spread the influential Pestalozzi-inspired Oswego instructional method and school reform movement.

Sheldon described three central principles of the new method. A child's education has to do with the natural development of human faculties. On the basis of the principle that only sense perception produces knowledge, instruction should be based on observation of concrete objects and events. Childhood education must cultivate the senses and the faculties of the mind, not simply communicate information. Teacher education in the Oswego method expressed these principles and the Oswego Movement flourished. Oswego organized and publicized Pestallozian principles in a transmittable format. The rather technical and narrow object method helped teachers, especially those who brought with them personal educational deficits, to develop teaching practices superior to those requiring textbook memorization and recitation. The object method eventually served as a bridge to more progressive, child-centered methods, as it addressed what were radical notions of individual differences and developmental aspects of learning. It foreshadowed nature studies through its observations of plants and animals; its concern for "doing" led to the development of industrial arts; and its inclusion of music, arts, physical education, and wellness into the elementary curriculum revolutionized life in schools.

The Oswego method focused on children as persons. It also made teaching more methodical, requiring planning lessons in advance. Consequently, teaching became a more distinguished occupation, a step toward professionalization. Oswego spread the call for teacher education, leading to the establishment of many normal schools offering modern education.

The influence of the Oswego Movement expanded through the work of teachers, many of whom wrote articles, textbooks, and manuals. Visitors to and from Oswego discussed and developed further applications of the object method. Graduates migrated everywhere. Of 948 teachers trained by 1886, more than half taught outside New York. Normal schools molded after Oswego's plan were founded in, among other places, Washington State, Iowa, Minnesota, Nebraska, Massachusetts, Maine, as well as Argentina, Mexico, and Japan. The modern educational system of Argentina was fashioned through the leadership of 65 women graduates of Oswego, who helped overhaul Argentinean teaching methods.

Many Oswego graduates were female. Such a large contingent of respectable professionals served as models, bringing sexism into question and contributing its share of women's rights activists. Graduates also worked in freedmen's schools, with Sheldon himself sending a memo advertising the need for teachers in the South. Through its graduates' work, the Oswego Movement made its impact on education in the United States and globally.

Tania Ramalho

See also Normal Schools; Pestalozzianism; Progressive Education

Further Readings

Rogers, D. (1961). *Oswego: Fountainhead of teacher education.* New York: Appleton-Century-Crofts.

Sheldon, E. A. (1911). *Autobiography of Edward Austin Sheldon.* New York: Ives-Butler.

PAIDEIA PROPOSAL

Grounded in the democratic principle of equality, the educational system known as the Paideia Proposal was set forth in philosopher and scholar Mortimer J. Adler's book, *The Paideia Proposal: An Educational Manifesto*. It was introduced at a time when the quality of the American educational system was coming under fierce attack. *A Nation at Risk* and other prominent documents of the time were drawing great attention to the deficits in public schools in the United States. In addition to the increasing awareness of mediocrity were glaring images of the inequality in educational opportunities and outcomes. Amidst this furor, a growing movement of whole-school reform efforts was building with the hope that restructuring education would ameliorate the inequities within the system. This entry reviews the Paideia Proposal, presenting the foundational philosophy, the structure of the curriculum proposed, and its current use in schools today.

In 1982, Adler, on behalf of the members of the Paideia Group, presented his plan for whole-school reform in *The Paideia Proposal: An Educational Manifesto* (*Paideia*, py-*dee*-a; Greek: the upbringing or education of a child). In this volume, Adler, who served as chairman of the Editorial Board of the *Encyclopaedia Britannica*, linked the ideals of democracy with the purpose of basic schooling, just as John Dewey had more than a half century earlier. Adler argued that a truly democratic civilization is a politically classless society and therefore requires an educationally classless social order. Democracy, Adler states, is dependent on the participation of all its citizens, as the full citizenry is the ruling class. Therefore, in order to develop an engaged and informed citizenry that can participate fully in the democratic process, the educational system must provide equitable educational experiences and outcomes for all children. Adler claimed that while the American educational system had reached equality in terms of quantity of schooling, with number of years of compulsory schooling and similar length of school calendars, its individualistic, competitive, tier structure was far from providing an equal quality of education for all children.

In *The Paideia Proposal*, Adler introduces a vision for an equitable, quality education for all. Adler developed this vision in collaboration with a philosophically diverse group of prominent educators who became known as the Paideia Group. Along with Adler, who was the chairman and author of the group's books, the group included such people as Jacques Barzun, Otto Bird, Leon Botstein, Ernest Boyer, Nicholas Caputi, Douglass Cater, Donald Cowan, Alonzo Crim, Clifton Fadiman, Dennis Gray, Richard Hunt, Ruth Love, James Nelson, James O'Toole, Theodore Puck, Adolph Schmidt, Adele Simmons, Theodore R. Sizer, Charles Van Doren, Geraldine Van Doren, and John Van Doren. Together, this diverse group contributed to and endorsed Adler's proposal for an equitable educational system.

The vision of equal quality of education presented in *The Paideia Proposal* begins by distinguishing between education and schooling. The education of an individual takes a lifetime, beginning with the earliest learning of an infant and ending only at the end of life. Within this lifetime of education, the purpose of schooling has three essential goals for all: to prepare individuals for lifelong personal and professional growth that will continue after schooling, to prepare individuals to be fully responsible citizens within the democracy, and to prepare individuals for earning a living. These three goals of schooling pertain to all individuals and form the educational objectives for Adler's vision of basic schooling.

The Paideia Curriculum

The heart of Adler's plan for education reform is the belief that all students can and should learn a challenging curriculum. Because the three objectives of schooling are common to all individuals, Adler claims that this challenging curriculum should include the same course of study for all. Although no specific coursework is endorsed, the common course of study proposed by Adler is based on a general, liberal arts curriculum. *The Proposal* eliminates all electives (except the choice of which foreign language to study), all academic tracks, and all specific vocational training.

The unique plan for the common course of study endorsed in *The Paideia Proposal* resides in the structure of the curriculum. The curriculum is organized into three columns representing three modes of teaching and learning. The first column is dedicated to the acquisition of organized knowledge. While no specific courses are endorsed, Adler suggests that the acquisition of knowledge should include the study of language, literature, and the fine arts; mathematics and the natural sciences; and history, geography, and social studies. Further, he proposes that acquisition of organized knowledge best occurs through didactic instruction with the use of lecture and response and the aid of textbooks.

The second column focuses on the development of intellectual skills, or skills required for further learning. In this column Adler includes skills related to the areas of study in the first column: reading, writing, speaking, and listening; calculating, problem solving, observing, measuring, and estimating; and exercising critical judgment. Adler

suggests that these skills be developed through instruction based on a coaching model in which teachers guide students through practice in using the skills until they become proficient and independent in their execution.

The final column of the Paideia curriculum is devoted to the development of an enlarged understanding of ideas and values. Adler suggests that the exploration of ideas and values should occur through Socratic questioning within the structure of a seminar. Within the seminar, primary documents in all areas of study, literature, and works of art become the focus for questioning and discussion among participants. While no specific works are recommended within *The Paideia Proposal*, its companion, *The Paideia Program: An Educational Syllabus*, suggests a selection of "great books" to be used for seminars. The Socratic seminar is one of the distinguishing hallmarks of the Paideia curriculum.

Paideia Schools Today

Since its publication, the ideas introduced in *The Paideia Proposal* have been put into practice in many schools in the United States and abroad. In 1988, the National Paideia Center was established at the University of North Carolina to foster and implement Adler's ideas. Today, the Center, directed by Dr. Terry Roberts, works with more than 100 partner schools annually, providing support, professional development, and resources to schools adopting the principles of *The Paideia Proposal*.

Mary Kay Kelly

See also Coalition of Essential Schools; Curriculum Controversies; Direct Instruction; Effective Schools Movement; Equity; High Schools That Work; Sizer, Theodore R.

Further Readings

Adler, M. J. (1982). *The Paideia Proposal: An educational manifesto.* New York: Macmillan.
Adler, M. J. (1983). *Paideia problems and possibilities.* New York: Macmillan.
Paideia Group. (1984). *The Paideia program: An educational syllabus.* New York: Macmillan.
Roberts, T. (1999). *The Paideia classroom: Teaching for understanding.* Larchmont, NY: Eye On Education.

Roberts, T., & The National Paideia Center. (1998). *The power of Paideia schools: Defining lives through learning.* Alexandria, VA: Association for Supervision and Curriculum Development.

PARENTAL RIGHTS

See Pierce v. Society of Sisters

PARENT TEACHER ASSOCIATION

With over 6 million members, the National Parent Teacher Association (PTA) is the largest child advocacy organization in the United States. There are organizations in all 50 states, the District of Columbia, the U.S. Virgin Islands, and in the Department of Defense schools in Europe and the Pacific. The declared mission of the PTA is to be a powerful voice for all children, to be a relevant resource for families and communities, and to be a strong advocate for the education and well-being of every child.

The founders, Alice McLellan Birney and Phoebe Apperson Hearst, began the organization at a time when American women were denied the vote. This single act of courage had the effect of opening the door for a number of social reforms. Recognizing that there is no stronger bond than that between mother and child, the founders believed that it was up to the mothers in the United States to eliminate the threats that endangered children. In its initial meetings, more than 2,000 people responded—all with a commitment to children. Problems were identified and strategies devised to resolve them. Dissent and reform were the hallmarks of this organization from its inception.

The swift growth of the organization implied that it filled a strong need for advocacy for America's children. Among the issues that the PTA has addressed over the years was its insistence on the formation of child labor laws in America. The political climate of the United States, highly favorable to the growth of big business in the early 20th century, was not eager to hear that children in the workforce were being exploited. Despite this, PTAs around the country stood firm on their support for enactment of laws to benefit children.

In addition, in the 1940s, the global devastation of World War II spearheaded the organization's determination to find a new and better way to resolve conflicts before they erupted into violence and destruction. The National PTA was one of the first organizations to support the fledgling United Nations.

In the 1950s, the PTA began to recognize and address the issues of America's affinity for prescription and over-the-counter medications and to call for a national conference to address narcotics and drug addiction in youth. In addition, one of the most high-profile projects in PTA history was the organization's participation in the field testing of the Salk polio vaccine, leading to securing the polio vaccination for all schoolchildren.

During the rise of the counterculture movement of the 1960s, reform efforts on the part of the PTA called for schools to focus on the risks involved with drug abuse; it also created public service messages to educate parents and the general public about the dangers of addiction.

Efforts to protect America's children continued in the 1970s, when the increase of violence on television spurred the PTA to action regarding the effects of such programming on children. Today, programs such as critical viewing skills workshops, which are developed by the National PTA, are held around the country.

In the 1980s, the rise of AIDS and sexually transmitted diseases found the PTA again at the forefront in advocating that comprehensive information about the diseases be made available at school and in the home.

In the 1990s, educational reform became the battle cry of PTAs. The population of the United States was becoming increasingly diverse. Opportunity existed for those with the education and training to take advantage of it, but for those with few skills, the gap grew greater than ever. The idea that parents needed more of a say in the education of this country's children was the cornerstone of the PTA's political involvement in that decade. In 1994, the PTA's advocacy skills culminated in the Goals 2000 Educate America legislation that, among many reforms, called for local school districts to make parents equal partners on issues affecting their children's education.

In 2000, National PTA published the book, *Building Successful Partnerships: A Guide for Developing Parent and Family Involvement Programs*. In January of that year, the organization provided field-tested strategies for developing successful parent involvement programs.

The increasing popularity of video games with sexually explicit and violence-laced content is the focus of a recent reform effort by the PTA. In 2008, the PTA and Entertainment Software Rating Board (ESRB) launched a nationwide education campaign through which a new booklet, *A Parent's Guide to Video Games, Parental Controls and Online Safety*, was distributed to all 26,000 PTAs in the United States. The campaign enables and encourages PTAs to educate their community's parents about the ESRB rating system and parental control technology available on the various game systems, as well as the concerns that exist when games are played over an Internet connection and what parents can do to mitigate those concerns. The booklets offer a step-by-step guide to setting up parental controls as well as an article about online safety.

Carol Engler

See also Community Control; Local Control; National Education Association (NEA)

Further Readings

Kowalski, T. J. (2008). *Public relations in schools* (4th ed.). Columbus, OH: Pearson.

National PTA: http://www.pta.org

National PTA. (2008). *A parent's guide to video games, parental controls and online safety.* Retrieved July 23, 2009, from http://www.pta.org/Documents/Video_Game__FINAL_WEB.pdf

National PTA. (n.d.). *Building successful partnerships: Best practices.* Retrieved July 23, 2009, from http://www.pta.org/documents/icebreakers%20and%20activities.pdf

PTO Today: http://www.ptotoday.com

PAY FOR PERFORMANCE

See Merit Pay

PEABODY, ELIZABETH PALMER (1804–1890)

Elizabeth Palmer Peabody devoted herself to a variety of causes and movements to reform society by improving the individual. Her greatest contribution was to early childhood education, most significantly her establishment and promotion of English-speaking kindergartens.

Born in Massachusetts in 1804, Elizabeth Peabody spent her early years in New England. Although she never married, her circle of friends included men whose careers she helped promote. Her friends Horace Mann and Nathaniel Hawthorne married her sisters Mary and Sophia, respectively. Unitarian minister William Ellery Channing and transcendentalists Ralph Waldo Emerson, Theodore Parker, Bronson Alcott, and George Ripley were also part of her circle.

Despite her friendship with women's rights advocate and transcendentalist Margaret Fuller, Peabody had little interest in the women's rights movement. She accepted the limitations that society placed on women while believing that women could do whatever they wanted.

A self-educated intellectual, Peabody started teaching in private schools when she was 17. Her best-known teaching position was as Bronson Alcott's assistant at his Temple School in Boston in the mid-1830s. Devoted to developing the talents of the individual, the school's approach was quite different from the rote learning typical of that period. In 1835 Peabody published *Record of a School*, describing Bronson's dialogues with students.

In 1840 Peabody opened her Boston bookstore and circulation library, specializing in books and journals from Europe. It served as a meeting place for the transcendentalists, for whom her publishing company produced *The Dial* for 2 years.

In the late 1840s and 1850s, she traveled to promote the use of chronological charts to teach history. During the 1850s, she also taught for a time at a private New Jersey school headed by antislavery advocate Theodore Dwight Weld, whose wife Angelina Grimke and her sister Sarah also taught there.

In 1859 Peabody met Republican politician Karl Schurz's wife Margareth, who had started a German-speaking kindergarten in Watertown,

Wisconsin, in 1856. Before fleeing Germany, Margareth Schurz had heard Friedrich Froebel lecture about his ideas on kindergarten. In 1860, in Boston, Peabody opened the first English-speaking kindergarten in the United States. The private school's organized curriculum interspersed with supervised play was meant to bridge the gap between preschool and primary school by focusing on the moral, physical, and intellectual growth of the child. Teachers were trained women who actively engaged in the child's development.

In 1867 and again in 1871 Peabody made lengthy trips to Europe, where she visited kindergartens. Her subsequent conviction that teaching reading did not belong in a Froebel kindergarten led to controversy and conflict with advocates for the American kindergarten movement who supported the teaching of reading.

Despite her increasing age, in the 1870s and 1880s she worked to promote her views about kindergarten with publications and lectures across the United States. She was instrumental in convincing St. Louis Superintendent William Torrey Harris to start the first English-speaking kindergarten attached to a public school in 1873.

Ann Hassenpflug

See also Infant Schools; Kindergarten; Montessori Schools; Phonics; Play School Movement; Reading First; *Sesame Street*

Further Reading

Marshall, M. (2005). *The Peabody sisters*. New York: Houghton Mifflin.

Ronda, B. (1999). *Elizabeth Palmer Peabody: A reformer on her own terms*. Cambridge, MA: Harvard University Press.

PEABODY FUND

In the years after the Civil War, a number of northern philanthropists and progressive Southerners took an interest in supporting free, public education in the South. One of the most prominent of the philanthropists was George Peabody (1795–1869), who established the Peabody Education Fund in 1867 to rebuild and improve Southern schools. The fund gave a total of $2,478,000 to strengthen education in the former Confederacy and West Virginia during the 30 years between 1867 and 1898. Because the resources of the fund were directed toward strengthening existing schools, no money went to the education of freed Blacks in the early years. Later, after Black schools had been established, the trustees adopted a deliberate policy of directing the majority of the grants to White schools, thereby playing a significant part in establishing a segregated system of education across the South. Even though the fund did very little to improve educational prospects for Black children, it contributed to significant reform of White schools and helped overcome resistance to free, public schooling in the South. When the fund was dissolved in 1898, the remaining money was given to George Peabody College for Teachers.

Despite sporadic attempts to establish public schools, most notably in North Carolina, the idea of free, state-sponsored public education did not take firm root in the South prior to the Civil War. Since the establishment of public school systems for both Blacks and Whites was a condition for readmission to the Union, southern states were forced to confront the issue during Reconstruction. The former Confederacy was so deeply impoverished, however, that there was little likelihood that anything resembling quality public education would be possible. In addition, public sentiment for universal education was sorely lacking. The South had a tradition of private education for those who could afford it, and common schools were few and far between. Clearly the South needed help if free, public education were to become a reality.

In 1866 George Peabody, a wealthy American émigré who made his home in London, toured the South and was appalled by the conditions he observed there. Becoming convinced that public education was the most effective means of rebuilding the southern economy and promoting reunification, Peabody established a philanthropic trust to improve public schools and support teacher education. The Peabody Education Fund (PEF) was governed by a board of trustees made up of prominent gentlemen from the North and South, including General Ulysses S. Grant,

Admiral David C. Farragut, and the former governors of North and South Carolina. Barnas Sears, who had succeeded Horace Mann as Secretary of the Massachusetts Board of Education and later served as president of Brown University, was appointed to manage the Fund.

From its beginning, the resources of the PEF were targeted almost entirely at schools for White children. Sears urged the trustees to establish model schools by giving money to improve existing public schools, which, in the early days of the Fund, were almost invariably White. This policy was seen as a more effective way to promote quality education than spreading the money more thinly to create new schools across the South. Later, Sears persuaded the trustees to award funds to Black schools at a level one-third of that for White schools. He justified this by observing that it cost much less to maintain the inferior schools that became the norm for Black children. Sears also advocated the use of PEF monies to support only segregated schools, and again the trustees agreed. When Louisiana and South Carolina made brief, abortive attempts to establish integrated schools during the Radical Reconstruction period, the Fund contributed $17,000 to private, Whites-only schools on the grounds that White children would not attend mixed-race schools. Sears also took an active role in successfully opposing Senator Charles Sumner's efforts to mandate mixed schools as part of the Civil Rights Bill of 1875. Sears's judicious application of PEF money and political influence to promote segregated schools decoupled public schooling from mixed-race schooling and helped remove the Reconstruction taint from the idea of free, public education. Educational reform supported by the PEF was a Whites-only enterprise. During the 30 years of its existence, the PEF played a significant role in establishing segregated schooling as the foundation of southern public education.

In addition to its donations to elementary and secondary education, the PEF supported teacher institutes and partnered with the University of Nashville to establish a normal school. The State Normal School opened in 1875 and was quickly renamed Peabody Normal College. In addition to its support for the institution, the Fund provided scholarships for 3,645 teacher candidates between 1877 and 1904. When the Fund was dissolved in 1898, $1.5 million of the remaining assets were used as matching funds to transform Peabody Normal College into George Peabody College for Teachers. The new college was built across the street from Vanderbilt University and in 1979 became Peabody College of Vanderbilt University.

The Peabody Education Fund is regarded as one of the first modern philanthropic efforts because it used a technique of leveraging relatively modest sums through challenge grants. PEF grants were contingent on matching funds being raised by local communities, often through taxes. This self-help model meant that the PEF strengthened the authority of local school officials and state superintendents. Consequently, the Fund wielded an influence far beyond what its relatively modest endowment would suggest. Peabody's trust also became the forerunner of other philanthropic efforts by individuals such as John F. Slater, Anna T. Jeans, and Julius Rosenwald.

Elizabeth P. Harper

See also General Education Board; Normal Schools; Southern Education Board

Further Readings

Anderson, J. D. (1988). *The education of Blacks in the south, 1860–1935.* Chapel Hill: University of North Carolina.

Black, M. W. (1961). Private aid to public schools. *History of Education Quarterly, 1,* 38–42.

Parker, F., & Parker, B. J. (1998). Peabody Education Fund in Tennessee. *The Tennessee encyclopedia of history and culture* [Online]. Retrieved September 9, 2008, from http://tennesseeencyclopedia.net/imagegallery.php?EntryID=P013

Urban, W., & Wagoner, J. L. (1996). *American education: A history.* New York: McGraw-Hill.

PEACE EDUCATION

Conflict is a natural part of human existence. Peace is the outcome of an agreeable resolution to conflict, and peace education is the process of learning about peace. The purpose of peace education is for people to gain knowledge, skills, dispositions, and values that will allow peaceful resolution of conflict. Never in the history of the human race has there been a more critical need for peace education than exists in the modern globalized world. Those focused on reform understand that the school curriculum necessarily must focus on issues of fairness and multiculturalism as a way of mitigating the injustice that so often results in acts of violence.

Violent acts and threats of violence have always existed, but the potential for total annihilation due to weapons of mass destruction, biowarfare, and terrorism make peace education a priority for all who are seriously focused on questions of educational reform. Personal acts of violence in our homes and neighborhoods prioritize safety as a major concern for our children within the school environment. Peace education is not a 21st-century innovation, but it is increasingly addressed by those who care deeply about the political and social well-being for future generations.

The advent of peace education coincides with the advent of civilization and war sanctioning the violence as a means of solving problems. Individuals have historically relied on each other for survival, which has spawned cultural values of competitiveness, dominance, and self-centeredness. Such values laid the foundation for social injustices evident in the modern world. It was at the turn of the 20th century, through the efforts of Alfred Nobel (1833–1896), capitalizing on the international movement against war, that the world began to recognize those who truly contributed to the advancement of a peaceful society. Even so, it is in the past 100 years that society has experienced the greatest devastation from warring countries and the perpetuation of violence that permeates all levels of society. One hundred years of an international antiwar movement could not stop the invasion of social injustices and extreme violence into our schools and into American culture. The escalating violence witnessed by children in schools throughout the United States at the end of the 20th century has initiated a sense of urgency for peace education. The call for social change through peace education has never been more critical than it is today, with educators seeking reform relative to sex bias and gender stereotyping, the type of programming permitted on television, and the ways in which the media deal with conflict and conflict resolution.

Recent and current world leaders such as Mohandas K. (Mahatma) Gandhi (1869–1948), Mother Teresa (1910–1997), Nelson Mandela (1918–), and the Fourteenth Dalai Lama (1935–) spent or are spending much of their lives advocating nonviolence and peace building. Addressing poverty, racism, and other forms of social injustice, they endeavored to facilitate social change through peace. Their concern for the well-being of all serves as the foundational model for others to follow. Peace education has evolved to encompass a much broader perspective to include global education, human rights education, and conflict resolution as a means of violence prevention. In the United States, political leaders such as Martin Luther King, Jr., building on the ideas of Gandhi and others, have articulated the different ways in which American society can more fully embrace issues of justice.

Echoing the same, educational leaders including John Dewey (1859–1952), Maria Montessori (1887–1952), Maxine Greene (1918–), Nel Noddings (1929–), and Vivian Paley (1929–) have emphasized that a peaceful society starts with education, particularly the education of our children. Dewey established himself as an educational reformer by sharing his ideas on democracy and ethics in education. Montessori's research on child development and her work with young children led to a new pedagogy supporting social change through peace. Her model of education spans preschool through adolescence and is exemplified by her position that averting war is the responsibility of politicians and establishing peace the responsibility of educators. Greene highlights justice, equality, and freedom as a means to advance social justice, while Noddings's perspective on the ethics of caring adds another dimension to the ethic of justice. Similar to Montessori's, Paley's work with young children has focused on fairness, justice, and the need to teach kindness to our youngest children. Today, there are numerous programs and strategies built on the work of these educational leaders that aim to bring social change through peace education.

Numerous program models range from a focus on violence prevention to an emphasis on peace education and typically include multicultural education with a global worldview; human rights education; conflict resolution centered on cooperation, mediation, and negotiation; problem solving; environmental responsibility; and social skill development that includes listening and reflection. Various concepts are integrated throughout the different curricula, such as kindness, caring, trust, respect, empathy, and service to others. Conflict as a normal aspect of social living is an underlying concept emphasizing cooperation over competition. Some leading research-based programs include Second Step, Tribes Learning Community, Character Counts, Peace Making Skills for Little Kids, Associated School's Project, Earth Charter Education, Teaching Students to Be Peacemakers, and Resolving Conflict Creatively Program, to name a few.

Cooperative learning and conflict resolution are the common threads in peace education programs. David and Roger Johnson's research and publications on cooperative learning and conflict resolution are the core of many programs and strategies taught in schools across the United States and internationally. They address five essential elements for sustaining peace through education: compulsory integrated attendance so children have an opportunity to interact with a variety of people, established mutual goals for unifying people, structured procedures for effective decision making to resolve controversy, conflict resolution skills for successful mediation and negotiation, and civic values that support the common good. These five elements, although not consistently labeled, have been established as critical components for successful peace education programs. Peace education is important for all members of society, but maintaining peace will happen only when our children have the necessary knowledge, skills, dispositions, and values required for sustaining peaceful communities and fostering peaceful resolution to inevitable human conflicts.

Celia E. Johnson

See also Character Education; Conflict Management; Cooperative Learning; Moral Education; Multicultural Education

Further Readings

Harris, I. M. (2003). Peace education at the end of a bloody century. *Educational Studies, 34,* 336–351.
Harris, I. M. (2004). Peace education theory. *Journal of Peace Education, 1*(1), 5–16.
Johnson, D. W., & Johnson, R. T. (2005). Essential components of peace education. *Theory Into Practice, 44*(4), 280–292.
Salomon, G., & Nevo, B. (Eds.). (2002). *Peace education: The concept, principles, and practices around the world.* Philadelphia: Erlbaum.

PENNSYLVANIA STUDY, THE

The Pennsylvania Study of the Relation of Secondary and Higher Education, sponsored by the Carnegie Foundation for the Advancement of Teaching, was conducted between 1925 and 1938 and examined the academic careers of 45,000 Pennsylvania high school and college students. The intent of the study was to shift the definition of academic progress from the passing of time (the Carnegie unit as "the package method of academic advancement") to a student's demonstration of knowledge as ascertained by innovative standardized tests. While the Carnegie unit continued to dominate the secondary school curriculum, The Pennsylvania Study greatly influenced college administrators' acceptance of standardized tests and, in so doing, expanded expectations for college applications and reformed the college admissions process.

By the mid-1920s, advances in tests and measurements prompted some educators to question the value of the Carnegie unit as the leading indicator of a student's readiness for postsecondary studies. The field of college admissions was undergoing a transformation as admission officers asked whether capable students, particularly those from less privileged settings and/or from rural backgrounds, were being overlooked due to their inability to fulfill certain Carnegie unit requirements. In addition, secondary school programs varied dramatically in academic quality, and Carnegie units were not commensurate across the country. Hopes ran high for standardized testing—the new science of measurement—to be able to reduce the high drop-out rate among college students by ensuring more accurate placement and by identifying able students regardless of their family background. These leaders believed that widespread testing to identify talent would open opportunities for students, and this would be done not by content-oriented tests, such as the traditional College Board (content-oriented) examinations, but by an innovative new type of college-oriented aptitude test. Standardized testing was at this time not viewed as "high-stakes testing," but instead associated with democracy, fairness, and opportunity since all students could now be considered for admissions to college on the grounds of intelligence rather than the accessibility to college preparatory programs. The question became what type of testing should be used: scholastic aptitude tests, traditional college (subjective essay) tests, or newly conceived objective (multiple-choice) achievement tests?

Directed by William Learned of the Carnegie Foundation's Division of Educational Enquiry, with assistance from Ben Wood, director of the American Council of Education's Cooperative Test Service, the Pennsylvania Study's fundamental thesis maintained that educational reform should be based on the needs of students rather than new administrative techniques and that the acquisition of knowledge remained the dominating focus of schooling. High school achievement tests were administered to more than 45,000 high school and college students, approximately 70% of all senior secondary students in the state of Pennsylvania, with some students tested every 2 years for a 6-year period. In 1928 alone, tests were given to 27,000 high school seniors. The Study was conceived to examine the 7-year progress of a group of sixth-grade children through high school; the 5-year progress of 40,000 high school seniors through college; and 1-year progress of 5,000 college seniors.

Learned had devised a new type of test consisting of multiple-choice, true-false, and matching items. This innovative format represented a major breakthrough in standardization because instruments could now be scored quickly and objectively. IBM collaborated with the Cooperative Test Service and developed means for scoring the Pennsylvania Study's exam sheets electronically. Thousands of tests were administered with the intent to accumulate reliable and valid data for students throughout their academic careers. The Cooperative Test Service, formed in 1930, became a factory for the standardized, objective achievement test and provided high school and college tests for the Pennsylvania Study and, originally planned by Learned and Wood, for the Progressive Education Association's Commission on the Relation of School and College (the Eight-Year Study).

Wood believed that by administering standard intelligence tests with achievement tests, school faculties could assist students to become more aware of their capabilities as a way to help plan their futures. Learned was able to introduce an extensive student sampling procedure to begin planning a statewide system that would result in a cumulative record of all students' "knowledge attainment." They believed that 6 years of cumulative records would provide adequate information for admissions to Pennsylvania colleges and ultimately would have greater predictive value than any single college entrance exam. Learned attempted to establish a system in which each student's cumulative record would become part of a national database college admissions officers throughout the United States could draw upon.

Craig Kridel

See also Carnegie Foundation for the Advancement of Teaching; Carnegie Unit; Eight-Year Study; Progressive Education; Progressive Education Association (PEA); Standardized Tests

Further Readings

Kridel, C., & Bullough, R. V., Jr. (2007). *Stories of the Eight-Year Study*. Albany: State University of New York Press.

Learned, W. S., & Wood, B. D. (1938). *The student and his knowledge*. New York: Carnegie Foundation for the Advancement of Teaching.

Lemann, N. (1999). *The big test*. New York: Farrar, Straus, and Giroux.

PEOPLE FOR THE AMERICAN WAY

In 1981, Norman Lear, the successful television producer of *All in the Family, Maude,* and *The Jeffersons,* led an effort by concerned citizens from political, religious, entertainment, and progressive corporations to counter what they considered one-sided leadership and lobbying by the political Far Right (e.g., Heritage Foundation,

Citizens for Excellence in Education, Concerned Women for America, Eagle Forum, Focus on the Family, Liberty Legal Institute, Christian Coalition, the Moral Majority). Lear, Congresswoman Barbara Jordan, Notre Dame president Father Theodore Hesburgh, and others joined together to help fund and launch People For the American Way (PFAW) as a liberal-leaning think tank to confront attacks from what PFAW identified as right-wing extremist groups, like those examples named above. Lear and other PFAW leaders and supporters believed that liberal advocacy must confront the power and influence of the religious Right, and the forces supporting the agenda of the extreme right wing.

PFAW's founding purpose sought to give a voice to "the American Way." Specifically, PFAW stated that the true American Way should promote pluralism; individuality; freedom of thought, expression, and religion; a sense of community; and tolerance and compassion for others. PFAW claimed an agenda that would reduce social tension and polarizations, encourage community participation, foster understanding and appreciation of diversity, and increase the level and quality of public dialogue. PFAW states that its highest purpose is to nurture a national climate that encourages and enhances the human spirit rather than one that divides people into hostile camps.

Critics of PFAW have suggested that its aggressive pursuit of its liberal agenda has also contributed to the culture wars and divided America. PFAW supporters will point to its victories in courts, among policymakers, and in the arena of public opinion as evidence of achieving its purpose of enriching the quality of public dialogue, debate, and decisions.

The PFAW has identified the following as major initiatives:

- Equality for all
- Fair and just courts
- Fighting the religious right
- Freedom of speech
- Religious liberty
- The right to vote

PFAW has often found itself involved in public school issues in pursuit of the above initiatives. As part of their partnership with public schools, PFAW has led legislative and litigated court fights against vouchers and any other efforts to privatize public education. Through efforts to educate the public and lobby policymakers, PFAW published reports like *Voucher Veneer: The Deeper Agenda to Privatize Public Education*. PFAW has also used the federal courts to challenge voucher initiatives and school boards' efforts to promote pro-Protestant Bible curriculum as an elective in public schools.

In advocating for religious liberty and freedom of speech, PFAW has taken on issues of Bibles in the classroom, prayers in public schools, and attempts to censor what students may read and learn. PFAW publishes an annual state-by-state report, *Attacks on the Freedom to Learn*, documenting attempts to restrict or censor public school curriculum and instruction as well as attacks on public school and public library materials. Conservative right-wing groups have claimed that public schools and liberal federal judges endorse what they characterize as a "new religion" in public schools, secular humanism. Such claims have led the conservative groups to challenge whole language teaching methods as promoting secular humanism, new age theology, and a New World Order. PFAW has mobilized local efforts to combat such right-wing attacks. In the past few years, PFAW has established state offices throughout the United States. The state affiliates and national offices have conducted extensive education programs to inform the general public and mobilize membership and supporters to fight attacks from the religious Right and other conservative activists.

PFAW has become famous for its opposition to the appointment of right-wing judges to the federal courts. Prior to major elections, such as presidential campaigns, PFAW has published special reports, such as *Courting Disaster: How a Scalia–Thomas Supreme Court Would Endanger Our Rights and Freedoms*, and *Confirmed Judges, Confirmed Fears*. Supporting federal judges and Supreme Court justices sensitive to PFAW's mission is important because PFAW has used the federal courts to challenge voucher initiatives, school boards' efforts to promote pro-Protestant Bible curriculum as an elective in public schools, and other issues where it believes the religious Right has attempted to disrupt or destroy public education as a force for democracy.

PFAW has taken on the National Council on Bible Curriculum in Public Schools (NCBCPS) as it attempts to elect school board candidates and promote the establishment of Bible courses of study in public schools. PFAW has mobilized educational and constitutional scholars to testify against the NCBCPS Bible curriculum, exposing its promotion of Protestant proselytizing and anti-evolution messages. NCBCPS had promoted its curriculum as being used throughout Texas public schools. PFAW, along with the American Civil Liberties Union (ACLU), challenged such curricula in places like Ector County Independent Schools in West Texas. NCBCPS and other conservative Christian right-wing advocates had attempted to get a state law passed that would require all Texas public school districts to offer a Bible elective course based on the NCBCPS. PFAW, along with its allies, like the ACLU and the Texas Freedom Network, challenged this legislative initiative. PFAW and its allies were able to modify the proposed legislation so it basically allowed school districts to offer electives in religious literacy, following the guidelines developed by major educational and First Amendment associations. Ector County educational authorities agreed to change their NCBCPS curriculum to comply with the new state guidelines, and all of the Ector County School Board members who had pushed through the NCBCPS Bible curriculum were defeated in the next round of school board elections. The new Texas religious literacy elective law may serve as a model for integrating religious studies into secondary schools in a constitutionally and educationally sound approach. The national PFAW and PFAW of Texas, along with its allies, are working to make the implementation of this law a model for religious liberty and progressive school reform.

Steve Jenkins

See also Concerned Women for America (CWA); Creationism; Religion and the Curriculum; Secular Humanism

Further Readings

Deckman, M. (2004). *School board battles: The Christian right in local politics.* Washington, DC: Georgetown University Press.

Gaddy, B., Hall, T. W., & Marzano, R. (1996). *School wars: Resolving our conflicts over religion & values.* San Francisco: Jossey-Bass.

Haynes, C., & Thomas, O. (2001). *Finding common ground: A guide to religious liberty in public schools.* Nashville, TN: First Amendment Center.

Hunter, J. D. (1991). *Culture wars: The struggle to define America.* New York: Basic Books.

Nord, W. (1995). *Religion & American education: Rethinking a national dilemma.* Chapel Hill: University of North Carolina Press.

Nord, W., & Haynes, C. (1998). *Taking religion seriously across the curriculum.* Alexandria, VA: Association for Supervision and Curriculum Development.

PERFORMANCE-BASED ASSESSMENT

Educational reform in how and what students are taught has also led to reform in how students are assessed to determine content knowledge and skills. This entry provides information on one alternative model of assessment, performance-based assessment, which requires students to demonstrate their level of knowledge through the actual performance of an activity.

Selected-response tests have been the norm in schools for many years. Formats such as multiple choice, true/false, and matching allowed the teacher to quickly assess student knowledge, with high reliability and objective scoring. This was acceptable for determining a student's factual knowledge, but did not allow for an in-depth analysis of a student's higher-order thinking skills or problem-solving ability, and often did not work well for documenting state standards. A different method of assessment was needed, one that allowed students to demonstrate their knowledge through both the product and the process of developing the product. This led to the use of performance-based assessment.

This type of assessment has also been known as "authentic assessment," as the student completed a "real" task; "alternative assessment," as this was different from the traditional selected-response tests; "direct assessment," as students were assessed on their ability to actually do the task; and finally "performance-based assessment," as the emphasis was on student performance to demonstrate their understanding of the content. While these titles are not interchangeable, they all refer to allowing students to demonstrate their knowledge through a method different from the traditional paper-and-pencil format of answering teacher-designed questions.

Performance-based assessments allow for the integration of knowledge, skills, and abilities. With performance-based assessments, the emphasis is on both the process of completing the assignment and the final product. The assessment of students is often tied to the instruction, with realistic problem-solving situations used to allow for active construction of meaning. Complex performance-based assignments are considered to be a better choice for assessing student problem-solving and thinking skills than selected-response tests and more appropriate for current learning theory, which emphasizes that students learn best by being involved in the learning process and by using previous knowledge to build new knowledge through active involvement and inquiry.

Lynn Fuchs offered three key elements of performance-based assessments. The first was students constructing their own responses, in contrast to the teacher providing responses for the student to choose from. The second element was that teachers could observe students' performance as they participated in authentic tasks to assess how individual students were arriving at the answer. The last element was that a student's responses could provide information on the student's thinking and learning, not just documenting whether the student reported the correct answer.

Problems with performance-based assessment include the time required to construct and score the assessment. To construct a performance-based assessment, the teacher first needs to start with a clear objective of what the student is to learn. This often comes from state standards, with a more general objective then defined by specific learning outcomes. The outcomes need to be presented in observable, measurable language that allows both teacher and students to know exactly what is required. Once the outcomes are defined, a feasible and authentic type of product capable of being scored is defined. This must be "doable" within the settings available, similar to what might be expected in real-life situations when out of school,

with observable process steps or a product that can be reliably scored.

This type of assessment is often considered to be subjective in scoring, although the second part of developing a performance-based assessment is the construction of clearly defined guidelines for evaluation, thus ensuring some measure of objectivity to the grading process. Developing a scoring guide or rubric before beginning the task is critical to understanding exactly what the student is to know following participation in instruction and relevant activities. Steps to reach the final product must also be assessed to provide feedback and continued growth for the student. Waiting to review/grade a final product will not allow the teacher and student to collaborate on how to extend the student's knowledge and skills.

Involving students in the process of evaluation and grading is encouraged with performance-based assessment. While teachers need to determine what to assess, based on the standard being taught, having the students help determine what an acceptable performance is will motivate them to reach the standards set and to evaluate their own work as they participate in the assignment. Knowledge of the criteria and standards against which the product will be judged helps students focus their product toward those standards.

Performance-based assessment has been utilized in programs for students with special needs for a number of years. Students were taught specific skills based on performance objectives that would allow them to be more functionally independent, or would teach them specific skills to be able to function within the general education curriculum. The move to bring performance-based assessment into the general education classrooms has allowed for more successful inclusion of students with special needs in the general education classroom.

The performance-based assessment movement has also affected how institutions of higher education develop and assess their teacher education programs. Professional organizations that are responsible for accrediting programs (e.g., National Association of Colleges of Teacher Education, National Council of Teachers of Mathematics, etc.) have adopted a performance-based assessment system where programs must demonstrate that their teacher candidates are meeting the standards of the organizations. In the course of state licensing, boards are also aligning with the professional standards; institutions of higher education also have been required to revise their teacher education programs to be more performance based.

Performance-based assessment has proven to be a viable method of documenting growth and learning for all students, from preschool to higher education. The strengths outweigh the limitations, but the time required to develop and score performance-based assessments and the perceived subjectivity of grading will remain controversial topics for educators.

Joni L. Baldwin

See also Alternative Assessment; Assessment; Constructivism; Inclusion; Standards Movement

Further Readings

Fuchs, L. S. (1994). *Connecting performance assessment to instruction.* Reston, VA: Council for Exceptional Children.
Miller, M. D., Linn, R. L., & Gronlund, N. E. (2009). *Measurement and assessment in teaching* (10th ed.). Upper Saddle River, NJ: Pearson Education.

PERFORMANCE CONTRACTING

Performance contracting is a process that permits companies to investigate alternatives for increasing utility efficiency or exploring innovative educational reform initiatives without bearing the full cost of those endeavors. Educational organizations usually demonstrate examples of efficiency, shared-savings, or cost-savings performance contracting and educational performance contracting. Schools employ *efficiency* performance contracting to upgrade or replace inadequate outdated organizational operations—for example, to replace boilers and install computerized environmental (climate) controls or energy management systems—whereas *educational* performance contracting facilitates field testing or the implementation of new alternative learning systems. Also, schools use performance contracting to document their efforts to meet federal, state, and local expectations of accountability, as well as to demonstrate good stewardship of taxpayer monies.

Contract periods range from 1 to 12 years, and payment, based on a guaranteed rate that is greater than or equal to the district's current expenditures for those services, is linked to the attainment of targeted outcomes and to the cost savings associated with the total project. Efficiency performance contract periods are generally long term (8–12 years), while educational performance contracts are apt to be shorter (1–3 years). School districts may undertake contracts with more than one company for a particular project and can enter agreements with both private and public organizations, including teachers' unions. Contracts between school districts and teachers' unions may denote some form of differentiated staffing or merit pay. Despite the tendency for outside companies to engage in performance contracting more frequently, teachers and administrators also participate. Compensation, determined by formulas or indicated as a fixed amount, may be disbursed in part or in full prior to the delivery of services. Federal funds, school or state bonds, and financial institutions finance performance contracting enterprises. This entry presents an overview of the performance contracting strategy in the field of education, describes the benefits and shortcomings of performance contracting, and summarizes the basic components of the performance contracting process.

Performance Contracting in Education

Scarce resources and the public's increased emphasis on outcomes and accountability prompted government agencies, such as the U.S. Department of Defense, to explore the applicability of performance contracting in the 1960s, prior to education agencies contemplating its use. From 1906 to 1911, Cleveland, Ohio, public school administrators explored measuring performance outcomes in the area of spelling as a means of increasing the quality and cost efficiency of the education they provided their students. Yet it was not until the late 1960s that the federal government viewed performance contracting, in its true form, as a viable means of achieving educational accountability and allocated Office of Economic Opportunity and Elementary and Secondary Education Act (ESEA) funds to support the process. After contemplating the impact that consolidating students with widely divergent academic achievement levels would have upon an already high dropout rate and considering the current national and local political and social climates, the Arkansas School District also deemed the time suitable for investigating the concept of performance contracting.

On September 10, 1969, Arkansas School District 7 partnered with the U.S. Office of Education and, using ESEA funds, entered an agreement with Dorsett Educational Systems, Inc., for the Texarkana Dropout Prevention Program. It was the first school district to employ performance contracting. The program, also known as the Texarkana Project, provided basic reading, math, and study skills instruction to at least 200 regular education students in Grades 7 through 12 who were functioning below (two or more grade levels) their assigned grade levels in the areas of reading and math. Project staff administered either the Iowa Test of Basic Skills or the Science Research Association test to students to determine their levels of performance at program entry and to determine their exit level achievement. The district agreed to pay Dorsett Educational Systems a prorated sum not to exceed $135,000 to increase per-student performance by one grade level in each subject within 60 to 167 hours of instruction. Incentives offered to students who completed their lessons included radios, premium stamps redeemable for gifts at a redemption center, and a television for the top student. Implementation inconsistencies rendered the Project's test results invalid. However, the district purchased the Project equipment and extended the Project for 2 additional years by entering a second performance contract with a different contractor, Educational Development Laboratories, Inc. The enterprise did not achieve definitive results regarding the effectiveness of performance contracting as a tool to increase student achievement.

Notwithstanding the unfavorable results of the Texarkana Project, the Office of Economic Opportunity's (OEO) desire to provide guidance to other school districts interested in performance contracting did not abate. OEO staff visited the Texarkana Project in the spring of 1970, and in the fall of the same year OEO launched its study of performance contracting by selecting six different contractors to deliver services in 18 school districts. OEO hired Battelle Laboratories as the independent contractor to complete the study's evaluation component. The research failed to discover any significant differences in achievement or cost between the experimental and control groups. In 1974, the federal government awarded funds to the RAND Corporation and the Government Accounting Office for each to examine the results of the OEO study. The RAND Corporation and the Government Accounting Office findings were consistent with those of Battelle's earlier research.

Legislation in a number of states, Texas, Indiana, New York, and Washington among them, require or enable governmental entities, PreK–12 schools, and universities to use different types of performance contracting. Federal and state agencies offer financial and/or technical assistance to school districts interested in exploring the use of performance contracting (e.g., Rebuild America, State Energy Conservation Offices, and State Departments of Education).

Benefits and Shortcomings

Performance contracting affords school districts the opportunity to realize potential benefits by achieving accountability through performance measurement, program evaluation, and cost-effectiveness measures. The process stimulates competition, serves as a vehicle for innovative change, and provides an avenue for new companies to introduce unique learning systems designed to increase the achievement of low-performing students. The success generated by performance contracting in the field of education fell short of its proponents' hopes and revealed a number of shortcomings: Several relate to program administration, program quality, testing and measurement, and professional development. Since, in some instances, schools maintain ultimate responsibility for performance contracting projects that someone else organizes and implements, supervision of the projects poses difficulties for school administrators. The scope of the curriculum diminishes when planned instructional activities focus exclusively on targeted curricular areas. Additionally, tests and other measurement instruments used to evaluate achievement in performance contracting prove challenging and in some cases are inadequate, depending on instrument selection and interpretation. Moreover, hiring outside contractors to deliver services traditionally provided by certified staff can potentially eliminate a school's motivation to assist teachers and administrators in developing the requisite skills for increasing student achievement. Further, teachers' unions tend to view educational performance contracting unfavorably, citing the process as encouraging the perception of teacher incompetence. For example, the Gary Teachers' Union threatened to strike in 1971 to demonstrate its opposition to a performance contract between the Gary Community School Corporation and Behavioral Research Laboratories, an action that contributed to the state of Indiana's decision not to recognize Banneker as one of the district's schools for a period of one month.

Performance Contracting Process

Two critical elements of performance contracting involve completing a needs assessment and designing the evaluation. Although additional components vary depending on organizational context and statutory requirements, the list generally includes a request for proposals (RFP), a contract, and activities commonly associated with performance measurement or program evaluation. The needs assessment results determine the project purpose. For example, in the case of efficiency performance contracting, districts identify areas of need and ascertain the extent to which opportunities exist for energy-saving improvements. Prior to settling on a project purpose, the district ensures that the proposed purpose aligns with funding source guidelines and the district's vision, mission, and goals. The next step is to develop performance specifications that address the district's unique needs; identify the project's constraints; and, if applicable, indicate the district's intent to adopt the initiative or efficiency procedures to maintain the cost savings or increased performance outcomes after the project is completed. The district prepares and advertises an RFP, which can include distributing it to preselected companies. After receiving and reviewing proposals, the district selects and works with the contractor to finalize an agreement. Project evaluation is integral to performance contracting; this component specifies the procedures for monitoring the project, measuring the achievement of predetermined outcomes, and calculating actual cost savings.

Judith Ann Green

See also Accountability Era; Collective Bargaining; Office of Economic Opportunity (OEO); School Finance; Unionization of Teachers

Further Readings

Ascher, C. (1996). Performance contracting: A forgotten experiment in school privatization. *Phi Delta Kappan, 77*, 615–622.

Gramlich, E. M., & Koshel, P. P. (1975). *Educational performance contracting.* Washington, DC: Brookings Institution.

Hansen, S. J. (1993). *Performance contracting for energy and environmental systems.* Lilburn, GA: Fairmont.

Mecklenburger, J. (1972). *Performance contracting.* Wortington, OH: Charles A. Jones.

Stucker, J. P., & Hall, G. R. (1971). *The performance contracting concept in education.* Santa Monica, CA: RAND.

PESTALOZZIANISM

The Pestalozzian movement of the 19th century represented the ideas of Swiss educator Johann Heinrich Pestalozzi (1746–1827) and was based on the premise that learning occurs most effectively in an emotionally secure environment where knowledge is acquired by sense perception. Influenced by Jean-Jacques Rousseau, Pestalozzi introduced psychology into education and was the first to systematize the science of teaching. Though known predominantly for the object lesson, Pestalozzianism led to transformational reform of elementary schools and ushered in the teacher licensure movement.

After the death of his father when Pestalozzi was only 5 years old, his mother brought him up in a loving but sheltered environment where outdoor excursions and interactions with other children were limited. His grandfather, a pastor, cultivated in him a concern for social justice, which was developed further in 1762 when he joined the Helvetic Society, a group of social activists. These early influences later impacted Pestalozzi's educational theory and practice.

Pestalozzi married a wealthy lady from Zurich in 1769. He considered following his grandfather into the ministry but chose to study law, only to decide later to try farming. He bought Neuhof, a farm with a large farmhouse, where he opened the first industrial school, which became home for more than 50 underprivileged boys. They were an undisciplined lot, many of whom took advantage of Pestalozzi's generosity by running off after receiving food and clothing. The first in a series of administrative bungles, Neuhof went bankrupt. Although reduced to poverty, Pestalozzi did not consider the 6-year experiment a complete failure. Leaving the Neuhof experience with a stronger conviction than ever, he began writing.

From 1780 to 1798, he gained prominence as a novelist, positioning himself for future success to promulgate his educational agenda. A novel about the original goodness of human nature, his 1781 *Leonard and Gertrude* gained him the most acclaim. Emphasizing the role of mothers in education, this novel served a double purpose for Pestalozzi. It promoted his concept of the ideal educational system and also pointed out the need for social reforms.

Although drawing heavily on Rousseauan principles regarding the inherent goodness of children and their need to develop freely, Pestalozzi's writings displayed three noteworthy differences. First, Pestalozzi did not support the glorification of nature as a utopia. He observed that nature can often be brutish, necessitating intentionality, especially in the moral instruction of children. Second, he was concerned about the education of the poor while Rousseau did not see such a need. Third, he applied theory to practice whereas Rousseau's ideology remained chiefly abstract. Unlike Rousseau, who relinquished his children to an orphanage, Pestalozzi educated his own son, implementing principles from *Émile*. Through application, Pestalozzi tempered Rousseau's ideas while refining his own praxis.

As he gained recognition for his writings, Pestalozzi also became identified as sympathizing with the French Revolution. He became convinced that the French regime could bring about moral regeneration and social reform. With funds from France's new government (France had invaded Switzerland), an orphan asylum was opened in Stans, Switzerland, with Pestalozzi as headmaster and sole teacher. Locals, who were predominantly Catholic, expressed hostility to the Protestant Pestalozzi and were resentful of his ties to the

French government. Despite its difficulties, however, Stans earned the reputation of being "The Cradle of the Modern Elementary School."

At Stans, the theories in Pestalozzi's writings were first implemented systematically. Even with 80 students and only one assistant, an atmosphere of familial love was cultivated. No books were used, as instruction was based on sense impression. Rather than traditional recitation of meaningless words, Pestalozzi's goal was to develop the students' powers of attentiveness, carefulness, and reliability. He viewed the strengthening of these skills at a young age as much more significant for later learning than what typically occurred in traditional classrooms. He refused to operate Stans on the broadly held assumptions that the purpose of school was to teach the written word, that children were innately bad and should be punished for not meeting academic expectations, and that education was inessential for the poor. After only 5 months, this successful experiment ended abruptly when French soldiers retreating from Austria sequestered the facility to establish a hospital.

Shortly thereafter, Pestalozzi moved to the Burgdorf castle where he began to fuse psychology and education and where he developed the first teachers' college. Using the German word *Anschauung* to refer to the acquisition of knowledge, he taught that no words should be used for instruction until after students had engaged in a process of sense impression. Inadequately translated as intuition, observation, sense experience, perception, or contemplation, *Anschauung* was defined by Pestalozzi as "things before words, concrete before abstract." This concept served as the framework for what popularly became known as the object lesson.

Students at Burgdorf engaged in field trips to the countryside, woods, or seashore where they collected specimens for object lessons. They closely examined the items, drawing and talking about their observations. They were then instructed to write about their objects and to read to others what they had written. Only after a process involving such concrete observations were teachers permitted to introduce vocabulary or concepts previously unfamiliar to the students. In addition to advancing the object lesson at Burgdorf, Pestalozzi refined and promoted such methods as movable letters, tactile arithmetic aids, slates, oral group answers, increased student–teacher interaction, and physical education.

Another psychological principle Pestalozzi advocated at Burgdorf was the need for balanced instruction in intellectual, moral, and physical development. Harmony among these powers was essential for proper growth and led Pestalozzi to include innovative activities such as drawing, singing, and physical exercise. Also radical for his time was the notion of the affective pedagogical element, that teachers should love their students. He identified the following dispositions as essential for effective teachers: fatherliness, cheerfulness, affection, and kindness.

Burgdorf closed due to a lack of funds in 1801. Though his ineptitude as an administrator led to several school failings, Pestalozzi continued to gain prominence as an innovative educator, especially during his 20-year tenure at Yverdon. Among international visitors to Yverdon were Friedrich Froebel, Johann Herbart, and William Maclure. Through these and many other visitors, Pestalozzianism spread to Germany, the United States, and other countries, influencing the following developments: kindergarten, scientific pedagogy, the New Harmony experiment, the common school movement, the Oswego Movement, and normal school training for teachers.

Critics indicate the enigmatic nature of Pestalozzi's method, arguing that it fragmented the sciences and neglected history and literature. Unfortunately, the object lesson was later so formalized that it became widely misunderstood, no longer representing the theoretical framework of its originator. Nevertheless, Pestalozzi's influence wrought considerable change in the emphasis given to student interest, respect for the child's natural development, and the overall tone of the modern elementary school.

Samuel James Smith

See also Herbartian Movement; Kindergarten; Normal Schools; Oswego Movement

Further Readings

Anderson, L. F. (1931). *Pestalozzi.* New York: AMS Press.
Gutek, G. L. (1968). *Pestalozzi and education.* New York: Random House.
Pestalozzi, J. H. (1898). *How Gertrude teaches her children* (L. E. Holland & F. C. Turner, Trans.). Syracuse, NY: C. W. Bardeen. (Original work published 1801)
Silber, K. (1960). *Pestalozzi: The man and his work.* London: Routledge & Kegan Paul.

PHILANTHROPY IN EDUCATION

Philanthropy entails funding dedicated to a specific cause with expectations that the gifts, especially financial gifts, will produce change to such a degree that it is measurable and recognized as a product of the gift. As such, the cause must be defined, the amount of donated resources extensive, and the gift should be sustainable over a period of time. Such criteria often require massive amounts of wealth; thus the association between philanthropy and the wealthy, and the disassociation between philanthropy and general charitable giving.

In education, philanthropy is likely to include donations of money, services, time, or materials to support the goals and objectives perceived to have value in educational settings. Those settings range from preschool settings to postsecondary institutions. The donors give without expectation of material reward for their gifts.

Development of Modern Philanthropy

Charitable giving in America can be traced to the early colonists. Although their altruism may have been somewhat associated with a desire to memorialize themselves, the giving was substantial and served society's needs. Giving in America mirrored the traditional giving of civilization at the time. Paul Boyer credited Benjamin Franklin with advocating that both the rich and the less well off should engage in philanthropic activities. Boyer wrote that by the mid-1770s, giving from one's own stores of wealth, whatever they might be, to the needy was an entrenched disposition in New England communities. As the country developed in the 1800s, citizens expanded their gift giving by creating private associations, such as orphanages, and maintaining contributions to schools and alms houses. Women were a critical component of multiple philanthropic institutions. For example, Dorothea

Dix sought treatment for the mentally ill; Jane Addams and Lillian Wald established settlement houses for immigrants. These reformers who focused on social responsibility promoted assistance efforts to remedy multiple social woes and obtained funding to support their endeavors.

One critical concern is related to when charitable giving became differentiated from philanthropy. The economic growth in the United States in the late 1800s, a source of great wealth for industrialists of the time, was the likely catalyst. The development of the business corporation model emerged in this period and eventually served as the model for philanthropic development.

Philanthropic giving can be traced to the turn of the 20th century and the efforts of men like Andrew Carnegie, John D. Rockefeller, Sr., John D. Rockefeller, Jr., Henry Ford, and Andrew Mellon. These industrial giants adhered to beliefs that the rich were trustees of wealth and that such wealth should address social issues and contribute to the alleviation of identified ills. Philanthropy (the word is derived from the Greek, meaning *to love people*) offered the wealthy a means to distribute grand sums to a wider range of recipients than did the traditional charitable giving of the time. Through the creation of organizations modeled on the successful business model (establishing trust and endowment funds) of the late 1800s, donors were able to gift large sums of wealth to address causes and effects of specific societal phenomena. These founders of modern American philanthropy established a format for giving by the wealthy for the 20th century. By 1930, approximately 150 foundations were active in the United States; Boyer reported that by 2000, more than 42,000 foundations existed. Of course the subset of philanthropic foundations supported by high-profile business wealth remains active in society, but the majority of active foundation support is a group of smaller organizations created by wealthy families at local levels. The recipients are also local; in this respect, these private foundations supplement the community foundations.

In the years ahead, the stage for philanthropy—one that has changed little in the last 100 years—may be structured to confront an even wider array of challenges and opportunities in the 21st century. Indeed, it is clear that education policy and practice is being influenced by the reform agendas of many high-profile philanthropic organizations, such as the Gates Foundation.

How Do Foundations Serve Philanthropists?

Philanthropists can gift others in multiple ways: trusts, outright gifts, and endowments are common methods of sharing wealth. Endowments are a particularly effective way to transfer wealth to others for specific purposes. The creation of foundations is essential for managing endowments for charitable purposes. Stanley Katz credits Carnegie and Rockefeller, considered among the country's foremost philanthropists, with creating the concept of the private foundation in order to distribute large amounts of wealth to meet social needs. A foundation, a legal entity, is a nonprofit organization that may either donate funds and support to other organizations, or provide the sole source of funding for its own giving. A foundation creates a constitution of sorts that outlines its general purposes, delineates its guidelines for operation, and maintains assets in the name of the foundation. The private foundation is governed by a board of trustees that may include the philanthropist and family members and close associates. By law, foundations must distribute at least 5% of their assets annually as gifts.

Development of the Foundation

Katz reports that the founding foundations in the early 1900s relied on business organizational structures and depended on a chief executive officer and staff to manage program areas, to address grant giving, and to collaborate with grant seekers to determine specifics and procedures that reflected the goals of their private foundations. These foundations can be thought of as general foundations because they concentrate on multiple societal needs and present a history of redirecting emphasis over time, thus impacting a variety of support; for example, education, poverty, arts, and humanities.

Many philanthropic and charitable organizations are foundations. The government differentiates between private foundations and community foundations. Private foundations, like those that Carnegie, Rockefeller, Ford, and Mellon established, are linked to individuals, families, or corporations and are subject to substantial governmental control and few tax benefits. Community foundations and other nonprofit groups that raise money from the general public receive a broader range of tax relief for their charitable work.

The community foundation took root in local social activism in the 1920s just after the close of World War I. The emphasis was local. The purpose was to seek endowments from multiple wealthy sources with the goal of creating a merged set of funds to be managed by the single foundation; the assets from investment could then be offered as grants to a significant number of local nonprofit entities. In essence, the foundation that managed the investments also was knowledgeable about the community's needs and the parameters and history of distribution of funds to causes. Multiple grant seekers could seek assistance locally and be somewhat assured of consideration—a phenomenon not as likely to occur at the national scale with the large private foundations.

The corporate foundation, sometimes classified as a type of private foundation, has the unique characteristic of being funded, not through endowments of individual wealthy donors, but by annual contributions from a corporation. Stanley Katz reported that the corporate foundation was established in the mid-1940s and appeared to flourish for some time. Recently, however, corporate philanthropy has declined.

Philanthropy in Education

John Harvard bequeathed a collection of hundreds of books and a sum of money to a new college in Cambridge, Massachusetts, in the mid-1600s; the college was renamed in his honor. Boyer and others assert that such giving established the pattern for much early giving to the educational community. A philanthropist in the 1800s, George Peabody provided in excess of $2 million to promote education in the South; his reward was the George Peabody College for Teachers in Tennessee, now affiliated with Vanderbilt University. He made further contributions to museums and libraries across the United States, including endowments to the museums at Harvard University and Yale University. Another 19th-century philanthropist, Anthony Drexel, provided substantial funds to establish Drexel University in 1892. Grace Dodge influenced the founding of the Teachers College of

Columbia University. The wealthiest philanthropists of the 20th century made education a target for shares of their wealth; their contributions contributed to their name recognition and ultimately brought additional attention to their foundations. According to the Foundation Center, about 25% of all annual giving on the part of foundations is devoted to education. Elementary, secondary, and postsecondary institutions, both public and private, are recipients of philanthropic gifts.

Colleges and Universities

As has been noted, institutions of higher education long have been recipients of endowments from the wealthy. The amounts and annual growth during economic growth periods is typically substantial. The National Center for Education Statistics (NCES) published survey data collected by the National Association of College and University Business Officers. Participating institutions were ranked by annual endowments, and the results indicated that Harvard University, in each of 2 years (2005 and 2006), had the largest endowment. Furthermore, the growth for Harvard from 2005 to 2006 was $3.5 billion. Although the highest ranking institutions are private universities, both public and private institutions were represented in the array placing in the top 20 endowments; the range in 2006 was from $3.6 billion to $28.9 billion.

The work of colleges and universities is supported by restricted gifts for particular purposes. One popular restricted gift is the scholarship program for promoting student access, retention, and success in the postsecondary environment, often in specific professional areas. Research projects often receive grants for a specified period of time; these may originate from the institution's foundation but more often are gifts of other foundations or corporations.

Elementary and Secondary Education

More than $500 billion is spent on elementary and secondary schooling annually in the United States, and the bulk of that revenue originates with taxpayers. An estimate of annual spending on elementary and secondary education in the United States by philanthropists is about $4 billion. The Bill & Melinda Gates Foundation is a private foundation created in 2001 as an amalgamation of two already established Gates foundations. Its assets are currently in excess of $29.1 billion, and the foundation is the recipient of a pledge from investor and businessman Warren Buffet for a $30.7 billion donation, making this foundation the richest in resources in the United States. It made its first education donations in 2000 and has since donated more than $350 million annually to schools. The Bill & Melinda Gates Foundation is committed to education philanthropy in K–12 schooling, and its current emphasis is on creating small high schools. Substantial funding has provided funds to charter initiatives; city districts of Boston, Milwaukee, Kansas City, and New York; and state schools in Michigan and Maine. Tom Van Ark, a key administrator of the Gates Foundation, reported in 2003 that upward of 2 years of planning can be devoted to crafting the plans and the goals for funded projects.

A wide array of philanthropies contributes to the elementary and secondary sector of education. One unique philanthropic support initiative in the early years of the millennium involved a cross-sector partnership between a philanthropy and the federal government to improve national collection of school site data. Other initiatives from yet additional foundations include specific funding to particular programs, such as early childhood education. Another thrust of philanthropic support has been aimed at teacher preparation for new millennium schools and administrator preparation. Old grant-giving models might have provided funding to colleges and universities to encourage more teachers to enter the field, for example, or to help prepare teachers for specific curricula. Current models include grants to private organizations that are forming for the express purpose of preparing teachers and leaders apart from the university and college preparation formats.

On the Horizon

Conflicts may be on the horizon for the present-day philanthropists. At least two factors may materialize. First, the sheer magnitude of the value of the resources associated with the top ranking, relatively newly formed private foundation may influence the behavior of the more established philanthropies of the 20th century. Second, if foundational support becomes more collaborative with multiple organizational partnerships and active participation on the part of the private foundation becomes an expected phenomenon, the more established foundations may consider shifts in their ways of doing business. The old guard has an established pattern for grant giving and sustaining the grant over periods of time; the new guard is showing signs of more assertive interaction with causes of social hardships.

Philanthropy has its supporters and critics. Some view philanthropy as benevolent and charitable only for the oppressed or needy. Some see it as an act of altruism that can impact positively the quality of life and ameliorate depraved social conditions. Nevertheless, the foundation sector in the United States represents a sizable store of wealth and a well-maintained and effective structure for pursuing social responsibility with those resources. Corporations may come to consider philanthropy—known as corporation social responsibility (CSR)—as providing a service that is not served by the market. Business leaders today argue the merits of CSR versus pure capitalism.

Given the intense interest of Bill Gates in philanthropy and his past influence in the business arena, corporate foundations may emerge as a more dominant player than in the recent past. Gates, founder of the computer software giant Microsoft and an entrepreneur with whom a majority of the population can identify, challenged a group of elite business leaders at a 2007 private business meeting to ponder what he terms "creative capitalism." He suggested multiple strategies that might bolster corporate position on social responsibility.

In resurrecting the role of corporate philanthropy, Gates urged capitalists to consider thinking beyond the parameters of current corporate giving; in one example, he asked leaders of current businesses to think outside the box and consider diversion of a small percentage of profits to assist social responsibility issues. Michael Kinsley used the contents of the speech as a catalyst to create an electronic conversation with economic leaders to assess the breadth of responses to the challenge. One frequent criticism offered by the economic leaders was that the strategies made up the maximization of profits for a corporation, their ultimate reason for existing. Yet a body of responses did accede to the possibility that corporations of the future might find room to blend profit taking with profit sharing.

Improving Understanding of Philanthropies

Katz, in 2007, maintained that for much of the 20th century, philanthropy had not received significant exposure; that lack of exposure resulted in minimal informed understanding of the field. Internet access has provided a pathway to information about philanthropic institutions. National directories of foundations exist, a central data bank is housed at the Foundation Center, and Indiana University has created a Center on Philanthropy.

Frederick Hess and others have captured ideas about the importance of philanthropy in K–12 education and about the impact such philanthropy has on advancing reform agendas. Hess asserts that education philanthropy has generally been "disorderly, visible, and little studied." The result of this circumstance is that people have given both credit and direct criticism to foundations that provide philanthropic dollars because people fail to understand fully the direct and indirect ways in which foundations insinuate themselves into the educational reform process. Philanthropy is clearly one of those areas that is impacting American education. It is a phenomenon that will continue to be an important part of the reform landscape as long as substantial dollars are being directed toward change efforts.

Barbara Y. LaCost

See also Gates Foundation; Peabody Fund

Further Readings

Anheier, H. K., & Leat, D. (2006). *Creative philanthropy: Toward a new philanthropy for the twenty-first century*. New York: Routledge.

Bishop, M., & Green, M. (2008). *Philanthrocapitalism: How the rich can save the world*. New York: Simon & Schuster.

Boyer, P. S. (2001). Philanthropy and philanthropic foundations. In *Oxford companion to United States history*. New York: Oxford University Press.

Fleishman, J. L. (2007). *The foundation: A great American secret: How private wealth is changing the world*. New York: Public Affairs.

Foundation Center. (2003). *Newsmakers: An interview with Tom Vander Ark*. Retrieved October 23, 2008, from http://foundationcenter.org

Frumkin, P. (2006). *Strategic giving: The art and science of philanthropy*. Chicago: University of Chicago Press.

Hess, F. M. (2005). *With the best of intentions: How philanthropy is reshaping K–12 education*. Cambridge, MA: Harvard Education Press.

Katz, S. N. (2007, February 7). Philanthropy's new math. *Chronicle of Higher Education*, p. B6.

Kinsley, M. (2008). (Ed.). *Creative capitalism: A conversation with Bill Gates, Warren Buffet, and other economic leaders*. New York: Simon & Schuster.

National Center for Education Statistics. (2007). *Digest of education statistics, 2006*. Washington, DC: U.S. Department of Education.

National Center for Education Statistics. (2008). *Digest of education statistics, 2007*. Washington, DC: U.S. Department of Education.

PHONICS

Phonics is considered by many as one of the most controversial topics in the field of reading. By definition, *phonics* is the collection of instructional approaches designed to teach children the connection between letters and sounds. Phonics plays an essential role in the teaching of reading. The historical role of phonics in the teaching of reading has been referred to as a pendulum, swinging back and forth from one extreme to the other. Phonics is an integral aspect of the teaching of reading, but the form it has taken and its emphasis have changed dramatically. This entry is intended to illuminate the history, current theories, and controversy surrounding the role of phonics in the teaching of reading.

A great deal of confusion exists in the field concerning the interconnected nature of certain key terms. *Phonological awareness* refers to the sound structure of language, of which there are many aspects. One of these aspects is *phonemic awareness*. Phonological awareness encompasses several different levels of understanding, and phonemic awareness is the most sophisticated of these levels. Phonemic awareness, also known as phoneme awareness, is the awareness of individual sound units, or phonemes, in spoken words. Phonemes are the smallest unit of sound in language. *Phonics* refers to the connection between sound and letter. Letter–sound correspondence involves the practice of phonics. Once a child is phonologically aware, phonics instruction may begin.

In the early years of formal reading instruction, phonics instruction in the form of skill and drill exercises was emphasized. The look–say method, emphasizing recognition of whole words, came into prominence in the 1920s. Beginning in the 1950s with Rudolph Flesch's *Why Johnny Can't Read,* phonics was identified as an essential, yet absent, component of reading. In 1967, Jeanne Chall put forth a model of the reading process that identified phonics as a critical prerequisite skill for advancing to higher levels of reading. In 1990, Marilyn Adams provided further support for the value of phonics to the teaching of reading in her work, *Beginning to Read: Thinking and Learning About Print.* These research studies and reports, along with numerous others, set the stage for the controversy surrounding how and when to include phonics instruction in the teaching of reading. Each emphasized the critical nature of phonics instruction, but failed to agree on a single method.

Adams's work coincided with the emergence and dominance of the *whole language* movement. Whole language is a method of teaching reading that emphasizes the use of authentic literature to teach reading skills. Whole language became a dominant method of teaching reading in the 1990s, and explicit, systematic teaching of phonics skills in particular, was not emphasized. In 2000, the National Reading Panel published a report that identified the importance of systematic, explicit phonics instruction over the contextual phonics instruction provided by whole language. Countless research studies have provided additional support for the importance of systematic, explicit phonics instruction in learning to read, though not without controversy and dissension.

It is important to note that systematic, explicit approaches to phonics instruction can differ widely. Phonics instruction can be taught using a variety of approaches, including synthetic, analytic, and embedded. Synthetic phonics instruction involves students in first identifying letters and sounds, then blending these together to form words. It is a part-to-whole approach to phonics. Analytic approaches to teaching phonics involve students in first reading words, then breaking these words down into their individual letters and sounds. This is a whole-to-part approach to phonics. Embedded approaches to teaching phonics involve students in learning phonics skills by reading authentic texts. This approach may be compared to whole language; however, embedded phonics involves planned skills taught within the context of authentic literature. Embedded phonics formed in response to the intense criticism experienced by the whole language movement, and highlights the role of phonics instruction within the context of authentic literature.

Systematic phonics instruction does not necessitate a synthetic approach. Analytic, embedded, and synthetic approaches can be systematic and explicit when they are carefully planned and taught to students as one component of the complex process of reading. A review of reading programs in elementary schools will reveal a wide variety of synthetic, analytic, and embedded approaches to teaching phonics, including a blending of the three approaches. Systematic, explicit phonics instruction means that instruction, relying on whatever approach is deemed appropriate by the teacher, is planned and taught to students in a sequential fashion. Deciding on an appropriate approach should be done in consultation with recent, relevant research in the teaching of phonics, as well as an assessment of the teaching context.

The importance of phonics knowledge in learning to read is not the fuel behind the controversy. Most reading professionals agree phonics knowledge is a critical component of the reading process. Rather, the controversy exists over how and when to teach phonics to children. The goal of reading is the construction of meaning. The graphophonic system (letter-sounds) works in conjunction with the semantic (background of experience), syntactic (language structure, grammar), and pragmatic (culture) systems, not in isolation. Research points to the importance of authentic activities highlighting transfer of skills, emphasizing patterns and analogy as a method of decoding unknown words. The role of phonics in the reading process is critical and widely accepted, but the debate continues regarding the most effective method of teaching phonics to children.

Mary-Kate Sableski

See also Flesch, Rudol; Reading First; Reading Recovery; Reading Reform; Whole Language

Further Readings

Adams, M. J. (1990). *Beginning to read: Thinking and learning about print*. Cambridge: MIT Press.

Chall, J. (1967). *Learning to read: The great debate*. New York: McGraw-Hill.

Dahl, K., Scharer, P., Lawson, L., & Grogan, P. (2001). *Rethinking phonics: Making the best teaching decisions*. Portsmouth, NH: Heinemann.

Cunningham, P. M., & Cunningham, J. W. (2002). What we know about how to teach phonics. In A. J. Farstrup & S. J. Samuels (Eds.), *What research has to say about reading instruction* (pp. 87–109). Newark, DE: International Reading Association.

Flesch, R. (1955). *Why Johnny can't read: And what you can do about it*. New York: Harper & Row.

PHYSICAL EDUCATION

The explosion of personal technology at the turn of the 21st century has been attended by increases in sedentary lifestyles and unprecedented levels of obesity in our nation's youth (17% of U.S. children aged 6–19 are obese). In response, physical educators at all levels across the country are again heeding the call to return to the profession's historical roots, which were originally grounded in the fields of medicine and public health. Founded in 1885 by physicians concerned with the ill effects of urbanization and industrialization, the American Association for the Advancement of Physical Education (AAAPE, the forerunner of the contemporary American Alliance for Health, Physical Education, Recreation and Dance, AAHPERD), was led by prominent physicians of the time, including Drs. William Anderson, Edward Hitchcock, and Dudley A. Sargent. Warning of the health risks associated with the transformation of America from a rural–agrarian land to urban–industrial country at the turn of the 19th century, Sargent, in 1904, wrote that "the problem is to retain our acquired health, strength, and power under the conditions imposed by modern progress . . . this advancement has resulted in the fact that it is possible to earn a living at the present time by the use of a very few muscles and faculties" (p. 6).

Prophetic indeed was Sargent, whose voice has been heard anew by modern-day physical educators and other professionals concerned with the health and fitness of the nation's youth. In returning to the founders' intent, three recent major reform efforts are providing students with increased opportunities for education both of and through the physical, which, in view of the national epidemic of obesity and sedentary lifestyles, are more essential now than at any point in history. The purpose of this entry is to identify, describe, and delineate those reform efforts and their impact on the field of physical education at the beginning of the 21st century.

Reform No. 1: Standards-Based Physical Education

Published first in 1995 and then revised in 2004 by the National Association for Sport and Physical Education (NASPE, an association of AAHPERD), *Moving Into the Future: National Standards for Physical Education* provided physical education professionals with their first nationally endorsed and coherent content standards and guidelines for assessment. A consensus document reflecting the collective expertise and experience of a group of the nation's most highly regarded physical education professionals from higher education and the public schools, the standards outline developmentally appropriate learning outcomes and assessment strategies from the cognitive, affective, and psychomotor domains across all grade levels (K–12). Utilized by physical educators, school district boards and administrators, members of the professoriate, and state organizations to guide the development and/or adaptation of innovative curricula, expert pedagogy, and authentic assessment, the standards are based on the most recent research on physical activity and best practices in physical education pedagogy. Identifying specifically what students need to know and should be able to do in the form of outcomes and benchmarks related to high-quality physical education programs, the NASPE National Standards for Physical Education continue to catalyze reform across the nation: 49 states now have content standards–based curricula.

Summarized below are the philosophical, operational–definitional components of the 2004 NASPE standards as well as the actual standards themselves.

Philosophical Underpinnings

The National Standards for Physical Education are intended to provide a framework from which students may learn the skills and practices required to live healthy, physically active lifestyles for a lifetime. The standards set guidelines for the acquisition and promotion of knowledge and skills necessary for students to be able to make informed decisions for participation in all forms of physical activity, including rhythms, dance, games, sports, gymnastics, and fitness activities focusing on all aspects of health-related fitness (i.e., cardiovascular endurance, muscular strength, muscular endurance, flexibility, and body composition) as well as the components of motor skill development (i.e., agility, coordination, reaction time, speed, power, and balance). Optimally, students benefiting from high-quality physical education guided by the National Standards will be physically fit and possess positive dispositions that value and pursue opportunities to be physically active for a lifetime.

Operational Definitions

High-quality physical education programs ensure that students receive the following:

- Opportunities to learn in the form of instructional periods totaling a minimum of 150 minutes per week at the elementary level and 225 minutes per week at the middle and secondary levels.
- Appropriate instruction featuring (a) full inclusion of all students, (b) maximum practice opportunities for class activities, (c) well-designed lessons facilitating student learning, (d) out-of-school assignments that support learning, practice, and the establishment of lifelong habits, (e) regular and authentic assessment to monitor, reinforce, and plan for instruction, and (f) instruction free of the use of physical activity as punishment.
- Content delivered by qualified physical education specialists providing a developmentally appropriate program.
- Meaningful content via instruction across a variety of motor skills designed to enhance the

physical, mental, and social/emotional development of every child.
- Fitness education and assessment to help children understand, improve, and/or maintain their physical well-being.
- Development of cognitive concepts about motor skills and fitness.
- Opportunities to improve their emerging social and cooperative skills and gain a multicultural perspective. (NASPE, 2004b)

NASPE Content Standards

Standard 1. Demonstrates competency in motor skills and movement patterns needed to perform a variety of physical activities.

Standard 2. Demonstrates understanding of movement concepts, principles, strategies, and tactics as they apply to the learning and performance of physical activities.

Standard 3. Participates regularly in physical activity.

Standard 4. Achieves and maintains a health-enhancing level of physical fitness.

Standard 5. Exhibits responsible personal and social behavior that respects self and others in physical activity settings.

Standard 6. Values physical activity for health, enjoyment, challenge, self-expression, and/or social interaction. (NASPE, 2004b)

Reform No. 2: Promotion and Proliferation of Sport Education

First introduced in the United States in 1995 by Daryl Siedentop of the Ohio State University, the sport education curriculum model (SEM) has contributed significantly to the preservation and improvement of physical education programs where a traditional sport-based culture is prevalent. Originally developed out of Siedentop's frustration at witnessing sport and physical education being taught insufficiently, the SEM provides students with sport and physical activity experiences that are more realistic, context specific, challenging, and enjoyable than those presented via conventional curricula. Resembling more realistically the actual essence of experiences in sport/physical activity by delivering content seasons/sessions of longer duration vis-à-vis units, allowing for continuous team/group affiliation rather than assignment to squads, and allowing for full student participation as players/athletes and also as coaches, officials, statisticians, choreographers, trainers, and so forth, the SEM is an all-inclusive and entirely student-centered approach to teaching physical education, aimed at reform and change but capable of preserving the best aspects of a school program's existing sport culture.

Based on the 2004 original work of Siedentop, Hastie, and van der Mars, the objectives of sport education follow. Students will

- Develop skills and fitness specific to particular sports
- Appreciate and be able to execute strategic play in sports
- Participate at a level appropriate for their stage of development
- Share in the planning and administration of sport experiences
- Provide responsible leadership
- Work effectively within a group toward common goals
- Appreciate the rituals and conventions that give particular sports their unique meanings
- Develop the capacity to make reasoned decisions about sport issues
- Develop and apply knowledge about umpiring, refereeing, and training
- Decide voluntarily to become involved in after-school sports

Research seeking to demonstrate the efficacy of curriculum reform efforts featuring sport education has been conducted in diverse settings and generated favorable results. Implementation of sport education has successfully promoted both content and pedagogical practices consistent with those delineated in all six NASPE Physical Education Content Standards (2004), particularly in the cultivation of responsible personal and social behavior that respects self and others in physical activity settings and in teaching students to value physical activity for health, enjoyment, challenge, self-expression, and/or social interaction. Sport education research has also been shown to (a) ameliorate the effects of—and in some cases, reverse—teacher burnout, (b) promote higher levels of physical activity, (c) enhance student learning of subject matter content, and (d) provide a teaching–learning environment more conducive to gender equity, personal and social responsibility, and enjoyment for all participants.

Reform No. 3: Teaching Personal and Social Responsibility Through Physical Activity

The lifelong pursuit of Don Hellison, of the University of Illinois of Chicago, whose work with underserved youth in urban areas has earned international acclaim over the span of 3 decades, has been physical-education reform featuring his teaching personal and social responsibility model (TPSR). Having gained widespread acceptance in physical-education programs, teacher-education programs and school districts across the country, Hellison's work has consistently demonstrated the efficacy of utilizing high-quality standards-based physical activity to promote personal and social responsibility, classically known as education through the physical. Research conducted by Hellison, his colleagues, and others has shown that students guided by his TPSR model in school as well as in community-based settings, and in academic as well as physical activity settings, facilitated (a) increased levels of participation, (b) improved attendance, (c) anger management and conflict resolution, and (d) improved group dynamics and community building.

Based on Hellison's (2003) original work, the TPSR model appears below in synthesis.

Level 0—Irresponsibility. Students operating at Level Zero make excuses, blame others for their behavior, and deny personal responsibility for what they do or fail to do.

Level 1—Respect. Students at Level 1 may not participate in the day's activities or show much mastery or improvement, but they are able to control their behavior enough so that they do not interfere with other students' right to learn or teachers' right to teach. They do this without much prompting by the teacher and without constant supervision.

Level 2—Participation. Students at Level 2 not only show at least minimal respect for others but also willingly play, accept challenges, practice motor skills, and train for fitness under the teacher's supervision.

Level 3—Self-Direction. Students at Level 3 not only show respect and participate, but they are also able to work without direct supervision. They can identify their own needs and begin to plan and carry out their own physical education programs.

Level 4—Helping-Caring. In addition to respecting others, participating, and being self-directed, students are motivated to extend their sense of responsibility beyond themselves by cooperating, giving support, showing concern, and helping.

Level 5—Outside the Gym-Classroom. Students transfer the concepts learned in the first four levels and apply them at home, on the playground, and/or in the community. In doing so, they become role models for their peers.

Conclusion

In returning to the profession's historical mission to provide education of and through the physical, the reformers whose work has been featured in this entry have successfully presented viable options to combat the epidemic of obesity and the pervasiveness of sedentary lifestyles affecting our nation's youth. Resulting in research demonstrating the efficacy of standards-based physical education, sport education, and teaching personal and social responsibility, the curricular reforms described herein are indeed worthy of continued embrace and implementation.

George Mario Paul DeMarco, Jr.

See also Ability Grouping; Assessment; Co-Curricular Activities; Coeducation; Differentiated Instruction; Experiential Learning; Extracurricular Activities; Performance-Based Assessment

Further Readings

Hellison, D. (2003). *Teaching responsibility through physical activity* (2nd ed.). Champaign, IL: Human Kinetics.

National Association for Sport and Physical Education. (1995). *Moving into the future: National standards for physical education.* Reston, VA: Author.

National Association for Sport and Physical Education. (2004a). *Appropriate practices for high school physical education.* Reston, VA: Author.

National Association for Sport and Physical Education. (2004b). *Moving into the future: National standards for physical education* (2nd ed.). Reston, VA: Author.

National Association for Sport and Physical Education. (2006). *Shape of the nation report: Status of physical education in the USA.* Reston, VA: Author.

Sargent, D. A. (1904). *Health, strength & power.* New York: Dodge Publishing.

Siedentop, D., Hastie, P., & van der Mars, H. (2004). *Complete guide to sport education.* Champaign, IL: Human Kinetics.

PIAGET, JEAN (1896–1980)

The Swiss psychologist Jean Piaget, whose work in cognitive and developmental psychology caused many significant changes in elementary education, was one of the most influential theorists of the 20th century. Educators in the latter part of the 20th century relied heavily on his ideas as they thought about how to structure classrooms and how to deliver curriculum in ways that would foster the intellectual development of young people.

Piaget proposed that the cognitive development of children occurred in sequential developmental stages: sensorimotor, preoperational, concrete operational, and formal operational. Each stage represented a specific type of cognitive functioning that was caused by the individual's level of biological maturation. Piaget believed that all individuals pass through these stages, and within each stage organize the information that they learn into stage-specific structures he called *schemes.* Piaget theorized that as individuals matured and their environment changed, they would adapt to the changes either by assimilating the changes into their current schemes or by accommodating the changes by reorganizing their schemes. The function of assimilation and accommodation is to maintain a balance, through the process of equilibration, between one's scheme and changes within the environment.

Contributions to Education Reform

Piaget significantly influenced elementary education with the idea that individuals construct their own understanding of reality. His understanding that individuals are active learners who modify and transform information through their engagement with that knowledge provides the foundation for the pervasive constructivist movement in contemporary education, which constituted one of the most significant and controversial reform efforts of the late 20th century. In Piagetian theory, children are not passive recipients of information, but active participants in the learning process who construct their own meaning.

Piaget influenced elementary education in a number of ways. First, the children's stage of development limits what they can learn. For instance, children cannot solve abstract problems until the last cognitive stage, formal operational, that begins around the age of 11. Second, what children learn in later stages is affected by what they learned and the cognitive structures that they developed in the earlier stages. Therefore, opportunities must be provided that facilitate the full cognitive development of the child in each stage. Third, the important part of a child's learning is the child's ability to apply or transfer what was already learned to the new information. Fourth, children cannot apply what they learned in a previous stage until they have developed the physical brain structures that will allow the next level of learning to take place. Finally, requiring students to learn information that is beyond their stage of cognitive development is a futile learning experience. For instance, no amount of practice in learning algebra will help middle-school students who are not yet in the formal operational stage.

Constructivist education takes its name from Piaget's research showing that children actively create—construct—new knowledge from their experiences that goes beyond what they already know. The following main ideas from Piaget's research and theory are relevant to education:

- Children construct knowledge.
- Interest is necessary for the constructive process to begin and continue.
- Experimentation with physical phenomena is essential to the constructive process.
- Cooperation characterizes the interpersonal atmosphere in which the constructive process thrives.

A challenge for constructivist teachers is to identify content that intrigues children and arouses their curiosity. Cooperation, according to Piaget, refers to the type of social context necessary for optimal development of intelligence or knowledge, and of emotional, social, and moral aspects of personality. By "cooperation," Piaget did not mean submissive compliance. For Piaget, cooperation is an essential characteristic of active education that respects the ways in which children think and the ways they transform their thinking by making new mental relationships. Mutual respect creates the basic dynamic in which individuals want and try to cooperate—that is, to operate in terms of one another's desires and ideas.

Each classroom and school has a sociomoral atmosphere. This is made up of the entire network of interpersonal relationships among children and between adults and children. In this atmosphere, children feel safe, securely attached to the teacher, and free to be mentally active. The first principle of constructivist education is that the teacher must establish a cooperative sociomoral atmosphere in which mutual respect is continually practiced.

A constructivist teacher tries to help children put aside their usual view of adults by relating to children as a companion or guide. Constructivist teachers express respect for children in a variety of ways: (a) having class meetings to discuss and evaluate how their classroom is structured, (b) allowing children to make selected decisions about classroom procedures and curriculum, (c) encouraging children to discuss and make rules they feel are necessary to prevent or solve problems, (d) conducting social and moral discussions about interpersonal problems in children's literature and problems arising in the classroom, and (e) engaging children in conflict resolution with the goal of children learning to take account of another's point of view and resolve their own conflicts.

Cooperating with children means that the constructivist teacher refrains from unnecessarily controlling children. Many people misunderstand this principle as permissiveness—that is, allowing children to do anything. The constructivist teacher is not permissive. Sometimes external control is necessary. When the teacher has to exercise external control, its negative effects can be minimized by empathizing with the child's feelings, explaining why the child must comply, and being firm but not harsh. The goal of the constructivist teacher is to minimize external control to the extent possible and practical and to promote the child's internal control. In other words, teachers help children help themselves.

The constructivist classroom context embodies the characteristics of respect mentioned above. Teachers respect children's interests by giving children choices during activity time among such activities as pretend play; reading books; painting; listening to and acting out stories; playing musical instruments; and water, sand, and block building or woodworking. Constructivist activities added to this traditional curriculum in early education include physical knowledge activities. In physical knowledge activities, children engage with physical phenomena involving movement (physics) or changes (chemistry) in objects. They also engage in group games that require cooperation, even for competitive games. In all these activities, teachers plan, intervene, and evaluate in terms of mental relationships children have the possibility to make. For example, in a physical knowledge activity involving making marble pathways with lengths of wood having a groove down the middle, children can make the mental relationship between height of support (a block or box) and speed of the marble or distance the marble travels off the end of an incline. In a game of tag, children have the possibility to make the reciprocal relationship between chaser and one who is chased— between the intention to tag and the intention to avoid being tagged. All children's activities are thus evaluated in terms of what mental relationships children are making, including those that are social, emotional, and moral as well as intellectual.

Conclusion

Research has established the limitations of Piagetian theory. Various researchers have challenged the existence of four separate stages of thinking even though many agree that children do pass through the changes in cognition identified by Piaget. Also, research does not support various aspects of Piagetian theory such as the developmental constraints on learning in the concrete–operational stage. Also, Piagetian theory does not explain how very young children can perform certain highly complex tasks. However, neo-Piagetian theories have combined Piaget's ideas with new information about cognitive development to better understand how children think and construct knowledge.

Piaget's ideas continue to shape a lot of what happens in classrooms throughout the United States. His work led to a variety of signficiant reforms in the early childhood education area and especially contributed to enhanced attention to the ways in which student curiosity and critical learning could occur during the early learning years.

Thomas P. Jandris

See also Constructivism; Early Childhood Education; Inquiry-Based Learning

Further Readings

Peterson, R., & Felton-Collins, V. (1986). *The Piaget handbook for teachers and parents*. New York: Teachers College Press.

Piaget, J. (1958). *Logic and psychology*. New York: Basic Books.

Piaget, J. (1973). *To understand is to invent: The future of education*. New York: Grossman.

Piaget, J., & Inhelder, B. (1969). *The psychology of the child*. New York: Basic Books.

PIERCE V. SOCIETY OF SISTERS

In 1925, the U.S. Supreme Court rendered a decision that was to have a dramatic impact on schooling in America and the relative authority of the state and parents to guide the education of children. That decision was *Pierce v. Society of Sisters*. This entry reviews the historic context of the controversy, identifies the parties to the dispute, outlines the legal issues involved, and describes the decision and the reasoning of the Court, as well as the significance of the decision on educational policy, then and today.

Origin of Compulsory Attendance Policies

Beginning with the common school crusade in the mid-1800s, states began encouraging the creation of systems of primary education; and by the 1880s, the authority of school systems to offer secondary education had been confirmed. Starting about the same time and continuing through the turn of the 20th century, a confluence of factors, both political and economic, contributed to the adoption of laws making schooling compulsory, for most, although not necessarily all, children. These factors included the influx of large numbers of nonwestern European immigrants with cultures, languages, and religions different from the then dominant population, which spawned laws and policies designed to ensure the assimilation and allegiance of these new arrivals to their adopted land. Compulsory education was one such law, as were laws dictating English as the language of instruction and the practice of patriotic exercises in the schools. A second factor contributing to the adoption of compulsory school attendance was the Industrial Revolution. It contributed to the exploitation of children as a cheap source of labor, which also resulted in unacceptably high unemployment rates among older and more costly workers, both of which augured for compulsory school attendance for the young.

The Controversy in *Pierce:* A Particularly Stringent State Policy

It was primarily the former of these two factors that, after a public referendum advocated for essentially by the Ku Klux Klan and the Scottish Rite Masons, led to the adoption in 1922 of a particularly stringent form of compulsory education law in the state of Washington. The Compulsory Education Act (1922) required every parent or guardian in charge of a child between 8 and 16 years of age to send their children to a public school, making attendance at a public school the exclusive means of satisfying the state's mandate that all children be educated through the eighth grade.

The operators of two private schools, one a parochial school owned by the Society of Sisters, and the other a private military school, Hill Academy, brought a federal court action challenging the Washington state law. The school owners variously contended that the compulsory education law threatened their business or property interests and conflicted with the liberty interests of parents to choose where their children would receive their education and religious training. The private schools also argued that the Act would infringe on the right of children to influence their parents' choice of schools and the right of teachers to pursue their profession.

The Supreme Court's Ruling and Rationale

The Supreme Court found this particular form of compulsory attendance law to be a violation of the substantive due process provision of the Fourteenth Amendment that bars states from depriving one of life, liberty, or property without due process of law. In this situation, the Court concluded that the Washington law unreasonably interfered with the

liberty interest of parents and guardians to direct the upbringing and education of their children and represented an arbitrary, unreasonable, and unlawful interference with the patrons of the school, resulting in the destruction of the business and property of the operators of the private schools. The Court consequently enjoined the enforcement of this particular compulsory education law.

In arriving at its decision, the Court observed that the schools were not engaged in an inherently harmful undertaking, but rather one long regarded as useful and meritorious. It further noted that there was no evidence that the schools had failed to discharge their obligations to patrons, students, or the state. Given that the schools were satisfying the state's interest in producing educated citizens, the Court concluded that the law effectively prohibiting attendance at such private schools could not be characterized as reasonable. The Court chided the state, observing that "the child is not the mere creature of the state; those who nurture him and direct his destiny have the right, coupled with the high duty, to recognize and prepare him for additional obligations."

A Compromise of Sorts

The Court, however, went on to point out that this ruling should not be read to suggest that the state is powerless to regulate private schools. Specifically, the Court stated that individual states have considerable power to supervise their schools. It is clear in the Court's view that a state can reasonably regulate all schools. In addition, the state can inspect, supervise, and otherwise examine them. The state can also expect appropriate supervision of teachers and pupils and can require employees and schools to meet certain standards.

And while the rights of parents prevailed given the unique facts of this case, the Supreme Court's decision did not appreciably diminish the state's legal authority under the doctrine of *parens patriae* to effectively contest parental decisions that threaten the welfare of their children. Practically, the requirement that private schools provide comparable or equivalent education to that afforded by public schools illustrates the state's legitimate interest and continuing authority to protect children from ill-advised decisions of their parents.

The Importance of *Pierce*

Pierce is thus a historically noteworthy case. It served to clarify the relative legal authority of the state, the schools, and the family. It established that while compulsory education laws were legally permissible, public schools would not have a monopoly on the provision of educational services in American society, and that children would not necessarily face standardization at the hand of government schooling. At the same time, private schools, while they could promote values and training different from the public schools, would have to satisfy certain reasonable, state-prescribed standards designed to ensure an educated citizenry.

Finally, *Pierce* demonstrates the enduring significance that Supreme Court rulings may have on the course of educational policy and schools and schooling in America. For it is the precedent of *Pierce*, and its recognition of the liberty interests of parents regarding their children's education, that has served as the legal anchor for the contemporary school choice movement, contributing to the increasingly diverse array of governmentally recognized educational alternatives that characterize the educational landscape in the first decade of the 21st century.

Charles B. Vergon

See also Alliance for the Separation of School & State; Americanization; Catholic Schools; Common School Movement; Compulsory Attendance; National Association of Independent Schools; School Choice; Vouchers

Further Readings

Cremin, L. A. (1988.) *American education: The metropolitan experience, 1876–1980*. New York: Harper & Row.

Ensign, F. C. (1921). *Compulsory school attendance and child labor*. Iowa City, IA: Athens Press.

Katz, M. S. (1976). *A history of compulsory education laws*. Bloomington, IN: Phi Delta Kappa Educational Foundation.

Pierce v. Society of Sisters, 268 U.S. 510 (1925).

Tyack, D. (1974). *The one best system: A history of American urban education*. Cambridge, MA: Harvard University Press.

PINAR, WILLIAM

See Reconceptualists

PLAY SCHOOL MOVEMENT

The play school movement was born from the work of Caroline Pratt (1867–1954). Pratt was an innovative educator at the forefront of American educational reform, the period of progressive education as well as the nursery school movement. Understanding that education is a multisensory endeavor, she opened the Play School in New York City in the autumn of 1914. She named her school the Play School owing to her belief that children created and tested their knowledge of the world through play. Pratt was considered progressive due to her beliefs that not only were women's experiences critical to shaping democracy, but so too were children's—a concept certainly novel at the time.

Pratt's philosophy of intrinsic motivation and belief in allowing children to construct meaning through play was influenced by Jean Piaget (1896–1980) and his cognitive–interactionist theory, which supported the principle that not only inherited traits, but also environmental opportunities to engage in the world around them contributed to children's learning and development. As a friend and teacher, John Dewey (1859–1952) also inspired Pratt to extend the notion of not just teaching children about democracy but allowing them to create a democratic society through play. Joining Pratt in the work at her school and also supporting her pragmatist philosophy of child-directed learning was her colleague Lucy Sprague Mitchell (1878–1967). Mitchell began the Bureau of Educational Experiments (BEE), which was dedicated to the scientific study of children's nature and growth using the natural setting of Pratt's Play School as the laboratory. Together, Pratt and Mitchell collected extensive data regarding childhood development. The BEE later evolved into what is today the Bank Street College of Education in New York City.

City and Country School

Pratt's legacy lives on today through the continuation of the school she founded. The school that began as the Play School was later renamed the City and Country School. It originally opened in a three-room apartment in Greenwich Village and was later moved to its present location on West 12th and 13th streets, using funds from Lucy Sprague Mitchell. Children between the ages of 2 and 13 are admitted through an application process. Considered to be the oldest continuously operating progressive elementary school in New York State, City and Country School maintains the philosophy of providing multisensory experiences where children learn to solve problems using an integrated curriculum with an emphasis on community and democratic citizenship. As the foundation of the curriculum, social studies is integrated throughout other subjects that are offered, including the traditional subjects of math, language arts, science, foreign language, music, and art. However, there are several offerings which are particular to City and Country. The Rhythms Program, developed at the school in the 1920s, allows children to act out what they are learning through movement. Topics from academic content areas are transformed into skits and plays in order to bring them to life to allow the children to develop their coordination as well as their creativity. The Jobs Program, developed for students ages 8 through 13, assigns a specific job to each child that is pertinent to the school's functioning as a whole. Shop, woodworking, and technology classes provide opportunities for students to create items relevant to their jobs as well as the larger curriculum. The Block Yard Program, also developed by Pratt in conjunction with the help of a pediatrician, was designed to strengthen gross motor skills as well as to provide an opportunity for children to practice good sportsmanship. Present in the Block Yard are the signature blocks for which Caroline Pratt was known and that are still instrumental in classrooms today.

Blocks

Caroline Pratt is credited with designing the wooden unit blocks that are a staple of many early childhood education programs throughout the world today. Certainly she was inspired by Friedrich Froebel (1782–1852), the father of kindergarten, and the blocks that were part of what he referred to as "gifts" to be presented to children. The purpose of the blocks and the other gifts was to allow children to engage in self-directed play in order to learn to use their environment as an educational aid. Pratt chose the blocks due to their durability and flexibility. She saw wooden blocks as a basic, open-ended tool for children to create a community and to re-create the world around them.

Catherine D. Krammer

See also Constructivism; Dewey, John; Early Childhood Education; Head Start; Infant Schools; Laboratory Schools; National Association for the Education of Young Children; Piaget, Jean; Progressive Education

Further Readings

Driscoll, A., & Nagel, N. G. (2005). *Early childhood education birth–8* (3rd ed.). Boston: Pearson.

Follari, L. M. (2007). *Foundations and best practices in early childhood education.* Upper Saddle River, NJ: Pearson.

Hendry, P. M. (2008). Learning from Caroline Pratt. *Journal of the American Association for the Advancement of Curriculum Studies, 4.* Retrieved November 1, 2008, from http://www.uwstout.edu/soe/jaaacs/vol4/hendry.pdf

Jacobson, L. (2000, May 24). Elementary schools using blocks to build students' skills. *Education Week.* Retrieved July 23, 2009, from http://www.edweek.org

POLITICS OF CURRICULUM

Elementary and secondary education in the United States is a state function sanctioned through each state's constitution. As such, primary authority over curriculum content rests with state legislatures. To varying degrees, all state legislatures share their control of the curriculum with state and local school boards. The broader contours of public school curriculum are dictated through state statutes and board (both state and local) policies. Contemporarily, these contours may be influenced by a variety of factors, including state and national standards, federal legislation such as the No Child Left Behind Act (Public Law 107-110), and citizen advocacy such as efforts to promote or to exclude the teaching of evolution in public school science curricula. Because of such variables, the issue of academic freedom and the curriculum within schools has become a focus for educators, parents, and the wide variety of constituents with concerns about what is taught in schools.

Educators are required to teach the curriculum as prescribed by the state legislature, the state board of education, and the local board of education. Educators' rights to academic freedom are limited in this domain. Academic freedom more broadly encompasses the rights of educators and educational institutions to decide who may teach, what may be taught, how it may be taught, and what students are permitted to study in that institution. With regard to public elementary and secondary education, academic freedom has been curtailed to the "how" of teaching—pedagogy. Teacher academic freedom over pedagogy is subject to district review and can be curtailed if found to be offensive or otherwise inappropriate.

Broader conceptions of academic freedom vis-à-vis curriculum issues have been recognized in the U.S. Supreme Court, but only in the context of higher education. In higher education, "the robust exchange of ideas" is a central component of the educational experience. This uniqueness of higher education was reiterated in Justice Roberts's plurality opinion in *Parents Involved in Community Schools v. Seattle School District*. He distinguished the purposes of voluntary desegregation plans challenged in Seattle and in Jefferson County, Kentucky, from a law school's affirmative action admissions plan upheld in *Grutter v. Bollinger*.

While defining the higher education context as unique, however, the Court has been limited in its articulation of the contours of academic freedom in curricular content, particularly in regard to elementary and secondary education. Although teachers generally are free to teach within the contours of the prescribed curriculum, unilateral omission of curricular components can result in termination of employment. Moreover, teaching beyond the prescribed curriculum may incur increased liability risks, especially in the areas of religion and politics. Following the Supreme Court's precedent in

Garcetti v. Ceballos, lower courts have extended the curtailment of employee speech and expression rights in the classroom. Most recently, the Seventh Circuit upheld the nonrenewal of a probationary teacher's contract for relaying to students her intent to attend an antiwar rally. While the conveyance of such information could potentially spark debate among students and encourage the development of critical thinking skills, such a "robust exchange of ideas" at elementary and secondary levels appears to be outweighed by judicial concerns over teacher-to-student political (or religious) inculcation not clearly aligned with state and local sanctioned curriculum content. Educator First Amendment speech rights are limited to curricula approved by the state and local board. A teacher's permission to bring controversial current events into his or her classroom to spark discussions and help students develop critical thinking skills appears to be more limited as a result of recent court decisions that limit teacher speech to the approved curriculum. This may curtail the ability of educators at the elementary and secondary levels to develop student critical-thinking abilities.

Parent and School Board Influences Over Curriculum

Contemporary developments restricting teacher-initiated discussions beyond prescribed content aside, historically courts have been the protectors of schools as marketplaces for ideas. In this vein, state regulations and parental intrusions into the curriculum are frowned upon, especially as articulated in the *Keyishan v. Board of Regents* decision, when encroachments "cast a pall of orthodoxy over the classroom."

Parents as individuals can request exemption for their children from some parts of the curriculum they deem inappropriate in consideration of their religious beliefs. Schools are required to make reasonable accommodations of these requests. Schools are not, however, required to make accommodations beyond that which is reasonable. For example, in *Mozert v. Hawkins County Board of Education*, the plaintiff's request to ban the use of a basic reading series for religious reasons was denied. Subsequently, plaintiff began to withdraw her child from reading classes repeatedly and provided instruction in the family car. On multiple occasions she was warned by the principal that her actions were contrary to school policy, and she was eventually arrested for trespass. The Sixth Circuit upheld the actions of both the district and the police department in *Frost v. Hawkins County Board of Education.*

While parents can request curricular exemptions for their individual children, parental and taxpayer curricular protests generally have not been allowed to cause curricular change. Courts, however, have been supportive of a school district's authority to shape curriculum in conformity with community norms and values. Courts will permit local authorities to regulate even when they do not agree. For example, in *Virgil v. School Board of Columbia County, Florida,* the school board removed a textbook on classical Western literature previously approved for an upper-division high-school elective upon parental complaints about vulgarity and sexual content contained within two of the book's selections. The court upheld the school board's removal of a textbook, but noted disagreement with the board's action: "Like the district court, we seriously question how young persons just below the age of majority can be harmed by these masterpieces of Western literature." Hence, parents disaffected by school curricula are better poised to influence change when working through their school board representative.

School board power over curriculum is not plenary. For example, districts cannot make blanket bans against political speakers without an assessment of whether what an individual speaker would present would be disruptive. In addition, school boards cannot censor library books previously approved for student use. Moreover, while districts have the right to evaluate teacher pedagogy, boards must respect teacher academic freedom over instructional strategies reasonably tailored toward influencing student learning.

Citizen and Special Interest Group Influences Over Curriculum

Curriculum content is the primary responsibility of states and school boards (state and local). The factors influencing curricular decisions within the political context of elected legislatures and boards have, however, drawn the courts into disputes over curriculum content.

State statutes vary greatly regarding curriculum content requirements and the means by which citizens may influence its creation. Current statutes require a variety of subjects, including the teaching of English, bicultural and bilingual education, requirements to teach specific subjects, and other requirements that are unique to each state. Two states actually provide citizen access to curriculum content by statute. Massachusetts statutes require that courses requested by at least 30 parents in schools of 150 pupils or more and in which a qualified teacher is available be taught. Iowa allows voters at regular elections to "determine upon additional branches that shall be taught."

Citizens and special interest groups including religious groups have used a variety of means to influence curriculum content. These have included political activity during elections, and lobbying and other means designed to get specific candidates elected or to gain support for a specific curriculum change. One of the most persistent curriculum issues is the teaching of biological evolution. This issue has endured since the Scopes monkey trial of 1925. The courts have generally supported the teaching of evolution and banned from the science curriculum the teaching of other explanations of life that are more aligned with religious teaching (creationism and intelligent design).

In his March 14, 2005, article in *The Washington Post,* Peter Slevin described efforts being made by activists trying to change state statutes regulating teaching about life's origins. In essence, Slevin captured in writing the active debate about evolution and about how schools deal with the difficult issues associated with teaching the origins of life when there are such diverse perspectives about the efficacy of evolution.

Evolution and topics like it will continue to frame debates about what should be taught in classrooms across several states. Clearly, citizens and special interest groups have influenced curriculum content through the democratic process. It is likely they will continue to play a role in curriculum decision making in the future. Their success and the final impact of their actions will ultimately be decided by the courts, but curriculum will also be influenced by the actions of a wide variety of reforms that are committed to change in American schools.

Crystal Renee Chambers and Kermit Buckner

See also Civic Education; Creationism; Curriculum
Controversies; Local Control; Neoconservatives;
Religion and the Curriculum

Further Readings

Ravitch, D. (2000). *Left back: A century of failed school
reforms*. New York: Simon & Schuster.
Shaker, P., & Heilman, E. (2008). *Reclaiming education
for democracy: Thinking beyond No Child Left
Behind*. New York: Routledge.
Spring, J. (1989). *American education: An introduction
to social and political aspects*. White Plains, NY:
Longman.

POSTMODERNISM

The cultural and intellectual trend known as post-modernism developed out of a climate of dissent from modernism, the broad cultural movement in art and literature that had emerged from the Age of Enlightenment. Often identified or associated with other terms such as poststructuralism, deconstructivism, social constructionism, and postcolonialism, postmodernism developed in reaction to modernism and is sometimes seen as a rejection of the notion that there is such a thing as truth "out there" in favor of the view that truth is *created* rather than *discovered*.

According to some theorists, the very act of trying to define postmodernism constitutes an act of modernism imposed on postmodernity. The spirit of postmodernism is inhospitable to such endeavors as the establishment of authoritative definitions or, for that matter, the compiling of encyclopedias. The project of collecting, codifying, and publishing exhaustive bodies of knowledge characterized the Enlightenment or modernist position. The epistemological position of modernism is consistent with the idea that truth is objective and can be defined according to principles of technical and scientific rationality. This idea is rejected by postmodernism; thus, attempts to define or state the essence of postmodernism go against the grain of postmodernist thought. Rather, postmodernism attempts to describe "what is" with an emphasis on subjectivity. Modernism, by contrast, prefers to emphasize that which is held to

be the case by applying objective standards and procedures. An element of a postmodern position is the activity of dissent from "what is."

The origins of postmodernism have been vigorously debated by prominent postmodern theorists such as Jean Baudrillard, Jean-François Lyotard, Michel Foucault, Jacques Derrida, Thomas Kuhn, Richard Rorty, and their respective followers. Some claim that postmodernism began with the Industrial Revolution, or after World War I or World War II, or even more recently, in the 1960s. Other theorists claim that it began in the arenas of art, music, and literature, while others claim that postmodernism began as part of philosophical or sociological discourse, or in the field of architecture.

No matter what label or historical moment or discipline is claimed as the root of postmodernism, any attempt to represent its nature must contend with the many differences among theorists over what its constitutive elements are. The resulting lack of clarity seems to characterize not only the world of the early 21st century, but also recent and contemporary acts of reform and dissent within both society generally and the discourse of education in particular.

In dissenting from modernity's attempts to create metanarratives as sources of truth, usually from a European and American perspective, postmodernism rejects such metanarratives. Postmodernism moves away from the modernist concepts of a democratic society and individuals' social responsibilities and toward understanding these phenomena from the perspective of those voices and histories that previously had been excluded from Eurocentric metanarratives. Starting from the premise that there can be no validity to any claim for a particular location to be privileged as the center of truth and meaning, or the center of the world, postmodernism departs from common notions of East and West (East and west of *what central point?*). Thus the memories of those who were historically colonized and oppressed now play a major role in understanding reality, be it from a historical, cultural, sociological, or religious perspective.

Modernism understands knowledge as totalizing narratives identified with the development of reason, science, and technology, thus valuing high culture over popular culture. By contrast, postmodernism values popular taste and the everyday in the lives of people as vital to shaping and understanding culture, celebrating diversity and pluralism. Concerning knowledge, postmodernism begins to raise questions about how knowledge is constructed, whose interests knowledge serves, and what values and assumptions underscore this knowledge. Even the very notion of what it means to be a human person continues to evolve and becomes more and more inclusive rather than being confined by boundaries and a list of essential characteristics, as developed by the human sciences of modernism, which established new metanarratives to understand social realities and the person's role within them.

Recent reform practices in schooling mirror the presence of postmodernism in contemporary society. For example, many teachers value as part of the curriculum multicultural histories, literary texts, and experiences, especially of those peoples and cultures that were once oppressed and marginalized, thereby emphasizing the value of plurality and diversity rather than simply handing down a Eurocentric metanarrative. Teachers help students critique the development of knowledge by having students analyze popular culture and current events from the perspectives of who benefits and whose story is being told, and where the sense of social justice with equality for all peoples is. Classrooms are characterized by diverse learners culturally as well as by students with diverse learning abilities and physical abilities.

The belief that every child can learn is embodied in teachers' use of a variety of instructional strategies that recognize diversity in learning styles and preferences. Classroom practices are characterized as being inclusive, and instruction as being differentiated and in a mode of inquiry and cooperative learning. These schooling practices are no longer viewed as acts of dissent by subversive teachers but as the norm of reforming pedagogical practices that lead to developing a critical pedagogy. Critical educators continue to be an active voice in critiquing educational policies in view of reforms that would benefit all students, literally leaving no child behind in the learning process.

More than a philosophical or sociological position, a reaction to modernism, and a label for that which has come after modernism, postmodernism also includes the critiques and reform efforts by teachers and educational leaders currently taking place in response to changing societal realities and the diversity of today's learners.

Thomas Oldenski

See also Critical Literacy; Critical Theory; Giroux, Henry A.

Further Readings

Connor, S. (Ed.). (2004). *The Cambridge companion to postmodernism*. Cambridge, UK: Cambridge University Press.

Glanz, J., & Behar-Horenstein, L. S. (Eds.). (2000). *Paradigm debate in curriculum and supervision: Modern and postmodern perspective*. Westport, CT: Bergin & Garvey.

Sim, S. (Ed.). (2004). *The Routledge companion to postmodernism*. New York: Routledge.

Slattery, P. (2006). *Curriculum development in the postmodern era* (2nd ed.). New York: Routledge.

POSTSECONDARY OPTIONS

See Dual Enrollment

POUGHKEEPSIE PLAN

The Poughkeepsie Plan was an imaginative educational collaboration between Catholic parishes and local public schools to educate Catholic children at little or no cost to their parents or the parishes. Although named for the city of Poughkeepsie in New York, the Plan was manifested in several different forms in a number of states. It also must be said that the Plan generated the most controversy and educated the fewest students of any of the many efforts to educate Catholic children in the United States.

From 1831 to 1916, Catholics in at least 21 communities in 14 states attempted to bridge the gap between parochial and public education. Although the specific terms of these agreements varied slightly from community to community, the most common plan called for school boards to lease school buildings from local parishes for nominal sums and pay the salaries of teachers who taught in those schools. The teachers were selected jointly by school boards and parish pastors. The board regulated the curriculum, selected the schoolbooks, and conducted periodic examinations, but parish pastors had the right to ensure that all of the elements of the curriculum were acceptable to the Catholic Church. Most important, however, was the fact that the school day at these publicly supported Catholic schools was the same as at any other public school. No religious instruction was conducted until after classes were dismissed.

These schools were experimental and in most communities the experiment was short-lived. But in three communities—Lowell, Massachusetts, from 1831 to 1852; Savannah, Georgia, from 1870 to 1916; and Poughkeepsie, New York, from 1873 to 1898—publicly supported parochial schools educated several generations of Catholic children. Even though the number of Catholic children educated in these schools was small, the publicly supported Catholic school was an important grassroots effort to resolve the outstanding differences that separated many Catholics from public education.

The publicly supported parish school in Poughkeepsie is worthy of closer attention not only because of its longevity, but also because it received national attention as the representative example of cooperative education efforts in other communities.

The "Poughkeepsie Plan," as the cooperative effort came to be known, began when the pastor of a parish in Poughkeepsie informed the local school board in the spring of 1873 that his parishioners could no longer afford to maintain the parish's two schools. Starting in the fall, the 800 children who had attended those two schools would enter the public school system.

But the pastor not only precipitated the problem, he also had a solution. He proposed that the school board lease his parish buildings to conduct public school classes for the parish children. Religious instruction would not be part of the public school curriculum, but would be conducted in the building after normal school hours. Participation in religious exercises would be completely voluntary for all students.

The new public schools were to be staffed by teachers selected, employed, and paid by the board. But the pastor made it clear that the board should hire Catholic teachers for the schools so long as they met school board requirements. The board agreed to the terms and further agreed that the parish school would retain unrestricted use of the building outside of regular school hours. A lease agreement was signed on August 21, 1873.

Not everyone was happy with this arrangement, however. Protestant ministers objected to the plan and to the board's decision to abandon Bible reading in these schools. The ministers appealed to the board for a return to the "secular education" that emphasized religion and morality as taught in the Bible.

But local criticism of the plan faded in the face of the communitywide goal of assimilating the foreign born into American society. The agreement between the school board and the parish continued year after year without further criticism from the general public.

The agreement held fast until the late 1890s when the state school superintendent ordered the Poughkeepsie school board to break the agreement or lose state aid. He based his actions on two grounds: the wearing of religious garb by the nuns who taught in the parish schools, and the long-term rental of parish buildings for the purpose of public education. Thus ended in January of 1899 the most innovative and visible effort to bridge the gap between parochial and public education.

Timothy Walch

See also Catholic Schools; Faribault-Stillwater Plan; Gibbons, James Cardinal; Ireland, John; Lowell Plan

Further Readings

Griffin, C., & Griffin, S. (1978). *Natives and newcomers: The ordering of opportunity in mid-nineteenth century Poughkeepsie.* Cambridge, MA: Harvard University Press.

Reilly, D. (1969). *The school controversy, 1891–1893.* New York: Arno Press.

Walch, T. (2003). *Parish school: American Catholic parochial education from colonial times to the present.* Washington, DC: National Catholic Educational Association.

PRAYER IN SCHOOL

See Engel v. Vitale

PRESAGE PRODUCT RESEARCH

See Process–Product Research

PRESIDENTS AND EDUCATIONAL REFORM

The principal domestic task of the president of the United States is stated in Article II, section 3 of the U.S. Constitution, which calls on him or her to take care that the laws are faithfully executed. In other words, the Constitution provides almost no explicit role for the president in the policymaking process. The president's job, as stated, is to carry out the will of the legislature and enforce the decisions of the courts.

Over the course of 2 centuries, the role of the president has gradually changed. Today, the American people expect their chief executive to come into office with a full-blown set of policy objectives and positions regarding virtually every major facet of American life. Despite a complicated history, education policy is no different. For better or worse, educational reform has become a national priority and, as such, a serious presidential concern. This entry explores the history and nature of the relationship between the American presidency, the presidents themselves, and educational policy and reform.

Education and the U.S. Constitution

The U.S. Constitution is federal by design. What this means in practice is that we have a complicated political system of separate and yet overlapping and competing sovereign political entities in the form of the federal government and the governments of particular states and locales. Questions of jurisdiction, competency, and prerogative among the various governmental levels

have been painstakingly worked out in the courts and even on the battlefield over the course of the nation's more than 220-year history. In the area of education, the long-standing consensus was that states and local governments were the appropriate and prevailing authorities. This view was buttressed constitutionally by the Tenth Amendment, which says that all powers not delegated to the national government nor prohibited by it to the states are reserved to the states or the American people themselves. Because the Constitution is silent on the question of education, control over it defaults automatically to the states. Many states, in turn, delegated by law or neglect much of their authority regarding education to either local governments or even families themselves in the early years of the republic.

As part of their traditional police powers to regulate for the health, safety, and moral well-being of their citizenry, states approached education in widely varying ways, based on their particular political culture, history, level of resources, and stage of economic development. This devotion to states' rights and localism was sustained by both practical reasoning and a set of ideological commitments that, when coupled with the fact of pluralism and the existence of the Tenth Amendment, made national intervention in the area of education policy extremely problematic. Indeed, despite the national government's enlarged role in this domain today, these factors and others continue to frustrate those who would like to treat educational reform as a national question or issue.

Early Presidents

American statesmen in the early republic understood that a functional democratic regime required a certain degree of virtue and self-control on the part of the citizenry. As intellectual children of the Enlightenment, presidents Washington, Adams, Jefferson, and Madison believed that virtue and self-control were the by-products of reason and learning. Education for them and other leading figures of the day was the key to good republican citizenship. Such education, however, was primarily seen as moral or character education designed to produce certain habits, dispositions, and virtues in the citizenry. Though Jefferson advocated for a constitutional amendment to establish a federal role for education and even went so far as to push for the creation of coeducational elementary schools in his home state of Virginia, there was in the end little real achievement in this area.

The same is true for the early presidents, such as James Madison, who pushed for the creation of a national university. Time and again the political culture and the constitutional questions proved too much and presidents by and large were left to pay lip service to the cause of education. Notable exceptions to this in the 19th century would have to include Lincoln's support for the Morrill Land Grant Act of 1862, which created the first system of agricultural colleges in the United States, and James Garfield's work while in Congress to create the first U.S. Office of Education. A teacher before he turned to politics, it is unclear what impact Garfield may have had if he had not been assassinated so early into his presidency.

The early years of the 20th century saw some movement in the direction of an increased role for the national government in the area of education. With the support of the Wilson administration, Congress passed the Smith-Lever Act of 1914, which extended agricultural education, and the Smith-Hughes Act of 1917, which asserted a federal role and interest in vocational education. The latter act also established the Federal Vocational Board of Education. However, most of Woodrow Wilson's presidency was dominated by World War I and foreign affairs. It was President Herbert Hoover who would attempt to have the Office of Education elevated to a cabinet-level position after convening the first-ever National Advisory Committee on Education. That proposal, however, was rejected by Congress for the standard political and constitutional reasons. By the end of the Hoover presidency, though, change was in the air.

Education and the Modern Presidency

The election of Franklin Delano Roosevelt (FDR) in 1932 marks the beginning of what many scholars call the modern presidency. As a direct result of the Great Depression and World War II, the size and scope of the federal government increased dramatically. Along with that increase came an expansion of the power and stature of the president in the domestic policy arena. When coupled with the increasing sophistication and technological demands of the American economy and the nation's postwar ascendancy in world affairs, the time was ripe for greater federal intervention in American education. Asserting that a right to an education was among the so-called new rights that should be guaranteed to all Americans, FDR's greatest contribution to the American educational landscape was setting the G.I. Bill of Rights into motion. Eventually this piece of public policy would see well over 2 million returning veterans attend colleges and universities. Though the "right to education" was later rejected by the U.S. Supreme Court and deemed instead a "privilege," the momentum for increased federal investment and involvement in education was growing quickly.

While the rapid growth in the American economy certainly increased the level of attention paid to education by the federal government and the presidents, it was the growing intensity of the Cold War that proved to be the real impetus for federal intervention. Noting both the need for greater technical capacity and the assumed ideological benefits of increased levels of education for thwarting communism, President Truman sponsored bills in 1947 and again in 1949 that would have begun providing federal aid to precollegiate education. Both times, however, Congress rejected the attempted "intrusion" into education policy by the national government in the name of the Constitution and states' rights. However, on October 4, 1957, everything changed.

On that date, the Soviet Union launched *Sputnik*, the world's first artificial satellite, and thereby beat the United States into outer space. Not only did this event exponentially increase the magnitude of the cold war, but it also provided an acute sense of urgency within the ranks of American social and political leadership. Although not particularly interested in the education question, President Eisenhower grasped in short order that something needed to be done to counter the fear and loss of confidence that was enveloping the American people. Calling the situation an "emergency" that required an unprecedented federal response, he pushed American educators and educational institutions to respond forcefully and immediately to the challenge of the Soviet Union's technological edge. Joining the emerging conservative chorus in decrying "progressive education," the administration pushed for increased attention to the hard sciences and technical education in American schools and universities. In 1958, The National Defense Education Act was passed. This Act increased federal spending on education in the form of low-cost loans for students pursuing degrees in the chosen fields. In keeping with precedent, though, Congress explicitly prohibited any semblance of federal control within the educational institutions themselves.

While retaining Eisenhower's commitment to cold war initiatives and pushing the U.S. space program, his successor, John F. Kennedy, began calling for a more robust federal role in American education. In particular, he called for raising teachers' salaries, providing money for school construction, and making it possible for those in need to attend college with scholarship dollars. In his New Frontier, Kennedy named federal aid to education as his principal domestic concern. While he would not find a welcome reception for this idea in Congress during his tragically brief tenure as president, his agenda was picked up with great vigor by the Johnson administration. In the wake of the assassination and the national mood that followed, Lyndon B. Johnson (LBJ) found a legislature that was much more pliable on the issues that had been near to Kennedy's heart.

A more forceful and skillful politician than most of his presidential predecessors, Johnson seized the historical moment and managed to link a number of issue streams together in the most aggressive set of federal initiatives since Roosevelt's New Deal. The three pillars of Johnson's Great Society would be education, social welfare, and civil rights. Driven by work like Michael Harrington's 1962 book *The Other America* and the civil rights movement, the issue of poverty had become prominent in the early 1960s. Johnson saw education as the solution to the problem of poverty and as an important piece of the civil rights puzzle as well. Under the banner of the equity reform movement, LBJ would become the first U.S. president to sign into law a bill containing direct federal aid for education. There would be dozens of other bills related to this reform movement also adopted. Among the most important pieces of legislation would be the Economic Opportunity Act of 1964, which would create the program known as Head Start; the Elementary and Secondary School Act of 1965, whose Title I provided categorical aid to the children of the poor (an

act that many, including Johnson himself, would say was the most important education bill ever passed by Congress and signed into law); and the Higher Education Act of 1965. The latter Act provided low-interest loans for needy students and created the work–study programs that persist to this day, as well as providing direct aid in the form of scholarships and grants.

Though there had been fits and starts in the area of educational reform from other presidents prior to the accomplishments of Johnson's administration, it was on his watch that education became firmly entrenched in the national arena as a federal concern. Aside from the signature pieces of legislation, he also expanded the U.S. Office of Education and increased the level of educational research being done. However, as the Vietnam War heated up and the related domestic turmoil ensued, significant attention was diverted away from central areas of concern for Johnson. Those issues would come to dominate presidential politics at the end of the decade and into the 1970s. As such, Richard Nixon spent little time on education issues beyond the creation of the National Institute on Education, which was intended to expand and encourage basic educational research. President Ford as well did little to thwart or further the Great Society initiatives, though he was traditional in his belief that education was best left in the hands of the states. Although Jimmy Carter was among the most educated presidents himself, he too had very little interest in educational reform. While it is true that it was his administration that managed to elevate the U.S. Office of Education to departmental status in 1979, this move is widely viewed simply as a political ploy designed to placate the National Education Association (the largest teachers' union and major financial supporter of the Democratic Party). It was not until the Reagan administration that education would again move to the national stage in a highly visible manner.

Though he was a major cold-warrior at heart, the challenges Ronald Reagan faced were economic as much as ideological. American competitiveness, especially with regard to the Japanese, was being seriously questioned, and the American educational system was once again under scrutiny. Because he had run on a platform that called for significantly decreasing the size and scope of the federal government domestically—including the abolishment of the Department of Education—Reagan put forward no educational initiatives that required new or increased federal spending. Indeed, under his administration, resources diminished significantly. Despite that fact, Reagan did develop a keen interest in educational reform. Upon entering office, Reagan's basic orientation to education was steeped in three general ideas. First, that states should set educational policy, not the federal government. Second, that school prayer should be reestablished. And, third that private education should be supported through the issuing of vouchers and through the opportunity for parental choice sustained by tax credits and tuition write-offs.

The turning point, however, arrived unexpectedly in the form of a study commissioned by his secretary of education, Terrell Bell, which was published in 1983 under the title *A Nation at Risk: The Imperative for Education Reform*. This document provided the phrase "a rising tide of mediocrity" to the national education debates and paved the way for what would come to be called the excellence reform movement. This movement aligned well with Reagan's conservative principles since what the reform demanded was at the foundational rather than the programmatic level. No new federal money would be needed, but instead the movement called for raising academic standards for both teachers and students, the return to a rigorous core curriculum, the promotion of cultural literacy, and a recentering of the role of families and parents in the educational process. Though Bell's own tenure was short lived, this movement produced a pivotal figure in the educational culture wars that soon ensued in the person of William J. Bennett.

Ideologically aligned with Reagan on the question of education, George H. W. Bush continued to push the excellence reform movement and championed school choice coupled with the ideal of national standards. Education, however, was to remain a state responsibility overall. Calling for an education summit with the nation's governors in 1989, Bush's educational vision was projected in what has been called the Jefferson Compact that emerged from those conversations. However, despite calls for raising standards, developing technology, reducing illiteracy, and having children enter school prepared to learn, most of the economic burden still fell to the states. With the

underlying rationale being American competitiveness, Bush's administration pushed for national testing and connected the idea of school choice to those scores.

Among the more active and influential governors at the Bush education summit was Governor Bill Clinton of Arkansas. So when he was elected president a couple of years later it is not surprising that many of the elements that emerged from that process were retained. In their revised plan, Goals 2000: Educate America Act (1994), the Clinton administration provided a blueprint that would be used to focus all federal education programs on national standards. Although the standards were voluntary, the linkage to federal dollars funneled through the Department of Education made compliance a necessity for most states. Under this Act, three important entities were created: the National Education Standards Improvement Council, the National Skills Board, and the National Educational Goals Panel were all three to monitor school reform. In 1994, the Clinton administration oversaw the Reauthorization of the Elementary and Secondary Education Act or Improving America's Schools Act first passed in 1965. Here the benefits to the underprivileged were tied as well to performance standards and assessment. School choice also received a boost under the new provisions of Title I, whereby eligible students under the right conditions could transfer to other schools within a given school district.

During the Clinton years there were other significant pieces of educational reform passed, including the National and Community Service Trust Act, which created a national service program for students 17 and older that provided them with postservice education or training dollars in exchange for their efforts. The School-to-Work Opportunities Act allowed states to assist students in making the transition from school to work. And, the Education Flexibility Partnership Act: Ed-Flex, gave states unprecedented authority to encourage and grant waivers to localities interested in innovation and reform under Department of Education supervision. In 1999, the Clinton administration spearheaded the Educational Excellence for All Children Act, which failed. Nevertheless, it paved the way for what is probably the single most important piece of national educational reform ever: No Child Left Behind (2001).

No Child Left Behind (NCLB) was an act with broad bipartisan support more or less authored by the George W. Bush administration and proposed by President Bush on his first day in office. It became law in January of 2002. The Act built on previous standards-based approaches and called on states to set rigorous achievement standards and create measurable goals that can be assessed through standardized testing at certain grade levels. In exchange for increased levels of federal funding, the states must demonstrate progressive levels of student achievement across basic skills, especially in the area of reading. The Act also provided increased levels of parental choice and flexibility regarding what schools their children attend. While NCLB did not set national achievement standards per se, it did provide significant oversight tied to the use of federal monies such that one would expect certain levels of convergence between states' testing regimes. When signed into law, the Act also reauthorized a number of existing federal laws in the area of educational policy, including the Elementary and Secondary Education Act (1965). While details of the Act remain controversial in many places and the money provided to meet its ambitious goals is often called highly inadequate, political support for its larger framework and general thrust remained strong during the presidential campaigns of 2008 and the election of Barack Obama.

Christopher M. Duncan

See also Education Commission of the States (ECS); Elementary and Secondary Education Act; Federal Educational Reform; No Child Left Behind Act (NCLB)

Further Readings

Berube, M. R. (1991). *American presidents and education*. New York: Greenwood Press.
DeBray, E. (2006). *Politics, ideology, and education: Federal policy during the Clinton and Bush administrations*. New York: Teachers College Press.
Finn, C. E., Jr. (1977). *Education and the presidency*. Lexington, MA: Lexington Books.
Lapatia, A. D. (1975). *Education and the federal government*. New York: Mason/Charter.
McCluskey, N. P. (2007). *Feds in the classroom: How big government corrupts, cripples, and compromises American education*. Lanham, MD: Rowman & Littlefield.
McGuinn, P. J. (2006). *No Child Left Behind and the transformation of federal policy, 1965–2005*. Lawrence: University of Kansas Press.
U.S. Department of Education. (1983). *A nation at risk: The imperative for educational reform*. Washington, DC: Government Printing Office.

PROBLEM-BASED LEARNING

Problem-based learning (PBL) developed from innovations in health sciences curricula launched more than 3 decades ago. Traditional medical education, with its intensive pattern of basic science lectures followed by an equally exhaustive clinical teaching curriculum, was increasingly being seen as an unproductive and, some felt, punitively harsh way to prepare students, given the explosion in medical information and new technology and the rapidly changing demands of current practice. In response, the medical faculty at McMaster University in Canada introduced the tutorial process, not only as a specific instructional method but also as central to their philosophy for structuring an entire program of study promoting student-centered, multidisciplinary education, and lifelong learning in professional practice.

As a recognized leader in researching and refining the PBL approach, Howard Barrows clearly articulated that the process of patient diagnosis combined a hypothetical–deductive reasoning process with expert knowledge in multiple domains. Traditional approaches to medical education involved lectures on discipline-specific content domains that did little to provide learners with a context for the content or for its clinical application. Generally, the knowledge base a physician needed to master was limited to a memorization strategy. When rapid advances in science and medical technology dramatically expanded the required knowledge base, then lectures on information that was rapidly becoming dated were simply inadequate preparation for medical professionals. Problem-based learning evolved to address this deficiency.

Characteristics of the Problem-Based Learning Instructional Strategy

PBL is a pedagogical learner-centered approach that empowers students to conduct research, integrate theory and practice, and apply knowledge and skills to develop a viable solution to a defined problem. Critical to the success of the approach is the selection of ill-structured problems (often interdisciplinary) and a tutor who guides the learning process and conducts a thorough debriefing at the conclusion of the learning experience. Barbara Duch, Susan Groh, and Deborah Allen argue that PBL develops specific skills, including the ability to think critically; analyze and solve complex, real-world problems; to find, evaluate, and use appropriate learning resources; to work cooperatively; to demonstrate effective communication skills; and to use content knowledge and intellectual skills to become continual learners. Linda Torp and Sara Sage describe PBL as focused, experiential learning organized around the investigation and resolution of messy, real-world problems. They describe students as engaged problem solvers seeking to identify the root problem and the conditions needed for a good solution and in the process becoming self-directed learners. Cindy Hmelo-Silver describes PBL as an instructional method in which students learn through facilitated problem solving that centers on a complex problem that does not have a single correct answer. She notes that students work in collaborative groups to identify what they need to learn in order to solve a problem, engage in self-directed learning, apply their new knowledge to the problem, and reflect on what they learned and the effectiveness of the strategies employed.

Barrows has described a set of generic PBL essential characteristics including: students must have the responsibility for their own learning, the problem simulations used in problem-based learning must be ill-structured and allow for free inquiry, learning should be integrated from a wide range of disciplines or subjects, collaboration is essential, what students learn during their self-directed learning must be applied back to the problem with reanalysis and resolution, a closing analysis of what has been learned from work with the problem and a discussion of what concepts and principles have been learned is essential, self- and peer assessment should be carried out at the completion of each problem and at the end of every curricular unit, the activities carried out in problem-based learning must be those valued in the real world, student examinations must measure student progress toward the goals of problem-based

learning, and problem-based learning must be the pedagogical base in the curriculum and not part of a didactic curriculum.

The challenge for many instructors when they adopt a PBL approach is to make the transition from teacher as knowledge provider to tutor as manager and facilitator of learning. If teaching with PBL were as simple as presenting the learners with a problem and students could be relied upon to work consistently at a high level of cognitive self-monitoring and self-regulation, then many teachers would be taking early retirement. The reality is that learners who are new to PBL require significant instructional scaffolding to support the development of problem-solving skills, self-directed learning skills, and teamwork/collaboration skills to a level of self-sufficiency where the scaffolds can be removed. Teaching institutions that have adopted a PBL approach to curriculum and instruction (including those noted earlier) have developed extensive tutor training programs in recognition of the critical importance of this role in facilitating the PBL learning experience.

Diffusion of the Problem-Based Learning Instructional Strategy

During the 1980s and 1990s, PBL was adopted in medical schools across North America and in Europe as an accepted instructional approach. PBL has also been adopted in elementary schools, middle schools, high schools, universities, and professional schools. What follows is a partial list illustrative of the multiple contexts in which PBL is being utilized.

The University of Delaware has an active PBL program and conducts annual training institutes for instructors wanting to become tutors. Samford University in Birmingham, Alabama, has incorporated PBL into various undergraduate programs within the Schools of Arts and Sciences, Business, Education, Nursing, and Pharmacy. The Illinois Mathematics and Science Academy has been providing high school students with a complete PBL curriculum since 1985 and serves thousands of students and teachers as a center for research on problem-based learning. The Problem-Based Learning Institute (PBLI) has developed curricular materials (i.e., problems) and teacher-training programs in PBL for all core disciplines in high school.

PBL is used in multiple domains of medical education (dentists, nurses, paramedics, radiologists, etc.) and in content domains as diverse as M.B.A. programs), higher education, chemical engineering, economics, architecture, and pre-service teacher education.

Assessment of the Effectiveness of Problem-Based Learning

Given that physicians are highly respected and valued members of society, there has been intense interest in how doctors were educated and prepared for their careers. The primary research focus was a comparison to discover any differences between physicians trained using PBL and physicians trained using traditional approaches. In 1993, a meta-analysis of 20 years of PBL evaluation studies was conducted by Mark Albanese and S. A. Mitchell, and also by D. T. Vernon and R. L. Blake, and concluded that a problem-based approach to instruction was equal to traditional approaches in terms of conventional tests of knowledge (i.e., scores on medical board examinations), and that students who studied using PBL exhibited better clinical problem-solving skills. A smaller study of graduates of a physical therapy program that utilized PBL showed that graduates of the program performed equally well with PBL or traditional approaches but students reported a preference for the problem-centered approach.

A systematic review and meta-analysis conducted by Mark Newman on the effectiveness of PBL used in higher education programs for health professionals determined that accessible summaries of the field did not provide noteworthy verification with which to provide important answers to questions about the efficacy of PBL. Specifically, this analysis of research studies attempted to compare PBL with traditional approaches to discover if PBL increased performance in adapting to and participating in change; dealing with problems and making reasoned decisions in unfamiliar situations; reasoning critically and creatively; adopting a more universal or holistic approach; practicing empathy, appreciating the other person's point of view; collaborating productively in groups or teams; identifying own strengths and weaknesses and undertaking appropriate remediation (self-directed learning). A lack of well-designed studies

posed a challenge to this research analysis and an article on the same topic by Robert W. Sanson-Fisher and Marita Lynagh concluded that the evidence was methodologically flawed and offered little support for the advantage of PBL

The adoption of PBL and any instructional innovation in public education is a complicated undertaking. State-funded schools are constrained by a state-mandated curriculum and an expectation that they will produce a uniform product. Standardized testing encourages a "teach to the test" approach that relies on memorization, drill exercises, and practice tests as strategies. The instructional day is divided into specific blocks of time and organized around subjects, leaving scant time for teachers or students to immerse themselves in an engaging problem. However, there are many efforts underway to work around the constraints of a traditional classroom. Until future research studies can provide clear evidence of the effectiveness of using PBL with a range of learner populations, widespread adoption in K–12 education will be limited.

Problem-Based Learning and Other Experiential Approaches

Closely related learner-centered instructional strategies include case-based learning, project-based learning, and inquiry-based learning. Both case-based and project-based approaches promote active learning and engage the learners in higher-order thinking such as analysis and synthesis.

A well-constructed case will help learners to understand the important elements of the problem/situation so they are better prepared for similar situations in the future. Case studies can help learners develop critical thinking skills for assessing the information provided and identifying logic flaws or false assumptions. Working through a case study will help learners build discipline-/context-specific vocabulary/terminology, and an understanding of the relationships among elements presented in the case study. When a case study is done as a group project, learners may develop improved communication and collaboration skills. Cases may be used to assess student learning after instruction or as a practice exercise to prepare learners for a more authentic application of the skills and knowledge gained by working on the case.

With a project-based approach, the learning activities are organized around achieving a shared goal (project). Within a project-based approach, learners are usually provided with specifications for a desired end product (build a rocket, design a Web site, etc.) and the learning process is oriented more to following correct procedures than to completing a finished product. While working on a project, learners are likely to encounter several problems that generate teachable moments. Teachers are more likely to be instructors and coaches (rather than tutors) who provide expert guidance, feedback, and suggestions for better ways to achieve the final product. The teaching (modeling, scaffolding, questioning, etc.) is provided according to learner need and within the context of the project. As in case-based instruction, learners are able to add an experience to their memory that will serve them in future situations.

While cases and projects are excellent learner-centered instructional strategies, they tend to diminish the learner's role by setting the goals and outcomes for the problem. When the expected outcomes are clearly defined, there is less need or incentive for the learner to set his or her own parameters. In the real world it is important both to define the problem and to develop a solution or range of possible solutions.

Problem-based learning and inquiry-based learning are also very similar. Inquiry-based learning is grounded in the philosophy of John Dewey, who believed that education begins with the curiosity of the learner and is realized through the processes of reflection. Inquiry-based learning is a student-centered, active learning approach focused on questioning, critical thinking, and problem solving. Inquiry-based learning activities begin with asking a question, followed by investigating solutions, creating new knowledge as information is gathered and understood, discussing discoveries and experiences, and reflecting on newfound knowledge. Inquiry-based learning is frequently used in science education and encourages a hands-on approach where students practice the scientific method on authentic problems and/or questions.

The primary difference between PBL and inquiry-based learning relates to the role of the tutor. In an inquiry-based approach the tutor is both a facilitator of learning (encouraging/expecting higher-order thinking) and a provider of information. In a PBL approach, the tutor supports the process and expects learners to make their thinking clear, but the tutor does not provide information related to the problem; that is the responsibility of the learners.

Conclusion

Today there are more than enough problems from which to choose in a range of disciplines. Some of the apprehensions that encouraged the advance of problem-based learning in medical schools resonate today in collegiate education. Lectures delivered to huge classes characterize many courses at most universities and many colleges. While problem-based learning is well known in the medical field, it is unfamiliar to most undergraduate programs. It is vitally important that current and future generations of students experience a problem-based learning approach and engage in constructive solution-seeking activities. The bar has been raised as the 21st century gathers momentum and, more than ever, higher-order thinking skills, self-regulated learning habits, and problem-solving skills are necessary for *all* students.

John R. Savery

See also Alternative Assessment; Assessment; Bloom's Taxonomy; Curriculum Controversies; Evidence-Based Education (EBE); Experiential Learning; Inquiry-Based Learning; Learning Packages; Performance-Based Assessment

Further Readings

Albanese, M. A., & Mitchell, S. (1993). Problem-based learning: A review of the literature on its outcomes and implementation issues. *Academic Medicine, 68*(1), 52–81.

Barrows, H. S. (1996, Winter). Problem-based learning in medicine and beyond: A brief overview. In L. Wilkerson & W. Gijselaers (Eds.), *Bringing problem-based learning to higher education: Theory and practice* (New Directions for Teaching and Learning, Vol. 68, pp. 3–11). San Francisco: Jossey-Bass.

Barrows, H. S., & Kelson, A. (1993). *Problem-based learning in secondary education and the Problem-Based Learning Institute* [Monograph]. Springfield: Southern Illinois University School of Medicine.

Blumenfeld, P. C., Soloway, E., Marx, R. W., Krajcik, J. S., Guzdial, M., & Palinscar, A. (1991). Motivating project-based learning: Sustaining the doing, supporting the learning. *Educational Psychologist, 26*(3/4), 369–398.

Boud, D., & Feletti, G. (1997). *The challenge of problem-based learning* (2nd ed.). London: Kogan Page.

Bransford, J. D., Brown, A. L., & Cocking, R. R. (Eds.). (2000). *How people learn: Brain, mind, experience, and school.* Washington, DC: National Academy Press.

Bridges, E. M., & Hallinger, P. (1996, Winter). Problem-based learning in leadership education. In L. Wilkerson & W. Gijselaers (Eds.), *Bringing problem-based learning to higher education: Theory and practice* (New Directions for Teaching and Learning, Vol. 68, pp. 53–61). San Francisco: Jossey-Bass.

Denton, B. G., Adams, C. C., Blatt, P. J., & Lorish, C. D. (2000). Does the introduction of problem-based learning change graduate performance outcomes in a professional curriculum? *Journal on Excellence in College Teaching, 11*(2 & 3), 147–162.

Dewey, J. (1938). *Experience and education.* New York: Macmillan.

Duch, B. J., Groh, S. E., & Allen, D. E. (2001). Why problem-based learning? A case study of institutional change in undergraduate education. In B. Duch, S. Groh, & D. Allen (Eds.), *The power of problem-based learning* (pp. 3–11). Sterling, VA: Stylus.

Gijselaers, W. H. (1996, Winter). Connecting problem-based practices with educational theory. In L. Wilkerson & W. Gijselaers (Eds.), *Bringing problem-based learning to higher education: Theory and practice* (New Directions for Teaching and Learning, Vol. 68, pp. 13–21). San Francisco: Jossey-Bass.

Hmelo-Silver, C. E. (2004). Problem-based learning: What and how do students learn? *Educational Psychology Review, 16*(3), 235–266.

MacDonald, P. J. (1997). Selection of health problems for a problem-based curriculum. In D. Boud & G. Feletti (Eds.), *The challenge of problem-based learning* (2nd ed., pp. 93–102). London: Kogan Page.

Newman, M. (2003). *A pilot systematic review and meta-analysis on the effectiveness of problem based learning* (Special Report 2). Retrieved October 20, 2008, from http://www.ltsn-01.ac.uk/docs/pbl_report.pdf

Sanson-Fisher, R. W., & Lynagh, M. C. (2005). Problem-based learning: A dissemination success story? *Medical Journal of Australia, 183*(5), 258–260.

Savery, J. R. (1999). Enhancing motivation and learning through collaboration and the use of problems. In S. Fellows & K. Ahmet (Eds.), *Inspiring students: Case studies in motivating the learner* (pp. 33–42). London: Kogan Page.

Savery, J. R., & Duffy, T. M. (1995). Problem-based learning: An instructional model and its constructivist framework. In B. Wilson (Ed.), *Constructivist learning environments: Case studies in instructional design* (pp. 135–148). Englewood Cliffs, NJ: Educational Technology Publications.

Stinson, J. E., & Milter, R. G. (1996, Winter). Problem-based learning in business education: Curriculum design and implementation issues. In L. Wilkerson & W. H. Gijselaers (Eds.), *Bringing problem-based learning to higher education: Theory and practice* (New Directions for Teaching and Learning, Vol. 68, pp. 32–42). San Francisco: Jossey-Bass.

Torp, L., & Sage, S. (2002). *Problems as possibilities: Problem-based learning for K–16 education* (2nd ed.). Alexandria, VA: Association for Supervision and Curriculum Development.

White, H. B. (1996). Dan tries problem-based learning: A case study. In L. Richlin (Ed.), *To improve the academy* (Vol. 15, pp. 75–91). Stillwater, OK: New Forums Press and the Professional and Organizational Network in Higher Education.

Woods, D. R. (1994). *Problem-based learning: How to gain the most from PBL.* Waterdown, Ontario, Canada: Author.

PROCESS–PRODUCT RESEARCH

Process–product research is a term that is used to describe a line of studies that attempted to identify teacher behaviors that were correlated with student gains in achievement. The term *process–product* was first used by Donald M. Medley and Harold E. Mitzel in 1963. This research flourished from 1955 to 1980 and the results remain relevant today. Two summaries of this research can be found in the work of Jere Brophy and Thomas Good in 1986 and Barak Rosenshine and Robert Stevens in 1986. Process–product research has been used by practitioners interested in classroom dynamics as well as school reformers who are focused on enhanced student achievement.

Process–product (p–p) research begins by observing the "process" of teaching. Classroom observers rate or count teacher and student behaviors that might be important for student learning. In some studies the observers counted variables such as the number and type of questions that were asked, the correctness of a student's response, the teacher's response to a student's answer, the use of praise and criticism, and the amount of time spent practicing new material. In other studies, the observers rated a teacher's "clarity" or "warmth" or "enthusiasm" or "organization" on a 1–5 scale.

The second part of p–p research involved obtaining the "product," which entailed a measure of student achievement. Typically, this was done by giving two tests to the students in the classes in the study—one test, usually in reading or in mathematics, was given to students in all the classes at the start of the semester or at the beginning of a unit. A second test was given at the end of the unit or semester. The investigators then calculated the amount of achievement gain in each classroom after adjusting for where each class began. These achievement gain scores represented the "product" in process–product research.

The third and final step in p–p research involved computing the correlations between the process—the observed ratings or counts, and the product—the measure of student gain in each classroom. The significant results were then used to form a pattern of effective teaching. In many cases, the investigators continued their work by conducting experimental studies in which another group of teachers was taught to use the specific positive findings from the p–p research and other teachers were asked to continue with their usual teaching method. These experimental studies were summarized by Nathaniel Gage and Margaret Needels in 1989. The majority of these experimental studies validated the findings from the correlational research.

During the process–product or "teacher effects" era between 1955 and 1980, more than 100 correlational and experimental studies were conducted using a common design and the different observation instruments shared many common instructional procedures. Brophy and Good in 1986 provided detailed descriptions of individual studies. The p–p results might also be called "master teacher" results in that the results represent the classroom behaviors of those teachers whose students made the greatest achievement gain after adjusting for initial scores.

Major Findings

Rosenshine and Stevens in 1986 summarized the process–product research and concluded that

across a number of studies, the most effective teachers used the following procedures:

- Begin a lesson with a short review of previous learning.
- Begin a lesson with a short statement of goals.
- Present new material in small steps, providing for student practice after each step.
- Give clear and detailed instructions and explanations.
- Provide a high level of active practice for all students by asking a large number of questions, checking for student understanding, and obtaining responses from all students.
- Guide students during initial practice.
- Provide systematic feedback and corrections.
- Provide explicit instruction and practice for seatwork exercises and, where necessary, monitor students during seatwork.

Three of the most important findings from that research are (1) the importance of teaching in small steps, (2) the importance of guiding student practice, and (3) the importance of providing for extensive practice. These steps formed the foundation for an instructional process that began to shape how several teachers taught skills within the classroom context.

1. Present New Material in Small Steps

In many of these studies, the most effective teachers taught new material in small steps. That is, they presented only small parts of new material at a single time. Breaking material into small steps simplifies the task so that the students can succeed and not be overwhelmed by its difficulty. In contrast, those teachers whose students made the least gain presented a good deal of material at once and then passed out worksheets, told students to work the problems, and then walked around the room helping students who were having a problem.

The procedure of teaching in small steps fits well with the findings from cognitive psychology vis-à-vis the limitations of the working memory of learners. Working memory, where learners process information, is small. It can handle only five to seven bits of information at once; any additional information swamps it. The procedure of first teaching in small steps and then guiding student practice represents an appropriate way of dealing with the limitation of our small working memories.

2. Guide Student Practice

A second major finding from the p–p or teacher effects literature was the importance of guided practice. The more effective teachers spent more time guiding students' practice, and they did this by providing models and explanations, giving examples, asking questions to check for students' understanding, and reteaching material when necessary. This guidance often consisted of the teacher working a few problems at the board and discussing the steps out loud or asking students to come to the board, work problems, and discuss their procedures. Guided practice has also included asking students to work together, in pairs or in groups, to quiz and explain the material to each other. Guided practice may occur when a teacher questions and helps students with their work before assigning independent practice.

Researchers found that the less-effective teachers gave shorter presentations and explanations and asked fewer questions. The result of this insufficient preparation showed up during seatwork when it was found that the students who were not sufficiently prepared made more errors during independent practice.

Guiding practice also fits the cognitive processing findings on the need to provide for processing in order to store new material in a learner's long-term memory. Guided practice is the place where the students, working alone, with other students, or with the teacher, engage in the cognitive processing activities of organizing, reviewing, rehearsing, summarizing, comparing, and contrasting. In comparison, the least effective teachers often lectured, then asked a question, called on one student to answer, and then assumed that everyone had learned this point.

3. Provide for Extensive Practice

The most effective teachers also provided for extensive and successful practice. As noted in the cognitive processing research, students need extensive practice in order to develop well-connected networks. The most effective teachers made sure that such practice took place only after there has been sufficient guided practice, so that students were not practicing errors and misconceptions.

Results From Ratings of Teachers

Process–product research also included observing classrooms and rating teachers on a 1–5 scale. Four of the most persistent findings in this research were that the teachers whose students made the greatest gain in achievement were also rated high in clarity, enthusiasm, business-like classrooms, and variability. Variability, for example, meant that these teachers used a variety of methods to help students learn.

Conclusion

Process–product research is an empirical method for determining those instructional procedures that are most highly correlated with student achievement gain. The research flourished between 1955 and 1980, and studies in that tradition continue today. In 2008, Tim Konold and colleagues conducted a p–p study involving 90 teachers and concluded that the results, which measured student acquisition of content knowledge and application, favored teachers who provided support for instruction. They noted that "teachers gave clues and reminders, encouraged serious thought, broke problems into steps, provided examples, asked questions, gave feedback, and the like." In essence, their findings reinforced the importance of teaching behaviors that were responsive to students and focused on fostering independent learning.

Barak V. Rosenshine

See also Constructivism; Differentiated Instruction; Eight-Year Study; Time on Task

Further Readings

Brophy, J. E., & Good, T. L. (1986). Teacher behavior and student achievement. In M. C. Wittrock (Ed.), *Handbook of research on teaching* (3rd ed., pp. 328–375). New York: Macmillan.

Evertson, C. E., Anderson, C., Anderson, L., & Brophy, J. (1980). Relationship between classroom behaviors and student outcomes in junior high mathematics and English classes. *American Educational Research Journal, 17,* 43–60.

Gage, N. L., & Needels, M. C. (1989). Process–product research on teaching: A review of criticisms. *Elementary School Journal, 89,* 253–300.

Good, T. L., & Grouws, D. A. (1979). The Missouri Mathematics Effectiveness Project. *Journal of Educational Psychology, 71*, 143–155.

Konold, T., Jablonski, B., Nottingham, A., Kessler, L., Byrd, S., Scott Imig, S., et al. (2008). Adding value to public schools: Investigating teacher education, teaching, and pupil learning. *Journal of Teacher Education, 59*, 300–313.

Medley, D. M., & Mitzel, H. E. (1963). Measuring classroom behavior by systematic observation. In N. L. Gage (Ed.), *Handbook of research on teaching*. Chicago: Rand-McNally.

Rosenshine, B., & Stevens, R. (1986). Teaching functions. In M. C. Wittrock (Ed.), *Handbook of research on teaching* (3rd ed., pp. 376–391). New York: Macmillan.

PROFESSIONAL DEVELOPMENT

Professional development refers to continuous learning opportunities for teachers. Other terms for professional development include in-service, teacher learning, staff development, and professional learning. Teachers are at the epicenter of discussion and debate over systemwide reform initiatives. Because teachers are critical to student achievement, professional development has become the focal point for supporting teachers in deepening their knowledge and skills. Today, as schools strive to become more focused on learning, professional development includes teachers, support staff, and administrators. The delivery modes of professional development have shifted over the years. As we look at the state of professional development over time, we can characterize these changes as a shift from generic to specific, static to dynamic, solitary to collaborative, individualized to systemic. Optimally, effective professional development offerings should serve the needs of educational reform initiatives and result in improved student performance.

During the 1970s and 1980s, professional development delivery relied on outside expertise for conducting workshops and seminars. In workshops or seminars during this period, teachers usually traveled to off-site locations to listen to information presented by an expert. According to M. S. Garet and colleagues, existing research suggests that this style of passive learning may not translate into effective classroom practice.

These one-time offerings were often generic in nature and disconnected from a teacher's specific classroom and student needs. When considering that the professional development was offered as a single session that lacked follow-up meetings, it is clear that the content of the offering could not be readily integrated with the individual needs of students in a teacher's classroom.

While workshops and/or seminars may be valuable for expanding a teaching repertoire, Lee Shulman's formulation of pedagogical content knowledge has prompted the education community to respect the special knowledge and skills of specific content areas. Math and science teachers, in particular, require professional development that focuses on sustained content and methods training. Thus, professional development offerings have been informed by this research.

The reforms in professional development differ from these traditional offerings to include activities that take place during the school day and rely more on colleagues, rather than outside experts. Professional learning communities, action research, and mentoring/coaching are examples of these reform types of professional development. The descriptions here highlight the unique features of each. Teachers engaged in a professional learning community collaborate and reflect with fellow teachers. Learning through these peer-to-peer interactions and having a shared sense of responsibility for student learning is a departure from the long-held view of the teaching profession as isolated. A growing number of teachers have been pursuing these questions with their own students through action research. Action research is a form of professional development in which the teacher is engaged in continuous learning through the inquiry process. Mentoring and/or coaching involves observation and ongoing communication with other teachers. Numerous districts now have formalized programs with financial incentives for teachers to serve as mentors or coaches for novice teachers in order to help retain first-year teachers.

Since the late 1980s, professional development schools, collaborations between K–12 schools and universities, have offered a natural multipronged strategy for professional development. These schools are often referred to as "teaching hospitals" in that they offer a clinical setting for preservice teacher preparation programs. In addition to assisting pre-service teachers with their development, professional development schools provide an opportunity for experienced teachers to expand their responsibilities through being mentors for pre-service teachers and communicating directly with university researchers.

These various reforms in professional development have evolved gradually over the years as outgrowths of comprehensive strategic reforms and research advances. Other influential forces on the professional development landscape have been technology, the enactment of the No Child Left Behind (NCLB) legislation, and funding constraints. With the advent of online courses and learning communities, teachers are now able to use technology to support their continuous learning. Teachers can participate in courses as well as in virtual communities. In addition to enhanced accessibility, online professional development offers the added benefit of collaboration with teachers globally.

While little is known about the influence that NCLB has had on the delivery of professional development, the law does mandate that federally funded professional development is routinely evaluated. This mandate ensures that evaluation is considered during the professional development-program planning phase. However, linking professional development directly to student achievement can be stunted by limited capacities for data collection within district data systems. More work is required at district and state levels to link teacher records to student records.

Budgetary constraints on districts have demanded that more professional development-offerings be conducted at the school site. A direct benefit of providing professional development at the school site is that more teachers can participate as a team, along with their administrators. This team participation can then support systemwide implementation. Involving administrators in training sessions also builds the necessary support for integrating the training on a schoolwide basis.

Little is known about district expenditures for professional development. Internal data systems in most districts do not sufficiently capture the scattered costs of professional development borne at the school, department, and central office levels, so the spending may often exceed what the districts realize. Karen Hawley Miles and her colleagues examined five urban school districts and found that professional development expenditures ranged from 2% to more than 5% of total district expenditures. As more research is being done to understand the application of cost-benefit analyses in education, future reforms in professional development will be informed by the data systems linking teachers to students and an awareness of both overt and hidden costs of professional development for districts.

Pamela Ellis

See also Academic Freedom; American Association of Colleges for Teacher Education; Curriculum Controversies; National Council of Professors of Educational Administration (NCPEA); National Network for Educational Renewal (NNER); Shulman, Lee; State Departments of Education; U.S. Department of Education; What Works Clearinghouse

Further Readings

Darling-Hammond, L., & McLaughlin, M. W. (1995). Policies that support professional development in an era of reform. *Phi Delta Kappan, 76*(8), 597–604.

Fullan, M. G. (2007). *The new meaning of educational change* (4th ed.). New York: Teachers College Press.

Garet, M. S., Porter, A. C., Desimone, L., Birman, B. F., & Yoon, K. S. (2001). What makes professional development effective? Results from a national sample of teachers. *American Educational Research Journal, 38*(4), 915–945.

Joyce, B., & Showers, B. (2002). *Student achievement through staff development* (3rd ed.). Alexandria, VA: Association for Supervision and Curriculum Development.

National Commission on Teaching & America's Future. (1996). *What matters most: Teaching for America's future.* New York: Author.

PROFESSIONAL DEVELOPMENT SCHOOLS

American colleges and universities that prepare future teachers have collaborated with elementary schools, middle schools, and high schools throughout the nation's history to provide those future educators with appropriate real-life experiences, particularly during the penultimate, student teaching, semester, quarter, or year. These school–university partnerships have proven beneficial to both the PreK–12 schools, which get additional hands in their classrooms as well as a firsthand look at potential new hires, and to the colleges and universities, who rely upon the PreK–12 sites for an element of realism in their teacher preparation programs. They also provide an avenue for reforming the teacher education process.

Professional development schools (PDS), initiated in the mid-1980s by the Holmes Group (now the Holmes Partnership), expand the collaboration between PreK–12 sites and colleges and universities beyond the preparation of future teachers. Professional development school collaborations focus not only on the preparation of future teachers but also on the professional development of those already in the teaching field, on the importance of collaborative school–university research and inquiry in furthering the profession, and on the degree to which these collaborations positively impact PreK–12 student learning. On the scale of school–university partnerships, then, PDS represent a more complex kind of relationship than the simple placement of student teachers in elementary, middle, or high school classrooms. They involve, instead, ongoing collaborations between the PreK–12 school's faculty and staff and the college or university faculty.

Three events between 2001 and 2008 highlighted the significance of PDS as venues for furthering school–university collaborations. First, the National Council for Accreditation of Teacher Education (NCATE) in 2001 published PDS standards as a tool for evaluating the efficacy of a particular PDS and for determining the developmental stage of that PDS, from "beginning" to "developing" to "at standard" to "leading." Second, while a number of educational organizations included discussions of PDS as part of their overall agendas, the 2005 creation of the National Association for Professional Development Schools (NAPDS) offered the first vehicle focusing exclusively on the work of PDS. Finally, the NAPDS, in response to questions about the differences between PDSs and other types of school–university partnerships, published in 2008 a statement titled *What It Means to Be a Professional Development School.*

The NAPDS statement offered what the association called the Nine Essentials of PDS work and is perhaps the clearest explanation of both the philosophical foundations and the logistical requirements involved in this very specific form of school–university collaboration. The Essentials begin with the acknowledgment that the relationship between the PreK–12 site and the college or university hinges on "a comprehensive mission statement that is broader in its outreach and scope than the mission of any partner." All educational institutions have mission statements, but the PDS expectation is that the mission of the collaboration is more than the sum of the parts of each institution's mission. PDS participants, in short, are asked to give careful consideration to what each partner brings to the relationship and to craft the mission and goals of the collaboration, in part, on these relative contributions.

Beyond a shared mission statement, the NAPDS Essentials call upon PDS relationships to focus on both the professional preparation of future teachers and ongoing professional development of educators already in the field. Teacher candidates placed in PDS sites for their internship/student teaching experiences are fully integrated into the PreK–12 school community, with the faculty and staff in those schools taking on the collective responsibility of mentoring those candidates. College/university faculty, meanwhile, provide the school-based faculty and staff with professional development experiences in what the school has identified as areas of need. It is not uncommon to see college/university courses for teacher candidates offered on the school site, nor is it uncommon to see PreK–12 faculty and staff actively engaged in teaching courses at the college/university. In a PDS relationship, the lines separating PreK–12 and college/university spaces dissolve in the shared objective of promoting student learning. That shared objective hinges upon the PDS partners identifying and implementing in both the PreK–12 and college/university cultures mutually determined best practices in teaching and learning. Such collaboratively agreed upon practices are routinely reflected upon by all of the PDS partners and, in addition, are consistently shared with the broader community, both within and outside of the PDS.

How individual PDS relationships approach each of these philosophical foundations of PDS work is the decision of the specific school–university collaboration. So, too, is the manner in which each PDS relationship organizes the logistical requirements of PDS work as outlined in the NAPDS Essentials. These requirements include the creation of a formal written agreement, developed and signed by individuals representing each side of the relationship, delineating the obligations of each partner and describing the various roles to be played by the PDS participants. In addition to the formal written agreement, PDS relationships also require the creation of an organizational structure that guides the work of the PDS and allows for ongoing governance, reflection, and collaboration; PDS partners meet formally and informally on a regular basis for the purposes of decision making and sharing.

The final logistical Essential for PDS relationships involves resources, rewards, and recognition structures. The PreK–12 and college/university partners must each bring to the collaboration those resources (e.g., money, time, materials, physical space) that it has available that will strengthen the work of the PDS. The resources need not be equal but should reflect instead the ability and willingness of the partners to dedicate to the relationship those things that will enhance the collaborative work of the PDS, work that goes above and beyond the normal routines of both PreK–12 and college/university faculty. Because of the extraordinary efforts required in establishing and sustaining a PDS, individuals engaged in PDS collaborations must be formally rewarded and recognized for their work. The rewards and recognitions can take many forms, from consideration in the tenure and promotion process for college/university faculty, to release time for PreK–12 faculty, to funding for all participants to attend conferences or workshops that will help them do their work even more effectively.

At a time when U.S. teacher preparation programs and PreK–12 education in general were both being criticized for their inadequacies, PDS relationships were hailed by Arthur Levine as offering "perhaps the strongest bridge between teacher education and classroom outcomes, academics and clinical education, theory and practice, and schools and colleges" (p. 105). Perhaps because of such praise, PDS relationships spread throughout the United States in the closing decades of the 20th century and the beginning years of the 21st century, and as of 2008 existed in at least 43 of the 50 states. In addition, educators in other countries, including Canada, the Netherlands, Great Britain, China, and Japan, have taken steps to initiate PDS as part of their nations' educational experience.

Bruce E. Field

See also Holmes Group; National Council for Accreditation of Teacher Education (NCATE); Teacher Education

Further Readings

Brindley, R., Field, B., & Lessen, E. (2008). *What it means to be a professional development school.* Columbia, SC: National Association for Professional Development Schools.

Levine, A. (2006). *Educating school teachers.* Washington, DC: Educational Schools Project.

National Association for Professional Development Schools (NAPDS). (2008). *What it means to be a professional development school.* Retrieved July 25, 2009, from http://www.napds.org/9%20Essentials/statement.pdf

National Council for Accreditation of Teacher Education. (2001). *Standards for professional development schools.* Washington, DC: Author.

Robinson, S. (2007). *Responding to educating school teachers.* Washington, DC: American Association of Colleges for Teacher Education.

Teitel, L. (2003). *The professional development school handbook: Starting, sustaining, and assessing partnerships that improve student learning.* Thousand Oaks, CA: Corwin.

PROGRAMMED INSTRUCTION

The psychologist B. F. Skinner developed the teaching machine and programmed instruction in the early 1950s to provide systematic effective instruction in skills such as arithmetic and reading. Then the USSR's launch of the first artificial satellite, *Sputnik,* in 1957 precipitated both curriculum reform in public education and interest in technology for the classroom. The programmed instruction movement produced, paradoxically, both research in program design and many programs marketed to schools without adequate evaluation, a situation that contributed to the decline of programmed instruction in the next decade. Nevertheless, research on programmed instruction introduced a focus on anticipating and addressing probable learner difficulties during planning for instruction, and other related topics. In other words, programmed instruction contributed to shifting the focus in education to the learner and learner outcomes and away from teacher activities. Programmed instruction was one of the developments that emerged in response to the call for curriculum reform after *Sputnik*. Research on programmed instruction also initiated the field known as instructional design.

Program Characteristics

Skinner developed programmed instruction because he observed that a teacher with 20 or 30 children could not arrange either (a) sufficient opportunities for each student to interact verbally with the subject matter or (b) the accompanying appropriate consequences for verbal behavior. These consequences, referred to as *reinforcers*, are essential in developing learner skills because they increase the likelihood of the repetition of correct student responses. Skinner estimated that ensuring acquisition of basic arithmetic skills alone would require 50,000 reinforcements for each student.

Skinner's solution was to develop both programmed instruction from his learning principles and the teaching machine to present the instruction. Programmed instruction is a reproducible set of instructional events that is self-paced, does not require teacher intervention, and leads the learner to the acquisition of particular behaviors or skills. Skinner's programs, referred to as *response centered*, consist of a graded sequence of small steps or frames, each requiring a constructed response by the student. Reinforcements include immediate confirmation of a correct response, and the opportunity to move forward to new material, and to operate the equipment. Cues or prompts for correct answers are gradually withdrawn as the student begins to acquire the targeted skills. Skinner discouraged the use of a book format that placed the correct answer to a frame on a subsequent page. Problems include the possibilities that students may look ahead, skip frames, or lose their place in the material.

The assumption of response-centered programming is that behavior is learned only when it is emitted and reinforced. A different approach, initiated by Nelson Crowder, is *stimulus centered*. This branching format first presents a unit of material, usually a paragraph, and a multiple-choice question on the material. Incorrect alternatives in the multiple-choice question represent plausible misunderstandings. The student's selection of the correct answer leads to the next unit of material. Choosing a wrong answer is followed by feedback that indicates why the particular choice is wrong and directs the learner back to the paragraph to try again.

The rationale for branching programs is that learning is cognitive and the response fulfills a diagnostic or testing function. Skinner disagreed with this approach, however, because he believed that the student must recall rather than recognize information and realistic wrong answers to multiple-choice questions might be learned inadvertently.

Impact

Interest in programmed instruction led to a flood of products into the schools. Successes included, for example, a grammar program in one school system. Because it required less time than conventional instruction, additional time was available for composition. Many programs, however, superficially copied the programmed-instruction format but were ineffective in producing learning. They often left blanks in the material for unimportant words, rather than addressing key concepts. Other problems with programmed instruction in education included the following: (a) many programs addressed low-level skills, such as definitions and examples of new terms, rather than more complex behaviors; (b) teachers often did not receive an adequate orientation on ways to integrate self-paced programmed instruction with group-based instruction; and (c) long programs in courses became boring as students progressed through the material.

Although the programmed instruction movement was short lived, programs were developed for all educational levels, from elementary school to graduate courses. Also, Skinnerian programs in updated machines with earphones and voice feedback continued to provide remedial work in reading and mathematics. In addition, efforts to develop effective and efficient programmed instruction introduced new topics to education. Some became part of the subsequent field of instructional design, such as the 5-step design process for standalone instruction. These steps are (1) specify the competency or behavior the student is to acquire; (2) identify relevant student characteristics, including entry knowledge level; (3) conduct a behavioral analysis of the material to be learned; (4) construct the program; and (5) test the program on a student sample, and revise it until it is effective. This process led in turn to other new topics. Two that entered the educational mainstream are the specification of behavioral objectives as learning outcomes, and the major role played by prior knowledge in any learning situation. Other current parts of instructional design are task analysis, which involves identifying the components of a learning outcome; formative evaluation, which provides information for revising instruction; and the performance requirements that reflect mastery learning.

Margaret E. Gredler

See also Educational Technology; Skinner, B. F.

Further Readings

Glaser, R. (Ed.). (1965). *Teaching machines and programmed learning: II. Data and new directions.* Washington, DC: Association for Educational Communications and Technology.

Skinner, B. F. (1968). *A technology of teaching.* New York: Appleton-Century-Crofts.

PROGRESSIVE EDUCATION

When John Dewey wrote *My Pedagogic Creed* in 1896, he said, "I believe that education is the fundamental method of social progress and reform." This belief is clearly one—and perhaps the only—unifying thread of progressive education then and now. This is in part because of the substance of the theories and recommendations offered by the variety of educators who claim the progressive mantle and in part because the term itself has historical and philosophical referents, and in all cases, the referents have political dimensions. In a narrower sense, "progressive education" is used to invoke a palette of educational reform efforts in a particular chronological period from 1890 through 1920, or 1940, or even 1957. The term *progressive education* refers to any effort to reconstruct taken-for-granted educational practice for social purposes, but what links all the different positions is not a particular educational worldview, nor is it the simplistic notion that the progressive is the enemy of the traditional, but instead the faith articulated by Dewey that education is the premier path to social progress in a democracy.

Educational Reform in the Progressive Era

The Progressive era in American politics and social life was an embedded response to the corporate capitalism that followed fast on the heels of three well-documented features of life in mid–19th-century United States: immigration, industrialization, and urbanization. Any attempts to ameliorate social conditions, improving the economic and social lot of the poor, the worker, and even the middle class, can be understood as progressive.

Progressive education in this sense is the educational phase of American progressivism writ large. Not all progressive educational thought and action were associated with schooling, and much of the impetus for efforts at educational change came from concerns that were political, social, cultural, and communal—not strictly speaking pedagogical—in character. Liberal progressive Jane Addams's Hull House is probably the best example of an institution for adults and children created to improve social and economic conditions through the creation of educational community.

Not all educational reformers of the era shared Addams's liberalism. Conservative progressives sought not social justice (through equality and economic opportunity), but social order, an order that would ensure a worthy American community without altering the dominance of the economic status quo. Still, the quality of an American community was a common focus. In a time when laissez-faire individualism dominated the economic scene and when the fact of cultural diversity required acknowledgment of actual and potential conflict, schooling presented itself as a powerful tool to combat social decay.

Both strains of the progressive temper spread to the newly developed and rapidly expanding system of public schools throughout the United States. Educators were responding to schools whose enrollments were growing exponentially, to educational institutions that seemed modeled after dehumanizing factories, to obvious conditions of educational inequity, and to a school curriculum that was perceived as academically exclusive. If individual students had diverse talents, testing could identify aptitudes and then differentiated curricula, enacted by child-centered teachers, would develop them. And all of this would occur in scientifically managed schools whose graduates could, as some desired, "build a new social order." Clearly, this educational worldview was not without its tensions.

Framing the Agenda for Educational Reform, 1890–1920

It was Dewey who described Francis W. Parker as the "father of the progressive education movement," and it is a label that is quite appropriate given the way Parker's work exemplifies the potential contradictions of progressive education as it developed between 1890 and 1920. As the superintendent of schools in Boston and later in Cook County, Illinois, Parker employed efficiencies of scale that bureaucracy and growth demanded while articulating the child-centered focus that his European education in the theories of Pestalozzi and Froebel predicted. Parker was a proponent of teacher specialization and of ability grouping and curricular standardization, but opposed drill as a dominant pedagogy, and spurned tests and grades as indicators of children's learning. Further, Parker understood that the end of educational effort was the development of democratic society. Perhaps the only element of the Progressive period per se that Parker's work misses is the focus on the social scientific or psychological evaluation of individual students. Parker was departing the educational scene just as psychology and the practice of psychological testing was coming of age.

If Francis Parker's work marks one chronological endpoint of Progressive era education, William Heard Kilpatrick's writings mark the other. Kilpatrick, a Dewey colleague at Teachers College, Columbia University, is emblematic of the transition from the Progressive era to the Progressive Education Association (PEA) era in that he was not a teacher, nor an administrator, but an education school faculty member. Kilpatrick thought of himself as an educational translator of Dewey's philosophical ideas. Working both before and after the PEA came into being, Kilpatrick is best known for his advocacy of "the project method." Over time, he became increasingly hostile to organized subject matter, embracing instead teaching and learning organized around projects determined by student interest. His 1918 essay, "The Project Method," outlining this method was thought by some to be the clearest statement of the child-centered school movement.

As Parker did, Kilpatrick sounded the seemingly contradictory strains present in the progressive education movement. Learning was governed by laws, but teaching was responsive to the natural interests and development of the child. Schooling required the scientific approach of the authoritative pedagogue, but that pedagogue bowed to the anti-intellectualism of the social utilitarian.

Four Strains of Reform

Thus there are four ways that educational reformers imagined schools might contribute to revitalized social life. While not always distinguishable in progressive school practice, they are different enough in intent and focus to warrant clear statement.

Child Centered

The first and best-known strain is the understanding that the means and ends of education must derive from the child's needs. This was a reaction to what were perceived to be sterile, ineffective, and therefore, outmoded, pedagogies. But even here, there are liberal and conservative variants. Liberals understood the child's needs in process terms—freeing the self to interact socially, often though not always thinking in the light of the European romantics, Rousseau, Froebel, and Pestalozzi. Conservatives understood child-centeredness in outcome terms—identifying a child's talents and educating those talents for social (and economic) functioning. Still, child-centered progressives shared the belief that one learns by doing. That is, one learns through using material geared to one's interest, development, and prior knowledge. For the child-centered progressive, it is not the case that one learns, *then* uses, as was the taken-for-granted view of the time.

While many of the child-centered advocates experimented in private school settings—Margaret Naumberg's Walden School is an example—some set their mark on public schools as well. Ella Flagg Young, a Dewey colleague who served as superintendent of the Chicago schools from 1909 to 1915, supported instructional efforts that originated in an understanding of the learner's interests and prior knowledge.

Kilpatrick's articulation of the project method and Harold Rugg and Ann Shumaker's description of *The Child-Centered School* are probably the fullest statements of the romantic view of this progressive strain. In both texts the emphasis on freedom, activity, and creative expression all leading to "maximum child growth" is clear.

Scientific

Adherents of the second strain shared the view that educating is a scientific endeavor in which means, and perhaps ends, can and should be determined with precision. The scientific progressives diverged in interest and goals. Their motivations were also different, though bound by faith in the power of rapidly developing social sciences to solve human problems. The first group under the influence of Darwinism and the new discipline of individual psychology wanted to understand, wished to quantify, and hoped to control the development of individual students. The second group, under the influence of Frederick W. Taylor's "scientific management," sought to construct and administer schools and classrooms with efficiency according to principles of human behavior and bureaucratic function.

When G. Stanley Hall brought evolutionary concepts to psychology, others followed. A disciplined plan of "child study," laid out in his 1904 book, *Adolescence,* shifted educators' focus to the development of the child rather than the defined subject matter. Hall's position was balanced by William James's view that there was no naturalistic determinism to a child's development, and that the formation of habits could be understood in developmental ways. At about the same time, Edward L. Thorndike began experiments at Harvard University to determine laws of learning; that is, to associate

pedagogical stimuli with learning responses in ways that would develop into behavioral theory.

With the work of Hall, James, and Thorndike, the door was opened to test and classify states of and potential for development in individual students. Lewis M. Terman stepped through that door in 1916 with *Intelligence Tests and School Reorganization.* Terman, a former high school principal and then chair of Stanford University's psychology department, put forward a recommendation that was simple and dangerously appealing: let science determine a child's aptitude and then tailor the school structure and program to the needs of different children. Mental testing, the scientific characterization of learners, became firmly established in the firmament of schooling. Henry Goddard acknowledged that the use of mental testing would lead to an "aristocracy in democracy" in *Human Efficiency and Levels of Intelligence,* but was undaunted by that. To the contrary, Goddard suggested (not unlike Thomas Jefferson 2 centuries earlier) that all citizens of a democracy should welcome the identification of the most talented among us as a way to achieve a more efficient and productive society.

Adherents of scientific management shared Terman's and Goddard's commitment to tailoring school structure to scientific knowledge, but with a focus on commonalities of human behavior and control rather than individual student differences. The strongest statement of the scientific management view was John Franklin Bobbitt's 1912 essay, "Elimination of Waste in Education." But the best known of the scientific management efforts, documented in the Dewey's *Schools of Tomorrow,* was the Gary Plan. William Wirt, a student of Dewey's at the University of Chicago and a supporter of Hull House, became the superintendent of schools in Gary, Indiana. He brought to Gary a Deweyan vision of the school as a community within the larger community of Gary, one that ought not "waste" money, time, talent, or facilities. He also brought a strong sense of the logic of scientific management, the Taylor view that complete and intensive use ought to be made of all facilities and resources. He sought to develop the school system as a cooperatively run, economically responsible, efficiently managed, and pedagogically enriched institution that worked seamlessly within that community and for the benefit of that community's citizens.

Social Efficiency

The results of a scientific focus on schooling included tests that identified individual students' talents and school programs and schedules that acknowledged specific community needs. With these tools in hand, enthusiastic educators sought to match students' abilities and community needs in what was the third strain of progressive era reform, the social efficiency movement. This included more than the social efficiency per se championed by David Snedden. It included industrial and vocational education as it developed for immigrant White students in the North, championed by Charles Prosser, and for Black students in the South, championed by Booker T. Washington. It included programs for physical health and mental hygiene. And it included changes in the school curriculum and the creation of an extra curriculum that targeted what would later be called "life adjustment."

Binding these various responses together was the general sense that the traditional academic curriculum was inappropriate for some students on social and economic grounds. Corporate interests required skilled laborers, and the schools could train them. Educators wanted to justify themselves while contributing to the vibrancy of the community. From an earlier emphasis on wisdom and character through imagination to a developing focus on service and power through manual employment, the social efficiency movement altered the curriculum and with it, the structure and purpose of schooling. Preparation for life became preparation for work. Readiness to take one's place in society meant attention to health, citizenship, and leisure.

This focus was captured in the language of the National Education Association's (NEA) 1918 statement, *Cardinal Principles of Secondary Education*. In sharp contrast to the goals articulated in the same NEA's 1892 *Committee of Ten Report*, the *Cardinal Principles* identified health, command of fundamental processes, worthy home membership, vocation, civic education, worthy use of leisure, and ethical character as the outcomes of successful education. Mastery of academic subject matter was virtually absent. While one might characterize the 1892 advocacy of a traditional academic curriculum as a conservative position countered by the NEA's liberal 1918 position, one can see the latter as contributing to the conservation of the

established socioeconomic order. This is particularly true when one ponders the features of the comprehensive high school, including tracking, that remain in place today and that, while seeming to offer each student what he or she needs, keeps him or her in the place to which he or she has already been socialized.

Social Reconstruction

As suggested at the outset, a desire to reshape and reinvigorate social life using the schools as a tool is a commitment that marks all who come under the progressive umbrella. This view was manifested as a general mind-set and, occasionally, as a specific proposal. George S. Counts famously stated one of the more specific, and more controversial, proposals in his presidential address at the PEA meeting in 1932. Counts sternly called his fellows to task for failing to advocate education that was truly progressive. He argued that the focus on freeing the child's creative spirit did not go far enough in repudiating the tyranny of elitist subject matter. He complained that indoctrinating children for life in a planned society, a swipe at those who advocated social efficiency, constituted surrender to dominant economic interests. Instead, Counts advocated a self-conscious program of education for systemic socioeconomic change. He challenged the PEA to be progressive and he dared the schools to build a new social order in the face of the economic and social chaos of a corporate capitalism-caused depression.

Clearly, not all educators of the Progressive era shared Counts's radical reconstructionist views, but most agreed with his general point that educators should be more self-conscious and more constructive regarding the impact of the school on the society at large.

John Dewey and Progressive Education

No discussion of progressive education is complete without an exploration of the role philosopher John Dewey played in its development and articulation, though Dewey cannot bear sole responsibility for progressive education. It is true that he was closely involved with one well-known experimental school. He did publicize positively a variety of such experimental approaches in Schools of

Tomorrow. He did teach many educators and social reformers at the University of Chicago and at Teachers College, some who would go on to experiment with the ideas Dewey articulated and others who would claim to implement Dewey's ideas while misunderstanding significant features. But the various facets of Progressive era reform suggested above had sources and prompts independent of Dewey's work. What Dewey did was to make sense of these elements in a way that acknowledged apparent contradictions and then suggested an alternate reading of the task and practice of education.

Dewey's Chicago Laboratory School was designed to allow students to work wholeheartedly and actively to understand problems of interest to them as a means to "moving in the direction of what the expert already knows," that is, academic subject matter. Dewey argued in several talks to parents (later published as *The School and Society* and *The Child and the Curriculum*) that it was a mistake to pit the needs of the school against the demands of society, because the school was society's organ for self-recreation. He claimed that the child and the curriculum were simply two sides of the same coin, two perspectives for viewing the same activity.

Dewey included a talk (published in *The School and Society*) on "Waste in Education," a concern of those who advocated scientific management, but he expanded the meaning of *waste* to include the waste of human resources and energy. Dewey demanded that educators use all of the child's capacities—physical, emotional, and intellectual—in the development of his or her intelligence. For Dewey, hand training was not remedial or even vocational but always a means to an intellectual and moral end.

In 1916, Dewey brought these elements into an explicit philosophical statement of the role and reality of education in a democratic society. In *Democracy and Education* he argued that a democratic society demanded a democratic form and structure of education. Without such an education, students could not participate in democracy as a "mode of associated living." He addressed the specific issues of active learning, of interest, of the formation of subject matter, of the centrality of intelligence understood functionally and developmentally, and of the value of the vocational. His

view that a scientific approach to solving human problems is paradigmatic is well known, if widely misunderstood, and he referred to that way of thinking simply as the "method of intelligence."

Dewey became, over time, a critic of "progressive education," despite his association with the idea of progressive education in the public imagination. After 1920, Dewey faulted those who called themselves progressive educators for failing to understand that neither child-centeredness nor so-called scientific approaches nor attention to life circumstances nor social reconstruction were enough by themselves, that any new approach without a spirit of experimentalism could not succeed over time.

The Era of the Progressive Education Association

In 1919, as the Progressive era was ending, the PEA came into existence. The Association capitalized on but did not spur the main movements of progressive innovation from 1890 to 1920 as described previously. The group did, however, lay claim to the term *progressive education,* coined at that time to name this organization of educational reformers and supporters and to express their desire to revitalize traditional curriculum with child-centered and scientific methods. These concerns persisted through the life of the organization in the 1920s, 1930s, and 1940s. In the main, the PEA was an advocacy group for child-centered practice. However, members of the Association also disseminated and supported a whole host of efforts that appeared to focus on the needs and interests of the individual child, while construing those needs in terms that maintained the socioeconomic status quo.

Two initiatives solidified the PEA's impact on the public consciousness. The first was the *Progressive Education Journal.* Published for 30 years in a style accessible to anyone interested in progress in the schools, the *Journal* made a strong case for attending to children's creativity in school settings. The second was the Eight-Year Study, conducted from 1932 to 1940. This well-funded, carefully designed experiment in progressive education at the secondary level, demonstrated that students from progressive high schools were capable, adaptable learners and excelled in even the finest universities.

As the Eight-Year Study proceeded to a successful conclusion, the nation, moved by depression and then war, lost its progressive heart. At the same time, education as a field was being rapidly professionalized for the teachers in the schools through their unions, for school administrators through their professional organizations, and for faculty in schools of education. Professionalization seemed to move the progressive center of gravity away from either the development of the individual learner or the reconstruction of the social environment toward a focus on efficiency—tracking and sorting, life adjustment and vocational education.

In 1944, the National Education Association's Educational Policies Commission published *Education for All American Youth,* with the endorsement of the American Association of School Administrators and the National Association of Secondary School Principals. Here a newly developed educational establishment made clear a vision of the school as the site of social planning. Neither the traditional academic curriculum nor the interests and rhythms of learners occupied center stage.

Faculty members in schools of education adopted a professional language, often employing progressive terminology, and in the process excluded the broad participation of the community in educational matters. Both the fact of professionalization and the shift away from child-centeredness impacted the Progressive Education Association. Its status as a popularizing forum that welcomed all interested parties was jeopardized. By the time the Association closed up shop in 1955, the social efficiency/life adjustment branch of the early 20th-century progressive movement had become the status quo.

The Critics of Progressive Education

Critics of progressive education are easy to find. Curriculum traditionalists like Robert Maynard Hutchins, Irving Babbitt and William Bagley, and later James Bryant Conant, argued strongly that abandoning the classical curriculum founded in the liberal arts was a mistake that would undercut the very claim to being educated. They further rejected the notion that societal demands should shape educational experience, citing the liberating aspects of the traditional curriculum.

Other critics came from inside the ranks of those who might be called progressive. For example, Arthur Bestor experienced as a student the positive impact of a progressive education at the Lincoln School at Teachers College. Nonetheless, in *Educational Wastelands,* he joined Dewey's call for "disciplined intelligence" in arguing that progressive schools can actually be regressive (but not traditional) when they fail to attend to the central task of schooling—the academic and moral development of youth.

Dewey himself rarely referred to "progressive" education, preferring to contrast "new" with "old." When he did use the term progressive, as he did in the 1928 address to the Progressive Education Association and in *Experience and Education,* he was critical of the progressive tendency to think dichotomously about important educational realities, to be purely reactionary. Whether traditional or progressive, suggested Dewey, those who thought in terms of either the child *or* the curriculum, either the school *or* society, would fail to educate well.

Dewey's criticisms of the efforts of progressive educators were pointed but polite. Contemporary critics have been less tolerant of the wide-ranging progressive agenda. Historian Diane Ravitch makes a clear case in *The Troubled Crusade* when she argues that progressive education after 1918 was a "betrayal" of the kind of education called for by Dewey. Ravitch's concern, like Dewey's and Bestor's, is that progressive educators do not educate. Providing health care and vocational training may be worthwhile, but this is not the role of educational institutions.

Even more pointed, revisionist educational historians claim that the progressive agenda masks social control with talk about democratic empowerment. Samuel Bowles and Herbert Gintis, for example, rewrote the story of progressive education as a hijacking of schools by corporate capital. Some naively child-centered educationists like Elwood Cubberly criticized schools as factories while also accepting corporate funding for social efficiency programs that tracked and sorted students in the service of an efficient labor force for corporate enterprises. Cubberly may have been an unwitting tool of corporate interests, but other progressives clearly intended tracking and sorting and welcomed its winnowing effect. G. Stanley Hall and Lewis Terman are examples of support for social control.

The revisionists' questions are fair ones. Did the progressives' enthusiasm for the new science of psychology and their fervor as social reformers lead them to create a system that manipulates individual students toward community needs under the guise of individual, personal interests? Who benefits from such a system? How, for instance, did immigrants, Blacks, females, and the children of working families fare in schools marked by tracking, standardized testing, student councils, daily flag pledge, high school athletics, home economics courses, vocational–technical placements, and professional administration?

On the other hand, it is also fair to suggest that the elements cited above are bastardized versions of the experiments progressive educators undertook and disseminated. As small-scale efforts became large-scale programs controlled by professional administrators and business-oriented school boards, they took on a corporate quality unintended by the educators who developed them.

The Contemporary Face of Progressive Education

Educators with a progressive inclination today tend to maintain that progressivism, at least pedagogical progressivism, never really took hold in the public schools in the United States. Ellen Condiffe Lagemann's well-known claim that Thorndike won and Dewey lost the struggle for center stage in 20th-century educational practice, is a testimony to this point of view. Nonetheless, Thorndike was, as much as Dewey, part of the progressive tenor at the beginning of the 20th century. If Thorndike won, it was still a victory for progressivism of a kind. On balance, one might most accurately argue that the "winners" were the social efficiency and life adjustment progressives, a state of affairs that resists change despite criticism from both sides of the political divide.

The kind of pedagogical progressivism espoused by Dewey and others in the early part of the 20th century went out of fashion with the arrival of World War II and the subsequent cold war. But the changing social milieu of the 1960s opened the door to a renewal of progressive experiments and themes. Open classrooms, cooperative learning,

multiage approaches, whole language, experiential learning, values clarification, and even inquiry-based science instruction shared a progressive bent. Elliott Wigginton's Foxfire Project is an excellent example of a progressive educational experiment. Even in the face of the Reagan era's "back to basics" movement, progressive reforms appeared with some frequency. Theodore R. Sizer's Coalition of Essential Schools, of which Deborah Meier's student-centered Central Park East schools may be the best-known examples, are educational reforms in the Deweyan tradition. Their integrated focus on "habits of mind" as the vehicle for understanding both the school and society, both the child and the curriculum marks them as progressive. Perhaps the most consistent advocate of pedagogical progressivism today is Alfie Kohn. In nearly a dozen books published over the past decade, Kohn has responded to those elements of educational policy and practice that are, in his view, regressive.

As noted at the outset, progressive education can be understood as any effort to reconstruct social practice using schooling as the tool. Some contemporary examples of progressive educational thought and practice stem not (or only partly) from the pedagogical progressivism of John Dewey, but ally firmly with the more politically and economically minded George Counts. Many claim origin for their reconstructionist thinking in the critical pedagogy of Paulo Freire. Schooling, on this view, must be liberatory praxis.

Paul Goodman and George Dennison are exemplars of a more radical progressive strain that arose in the 1960s and resulted in proposals for "free schools." More recently, Bob Peterson and his colleagues sought to bring an explicit social justice perspective to urban schools with Freire's "problem-posing" method as a guide. Their journal *Rethinking Schools* remains today a viable organ for examining schooling from the viewpoint of participatory democracy and critical, socially engaged intelligence.

These educators have integrated the revisionist critique into their progressive claims, challenging the reproduction of inequitable practices, and seeking to balance critique and imagination in the processes of teaching and learning. That is, they acknowledge the schools' role in maintaining unjust socioeconomic arrangements but continue to believe that the education of teachers and students can go forward to resist injustice and to reenvision transformative practice. Jeannie Oakes is a University of California, Los Angeles, professor who has long sought to challenge the practice of tracking in schools. In *Teaching to Change the World,* she (with Martin Lipton) articulates for future teachers a vision of social justice and a theory of teaching and learning that brings the revisionist, reconstructionist commitments into conversation with a Deweyan understanding of educational processes.

What ties progressive educators one to the other is just this faith that the schools are and can be "the fundamental method of social progress and reform"—whatever the actual vision of social progress. This was true in Dewey's time and it remains true today.

Barbara S. Stengel

See also Addams, Jane; Cubberly, Ellwood; Dewey, John; Du Bois, W. E. B.; Freire, Paulo; Gary Plan; Hall, G. Stanley; Intelligence Testing; Open Education; Problem-Based Learning; Progressive Education Association (PEA); Project Learning; Ravitch, Diane; Rugg, Harold; Social Efficiency; Social Reconstructionism; Terman, Lewis M.; Thorndike, Edward L.; Washington, Booker T.

Further Readings

Addams, J. (1994). *On education.* Edison, NJ: Transaction Publishers.

Aikin, W. (1942). *The story of the Eight-Year Study.* New York: Harper.

Altenbaugh, R. (2003). *The American people and their education: A social history.* Upper Saddle River, NJ: Merrill Prentice Hall.

Bode, B. (1938). *Progressive education at the crossroads.* New York: Newson & Company.

Bestor, A. (1953). *Educational wastelands: The retreat from learning in our public schools.* Urbana: University of Illinois Press.

Bowles, S., & Gintis, H. (1976). *Schooling in capitalist America: Educational reform and the contradictions of economic life.* New York: Basic Books.

Cremin, L. (1961). *The transformation of the school.* New York: Knopf.

Dewey, J. (1938). *Experience and education.* New York: The Macmillan Company.

Dewey, J. (1990). *The school and society, and the child and the curriculum.* Chicago: University of Chicago Press.

Dewey, J., & Dewey, E. (1962). *Schools of tomorrow.* New York: E. P. Dutton.

Freire, P. (1960). *Pedagogy of the oppressed.* New York: Continuum International.

Graham, P. (1967). *Progressive education from Arcady to academe.* New York: Teachers College Press.

Kilpatrick, W. (1925). *Foundations of methods.* New York: Macmillan.

Kohn, A. (1999). *The schools our children deserve: Moving beyond traditional classrooms and "tougher standards"?* New York: Houghton Mifflin.

Oakes, J., & Lipton, M. (1998). *Teaching to change the world.* New York: McGraw-Hill.

Peterson, R. (1995). *Rethinking schools: An agenda for change.* New York: New Press.

Puckett, J. (1989). *Foxfire reconsidered: A twenty-year experiment in progressive education.* Urbana: University of Illinois Press.

Ravitch, D. (1983). *The troubled crusade: American education, 1945–1980.* New York: Basic Books.

Ravitch, D. (2000). *Left back: A century of battles over school reform.* New York: Simon & Shuster.

Rethinking Schools: http://www.rethinkingschools.org

Rugg, H., & Shumaker, A. (1928). *The child-centered school: An appraisal of the new education.* Yonkers-on-Hudson, NY: World Book.

Semel, S., & Sadovnik, A. (Eds.). (1998). *Schools of tomorrow, schools of today: What happened to progressive education.* New York: Peter Lang.

PROGRESSIVE EDUCATION ASSOCIATION (PEA)

Founded as a populist organization for those who identified themselves as educational reformers, the Progressive Education Association (PEA) enjoyed initial success but experienced declining influence after World War II. The demise of the organization has been attributed to a shift in mission and identity—from an association of persons interested in education and its impact on community life to a more narrowly drawn organization of professional educators. As the practice of education became more professionalized, which was one of the tenets of the progressivist movement, the PEA lost its reason for being.

The founding force behind the PEA was Stanwood Cobb, a Dartmouth College honors graduate with an M.A. degree from Harvard Divinity School, who, after teaching in Istanbul, headed the English Department at St. John's College and taught at the U.S. Naval Academy in Annapolis, Maryland. Cobb was impressed by the experiments in schooling chronicled in John and Evelyn Dewey's *Schools of Tomorrow*. Against the backdrop of progressive political reform and the educational experimentation that the Deweys documented, Cobb sought out Marietta Pierce Johnson, founder of the Organic School. With the help of Eugene Randolph Smith, headmaster of the Park School, philanthropist Laura C. Williams, and others, the Association was born in 1919.

By the time the PEA was founded, the Progressive era in American politics already had begun to wane; the founders of the Association were not, by and large, the pioneering figures who had spearheaded thinking about educational innovation. Yet if they were self-described educational "nobodies," they were nobodies associated with upper-middle-class roots, philanthropy, and eastern private schools. While they claimed ambitions to "reform the entire system," their focus was typically more limited: to infuse the traditional curriculum with vigor and creativity. That Harvard University president Charles W. Eliot—long a proponent of academic curriculum over social efficiency—signed on as honorary president is an indicator of the concerns and direction of the founders.

Still, the Association's original Statement of Purpose incorporated multiple strains of reformist thought and practice—child-centered teaching practice, the scientific study of students and the scientific administration of schooling, school as an instrument of democratic social reform, and even though unstated, social efficiency—enabling many to find a home within its borders. The members of the PEA were committed to children's freedom to develop naturally; interest as the motive for all work; the teacher's role and responsibility to be a guide, not a taskmaster; scientific study of pupil development; greater attention to all that affects the child's physical development; cooperation between school and home to meet the needs of a child's life; and the progressive school as the leader in educational movements.

In its initial decade, the PEA was successful in attracting a wide audience to the cause of educational reform. This can be attributed partly to the 1924 founding of the *Progressive Education Journal*, edited by Gertrude Hartmann. The journal put progressive educational experiments and thought squarely in public view, expanding understanding and creating new interest in education as a public commitment. Its focus on children's "creative expression" contributed to the public perception of progressive education that still persists, but that misses capturing the broader reality of that movement.

In 1926, the Association appointed its first executive director in a move that formalized its structure while beginning the trend toward professionalization that would lead to its eventual demise. But first, success would come in the way of popular influence and significant philanthropic funding for educational experimentation. The substantive highlight of the PEA's impact was prompted by a 1930 study. Specifically, The Commission on the Relation of School and College, chaired by Wilford M. Aiken, proposed an experiment in which 30 secondary schools would redesign their offerings to achieve improved teaching, expanded learning, the release of the creative energies of students, and coordination between education and community need. Called the Eight-Year Study, it extended from 1930 to 1942, and was richly funded by various philanthropic grants. It focused specifically on comparing two educational approaches: experimental, progressivist high schools with traditional high schools; the former school programs were more student centered, while the latter were more teacher centered.

While much is made of colleges' concessions to waive entrance requirements for students from the experimental schools, perhaps the most interesting aspect of the Study was Ralph Tyler's extensive assessment. Tyler studied 1,475 matched pairs of students from participant and nonparticipant high schools. He documented that the graduates of participant schools had a "higher degree of intellectual curiosity and drive," were "more precise, systematic and objective in their thinking," held more significant "ideas concerning the meaning of education," and demonstrated "resourcefulness in meeting new situations." In short, the schools participating in the study succeeded not in changing the structure of schooling but in revitalizing traditional subject matter, the main hope of the Association's founders.

The PEA was well into its second decade—and just beginning the Eight-Year Study—when, in 1932, President George S. Counts challenged the organization to lead schools to "build a new social order." He asked, "Dare the Progressive Education Association be progressive?" With the nation in the throes of a deepening economic depression, he called the membership to face the economic realities of the time and introduced a resolution intended to shake the self-satisfaction of the advocates of child-centeredness.

It is not clear whether Counts's efforts had any lasting impact on the Association or on educational policy and practice generally. Rather, it was the Eight-Year Study that both anchored the PEA during the decade of the 1930s and shifted its focus from popularizing to professionalizing.

Although educational philosopher John Dewey remains the face of the PEA in the contemporary educational imagination, Dewey was as much critic as supporter of the organization. Never an active member, he nonetheless accepted the honorary presidency in 1927 following Charles W. Eliot's death.

Several realities ushered the PEA into the 1940s. Primary was the success of the Eight-Year Study, overshadowed by the onset of WWII. The Eight-Year Study "worked," but it marked a significant shift in the nature and structure of the Association. As World War II came to a close, the Association struggled to carve out some role for itself. It was no longer, as Lawrence Cremin described it, "primarily an association of parents and others who [were] interested in education as it affects the community and the nation." As it became increasingly professional in orientation, it narrowed its base of support and constrained its own role in the educational conversation. In 1955, following withdrawal of support by the Carnegie Foundation and the Rockefeller Foundation, the Progressive Education Association went quietly out of existence, shortly after ceasing publication of *Progressive Education*.

Barbara S. Stengel

See also Dewey, John; Educational Reform During the Great Depression; Eight-Year Study; Eliot, Charles W.; Progressive Education

Further Readings

Aikin, W. (1942). *The story of the Eight-Year Study.* New York: Harper.

Cremin, L. (1961). *The transformation of the school.* New York: Alfred A. Knopf.

Dewey, J., & Dewey, E. (1915). *Schools of tomorrow.* New York: E. P. Dutton.

Graham, P. (1967). *Progressive education from Arcady to academe.* New York: Teachers College Press.

Karrier, C. (1970). Review of Patricia Albjerg Graham's *Progressive education from Arcady to academe. Educational Theory, 20*(2), 197–201.

Ravitch, D. (2000). *Left back: A century of battles over school reform.* New York: Simon & Shuster.

PROGRESSIVE POLICY INSTITUTE

The Progressive Policy Institute (PPI) is a Washington, D.C.–based think tank dedicated to policy innovation and the modernization of progressive politics. Founded in 1989, PPI subsequently was dubbed "Bill Clinton's idea mill," and many of its signature proposals (e.g., national service, public charter schools, community policing, and a work-centered approach to welfare) have been enacted into law.

Over the years, PPI's approach to education reform has revolved around a simple organizing principle: In public education, the interests of the children must take precedence over those of adults. Accordingly, PPI has earned a reputation as a rare progressive think tank willing to challenge the education establishment.

In 1990, the Institute published a pathbreaking report by Ted Kolderie on Minnesota's school-choice experiment. This report made the case for what later would become known as public charter schools. Even before the nation's first charter school in St. Paul, Minnesota, opened its doors, PPI was defining and refining the concept for progressive lawmakers. President Clinton embraced the concept and created the first national program to seed the development of charters around the country. Since then, PPI has produced a substantial body of work on the theory and practice of public charter schools. This includes a series of reports on leading state experiments with charters, as well as assessments of the factors that make independent charter school authorizers effective.

In 2006, Paul Hill of the University of Washington—a longtime collaborator with PPI on education reform—authored an important paper calling for the abandonment of the traditional "command-and-control" system of public school governance, and for the embrace of a new organizational model Hill called "portfolio management," in which "school boards would manage a diverse array of schools, some run by the school district and others by independent organizations, each designed to meet the different needs of students."

PPI is a nonpartisan, nonprofit organization, and its education prescriptions tend to fit the orthodoxies of neither Democrats nor Republicans. Broadly speaking, PPI has tended to favor expanded investments in education at all levels, and to favor an active role for the government (including the federal government) in improving educational outcomes for students at all age levels and from all economic strata.

PPI has consistently urged progressives to take up the cause of educational accountability as passionately as they support education spending. Andrew Rotherham's 1999 PPI paper on the need for reforming the federal role in education, *Toward Performance-Based Federal Education Funding*, provided the intellectual framework for a Democratic "Three R's" education-reform bill in Congress, from which President George W. Bush borrowed key elements for his No Child Left Behind (NCLB) legislation.

Although NCLB has been heavily criticized by policymakers, PPI believes it is essential not to abandon two key principles embedded in the law: first, that districts be required to measure the education performance of all kids, so that schools can be held accountable; and second, that the federal government should withhold funding from school systems that chronically fail to educate children.

PPI has helped generate some of the leading young thinkers on education reform policy, including Eduwonk blog-founder Andrew J. Rotherham and policy-expert Sara Mead.

It is perhaps indicative of PPI's interest in education reform that the first paper released in the organization's *2008 Memos to the Next President* series dealt not with that year's financial crisis or with either of the two wars the nation found itself in, but with the often-overlooked topic of urban education. The inaugural "memo," authored by Doug Ross, superintendent of University Preparatory Academy in Detroit, a successful inner-city public charter school, stipulated two main prerequisites for creating more high-performing schools: autonomy ("Virtually all…successful [urban] schools are managed by their principals and teachers") and "the abolition of tenure."

PPI authors have favored other means of breaking the administrative logjams that have hindered innovation and institutionalized failure in so many of our urban school systems. In 2007, Andrew Rotherham and David Harris co-wrote a PPI article that proposed allowing mayors to open charter schools: Harris himself had led Indianapolis Mayor Bart Peterson's charter school initiative from 2001 to 2006.

While organizational reform has been a lasting theme of PPI's educational work, it is by no means the only one. PPI has also been a persistent advocate of early childhood education, enhancement of teacher recruitment and retention, and broadened access to college and other forms of postsecondary education.

Such emphases derive from PPI's attempts to forge an updated identity for progressivism in the United States. In cooperation with like-minded center-left policy centers in Europe and Australia, PPI has sought to advance a principled, sustainable role for active government while simultaneously enhancing individual responsibility and broadening the scope of economic possibilities for the average citizen. In short, PPI has endeavored to build a progressivism that can be sustained in a 21st-century America that often tends to be distrustful of big government solutions to common problems.

Educational reform fits well with this post-Reagan progressivism. It represents a realm of public policy in which progressive government action, if exercised properly, can generate benefits that no mainstream conservative could quibble with—a stronger economy, robust communities, diminished crime rates, even a more effective military.

Therefore, education reform constitutes an amalgam of progressive and conservative values—a perfect mix for an organization that prides itself on "moving beyond the left–right debates of the last century."

Mark Ribbing

See also Charter Schools; No Child Left Behind Act
    (NCLB); Presidents and Educational Reform

Further Readings

Gau, R. (2006). *Trends in charter school authorizing.*
    Washington, DC: Thomas B. Fordham Institute.
Hess, F. M. (2008). *The future of educational
    entrepreneurship.* Cambridge, MA: Harvard
    Education Press.
Howell, W. G., & Peterson, P. E. (2002). *The education
    gap: Vouchers and urban schools.* Washington, DC:
    Brookings Institution.

PROJECT FOLLOW THROUGH

Project Follow Through was a federally funded study comparing the effects of nine major educational approaches to instruction. The first part of the study was begun in 1967 and included some of the major curricula and teaching strategies of the time. Project Follow Through continued as a service project through 1995, but most references to the project are to the initial large study and the discussion of those results. Project Follow Through was tied to President Lyndon Johnson's Great Society educational reform efforts and was used to identify programs that could extend the skills gained by young children after they exited Head Start programs—a project to "follow through" with educational improvement. The results of the Project, however, were controversial because they did not reflect the then-current trends in educational philosophy. Today, educators are looking back at the results of Project Follow Through as they search for an evidence base for teaching strategies and curricula. This large and expensive study continues to be referenced today as educators look for programs based on empirical support.

In the mid-1960s, the government was in the middle of the War on Poverty led by President Lyndon B. Johnson. Because of research indicating a link between poor reading achievement and poverty, a goal of early education programs was to reduce, if not eliminate, the educational gap between underachieving children and children achieving at or above grade level. Head Start programs were introduced to preschool-age children across the country. The government was also searching for appropriate educational programs that could support and bolster the academic performance of young children in the early elementary years, specifically, in Grades K–3.

As part of that search, the U.S. Department of Education sponsored a large experiment, Project Follow Through, designed to compare how effective certain programs would be in addressing the needs of underachieving students. The Project has been called the largest educational experiment in history. Nine programs, sponsored by developers, universities, and/or publishers, became candidates for the project. Schools across the country were asked to choose one of the nine programs. Each school then was matched with a control school that received none of the experimental interventions.

The programs used for the study fell into one of three categories: basic academic skills models, cognitive conceptual skills models, and affective skills models. The nine programs evaluated in Project Follow Through are shown below.

Basic Academic Skills Models

1. *Direct Instruction:* This model was sponsored by the University of Oregon and was based on explicit, sequenced instruction; controlled materials; and behavioral principles.

2. *Behavior Analysis Model:* This model was sponsored by the University of Kansas and used systematic classroom management based on reinforcement principles applied to academic learning.

3. *Language Development Model:* Southwest Educational Development Laboratory sponsored this programmed curriculum that focuses on language development of children and bilingual education.

Cognitive Conceptual Skills Models

4. *Tucson Early Education Model:* The University of Arizona sponsored this program that was based on the language experience approach and the unique learning styles of children.

5. *Parent Education Model:* This model was sponsored by the University of Florida and focused on training parents to be parent

educators and included placing parent educators in classrooms.

6. *Cognitively Oriented Curriculum:* Sponsored by High/Scope Educational Research Foundation, this model was based on Piaget's theories of child development and focused on encouraging the reasoning and concept development of children.

Affective Cognitive Skills Models

7. *Open Classroom Model:* This model was sponsored by the Educational Development Center and was based on the British infant school model, which stressed individual rates and ways of learning in supportive environments.

8. *Responsive Education Model:* The model was sponsored by Far West Laboratory for Education Research and was based on child-centered learning with a focus on cultural pluralism.

9. *The Bank Street Early Childhood Education Model:* The model was sponsored by the Bank Street College of Education and focused on whole child development, which stressed giving equal importance to academic and social/emotional development.

The study followed cohorts of children from kindergarten or first grade through third grade. A planned variation design was used to compare the effects of the various educational programs on student performance. Performance measures were taken on 9,000 students from the experimental schools and 6,500 students from control schools. These measures included tests of academic, cognitive, and affective behavior. The five assessment instruments used were: (1) Metropolitan Achievement Test, (2) Wide Range Achievement Test, (3) Raven's Colored Progressive Matrices, (4) Intellectual Achievement Responsibility Scale, and (5) Coopersmith Self-Esteem Inventory. These data were collected by the Stanford Research Institute and analyzed by Abt Associates.

The data were broken down into measures that reflected the three categories of academic, cognitive, and affective skills. The results of the experiment stunned many in the educational community. Most of the interventions showed no increases and some decreases in all three areas.

Only one program showed important increases in students' academic, social, and affective skills. That program was the Direct Instruction program created by Siegfried Engelmann and Wesley Becker. The only other program demonstrating academic gains was the behavior analysis model. Educators were shocked at these results because those programs reflecting preferred educational philosophies stressing child-centered learning, cognitive development, and fostering divergent learning styles, received no support from the data. Not only did the direct instruction model, with its programmed, structured, and scripted materials show great increases in academic skills, it also resulted in greater growth in cognitive skills and measures of self-esteem.

Because of the lack of data supporting most of the instructional program models, the project was considered to be a failure. Proponents of direct instruction argue that the data supporting that program were essentially suppressed because of the incompatibility of the results with the prevailing educational philosophies. Before the results were officially released, Ernest House was commissioned to reevaluate the data. His report dismissed the results because of methodological flaws in the study. Because of this reevaluation, the results of Project Follow Through were not used by the Department of Education to influence educational policy or to provide support for direct instruction. Nevertheless, Project Follow Through continues to be cited by authors of direct instruction curricula, publishers, and teachers as evidence of the effectiveness of direct instruction programs.

Kathleen Joan Marshall

See also Direct Instruction; Elementary and Secondary Education Act; Federal Educational Reform; Head Start; War on Poverty

Further Readings

Bock, G., Stebbins, L., & Proper, E. (1977). *Effects of Follow Through models* (Education as Experimentation: A Planned Variations Model, Vol. IV-A & B). Washington, DC: Abt.

House, E., Glass, G., McLean, L., & Walker, D. (1978). No simple answer: Critique of Follow Through evaluation. *Harvard Educational Review, 48,* 128–160.

PROJECT LEARNING

Project learning is a nontraditional instructional approach that has its roots in constructivist, constructionist, and progressive views of education. Project learning is also referred to as the *project approach*, a term popularized by Sylvia Chard, Judy Helm, and Lilian Katz. Another related term, often used interchangeably with project learning, is *project-based learning* (PBL). Rather than traditional teacher-directed instruction, project learning provides opportunities for long-term, interdisciplinary, student-centered, and integrated learning with real-world issues and practices.

For more than 100 years educators, perhaps most notably John Dewey, have heralded the benefits of experiential, hands-on, student-directed learning. More recently, project learning has generated interest in the wake of research in psychology and neuroscience on cognition and learning theories, as well as cognitive research on the nature of problem solving and the benefits of scaffolding and social learning. The fast pace at which the world is changing has highlighted a need for students who can become effective and proficient employees with the ability to solve problems and work collaboratively with others. Such process skills are supported by project learning. The current emphasis on standards and accountability has heightened the need for the creation of standards-focused projects defined by a primary question or authentic problem linked to content standards in the curriculum. Standards-based project learning emphasizes the importance of linking the project expectations and outcomes to the learning standards and making these explicit to the student.

Project learning concentrates on an in-depth investigation of a real-world topic that is worthy of students' attention and effort. The focus is on meaningful authentic learning situated in real problems or dilemmas. Project learning may be conducted by an entire class or by small groups of learners. Typically, project learning does not characterize an entire curricular approach, but rather is one type of learning opportunity included in the instructional program. Some projects may last only 1 or 2 weeks, while others may require 6 months to a year. Initially, a teacher may introduce the project or focus of the project learning, but, when

possible, students are invited to select and define issues or projects they find significant or meaningful. Project learning typically concludes with a presentation or product that demonstrates learning and provides an opportunity for students to showcase their project to an appropriate audience.

Project learning includes three phrases: the planning phase, the creating or implementing phase, and the processing phase. The planning phase includes choosing a topic, searching for resources, and organizing the work. The second phase is creating or implementing the project. Activities may include development and documentation of the project, coordinating and combining the contributions of project learners, and building the project. The processing phase includes sharing the project with others, obtaining feedback, and engaging reflection and follow-up on the project.

The role of the teacher in project learning is that of facilitator and guide. The teacher guides or coaches the students through the project by offering questions, suggestions, and resources as they work. One of the goals of project learning is student autonomy. Project learning also allows the teacher to be a co-learner or co-constructor of knowledge while discussing the products, plans, and steps required with the students. Teachers also document the learning process through photographs, recordings, notations, and the like. Project learning requires a teacher with strong instructional and organizational skills, as well as one who is able to manage the learning process, which includes inquiry, dialogue, and skill building.

A number of instructional strategies can be implemented to support project learning. These include, but are not limited to, making real-world connections, discovering and activating prior knowledge, making predictions, designing plans and experiments, collecting and analyzing data, asking higher-order questions, incorporation presentations to audiences, and integration of peer evaluation, self-evaluation, and portfolio evaluation.

Some of the benefits associated with project learning include increased student motivation, active involvement in learning, and application of learning in authentic and meaningful ways. Project learning often assists in motivating students by engaging them in their own learning. Project learning also allows students to relate their school learning to life outside the classroom as they apply fundamental skills, such as reading, writing, speaking, listening, and math, to pursuing their own interests and questions. Utilization of project learning provides an effective means for involving parents and community members in education. This involvement often creates more support and understanding of educational needs and issues as students work with adults in workplaces or in the community.

Rich opportunities for peer interaction and collaboration are characteristic of project learning as students make decisions, find answers, and solve problems. Students who participate in project learning are encouraged to research relevant topics and present their findings and learning in varied formats through interdisciplinary learning. Applying and integrating the content of different subject areas is not only permitted, but encouraged. Participating in project learning allows students opportunities to practice many real-world skills, such as working with others, taking initiatives, and solving complex problems, which are desired by employers. As learners improve their problem-solving skills, they also strengthen their critical-thinking skills. Using real resources and seeking information in project learning affords real opportunities for students to develop and strengthen their research skills.

Other characteristics associated with project learning include recognition of students' inherent desire and ability to learn, intentionality in engaging students' minds and bodies in meaningful learning through experience; in-depth exploration of authentic and important topics; utilization of tools and skills to accomplish learning; application of research, reasoning, and problem solving; implementation of performance-based assessments; and collaboration with others for completion and assessment of the project. Key components of project-based learning are a learner-centered environment, collaboration, integration of curriculum content based on standards, authentic tasks, multiple presentation modes, emphasis on time management, and assessment as a process of documenting student learning.

Project learning presents some challenges for both teachers and students. Project learning requires an extended time frame to allow students and teachers adequate time to plan, implement, revise, and reflect on their learning; however, teachers may actually have more time to work with individual students when the project is enacted. Additionally, project learning may require access to materials and resources not typically utilized in a traditional school classroom. Project learning also demands a different approach to assessment and documentation of student learning. A traditional teacher-constructed test does not adequately or accurately assess the students' learning in a project environment. Many teachers are not prepared to implement and facilitate project learning due to lack of familiarity with the approach or inability to loosen their control to allow students to direct the project as it unfolds.

Research evidence by Judy Helm and Lilian Katz supports the conclusion that project learning leads to higher-level cognitive development, and empirical studies suggest that project learning is equal to or slightly better than other instructional approaches for producing gains in academic achievement. Project learning provides engaging experiences that engage learners in complex and real-world projects through which they develop and apply skills and knowledge.

Beth Nason Quick

See also Constructivism; Cooperative Learning; Curriculum Controversies; Dewey, John; Experiential Learning; Inquiry-Based Learning; Learning Packages; Performance Contracting; Problem-Based Learning

Further Readings

Bransford, J. D., & Stein, B. S. (1993). *The IDEAL problem solver* (2nd ed.). New York: Freeman.

Helm, J. H., & Katz, L. (2001). *Young investigators: The project approach in the early years.* New York: Teachers College Press.

Thomas, H. W., Mergendoller, J. R., & Michaleson, A. (1999). *Project-based learning: A handbook for middle and high school teachers.* Novato, CA: Buck Institute for Education.

PURCHASE OF SECULAR SERVICES

See Lemon v. Kurtzman

Race- and Ethnic-Based Schooling

Race has been a significant issue in American educational policy and practice. It has also been the grounding for significant educational reform, especially throughout the 20th century. During America's earliest beginnings, it was illegal to provide education for African Americans. By the mid-1800s, however, significant changes had begun to occur in the education of African American youth. For example, in 1837 the Institute for Colored Youth was founded by Richard Humphreys; later it became Cheney University. In 1854, Ashmun Institute in Pennsylvania was opened as the first school of higher learning for young Black men and was later renamed Lincoln University after President Abraham Lincoln. Wilberforce University, founded by the African American Episcopal Church in 1876, was the first university owned and operated by African Americans. Howard University housed the nation's first Black law school (1869), and Meharry Medical College (1876) was the first Black medical school, founded by the Freedman's Aid Society of the African American Episcopal Church. The first college for Black women, Spelman College, was founded in 1881 by Sophia B. Packard and Harriet E. Giles. All of these institutions were founded for Black students and were segregated, and all were efforts to significantly reform the way in which African Americans could be educated in the United States.

After the Civil War and with the signing of the Emancipation Proclamation, educational institutions for Black Americans began to open up all over the country. The number of historically Black colleges and universities grew rapidly, most of them in the South, in an attempt to meet the thirst for knowledge that many persons of color had previously been denied. The reality was that schools, colleges, and universities were typically segregated, and the notion of separate but equal was codified in the landmark *Plessy v. Ferguson* (1896) Supreme Court ruling, which gave full legal standing to the concept that separate education and other forms of color separation were legal. While separate facilities and opportunities existed, equality in the context of separation was never achieved. Almost 60 years later, the Supreme Court, in *Brown v. Board of Education of Topeka, Kansas,* ruled unanimously that segregation in public schools is unconstitutional.

The implementation of the process built in the caveat of using "all deliberate speed" and was used by those unwilling to move forward as a "political crutch" to impede the reform process. Social and political battles to desegregate schools both north and south began, and the resistance was significant and deep in most parts of the country. There were remedies imposed in the 1960s and 1970s, usually by court order, including "busing" programs (as opposed to transportation programs that many districts used), redistricting, magnet schools, and other devices designed to bring students together in the same physical facility or within the same school district. The efforts seemed to assume that desegregation would lead to integration and that all students would receive an equal educational opportunity in schools. There were also struggles over deciding whether segregation was de facto, meaning simply a result of where people "happened" to live, or de jure, which meant that it was imposed intentionally and legally by a local board or other agency able to make such a ruling.

In 1967, President Lyndon B. Johnson signed Executive Order 11246 implementing affirmative action programs. Affirmative action was designed to right the historical wrongs imposed initially on Black Americans as a result of slavery and segregation. Many White Americans saw this as an attempt to provide an unfair advantage to persons who had hitherto been denied access to resources routinely available to White students. These differing views created greater social divides between and among many members of American society. Quality education was seen as one way of affording persons with the knowledge and skills that would allow them to play on a level field.

The results of segregation were significant. Data from various tests indicated a negative outcome for Black students when their performance was compared with that of their White counterparts. The racial achievement gap had some apologist scholars posit that these outcomes could be assigned to genetics, cultural disadvantages, or simply laziness on the part of the students, their families, and their communities. Researchers have since been able to document that there is a racial achievement gap as measured by existing standardized tests, and that gap is particularly pronounced in educationally segregated settings.

Other concerns emerged around the use of standardized tests to assess student performance. Specifically, there is a tendency to ignore how much of any standardized test contains subtle content that may be culturally specific and biased for some students. The issue of stereotype threat to test takers is too frequently overlooked. At the same time leading figures who serve as educational champions and researchers, including Linda Darling-Hammond, Jonathan Kozol, Glenn Singleton, and Randy Lindsey, have challenged education policymakers to examine the access to resources and identify and eliminate systemic forms of oppression that work against many students, particularly African American students.

There has been continued resistance to openly discussing the effects that race plays in the educational arena. When Attorney General Eric Holder asserted that Americans are cowards when it comes to talking about race, many folks became outraged. There have been myriad calls to have a national conversation about race, but this type of dialogue has never really happened. The fact that it is recognized as necessary, but no substantive action follows this recognition, seems to be a testament to how hard it is to focus on the issue of race and the problems of educating young people in a racially diverse culture. There clearly have been attempts to deal with the race issue. President Bill Clinton, for example, formed a commission to look into complex race issues. Race was a subtext and sometimes the dominant theme in the 2008 presidential election. As a presidential candidate, Barack Obama was forced to address the issue of race when the pastor of his church was taped making remarks that most African Americans thought rang true, while many Whites were outraged. So, just as race is ever present in the rest of U.S. social order, so it is ever present in the U.S. education system.

There are those who approach race as a Black issue. It is necessary to begin to seriously talk about race as something that White folks also have to confront. Clearly, ignoring racial issues has had deleterious effects on American culture. The most pernicious and persistent gap in achievement is the gap between African American students and their European American classmates. Scores on standardized tests over the past 40 years consistently reflect disparities between racial/ethnic minority groups and the dominant group. The emergence of the gap begins at the earliest ages of schooling, an age when students are clearly aware of race and many have developed feelings of inferiority or superiority based on race. Some who have studied the race issue point out that at these early educational stages, the overwhelming majority of teachers are European American females who are teaching a growing student population of African Americans and Latino/a students. They contend that because of both the structure of schools and the type of instruction occurring within classrooms, students of color end up with lower-than-average test scores and more than their proportion of discipline and special education referrals. They also have higher dropout rates and lower going-to-college percentages, and they are underrepresented in gifted and advanced-placement classes. These types of differential performance indicators form the basis for much of the reform work of creating more equitable educational opportunities for all students regardless of racial or ethnic background. In essence, there must be an understanding of the significant role that race plays in education. When this occurs, educators will begin to understand why some students are disconnected and underserved in the schooling process.

Facing race, talking about race, challenging current education practices and focusing on extant educational policies are necessary aspects of creating a more just and fair society for all people. Ensuring that all students, regardless of their educational background, have opportunities to achieve their full potential offers the best hope for addressing issues of race and education. It is through dialogue and continued educational reform that the social, cultural, and academic achievement gap will be closed.

Raymond Terrell

See also Affirmative Action; Afrocentric Schools; Diversity; Hispanic/Latino Education; No Child Left Behind Act (NCLB); Racism

Further Readings

Davis, B. (2006). *How to teach students who don't look like you.* Thousand Oaks, CA: Corwin.

Delpit, L. (2006). *Other people's children.* New York: New Press.

Lindsey, R. B., Robins, K. N., & Terrell, R. D. (2003). *Cultural proficiency: A manual for school leaders* (2nd ed.). Thousand Oaks, CA: Corwin.

Tatum, B. D. (2007). *Can we talk about race?* Boston: Beacon Press.

RACISM

The phenomenon of racism is not unique to any country but is encountered worldwide. For people of different ethnic backgrounds who have migrated to the United States, especially non-Caucasians, it has been, and remains, a societal issue. The words *racist* and *racism* have been used to describe U.S. society, and although there may be disagreement about how pervasive the problem is, the historical reality of racism and racist attitudes in America is a matter of record; consequently, race and racism are embedded in U.S. institutions and everyday life. People of color, particularly African Americans, have been subjects of both institutional and individual racism. Many individuals respond differently to people of color (as opposed to Caucasians) simply because of their race or ethnicity. The prevalence of racism has been the stimulus for many educational reforms, including significant calls for social justice in teacher preparation programs.

According to *Webster's New World Dictionary,* race is any biological division of humankind, distinguished by color and texture of hair, color of skin and eyes, stature, bodily proportions, and other physical characteristics. Many ethnologists concur in the identification of three primary divisions: the Caucasian, Negroid, and Mongoloid races. Within these three primary races are varying subgroups. The concept of race is a relatively recent human invention. The word *race,* interpreted to mean "of common descent," was introduced into English in about 1580, from the Old French *rasse.* It has evolved, however, from a biological term to a social, psychological, and cultural term, with people using it to classify others based on genetic traits shared by each group. As a number of social theorists have pointed out, however, the idea of race is primarily about culture, not biology. Although most people continue to think of the races as physically distinct populations, scientific advances in the 20th century demonstrated that human physical variations do not fit a "racial" model. There are in fact no genes that can identify distinct groups that accord with conventional race categories. Moreover, theorists have long understood that the concept of race as relating solely to phenotypic traits encompasses neither the social reality of race nor the phenomenon of racism.

Racism is an ideology, a belief that all members of each racial group possess characteristics or abilities specific to that race, especially to distinguish it as being either superior or inferior to another racial group or racial groups. Racism has existed throughout human history. It may be defined as the hatred of one person by another or the belief that another person is less than human because of skin color, language, customs, or place of birth. In U.S. society, African Americans tend to experience the highest rates of discrimination and racism.

By the early 19th century, racial ideology's influence was widespread. In many nations, leaders began to think of the ethnic components of their own societies, usually religious or language groups, in racial terms and to designate "higher" and "lower" races. Racism elicits hatred and distrust and precludes any attempt to understand the Other. For this reason, most modern human societies have concluded that racism is morally and socially wrong, at least in principle, and social trends have moved away from racist policies and practices. Many societies have begun to combat institutionalized racism by denouncing racist beliefs and practices and by promoting human understanding in public policies, as does the Universal Declaration of Human Rights, set forth by the United Nations in 1948.

J. Angelo Corlett, a philosopher specializing in ethics, argues that a racist is someone who discriminates, whether purposely or not, and that even if a person commits an act of racism only once, he or she is still essentially a racist. Based on Corlett's beliefs, then, one could gather that everyone is racist and that the practice is not limited to "other" people. Corlett identifies several forms of racism, such as individual, group, and institutional.

More than 50 years after the Supreme Court's decision in *Brown v. Board of Education* officially ended racial segregation in U.S. public schools nationwide, complaints of institutional racism in public schools continue to surface in different localities from time to time, garnering much public and media attention and often resulting in efforts by school and government officials to address underlying issues and implement necessary reforms.

A more fundamental approach to combating racism may perhaps be found in the variety of ongoing initiatives designed to educate students on how to combat racism, even as early as kindergarten. At the same time, teacher education curricula across the United States have incorporated a stronger emphasis on the theme of social justice.

Although the total eradication of racism may not be possible, reformers argue that educators can and should be instrumental in laying the foundation for greater social harmony and a more just society. It is therefore especially important for educators to make an effort to deal with racist attitudes, helping not only students but also new classroom professionals to understand more about other races, religions, cultures, and beliefs. These emerging practitioners in turn will become leaders in education by obtaining the knowledge they need to provide learning environments that are nurturing and intellectually challenging; that include stimulating and socially relevant content; that are instrumental in assisting all children and adults to become academically productive; and that allow educational personnel to become "classroom researchers," continually analyzing methods and seeking better ways of teaching and learning in ways that are race neutral.

James S. Norman

See also Affirmative Action; Civil Rights Act of 1964; De Facto Segregation; De Jure Segregation; Equity

Further Readings

Corlett, J. A. (2003). *Race, racism, and reparations*. New York: Cornell University Press.

Epstein, K. K. (2006). *A different view of urban schools: Civil rights, critical race theory, and unexplained realities*. New York: Peter Lang.

Feagin, J. R. (1991). The continuing significance of race: Anti-Black discrimination in public places. *American Sociological Review*, 56, 101–116.

Ward, J. K., & Lott, T. L. (Eds.). (2002). *Philosophers on race: Critical essays*. Malden, MA: Blackwell.

RAVITCH, DIANE (1938–)

Born in 1938 in Houston, Texas, Ravitch attended Wellesley College, thereafter earning her Ph.D. from Columbia University. Currently, she is a research professor of education at New York University. She served in the senior Bush administration and during the Clinton presidency. Ravitch was assistant secretary of education from 1991 to 1993. She is a nonresident senior fellow for both the Brookings Institution in Washington, D.C., and the Hoover Institution at Stanford University. Her numerous prestigious awards, board positions, as well as honorary doctorates have been in recognition of her substantial contributions to educational policy and reform.

Some label Ravitch an independent, whereas others view her as a moderate-conservative on the spectrum of politics. The themes of her prolific writings focus on American educational history and school standards. Her knowledge of New York City public schools is extensive. Additional areas of focus for Ravitch include ensuring that the United States has effectively educated its citizens, especially the young people matriculating through elementary and secondary schools. Ravitch has also focused attention on ensuring that teachers are intellectually and pedagogically equipped to effectively communicate disciplinary content. She credits Lawrence Cremin, noted educator, historian, and past president of Teachers College of Columbia University, for influencing her work. This entry highlights Ravitch's prominent position within American public education regarding the need for a standardized national curriculum, testing methods to determine what students actually learn, and the pitfalls of self-censorship and language control.

National Standardized Curriculum

Ravitch's numerous books, commentaries, and blog offer critiques of both left- and right-wing positions that are contrary to her view for the need of increased intellectual rigor or the opposition of self-censorship. As a policy analyst she is concerned with the need for a return of rigorous intellectualism in public education, whereby students systematically experience a curriculum oriented toward high academic standards. She opposes the absence of systematic, traditionalized approaches in disciplinary studies. Ravitch and Chester E. Finn, Jr., published a book titled *What Do Our 17-Year Olds Know?* (1987) in which they describe the importance of academically prepared teachers capable of delivering a rigorous curriculum in a thoughtful and systematic manner.

Ravitch takes the position that injudicious reforms prohibit the achievement of exact schooling in this country due to the prevalence of anti-intellectual progressive pedagogies, the infiltration of specialists, and a diluted curriculum. Ravitch attests that Congress is unrealistic in its mandate for bringing into fruition a goal of universal proficiency in America. Her claim is that accessible

goals need to be set in motion as well as a serious reexamination of federally funded school programs within public education. Otherwise, children will indeed be left behind, particularly those noted as disadvantaged or evidencing a particular exceptionality.

Testing Student Learning

Ravitch argues that the quest for creating tests that do not imply biases of any kind, or negatives against diverse lived experiences such as sex-gender, race, class, age, and culture, have impeded student testing to the point that it is difficult to determine what students are actually learning. She opposes designers and publishers of tests that are more concerned with not offending students and fail to focus on the measurement of student aptitude, intellectual acuity, and overall achievement. Ultimately, her concern is that existent testing methods measure what students can do and not what they have learned. Ravitch deems that it is the responsibility of each state to administer testing programs through the most ethical means possible.

Censorship

As an educational historian, Ravitch includes, as an area of focus, her stance against self-censorship and those whom she identifies as the "language police" comprising both right- and left-wing politics and policies that impact not only language but also school texts and exams, thereby restricting what educators teach and students learn. Ravitch especially disapproves of the sanitizing of history books used in public education, believing that this "sanitization" disallows the complete telling of a historical event or story. She advocates that the entire story be told whether good or bad. Further still, she asserts that teachers need to solidly educate themselves in the field of history if they are to teach the *truth*.

Ravitch has her detractors and critics who oppose, for example, her position taken that progressive pedagogies are anti-intellectual; her opposition to multiculturalism methods that encourage teaching social studies in lieu of history; and her positivist approaches in standards and measurements in education.

B. Lara Lee

See also Association for Supervision and Curriculum Development; Brookings Institution; Business and Educational Reform; Curriculum Controversies

Further Readings

Ravitch, D. (1974). *The great school wars*. New York: Basic Books.

Ravitch, D. (1983). *The troubled crusade*. New York: Basic Books.

Ravitch, D. (1985). *The schools we deserve*. New York: Basic Books.

Ravitch, D. (Ed.). (1991). *The American reader*. New York: HarperPerennial.

Ravitch, D. (2000). *Left back*. New York: Simon & Schuster.

Ravitch, D. (2003). *The language police*. New York: Knopf.

Ravitch, D., & Goodenow, R. (Eds.). (1981). *Educating an urban people*. New York: Teachers College Columbia University.

Ravitch, D., & Vinovskis, M. (1995). *Learning from the past*. Baltimore: Johns Hopkins University Press.

Ravitch, D., & Viteritti, J. (Eds.). (1997). *New schools for a new century*. New Haven, CT: Yale University Press.

READING FIRST

The teaching of reading in the United States was given renewed focus in 2001 in response to the No Child Left Behind Act. Title I (Part B, subpart 1) of the Act establishes the $1 billion-a-year federally funded Reading First program. The Reading First legislation was signed into law on January 8, 2002, and developed in response to the April 2000 *National Reading Report,* which identified deficiencies in current reading practices. The program is defined by its goal of providing funding to schools in correlation with teachers using proven methods of reading instruction and assessment in their classrooms. The program is intended to give the highest amount of funding to schools that demonstrate the most need. Reading First is designed to close the achievement gap for disadvantaged and minority students.

The Reading First program is markedly different from preexisting programs. In the past, remediation programs focused on helping older, struggling students after they displayed reading deficiencies. Reading First is characterized by its emphasis on early intervention (kindergarten through third grade) to help young readers before they can fall behind. Reading First is unique and controversial because it is prescriptive. To receive funding, schools and districts are required to develop a rationale for how instruction will be implemented and guided by research. Reading First provides formula grants to schools; to qualify for funding, states are required to submit applications, detailing the implementation of grant programs within their districts with the impetus of increasing reading proficiency in kindergarten through third grade in schools with low-performing, disadvantaged, and minority students. Reading First is supported by three technical assistance centers housed at universities. These technical assistance centers provide supervision of the implementation of the Reading First program. One million dollars a year is budgeted to monitor schools' implementation of Reading First and intervene when necessary.

With the establishment of Reading First came the expectation that all students, regardless of diverse demographics, will be able to read by third grade. Schools become eligible to receive funding in the program by incorporating essential components of reading instruction and using research-based reading strategies and programs. Essential reading components are defined as (a) reading comprehension strategies; (b) phonemic awareness, which is the ability to hear and reproduce or manipulate phonemes; (c) phonics; (d) vocabulary development; and (e) reading fluency, the ability to read text smoothly and correctly. Within the Reading First legislation, federal funds also support professional development for teachers to ensure that teachers are equipped with the skills necessary to effectively teach reading. Funds are also available for student screening to diagnose and prevent early reading difficulties.

More than 6 years following the implementation of Reading First and after the federally mandated evaluation of the program's effectiveness, widespread disagreement and controversy exists about the success of the program. The federally mandated evaluation examined first and second graders in 13 different states, totaling 248 schools and thousands of students. The findings of the evaluation have done little to resolve the debate surrounding the effectiveness of Reading First.

The Reading First Impact Study: Interim Report provided credibility to critics of the reading program. The report indicates that no statistical difference exists between the estimated reading comprehension gains experienced by students participating in the program compared to students in non–Reading First schools. Critics also point out that Reading First takes away key instructional time from other subjects with little or no validated results in reading. Although significantly more minutes a day are spent on reading instruction in Reading First schools than in non–Reading First schools, there is no difference in the level of achievement recorded on reading comprehension exams. Experts in the field of education report an increased amount of time spent on decoding skills and suggest enough time is not designated for reading comprehension. The report also found that the experience of schools with the Reading First program did not impact reading comprehension or classroom instruction. Critics refer to decreased federal appropriations as proof that Reading First is a failure. From 2003 to 2006 Reading First received an overwhelming $1 billion in funding. In 2008 funding was cut to $393 million.

Despite controversy, Reading First continues to garner support from many in the field of education. Margaret Spelling, the secretary of education under President George W. Bush, proclaimed the program as being as effective and successful as any program in the nation's history. Washington, Alabama, and Arizona are a few states among many reporting drastic increases in reading proficiency. Furthermore, survey results of state and local grant recipients support that Reading First, despite criticism, is successfully impacting the education of students. Reading First is reported to have led to changes in curriculum, instruction, and assessment. Also, the survey data illustrate that the majority of participating schools credit Reading First for student achievement they are currently experiencing. Nearly all districts receiving Reading First subgrants directly related the Reading First program to an increase in student achievement. This supports the finding that districts that spent more money per student from their Reading First money showed more achievement gains. An estimated increase of spending of $100 per student equated to an increase of 3 points on the comprehension tests that were given. This finding appears to contradict the present state of the program that will function on one-third ($393 million) of its previous budget ($1 billion). The drastic reduction in the Reading First budget may be directly related to concerns that have been raised about appropriate spending of funds within the program.

Both proponents and critics are calling for reevaluation of the Reading First program. The final report, published in early 2009, lists the key findings:

1. In grades one and two, Reading First produced a statistically significant, positive impact on the amount of instructional time spent on the five essential components of reading instruction promoted by the program (phonemic awareness, phonics, vocabulary, fluency, and comprehension).

2. The curriculum produced statistically significant, positive impacts on practices promoted by the program, including inservice in scientifically based reading instruction, support from reading coaches, amount of time in reading instruction, and providing support for struggling readers.

3. Reading First produced a statistically significant, positive impact on decoding skills among first grade students.

4. Reading First did not produce a statistically significant, positive impact on student reading comprehension test scores in grades one, two, or three.

Zachary G. Kassebaum

See also No Child Left Behind Act (NCLB); Presidents and Educational Reform; Reading Recovery; Reading Reform

Further Readings

Antunez, B. (2002). *A brief history of Reading First.* Retrieved August 1, 2008, from http://www .readingrockets.org/article/309

Barbash, S. (2008). The Reading First controversy: Promises and perils of federal leadership. *Education Next, 8*(3), 47–53.

eSchool News Staff. (2006, September 26). *Study: Reading First spurs achievement gains.* Retrieved August 1, 2008, from http://www.eschoolnews .com

Gamse, B. C., Jacob, R. T., Horst, M., Boulay, B., & Unlu, F. (2008). *Reading First impact study: Final report executive summary* (NCEE-4039). Washington, DC: National Center for Education Evaluation and Regional Assistance.

Glod, M. (2008, May 2). Study questions "No Child" Act's reading plan. *The Washington Post.* Retrieved

August 1, 2008, from http://www.washingtonpost
.com/wp-dyn/content/article/2008/05/01/AR200805010
1399.html

Manzon, K. K. (2008, May 7). Reading First doesn't help
pupils "get it." *Education Week*, pp. 12–13.

U.S. Department of Education. (2008). *Reading First impact
study: Interim report.* Washington, DC: National Center
for Education Evaluation and Regional Assistance.
(ERIC Document Reproduction Service No. ED501219)

READING RECOVERY

Reading Recovery is a school-based literacy intervention for first-grade students having the greatest difficulty learning to read and write. According to evidence from longitudinal research, children who struggle with reading in the early years are very likely to continue struggling in later years. As a result, these students frequently encounter school failure and often drop out of school. It is therefore necessary to redirect educational policy and school funding to the prevention of reading failure. Reading Recovery represents not only a significant reading intervention but also a significant reading reform because of its success in fostering enhanced comprehension and fluency.

The goal of Reading Recovery, as a first-grade literacy intervention, is to intervene early and spoil the predictions of failure that often accompany early difficulties with reading. The expert, intensive instruction delivered by Reading Recovery teachers helps children get back on course to recover their trajectory of reading development.

Having Reading Recovery lessons means that most children who begin the instruction with abilities far below the average of their classroom (lowest 20%) end the intervention in 12 to 20 weeks working within average reading and writing levels. They are able to make use of regular classroom instruction and continue to make progress.

Reading Recovery teachers become specialists in designing and delivering individual literacy lessons to first-grade students who are having the greatest difficulty learning to read and write. Professional development for Reading Recovery teachers is designed and delivered by literacy coaches called "teacher leaders." The teacher leaders participate in professional development designed by Reading Recovery faculty at the university level.

Reading Recovery has been implemented worldwide in five countries and developed in English, Spanish (*Descubriendo la Lectura*), and French. To date, Reading Recovery and *Descubriendo la Lectura* teachers have taught more than 1.7 million students in the United States alone. The 2008–2009 report stated that more than 91,000 first-grade students received Reading Recovery or *Descubriendo la Lectura* lessons in the United States from 10,820 teachers working in nearly 6,500 schools. Approximately 75% of those children who received a complete intervention reached average levels of reading and writing.

Reading Recovery is rarely a full-time teaching assignment because of the intensity of the teaching involved; therefore, Reading Recovery teachers usually work in some other role for part of the school day, most often as a Title I or classroom teacher. In 2007–2008, Reading Recovery/Title I teachers taught, on average, 45 students each during the school year, and the average Reading Recovery/classroom teacher taught 30 students during the year.

Brief History

Reading Recovery was first implemented in the United States by faculty at the Ohio State University, but it was developed in New Zealand as a result of research conducted at the University of Auckland by educational psychologist and educator Marie Clay.

Clay's 1966 doctoral dissertation, *Emergent Reading Behaviour,* described the reading behaviors of 100 children across their first year of school. Her sample included a range of children, from students making very good progress to students struggling to learn to read and write.

By 1960 Clay was already taking a different path from her fellow clinical child psychologists. In a presentation to the New Zealand Psychological Society in 1972, she questioned the prevailing view that a discrepancy criterion could identify children with learning disabilities. Clay later reflected on that 1972 presentation and expressed real concerns about the way in which young learners were being erroneously misdiagnosed as either learning disabled or dyslexic.

Clay published three volumes in the 1970s, *Sand* (1972), *The Early Detection of Reading Difficulties* (1979), and *The Patterning of Complex Behaviour* (1979), reflecting her growing interest in understanding and describing the reading process (what proficient readers do when they read) and also in children experiencing great difficulty beginning to read. As such, Clay's view of reading difficulties, how and why these difficulties develop and how best to teach these students, is firmly grounded in her literacy processing theory, which describes what proficient readers and writers do.

By 1976 Clay began developing teaching procedures for students having great difficulty learning to read and write. These teaching procedures were based on close observation of a teacher working one-on-one with beginning readers behind a one-way mirror. The initial field trials took place in five Auckland schools in 1978, and 100 teachers were trained the following year.

Faculty at the Ohio State University learned about Clay's research in 1982 and by 1984 they began implementation of Reading Recovery in Ohio schools. Since that time, Reading Recovery has been implemented in nearly every state in the United States and province in Canada, and widely implemented in Australia, the United Kingdom, and New Zealand.

Summary of Research

In 2007 the What Works Clearinghouse (WWC; U.S. Department of Education, Institute of Education Sciences) reviewed four studies of Reading Recovery that met the WWC evidence standards and one additional study that met these standards with reservations. From the effects of these studies together, Reading Recovery was found to have positive effects on students' alphabetics skills and general reading achievement outcomes. The program was found to have potentially positive effects on comprehension and fluency. As such, Reading Recovery is the WWC's top-rated reading intervention.

Reading Recovery as Part of a School's Comprehensive Literacy Plan

A comprehensive literacy plan involves two components: First, the plan must specify a method of delivering high-quality classroom instruction to all children. Good first instruction is an example of primary prevention in which all children develop sophisticated and effective reading and writing strategies in such a way as to prevent subsequent problems. Second, a comprehensive literacy plan

would specify the specific kinds of supplementary opportunities that must be provided for low-achieving children. One part of the supplementary instruction would include early safety nets, such as Reading Recovery for children who need more than good classroom teaching. In this way Reading Recovery operates as a secondary prevention in which a select group (lowest-performing first graders) is identified early and provided with treatment before problems become severe handicapping conditions. Supplementary instruction also includes a plan for providing long-term extra support for the few children who do not benefit from early prevention efforts and who need support throughout most of their school lives. Thus, secondary prevention programs such as Reading Recovery provide for two positive outcomes.

The first outcome is that most children (70% who receive a full program) reach average levels of achievement and can now benefit from classroom instruction alone, thereby saving costs for the school and district as these children will not need long-term services by specialized teachers. The second positive outcome of Reading Recovery is that a few children who do not respond to the instruction in Reading Recovery will be reliably identified for the costly long-term intervention. Without Reading Recovery, the chances that all of the lowest-performing children (bottom 20%) would end up in some form of supplemental and long-term instruction is greatly increased.

Clay's dissertation, and subsequent publications based on that research, shed light on children's literacy development not only in terms of what happens when the development is going well but also in terms of what struggling readers need to learn how to do. Clay observed in 2004 that the real focus should be on identifying what the brain is doing when the child is reading and writing successfully and not on what happens to readers when they come to parts of text that are difficult to understand.

If Clay's premise—that there is no one cause of reading difficulties and that most children can learn to read well provided educators design instruction that meets their needs—is accepted, then attention must go to instruction rather than diagnosis. The stable success of Reading Recovery provides evidence that teaching does make a difference. The long-term survival of Reading Recovery in school climates where innovations typically come and go suggests that in order to make a difference, teachers may need to sail in a different direction.

Emily M. Rodgers, Lea McGee,
and Gay Su Pinnell

See also Critical Literacy; No Child Left Behind Act (NCLB); Phonics; Reading First; Reading Reform

Further Readings

Clay, M. M. (1979). *The early detection of reading difficulties: A diagnostic survey with recovery procedures.* Auckland, New Zealand: Heinemann.

Clay, M. M. (1979). *Reading: The patterning of complex behaviour.* Auckland, New Zealand: Heinemann.

Clay, M. M. (2004). *Simply by sailing in a new direction you could enlarge the world: 53rd yearbook of the National Reading Conference.* Oak Creek, WI: National Reading Conference.

McGee, L. (2006). Research on Reading Recovery: What is the impact on early literacy research? *Literacy Teaching and Learning: An International Journal of Early Literacy, 10,* 1–50. Worthington, OH: Reading Recovery Council of North America.

Pinnell, G., DeFord, D., & Lyons, C. (1988). *Reading Recovery: Early intervention for at-risk first graders* (Educational Research Service Monograph). Arlington, VA: Educational Research Service.

Pinnell, G., Lyons, C., DeFord, D., Bryk, A., & Seltzer, M. (1994). Comparing instructional models for the literacy education of high-risk first graders. *Reading Research Quarterly, 29,* 8–39.

Reading Recovery Council of North America. (2000). *Reading Recovery in North America: An illustrated history.* Worthington, OH: Author.

Rodgers, E. M., & Ortega, S. (2008). *Reading Recovery in the United States: Executive summary 2007–2008* (NDEC Rep. No. 2009-02). Columbus: Ohio State University, National Data Evaluation Center. Retrieved August 2, 2009, from http://ndec.us

Schmidt, M., Askew, B., Fountas, I., Lyons, C., & Pinnell, G. (2005). *Changing futures: The influence of Reading Recovery in the United States.* Worthington, OH: Reading Recovery Council of North America.

Schwartz, R. (2005). Literacy learning of at-risk first-grade students in the Reading Recovery early intervention. *Journal of Educational Psychology, 97,* 257–267.

What Works Clearinghouse. (2008, December). *Intervention: Reading Recovery.* Retrieved December 5, 2008, from http://ies.ed.gov/ncee/wwc/reports/beginning_reading/reading_recovery

READING REFORM

The field of reading has undergone reform throughout the history of education, but particularly since the turn of the 21st century. These recent reform initiatives have been predominately driven by national initiatives. These initiatives have consequently influenced reading instruction at the state and local levels. A current climate of high-stakes testing has contributed to the increased importance of research-grounded instruction to inform the teaching of reading and the reforms driving that instruction. Major reform initiatives from the national, state, and local levels that have impacted reading instruction are discussed in this entry.

Title I

Title I is a reform initiative embedded in the Elementary and Secondary Education Act, issued first in 1965, then again in 2000. The issuing of the Act in 1965 marked the first distribution of federal funds for the compensatory education of students in poverty and struggling with reading. Compensatory reading instruction in 1965 under Title I was provided in a pull-out classroom by a reading specialist. In 2000, the Act was reissued and Title I was renewed. Significant reforms were made to the provisions of Title I, however, based on research showing underwhelming success rates. Under the revisions, there is a greater emphasis on providing high-quality classroom instruction as opposed to pull-out instruction. Under this provision, reading specialists can go into the classroom to work with children in need as well as coaching and supporting teachers in their environment.

The revision of the Title I initiative also reinforced the emphasis on the use of scientifically based research to inform instruction. This reform initiative affected the state and local settings as state departments of education and local school districts reexamined classroom practices and modified approaches to incorporate research-based educational programs. Finally, the reauthorization and reforms in the Title I program encouraged local districts to use informal assessment techniques to monitor student progress.

The changes in the Title I program opened new doors for state and local programs to consider how to use the reading specialists in their programs. Districts began implementing programs that facilitated literacy coaching. These programs provided advanced training to reading specialists to act as literacy coaches in their schools. Literacy coaches provide support to classroom teachers in designing high-quality instruction in reading within the classroom.

Elementary and Secondary Education Act

The Elementary and Secondary Education Act of 2000, along with additional political pressures, caused state programs to reevaluate and reform curriculum and standards. States began to reform their curricular programs for both elementary and secondary programs. At a national level, organizations such as the National Council of Teachers of English and the International Reading Association developed broad English/language arts and reading standards to guide and support state work. These new sets of curriculum and standards were then handed down to local school districts. New standards and curriculum drove further reform in school buildings as reading teachers, in particular, examined their teaching and the standards to be met in determining what would stay, what would go, and what would be added. This local and state reform was fueled by the national Reading Excellence Act of 1999, which secured funds for reading instruction staff development in states that based their standards on research that was scientifically rigorous.

National Reading Panel

In 1997, at the request of Congress, the National Reading Panel (NRP) was formed with the goal of reviewing and assessing reading research to determine the effectiveness of different approaches in teaching children to read. In 2000, the NRP published its meta-analysis of the available research in reading in their report titled *Teaching Children to Read*. Commissioned by the National Institute for Child Health and Human Development in 1997, the NRP pulled together researchers in the area of reading to review the available research on reading and make recommendations for instruction. This report focused upon eight critical areas in relation to literacy instruction: (1) phonemic awareness, (2) phonics instruction, (3) fluency instruction, (4) vocabulary instruction, (5) comprehension instruction, (6) independent reading, (7) computer assisted instruction, and (8) teacher professional development.

The NRP created a great deal of controversy and dissent over the decision to review only studies that were experimental or quasi-experimental in methodology design. Objections have been voiced regarding how the research was selected to review, with many feeling that key types of research were excluded. This decision greatly limited the depth and breadth of the NRP's review.

Despite the controversy, the NRP's findings have had a major impact upon reading instruction. Many teacher education programs, as well as state and local curriculum developers, now focus instruction around the five pillars that the NRP identified: (1) phonemic awareness, (2) phonics, (3) fluency, (4) vocabulary, and (5) comprehension. The NRP reported that there were too few empirical studies in the areas of independent reading and computer-assisted instruction for any recommendations regarding these topics to be made.

No Child Left Behind Act

In 2001, President George W. Bush signed into law the No Child Left Behind Act (NCLB), which is a reauthorization of the Elementary and Secondary Education Act of 1965. NCLB is a federal initiative aimed at improving education in America's public schools. NCLB centers upon standards-based educational reform and accountability through assessment. This major piece of government legislation has prompted reform throughout every level of school education.

President Bush announced that the NRP's work would serve as the foundation for the federal literacy policy, and as a result the NRP's work was used prominently in developing the Reading First program. This program is a $5 billion initiative that is one component of NCLB. Reading First is aimed at reading reform, and has been highly controversial. Targeting students in Grades K–3, Reading First distributes grants to states to reform reading instruction. The primary goal of the Reading First program is to ensure that all students are reading successfully by the end of the third grade. Through a bipartisan majority in Congress, over $900 million per year was allocated through a state-funding formula for states to implement reading reform initiatives in local school districts.

Controversy has arisen over how the grant money is distributed, in particular over requiring states to adopt specific reading programs designed to meet the requirements of Reading First. Emphasis is placed on providing scientifically based reading instruction to the neediest students, both economically and in terms of reading achievement. Reading First funds are controlled by state and local school leaders, but their use must meet the strict requirements of the grant. Professional development, assessment, and implementation of scientifically based instruction are areas designated for the funds to be allocated.

Dissent regarding this program has continued to grow, particularly with the release of the U.S. Department of Education Office of the Inspector General's report, which revealed that mismanagement and corruption were present throughout the federal program. This report revealed that states were often required to implement guidelines not established under NCLB and that particular commercial programs were given preference over others. In addition, a study released by the U.S. government in May 2008 further fueled the dissent over this program. The study, which had empirically studied the program, found that after 3 years of implementation, Reading First schools had no statistically significant impact on reading comprehension as compared to schools that did not participate in the program. Critics of the program quickly noted their belief that the program overemphasized explicit phonics instruction and did not do enough to foster comprehension.

Regardless of the dissent and controversy centered upon the Reading First program, NCLB has continued to initiate major reform at the state and local levels. As previously discussed, state and local educational programs had revised and renewed curriculum driven by NCLB. A cornerstone to NCLB is the accountability and assessment policies. States desiring to receive federal funding now were required to develop accountability plans in which each school district must report upon the annual yearly progress of each student, grade, and school. These plans must illustrate how each state plans to achieve full proficiency of their academic content standards. As a result of this federal requirement, state programs quickly reformed their testing policies and procedures to gather and report data required by NCLB.

Assessment Systems

One example of an assessment system put in place to meet the requirements of NCLB is the Dynamic Indicator of Basic Early Literacy Skills (DIBELS). DIBELS is an assessment developed by researchers at the University of Oregon to assess the five pillars of reading instruction, as identified by the NRP. The short amount of time in which DIBELS measures are administered and scored has brought controversy to this assessment, with critics citing a lack of thorough understanding of a child's full spectrum of reading skill after completing this assessment. DIBELS has been widely adopted by school districts across the country because of its accessibility, affordability, and accountability with the requirements of NCLB.

In addition, the National Assessment of Educational Progress, also known as the Nation's Report Card, is an assessment administered to a sample of students in Grades 4 and 8 every 2 years and is intended to gauge the progress of America's schools. Results of the National Assessment of Educational Progress are reported for each state and are used to fuel program improvement at the district, state, and federal level. Reading achievement is defined at three levels: basic, proficient, and advanced. Frameworks were developed and are employed to assess what students should know and be able to do at each level. The National Assessment of Educational Progress is used to inform progress related to Reading First and NCLB, and meets the requirement for ongoing, standardized assessment of the educational progress of the nation.

Conclusion

As a result of these accountability initiatives, serious dissent continues to grow against the mounting tide of testing that districts are required to complete each year. Adversaries of NCLB and the accountability initiative hold that significant hours of student instructional time is now spent administering tests and practice tests. Teachers now understand the dire nature of the annual yearly progress requirements and the Nation's Report

Cards delivered to the public. Under this significant pressure, teachers often teach specifically to the test to achieve district goals.

However, advocates of this latest national reform state that this legislation holds districts responsible for the success and achievement of every student. State and local districts now report accountability data to the public in a way completely unprecedented by previous initiatives. All districts receiving federal dollars have the charge to support every child in becoming a successful reader by the third grade. This latest reform initiative has caused much dissent in the field of reading, and only time will tell the true impact it will have on students and schools.

Mary-Kate Sableski and Jackie Marshall Arnold

See also Elementary and Secondary Education Act; No Child Left Behind Act (NCLB); Phonics; Reading First; Value-Added Education; Whole Language

Further Readings

Barone, D., Hardman, D., & Taylor, J. (2006). *Reading First in the classroom*. Boston: Pearson Education.

National Assessment of Educational Progress, The Nation's Report Card: http://nces.ed.gov/nationsreportcard

National Institute of Child Health and Human Development. (2000). *Report of the National Reading Panel. Teaching children to read: An evidence-based assessment of the scientific research literature on reading and its implications for reading instruction* (NIH Publication No. 00–4769). Washington, DC: U.S. Government Printing Office.

No Child Left Behind Act (NCLB): http://www.nclb.gov

RECONCEPTUALISTS

The curriculum, or what courses should be a part of schooling and what outcomes are appropriate for schools, has historically been a matter of considerable debate and controversy. In the 17th century, reading and the scriptures provided the basis for what should be taught in schools, with particular emphasis on Latin and Greek. In the 18th century, a gradual shift occurred with increased attention to subjects such as writing and arithmetic. Reading and religion, however, still dominated the curriculum. In the 19th century, more focus was placed on literacy, vocational competence, and democratic citizenship. In essence, as the United States matured as a democracy, a gradual expansion evolved of what was to be taught at both elementary and secondary levels.

The 20th century evidenced an explosion of ideas thought to be essential for inclusion in the elementary and secondary curriculum and a "reconceptualizing" of how schools should be structured to foster their emancipatory capacities. John Dewey, leader of the Progressive movement, caused educators to think more about the child's interests and curricular relevance and less about formal disciplinary study and teacher-centered instruction. Whereas educators in early America emphasized formal disciplinary study and rote memorization, John Dewey and those inclined toward Progressivist ideas began to explore and encourage curricular relevance and a focus on the child. Indeed, the Progressive era ushered in a time of prolonged focus on what types of topics and subjects should be covered in a society dedicated to universal schooling. It also laid the groundwork for the reform agenda of the reconceptualists, who began to systematically critique educational policy and practice during the second half of the 20th century, most particularly in the 1970s.

Curriculum content and structure are important because they are the "essence" of what knowledge is transmitted to successive generations of young people. Schools are primary cultural transmitters, and the curriculum is the accumulated wisdom or knowledge base that succeeding generations require for personal survival and development. The learner is the focus; the curriculum is offered to that learner with appropriate scope and sequence; the textbooks and other materials are the elements to be studied; and, finally, the teacher, who is responsible for mediating instruction, must be highly qualified for his or her assigned instructional role. It sounds quite simple; in fact, it is complex and political, and, for the reconceptualist, it is something that must be critically examined and structurally understood.

In the early 1970s a loosely coupled group of education thinkers and social critics began to challenge the heavy emphasis on "how to" or reductionistic curriculum development processes. Questions began to emerge as to what constitutes the primary goal of the educational process: Is it to prepare one "for the duties of life," which suggests one way of structuring what and how knowledge is communicated to young learners; or is it to "free the mind of the learner," which entails moving beyond traditional curricular structures? In addition, the reconceptualists placed more emphasis, indeed some might assert exclusive attention, on truly *understanding* the curriculum and doing so with reliance on significant disciplinary knowledge from the humanities.

Those associated with "traditional" delivery included, most notably, Ralph Tyler. Tyler thought about curriculum in terms of what the learner needs to know and how an educational program needs to be structured to foster defined outcomes. He focused on questions such as What educational goals should be focused on by schools and the schooling process? And what types of classroom or extra-classroom experiences need to be offered to assure that these goals are achieved? The Tyler approach, logical and sequenced, was a way for every educator to think about both what should be taught and how it should be communicated.

The reconceptualists began to question the assumptions of the Tyler rationale and of other "accepted" educational practices and argued that educators needed to move beyond the curriculum as a "how to" process and to examine it historically, politically, philosophically, and even theologically. Tyler and others embraced traditional curricular approaches and derived objectives from studies of the *learner, society,* and *subject-matter specialists.* On the surface, the approach seemed eminently rational. Problems emerge, however, when one begins to consider all the latent or tacit objectives that may not be stated in the explicit curriculum and that represent important political, ethical, or moral dimensions that must be understood.

The reconceptualists challenged not only the assumptions of the explicit curriculum and how it was developed but also the ways in which curricular content was understood and the types of educational structures in place for the delivery of the curriculum. For the reconceptualists the curriculum was necessarily much more than a simple mechanism for defining what content should

be taught and for transmitting such knowledge to students in ways that foster their emergence as "finished products." The curriculum, instead, was something that needed to be challenged, critiqued, understood, and even "freed" from its focus on turning the "raw student" into a "finished product" and toward an exploration of each school's and student's potential. The metaphors of traditionalists focused on production; those of the reconceptionalists emphasized understanding.

The reconceptualists placed more emphasis on intellectual empowerment. Learners construct personal meaning from the experiences they have in the classroom: Reconceptualists do not dismiss the importance of disciplinary knowledge, as defined by subject-matter specialists (through standards), but rather they emphasize the importance of how learners engage ideas and then use such understandings in personally constructed and imaginative ways. With the traditionalists, students tend to emerge with common understandings and tend to "look the same." With the reconceptionalists, the emphasis is on understanding what is, considering what might be, and emerging with potentialities that may be quite diverse in scope and nature.

A wide range of scholars could be described within the reconceptualist framework: William Pinar, James MacDonald, Maxine Greene, Philip Phenix, Dewayne Huebner, Henry Giroux, and Madeleine Grumet. All of their writings offer a critical view of schools and schooling. Like traditionalists or neoconservatives, they are focused on issues of morality, power, and excellence, but their attention is in support of an approach to curriculum delivery that empowers students (especially those who have been historically disenfranchised) and teachers to create and shape their own personal possibilities.

The voice of the reconceptualists began to diminish during the 1980s. Some argue that it was actually "silenced" in the 1980s, not by educational adversaries but rather because the reconceptualist movement was successful as evidenced by the warranting of personalization such as autobiographical studies and existential scholarship. But there may be a less "acceptable" explanation: With the emergence of renewed attention to the outcomes of schooling, especially academic outcomes, the curriculum as a political process began to dominate educational thought in the 1980s and 1990s (e.g., *A Nation at Risk*); the policy perspectives of neoconservatives then dominated the world of educational practice in the early 21st century (i.e., No Child Left Behind). Clearly, there are still reconceptualist thinkers who call on schools to be more than "knowledge factories," but equally clear is the fact that critical curricular voices calling for educational emancipation have been marginalized by ideological views that demand higher academic standards, enhanced assessment, and more accountability.

In summary, curriculum became an object of more formalized studies in the late 18th century. Over the past century a wide range of educational thinkers from John Dewey to Ralph Tyler have proffered ideas about the structure and substance of the curriculum. The reconceptualists became a part of this dialogue because they challenged the status quo and argued that schools should be emancipated in ways that fostered personal, enhanced understanding and focused on freeing the minds of students and teachers to think about and beyond the academic goals emphasized by schools and mandated by state policymakers. For the reconceptualists it was not about defining the curriculum "out there" but rather introspectively understanding oneself and that the outgrowth of that personal transformation is the emergence of a potential to change or "contribute to" others.

Thomas J. Lasley II

See also Academic Freedom; Comprehensive School Reform; Curriculum Controversies; Differentiated Instruction; Progressive Education

Further Readings

Huebner, D. (1975). Power and poetry: The politics of curricular development. In W. F. Pinar (Ed.), *Curriculum theorizing: The reconceptualists* (pp. 271–280). Berkeley, CA: McCutchan.

Giroux, H., & Purpel, D. (1983). *The hidden curriculum and moral education.* Berkeley, CA: McCutchan.

Pinar, W. F. (1975). *Curriculum theorizing: The reconceptualists.* Berkeley, CA: McCutchan.

Pinar, W. F., Reynolds, W. M., Slattery, P., & Taubman, P. M. (1995). *Understanding curriculum.* New York: Peter Lang.

REFORM SCHOOLS

In the 19th century, social reformers in America noted that there were negative connotations associated with the practice of treating juvenile offenders the same as adult criminals. Managing young offenders became a tremendous concern for the criminal justice system. These offenders were incarcerated with adult criminals and were often exploited by older inmates. Ironically, they also received instruction about advanced criminal activities from these cellmates. It was apparent that this was in direct opposition to the juvenile's best interest. In 1820, Boston, New York, and Philadelphia began to examine the penal system and created a "house of refuge" for juveniles. It was a part-school, part-prison institution and became a "holding pen" for offenders. In addition, it was used as a deterrent and precautionary measure for nonconvicted children. New York's program dealt mainly with children who were convicted criminals or who were considered vagrants. In 1886, Massachusetts created the Lyman School for Boys, a state reform school, specifically for males under the age of 16 who had been convicted of an offense. It was the school's responsibility to instruct the students in morality and provide training in a skill or occupation.

Reformatories for female offenders were also necessary. These institutions were usually smaller than the facilities for boys and involved the teaching of domestic skills. The goal of these institutions was to provide training to the residents in skills mastery, which appeared to be lacking in their education. Thus, by incorporating rehabilitation and education for its residents, the philosophy of the "reform school" was born.

The "curriculum" of these reform schools varied and was sometimes controversial. To ensure discipline, corporal punishment was used, and in some cases more extreme measures were practiced. These included vasectomy, castration, or sterilization in an effort to reduce and/or remediate sexual promiscuity. Minor offenses were not treated as harshly as major offenses, and the resident might be given a lesser punishment such as loss of recreation time or loss of a special activity; harsher punishment included the withholding of food or a period of solitary confinement. Some disciplinary actions progressed to beatings. Although the conditions were harsh and extreme, there were residents who "graduated" from the schools and lived productive lives. It was not without some psychological scarring, of course, and the term *productive* is used carefully in this context.

Guards were available if problems arose. Counselors would live within the facility and interact with the residents. A cottage master and a cottage matron would be expected to be on duty 24 hours a day. The counselor would be a role model or "big brother" for the residents and aid in their rehabilitation. Additionally, religious education, either Catholic or Protestant, was part of the day's requirements. No additional religious choices were available. Services provided to the boys were usually held in the spartan surroundings of an auditorium. The introduction of religion and hard work was conceived as a way to help the residents change their "bad behaviors."

Children were also used to provide free labor to farmers and would work the farms as long as they stayed healthy. If they became sick or could not do the work, they would be returned to the facility. Additional forms of labor included lawn maintenance, laundry, or working in the cafeteria. Trades or skills taught included carpentry, painting, masonry, plumbing and steam-fitting, and printing.

School reform witnessed a breakthrough when Cook County, Illinois, established a specialized criminal court system for delinquent, homeless, abandoned, and neglected children. The Illinois Juvenile Court Act of 1899 was passed with the establishment of a court for children who were neglected, dependent, or delinquent and under the age of 16. The law resolved conflicts and problems based upon individual needs and with a perspective related solely to children. Punishment was replaced by rehabilitation; records were kept in strict confidence and were stored separately from adult criminal records. The separation of children from adults symbolized a new view of youth offenders. The courts were called *juvenile courts* in recognition of this new age of reasoning. The idea became widespread across America. Colorado's juvenile court statute, for example, declared problem children as "juvenile disorderly persons." The emphasis moved toward a social responsibility for reforming children. The introduction of a juvenile

justice system contributed to the decline of the reform schools, as did the push by trade unions to institute nonunion labor for residents. If the residents were to be paid union wages, it would dramatically increase the cost of the programs. In Connecticut, the cost of maintaining each student at the institution would increase from $5,000 to $50,000 and would result in the closing of the Lyman School. The Lyman School closed in 1971 with little opposition.

The term *reform school* has passed into obsolescence. Contemporary equivalents include alternative schools, special-needs day care, independent private schools, therapeutic wilderness programs, and emotional growth boarding schools. These programs have attempted to offer the least restrictive environment for offending youth and continue to provide an individualized coeducational, safe, home-type environment for the least corrigible of juvenile offenders.

Mario C. Barbiere

See also Alternative Schools; Guidance and School Counseling; Life Adjustment Education

Further Readings

Brenzel, B. M. (1983). *Daughters of the state: A social portrait of the first reform school for girls in North America, 1856–1905*. Cambridge: MIT Press.

Friedman, L. M. (1993). *Crime and punishment in American history*. New York: Basic Books.

Hawes, J. (1971). *Children in urban society*. New York: Oxford University Press.

Schlossman, S. L. (2005). *Transforming juvenile justice: Reform ideals and institutional realities, 1825–1920*. DeKalb: Northern Illinois University Press.

RELIGION AND THE CURRICULUM

Efforts to understand the relationship between religion and the public school curriculum require a review of the larger issue of religious liberty. For the past 2 decades, religious liberty has intersected public education in America in ways more divisive than uniting. The polarization of conservative Christians seeking to advance particular interpretations of the Bible within the public school arena versus those citizens advocating for a religion-neutral and secular arena has grown wider and wider.

This entry reviews the current state of the debate concerning religion and the curriculum with a cursory look at the larger context of the debate—religious liberty. The two major groups participating in the debate are highlighted along with their arguments for and against religion in the public school curriculum. A recommendation to thoughtful reformers for a more balanced approach to religion and the public school curriculum concludes the entry.

Many American school systems and their communities are at odds over educational philosophy, faith-based curricula, the teaching of the Bible as a literary course, and the role of religion in U.S. public schools. The controversies have moved from the subject of the debate to the manner of the debate. The shrillness, anger, and antagonism have moved beyond dissent in a democratic society and become one more element of the so-called culture wars. The battlefield of choice for many Christians is the U.S. public schools.

Public schools face a difficult challenge from evangelical Christians who have made public education the rhetorical "devil" for their cause. For example, the Southern Baptist Convention, the nation's largest Baptist denomination, has agitated to remove Southern Baptist students from public schools. Some critics have pointed out that the underlying religious motives are tinged with racial attitudes that are, in some ways, as deeply entrenched as ever, in the South. The danger is that "religious liberty" will be used to make a scapegoat of the public schools.

There are two basic sides in the current debate over the relationship between religious liberty and the public school. One side insists that America was founded as, and continues to be, a Christian nation. Arguing on the basis of such beginnings, these Christians advocate prayer in public school, the teaching of the Bible in the curriculum, and the priority of Christianity over all other forms of religious instruction, including secularism and atheism. In addition, this side of the argument asks for the teaching of a particular Christian theology: fundamentalism as opposed to any of its alternatives.

The emotional argument of the conservative attempt to establish Christianity in the public schools of America is that the Supreme Court has "kicked God out of the public schools." In response to such statements, critics have pointed out that this is not only a presumptuous argument but a patently false one. What the Supreme Court actually did was to ban state-sponsored religion from public schools. Religious activity *is* allowed in public schools, and this includes voluntary prayer, studying religious holidays, Bible clubs, and certain religious attire. The majority of American denominations and religious bodies have officially adopted statements of support for voluntary use of religious activities in the public schools.

The intellectual argument for establishing Christianity in the public schools revolves around a revisionist history that promotes America as a "Christian nation." This approach concentrates on portraying the nation's founders as born-again, Bible-believing, evangelical Christians. Yet even a cursory reading of the history of the founding of the United States will show that the Founding Fathers were in fact a diverse group. Thomas Jefferson was a strong supporter of religious liberty. Benjamin Rush, a hero of many conservative Christians, became a Unitarian.

What is often overlooked in this increasingly bitter debate is that the First Amendment's protections for religious liberty were supported by evangelical dissenters—Baptists, Quakers, and Presbyterians. Ironically, Southern Baptists are now leading the charge to undo the settled law of the First Amendment.

The issue of religious liberty becomes muddled when there are so many truth claims that fail to pass the test of validity. For example, the claim that the United States is a Christian nation is untrue in any legal or theological sense. Our founders brought a variety of religious convictions to the table. Thomas Jefferson was a deist. Thomas Paine was attacked by Christian leaders for the perception that he was an atheist. George Washington refused to have a clergy person at his bedside when he was dying. President Washington referred to God as a deistic "Providence."

The U.S. Constitution never mentions Christianity, and the word *religious* is used only once, to disallow a religious test for public office. The Bill of Rights famously declares, "Congress shall make no law respecting an establishment of religion or pro-hibiting the exercise thereof." The United States of America as a constitutional democracy protected all religious beliefs. U.S. citizens enjoy freedom *of* religion and freedom *from* religion.

The charge made by some conservative Christians that "God has been removed from our public schools" appears to be grounded in the notion that by banning state-sponsored religion, the courts have somehow infringed upon religious liberty. In actuality, voluntary student religious expression is protected, with two qualifications: (1) The educational process cannot be disrupted, and (2) the rights of students *not* to participate must be protected.

In fact, a wide variety of voluntary religious practices are allowed in public schools. As noted earlier, among the approved religious activities in schools are voluntary prayer, instruction about religion, the study of religious holidays, Bible clubs, and certain kinds of religious attire. Religious expression, far from being removed from the public schools, has numerous permissible avenues of expression.

The second approach sees religion as having no role at all in public life and public education. The advocates for a religion-neutral public school arena see involvement of people of faith and the teaching of any faith content as a violation of the First Amendment. At times these arguments are strident. For example, some secular proponents regard religious arguments as naive and seek to embarrass and even harass people of faith. The weakness of this point of view is its denial of the powerful moral guidance of religious heritage upon the founding of the nation. As a point of clarification, seeing America as founded on guiding moral principles is not the same as the theory that America was founded as a Christian nation.

Neither a sectarian nor a religion-neutral approach to the curriculum offers students a fair and balanced opportunity to learn about religion in unbiased and academically credible ways. A fair and just resolution may require a more balanced approach to religion and the curriculum in public schools, and such an approach requires thoughtful reform in terms of what curriculum is taught.

Two primary organizations have developed textbooks for teaching the Bible in public schools. The National Council on Bible Curriculum in

Public Schools and the Bible Literacy Project. A review of these widely different approaches to religion curriculum will indicate the severity of the challenge to teach the Bible in public schools.

The National Council on Bible Curriculum in Public Schools, a conservative Christian organization, has produced a textbook, *The Bible in History and Literature,* which presents a clear apology for Christian fundamentalism. The material, gathered from numerous uncited sources, was criticized for containing numerous factual errors. As a result of these criticisms, the National Council on Bible Curriculum in Public Schools released a revised version of the textbook in August 2005. The revised textbook remains, however, a sectarian project from beginning to end. The political attempt to Christianize America is still evident.

In response to *The Bible in History and Literature*, the Bible Literacy Project published *The Bible and Its Influence*. This curriculum contains a teaching manual and a university, online teacher-training component. This textbook has been produced from a broader and more diverse group of consultants, including Jews and Christians of a variety of denominations. The purpose of this curriculum is not to teach a sectarian set of Christian doctrines but to insist that education in the humanities should include a study of religion. The overall approach of the authors of *The Bible and Its Influence* is unbiased, informed, and scholarly.

The offshoot of these competing curricula is a growing recognition that the public schools are once again being pressured from all sides to fill in the gaps left by uninvolved and uninformed parents. When surveys indicate that only 10% of teenagers can name all five of the world's major religions and 20% do not know the meaning of Easter, it is presumptuous to believe that public school teachers can do much to close this gap. In fact, a larger concern may be that the Bible as part of the public school curriculum may be a generation too late. The ignorance of religious content among today's students goes far beyond the Bible and includes the entire scope of Western culture and history. This indicates that the matter of religion and the curriculum remains political in nature rather than genuinely pedagogical.

Although public schools will remain a primary battleground in the culture wars between defenders of religion and opponents of religion, there are reform guidelines for public school boards, administrators, and teachers. Among those guidelines is the need to be fair, balanced, and unbiased. No favoritism should be shown to any specific version of Christianity. Curriculum should include Roman Catholic, Orthodox Christian, Protestant, and Free Church primary sources. The effectiveness of the curriculum will depend mostly on the abilities and the tolerance of the teachers. Specifically, teachers need to rise to the challenge of informing a mostly uninformed and biblically illiterate generation of students of the way generations of Americans have historically been shaped by the Bible. Enlightened reformers are focused on this higher-order understanding about religion and schools; they are not focused on teaching particular sectarian views.

Rodney Wallace Kennedy

See also Edgerton Bible Case; Episcopal Schools; Separation of Church and State; Society of Friends Schools

Further Readings

Mapp, A. J., Jr. (2003). *The faiths of our fathers: What America's founders really believed.* Lanham, MD: Rowman & Littlefield.

Meacham, J. (2007). *American gospel: God, the Founding Fathers, and the making of a nation.* New York: Random House.

Nord, W. A. (2005). *Religion and American education: Rethinking a national dilemma.* Chapel Hill: University of North Carolina Press.

Paige, R. (2003). *Guidance on constitutionally protected prayer in public elementary and secondary schools.* Washington, DC: U.S. Department of Education.

RICE, JOSEPH MAYER (1857–1934)

Joseph Mayer Rice is viewed as one of the first muckraking journalists to turn his attention to the field of education and describe the deplorable conditions, inept administration, and tedious teaching practices of schools. A knowledgeable educational reformer, researcher, and trained physician,

Rice generated public attention to the dismal state of affairs of education in the late 19th century through his magazine articles. His work contributed significantly to school reform in the Progressive era.

Rice, practicing medicine in New York City in the 1880s, became interested in the physical fitness programs offered in the city schools. This led to his decision to leave medical practice and to travel to Germany in 1888 where, for the next 2 years, he studied psychology and pedagogy at the universities in Jena and Leipzig and traveled throughout Europe observing school systems and pedagogical practices. Rice would observe the first laboratory of experimental psychology, directed by Wilhelm Wundt, and learned of Herbartianism as it was taught at the University of Jena and its laboratory schools. Rice returned to the United States in 1890 with strong views for the reform of elementary education. He began writing for the public press and published several articles in *The Forum*, a New York monthly magazine owned by his brother, Issac Leopold Rice. His recommendations for American education, striking a resonate chord during the late-19th-century Populist and Progressive eras, included better training of teachers, a curriculum based on sound psychological principles, and the scientific management of education in which clearly defined goals and standards mandated the scientific measurement of outcomes.

The editor of *The Forum*, Walter Hines Page (later editor of *The Atlantic Monthly* and U.S. ambassador to England during World War I), became intrigued with Rice's German experiences and his critique of American schools and, seeing an opportunity to publicly expose a little-examined system, proposed that Rice conduct a school survey–study tour for *The Forum*. Rice began the 6-month project in 1892 and traveled to 36 cities, visiting 6 to 8 schools in each city. He observed classrooms, talked to approximately 1,200 teachers, met with school officials and school boards, interviewed parents, and visited 20 teacher-training institutions. Rice's research compared traditional schools, with their narrow curricula and recitation, with that of the progressive "new pedagogy" of modern schools, characterized by an integrated approach to curriculum and instruction. From 1892 to 1893, Rice published a series of nine articles in *The Forum*, now considered an example of muckraking, which created an outrage among the general public, who had previously maintained faith in the education system.

Rice's articles reported some of the most tedious, pedantic teaching imaginable in the traditional schools. He described unassisted superintendents responsible for the supervision of hundreds of teachers, and he quoted at length from board of education reports portraying the deplorable conditions of schools and the senselessness and ineffectiveness of educational practices. The general public became outraged at educators with each succeeding *Forum* essay. Lawrence Cremin described professional educators' reactions to Rice as ranging from "chilling disdain to near-hysteria."

Rice conducted a second survey tour in the spring of 1893, exposing the deplorable conditions of education in additional traditional schools, and a third *Forum*-sponsored tour of classrooms (in 1895) included a school/student survey representing what is considered to be one of the first comparative tests used in American education. This 16-month survey examined approximately 33,000 fourth- to eighth-grade students, tabulating age, nationality, environment, and type of school system. One aspect of the research examined the pedagogy of spelling, deemed by Rice as the "futility of the spelling grind," and concluded that there was no correlation between the amount of spelling drill and the degree of success in the actual act of spelling. This comparative test was widely applauded and, although the results were not universally supported by educators, Rice received acknowledgment for helping to initiate a research movement that advocated objective study of education. Rice's methods portrayed a scientific and progressive methodology for the pedagogy of spelling and the "passing of recitation"—a methodology that was well ahead of its time.

In 1897, Rice assumed the editorship of *The Forum* and served in that capacity until 1907, ultimately retiring from the journal in 1915. He published his last work in that year and expressed some regret for not being acknowledged as one of the founders of educational research in America.

Craig Kridel

See also Elementary Curricular Reform; Herbartian Movement; Progressive Education

Further Readings

Cremin, L. A. (1961). *The transformation of the school.* New York: Knopf.

Rice, J. M. (1893). *The public-school system of the United States.* New York: Century.

Stanley, J. C. (1966). Rice as a pioneer educational researcher. *Journal of Educational Measurement, 3,* 135–139.

Travers, R. M. W. (1983). *How research has changed American schools.* Kalamazoo, MI: Mythos Press.

RICKOVER, HYMAN (1900–1986)

In his *Education and Freedom*, Admiral Hyman Rickover stated that "only massive upgrading of the scholastic standards of our schools will guarantee the future prosperity and freedom of the Republic. This is the conclusion which I have reached as a result of my personal experience with developing a new source of power—nuclear fission."

This quote presents a good summary of Rickover's education ideas. Although not, in his words, an "educationalist," his dissent struck a chord in Congress and in the nation. The tone of his 1959 work *Education and Freedom* is controversial, and even a supporter, Charles Van Doren, describes him as "truculent." He established his credentials because of the educational program he developed for training officers. He also stated, "I should like every American to get into battle for better schools."

Rickover was noted for his development of nuclear-powered submarines and for his work at the Atomic Energy Commission. He was able to cut through red tape to accomplish the development and production of nuclear-powered submarines and ships. Because this field was new, he needed to develop new programs in leadership and technology. For this, he needed educated people. He found that the U.S. educational system was not producing graduates who could step up to the challenges of implementing civilian and military nuclear power plants. He was well known to both supporters and detractors in Congress, and to presidents, including Jimmy Carter. His book *Education and Freedom* discusses the challenges faced as society becomes increasingly complex and technological. Read in the early 21st century, his chapter on "Energy Resources and Our Future" seems almost prescient. His other books on education include *Swiss Schools and Ours: Why Theirs Are Better* (1962) and *American Education, a National Failure: The Problem of Our Schools and What We Can Learn From England* (1963).

The launch of the world's first artificial satellite, *Sputnik*, by the Soviet Union in 1957 caused widespread shock in the United States. Rickover used that event as a catalyst for a call to change in the U.S. educational system. His testimony to Congress contributed to the passing of the National Defense Education Act of 1958. Rickover stated: "*Sputnik* has been seen as the triumph of Russian education, and rightly so." Viewing education through the lens of national defense, Rickover contended that the Soviet Union's lead in the space race, as demonstrated by its successful launch of *Sputnik*, was not the fault of the National Advisory Committee for Aeronautics, the predecessor to the National Aeronautics and Space Administration, nor was it the fault of the American military or U.S. rocket manufacturers. Rather, it was the fault of the schools. The positive effect of the National Defense Education Act was that money was invested in the schools. *Sputnik* sent a wakeup call to the United States, and the space race was on, with a focus on technical education as a key to that race.

Rickover's educational platform was in favor of a rigorous liberal arts and solid technological education, calling for more attention to be directed toward gifted students. A backer of ability grouping, Rickover criticized what he felt were the "watered-down" standards of the comprehensive high school. He advocated observing European and Russian schools and learning from them. He was in favor of national testing standards. As he stated, "The man of the future on whom we shall depend more and more is the technical expert." He was critical of the theories of John Dewey and their focus on life skills, distrustful of the educational establishment, and opposed to letting professional educators be in control of American schooling. After Rickover's testimony about the superiority of the Soviet schools, the U.S. commissioner of education, Lawrence G. Derthick, testified before Congress to dispute Rickover's interpretation. He felt that the top salesmen of the Soviet schools had misled Rickover and that the

Soviet Union had very different societal aims than those of the United States.

Biographers Norman Polmar and Thomas B. Allen stated that Rickover had an inner vision of what was wrong with American education and how it could be changed. They described his efforts as a "quixotic crusade." He was a dissenter who used his experiences in the development of nuclear power as a platform to call for reform. After a long career in the U.S. Navy, Rickover retired at age 82.

Jack O'Gorman

See also Ability Grouping; Comprehensive High Schools; Conant, James Bryant; Council for Basic Education; Life Adjustment Education; National Defense Education Act (NDEA)

Further Readings
Polmar, N., & Allen, T. (1982) *Rickover, controversy and genius: A biography*. New York: Simon & Schuster.
Rickover, H. (1959). *Education and freedom*. New York: E. P. Dutton.
Rickover, H. (1962). *Swiss schools and ours: Why theirs are better*. Boston: Little, Brown.
Rickover, H. (1963). *American education, a national failure: The problem of our schools and what we can learn from England*. New York: E. P. Dutton.

RUFFNER, WILLIAM HENRY (1824–1908)

Born on February 11, 1824, William Henry Ruffner pursued careers as a geologist and preacher before turning to education. An ordained Presbyterian minister, Ruffner was selected as the first superintendent of public education in Virginia in 1870 by the Virginia legislature, with the backing of Robert E. Lee. He was given 30 days to come up with a plan for public schooling in Virginia, which he did with the help of several notables, including William Holmes McGuffey. He traveled thousands of miles on horseback on behalf of the nascent public schools in Virginia during his tenure as superintendent, which lasted until 1882. He is justly regarded as a reformer; in fact, some have referred to him as the "Horace Mann of the South."

Three major challenges that Ruffner faced during his tenure are addressed in this entry. The first is the establishment of a system of public education. The second is the difficulties associated with questions of race in the recently formed public schools. (These two challenges were mixed with religious quarrels and intertwined, at times, with each other.) The third, and last, is the issue of funding the schools, the issue that led to his dismissal.

Efforts to establish public schools in Virginia had been made by a number of individuals and groups prior to the Civil War. The best known of those were by Thomas Jefferson in the late 18th and early 19th centuries. Charles Fenton Mercer, in the second and third decades of the 19th century, was another advocate of public schooling. He differed from Jefferson in that he wanted the schools controlled by the state, whereas Jefferson opted for local control. They were followed by Ruffner's father, Henry, in the 1840s. None of these efforts was successful at the state level, although there were some, less than a dozen, local school divisions in existence prior to the war.

The state school system was brought into existence when Governor Gilbert C. Walker signed a bill to "establish and maintain a uniform system of free public schools" in July 1870. Critics of this action abounded, and their criticism was vocal, strong, and sustained. Some charged that the law replaced the parents, educators of their children by God's will, with the "Godless" state. Others contended that the system interfered with parental liberty. Ruffner's long-time friend and colleague and a fellow Presbyterian minister who also had been educated at Union Theological Seminary in Richmond, Robert L. Dabney, also denounced the public school system. Among the charges he leveled at it was that it was the result of "Yankee" influence. Dabney also emphasized the primacy of the parent in the educational process and that it was the state's duty to protect the family's rights, not usurp them. True education, some of Ruffner's opponents held, demanded that it be Christian, and that the state, as a secular entity, was totally inadequate to educate. Ruffner argued that the public school system was religious and moral, indeed Christian, but not sectarian. It advanced a

"common religion" that would unite all citizens and bring about moral and social unity.

Many of Ruffner's critics included racial salvos in their arsenal. The freedmen were described as being of low character and morals, ignorant, indolent, and devoid of ambition—in short, incapable of being educated. Ruffner argued that public education would improve the Black race in citizenship and reduce crime and pauperism. He opposed mixed race schools, on the pragmatic grounds that southern Whites would not accept them. In this he was joined by Barnas Sears, the agent for the Peabody Fund, and influential Virginians. Time was the only means that would erase the Whites' belief that the freedmen were morally, intellectually, and culturally inferior.

Well into his term as superintendent, Ruffner was caught up in the political debate over what to do with Virginia's massive $45,000,000 war debt. He had steadfastly urged the legislature to support public schooling throughout the 1870s for all of Virginia's children, while professing that education should be free of politics. Nonetheless, he became caught in the fight between the "funder" position, which held that the debt should be paid in full, and the "readjusters," who maintained it should be readjusted, as advocated by Governor William Mahone. The readjuster party became dominant in the legislature, and Ruffner, along with many local superintendents, became a casualty and left office in 1882.

After leaving the superintendency, Ruffner returned to geological surveying and farming, before assuming the presidency of the State Female Seminary, now Longwood College, in 1884. He left that position for retirement in 1887 and died in 1908.

Thomas C. Hunt

See also Dabney, Robert L.; General Education Board; Peabody Fund; Southern Education Board

Further Readings

Dabney, C, W. (1936). *Universal education in the south, I.* Chapel Hill: University of North Carolina Press.

Fraser, W. J., Jr. (1970). *William Henry Ruffner: A liberal in the old and new South.* Unpublished doctoral dissertation, University of Tennessee.

Fraser, W. J., Jr. (1971). William Henry Ruffner and the establishment of Virginia's public school system, 1870–1874. *The Virginia Magazine of History and Biography, 79*(July), 259–279.

Hunt, T., & Wagoner, J., Jr. (1988). Race, religion, and redemption: William Henry Ruffner and the moral foundations of education in Virginia. *American Presbyterians, 66*(1), 1–9.

Rugg, Harold (1886–1960)

During his varied career, Harold Ordway Rugg was a key member of the Progressive education movement and worked on a wide range of topics, including measurement and statistics, social studies, teacher education, and the creative process. Whereas all members of the Progressive Education Association sought reform in American education, Rugg had a direct impact on schools across the United States through his social studies textbook series, *Man and His Changing Society*. His texts were used in all types of schools, not just those operated by the Progressives. His ideas of social reconstruction shaped the pedagogy of the series around the study of real social problems and their solutions. Attacks on his approach to education grew during the 1930s, and his textbooks fell out of favor during World War II.

After completing his doctoral degree in 1915 at the University of Illinois, Rugg initially focused his attention on the areas of measurement and statistics. He worked first with Charles Judd at the University of Chicago and then with Edward Thorndike in the widespread use of standardized tests among soldiers in the U.S. Army. Rugg, however, seemed to undergo a metamorphosis after his move in 1920 to Teachers College, Columbia University, and its related laboratory for educational reform, the Lincoln School. Living in Greenwich Village and working at Columbia exposed him to a wide range of colleagues and new ideas, particularly ideas related to social concerns. This gave him a new direction to pursue the reform of social studies education and, through it, the reform of society.

By 1921 Rugg published his first article on the reconstruction of the social studies curriculum. In it he called for the integration of the different branches of the social studies—history, geography, economics, and political science—into a coherent program that would be more meaningful for children and less burdensome for teachers. He also advocated focusing the curriculum on student investigation of social problems and issues. An advocate of social planning, Rugg believed students would become engaged in the social studies through social justice, identifying problems and planning for their solution. Although supportive of the Progressive Education Association's emphasis on child-centered schools (he published an "appraisal," or evaluation, of such schools in 1928), he pushed the organization to become more engaged in social action and justice.

As a way of leading by example, he began work in 1921 on perhaps his most influential writing, his textbook series *Man and His Changing Society*. Initially begun as a pamphlet series, it contained a pedagogy that was radically different from anything else available. Rather than providing an "official" version of national history, Rugg's books focused on social issues and problems in the United States. Students were then encouraged to explore potential solutions to these problems. During 9 years of research and development, Rugg sold more than 750,000 copies of his pamphlets. Based on their widespread acceptance, the pamphlets were turned into a textbook series. Commercial distribution by Ginn and Company began in 1929. In spite of the Great Depression, Rugg's textbooks sold well across the nation.

As early as 1934, however, Rugg was attacked for his approach to social studies education and his textbook series. While this was partially due to his initial fascination with the Soviet "experiment," it was primarily due to his core pedagogy: the study of social problems in the United States. As the 1930s progressed toward international conflict and war, the investigation of social ills and problems in American society, even with an eye toward their solutions, was seen by some as unpatriotic. Rugg became the target of those who labeled him extremist and anti-American. His colleagues were quick to support him and his textbooks. He defended himself in *That Men May Understand* (1941). These actions did not stem the changing tide of public sentiment. The most serious charges were eventually retracted by his critics, but his textbooks quickly fell out of favor and use.

Rugg was a founding member of the John Dewey Society and one of the founders of the National Council for the Social Studies. He was editor for *Frontiers of Democracy*, the *Journal of Educational Psychology*, and social studies editor for *Senior Scholastic*. In his final 20 years, Rugg continued to write prolifically, still promoting social reform, though with perhaps a more constrained voice. His last works clustered around three areas: school redesign, teacher education, and creative imagination.

Larry D. Burton

See also Counts, George S.; Progressive Education; Progressive Education Association (PEA); Social Reconstructionism; Thorndike, Edward L.

Further Readings

Kliebard, H. M. (2004). *The struggle for the American curriculum: 1893–1958* (3rd ed.). New York: RoutledgeFalmer.

Rugg, H. O. (1947). *Foundations for American education*. Yonkers-on-Hudson, NY: World Book.

Rugg, H. O., & Shumaker, A. (1928). *The child-centered school: An appraisal of the new education*. Yonkers-on-Hudson, NY: World Book.

RURAL EDUCATION

Rural education, also known as country and nonmetro education, has been a target for reform and a site of resistance and dissent for well over a century. The one-room public school, once the dominant educational experience for most rural children, has given way to larger, multigrade country schools. Today, one-fifth of all public school students are enrolled in rural districts. This entry begins with a definition of rural schools, followed by a snapshot of current rural enrollments and demographics. Next, the entry reviews efforts at systemic reform, and the accompanying resistance to these policies, with a focus on school consolidation, closure, and cultural transformation. The entry concludes with an overview of two enduring challenges to rural schools: teacher recruitment and equitable finance.

Defining Rural Education

Definitions of rural education have varied widely since the mid-1800s. States have categorized a school or district as "rural" based on population density (number of students per square mile); remoteness (the percentage of rural communities within a county); or the number of students in the grade, school, or district. Researchers and advocates have also identified rural communities and schools according to other defining features, including local language, shared values, and culture. The lack of universal criteria to classify rural schools has led to widely varying counts of the number of rural students and schools and calls for the creation of a common, standard measurement system. In 2006, the U.S. Department of Education attempted to institute uniformity in the identification and categorization of rural schools. Under the new system, rural schools are distinguished by their proximity to urban centers and subidentified as institutions in fringe, distant, and remote rural areas.

Based on this new classification system, the National Center for Education Statistics reported in 2007 that 56% of districts, 30% of schools, and 22% of students, approximately 10 million, were rural. Although a dozen states (Alaska, Arkansas, Iowa, Kentucky, Maine, Mississippi, Nebraska, New Hampshire, South Dakota, Vermont, West Virginia, and Wyoming) have a majority of their public elementary and secondary school students classified as rural, the greatest number of rural students are enrolled in the high-population states of Texas, North Carolina, and California. Rural school enrollment has increased in the 21st century: From 2002–2003 to 2004–2005, the number of rural students has increased by 15%, or 1.3 million students, in stark contrast to a decline in urban and suburban enrollments during the same period.

Rural education is a diverse phenomenon in the United States. The demographic profile of rural schools varies across and within regions. In some states, like Hawai'i and Alaska, most rural students are indigenous, whereas in the Southeast, African Americans constitute the majority. In the South and West, particularly in New Mexico and Arizona, the rural population is predominantly Latino/a and Native American. Poverty is a defining characteristic of many rural students. In 2002,

14.2% of the rural population, approximately 7.5 million people, was poor, with child poverty rates exceeding 35%. While all ethnic and racial groups had higher poverty rates in rural locales, Blacks (33%), Hispanics (26%), and Native Americans (34%) had the highest rates among the nonmetro population in 2002. Among the challenges deep poverty brings to rural schools are weak local tax bases for educational funding, children who have yet to learn foundational skills, and limited resources to recruit and retain quality teachers.

Closure and Consolidation

Educational reformers, guided by notions of cost-effectiveness, efficiency, and improved educational quality, began targeting rural schools in the late 19th century for systemic change. As American society shifted from a predominantly agrarian to an industrial base, calls intensified for significant reform, including rural school and district consolidation. Reform efforts gained strength following the findings of the Country Life Commission, which President Theodore Roosevelt founded in 1907 to explore ways to improve rural life. The Commission found rural schools, with their poorly trained teachers, loosely developed curricula, and inadequate structures, were inefficient and detrimental to local communities. Administrative Progressives such as Ellwood Cubberley delivered sharp critiques of rural schools, describing them as backward and at the heart of the rural-life "problem." The Commission proposed rural school consolidation, curriculum standardization, and teacher professionalism as viable solutions for the improvement of the rural condition.

As a result of these varied reform efforts and demographic shifts, the one-room schoolhouse, once a common institution in rural communities serving mixed-age student groups, began to give way to multiroom, graded schools. Starting in 1920 and continuing over a decade, approximately 4,000 one-room schoolhouses were closed annually, while the number of consolidated schools doubled from 10,000 to 20,000 during that same period. Consolidation was facilitated in large part by the improvement of the country road system, availability of buses, and the use of standardized tests to compare the academic achievement of one-room schools versus their consolidated and urban counterparts. During the decades immediately following World War II, attempts to achieve economies of scale led to the almost complete eradication of one-room schools and a further push to consolidate small schools. In the late 20th and early 21st centuries, efforts to reform and sustain rural schools continued to revolve around the disputed merits of a smaller educational institution. States, confronted with severe budget cutbacks, have looked to reduce the number of districts in an effort to be more cost-effective. The most common methods to promote consolidation include the imposition of minimum size limits (i.e., number of pupils), the use of state-funding formulas to better fund larger schools and districts, unfunded mandates, and financial inducements.

Rural communities have staged significant resistance to school closure and consolidation efforts. In the 19th and early 20th centuries, country schools represented the heart of rural towns. As community schoolhouses, these rural institutions served as central meeting points for educators, politicians, religious leaders, and social organizers. Opposition to consolidation was particularly strong in the rural Midwest, where local farmers in Iowa organized in the early 20th century to resist with much success the mass closure of one-room, ungraded schools. Rural school consolidation and closure continue to pose one of the greatest threats to the vitality of small, 21st-century country schools. Resistance to current efforts at school consolidation continues, with advocacy groups, researchers, and community activists drawing attention to the positive aspects of rural schooling: higher graduation rates, comparable academic achievement to urban counterparts, and high levels of extracurricular involvement. Anticonsolidation and decentralization advocates point to the vital small-school movement in urban areas as further evidence in support of smaller institutions. This movement aims to restructure and break up large city high schools into smaller learning communities for increased student well-being and achievement. In addition to grassroots, community-driven resistance to consolidation, three state governments—Louisiana, Oklahoma, and Wyoming—have worked to sustain small rural schools through active state support, proposed constitutional amendments, and adjusted finance formulas.

Cultural Reform

Education reform has also targeted rural culture. The settlement movement of the late 19th and early 20th centuries concentrated on addressing, in Allen Davis's terms, the "poverty of opportunity," particularly in rural Appalachia. Local communities generally welcomed these educational reforms, as evidenced by the donation of land and materials for the schools. Drawing on the principles and practices used in urban settlements, like Jane Addams's Hull House, graduates from northeastern, elite women's colleges traveled to rural areas of eastern Kentucky, Tennessee, and North Carolina to establish schools. Settlement schools strove to alter the behavior of rural people through citizenship, health, and family education. Notably, settlement educators recognized the value of select elements of rural, mountain culture, including music and handicrafts, and attempted to preserve these skills through a tailored arts curriculum at the schools.

Throughout the 20th century, rural school reform continued to be directed at rural culture. In order to cultivate students who could capitalize on employment opportunities in urban locales, a nationally and internationally oriented curriculum took precedence over one infused with local histories and elements. Paul Theobald emerged in the 20th century as a vocal critic of the market orientation and emphasis in the curricula of rural schools. In an effort to resist the homogenization of rural schools and sustain the vitality of rural communities, educational reformers have called for a curricular transformation. Wendell Berry, the educational philosopher, has argued in support of a liberal arts curriculum for country schools that incorporates rural knowledge. Likewise, the development of place-based education in the latter 20th century represents, in part, a corrective action to the marginalization of local experience in rural schools. Place-based education attempts to connect schoolchildren with their rural environs and re-create an affiliation with community through local historical, environmental, and cultural study and research.

Enduring Challenges

One enduring challenge for rural schools, and an area targeted for significant reform, is the recruitment and retention of qualified teachers. Lower salaries, geographic isolation, and poor school facilities complicate attempts to develop and improve the teaching and administrative force in rural schools. According to the National Center for Education Statistics, rural public school teachers earn less, on average, than their urban and suburban counterparts. The difficulty in attracting qualified teachers has become more intense under the requirements of the No Child Left Behind Act, which demands all teachers meet a common state definition of the characteristic "highly qualified." In hard-to-staff rural schools, where teachers commonly teach more than one subject especially in science and mathematics, the "highly qualified" designation has been elusive. To address these challenges, states, such as Mississippi, have offered salary incentives to qualified teachers to work in subjects and schools with the greatest shortages. The federal government's Rural Education Achievement Program intends to address further the additional financial hardship that rural communities face in meeting the No Child Left Behind requirements through funneling additional resources to rural districts.

Persistent problems with school funding present an additional challenge to rural schools and districts. Rural education advocates find especially problematic inequitable state-funding formulas and inadequate federal aid levels to students in need. In both cases, critics argue that a size bias exists in favor of larger, urban districts over their smaller, rural counterparts. In most cases, rural educators claim that state and federal governments disregard the varying needs and circumstances of rural communities. As evidence of the unique financial position of their rural schools and districts, rural advocates draw attention to the low tax base in rural communities, which complicates attempts to increase school revenues through property taxation. Additional budgetary strain is generated by rural transportation demands and the poor condition of rural schools, which requires increased expenditures on building maintenance, temperature control, and safety upgrades. Funding adequacy lawsuits have challenged some of these fiscal inequities at the state level, with several courts declaring the state school-funding system as unconstitutional. Grassroots efforts to draw attention to the plight of rural schools via documentaries and online petitions have also become popular in the Southeast and Midwest.

Kara D. Brown

See also Addams, Jane; Consolidation of School Districts; Cubberley, Ellwood; Local Control; No Child Left Behind Act (NCLB); School Size; Small-School Movement

Further Readings

Berry, W. (1990). *What are people for?* San Francisco: North Point Press.

Cubberley, E. P. (1914). *Rural life and education.* Cambridge, MA: Riverside Press.

Davis, A. F. (1967). *Spearheads for reform: The social settlements and the Progressive movement, 1890–1914.* New York: Oxford University Press.

DeYoung, A. J. (Ed.). (1991). *Rural education: Issues and practice.* New York: Garland.

Fuller, W. E. (1982). *The old country school: The story of rural education in the Middle West.* Chicago: University of Chicago Press.

Provasnik, S., KewalRemani, A., Coleman, M. M., Gilbertson, L., Herring, W., & Xie, Q. (2007). *Status of education in rural America* (NCES 2007–040). Washington, DC: National Center for Education Statistics.

Reynolds, D. R. (1999). *There goes the neighborhood: Rural school consolidation at the grassroots in early twentieth-century Iowa.* Iowa City: University of Iowa Press.

Sher, J. P. (Ed.). (1977). *Education in rural America: A reassessment of conventional wisdom.* Boulder, CO: Westview Press.

Theobald, P. (1995). *Call school: Rural education in the Midwest to 1918.* Carbondale: Southern Illinois University Press.

RUSH, BENJAMIN (1745–1813)

Benjamin Rush was a Founding Father and a signer of the Declaration of Independence. Rush contributed widely to the development of the United States as a republic. The scope of his impact and interests included education, medicine, psychiatry, mental illness interventions, the American penal system, and slavery abolition. Whereas Rush is known as a physician in the early republic, he is less familiar as an advocate for public education yet was instrumental in developing a plan for a unified school system in Pennsylvania. The plan called for one university and four colleges throughout the state, an academy in each county, and a free school in each town consisting of at least 100 families. His thoughts on public education were reflected in his plans for a unified educational system.

Raised in Philadelphia, Rush attended the West Nottingham Academy in Maryland and the College of New Jersey, which would later become Princeton University. Having earned a medical degree from the University of Edinburgh, Rush taught chemistry at the College of Philadelphia after having returned to the United States. He eventually founded Dickinson College in Carlisle, Pennsylvania, in 1783, having begun a primary school there 10 years earlier.

Like many of his contemporaries, Rush saw education as a means of preparing Americans for civic life. In *Punishment, Prisons, and Patriarchy: Liberty and Power in the Early American Republic,* Mark Kann explores the tension Rush felt between his commitment to liberty and his fear that citizens could use liberty as a justification for rebellion. Rush, according to Kann, viewed liberty as the freedom to yield completely to a well-run government. Education was the primary means of indoctrinating a free but submissive populace. This perspective is consistent with Rush Welter's depiction of Benjamin Rush's philosophy of education. In *Popular Education and Democratic Thought in America,* Welter notes that republican education in the 19th century was meant to inform the citizenry of their rights and freedom, but the Founders did not expect the people to define those liberties beyond their original scope. John Holder offers a more generous view of Rush's intentions for public education. Holder notes that according to Rush, an educated population was more productive, happier, and therefore more likely to be sustained.

Rush saw his plan for public education as a way of connecting the state of Pennsylvania by one system, including a university, which would provide teachers for the colleges, from which teachers for the academies and free schools would come. The academies and free schools would reciprocate with students for the colleges and university. Yet education, particularly higher education, was available primarily to males. Education beyond the early primary grades provided in the free schools was often limited to boys from families who could afford to pay. Furthermore, it was Rush's opinion that anyone serving in government had to have been university trained. The implication of this reality is that those who were financially limited to the free schools would not be qualified to engage in the process of actually governing but would instead always be governed.

Rush was somewhat progressive for his time in that he believed women should be educated. He applied a utilitarian perspective to education for females as well as males, albeit for different purposes. Advocating for education of women was important to Rush, as he saw women as instrumental in furthering the development of a rapidly growing republic. A learned woman could successfully manage a household and support her husband in his business. Because men were engaged in civic and professional endeavors outside of the home, it would be mothers who provided early instruction for children. More precisely, women would have the primary responsibility in raising males and therefore teaching them the virtues and responsibilities of American liberties. Because American women tended to marry young, education for females needed to be efficient and skill based. Subjects women should be taught, according to Rush, included the arts, religious texts, English, bookkeeping, and some history and philosophy.

Alison Jackson Tabor

See also Common School Movement; Franklin, Benjamin; Jefferson, Thomas; Northwest Ordinance; Webster, Noah

Further Readings

Cott, N. (1977). *The bonds of womanhood*. New Haven, CT: Yale University Press.

Holder, J. (1988). The political and educational philosophy of Benjamin Rush. *Transactions of the Charles S. Pierce Society, 24,* 409–422.

Kann, M. E. (2005). Benjamin Rush: Patriarch of penal reform. In *Punishment, prisons, and patriarchy: Liberty and power in the early American Republic* (pp. 89–109). New York: New York University Press.

Matthews, B. (2001). Women, education and history. *Theory Into Practice, 15,* 47–53.

Rush, B. (1965). *Thoughts upon female education, accommodated to the present state of society, manners, and government in the United States of America* In F. Rudolph (Ed.), *Essays on education in the early republic* (pp. 27–40). Cambridge, MA: Belknap Press. (Original work published 1787)

Rush, B. (1965). Thoughts upon the mode of education proper in a republic. In F. Rudolph (Ed.), *Essays on education in the early republic* (pp. 9–23). Cambridge, MA: Belknap Press. (Original work published 1786)

Straub, J. S. (1967). Benjamin Rush's view on women's education. *Pennsylvania History, 34,* 147–157.

Welter, R. (1962). *Popular education and democratic thought in America.* New York: Columbia University Press.

RUSHDOONY, ROUSAS (1916–2001)

Rousas J. Rushdoony's writings, addresses, and political activism have had a profound influence on the Christian day school and homeschooling movements from the 1960s to his death in 2001, making him one of the 20th century's most important dissenters against the U.S. public school paradigm. Born in 1916 to Presbyterian Armenian immigrants who had narrowly escaped the Armenian genocide during World War I, Rushdoony earned his B.A. and an M.A. in education from the University of California at Berkeley. After further study in divinity, Rushdoony was ordained in the Presbyterian Church, USA. He spent 8 years as a missionary preacher to Native Americans in Nevada, during which time he came under the influence of Calvinist philosopher Cornelius Van Til, whose "Biblical presuppositionalism" argued that the Bible's veracity cannot be debated but must be either accepted or rejected a priori. Building on this claim, Rushdoony spent decades unpacking a biblical view of law, politics, economics, history, family, and education under the auspices of the Chalcedon Foundation, which he founded in 1965.

Three of his views have proven especially influential among conservative Protestants. First, Rushdoony is often cited as the father of "providentialist history," the view that history rightly told reveals God's guiding hand and that the

United States has played, and should still play, a key role in God's divine plan. Rushdoony's account of America's Christian founding, its subsequent betrayal by the forces of secular humanism, and its inevitable restoration as Christians rise up and take back the land that is rightfully theirs exerted profound influence on many of the leaders of the Christian Right in the 1970s and 1980s, notably Francis Schaeffer, Timothy LaHaye, the Rutherford Institute's John Whitehead, and the Home School Legal Defense Association's Chris Klicka and Michael Farris. It has spawned a growth industry of popular historical works that celebrate the United States' "godly heritage" and Christian roots. Second, Rushdoony's claim that the Bible's moral precepts should be the law of nations today has inspired a small but vocal political movement often dubbed "Christian reconstructionism" or "theonomy," which works toward a preordained future when the United States and eventually all the world will be governed by biblical law. Finally, Rushdoony claimed that the restoration of Christian America must begin with "dedicated minorities" who remove their children from public schools that espouse secular humanism and instead teach them in authentically Christian environments, be they Christian schools or homeschools. Two of Rushdoony's books on education, *The Messianic Character of American Education* (1963) and *The Philosophy of the Christian Curriculum* (1981), achieved a readership far beyond his Calvinist base. The first examines the history of public schools in the United States through the educational writings of leading reformers of the 19th and 20th centuries, concluding that the "religion" of secular humanism is the official dogma of public education. The second provides one of the most vigorous and creative accounts ever penned of precisely what a distinctively Christian curriculum should entail. Rushdoony popularized his message through several decades of public speaking at Christian venues and expert testimony in court cases and public hearings defending the rights of Christian schools and homeschools to exist free of government entanglement.

Milton Gaither

See also Christian Day Schools; Homeschooling and the Home School Legal Defense Association; Secular Humanism

Further Readings

Gaither, M. (2008). *Homeschool: An American history*. New York: Palgrave Macmillan.

SAN ANTONIO INDEPENDENT SCHOOL DISTRICT V. RODRIGUEZ

A class action suit was brought against the Texas school financing system, in 1968, by poor families of children attending schools in districts with low property wealth. The plaintiffs alleged that the school financing system, approximately half of whose revenue came from the state and the other half from local property taxes, violated equal protection because it favored property-rich districts.

The federal district court found for the parents and children. The district court ruled that wealth was a suspect classification and that education was a fundamental right under the U.S. Constitution. Because the court ruled education a fundamental right and wealth a suspect classification, the finance system was examined under strict judicial scrutiny and the state was required to show a compelling state interest in distributing school revenue. The court then ruled the state did not meet the compelling interest test as required by the strict scrutiny test for distributing school revenue. The court further stated that the system was not rational nor reasonable, therefore it could not possibly meet the compelling interest test.

In 1973 the U.S. Supreme Court reversed the federal district court. In a 5–4 decision, with Justice Powell writing the opinion, all the lower court arguments were reversed. Justice Powell wrote, "Nor does the Texas school financing system impermissibly interfere with the exercise of a 'fundamental' right or liberty, though education is one of the most important services performed by the state, it is not within the limited category of rights recognized by this court guaranteed by the Constitution." Also, the Court noted that wealth was not a suspect classification, observing that, "This court has never heretofore held that wealth discrimination alone provides an adequate basis for invoking strict scrutiny."

Education is not specifically mentioned in the federal Constitution, therefore it is not explicitly or implicitly guaranteed by the Constitution. Although education is socially significant and extremely important, the Court further stated, "The undisputed importance of education will not alone cause this Court to depart from the usual standard for reviewing a state's social or economic legislation."

Even though great disparities existed in the Texas school financing scheme, they did not violate the federal Constitution. This case was pivotal because it closed the doors of the federal courts to school financing litigation. School financing litigation therefore moved back to the state courts where challenges were made to educational provisions of the state constitutions. Several states have ruled that education is a fundamental right under their state's constitution, compelling the state legislatures to provide equitable and adequate education for the children of those states. Other states have ruled education not to be a fundamental right under their state constitution, thereby continuing fiscal disparities within those states.

Michael David Alexander

781

See also De facto Segregation; Hispanic/Latino
   Education; Serrano v. Priest

Further Readings

Alexander, K., & Alexander, M. D. (2009). *American
   public school law* (7th ed., chap. 20). Belmont, CA:
   Wadsworth Cengage Learning.
Committee for Educational Rights v. Edgar, 672 N.E. 2d.
   1178 S. Ct. Illinois (1996).
DeRolph v. State, 677 N.E.2d.733. S. Ct. Ohio (1997).
Edgewood Independent School District v. Kirby, 777
   S.W. 2d. 391 S. Ct. Texas (1989).
Rose v. Council for Better Education, Inc, 790 S.W. 2d
   186 S. Ct. Kentucky (1989).
San Antonio Independent School District v. Rodriguez,
   411 U.S. 1, 93 S. Ct. 1278 (1973).
Serrano v. Priest, 487 P. 2d 1241 S. Ct. California
   (1971).

SCHOOL-BASED DECISION MAKING

See Site-Based Management

SCHOOL CHOICE

Policies that deliberately promote parental choice of schools, the focus of this entry, are only a very small part of the school choice universe. Such policies are playing an increasingly significant role in educational policy debates in the United States, just as they have over many decades in other Western nations.

The policy debate should be seen against the background of everyday school choice. In our mobile society, the reputation of local schools is a major factor in choice of residence on the part of those who can afford to make such choices. It is common for public secondary schools to offer a variety of programs and courses among which students can choose, often with major consequences for their subsequent opportunities in education and in life. Some of these are vocational (and of course choice among schools may also be for vocational reasons), others respond in large measure to

how willing students are to work hard. In fact, choice is constantly exercised within public education in ways that fundamentally subvert the idea of the "common school" in which a random assortment of young citizens are educated together.

Historical Background

During the middle decades of the 20th century there was an effort, in a number of Western democracies, to extend the undifferentiated elementary school model into secondary education—comprehensive schools in England and the United States, *l'école unique* in France, the *Gesamtschule* in parts of Germany—with what can charitably be called mixed results.

More recently, education reformers have recognized that one size does not fit all in education and that schools with a clear and distinctive focus can in fact be more effective than the "shopping-mall high school." Policies to promote parental choice of distinctive schools have been adopted in New Zealand, Chile, and Colombia, in England, France, Sweden, and Italy, in the United States and Canada, and in other countries.

Such policies are distinct from the long-standing practice of public funding of independent religious schools as an alternative to government-operated schools, a practice that was well established in the 19th century in Belgium, the Netherlands, England, and Canada, and has been adopted more recently in Australia, Spain, Portugal, Germany, and other countries. This has been generally a response to the role churches play in providing schooling for their members, often adopted after decades of political struggle as a concession to the right of religious freedom.

The various international conventions protecting human rights adopted after World War II included provisions recognizing that, in the words of the Universal Declaration of Human Rights (1948), "parents have a prior right to choose the kind of education that shall be given to their children" (article 26, 3). According to the International Covenant on Economic, Social and Cultural Rights (1966),

> the States Parties to the present Covenant undertake to have respect for the liberty of parents . . . to choose for their children schools, other than

those established by public authorities, which conform to such minimum educational standards as may be laid down or approved by the State and to ensure the religious and moral education of their children in conformity with their own convictions. (article 13, 3)

As this Covenant—ratified by the United States—recognizes, religious and moral concerns are the most frequent motivations for establishing and supporting (often sacrificially) nonpublic schools. In the 2001–2002 school year, 83.1% of the pupils attending nonpublic schools in the United States were in schools with a religious character. Nearly half (47.1%) were in Catholic schools and more than one-quarter (28.5%) in schools of a generally evangelical Protestant character. The balance of the pupils were in liberal Protestant, Jewish, Islamic, and Greek Orthodox schools, with only one in six (16.9%) in nonpublic schools with no religious identity.

Since the 1925 U.S. Supreme Court decision *Pierce v. Society of Sisters*, American law has protected the right to operate and to choose schools that are not part of the public system. Unlike in most other Western democracies, however, public funds have not generally been provided to support those parental choices. This is a result of the lingering effects, in state laws and constitutions, of the prejudice against Catholic schools in the 19th century, as well as of the restrictive interpretation of the First Amendment to the Constitution that developed after World War II. As we will see, more recent developments that have nothing to do with a concern for religious freedom have in fact begun in a small way to bring American policies in line with international norms.

These recent developments can primarily be attributed to frustration with American public school systems, particularly though not exclusively in the hyper-bureaucratized form that they take in cities and heavily populated counties. Local school systems have enjoyed a monopoly on publicly funded schooling, resulting in a strong competitive advantage in comparison with nonpublic rivals, and permitting them to assign children to particular public schools on the basis of administrative convenience without concern for the preferences of parents. This began to change in the 1960s. Parental choice within public education developed

largely spontaneously at first, until public officials began to recognize that such choices should function within policies promoting accountability and equal opportunity.

Alternative, Magnet, and Charter Schools

First there was a brief flourishing of "alternative schools," responding to the demands of countercultural parents, followed by public "magnet schools," developed to promote racial integration through attracting racially mixed student populations on a voluntary basis as a way to meet the requirements of court-ordered desegregation without the accompanying controversy of mandatory reassignments. In order to attract White parents to enroll their children in schools with a substantial proportion of Black pupils, magnet schools developed themes such as the arts or language immersion or career exploration. Though still lodged within public school systems, with restrictions on personnel and curriculum, magnet schools frequently developed a distinctive character that showed that public schooling did not have to be monotonously uniform. They also created the expectation that parents could choose schools without changing residence or paying tuition. In some communities "controlled choice" policies were put in place, abolishing attendance zones, so that every school enrolled pupils on the basis of parental choice.

By 1990, however, it had become apparent that magnet schools and controlled choice did not allow enough scope for real diversity and school-level autonomy. Beginning in Minnesota and soon spreading to 40 states, public charter schools became the most fundamental structural change in American education in more than a century. Although state laws differ, the fundamental pattern is that anyone may propose a charter school, spelling out in detail whom it will serve, how it will operate, and how its results will be assessed. If a charter is granted by whatever body is authorized by the state legislation, the school operates as a publicly funded school under its own board or sponsoring organization, subject only to producing the promised results. If it fails to do so after several years, the charter will usually be withdrawn, forcing it to close. Thus with the freedom comes accountability for results of a sort not characteristic of regular public schools.

The state-level laws and the local initiatives that have created more than 4,000 such schools nationwide have made it difficult to generalize about charter schools. The Web site of the Education Commission of the States (www.ecs.org) provides information on how each of 42 jurisdictions deals with each of 25 questions with policy implications. The answers to these questions may vary widely among the states. The details are important, and may make a great deal of difference in how effective charter schools are in a particular state, but of course the overall educational culture of a state, the manner in which the charter school law is implemented, and other factors also have a major effect.

Charter schools have proved extremely popular with teachers (despite union opposition) and with parents, to such an extent that they are a serious threat to faith-based schools. Most state charter school laws explicitly forbid charter schools to have a religious character, but the strong demand from parents for schooling consistent with their own deep convictions has led to a variety of accommodations, and we can expect more in the future.

Vouchers and Tax Credit Programs

The forms of government policy best adapted to satisfying the demand of many parents for schooling with an explicitly religious character—as in most Western democracies—are vouchers and tax credits. Vouchers are certificates for a fixed tuition amount, issued to parents and used by them to "purchase" enrollment of their children at schools of their choice, public or nonpublic, faith-based or not. The idea was proposed by economist Milton Friedman in a 1955 article, later incorporated into *Capitalism and Freedom* (1962), as a way to unleash the "competitive enterprise" that, he argued, would be far more efficient than government in responding to demand for education.

A somewhat different rationale lay behind the adoption of the few voucher programs in the United States: a concern to make it possible for pupils—mostly Black—assigned to failing urban public schools to escape. As with Friedman's proposal, vouchers in Milwaukee, Cleveland, Washington, D.C., and Florida have not been designed explicitly to respond to the religious freedom rights of parents as defined by international law. Litigation about

vouchers has, however, opened the door to public funds for the tuition costs of faith-based and other nonpublic schools. Since the decision about where the voucher will be spent is made by the parent, the U.S. Supreme Court held, in *Zelman v. Simmons-Harris* (2002), that

> the program challenged here is a program of true private choice . . . and thus constitutional. . . . the Ohio program is neutral in all respects toward religion. It is part of a general and multifaceted undertaking by the state of Ohio to provide educational opportunities to the children of a failed school district. (536 U.S. 639)

It is important to note that the Court did not find that parents have a *right* to public funding for their school choices, as in the case in the constitutions of a number of countries, so in the United States it remains entirely up to state legislatures whether to adopt such programs. In addition, their consistency with state constitutional prohibitions of aid to religious schools has not been resolved, though various cases are moving forward on this point.

There are also dangers that a state could attach requirements to use vouchers that would significantly reduce the autonomy of nonpublic schools accepting them; this concern has led to support for the alternative of "tuition tax credits," which would allow parents simply to deduct from their tax obligations all or part of the tuition paid for their children.

Expanding School Choice

Whatever the exact arrangements—and this discussion has not been exhaustive—it is evident that there is a steady trend in the United States toward recognizing that the right of parents to choose the schools which their children attend should, as in other free societies, be supported by public policies and funding. The pressing question now is whether, as has occurred in other countries, increased government support for the choices of parents will come with conditions that limit the real distinctiveness and distort the mission of the schools they choose.

Four primary arguments are used by those urging public policies to expand parent choice of schools in the United States; we are promised

1. that being allowed to shape the education of one's children through school choice is a fundamental matter of liberty guaranteed by various international human rights covenants and by the U.S. Supreme Court;

2. that publicly funded school choice is a matter of justice for poor parents, since more affluent parents already have choice of schools, and provides the only realistic prospect for racial integration in education;

3. that market pressures, freedom from bureaucracy, and freedom to be focused around a clearly defined educational mission will make schools more effective;

4. that variety in the forms of schooling is inherently a good thing, given that pupils have differing strengths and needs and respond well to different approaches.

There are also four primary arguments used against school choice, apart from the seldom-mentioned but very powerful motivation for opposition on the part of the education establishment (including teacher unions), that expanded choice threatens present arrangements and interests within the American educational system. We are warned

1. that school choice will lead to increased racial and social class segregation;

2. that choice will lead to a (further) degradation of the public educational system (or, in the case of choice limited to public schools, to the schools that are already least successful), and thus to worse education for those who do not participate;

3. that choice will lead to new injustices since the poor will not be able to participate on equal terms;

4. that choice will lead to conflict among groups that will not have been socialized by the common public school, but have instead been exposed to dangerous and divisive ideas in religious and other nonpublic schools.

Most thoughtful advocates of expanded school choice concede that all of these possibilities are real and serious, unless choice is organized effectively. Some thoughtful opponents agree that it is possible to organize choice so that these negative effects will not occur. The conflict often comes down to whether it is realistic to expect that, once the genie of choice is let out of the bottle, it will be politically and practically possible to take advantage of its positive effects while preventing negative ones.

Conclusion

In summary, the school choice movement represents a confluence of two sets of motivations. One is concerned with *educational freedom* as a fundamental right of parents to guide the development of their own children and therefore to choose a school in which they have full confidence. For many parents, this will mean a school that shares their own views about what is most important in life: their religious or philosophical worldview. To deny parental choice, or to make it impossibly difficult for parents of modest means, proponents say, is unjust and unworthy of a free society.

The other set of motivations seeks to make public education *more effective* through competition and also through differentiated, focused schools corresponding to the professional judgment of teachers and the varied strengths and interests of students. Such arguments for school choice have been expressed almost exclusively in English-speaking countries; only recently have countries with long-established policies of support for non-government schools begun to ask whether their commitment to the rights of parents may have unanticipated benefits for school quality.

Charles L. Glenn

See also Alliance for School Choice; Black Alliance for Educational Options; Charter Schools; Finn, Chester E., Jr.; Friedman, Milton; Magnet Schools; Tax Credits; Vouchers; *Zelman v. Simmons-Harris*

Further Readings

Enlow, R. (2006). *Liberty & learning: Milton Friedman's voucher idea at fifty.* Washington, DC: Cato Institute.

Finn, C. E., Jr., Manno, B. V., & Vanourek, G. (2001). *Charter schools in action: Renewing public education.* Princeton, NJ: Princeton University Press.

Glenn, C. L., & De Groof, J. (2005). *Balancing freedom, autonomy, and accountability in education* (3 vols.). Tilburg, the Netherlands: Wolf Legal Publishing.

Holmes, M. (1998). *The reformation of Canada's schools: Breaking the barriers to parental choice.* Toronto, Ontario, Canada: McGill-Queen's University Press.

Moe, T. M. (2002). *Schools, vouchers, and the American public.* Washington, DC: Brookings Institution.

Peterson, P. E. (Ed.). (2003). *The future of school choice.* Stanford, CA: Hoover Institution Press.

Peterson, P. E., & Campbell, D. E. (Eds.). (2001). *Charters, vouchers and public education.* Washington, DC: Brookings Institution.

Walberg, H. J. (2007). *School choice: The findings.* Washington, DC: Cato Institute.

Weinberg, L. D. (2007). *Religious charter schools: Legalities and practicalities.* Charlotte, NC: Information Age.

Wolfe, A. (2003). *School choice: The moral debate.* Princeton, NJ: Princeton University Press.

SCHOOL CLIMATE

There is not one accepted, concise definition of school climate. *School climate* refers to the intangibles that can affect the feelings and attitudes of the students, teachers, staff, and parents. It is the way people *feel* about being in the school. More specifically, school climate refers to the physical and psychological aspects of a school that provide the environment necessary for teaching and learning to take place. In recent years, school climate has been acknowledged to have a relationship with student achievement. The fact that more schools are developing improvement plans to foster a positive school climate is a good example of a reform in school improvement strategies. This entry gives a historical perspective of the awareness of school climate, provides four general domains embodied in most definitions of school climate, and identifies options for measuring school climate.

The first educational leader to address school climate in the literature was Arthur C. Perry in his 1907 work, *The Management of a City School.* The book, a guide for future principals, refers to the importance of the feelings of students, staff, and parents. It includes a frank discussion of the importance of the home–school relationship and the students' feeling of safety. Perry also addresses the importance of the moral/ethical development of the child.

In the 1980s a systematic study of school climate was undertaken, following the publication of numerous studies of business organizational climate. Since the 1980s, educational research has documented the positive relationship between school climate and numerous school and nonschool factors. In the move toward more school accountability and transparency, school climate has become recognized as a school reform that contributes to success for all stakeholders.

How School Climate Is Embodied

A review of research suggests that there are four broad areas that embody school climate: relationships, teaching and learning, safety, and the environment. These areas of school climate can be represented by four domains: physical, social, affective, and academic. For a school to have a positive school climate these domains have the following characteristics:

1. *Physical* (Safety): A physical environment that is safe, welcoming, and conducive to teaching and learning

2. *Social* (Relationships): A social environment that promotes communication and interaction among students and among staff and among the community

3. *Emotional* (Environment): An affective environment that promotes a sense of belonging and self-esteem among students and staff and community

4. *Academic* (Teaching and Learning): An academic environment that promotes learning and self-fulfillment for students and staff

Instead of focusing on a specific definition for school climate, common practice describes what a positive school climate looks like. The implication is that a negative school climate is the opposite of the positive. All positive climate descriptions proposed agree that a positive school climate allows principals, staff, students, and parents to focus on the mission of schools rather than expend energy on negative influences. The negative influences and the interactions among them are significant deterrents to successful schools.

But school climate is more than individual experience: It is a group phenomenon. Positive school climate is associated with and/or predictive of academic achievement, effective risk prevention efforts, and healthy youth development, as a group. Positive school climate creates environments where young people can discover how to be lifelong learners, friends, and contributing members of society.

The research relating school climate to student achievement also reveals that risky student behavior is less frequent in schools with positive school climate. Less risky behavior is also related to higher student achievement. Student risky behavior is part of the emotional and social domains of school climate.

In addition, for staff members, a positive school climate is an indication of the trust between the principal and teachers (social domain). Higher scores for school climate indicate higher trust levels among all stakeholders. Another finding is that the better the school climate, the lower the turnover in staff (emotional domain). Positive climate impacts the staff, which in turn impacts student achievement.

Since an open and healthy environment is known to contribute to student achievement, fewer student risky behaviors, and higher teacher retention, overall school improvement can be enhanced by monitoring the school's organizational climate. The most frequently used method to measure school climate is a survey of the school community regarding its perceptions of school life. The results of the surveys can be analyzed to identify areas within the domains that need improvement. The survey results can be used as one source of data in an overall school improvement plan.

School Climate Survey Instruments

There are three dominant school climate instruments: *The Comprehensive Assessment of School Environments* (Kelley, Schmitt, & Loher, 1986); the Organization Health Inventory (OHI; Hoy & Sabo, 1998; Hoy, Tarter, & Kottkamp, 1991), and Organizational Climate Descriptive Questionnaire (OCDQ; Hoy & Sabo, 1998; Hoy et al., 1991).

The CASE survey is part of a package product (CASE–Information Management System [IMS])

for schools to study climate. The survey can be used as a stand-alone survey, not using the IMS options. The package product (CASE-IMS) provides the survey as well as predictive tools and suggestions for interventions that can be used in developing school improvement plans. CASE-IMS is an example of a reform designed by principals for principals. The survey contains 55 items and is administered only to students in Grades 6 through 12, their teachers, and their parents. Reliability and validity of the instruments are not strong; they are still being studied.

The OHI and the OCDQ have separate instruments that are for use in elementary, middle, and high schools. There are between 34 and 50 items, depending on the instrument (OHI/ OCDQ) and the version (elementary, middle, and secondary). The instruments are designed for use with students, teachers, principals, and parents. Reliability and validity estimates vary, with extensive work continuing to be done to document both.

Conclusion

Evaluation of school climate is a springboard for one aspect of school improvement. The results of climate surveys drive the reforms developed and implemented by the administration. Longitudinal data on school climate are used to track such improvements. Making a commitment to improve school climate is doing much more than promoting academic achievement. It is also related to effective risk prevention efforts, healthy work environment, and healthy youth development.

Myra Suzanne Franco

See also Character Education; Co-Curricular Activities; Culturally Relevant Teaching; Moral Development; Moral Education

Further Readings

Center for Social and Emotional Education: http://portal.schoolclimate.net
Cohen, J. (2006). Social, emotional, ethical and academic education: Creating a climate for learning, participation in democracy and well-being. *Harvard Educational Review*, 76(2), 201–237.

Hoy, W. K., & Sabo, D. J. (1998). *Quality middle schools: Open and healthy.* Thousand Oaks, CA: Sage.

Hoy, W. K., Smith, P. A., & Sweetland, S. R. (2002). The development of the organizational climate index for high schools: Its measure and relationship to faculty trust. *High School Journal, 86*(2), 38–49.

Hoy, W. K., Tarter, C. J., & Kottkamp, R. B. (1991). *Open schools/healthy schools: Measuring organizational climate.* Newbury Park, CA: Sage.

Kelley, E. A., Schmitt, N., & Loher, B. (1986). *Comprehensive assessment of school environments.* Reston, VA: National Association of Secondary School Principals.

National School Climate Center: http://www.nscc.csee.net

SCHOOL DISTRICT OF ABINGTON TOWNSHIP V. SCHEMPP

The case of *School District of Abington Township v. Schempp* was consolidated with the case of *Murray v. Curlett* and heard by the U.S. Supreme Court in 1963. These two companion cases were from Pennsylvania and Maryland, respectively. The issue in both was the constitutionality of prayer and Bible reading in the public schools.

The Commonwealth of Pennsylvania had enacted a statute that required "At least ten verses from the Holy Bible shall be read, without comment, at the opening of each public school on each school day." The King James, the Douay Revised, and the Revised Standard versions of the Bible and the Jewish Holy Scripture were texts that were read. After the reading of the Bible, the Lord's Prayer was to be recited. Children were permitted to be excused from these activities with written permission of their parent.

The Schempp family regularly attended the Unitarian Church in Germantown, Pennsylvania. Edward Schempp, the father, brought suit, contending that his rights under the First Amendment were being violated by continuing enforcement in the schools of the statute mentioned above.

The second case originated in Baltimore, Maryland. The Board of School Commissioners of Baltimore City had adopted a rule pursuant to the code of Maryland, which provided that each school in the city "would read a chapter from the bible and/or recite the Lord's Prayer, these activities were to be conducted without comment." Ms. Madalyn Murray, a professed atheist, filed on behalf of her son William a suit claiming her rights under the First and Fourteenth amendments were violated. As in the Pennsylvania case, the children could be excused upon request of the parents.

The U.S. Supreme Court ruled that both of the practices violated the First Amendment of the U.S. Constitution. Using a historical context, the Court explained how religion was interwoven into the American culture. "The history of man is inseparable from the history of religion" as "we are a religious people whose institutions presuppose a Supreme Being." Before ruling, the Court reviewed the history of religion and the U.S. Constitution. The Court explained that some "twenty-three years" before, in 1940, the Supreme Court had ruled, in *Cantwell v. Connecticut,* that states were required to recognize the Establishment Clause of the First Amendment under the Liberty Clause of the Fourteenth Amendment.

The Court then addressed the interrelationship of the two religious clauses of the First Amendment: the Establishment Clause and the Free Exercise Clause. It cited the opinion of Justice Roberts from *Cantwell,*

> The Court in *Cantwell v. Connecticut* . . . where it was said that their 'inhibition of legislation' had "a double aspect." On the one hand, it forestalls compulsion by law of the acceptance of any creed or the practice of any form of worship. Freedom of conscience and freedom to adhere to such religious organization or form of worship as the individual may choose cannot be restricted by law. On the other hand, it safeguards the free exercise of the chosen form of religion. Thus the Amendment embraces two concepts, freedom to believe and freedom to act. The "first is absolute but, in the nature of things, the second cannot be."

Again citing a previous case, this time *Everson v. Board of Education,* Justice Black stated that the "scope of the First Amendment was designed forever to suppress the establishment of religion or the prohibition of the free exercise thereof." In short, the Court held that the First Amendment "requires the state to be neutral in its relations with groups of religious believers and non-believers; it does not require the state to be their adversary. State power is no more to be used so as to handicap religions, than it is to favor them."

The two clauses overlap. The Establishment Clause had been considered by the Court some eight times in the 10 years before the *Schempp* and *Curlett* cases, and, with the exception of one dissent, the Court had always held that legislative power could not be used respecting a religious belief or expression. Then, the Court discussed the test to be used when addressing Establishment Clause cases. The Court's test enunciated in *Schempp* and *Curlett* later became known as "the famous test of religious neutrality." The test used in *Schempp* states that legislation must (a) be secular and (b) that the primary effect is not to advance or prohibit religion.

The Court in *Schempp* and *Curlett* stated, "Applying the Establishment Clause principle, at bar we find that the states are requiring the selection and reading at the opening of the school of verses from the Holy Bible and recitation of the Lord's Prayer by students in unison . . . in violation of the Establishment Clause." Both cases had laws requiring religious exercises and these exercises were not mitigated by the excusal system. Even with the consent of the majority "it has never meant that a majority could use the machinery of the state to practice its beliefs" and in the process violate the free exercise rights of individuals.

In a final note, the Court stated, "the Bible can be studied for its literary and historical qualities, nothing we have said here indicates that such study of Bible or of religion, when presented as a part of a secular program of education, may not be consistent with the First Amendment." Therefore, the public school could teach the Bible from a historical or literary perspective as long as the class was conducted in a secular manner.

Michael David Alexander

See also Edgerton Bible Case; *Engel v. Vitale; Everson v. Board of Education; Lemon v. Kurtzman;* Religion and the Curriculum; Separation of Church and State

Further Readings

Alexander, K., & Alexander, M. D. (2009). *American public school law* (7th ed., chap. 5). Belmont, CA: Wadsworth.

Everson v. Board of Education, 330 U.S. 1, 67 S. Ct. 504 (1947).
Lemon v. Kurtzman, 403 U.S. 602, 91 S. Ct. 2105 (1971).
Illinois ex rel. McCollum v. Board of Education of School District No. 71, Champaign County, Illinois, 333 U.S. 203, 68 S. Ct. 461 (1948).
Lee v. Weisman, 505 U.S. 577, 112 S Ct. 2649 (1992).
Santa Fe Independent School District v. Doe (2000), 530 U.S. 290, 120 S. Ct. 2266.
School District of Abington Township v. Schempp, Murray v. Curlett, 374 U. S. 203, 83 S. Ct. 1560 (1963).

SCHOOL FINANCE

School finance is concerned with the amount of funding available, the way those funds are collected, the way those funds are allocated, and the resources they provide to public education. It is concerned with the equitable distribution of the burden to taxpayers and the benefits to students. This entry reviews the history of school finance in the United States and concludes with a discussion of current practices and issues surrounding school finance.

From the Colonial Period to 1900

The period from the mid-1600s through the very early 1800s is considered the pre-public era in school finance in America. In general, this era saw most education paid for privately; there was little public financial responsibility for schooling. The earliest education in the Colonies in the 1600s in Massachusetts was in the form of apprenticeships for young men only. They not only learned a trade, but also studied religious principles and the law. This education was paid for by the apprentice, himself, in the form of labor services to the "teacher." The "dame" schools, schools that taught both boys and girls, were supported by neighbors who hired a local woman to teach the alphabet and reading (and homemaking to girls). "Common" schools that taught writing, paid for by the families of children who attended, also appeared at this time. At this time the only tax-supported public schools were for the poor. The first widespread education in the Colonies was primarily the responsibility of the churches and supported financially by the churches.

In 1647, Massachusetts passed the first mandatory education law. It required payment by the parents or master of the student or by all the community members, allowing for both private and public financing, thus authorizing the collection of taxes for schools and establishing the framework for using property to fund education. New Hampshire followed suit in 1693, with both the facility and the teacher supported with taxes paid by all citizens. This was the beginning of the first tax-supported schools in America; thus, the first public schools.

By the end of the 17th century, as the population in the Colonies grew and people began moving farther from central areas, they began demanding their own schools and taxed themselves to support the schools. Tax-supported public schools spread through New England, while schools throughout other parts of the Colonies continued to be supported by tuition-type payments. Even as early as colonial days, opposition to school funding existed. As the population centers changed, the people demanded that their tax money go to education in their specific districts rather than to the clergy or church in the central communities. They no longer wanted to pay for a traveling teacher. They wanted their own full-time schools and were willing to pay for them with taxes.

Although public support of education had been introduced, generally, throughout the 1700s most education was still privately funded. By 1791, 4 of the 14 states having their own constitutions had specific education clauses. By this time, academies had replaced many of the earlier Latin grammar schools. The academies taught more practical subjects necessary to maintain the growing economy. The federal government's first effort to fund education occurred during the last quarter of the 1700s. Federal ordinances required land be set aside and either used for educational purposes or sold, the proceeds to be used to finance public education. A short time later, in 1788, with the ratification of the U.S. Constitution, individual state's responsibility for public education was established. After great dissension by early policymakers over where responsibility for education rested, they compromised by including Article X,

which states that that which is not identified as a federal duty will be the obligation of the states. However, despite the growing recognition of the need for everyone to be educated and promotion of "free" public education by such prominent Americans as Thomas Jefferson, Benjamin Franklin, and George Washington, most schools continued to be funded privately by parents, charitable organizations, or religious groups. The first law making all elementary grades available to all students "free" of charge passed in 1827 in Massachusetts, and the first publicly supported high school opened in 1820 in Kalamazoo, Michigan.

By this same year, 23 states had constitutional provisions recognizing the state's responsibility for providing public education and identifying greater state oversight of education than had occurred previously. Industrialization and urbanization exposed inequities much more severe than had been recognized previously. Although compulsory attendance laws existed, there was little uniformity in financing. This was the beginning of the foundation era in school funding. By the mid-1850s, education was the subject of major public interest debates. During this era, the foundation for current funding programs was laid.

Nonetheless, education continued to be available primarily to the wealthy through the middle of the 19th century. Growing opposition to private schooling for the elite, led by people referred to as "common-school reformers," and labeled the common school movement resulted in "free" public elementary education available to all children by the end of the century. Dissent also arose in the post–Civil War South, where Blacks organized and advocated for publicly financed universal education. Additional funding controversy focused on the separation of church and state, that is, the funding of church schools with public state monies. In 1842, New York led the way by approving legislation that prohibited use of state money to finance any school that taught or practiced any religious doctrine. Other states quickly followed New York's lead. The foundation era also saw one of the first legal cases addressing state support of education. In a case commonly referred to as the Kalamazoo case (1874), the Michigan Supreme Court decided the state had the right to levy taxes for support of a complete system of public education.

From 1900 to the Present Day

The Formative Era

The period from 1900 through the 1930s, referred to as the *formative era,* was the period when most state aid programs that exist today were established. This era saw the introduction of formal state-aid programs throughout the country. Similar to the mid-1800s, further industrialization and urbanization exposed major intrastate inequities in education funding. States became involved in an effort to reduce these inequities; they recognized that spending and wealth varied considerably from district to district. Thus, substantial financial responsibility for education began to shift to the state from the local districts and private sources (individuals and churches) of the previous period. For the 1919–1920 school year, an average 83.2% of the funding for public elementary and secondary schools nationwide came from local (and to a very small extent, private) sources, while only 16.5% was from states. By 1939–1940, funding sources had shifted such that 68% came from local governments and 30.3% from states.

The first type of state funding was in the form of flat grants. They provided minimal funding per student, per teacher, or per classroom. Furthermore, as the name suggests, the amount of money was the same for all units across a state. As a result, the inequities that created the impetus for state involvement were not addressed by flat grants. Foundation programs designed to equalize unequal spending patterns due to differences in local wealth were introduced during this era.

This period also saw increases in federal government involvement in financing education. The 1917 Smith-Hughes Act provided grants to states to support vocational education. Initial federal legislation that eventually became known as the School Lunch Program began during this period. From 1919 to 1940, federal government financial support for public elementary and secondary education increased sixfold from 0.3% to 1.8%.

The Special Needs Era

The *special needs era* in school finance spanned from 1940 through 1965. This period marked the formal beginning of concern for equity in funding. National recognition of unfunded or underfunded education for special populations or special program needs was recognized at the federal level. Prior to this time, all students were considered homogeneous except with respect to their district's local capacity to support education. Several national issues were in the forefront, issues that had a major impact on federal funding of education because of their focus on special needs. This era ushered in a focus on vertical equity issues. That is, extra financial support was provided for student and program needs outside of the traditional education framework.

The federal government's role in school finance focused on building and maintaining the nation's defense system and expanding educational opportunities to everyone. As a result of Russia's successful launch in 1957 of *Sputnik,* the world's first artificial satellite, the National Defense Education Act of 1958 provided federal money for the stepped-up teaching of mathematics, science, and foreign languages, and funded other programs critical to the nation's success in the world arena. The Civil Rights Act of 1965 recognized the equal rights of all people regardless of race, religion, or national origin and provided support to school districts in their efforts to eliminate segregation within their systems. This action formalized in law what had already been determined by the courts in *Brown v. Board of Education of Topeka* in 1954 that "separate is not equal" with respect to education. In 1965, the first Elementary and Secondary Education Act was passed; it provided grants for elementary and secondary school programs for children from low income families. Federal assistance was also authorized for training teachers of the disabled, another special needs group, in 1958 by the Education of Mentally Retarded Children Act. By the end of this era, an average of 7.9% of public elementary and secondary revenues came from the federal government.

During the special needs era, states were designing funding programs to coincide with student education needs and taxpayers' ability to pay. Between 1940 and 1965, on average, state funding increased from 30.3% of all elementary and secondary education funding to 39.1%. States continued to fund school districts based on the residents' ability to support them, primarily based on property wealth. In 2004–2005, the state of Vermont funded the highest proportion of district education at 85%, while Nevada funded the lowest proportion at 27.1%. Generally, state financial support is for purposes of horizontal equity; that is, it is an effort to equalize revenues across school districts having differing property values. Meanwhile, most local districts were trying to get residents to vote to increase taxes on their property in order to generate more local money.

The Evaluation Era

The *evaluation era,* between 1965 and 1990, was a period of detailed analysis of the results of public K–12 education. When schools reached out to educate and fund the previously neglected populations, the costs increased and achievement decreased. Arguably the most controversial of these assessments was *A Nation at Risk.* It was during this era that scholars began to question how greatly money mattered with respect to student achievement. It was also during this era that dissenters began to raise intrastate equity issues. No fewer than 28 lawsuits were filed during the period, generally arguing that horizontal equity was not being maintained in the given state. These legal cases most often claimed that the state was not fulfilling its obligation to provide an equitable education to all students according to the state constitution. By the end of this era, state funding had increased to an average of 47.1% of all elementary and secondary school district revenue. Taxpayer revolts also began during this era. California's Proposition 13 in 1978 capped the property tax at 1% of the full cash value of the property.

The Reform Era

The evaluations of the previous period led to the *reform era,* extending from 1990 to 2000. Much legislation directed toward academic improvement was passed during this period, including Goals 2000: Educate America Act, which provided grants to states and local school districts to reform the nation's education system. However, dissension accompanied reform. In order to improve the quality of education deemed to be lacking in the previous era, the federal government as well as state education agencies and state legislatures developed standards to be met by all students in order to progress through the education

system. Dissension grew as education leaders, both scholars and practitioners, objected to the imposition of unfunded mandates. Equity legal cases gave way to adequacy lawsuits. School districts were expected to teach to newly devised standards that purportedly, once met, would provide an adequate education to all students. However, the funding was inadequate to provide the mandated education. At least one adequacy lawsuit was filed in 20 states during this period.

The taxpayer revolt that began in California extended to other states. In 1992, Colorado citizens voted to revoke the state's authority to impose mills ($1.00 per $1,000.00 of assessed value) for property tax or increase income tax without a vote of the public. The Michigan electorate voted to replace property tax for funding schools with increased sales tax and an increased cigarette tax in 1994. This resulted in a shift in state and local funding shares. The state's share went from 37% to 80%; the local share experienced an equivalent decrease. As the result of the court findings in a legal case in 1998, Vermont replaced the local district property tax with a statewide property tax or income tax, depending on specific situations delineated in the law.

The Accountability Era

The present era in public school finance, beginning in approximately the year 2000, has been called the *accountability era.* The No Child Left Behind Act holds all school districts accountable for educating every child to state standards by 2014. Adequacy legal cases continued into the 21st century as school districts argued for money to develop education programs and strategies to teach all students to state standards.

Issues in School Finance

Revenues, as described above, create more dissension than do expenditures. Revenues must meet or exceed expenditures. Lawsuits discussed above were often filed based on expenditure per pupil. Plaintiffs in equity lawsuits argue that more money is spent on students in some districts than on students in other districts in the state. Plaintiffs in adequacy lawsuits argue that the expenditure per pupil in a specific district is inadequate to teach students to high standards. Expenditure per pupil is related to a district's ability (property wealth) and willingness (often considered income though sometimes measured in terms of local tax rate) to tax itself.

Expenditure also refers to how each school district allocates its money to the various budget items. Scholars disagree regarding the importance of expenditure allocations. Some argue that the amount of money received by most school districts is adequate; what is needed is a more efficient allocation of funds. That is, restructure the budget to spend money in ways that have proven to improve student achievement. Others contend that the problem remains one of inadequate funds. Slightly more than 55% of current (excludes capital expenditures) elementary and secondary public school expenditures were consumed by teacher salaries and benefits in 2004–2005. Researchers, such as Linda Darling-Hammond, have shown that teachers are the most important component of student achievement. Since student achievement has gained national attention as described above, policymakers questioned the inconsistency between the high proportion of expenditures going to teacher compensation and the low achievement levels. Attention to this matter led to increased dollars going to faculty development from both the federal government and the states in an effort to improve student performance.

Also in 2004–2005, about 4.6% of current expenditures went to salaries and benefits of student support staff, including counselors, social workers, and the like. Scholars and practitioners argue that because minority and low-income children have the lowest achievement, and research has shown that this stems from lack of preparedness when they enter school as well as from home and family problems they carry with them to school, then it follows that more dollars allocated to more, and perhaps better, support staff could help solve the problem. On average, nationwide, about 10% of all elementary and secondary education current expenditures are for administration. Many school districts spend much more than this and many spend less. Discussions will likely continue on the ideal proportion of budgets allocated to administration and the relationship between administrative expenditures and student achievement.

Besides revenues and expenditures, school finance scholars also study various budgeting patterns: incremental; line-item; program, planning, evaluating; zero-based; and site-based. In an environment of federal and state mandates for student performance, many argue for imposing free market strategies wherever possible. With respect to budgeting, that means site-based. The assumption is that the site administrator is in the best position to make expenditure decisions about her or his building and that competition among site administrators will result in not only more efficient use of money, but also improved student performance. Dissenters contend that site administrators are not prepared for fiscal management responsibilities, and furthermore, traditionally have been the instructional leaders, not the financial leaders. Seattle, Denver, and Cincinnati are a few districts that have tried this approach to budgeting. Cincinnati abandoned it for several reasons, one of which was the argument presented above. Researchers continue to study this issue.

Dissent among school finance scholars has focused on the unit to be studied. Much research has centered on federal and state finance issues. However, because education takes place at the local level and there are many variables involved, most scholars agree that research relating to finance, particularly when looking for the linkages between finance and student achievement, should be done at the school district level. In fact, some even argue, studies at the building and even student level would be most enlightening for making inferences on practice. It is likely that all levels must be studied to get an accurate picture of school finance policies, practices, and needs.

Barbara M. De Luca

See also Adequacy; Equity; Local Control; *San Antonio Independent School District v. Rodriguez; Serrano v. Priest;* Site-Based Management; Tax Credits; Vouchers

Further Readings

Clausen, H. C. (1979). *Why public schools?* San Diego, CA: Supreme Council, 33 Ancient and Accepted Scottish Rite of Freemasonry, Mother Jurisdiction of the World.

Cubberley, E. (1920). *The history of education.* Boston: Houghton Mifflin.

Ladd, H. F., & Jansen, J. S. (Eds.). (1999). *Making money matter: Financing America's schools.* Washington, DC: National Academy Press.

National Center for Education Statistics. (2008). *Digest of education statistics: 2007.* Retrieved August 12, 2008, from http://nces.ed.gov/programs/digest/d07

National Commission on Excellence in Education. (1983). *A nation at risk.* Washington, DC: U.S. Department of Education.

Odden, A. R., & Picus, L. O. (2008). *School finance: A policy perspective.* Boston: McGraw-Hill.

Owings, W. A., & Kaplan, L. S. (2006). *American public school finance.* Belmont, CA: Thomson Wadsworth.

Thompson, D. C., Wood, R. C., & Honeyman, D. S. (1994). *Fiscal leadership for schools: Concepts and practices.* New York: Longman.

Watras, J. (2008). *A history of American education.* Boston: Pearson.

School Size

In the early years of schooling in the United States, schools tended to be very small. Starting almost immediately following the passage of laws making school attendance compulsory, however, reformers began to press for school consolidation as a way to make schools larger and more efficient. Nevertheless, until the 1930s when efforts to consolidate schools became widespread, local school boards did not heed the recommendations of these reforms. By the late 1950s the conventional wisdom of bigger is better had gained acceptance among those seeking to improve schools, including state officials, local school administrators, and educational researchers. Former Harvard University president James Bryant Conant, for example, argued for "comprehensive" high schools that would enroll no fewer than 400 students. In the several decades following the publication of Conant's influential *The American High School Today,* communities, especially those in cities and suburbs, began to build schools that could enroll larger and larger numbers of students. As a result of these mid-century reforms, school sizes increased almost fourfold between 1950 and 1970.

Despite the sharp upward trend in school size, variability still exists. The fierce opposition to consolidation in many rural communities and small towns contributes to this circumstance.

Parents in such communities not only recognize that consolidation breaks the bond between school and community; they also believe that their children fare less well in more remote and impersonal consolidated schools.

Because variability in school size persists, researchers are able to evaluate the influence of school size on outcomes such as students' self-esteem, discipline referrals, school completion rates, participation in extracurricular activities, academic achievement, and career success. According to some commentators, this research overwhelmingly favors smaller schools. Others suggest that the pattern is less clear, particularly with respect to student achievement. A small body of qualitative research, moreover—such as studies focusing on differences in the organizational cultures of private, Catholic, and public schools—appears to support the claim that smaller schools promote healthier relationships, thereby cultivating the engagement of teachers, students, and families. Nevertheless, some studies suggest that small schools can become stagnant or replicate community inequities.

Furthermore, even the research demonstrating the advantages of small schools does not necessarily support a reform package based on the conversion of larger schools to smaller ones. Much of this research takes a structural approach to examining relationships between school size and valued outcomes. Studies in this tradition have demonstrated positive associations between small school size and (a) student attendance, (b) the achievement of students from lower socioeconomic groups, and (c) students' eventual earning. These studies speak directly to the practice of closing existing small schools, but much less directly to the practice of restructuring larger schools into smaller learning communities.

Although reformers in the contemporary small-school movement draw on the structural literature to support their recommendations, they are not convinced that structure alone has a determining influence. In fact, they tend to see smaller school size simply as a preexisting condition permitting a package of small-school reforms to take hold. Proponents of small-school reform, moreover, see this approach as an urban innovation and show little concern for the naturally small schools in rural communities that are being consolidated out of existence.

If small size does not itself characterize small-school reform, what does? Various advocates of this approach recommend practices that they see as critical. Darling-Hammond and colleagues, for example, suggest that small-school reform requires the following practices: small classes and reduced pupil load, advisement structures, coherent and purposeful curriculum, explicit teaching of academic skills, multiple strategies for active learning, real-world connections, performance assessment, flexible supports, and collaborative planning and professional development. Kathleen Cotton provides a somewhat different list, which includes among other key features: autonomy, self-selection of teachers and students, flexible scheduling, clear vision and mission, focus on student learning, detailed planning, personalization, and support for teaching. Despite differences in how they define the practices that characterize the innovation, small-school reformers seem to believe that their approach is likely to produce positive outcomes across a range of settings—small theme schools, large-schools broken up into smaller houses or learning communities, freshman academies, career academies, and alternative schools. Ironically, this faith in the strength of the reform package leads to the implementation of small-school reform in schools that, in structural terms, are quite large.

Unlike many other approaches to school improvement, the small-school movement has received high levels of financial support in the form of grants from the Bill & Melinda Gates Foundation and from the U.S. Department of Education. According to a report sponsored by the Department of Education, the Gates Foundation spent more than $600 million to support this approach, enabling 2,000 high schools in cities across the United States to undertake small-school conversions. Of these schools, 800 remained large structurally but divided students into separate houses. In addition to this support, Congress also allocated $45 million to sponsor small learning communities in 125 schools.

Even with high levels of support, small-school conversions do not seem to be living up to their promise. Varying levels of implementation fidelity may have something to do with the fact that schools adopting small-school reforms do not seem to boost achievement in spite of some apparent improvements in school culture. Findings from a study of Chicago's small schools suggest that, despite increased professional collegiality in these schools, teachers were not changing their methods of teaching. Findings such as these may be responsible for the shift in focus of the Gates Foundation, away from small-school reforms and toward teaching quality.

Nevertheless, the expectation that small-school conversions would result in improved performance over the short term may be unrealistic. After all, the schools undertaking the reforms are facing daunting challenges, including extensive and worsening poverty, bureaucratic impediments, and burned-out teachers. At a deeper level, moreover, the theory of change undergirding small-school reform may be optimistic in its assumption that the culture of trust that researchers report existing in many naturally occurring small schools would be likely to carry over to newly established small-school conversions. As research in rural and small-town schools demonstrates, the trust established between a community and its school is long in the making and easily destroyed.

Aimee Howley

See also Consolidation of School Districts; League of Small Democratic Schools; Rural Education; School Climate; Site-Based Management; Small-School Movement; What Works Clearinghouse

Further Readings

Bard, J., Gardener, C., & Wieland, R. (2006). Rural school consolidation: History, research summary, conclusions, and recommendations. *Rural Educator, 27*(2), 40–48.

Bernstein, L., Millsap, M. A., Schimmenti, J., & Page, L. (2008). *Implementation study of smaller learning communities.* Washington, DC: U.S. Department of Education.

Berry, C., & West, M. (2007). *Growing pains: The school consolidation movement and student outcomes* (Harris School Working Paper: Series 07.03). Chicago: University of Chicago. Retrieved September 12, 2008, from http://harrisschool.uchicago.edu/About/publications/working-papers/abstract.asp?paper_no=07.03

Cotton, K. (1996). *Affective and social benefits of small-scale schooling.* Charleston, WV: ERIC Clearinghouse on Rural Education and Small Schools. (ERIC Document Reproduction Service No. ED 401 088)

Cotton, K. (2001). *New small learning communities: Findings from recent literature.* Portland, OR: Northwest Regional Educational Lab. (ERIC Document Reproduction Service No. ED 459 593)

Cox, D. (2002). *Big trouble: Solving education problems means rethinking super-size schools and districts.* Salt Lake City, UT: Sutherland Institute. (ERIC Document Reproduction Service No. ED 462 221)

Darling-Hammond, L., Ancess, J., & Ort, S. (2002). Reinventing high school: Outcomes of the Coalition Campus Schools Project. *American Educational Research Journal, 39*(3), 639–673.

Gladden, R. (1998). The small school movement: A review of the literature. In M. Fine & J. I. Summerville (Eds.), *Small schools, big imaginations: A creative look at urban public schools* (pp. 113–133). Chicago: Cross City Campaign for Urban School Reform.

Hampel, R. L. (2002). Historical perspectives on small schools. *Phi Delta Kappan, 83*(5), 357–363.

Howley, C. (1996). *On-going dilemmas of school size: A short story* (EDO RC-96-6). Charleston, WV: ERIC Clearinghouse on Rural Education and Small Schools. (ERIC Document Reproduction Service No. ED 401 089)

Howley, C. B., & Howley, A. (2004). School size and the influence of socioeconomic status on student achievement: Confronting the threat of size bias in national data sets. *Education Policy Analysis Archives, 12*(52). Retrieved January 20, 2005, from http://epaa.asu.edu/epaa/v12n52

Howley, A., & Howley, C. B. (2006). Small schools and the pressure to consolidate. *Education Policy Analysis Archives, 14*(10). Retrieved September 30, 2008, from http://epaa.asu.edu/epaa/v14n10

Kahne, J. E., Sporte, S. E., de la Torre, M., & Easton, J. Q. (2008). Small high schools on a larger scale: The impact of school conversions in Chicago. *Educational Evaluation and Policy Analysis, 33*(3), 281–315.

Kuziemko, I. (2006). Using shocks to school enrollment to estimate the effect of school size on student achievement. *Economics of Education Review, 25,* 63–75.

Meier, D. (2002). *In schools we trust: Creating communities of learning in an era of testing and standardization.* Boston: Beacon.

Peshkin, A. (1982). *The imperfect union: School consolidation and community conflict.* Chicago: University of Chicago Press.

School Social Services

Among the many barriers that may prevent children from being successful students are societal and familial disturbances that interfere with their learning. These often include issues such as emotional difficulties resulting from grief and loss of a parent due to death, divorce, military deployment, or incarceration. Many children are being raised by their grandparents or are living in foster care placements. Other major psychosocial problems students deal with include exposure to domestic violence, substance abuse, suicide, teen pregnancy, poverty, hunger, inadequate housing, parental mental illness, and homelessness. Due to the demands placed on educators' schedules, even the most well-intentioned school personnel do not have time to address all the social and emotional needs their students face. It is imperative that they collaborate and communicate effectively with social service providers to meet the plethora of needs children bring with them to school.

School social services can be defined as all resources or programs that are provided for students and their families to address social and emotional issues that cannot be sufficiently addressed by school personnel. School systems hire teachers, counselors, and administrators to provide educational opportunities for students. The main focus of school personnel typically is to provide excellent academic and career opportunities for students. School social services programs vary according to school setting. Regardless of setting, the key to all effective social service programs offered is collaboration efforts between school personnel and social service providers.

Collaboration

Collaboration between social service providers and school personnel is vital to prevent school failure and dropout and to increase academic success for children who are experiencing social and family problems. Typically either an administrator or a school counselor takes on the role as key spokesperson for the school. This person then serves to articulate the needs of the students in his or her building to local community agencies to determine which programs can and should be offered to the students within the school. Collaborative efforts take a great deal of time, yet are very rewarding when students and families benefit from their involvement.

Basic collaboration tips for educators include, but are not limited to (a) conduct a needs assessment, (b) acquire knowledge of social services agencies in one's area, (c) develop positive relationships with social service agency providers, (d) agree on common goals, (e) identify priorities based on needs, and (f) develop a strategic plan to carry out objectives. If collaborative efforts are successful, students and their families will benefit immensely from the assortment of programs offered. Following is a sampling of some common social service programs found in schools at various levels.

Elementary

At the elementary level, one can expect to find many school social service programs. In addition to having school counselors who address personal and social issues of students, some elementary schools also have nurses. Nurses are essential in that they provide necessary social services, from administering medications to collaborating with Children and Family Social Service agencies to prevent and/or report child abuse. Additionally, nurses often work with school counselors to provide sexual abuse prevention programs, substance abuse prevention programs, and character education, anti-bullying, and/or conflict management programs for children.

Some schools also hire social workers to help families obtain the services they need. School social workers visit families in their homes to determine which community services might be most beneficial. School social workers also communicate with school administrators and counselors in efforts to avoid overlap of services between school and community providers. Some school social workers also offer small-group counseling sessions and parenting seminars on areas of greatest need.

Additionally, attendance or truant officers can be found in some school districts. They are vital social service agents as they work with families to make sure students attend school on a regular basis. They assist with providing transportation if needed.

Due to the rise in homeless families in the past 2 decades, programs that address this issue are available to students and their families such as Project HOPE, Project CONNECT, and the HEART project. Many school personnel look to outside agencies and community organizations to fund specific needs for students and their families.

School counselors, teachers, and administrators often turn to churches and area food banks to provide clothing, food, and furniture for families in need. They also work with homeless shelters and departments of children and family services to determine how to meet housing needs of students and their families.

Finally, school personnel also contact their local department of children and family services for other programs available to families within the community. Many departments of children and family services offer cluster programs that provide free counseling services for families in crisis. It is crucial that social service programs be infused at the elementary level.

Middle School

Social services programs in the middle school mirror those found in the elementary setting. However, as children develop and move into adolescence, the need for additional social services programs becomes more prevalent. Many problems that high school students encountered a generation ago are now visible in middle school, such as peer pressure, sexual identity issues, dating, sex, teenage pregnancy, drug abuse, gang involvement, bullying, criminal activity, suicide, self-injurious behaviors, eating disorders, and other mental health diagnoses. Due to their overwhelming job responsibilities, school counselors are not always able to provide the social and emotional support that students need. Therefore, school districts often hire community mental health counselors and/or social workers to provide small-group counseling sessions on topics such as anger management, violence prevention, self-esteem, healthy lifestyles, and gender and/or identity issues. School social workers and community counselors who provide social services in the schools often do so while in close contact with school counselors, teachers, and administrators. Drug prevention programs such as DARE are often offered to middle school students by local law enforcement agencies. Furthermore, some school systems provide suicide prevention, character development, conflict resolution, and peer mediation training to students that are led by an outside social service provider. There are many evidence-based programs available for educators to utilize on the topics listed above.

High School

Additional social services programs are available for high school students to address their unique needs. There is a vast amount of transition planning that happens at the high school level. Students may need vocational guidance for future careers and assistance obtaining credits to graduate rather than drop out of school. Many students need help determining which college to attend, while others need help dealing with parenthood issues. Special programs for expecting teenage mothers and fathers, such as GRADS, are one such example of a school social services program available to students at this level. Other school social services provided at the high school level include: credit recovery programs, alternative schools, Adopt a Family, and parenting programs available through the Juvenile Court System and/or offered by community mental health agencies. Probation officers also are utilized by school personnel to assist teens in legal trouble address their problems and encourage them to remain in school.

Conclusion

Children are faced with a multitude of societal and family problems that may distract and impede them from being successful students. School personnel have a huge responsibility to prepare students academically to transition into the world of work or on to college. They also have an enormous responsibility to prepare students to utilize appropriate personal and social skills that will enable them to be thriving, contributing members of society. Hence, there are numerous reasons why it is beneficial for school counselors, administrators, and teachers to utilize social service programs within their communities.

Kelli Jo Arndt

See also Alternative Schools; Character Education; Conflict Management; Council for Exceptional Children; Guidance and School Counseling; War on Poverty

Further Readings

Allen-Meares, P. (2007). *Social work services in schools.* Boston: Pearson Allyn & Bacon.
Altshuler, S. (2003). From barriers to successful collaboration: Public schools and child welfare working together. *Social Work, 48*(1), 52–63.
Franklin, C., Harris, M., & Allen-Meares, P. (2006). *The school services sourcebook: A guide for school-based professionals.* New York: Oxford University Press.
Moore, J. (2005). *Collaborations of schools and social service agencies.* Greensboro, NC: National Center for Homeless Education at SERVE.
Taylor, L., & Adelman, H. (2000). Connecting schools, families, and communities. *Professional School Counseling, 3*(5), 298–307.

SCHOOLS OF EDUCATION

Teacher education includes the practices, guidelines, and procedures developed for persons aspiring to be teachers with the knowledge, skills, attitudes, and behaviors to be successful in school classrooms and to increase student learning. Universities and colleges that prepare teachers generally have a separate department (school or college) for teacher education. Understanding teacher education includes understanding the history of teaching in the United States. Ensuring and improving the quality of teacher education has always been a concern for school reformers.

Historical Perspectives

In colonial times there was little or no preparation for teachers, especially teachers of young children. Teachers were often hired because they were available and had some education. Teachers of older children often had some advanced subject knowledge but few had any formal training in teaching skills. A normal school was first established by the Reverend Samuel Hall in 1823 in Concord, Vermont, to prepare elementary teachers for classroom responsibilities. This normal school represented the beginning of teacher education in America.

Normal schools generally provided a 2-year program that included subject knowledge as well as teaching strategies. Some students within these normal schools had only an elementary education while others possessed a secondary education diploma. Elementary teachers were encouraged to have some high school education while secondary teachers who evidenced some college education were preferred. Due to the low standards for accepting students into normal schools and the limited program provided, teachers trained through normal schools were not given college credit.

In the early 1900s, normal schools were the major providers of the training for teachers. This training was limited in scope and resulted in teaching not being considered a profession. This perception was also due to the fact that in the early 1900s, the majority of the teachers were women, who at that time were not held in high esteem (indeed, did not have the right to vote). By the middle of the 1900s teaching had come to be regarded as more of a semi-profession: evidenced by lower occupational status, less autonomy for practitioners, and a greater reliance on women in staffing the schools.

Professionalizing Teaching

As the 20th century progressed and more students were enrolled in schools (compulsory education laws were enforced), teacher training and teacher professionalism became more important. This was the beginning of teacher education programs being offered by private colleges and universities, and normal schools offering 2-year programs were beginning to offer 3- and 4-year programs, with many normal schools becoming state teachers colleges. The assumptions of teacher preparation in normal schools included teaching skills, the learning process, and child development; these assumptions greatly influenced teacher training in future teacher education programs, especially at the elementary level. State teacher colleges, however, began to offer more professional education courses and to require extensive teacher training.

There was a difference in the way elementary teachers were prepared and the way secondary teachers were prepared. Elementary teachers were expected to know subject areas as well as how to teach those subjects, while secondary teachers were expected to have a background in a specific subject area but not necessarily to have undergone teacher preparation courses. Many secondary teachers gained their knowledge through liberal arts colleges where they concentrated on one subject area. Three changes in secondary education led to further teacher training at the secondary

level and more courses being offered through teacher education programs. The first change was the offering of courses at the secondary level that were vocational in design, such as home economics and agriculture. Secondary teachers were unable to take courses at a liberal arts university that would prepare them to teach vocational courses. Secondary teachers could find these courses only through teacher education programs.

The second change in secondary education was the mandatory attendance laws, which resulted in not only more secondary students but a more diverse student population in American classrooms. This change influenced the need for specially trained secondary teachers.

The third change was the development of the junior high school. There was a disagreement regarding who should teach seventh- and eighth-grade students. The elementary educators argued that junior high teachers should be prepared in the same tradition as elementary teachers. Secondary educators argued that junior high school teachers should have a liberal arts background. There was some agreement that junior high school students should be taught by teachers educated at liberal arts colleges as well as having training based on normal school assumptions. Normal schools began to work toward including preparing secondary teachers as well as elementary and junior high school teachers. This also led to normal schools becoming state teachers colleges.

These changes meant that more and better prepared teachers were needed in classrooms throughout the United States, and it was at this time that universities began to create schools or colleges of education at the undergraduate level. Prospective elementary teachers and persons wanting to teach nonacademic subjects populated these schools or colleges of education. Persons wanting to teach academic subjects stayed at the liberal arts colleges and were perceived to be more academically prepared. Once again this led to teacher preparation programs being seen as not as intellectually distinguished as other academic areas. The debate over whether teaching is a profession or a semi-profession continues into the 21st century.

The Holmes Group initiative (in 1986) and the use of evidence to ground teacher preparation practices fostered a real move toward professionalizing teaching. The Holmes Group focused on a 5-year program (postbaccalaureate preparation) and the emphasis on evidence was intended to ensure that teaching, like other professions, was grounded in specialized knowledge.

Teacher Testing

Teacher quality has always been a concern to school reformers. Indeed, a significant part of the No Child Left Behind legislation of 2002 related to ensuring that a highly qualified teacher was present in every American classroom. One mechanism for measuring teacher quality has been the use of licensure exams. Those exams have focused on a wide range of skills, including basic skills such as reading, writing, and math as well as pedagogical and academic content skills. States often use the same tests (e.g., the Education Testing Service Praxis Exams), but they establish different passing scores for those exams. Policy reform advocates have questioned whether the tests have really been effective in separating competent from incompetent teachers. They have argued that the tests were too easy and did not focus sufficiently on the academic disciplinary knowledge that teachers needed in order to be successful.

Teacher education institutions and educational reformers have consistently struggled with what it means to educate for teacher quality. Over the past century there has been an emphasis on ensuring that teachers "personify virtue" and have an ability to transmit the civic culture to the young people in their classrooms. These points of focus are still important, but increased attention is now being given to whether teachers know how to foster student learning and whether they possess a deep knowledge of the content they are expected to teach. As a result, licensure exams that measure teacher knowledge of essential pedagogical concepts and disciplinary content have become prevalent in almost all 50 states. What remains unanswered is the connection between how prospective teachers perform on these exams and how well their students subsequently perform on the standardized and high-stakes tests that they are expected to take. In essence, teacher testing is clearly keeping some people out of the profession, but it is also quite clear that reformers have been unable to determine what type of testing can be instituted to ensure that teachers who pass required

licensure exams are also fully qualified to create value-added classroom environments.

Mary Lou Andrews

See also Effective Schools Movement; Junior High School; Kindergarten; Normal Schools; State Departments of Education

Further Readings

Howsam, R. B., Corrigan, D. C., Denemark, G. W., & Nash, R. J. (1976). *Educating a profession.* Washington, DC: American Association of Colleges for Teacher Education.
National Research Council. (2001). *Testing teacher candidates: The role of licensure tests in improving teacher quality.* Washington, DC: National Academy Press.
Sadker, D. M., & Zittleman, K. R. (2007). *Teachers, schools, and society.* New York: McGraw-Hill.
Sikula, J., Buttery, T. J., & Guyton, E. (Eds.). (1996). *Handbook of research on teacher education* (2nd ed.). New York: Simon & Schuster Macmillan.
Smith, E. R. (Ed.). (1962). *Teacher education: A reappraisal.* New York: Harper & Row.

SCHOOL-TO-WORK

School-to-Work was a national effort to develop an educational system that would assist students in the transition from their local schools to the adult workforce. This effort grew out of the School-to-Work Opportunities Act (SWOA) of 1994, signed into law by President Bill Clinton in May 1994. The SWOA provided national financial support for states to develop statewide systems to assist in this effort. Congress was concerned because nearly three-fourths of high school graduates entered the workforce without a college degree. Congress also had grave concerns because most students entering the workforce could not meet the changing academic requirements for entry-level positions.

U.S. employment statistics clearly show that young workers with only high school educations earn considerably less than college graduates and in general are the first to lose their positions in a down economy. The School-to-Work Act was designed to encourage youths to further their postsecondary education while receiving on-the-job experience.

School-to-Work required partnerships between and among many sectors of the local, state, and national population. Business/industry, educators, labor representatives, parents, students, and other community-based organizations were some examples of partnering groups. It was mandatory that three components were in place to receive funding: work-based learning, school-based learning, and activities designed to provide a link between the two.

School-to-work learning is modeled after the old apprenticeship concept, which integrates classroom learning with on-the-job training. This approach, integrating school or theory-based and work or experience-based development, can be an effective way to keep students engaged in learning and skill acquisition. It is similar to the collegiate model of internships. In addition to keeping the students in school, results indicate that the students develop improved school attendance and work attitudes.

Justin Perry and others conducted a study that looked at the self-efficacy of ninth-grade urban youth enrolled in a school-to-work program. In general, the project studied students' perceived confidence in their ability to perform actions to attain specific academic goals. School-to-work programs are designed to make career exploration and career decision making possible. The goal is to help students understand the purpose of school as it relates to their future with the intent of improving motivation to achieve while in school. While the findings of this study produced only two indicators of eight that were statistically significant, there were both qualitative and quantitative indicators to support the school-to-work programs.

School-to-Work sought to make students aware of career opportunities and encouraged lifelong learning. Many students and school districts benefited over the course of its existence; however, in the late 1990s School-to-Work became linked with outcome-based education and, as such, was seen more often as an example of the national government micromanaging the lives and careers of families and the impressionable youth of America. Resources were believed to be directed away from raising standards, improving discipline, and strengthening the core curriculum and moved toward

careers in business and industry, local partnerships, and other collaboration.

School-to-Work was one of the few national efforts to support high school students choosing to follow a career or technical path after high school since the Smith-Hughes Act of 1917, which provided funds to train individuals who had chosen to work on the farm as their career. It forced states to develop state boards of vocational education in order to receive funds. Funds could be used for salaries for vocational teachers, but could not be used for academic teacher salaries. Though the intention was not to segregate systems of education, the result was a separate and more isolated and distinct vocational system of education.

Another program that has integrated vocational curriculum with more comprehensive academic curriculum and provided a seamless link with 2-year postsecondary institutions is Tech Prep. This program evolved from the Carl D. Perkins Applied Technology and Vocational Education Act, most recently reauthorized as the Carl D. Perkins Vocational and Technical Education Act of 1998. Unlike School-to-Work, Tech Prep attempts to attract all students, whether they are vocationally or academically focused.

The change in U.S. national presidential leadership in 2001, however, brought a change in federal educational focus. Funding shifted to No Child Left Behind. As a result, School-to-Work initiatives ended abruptly in some states and more gradually in others.

Daniel J. Milz

See also Business and Educational Reform; Career Education; Compensatory Education; Competency-Based Education; Continuation Schools; Differentiated Instruction; Experiential Learning; General Education; High Schools That Work; Job Corps; Life Adjustment Education; Manual Training; Service Learning

Further Readings

Arbona, C. (2000). The development of academic achievement in school-aged children: Precursors to career development. In S. D. Brown & R. W. Lent (Eds.), *Handbook of counseling psychology* (3rd ed., pp. 270–309). New York: Wiley.

Blustein, D. L., Juntunen, C. L., & Worthington, R. L. (2000). The school-to-work transition: Adjustment challenges of the forgotten half. In S. D. Brown & R. W. Lent (Eds.), *Handbook of counseling psychology* (3rd ed., pp. 435–470). New York: Wiley.

Blustein, D. L., Perry, J. C., & DeWine, D. (2004). School-to-work transition. In C. Speilberger (Ed.), *Encyclopedia of applied psychology* (Vol. 3, pp. 351–353). San Diego, CA: Academic Press.

Carl D. Perkins Vocational and Technical Education Act of 1998, Pub. L. No. 1-5-332 (1998). Retrieved February 10, 2009, from http://www.ed.gov/offices .OVAE/CTE/legis.html

The National Vocational Education (Smith-Hughes) Act, Pub. L. No. 347 (1917). Retrieved March 1, 2009, from http://www.cals.ncsu.edu/agexed/sae/smithugh.html

Paris, K. (1994). *A leadership model for planning and implementing change*. Madison: University of Wisconsin–Madison, Center on Education and Work.

Perry, J., DeWine, D., Duffy, R., & Vance, K. (2007). The academic self-efficacy of urban youth. *Journal of Career Development, 3,* 103–126.

School-to-Work Opportunities Act of 1994, Pub. L. No. 103-239,108 Stat.568 (1994). Retrieved March 17, 2009, from http://www.seanet.com/~barkonwd/school/ STWOACT.HTM

SCIENTIFICALLY BASED RESEARCH

Scientifically based research is the systematic application of the scientific method resulting in reliable and valid information with the potential to improve educational practice. At the level of practice, scientifically based research is the clear development of best practice, as determined by rigorous and replicable empirical research. Scientifically based research became especially significant with the adoption of the No Child Left Behind (NCLB) legislation and represented one of the most significant aspects of the proposed NCLB reforms.

Although there are many formal definitions of scientifically based research (e.g., the American Educational Research Association, the Center for Comprehensive School Reform and Improvement), arguably the most influential definition appeared in 2001 when President Bush authorized the No Child Left Behind Act. Scientifically based research, according to the No Child Left Behind Act, "means research that involves the application of rigorous, systematic, and objective procedures to obtain reliable and valid knowledge relevant to education activities and programs." Most formal definitions of scientifically based research, including that in the No Child Left Behind Act, include specific characteristics:

Explores meaningful questions. Scientifically based research must seek answers to questions that are socially relevant to students and practitioners in today's schools and must be framed in such a way that allows the results to be generalized beyond the sample studied.

Defines replicable procedures. Scientifically based research must include sufficient detail in its description of the dependent variables and steps for implementation so that other researchers can reproduce the research or build on the findings with further investigations.

Uses valid and reliable measures and/or observational techniques. Scientifically based research must use sound and objective means of collecting the data, relying on established measures and observational techniques.

Relies on appropriate design and analyses. Scientifically based research must thoughtfully match the research methodology to the question and apply appropriate data analysis strategies to draw valid conclusions.

Allows independent review. Scientifically based research must allow for rigorous examination of the research methodology, tools, and conclusions, by qualified researchers not connected to, or invested in, the project's outcome.

Critics of scientifically based research have taken issue with both foundational and practical components. For instance, some have argued against the notion that one has the ability to know anything objectively. According to these critics, since creating definitions is in itself a subjective experience, there is no sensible way to objectively define the methodology or describe the research tools with the precision required for replication. More practical criticisms have been leveled at the value placed on different research methodologies. Since the Institute of Education Sciences values randomized trials (i.e., the random assignment of research subjects to treatment and control groups) as the "gold standard," some researchers have felt that other methodologies (usually those that are more qualitative in design) are not seen as useful or valuable.

For example, there is little recognition by the Institute of Education Sciences that qualitative or single-subject design models contribute to the scientifically based research base of knowledge. Because scientifically based research is primarily concerned with establishing causal relationships (i.e., this intervention leads to this outcome), the focus must be on ensuring that the empirical investigation is of the highest quality, rather than narrowly focusing on the specific methodology. As Robert Horner and colleagues have clearly articulated, however, well-designed and -executed single-subject research can be appropriate and even desirable for establishing initial causal relationships when the affected population is small and strict controls and procedures are in place. As with any research, establishing a firm causal relationship requires that research be replicated over time, with a wide variety of subjects and in diverse settings. Recall in the medical field that the generally accepted "causal" relationship between smoking and cancer in humans was initially suggested by correlational investigations that demonstrated that smokers were much more likely to develop cancer of the lung, oral cavity, pharynx, larynx, and esophagus.

Under the leadership of the U.S. Department of Education, the field of education is in the early stages of utilizing scientifically based research. The Institute of Education Sciences moderates the What Works Clearinghouse, one of the first attempts to systematically review and disseminate scientifically based research. Established in 2002, the What Works Clearinghouse is designed to offer standards for reviewing research in education, to provide practitioner-friendly guides for effective practice, and to present guidelines for program evaluation and decision making. The Johns Hopkins University School of Education's Center for Data-Driven Reform in Education (CDDRE) operates a similar resource of scientifically based research; the *Best Evidence Encyclopedia* (BEE). With grant support from the Institute of Education Sciences, the *Best Evidence Encyclopedia* provides comprehensive information regarding the empirical support for a wide range of educational programs, designed specifically to address K–12 interventions.

Michael Rozalski

See also Evidence-Based Education (EBE); Individuals with Disabilities Education Act (IDEA); No Child Left Behind Act (NCLB); Reading First; What Works Clearinghouse

Further Readings

Algozzine, B. (2003). Scientifically based research: Who let the dogs out? *Research and Practice for Persons With Severe Disabilities, 28*(3), 156–160.

Eisenhart, M., & Towne, L. (2003). Contestation and change in national policy on "scientifically based" education research. *Educational Researcher, 32*(7), 31–38.

Horner, R. H., Carr, E. G., Halle, J., McGee, G., Odom, S., & Wolery, M. (2005). The use of single-subject research to identify evidence-based practice in special education. *Exceptional Children, 71*(2), 165–179.

Odom, S. L., Brantlinger, E., Gersten, R., Horner, R. H., Thompson, B., & Harris, K. R. (2005). Research in special education: Scientific methods and evidence-based practices. *Exceptional Children, 71*(2), 137–148.

Shaker, P., & Ruitenberg, C. (2007). Scientifically based research: The art of politics and the distortion of science. *International Journal of Research & Method in Education, 30*(2), 207–219.

Smith, A. (2003). Scientifically based research and evidence-based education: A federal policy context. *Research and Practice for Persons With Severe Disabilities, 28*(3), 126–132.

SCOPES MONKEY TRIAL

See Creationism

SECONDARY CURRICULAR REFORM

The history of American education demonstrates how nonlinear the process is of determining the best means of delivering basic education to young people in the United States. Initially most of the emphasis was on how to educate those students who were of elementary age, and by 1880 almost 10 million young people were enrolled in some type of elementary experience. In the late 1800s, secondary schools as well as colleges and universities were just emerging as a reality. As the nation moved from rural to urban living and as the United States became much more industrial, the skills needed to drive the economy required an increasingly educated workforce. Educational reformers sought to provide that workforce through a series of systematic reforms, all oriented to educating the masses and to ensuring that each student had an opportunity to achieve his or her full intellectual potential.

Beginnings

One of the first high schools to be established was the Boston English Classical School. Public high schools were not a reality in the early 1800s. Secondary education was delivered through private academies, and most of the early secondary schools that did exist charged a tuition fee. By the mid-1800s there were several thousand private academies throughout the United States. No single curriculum existed across these schools or academies. Some prepared students for college and others offered a more general curriculum. Clearly, paying tuition represented a significant problem for many students. The Kalamazoo Court Case in 1874 was significant because it ruled that taxes collected to support public schools represented a legal way of delivering secondary education. In many respects the modern secondary school was a result of the Kalamazoo decision. Once it became possible to fund secondary schools with taxes, it then became possible for communities around the United States to find ways to educate their older youth. Still, the evolution of the modern high school occurred slowly and it was not until the 1930s and 1940s that public high schools became widespread across the United States.

Conant, the SAT, and the Committee of Ten

One of the chief architects of the modern public secondary school was James Bryant Conant. He was a strong advocate for public school reform, and he assertively argued that with enhanced and redesigned educational structures the United States would become a better and safer place for everyone to live. That is, democracy could be preserved. Conant was also instrumental in implementing the use of the SAT as a way of removing some of the

historic favoritism that had been granted to those who came from privileged backgrounds. Specifically, colleges and universities needed a better and fairer means of determining which students could succeed in and should be admitted to college. Conant was able to articulate through his leadership the way in which children should be educated from the earliest grades through college. He wanted to create a seamless educational process that would allow all of America's youth to explore their full potential and that would essentially sort students according to their academic abilities. The SAT was a part of that sorting process. Conant wanted the best and brightest to be prepared for the most responsible positions within communities, but he wanted all young people to be educated so that they could be full participants in the maturing democratic experience.

The Committee of Ten was established in 1892 by the National Education Association, and its focus was on the development of national policy relative to the structure of high schools. The Committee was composed primarily of college professionals, and its goal was to create a curriculum to help young people be better prepared for college academic work. The Committee's recommendations were significant and consisted, for example, of ensuring that some traditional and classical courses would be taught sequentially and that Carnegie Units (i.e., student seat time) would be used to assess student progress.

The *Cardinal Principles*

The Committee of Ten was a precursor to the work of another commission, the Commission on the Reorganization of Secondary Education, which issued the *Cardinal Principles of Secondary Education,* published in 1918. The *Cardinal Principles* are significant because they laid the foundation for the development of comprehensive high schools that would offer a variety of curricula based on the needs of diverse student populations within the new high schools. In essence, through the *Cardinal Principles* the modern high school emerged and the education of all young people became more of a reality. Since that time, there have been a variety of experiments about how to be more successful in actually educating young people to reach their potential. Clearly, many teenagers experienced success within the comprehensive high school context. Equally true, many young people found that the environment did not engage them, and especially in urban areas the dropout rates were often alarmingly high. Indeed, the second half of the 20th century evidenced a spate of reports on how to reform comprehensive high schools to better ensure the success of all students.

Effect of Compulsory Attendance

According to the U.S. Department of Education, in 1890 about 6% of eligible youths were attending high school and 4% were graduating. By 2000, the success of the United States in matriculating students in high school programs could be seen through some compelling and dramatic changes in student attendance rates: 96% were attending high school and 73% were graduating. Part of the dramatic change in the attendance was the result of compulsory attendance laws, which first appeared in the mid-1800s. By 1900 approximately 30 states had compulsory attendance laws in place, and by 1918 every state evidenced compulsory attendance for students aged 5 through 13.

Fundamental Issues

Educators and policymakers throughout the 20th century grappled with three fundamental issues, and they looked to schools to help solve the associated problems. First, educators were looking for ways to assimilate young people from diverse backgrounds into American society. Second, they were dealing with fundamental issues about whether and how students, because of racial or cultural differences, should be separated for educational purposes. At the beginning of the century, "separate but equal" was permitted (*Plessy v. Ferguson*), but in 1954 (the Brown decision) it was declared unconstitutional. Finally, educators struggled with what it meant to create schools that could deal with the pluralistic nature of American society. These three problems surfaced in many different ways and resulted in attempts by educators to find ways to educate every child to his or her full potential. They also resulted in heated debates about the nature of the school curriculum and the attendance patterns of students within American schools.

Curriculum Delivery and Student Competence

Toward the end of the 20th century, policymakers began to focus more on what students were actually learning. That is, many of the 20th-century fights were about where young people should be educated (i.e., should African American students be integrated into traditional comprehensive high schools), but by the end of the 20th century the battles began to focus on what students of all races and ethnic groups needed to know in order to be successful adults. As a result, states began to mandate comprehensive minimum competency exams, and the questions that surfaced related to how different types of schools performed in terms of ensuring that students were able to graduate with the minimum competencies needed to be economically and socially competitive.

In essence, once secondary schools became an established part of the educational landscape they first focused on ensuring student attendance and then on having students complete a certain number of Carnegie Units as a condition of graduation. If students attended school and completed the units, they could graduate. By the beginning of the 21st century the end game had changed and policymakers were now looking at ways to ensure that students actually possessed the understandings needed for them to be successful in college or in a job. By 2002, 18 states had some form of exit testing as a condition for graduation and by 2008, 23 states evidenced the use of either minimum competency exams, comprehensive exams, or end-of-course exams.

Helping students acquire the essential basic skills and intellectual dispositions meant that reformers were looking at the different ways in which the secondary curriculum could be delivered. More and more people were questioning whether the comprehensive high school represented the best structural design for the delivery of secondary content. Leon Bottstein, for example, questioned the traditional 4-year high school experience and argued for a new design that would accommodate the types of developmental differences evidenced in young people across the United States. The Gates Foundation expressed concern over the large number of dropouts and proffered the "small-school" solution. The small-school approach was grounded on the assumption that comprehensive high schools were simply too large and as a result student anonymity was too prevalent. By designing high schools of 300–500 students, educators could better ensure that each secondary student's needs would be addressed and that each secondary student would actually be known by a teacher.

Conclusion

The history of educational reform at the secondary level illustrates the move from simply creating structures where all students could receive an education to creating structures where all students could receive the knowledge they need to be successful. In some ways the reforms have been very successful and in other ways far too many students, especially those in urban areas, are still being left behind. The current secondary reforms are addressing questions around how to help urban and rural students be successful who up to this time have had mixed success within secondary education models that are available in their respective communities. Reforms of the next decade will likely continue to look at alternative structures that can be used in helping each student acquire the knowledge and skills needed to become economically competitive as an adult.

Thomas J. Lasley II

See also ACT and SAT Tests; Cardinal Principles Report; Carnegie Unit; Committee of Ten; Conant, James Bryant; Early College High Schools

Further Readings

Ferguson, A. (2009, May). The SAT and its enemies. Fear and loathing in college admissions. *Weekly Standard*, pp. 18–27.

Krug, E. A. (1969). *The shaping of the American high school, 1880–1920*. Madison: University of Wisconsin Press.

Newman, J. W. (1998). *America's teachers: An introduction to education*. New York: Longman.

Sadker, M. P., & Sadker, D. M. (1994). *Teachers, schools, and society*. New York: McGraw-Hill.

Spring, J. (1989). *American education: An introduction to social and political aspects*. New York: Longman.

SECTION 504 OF THE REHABILITATION ACT

Section 504 of the Rehabilitation Act of 1973, Public Law 93-112, 87 Stat. 394 (Sept. 26, 1973), codified at 29 U.S.C. § 701 et seq., is a civil rights law that prohibits discrimination against individuals with disabilities. The U.S. Rehabilitation Act of 1973 prohibits discrimination in programs conducted by federal agencies, in programs receiving federal funds, in federal employment, and in the employment practices of federal contractors on the basis of disability. There are four key sections of the Act, Sections 501, 503, 504, and 508. Section 504 states that "no qualified individual with a disability in the United States shall be excluded from, denied the benefits of, or be subjected to discrimination under" any program or activity that receives federal funds, public or private, or that is conducted by any federal executive agency or the U.S. Postal Service. Section 504 is considered to be the first civil rights statute for persons with disabilities. It extends to individuals with disabilities the same kinds of protections Congress extended to persons discriminated against because of race and sex. It protects children and adults with disabilities from exclusion, and from unequal treatment in schools, jobs, and the community. Section 504 was a first step in educational reform for students with disabilities as it ensured access to public education and it also set the stage for future litigation and legislation that has improved the lives of persons with disabilities. Unfortunately, it took 4 years and civil disobedience in the form of citizen protests and sit-ins before the regulations were endorsed and compliance with the law was enforced.

Protections and Enforcement

The protections under Section 504 extended to any person who (i) has a physical or mental impairment that substantially limit one or more of such person's major life activities, (ii) has a record of such impairment, or (iii) is regarded as having such impairment. A physical impairment is defined as: any physiological disorder or condition, cosmetic disfigurement, or anatomical loss affecting one or more body systems. Examples include epilepsy, AIDS and HIV, allergies, arthritis, broken limbs, cancer, cerebral palsy, diabetes, hemophilia, heart disease, Tourette's syndrome, and visual impairment. A mental impairment is defined as any mental or psychological disorder, such as mental retardation, organic brain disorder, emotional or mental illness, and specific learning disability. Examples include attention deficit disorder/attention deficit hyperactivity disorder (ADD/ADHD), conduct disorder, depression, eating disorders, and social maladjustment. Major life activities include caring for oneself, seeing, hearing, speaking, breathing, walking, performing manual tasks, learning, and working. The person also must be qualified for the services or job in spite of his or her disability. For example, to qualify for services in a public school a person must be of public school age.

The Disability Rights Section in the Civil Rights Division of the Department of Justice carries out responsibilities under Section 504, and each federal agency has its own set of Section 504 regulations that apply to its own programs. Agencies that provide federal financial assistance also have 504 regulations covering those entities that receive federal aid. Some common requirements of these regulations include accommodation for employees; program accessibility; effective communication with individuals who have visual or hearing disabilities; and accessible new construction and alterations. Each agency also is responsible for enforcing its own regulations.

Although the Rehabilitation Act was signed into law in 1973, compliance and enforcement of it was weak because the regulations still needed to be endorsed by the Department of Health, Education and Welfare (HEW). In addition, Congress did not provide any funding for this legislation and encouraged compliance only by threatening to withhold future funds for noncompliance. Frustration mounted and in 1977 the American Coalition of Citizens with Disabilities (ACCD) staged protests in a number of cities around the country, demanding that the regulations be signed. On April 28, nearly 4 weeks into a sit-in in San Francisco, HEW Secretary Joseph Califano finally endorsed the regulations.

Impact on Public Education

Over the years, Section 504 has had a significant impact on public education reform as it guarantees students with disabilities equal opportunities to benefit from educational programs and facilities. Prior to this law the burden of accessibility was on the child and family, and many children with disabilities were not able to attend public schools. Schools have complied with Section 504 by providing ramps, enlarging restrooms, and otherwise removing physical barriers. More recently, schools were challenged to take responsibility under this law to remove barriers that may impede learning. For example, a child may need special seating because of a hearing or vision problem. Another child may require an alternative (or additional) way of receiving instruction, such as taped lectures or large-print books, or of being tested orally over the coursework or using non-timed tests.

Section 504 regulations require that school districts provide a *free appropriate public education* (FAPE) to any qualified person with a disability within the district's jurisdiction. In addition, section 504 provides for the rights of students with disabilities for issues outside of the school day such as extracurricular activities, sports, and after-school care. Section 504 also provides for a placement evaluation involving multiple assessment tools to assess specific areas of educational need. Service decisions must be made by a team of persons familiar with the student and who understand the evaluation information and options. Students served under Section 504 also must have an individualized accommodation plan that details the services provided. In public schools, 504 accommodation plans are developed for students with a variety of conditions, such as ADD/ADHD and conduct disorder. Due process procedures also must be provided by the district with an impartial hearing for a parent who disagrees with the identification, evaluation, programming, or placement of his or her child under Section 504. Examples of noncompliance that have been found in schools include: failing to provide physical access to programs or facilities; imposing double standards for eligibility for extracurricular activities; and failing to design regular classroom programs to meet a student's individual needs as adequately as the needs of other students.

Section 504 accommodations began as mainly providing physical access for persons with disabilities and now entail many various accommodations beyond physical access, such educational opportunities. The Disability Rights Section of the Civil

Rights Division of the Department of Justice estimates that their activities affect 49 million people with disabilities, 80,000 units of local and state government, 100 federal agencies and commissions in the executive branch, and 6 million businesses and nonprofit agencies.

Criticisms

Criticism of Section 504 stems from the issues of no federal funding for schools to provide accommodations and the vagueness of the language in the law and regulations. Costs for school districts include the staff time spent working directly with students as well as for planning and advocating for students' needs. Additional costs have been incurred from the thousands of lawsuits filed since the early 1970s between parents and school districts. This lack of funding may be causing dissension toward the very group it is intended to help.

In addition, the language of Section 504 is vague, and school personnel have been confused as to their responsibilities. Problems with Section 504 gave rise to further reform in educating children with disabilities, and in 1975 the Education for All Handicapped Children Act was enacted. It mandated all school districts to educate students with disabilities and it provided federal funding. In 1990, this law was amended and is now called the Individuals with Disabilities Education Act (IDEA). In 2004, IDEA was reauthorized and called for more accountability at the state and local levels for student outcomes.

Christine Ann Christle

See also Civil Rights Act of 1964; Individuals with Disabilities Education Act (IDEA); Special Needs Education

Further Readings

Katsiyannis, A., & Conderman, G. (1994). Section 504 policies and procedures: An established necessity. *Remedial and Special Education, 15,* 311–318.

U.S. Department of Education, Office for Civil Rights. (2007). *Free appropriate public education for students with disabilities: Requirements under Section 504 of the Rehabilitation Act of 1973.* Washington, DC: Department of Education.

Yell, M. L. (2006). *The law and special education* (2nd ed.). Upper Saddle River, NJ: Pearson Prentice Hall.

SECULAR HUMANISM

Secular humanism is a worldview that shares a common heritage with similar philosophies and worldviews, including Renaissance humanism and traditional humanism. Secular humanism is consistent with rationalism, agnosticism, and atheism in that adherents do not subscribe to biblical doctrines but regard human nature as pure and the world understandable through the power of reason, thus precluding a need for, or interest in, the supernatural. Secular humanists often contend that religion is a private matter and has no place in the public square or the public schools. This often puts secular humanists in conflict with conservative Christians, who believe that Christianity should have a prominent place in public life. These disputes often take place in the public school arena as secularists dissent from certain policies and proposed reforms that seem to them to advance religion, such as proposals to include creationism or intelligent design in the science curriculum, or to eliminate treatment of homosexuality from discussions of human sexuality.

Renaissance Humanism

Renaissance humanism originated in the late 14th century as an intellectual movement that developed as European scholars rediscovered ancient Latin and Greek texts. Originally, a humanist was a teacher of Latin literature, but by the mid-15th century, Renaissance humanism promoted the study of the ancient world, specifically Greece and Rome, because it was seen as the pinnacle of human achievement and should be taken as a model by contemporary Europeans.

Renaissance humanism offered to the European world emerging from the so-called dark ages the necessary intellectual and philological tools for textual analysis, including textual criticism of Biblical texts, creating a controversy with the church. This crisis came to a head with the trial of the scientist Galileo Galilei (1633), which pitted the authority of a belief in one's own observations against the authority of religious teaching. The trial made the contradictions visibly apparent, and humanism was branded a "dangerous doctrine" by the church authorities. It became, therefore, very difficult and somewhat dangerous to openly espouse a belief in humanism.

To avoid conflicts between humanist beliefs and the church, intellectuals made great attempts to meld the works of Antiquity with Christian values in a type of Christian humanism. This allowed ethics to be taught independently of theology. Through this bending of tradition, the authority of the church was tacitly transferred to the reasoning logic of the educated individual. Nevertheless, humanists were still constantly in danger of being labeled as heretics by the church. Interestingly, it was the Renaissance humanist emphasis on returning to the original sources that contributed greatly to the Protestant Reformation. One of the key points of the Reformation was the belief in a more accurate translation of Biblical texts. Early religious humanists included Desiderius Erasmus, a Dutch Catholic priest, and Sir Thomas More, a devout Catholic from London.

Modern Humanism

Organizations espousing humanism began to appear in the United States in the 1920s. The First Humanist Society of New York was organized in 1929, and the American Humanist Association was organized in 1941. There have been three documents published under the title *Humanist Manifesto* (1933, 1973, and 2003) that outline the tenets of modern humanism. Each new version updates and replaces the previous edition.

Humanism is generally compatible with atheism and agnosticism, but neither position is required. Although secular humanism rejects all endorsement of supernatural beliefs in resolving human affairs, those beliefs themselves are not necessarily rejected. Because humanism includes intellectuals from a variety of fields of thought, there are groups of humanists that function in a role analogous to that of a religious organization. There are a number of countries that, for the purpose of laws, give rights to "religions." In these countries, humanist organizations have become legally recognized as equivalent to a "religion" for legal purposes. In the United States, the U.S. Supreme Court, through a

footnote to *Torcaso v. Watkins* (1961), recognized humanism as equivalent to a "religion" in the limited sense of authorizing humanist groups to conduct ceremonies commonly carried out by officials of religious groups. Contrary to a popular belief, however, this case did not officially classify humanism as a religion in this country.

Religious humanists hold to three basic propositions: honest and serious scholarship; belief that human affairs are immanent, not transcendent; and a commitment to practice religious teachings. They often embrace some form of theism, deism, or supernaturalism without being aligned with any organized religion. Religious humanists do not hold supernatural assertions as a necessary source for their moral values. Human beings are central, and all moral value and authority comes from the centrality of humans for religious humanists. One of the attractive features of religious humanism is that it allows for the full expression of human emotions, a concept that is sometimes ignored by other humanists. Religious humanism has been most closely associated with the Unitarian Universalist denomination, which publishes the *Religious Humanism* periodical. There is also an organized group of Jewish humanists.

Secular humanists reject all theistic religious beliefs and any belief in the existence of a supernatural world. They base their beliefs on the assumption that supernatural beliefs cannot be supported using rational arguments and therefore they must be completely rejected. Many secular humanists are strongly antireligious and tend to dismiss all other groups as not qualifying to be labeled as true humanists. Secular humanists have been officially organized as a separate group since 1979. There have also been student organizations formed on college campuses in recent years. Since there are multiple religious organizations on the typical college campus, organizers believed it was important that a free-thought organization also be formed on every campus.

Humanism Today

The late Rev. Jerry Falwell, an evangelical Christian pastor and conservative commentator, blamed many contemporary problems in U.S. society on the influence of secular humanism. These included abortion on demand, public acceptance of homosexuality, the growth of the pornography industry, widespread use of illicit drugs, the decline of public education, and the legalization of prostitution and gambling. This accusation led to a common assumption, especially among conservative religious groups, that secular humanists were nonbelieving, immoral God-haters; the initial effect of such attacks was a decline in activism among humanists. In recent years, however, a backlash against the conservative Right has invigorated a new generation of humanists. The problem humanists still face, though, is the common notion that all humanists are atheists; more than half of all Americans view atheists unfavorably, according to a 2002 Pew Forum on Religion and Public Life survey.

A potentially more serious problem for secular humanists is an apparent erosion of evidence for a basic tenet of humanism; namely, that as the world's population becomes richer and better educated, it will become less and less religious. A corollary axiom is that science should increasingly displace dogma, and reason should completely replace unthinking religious obedience. This, however, does not appear to be the case. Conservative religion, both Christian and Islamic, is growing rapidly around the world, even as humankind experiences a great period of scientific progress and the creation of much wealth. Interestingly, the fastest growing Christian denominations are those that have refused to accept and adapt to secularism; at the same time, denominations that have tried to be "modern" and "relevant" are losing members. The Christian population in Africa alone is expected to double to 630 million by 2025, with conservative denominations and organizations leading the way.

Secular Humanism and Public Education

The most common points of contention for secular humanists over activities in public schools today are in two areas. The first is the constitutional principle of separation of church and state. In this area, secular humanists appear to be prevailing as court case after court case has removed more manifestations of state-sanctioned religion from the public schools, including government-sponsored prayer, devotional Bible reading, Ten Commandments displays, the teaching of creationism in science classes, and clergy-led prayer at graduation ceremonies. Student-led religious activity, however, continues to enjoy broad constitutional protection. The second area is the teaching of biological evolution, which secular humanism insists must be free of arguments that depend on the supernatural and are thus by definition unscientific. On these grounds, secular humanists are opposed to the teaching of the rival theory of creationism, or what they believe to be its thinly disguised twin, intelligent design or ID. The teaching of these theories in the context of science classes is viewed as an intrusion of religion on the legitimate province of science. As more religious conservatives get involved in political life and become more active in local schools, this clash will most likely intensify. Clearly, secular humanism and its adherents will continue to be involved in heated debates in the public school arena, sometimes as dissenters from practices they abhor, such as including the phrase "under God" in the Pledge of Allegiance, and sometimes as advocates of reforms they favor, such as a greater emphasis on evolutionary biology in science classes.

Herbert L. Steffy

See also Creationism; Ethical Theories; Intelligent Design; Religion and the Curriculum

Further Readings

Bowers, M. (2007). *Secular humanism: The official religion of the United States of America.* Frederick, MD: PublishAmerica.

Johnson, P. E. (1998). *Reason in the balance: The case against naturalism in science, law & education.* Downers Grove, IL: Intervarsity.

McDowell, J. D., Hostetler, B., & Bellis, D. H. (2002). *Beyond belief to convictions.* Carol Stream, IL: Tyndale.

Mohler, R. A., Jr. (2008). *Desire and deceit: The real cost of the new sexual tolerance.* Phoenix, AZ: Multnomah.

Sears, A., & Osten, C. (2005). *The ACLU vs. America: Exposing the agenda to redefine moral values.* Nashville, TN: B & H.

SEPARATION OF CHURCH AND STATE

The issue of separation of church and state is an umbrella for a variety of disputes in the marketplace of ideas in the United States. For example, the separation of church and state prohibits churches from endorsing candidates for political office. Any church, temple, or mosque that specifically endorses a candidate stands to lose its tax-exempt status. Specifically related to public schools, the issues include prayer in schools, intelligent design, the Ten Commandments, the Pledge of Allegiance to the American flag, school vouchers, and the teaching of the Bible in the curriculum. This entry reviews the arguments about the separation of church and state as it pertains to the First Amendment, outlines the significant U.S. Supreme Court rulings that have consistently upheld the separation of church and state, and suggests ways that school boards can be proactive in dealing with challenges to the separation of church and state.

Ninety percent of the children of the United States attend public schools. The diversity of religious beliefs among these children and their families defies description. The more diverse the country becomes, the more important the principle of the separation of church and state. The idea of separating church and state includes, but is not limited to, the First Amendment's insistence that no one church would be privileged in America. Thus, the United States does not have an established church. In addition, the First Amendment protects all citizens from the intrusion of religious beliefs into the public arena, especially the public schools.

On one side of the pressure to tear down the wall of separation of church and state are Christians who believe that the United States is a nation under divine authority, founded as a Christian nation, and intended by our founding fathers to be aligned with Christianity. The emotion-laden, reductionistic arguments that God has been outlawed from the public school, or prayer has been banned, have led to assertions about the moral demise of the nation in general and of schools in particular. Once again, as in the debates over intelligent design, the Bible taught in the schools, prayer, and the Ten Commandments, the public schools have been the target of attack; they are viewed as valueless institutions that are failing to teach both explicitly and implicitly the values young people need as they mature and grow.

The conservative religious reform argument that public schools are responsible for the moral fiber of the United States represents a common fallacy of

logic: "After this, therefore on account of this— *post hoc ergo propter hoc.*" Some religious reformers want the church–state separation mitigated, or at least returned to the halcyon days of their own early educational experience.

On the other side are advocates for maintaining the wall of separation first envisioned by Thomas Jefferson with help from James Madison and a Baptist preacher, Isaac Backus. Since we are a diverse country, the church should attend to religious education, not the public schools. Some of these modern "separationists" are determined to have a religion-neutral and completely secular public school. Opponents of this stance argue that this approach denies the significant role played by faith in the development of this country. Americans, it is argued, are a very religious people, and a public education scrubbed of all references to God, faith, and religion would diminish the value of education. Consequently, we need reminders of our religious heritage and tradition.

There are common misperceptions about the proper role of religion in public schools. Conservative Christians, for example, argue that prayer has been expelled from the schools. That is not true. The Supreme Court did not expel prayer, but said that school officials could not compose prayers for students to recite. The Court removed government-sponsored worship. Another misleading claim is that Bible reading has been banned from public schools. In fact, it is perfectly acceptable for students to read the Bible on a voluntary basis during recess and before and after school. A third misleading claim is that teachers must avoid all mention of religion. The actuality: Schools are allowed to take religion seriously in the curriculum and, at the same time, meet the Free Exercise needs of students.

In short, God has not been expelled from public schools; prayer has not been outlawed; we do have separation of church and state as "settled law" in America; we have freedom of religion as well as freedom from religion; the First Amendment applies to the states. Voluntary student participation in religious activities is protected. The only prohibition that relates to the public schools is that state-sponsored religion has been banned. Public schools are not allowed to promote nor prohibit religious belief or nonbelief. Public schools are obligated to protect the freedom of conscience of every student.

The Supreme Court has provided guidance to schools and churches in its interpretations of the First Amendment. In 1963, in *Abington School District v. Schempp,* the court banned school-directed recital of the Lord's Prayer and reading of Bible passages as part of "devotional exercises" in public schools. *Stone v. Graham,* a 1980 case, banned the posting of the Ten Commandments on public school classroom walls. In 1985, the Court ruled, in *Wallace v. Jafree,* that "daily moments of silence" were illegal when students were encouraged to pray during the silent periods. A 1990 case, *Westside Community Board of Education v. Mergens,* held that schools must allow student prayer groups to organize and worship if other nonreligious clubs are also permitted to meet on school property and time. In 1992, *Lee v. Weisman,* the Supreme Court outlawed prayers led by members of the clergy at public school graduation ceremonies. In 2000, the Court ruled, in *Santa Fe Independent School District v. Doe,* that student-led pregame prayers at public high school football games would not be allowed.

The complexity of the cases involving the separation of church and state creates special challenges for school boards and local school principals. Some educational reformers may be swayed by a personal religious desire to return to the schools of an earlier time when Christianity was the majority faith and thus was accorded priority with morning prayer and Bible study. Others will be tempted to create a school environment where every vestige of religion is stripped away. Both of these extremes are unconstitutional.

Within these polarities it is imperative that school leaders take religion seriously in the curriculum, make sure they do not promote religion, and protect and honor the Free Exercise activities of their students. Indeed, this may represent the true face of reform: the exercise of religious belief that is personal rather than corporate. Toward that end, perhaps the most important contribution that public school educators can make to the principle of separation of church and state is to engage their students in a study of the First Amendment to the Constitution. Surveys indicate that a majority of American high school students give little or no value to the rights guaranteed in the First Amendment. Teaching students the value of the First Amendment is not the same as teaching them a particular version of the Christian faith. It is a safeguard against those who are agitating for a "Christian" public school system and those arguing for a "secular" public school system.

Rodney Wallace Kennedy

See also Amish and Mennonite Schools; Catholic Schools; Edgerton Bible Case; Episcopal Schools; Islamic Schools; Jewish Schools; Religion and the Curriculum

Further Readings

Feldman, N. (2005). *Divided by God: America's church–state problem—and what we should do about it.* New York: Farrar, Straus, & Giroux.

Gaustad, E. S. (1999). *Church and state in America.* New York: Oxford University Press.

Nord, W. (1995). *Religion and American education: Rethinking an American dilemma.* Chapel Hill: University of North Carolina Press.

Taylor, C. (2007). *A secular age.* Cambridge, MA: Belknap Press.

SERRANO V. PRIEST

In the case of *Serrano v. Priest,* 487 P. 2d 1241 (S.Ct. California, 1971), the plaintiff sued contending that the California system of funding public schools violated the Fourteenth Amendment to the U.S. Constitution. The complaint alleged (a) the quality of a child's education was a function of the property wealth where the child lives, (b) the quality of the education was a function of the geography depending on the district where the child resides, (c) the educational needs were not taken into account because generally poor children have greater and more costly educational needs, and (d) the inequitable apportionment of state resources creates great disparities in educational quality.

In 1968–1969, 55.7% of California's school revenues came from local property taxes, 35.5% from state sources, 6.1% from federal sources, and 2.7% from miscellaneous funds. Since the majority of funding came from local property taxes, the amount of revenue generated from property taxes depended on the property wealth of the district. In 1969–1970, the property wealth or assessed valuation per student ranged from a low of $103 per pupil in the poorest district to $952,156 in the wealthiest district. This was a ratio of approximately 10,000 to 1.

The court rejected the plaintiff's argument that the school finance system violated the California state constitution. The court stated "we reject . . . [the] argument that the provision in Section 5 [California State Constitution] for a 'system of common schools' requires uniform educational expenditures."

The court then addressed the issue of whether the financing program violated the Fourteenth Amendment of the U.S. Constitution by questioning whether wealth was a suspect classification. The court stated, "Plaintiffs contend that the school financing system classifies on the basis of wealth. We find this proposition irrefutable." Therefore, the court found that funding formulae discriminated against children living in property-poor districts since these districts had a high dependence on local property taxes. There were great funding disparities among school districts and, since the California court declared education a fundamental interest, the state was compelled, under strict judicial scrutiny, to justify the method of public school financing in California. In 1973, the U.S. Supreme Court would reject the argument that wealth is a suspect classification, thereby requiring only a rationale basis for distributing educational financing and not the strict scrutiny where the state would be required to show a compelling reason for justifying the distribution of school funds (*San Antonio Independent School District v. Rodriquez*, 411 U.S. 1 93 S. Ct. 1278, 1973).

Although the *Serrano* decision, with respect to the Fourteenth Amendment to the U.S. Constitution, was reversed by the Court in *Rodriquez*, the *Serrano* decision was the beginning of school finance litigation. After the *Rodriquez* case plaintiffs challenged school finance funding under the state constitution provisions.

M. David Alexander

See also Equal Education Opportunity; *San Antonio Independent School District v. Rodriguez*

Further Readings

Alexander, K., & Alexander, M. D. (2008). *American public school law* (7th ed.). Belmont, CA: Wadsworth Cengage Learning.

Committee for Educational Rights v. Edgar, 672 N.E. 2d 1178. S. Ct. Illinois (1996).

DeRolph v. State, (1997). 677 N.E. 2d 733. S. Ct. Ohio.

Edgewood Independent School District v. Kirby, (1989). 777 S.W. 2d 391 S. Ct. Texas (1989).

Rose v. Council for Better Education, Inc., 790 S.W. 2d 186 S. Ct. Kentucky (1989).

San Antonia Independent School District v. Rodriquez, 411 U.S. 1, 93 S. Ct. 1278 (1973).

Service Learning

Service learning, a form of experiential education, has its roots in the ideas and writings of educational philosopher John Dewey. Dewey declared that the aim of community effectiveness calls attention to the fact that authority must be relative to doing something worthwhile, and to the reality that the things most in need of being done are things that entail one's connection with others. Furthermore, social efficiency includes that which makes a person's experience more meaningful to others, as well as that which enables one to contribute more completely in the experiences of contemporaries. As a result of Dewey's work and that of the National Society for Experiential Education (NSEE), many forms of experiential learning can be found in Grades K–16 in public as well as in private education. Some examples include: tutoring, mentoring, cooperative learning, collaborative learning, internships, public service, and youth service.

Service learning as a term first appears in the late 1960s in the publications of the Southern Regional Education Board whose primary writers were Robert Sigmon and William Ramsay. In 1969, the Office of Economic Opportunity established the National Student Volunteer Program, which later became the National Center for Service Learning. In 1971, this program and two others—Peace Corps and VISTA—combined to form the federal agency ACTION.

Service learning was introduced to and present on many college campuses during the late 1960s and the 1970s. From the mid-1980s, service learning on campuses increased in popularity. In 1985 the Education Commission of the States began Campus Compact or the Project for Public and Community Service. Today, this is a national coalition of more than 1,100 college and university presidents—traditionally involving more than 20 million students—devoted to promoting community service, civic engagement, and service learning in university education.

As a result of community service and the spread of service-learning programs, the NSEE began to establish a set of principles of good practice in 1987. This effort culminated in a 1989 Wingspread conference hosted by the Johnson Foundation at which the Principles of Good Practice in Combining Service and Learning were articulated. Wingspread offered the ideal that any definition of service learning must represent service combined with learning, which adds value to each and transforms both.

After this conference Kendall and Associates published the classic three-volume set, *Combining Service and Learning*, under the auspices of the NSEE and in collaboration with 91 national and regional associations. The document contains a wide range of resources on service learning in K–12 and higher education plus an annotated bibliography on service-learning literature.

NSEE hosted another Wingspread conference in 1991. As a result of the push for research on the benefits and effects of service learning, the *Michigan Journal of Community Service Learning* was launched in late 1994.

In recognition of the need for a widely agreed-on definition of service learning and a set of standards by which to judge programs, a diverse group of service-learning educators formed the Alliance for Service Learning in Education Reform, or ASLER. They defined service learning in 1993 as a system by which young people discover and extend through active involvement in thoughtfully organized service experiences that

- meet actual community needs,
- are coordinated in collaboration with school and community,
- are integrated into each young person's academic curriculum,
- provide structured time for a young person to think, talk, and write about what he/she did and saw during the actual service activity,

- provide young people with opportunities to use newly acquired academic skills and knowledge in real life situations in their own communities,
- enhance what is taught in the school by extending student learning beyond the classroom, and
- help foster the development of a sense of caring for others.

The federal government's interest in and support of service learning increased dramatically in the 1990s as well. This was due in large measure to the passage of the National and Community Service Act of 1990. This Act reflected President George H. W. Bush's campaign pledge of a "thousand points of light," and led to the creation of the first White House Office of National Service and the Points of Light Foundation. President Bill Clinton's campaign stressed the establishment of a national "service" program that culminated—after much debate—in the passage of the National and Community Service Trust Act of 1993. This legislation brought together the Commission of National and Community Service, ACTION, and the newly established National Civilian Community Corps that merged to form the Corporation for National and Community Service, known as the Corporation for National Service (CNS).

This corporation is responsible for the establishment and maintenance of three major volunteer, community service, and/or service-learning programs: Senior Corps, AmeriCorps, and Learn and Serve America. The goal of all three groups or programs is to provide opportunities for Americans of all ages and backgrounds to *serve* their communities and country.

In early 1999, the National Center for Education Statistics (NCES) of the U.S. Department of Education conducted the first National Student Service-Learning and Community Service Survey. This survey provided consistent nationwide estimates of the proportion of schools, elementary through high school, that introduced service learning into their curriculum. In addition, the most recent data on schools engaged in community service were collected.

Throughout the short history of service learning, there still appears to be divided opinion as to its definition and some confusion distinguishing it from community service. In the above-cited NCES survey, community service was defined as activities that are noncurriculum-based and are recognized by and/or arranged through the school. The study defined service learning as curriculum-based neighborhood or community service that

- incorporates classroom training with community service projects organized in relation to a school-based curriculum, with plainly stated objectives;
- addresses an authentic community request;
- lasts over a period of time; and
- assists participants in drawing lessons from the service through frequently scheduled, organized reflections or critical analysis of activities, such as discussions, presentations, or reflective writing.

Thomas A. Kessinger

See also Civic Education; Cooperative Learning; Curricular Controversies; Dewey, John; Experiential Learning; National Center for Education Statistics (NCES); National Council for the Social Studies; Presidents and Educational Reform; Progressive Education; U.S. Department of Education

Further Readings

Alliance for Service-Learning in Education Reform. (1993). *Standards of quality for* school-based service-learning. Chester, VT: Author.

Campus Compact: http://www.compact.org

Corporation for National Service. (1993). *The National and Community Service Trust Act of 1993.* Washington, DC: Author.

Dewey, J. (1930). *Democracy and education: An introduction to the philosophy of education.* New York: Macmillan.

Kendall, J. C., & Associates. (Eds.). (1990). *Combining service and learning: A resource book for community and public service* (Vols. 1, 2). Raleigh, NC: National Society for Internships and Experiential Education.

National Council for the Social Studies. (2000). Service-learning: An essential component of citizenship education. *Social Education, 65*(4), 240–241.

Shumer, R. D. (1999). *Service, social studies, and citizenship: Connections for the new century.* Bloomington, IN: ERIC Clearinghouse for Social Studies/Social Science Education. (ERIC Document Reproduction Service No. ED 430 907)

Sigmon, R. (1994). *Linking service with learning in liberal arts education.* Washington, DC: Council of Independent Colleges.

SESAME STREET

Sesame Street, an educational television program for preschool children (ages 3–5), is one of the longest-running educational television shows. It debuted in 1969 and continues to run to the present day. *Sesame Street* is of interest not only for its longevity and popularity, but also for the unique contribution educational research makes in supporting its production. The show has reached iconic status and is familiar to a large proportion of the nation's population. Further, the show developed a strong international following and has been shown in 140 countries. The show has won more Emmy Awards than any other television series and continues to earn accolades and recognition.

Sesame Street's success has largely been attributed to its unique format. The show integrates live actors, puppets, and animation. The cast includes a set of familiar recurring characters (both actors and puppets). Initially, the show struggled for popular acceptance because the actors and puppets were kept in separate scenes on the basis of psychologists' recommendations to keep fantasy and reality elements separated; however, once scenes were rewritten to combine both elements, the show immediately attracted the attention of children. The approach allows children to be introduced to a variety of sensitive topics through nonthreatening and familiar characters. Through this tactic, young children are introduced to the alphabet, counting, and some basic words. Perhaps more important, children are taught the values of honesty, sharing, and community, as well as safety and health.

The show has specifically targeted inner-city, perhaps disadvantaged youth; however, it has been accepted and adopted by children from all backgrounds. Emerging on the heels of the Civil Rights movement, the show has been particularly sensitive to issues related to multiculturalism. The show is intentionally set in a diverse, urban setting.

Another unique aspect of the show's commitment to multiculturalism was the occasional introduction of Spanish words. These words were a conduit for teaching language skills as well as respect for different cultures and an appreciation of diversity. This technique has been adopted and used in shows such as *Dora the Explorer* and *Maya and Miguel.*

Sesame Street was launched by the Children's Television Workshop (CTW), an organization created specifically to provide sound programming for preschoolers, who had been underserved in the television era. The CTW's founders conducted research on the viewing patterns of children and discovered that kids learn best from the television when selections are kept short and when music and jingles are integrated into a show's segments. The same successful format was eventually used by other CTW created shows: *The Electric Company, 3-2-1 Contact,* and *Ghostwriter.*

Master puppeteer Jim Henson was brought in with his Muppets. Henson had coined the term *Muppet* to refer to his unique style of marionettes combined with puppets. The Muppets were a mix of people, outlandish characters, and animals. The Muppets were designed to allow children to connect with the characters on multiple levels. Iconic characters include Big Bird, an enormous yellow bird with a childlike naiveté; Oscar the Grouch, a perpetually cranky character who lives in a trash can; Grover, an irrepressible and enthusiastic character; Cookie Monster, with an insatiable appetite; Kermit the Frog, who offers a mature introspective voice; and Bert and Ernie, roommates who demonstrate conflict management skills; among many others. The Muppets provided a safe and entertaining method for exploring sensitive topics, as well as created an exciting atmosphere for learning. Each character has different dispositions and levels of maturity, allowing children an opportunity to see themselves in different characters as they confront different life issues.

Approximately 130 episodes have been produced each year. Each episode contains about 40 separate vignettes or skits on different topics. Each skit is designed to achieve specific educational goals and objectives. Each segment was tested for achievement of goals, as well as the attentiveness of the children and parents. Segments that did not satisfy the researchers on a number of fronts were dropped. The focus on these instructional variables helped the show compete for viewers who had other viewing options. In fact, the focus on attentiveness was pioneered in the show answering the question, "How can children's attention be captured through educational programming?" This research base included invaluable information, such as how long attention can be focused, what production techniques help maintain attention, and the influence of particular characters on particular types of content.

Hundreds of studies have been completed on *Sesame Street*'s cognitive effects. Since its beginnings the show has combined educational research to inform the content and implementation of the show. In fact, the show has its own education and research department. Scenes are created by a team of writers and then shared with the education and research department to ensure a healthy and educational experience. This is quite a different relationship from that which exists on many children's shows.

Successful shows prior to *Sesame Street*, such as *Captain Kangaroo,* had educational aspects but had not made the application of educational research a priority; educational segments were generally written by producers without formal expertise in education. Often, production experience and luck had been relied upon to create a successful show, without concern for empirical research. *Sesame Street* changed this relationship. In fact, the Educational Testing Service was recruited to perform summative research. Formative research was viewed as even more important than summative research and the commitment to it justified the in-house research department. A commitment to research, combined with the creative forces of television writers and producers, has made *Sesame Street* a continuing presence in our culture.

David Richard Moore

See also Educational Radio; Educational Television

Further Readings

Clark, D. A. (2008). *Sesame Street* and the reform of children's television by Robert W. Morrow. *History of Education Quarterly, 48*(3), 477–479.

Mandel, J. (2006). The production of a beloved community: *Sesame Street's* answer to America's inequalities. *Journal of American Culture, 29*(3), 3–13.

Rice, M. L., Huston, A. C., Truglio, R. T., & Wright, J. C. (1990). Words from "Sesame Street": Learning vocabulary while viewing. *Developmental Psychology, 26*(3), 421–428

Truglio, R. T., & Fisch, S. M. (2000). Introduction. In S. M. Fisch & R. T. Truglio (Eds.), *"G" is for growing: Thirty years of research on children and Sesame Street.* New York: Erlbaum.

SETON, ELIZABETH ANNE (1774–1821)

Elizabeth Anne Bayley Seton was the founder and first Mother Superior of the Sisters of Charity in the United States. She is often credited with establishing the first Catholic parochial school in the United States, but the claim is dubious. Without question, however, Seton should be credited with spreading and systemizing Catholic education in the first quarter of the 19th century and leaving a legacy that affected the development of Catholic education for the next 150 years.

Early Life

Seton was born in New York on August 28, 1774, the daughter of a surgeon, Richard Bayley, and Catherine Charleston. As a student, Seton showed real aptitude and was described as personable but introspective. She wed William Seton, Jr., in 1794 and was responsible for raising five children.

In 1798, Elizabeth and William inherited responsibility for both the family company and the welfare of his three young sisters. Elizabeth managed the care of both families in the Seton household and homeschooled her own children and her sisters-in-law.

The family fortunes took a turn for the worse in 1801 when the company went bankrupt and William showed signs of tuberculosis. In 1803 Elizabeth, William, and their oldest daughter traveled to Italy in an effort to restore his health. He died shortly after arrival and left Elizabeth a widow with five young children.

Conversion to Catholicism and the Religious Life

A family friend, Antonio Filicchi, and his wife provided gracious hospitality until the Setons could return to the United States the next spring. In fact, it was the Filicchis who introduced Elizabeth to Catholicism. Seton returned to the United States in 1804 and became a Catholic on March 14, 1805. Her initial years in the Church were marked by a community hostility that prevented her from beginning a school in New York.

The Sulpicians, an order of French priests, invited Seton to Baltimore in 1808 to establish a small school in the city for the education of Catholic children. Within a year, Seton took religious vows and established the Daughters (later Sisters) of Charity of Saint Joseph and was given the title "Mother Seton" by Archbishop John Carroll.

A wealthy seminarian and fellow convert gave Seton land for the establishment of a motherhouse near Emmitsburg, Maryland, and Elizabeth and her group arrived in the small community in June 1809. The Reverend John Dubois, founder of Mount Saint Mary's College and Seminary, also in Emmitsburg, offered his cabin on Saint Mary's Mountain for the women to use until they were able to move to their property. Elected by the members of the community to be the first Mother Superior of the Sisters of Charity in 1812, Seton was reelected successively and remained as Superior until her death.

The Sisters of Charity and the Education of Children

In February 1810, Elizabeth opened Saint Joseph's Free School for the education of "needy girls"; it was the first free Catholic school for girls in the country staffed by sisters. Saint Joseph's Academy began in May of that year. By boarding pupils who paid tuition, the Sisters of Charity subsidized their charitable free school operations.

The order grew in numbers during the first decade of its existence. Numerous women joined the Sisters of Charity. Of the 98 women who arrived at the convent in Elizabeth's lifetime, 86 candidates actually joined the order and 70% remained Sisters of Charity for life. Illness and early death were a constant in Elizabeth's life. In addition to two of her daughters and her sister-in-law, she buried 18 Sisters at Emmitsburg.

The Sisters of Charity intertwined social ministry with education in the faith and religious values in all they undertook in their mission. Elizabeth dispatched Sisters to Philadelphia to manage Saint Joseph's Asylum, the first Catholic orphanage in the United States in 1814. The next year she opened a mission at Mount Saint Mary's to oversee the infirmary and domestic services for the college and seminary near Emmitsburg. In 1817, Sisters from Saint Joseph's Valley went to New York to begin the New York City Orphan Asylum.

Impact on the Evolution of Catholic Education

It is hard to overestimate the importance of Seton and her order on the evolution of American Catholic parochial education. Indeed, Seton developed what would become the model for the typical Catholic parochial school in the United States for the next 150 years.

For the most part, Seton's schools were supported by tuition from Catholic parishes or communities; as such, these schools functioned as autonomous units on the local level. Thus the success of Seton's schools was heavily dependent on the financial support of the parents of the children in the classroom.

The success of Seton's schools also was dependent on a steady stream of religious vocations. Parochial school classrooms were staffed by Sisters who took the education as their religious charism. These women made enormous personal sacrifices that ensured the survival and success of the Seton model.

Finally, the Seton model implicitly imposed a curricular model that was decidedly American in culture, values, and content. To be sure, Catholic doctrine was a vital thread in the classroom day, but most of the instruction was conducted in English and concentrated on secular subjects. Without stating as much, Seton's model promised to prepare young Catholics for productive roles in American society.

Seton died January 4, 1821. Her remains repose in Emmitsburg, in a Basilica that bears her name. Her work of education and charity lives on in the order that she founded. James Cardinal Gibbons of Baltimore began the process of canonization for Seton in 1882. Pope John XXIII declared Seton "venerable" in December 1959, and also beatified her in March 1963. Pope Paul VI canonized Saint Elizabeth Ann Seton in September 1975.

Timothy Walch

See also Catholic Schools; Drexel, Katharine; Hughes, John

Further Readings

Dirvin, J. I. (1962). *Mrs. Seton: Foundress of the American Sisters of Charity*. New York: Farrar, Strauss, & Giroux.

Kelly, E. M., & Melville, A. M. (Eds.). (1987). *Elizabeth Seton: Selected writings*. Mahwah, NJ: Paulist Press.

Melville, A. M. (1951). *Elizabeth Bayley Seton, 1774–1821*. New York: Scribner's.

SEVENTH-DAY ADVENTIST SCHOOLS

The Seventh-day Adventist Church, a Christian denomination formed in 1861, operates a global system of schools from the preschool- through the graduate-level. Adventist schools emerged during the 19th century, a time of widespread calls for educational reform in the United States. The educational system developed by the Seventh-day Adventist Church was from its beginnings intent on reformation of existing school practices. This reform focused on providing a principle-based education in harmony with the church's Bible-based beliefs. From a lackluster beginning in the 1850s typified by starts and stops, the philosophy of Adventist education has since about 1900 developed into a coherent scheme of general and denominational-specific principles.

Purpose and Guiding Principles

The primary intellectual architect of Adventist schools was Ellen Gould White, a woman Adventists believe received visions from God on many matters, including education. White wrote *Proper Education*, her first position statement on education, in 1872. Until her death in 1915 she continued to explain and expand the ideas presented in this first work. Her views on education centered on the character and nature of God, particularly His love for humanity and His plan to restore His image in them. In this context she advocated love as the true foundation of education and declared that the work of education was to help God in His work of restoration. Further, education was not something that happened only in formal schools. For White, education was a life-long process. It began at home during infancy, and continued uninterrupted through formal schooling, the adult life, and throughout eternity in the afterlife. As would be expected in schools formed by a Christian denomination, the Bible was to be at the core of the curriculum. Its principles and wisdom were to be integrated in all fields of study. But study of the Holy Scriptures alone was an inadequate education. The whole being was to be developed: mental, spiritual, physical, and social. Not only were students to study and implement principles of healthful living, the school environment itself was to be healthful, with adequate heating, ventilation, lighting, child-sized furniture, and sufficient space for outdoor study and gardening.

Many schools of the time focused on rote memorization and training children to follow others, but White called for Adventists to teach their children to be critical thinkers who could use their own judgment and engage in original thought. This type of thinking was central to good decision making and strong character. The Adventist school was to engage children in experiential learning: in nature, in manual labor, and in study of the Bible. Head knowledge was deemed important but inadequate; practical, experiential knowledge of God and His creation was the objective. As Adventist schools were formally started to help provide workers for the growing church, it is not surprising that White emphasized service as a primary goal of education. However, service was not the goal only for church workers, but for every child in the school. Service, as well as learning, was viewed with an eternal perspective: beginning with service to our neighbors on earth and continuing throughout eternity.

First Educational Experiments

The first Adventist school was begun in 1853 at Buck's Bridge, New York, 8 years before the formal organization of the Seventh-day Adventist denomination. It was started by a small number of church families who wanted something better for their children than the local public school. The Buck's Bridge school was a family initiative rather than a church-supported school. Martha Byington, daughter of the local Adventist pastor, John Byington, served as the first teacher. After 3 years of operation, with a different teacher each year, the school closed.

Additional experiments with education continued after the formation of the Seventh-day Adventist Church, particularly in Battle Creek, Michigan, location of the new denomination's headquarters. Most of these experiments were short lived and not strongly supported by the church. However, in 1868 the Battle Creek Adventist Church officially employed Goodloe Harper Bell, a former student at reform-oriented Oberlin College, to begin a school. After one year the church withdrew its support, but Bell continued operating the school independently. By the time the first part of *Proper Education* appeared in December 1872, Bell's school had outgrown its meeting place and moved into the church. In the context of the publication of *Proper Education*, the school continued to grow and denominational leaders began to speak seriously about founding a college, primarily to prepare workers for the rapidly growing church.

Battle Creek College opened in 1874 with a charter to offer primary through college-level courses, although no formal college program yet existed. However, the College hardly reflected the reforms called for in *Proper Education*. Rather it reflected the classical training of its principal, Sydney Brownsberger, who held a master's degree in classics from the University of Michigan. The campus was small and in an urban setting. No manual labor or practical studies were part of the initial curriculum. And perhaps most telling of all, courses in the study of the Bible either did not exist or were optional. Over the next 25 years the Battle Creek College faculty struggled to fully implement the denomination's vision for Adventist education. Meanwhile, additional colleges and K–12 schools were established both in the United States and abroad. While ministering to the Adventist Church in Australia, White was instrumental in founding Avondale College, a conscious attempt at implementing an educational institution aligned with Adventist thought and practice. By 1901, the church organization decided a new start was needed for Battle Creek College to shift it into alignment with an Adventist philosophy of education. It was moved to a rural location in Berrien Springs, Michigan, and renamed Emmanuel Missionary College (now Andrews University).

Growing a Diverse Global Educational System

As Adventist education matured and grew, variations of schools emerged in addition to standard primary schools, secondary schools, and Bible training colleges. As a natural outgrowth of the

Adventist emphasis on healthful living, programs and schools, such as Loma Linda University, emerged that were focused on health care. In advancing an agenda of service, Adventists opened schools in the southern United States after the Civil War, such as Oakwood University, for African Americans, who had limited opportunities for education. Beginning in 1897 Adventist education in the United States experienced a surge of growth. This growth trend continued in the United States and expanded to other countries and all six inhabited continents during the 20th century. Throughout the growth years of the 20th century, Adventist schools continued to reflect common core principles and emphasize a curriculum focused on meeting societal needs, such as nursing, medicine, social work, or education. In 2006 the global Adventist Church educated 1,436,290 students in 7,284 schools, from elementary through university levels.

Larry D. Burton

See also Catholic Schools; Christian Day Schools; Episcopal Schools; Islamic Schools; Jewish Schools; Lutheran Schools

Further Readings

Greenleaf, F. (2005). *In passion for the world: A history of Seventh-day Adventist education*. Nampa, ID: Pacific Press Publishing Association.

Knight, G. R. (2001). The aims of Adventist education in historical perspective. *Journal of Research on Christian Education, 10*(Summer), 195–225.

White, E. G. (1952). *Education*. Nampa, ID: Pacific Press Publishing Association.

White, E. G. (1952). *Fundamentals of Christian education*. Nampa, ID: Pacific Press Publishing Association.

SEX EDUCATION

In the early 20th century, schooling played an increasingly large role in the lives of growing numbers of American children and adolescents, and the scope of curricula widened accordingly. Compulsory education and child-labor laws brought unprecedented numbers of children into the schoolhouse,

and Deweyite notions of educating the "whole child" expanded the purview of curriculum to address vocational and broader developmental questions. The presence of these children, often hailing from working-class ethnic families with unfamiliar social customs, the concurrent "invention" by influential psychologist G. Stanley Hall of "adolescence" as a sexually fraught and even perilous time, and this expanded pedagogical purpose, gave rise to the first sex education curricula. Over the course of the 20th century, sex education became a contested but consistent feature in the American schoolhouse, its emphasis evolving from social hygiene; to courtship, marriage, and the family more broadly; to comprehensive programs including homosexuality and contraception; to the most recent curricula that teach abstinence from sexual activity as adolescents' only reliable recourse against pregnancy and sexually transmitted disease. Unlike many contemporary education initiatives that rely primarily on federal support, sex education has largely emerged from local, state, and private impetus. For this reason, this controversial curricular question proves a rich site from which to explore the reformist impulses that animate everyday citizens to engage passionately in the construction—and often dismantling—of educational policy and practice.

Early History

Historians of education have recently pointed to "social control" as the ethos underlying various curricular innovations, and early forms of sex education amply support this claim. In 1913, the American Social Hygiene Association, finding "traditional institutions insufficient to guard youth from urban temptations," convened doctors and social engineers to design energetic curricula to counteract growing secularism, lax social examples set by immigrant parents, and the general cultural and moral dissolution embodied by the urbanizing, diversifying society. Social hygienists aimed to safeguard adolescent chastity by regulating teenagers' sexual desires during the expanding period between puberty and marriage. While these early sex educators condemned Victorian repression for inciting deviant sexuality, they confronted the same paradox that would vex conservatives, sex education activists, and opponents alike in the coming century: By openly discussing sexuality, weren't sex educators encouraging sexual exploration rather than limiting it? Conservative sex educators thus exalted specifically reproductive sexuality, safe within the nuptial home, and attempted to de-eroticize their subject matter by avoiding any discussion of sexual pleasure and emphasizing rational, scientific explanations of sexuality.

These strategies hardly served to stem controversy, which has attended sex education throughout its history. The central issues that immediately emerged in response to these programs—a crusade to purge "sex hygiene and personal purity education" from the Chicago public schools in 1913 is the most famous early example—remained largely consistent throughout the 20th century. Opponents complained that educators trespassed upon the domain of the family and church, and accused sex educators of "sneaking" sex education into science and health classes, undermining parental prerogative, and corrupting innocent youth. Even in these early battles over sex education, the fraught question of who other than parents was qualified to teach children about sexuality was central. As with any innovative pedagogy, early sex educators were inexperienced with new material, yet were dealing in highly sensitive questions of morality and sexuality. In an era when the role of the school grew in children's lives, sex education was a particularly delicate area, representing to many parents a threat to their control over their children's moral development.

Despite enduring attacks as perverts, many early sex educators actually strove to defend a social and moral order they sensed eroding in the face of demographic and cultural change. They sought to steer adolescents on a virtuous path clear of their own libidinous impulses and the vicious temptations of their ethnic, urban environments. Sex education has since its inception been a product of its historical moment. Similarly, during both world wars, when young Americans faced military service, sex educators emphasized disease prevention, highlighting the perils of contracting venereal disease from foreign women. Thus, though the American education system is famed for its localism, and sex education programs were largely developed independent of federal funding or policy mandates, national politics and culture persistently shaped these curricula.

The Post–World War II Era

In the postwar era, as the threat of venereal disease receded, the "family life era" in the history of sex education dawned. In this period, stretching through the 1950s and the sexual revolution until the advent of the AIDS virus in the early 1980s, sex educators expanded the purview of their curricula beyond disease prevention and mechanical explanations of reproduction. Instead, they treated broader questions of family life, gender, dating, and marriage. Within this expanded purview, many sex educators perpetuated the work of their conservative antecedents, shoring up normative values prizing chastity and the nuptial home, and encouraging shame for transgression of these mores. Sex educators in the San Diego schools, for example, prominently advertised their happy and prolific marriages as credentials for the job, and described their responsibility as imparting to students "the truth" about matters of gender and morality. Such curricula tended to enshrine the White, middle-class family as normative, and to pathologize or remain silent on all nonreproductive sexuality, particularly masturbation and homosexuality.

Programs generating controversy in this era were distinct primarily in that they fostered open conversation among students and teachers about values, sexuality, decision making, and even previously taboo questions. Still, even these more discursively open programs tended to draw moderate conclusions. One sex educator both reviled and celebrated for designing progressive curricula in the late 1960s explained that open discussion was encouraged expressly to steer adolescents toward marriage, and to warn girls to avoid the temptations of boys and of their own desires that might bring about their ruin. Programs administered in parochial schools arrived at similar conclusions, but relied primarily on moral and scriptural reasoning to impart these lessons. That in mid-1968 over 70% of American adults advocated some form of sex education in schools suggests the general moderation of most such curricula.

Despite the underlying conservatism of many such family life programs, those fostering open discussion of sexuality, even if to measured ends, sparked vitriolic controversy in the late 1960s. In one Southern California district, anti–sex education opponents took over the school board, and the administrators responsible for the program received death threats and ultimately resigned in distress. Northern California parents protested sex education so vehemently, garnering national attention, that Governor Ronald Reagan diagnosed a "moral crisis" and appointed a committee to devise an explicit moral code to be taught in public schools. Similar battles over sex education ensued nationwide in the late 1960s and early 1970s, even as programs spread across the nation to an estimated 50% of urban and suburban public schools. Private and parochial schools also participated in this expansion of sex education, though less consistently.

Again, both sex education and the response it inspired derived from the larger historical moment. The U.S. Supreme Court both narrowed the definition of obscenity and proscribed prayer in schools over the course of the 1960s. Immediately, provocative themes abounded in popular culture. Still worse for social conservatives, the Court then constrained schools from acting as a moral counterweight to these newly unregulated suggestive images and ideas permeating popular culture. Whether these legislative changes galvanized or constituted the sexual revolution that swept over campuses, cities, and bars by the end of the decade, American youth experienced what other scholars have styled a complete revolution in morality and comportment. Unrest over civil rights and the emergence of an ethos privileging self-fulfillment over traditional obligations to family contributed to the sense that the very tenets of society were in flux, and the era's family life and sex education programs were a mechanism to deal with these dislocations. Sex educators of all stripes—commensurate with the vision of early 20th-century reformers—conceived of curricula precisely as a method to manage adolescents' desires in the face of temptation. Increasingly vocal opponents, however, derided the programs as troubling outgrowths of the very trends they were devised to counteract.

At the core of the heated debate over sex education that flared in the late 1960s and early 1970s were two familiar concerns: The school was intruding upon parental rights to teach about sex, and any discussion of sexuality amounted to encouraging sexual experimentation. Even moderate speech would diminish the silence and shame that had supposedly kept previous generations

safe from moral ruin. Recent scholars have noted that sex education programs in this era, as moderate as they may seem in retrospect, were revolutionary in bringing the wider society's new openness about sexuality into one of the last bastions where sexual speech was silenced: the classroom. Countless students' recollections suggest that mentioning sex, even to shore up conventional morality, signified an upheaval of discursive norms. To local citizens' groups and national religious organizations, sex education embodied all that was wrong with the corrupt society sexual liberals and social progressives envisioned. Aside from countless homemade flyers disseminated locally, lurid propaganda such as the pamphlet "Is the Schoolhouse the Proper Place to Teach Raw Sex?" and the film *Pavlov's Children* circulated nationally, describing the nightmarish potential of sex education to rob children of their allegiance to family, country, and morality.

As sex education garnered both popularity and opprobrium, advocates strove with considerable success to win professional and public legitimacy. In 1964, only three medical schools in the country "barely mentioned sex education" in their curricula, according to one reformer. Yet by 1976, all the major medical schools provided such training, and diverse districts nationwide availed themselves of these resources. The American Association of Sex Educators and Counselors in 1974 announced a certification plan for sex educators, and a week in October 1975 was declared National Sex Education Week. Most important, however, was the 1964 establishment of a national organization expressly to disseminate information about sexuality, the Sexuality Information Education Council of the United States (SIECUS).

Though an invaluable resource to sex educators, SIECUS gave the growing ranks of sex education opponents the impression that these curricula were the machinations of a centralized authority. SIECUS in many ways fit seamlessly into an already familiar trope among conservatives of a large, outside organization harboring a nefarious agenda to undermine family authority. SIECUS had no authority and little influence over local curricula. Yet its identity as a top-down New York City institution, cofounded by Mary Calderone, a blueblood and alleged communist who had made a career at Planned Parenthood advocating contraception,

SIECUS raised hackles among those who believed sexual issues were best left unspoken, large outside organizations were not to be trusted, and the East Coast was vaguely corrupt. Though Calderone herself was hardly a radical, and even called abortion a "medical immorality," SIECUS provided sufficient grist for the Right to develop a powerful discourse around sex education that simultaneously silenced proponents while galvanizing social conservatives around a host of social and political questions for which sex education became a convenient shorthand.

When these "sex wars in the schools" ebbed, many local curricula had been dissolved, SIECUS retreated from being the lightning rod of K–12 programming, and opponents to some extent found new foci in the absence of this target. As national attention shifted from sex education and the feminist and gay rights movements grew, many family life and sex education programs in the 1970s evolved to reflect far less traditional ideas about gender, sexuality, and the body than the programs that had so recently incited such controversy. The popular 1973 women's health text *Our Bodies, Ourselves,* written "by women for women," and since translated into 20 languages, exemplifies how during the 1970s new attitudes about teaching sex took hold. Sex education certainly served as a rallying point for the emerging political Right, yet such activism, ostensibly in service of preserving silence around questions of sexuality, actually served to generate a louder and more inclusive discourse on these once-hushed themes.

The Era of AIDS

In the early 1980s the advent of the AIDS virus brought the "family life era" to a close, as panic over AIDS narrowed the focus of curricula once again to disease prevention. By 1990, all 50 states recommended or mandated AIDS education, while only 41 encouraged or required more comprehensive programs. In some ways, this public health crisis was a boon to conservative opponents to sex education who had unwittingly invigorated debates over what constituted appropriate sex education. Now that (especially homosexual) sex could literally be fatal—rather than merely leading to uncomfortable disease, unwanted pregnancy, or a tarnished reputation—social conservatives had

powerful material to support the newest form of sex education, which would become preeminent by the close of the 20th century: abstinence-only pedagogy.

Abstinence-only education dispenses with any notion that adolescents might make decisions about premarital sexuality based on their own value system, and exclusively teaches abstinence before marriage. Because this pedagogical approach forswears nonreproductive, premarital intercourse, students of abstinence-only education do not learn about birth control or safer sex practices. Conservative organizations such as Focus on the Family, which once balked at the presence of sexual speech in the schoolhouse, champion such abstinence-only programs as an instrument for imparting the "family values" the religious Right places at the forefront of its agenda. Even as such curricula continue to multiply in the United States, many health educators and medical professionals argue that abstinence-only programs are unrealistic and fail to teach teenagers how most effectively to cultivate their sexual health. A plank of contemporary criticism of sex education is that it legitimizes morally questionable lifestyles; thus the moral absolutism of abstinence-only programs has contributed tremendously to their success.

Conclusion

Sex education has become a mainstay of K–12 public education, even as it continues to inspire controversy. The conflict between parental and state prerogative is especially pronounced in the case of sex education, as parents have waged and won repeated battles to allow their children to "opt out" of such classes, a dynamic virtually unimaginable in other subject areas. As curricula have manifested differing emphases and support for programming has waxed and waned over the 20th century, sex education has generated an often-heated dialogue about youth, sexuality, civics, and morality that promises to persist in the new millennium.

Natalia Mehlman-Petrzela

See also Character Education; Hall, G. Stanley; Health Education; Lesbian, Gay, Bisexual, and Transgender (LGBT) Issues; Life Adjustment Education; Moral Development; Secular Humanism

Further Readings

Breasted, M. (1970). *Oh! Sex education!* New York: Praeger.

Carter, J. B. (2007). *The heart of whiteness: Normal sexuality and race in America, 1880–1940.* Durham, NC: Duke University Press.

Freeman, S. K. (2008). *Sex goes to school: Girls and sex education before the 1960s.* Urbana-Champaign: University of Illinois Press.

Irvine, J. M. (2002). *Talk about sex: The battles over sex education in the United States.* Berkeley: University of California Press.

Luker, K. (2006). *When sex goes to school: Warring views on sex—and sex education since the sixties.* New York: W. W. Norton.

Mehlman, N. (2007). Sex ed . . . and the reds? Reconsidering the Anaheim battle over sex education, 1962–1969. *History of Education Quarterly, 47,* 203–232.

Moran, J. (2000). *Teaching sex: The shaping of adolescence in the twentieth century.* Cambridge, MA: Harvard University Press.

Zimmerman, J. (2002). *Whose America? Culture wars in the public schools.* Cambridge, MA: Harvard University Press.

SHULMAN, LEE (1939–)

Lee Shulman is an educational psychologist, a teacher educator, and a reformer who has impacted the study of teaching and teacher education through his research and writings. He has held various roles and positions during his professional career. He holds the title of Professor Emeritus, the Charles E. Ducommun Professor of Education, from Stanford University, as well as Professor of Psychology Emeritus. While at Michigan State University, he held the position of Professor of Educational Psychology and Medical Education. He became the founder and codirector of the Institute for Research on Teaching (IRT), thus extending and codifying research on the study of teaching.

Shulman has served as president of the Carnegie Foundation for the Advancement of Teaching, the American Educational Research Association, and the National Academy of Education and has received numerous awards for his research and writings. The Carnegie Foundation is an independent policy and research center whose mission is to address the hardest problems faced in teaching at all levels and contexts: public schools, colleges, and universities. He received the Distinguished Contributions to Educational Research Award presented by the American Educational Research Association, and is also a recipient of the American Psychological Association's E. L. Thorndike Award for his many contributions to education. Lee Shulman received the Grawemeyer Award in 2006. This award is given to individuals in five different categories: music composition, education, ideas improving world order, religion, and psychology. Its purpose is to recognize individuals who demonstrate powerful ideas or creative works in the sciences, arts, and humanities. Shulman's research focused on what makes a good teacher, recognizing that an increase in knowledge among pre-service teachers is essential if teachers are to be prepared to make skills understandable to others. He also asserts that society is responsible for preparing and assessing the performance of teachers at all levels and for giving recognition as deserved.

Shulman's research and writing transcends professions exemplified by his work in the psychology of instruction in science, mathematics, and medicine, as well as his writings on signature pedagogies in the professions of law, medicine, engineering, and the clergy. His work transcends colleges through the study of teacher education and medical education; and transcends structures in both K–12 and higher education by focusing on quality instruction at all levels.

Shulman is credited with coining the phrase *"pedagogical content knowledge"* in relationship to the pre-service and in-service teachers' knowledge of their subject matter and the impact of strong content knowledge on successful teaching. From his research, a model of pedagogical reasoning was developed that details the cyclic nature of teaching and activities that engage the teacher in developing good teaching practice. This model purports that good teaching involves comprehension, understanding the purposes of the discipline and teaching; transformation, aligning content and pedagogy that meets the needs of the students; instruction, the act of teaching; evaluation, using tests and evaluation as an extension of teaching; reflection, critically analyzing one's teaching and making the necessary changes to become a better teacher; and new comprehension, understandings based on the above acts where the teacher gains new insights about the teaching process.

Building upon his research, Shulman is investigating signature pedagogies: the way professionals are trained for their profession. He views education as a synthesis of three apprenticeships: cognitive, practical, and moral. In the cognitive apprenticeship the pre-service teacher is learning to think like a professional. In the practical apprenticeship the pre-service teacher is learning to perform like a professional, and in the moral apprenticeship the pre-service teacher is learning to think and act in a responsible, ethical manner. Shulman maintains that professionals, whether they are in law, medicine, engineering, clergy, nursing, or education, must all be prepared to act, to perform, and to practice. Shulman divides signature pedagogies into three types: pedagogies of uncertainty, of engagement, and of formation. Pedagogies of uncertainty and engagement both depend on students' responses and active involvement, while pedagogies of formation build upon dispositions and values. Shulman believes that the study of signature pedagogies is a way of systematically following our pre-service and in-service teachers in the learning process and using the feedback to redesign our teacher education programs and professional development.

Connie Louise Bowman

See also Achievement Gap; Assessment; Carnegie Foundation for the Advancement of Teaching; Interstate New Teacher Assessment and Support Consortium (INTASC); National Commission on Teaching and America's Future (NCTAF); Problem-Based Learning; Teacher Education; Teacher Evaluation

Further Readings

Beyerbach, B., & Nassoiy, T. (2005). Where is equity in the national standards? A critical review of the INTASC, NCATE, and NBPTS standards. *Scholar-Practitioner Quarterly, 2*(4), 29–42

Falk, B. (2006). A conversation with Lee Shulman. Signature pedagogies for teacher education: Defining our practices and rethinking our preparation. *New Educator, 2*(1), 73–82.

Shulman, L. (1987). Knowledge and teaching: Foundations of the new reform. *Harvard Educational Review, 57*(1), 1–22.

Shulman, L. (2005). Signature pedagogies in the professions. *Daedalus, 134*(3), 52–57.

SINGAPORE MATH

In 1981, the Singapore Ministry of Education (MOE) created a project team identified as the Curriculum Development Institute of Singapore (now titled the Curriculum Planning Development Institute of Singapore) that composed a mathematics program for primary grades in Singapore. The goal of this mathematics curriculum was to create a labor force with technical skills that surpassed all others in the Third World. Ministry of Education primary grades translate to kindergarten through Grade 12 in the United States. The curriculum was published initially in 1982. The first edition focused on mathematical computation. The mathematics was presented at three levels of understanding: concrete, pictorial, and abstract. The intent was to have students develop meaningful mathematics skills with flexible thinking. Such a level of understanding would serve as a foundation for the study of mathematics in the high school years, thus enabling students to be well prepared for advanced mathematics at the university level.

The textbook series was revised in 1992 to have problem solving as the basis of the curriculum. A goal of this curriculum was to enable students to use mathematics in challenging situations as well as to know basic computation. In 1994, the Ministry of Education did not change the curriculum, but did reduce the amount of mathematical content in the textbook series to allow for subject mastery. By 1999, the Ministry of Education realized that the curriculum needed to be reduced in order for teachers to inject more thinking skills, technology, and the national education messages into the curriculum. The content that was removed from the curriculum included math that was just recall items, math that centered on technical details rather than conceptual understanding, and math that research had identified as too abstract for a given grade level. This was the third edition of the mathematics series.

International recognition of this curriculum began with the Third International Mathematics and Science Study results in 1995 when Singapore students scored in the number-one position when compared with 41 other industrial nations in their mathematical skills. The study group continued their work under the name of Trends in International Mathematics and Science Study (TIMSS); in 1999 and 2003, Singapore students maintained their top ranking in the world for mathematical proficiency.

While the Ministry of Education of Singapore identified the mathematics curriculum that they created as the *Primary Mathematics Series*, once the TIMSS results were distributed, educators in the United States and Canada began to identify the curriculum as "Singapore Math." The Primary Mathematics Series textbooks were privatized in 2001 in order to make changes to the series with greater speed.

The Ministry of Education recognized the change in teaching methodologies in 2001 with another curriculum revision, including newer cognitive approaches to teaching and learning along with different assessment modes. Since the Singapore government sponsored this series, it included citizenship skills and values as well as information technology. In response to market demand in 2003, an American version was published that used American currency and measurements. The most recent revision to the series came in 2007. The changes focused on the inclusion of calculator usage and a reduction in mental mathematics.

Singapore Math focuses on the use of "bar modeling" as a problem-solving tool. In a problem-solving situation, a bar—one or two long, thin rectangles—is used to represent what is known about a problem: the parts and/or the whole of a given situation. Within the bar, relative sizes of known information are labeled and from that representation students glean what the missing part is; this enables students to correctly select a mathematical process to solve the problem.

Pilot testing of the Singapore Math curriculum occurred in four locations in the United States: one in Massachusetts, one in New Jersey, and two in Maryland. Among issues identified by the pilots were that U.S. standards required statistics, probability, and data analysis to be taught, but these were not included in the Singapore curriculum. A lack of alignment with U.S. mathematics curricula requirements was identified as the main reason that three of the four pilot sites did not continue with the program even though student scores significantly improved. The Singapore curriculum required extensive professional development of U.S. classroom teachers for correct implementation. A deep understanding of mathematics by elementary level teachers was needed to correctly teach Singapore Math; thus an extensive professional development program was a part of using Singapore Math. This financial cost was identified as a reason not to use the curriculum. Many parents who homeschool their children turn to Singapore Math because it presents mathematics in a manner similar to the methods that were used when they were in grade school. However, homeschooling parents are cautioned to use an additional curriculum in order to meet all the state requirements for mathematics curricula. In 2008, California approved Singapore Math as a mathematics curriculum for students.

Janet M. Herrelko

See also Curriculum Controversies; National Council of Teachers of Mathematics; Trends in International Mathematics and Science Study (TIMSS)

Further Readings

Garelick, B. (2006, Fall). Miracle math. *Education Next*, pp. 39–45.

Flatow, I. (2004, December 17). *National Public Radio: Talk of the Nation: Singapore math method* [Radio broadcast]. Retrieved from http://www.npr.org/templates/story/story.php?storyId=4233324

Thomas, J., & Thomas, D. (2002). *The Singapore math story*. Retrieved August 4, 2008, from http://www/singaporemath.com/Singapore_Math_Story_s/10.htm

SINGLE-SEX SCHOOLS

Single-sex schools/education, also known as single-gender and same-sex schooling, is the practice of separating boys and girls for formal instruction. Policies and practices of single-gender education in the United States have undergone significant reform in the early 21st century. Public school, an institution with a strong tradition of coeducation dating from the mid-19th century, has increasingly become a site of experimentation with single-gender approaches once found primarily in parochial and private school networks. The No Child Left Behind Act of 2001 (NCLB) has helped to create new opportunities for this type of education in schools across the United States. The number of public schools offering some type of single-sex program has risen steadily from 3 in 1995 to 442 in 2008, with close to half of these programs located in South Carolina. These new public schooling arrangements to separate the education of boys and girls in hopes of bettering academic achievement represents one of the major new reforms of 21st-century public schools. This entry provides the policy context of single-gender education programs, reviews the purported benefits of this approach, and considers the critiques of these reforms.

Policy Context

A lively policy conversation regarding the potential benefits and drawbacks of segregating boys and girls for education has existed since the mid-20th century. While elementary schools have historically been coeducational institutions, experiments with differentiating the high school experience by sex gained momentum during the Progressive era. With few single-sex high schools remaining from the 1900s, advocates of differentiated secondary education focused on promoting a sex-segregated curriculum consisting primarily of physical education and elective courses such as home economics, sex education, and manual-vocational training. These reforms strove to prepare and benefit students entering a society where the roles of men and women were well defined and generally accepted.

The rise of the women's liberation movement in the 1960s launched a critique of the open and hidden sexism within American public schools. In this coeducational context, researchers found systematic bias against girls in textbooks, course scheduling, and teacher expectations, a bias believed to diminish academic performance in key subjects like math and science. Reformers aimed to address sexism through fights for increased equity within the coeducational context rather than through the separation of boys and girls. The commitment to this coeducational arrangement was cemented in the 1972 Title IX law, which prohibited discrimination by sex in schools receiving federal funds and largely

restricted single-sex education to particular classes, including sex education and physical education involving contact sports.

Changes in federal regulation and increased concerns about academic achievement have infused single-gender programming with new energy in the 21st century. Under Title IX, many states and school districts feared sex discrimination lawsuits and were reluctant to support single-sex schools. Single-gender education in public schools gained significant support under the NCLB law, which included a section urging the U.S. Department of Education (DoE) to promote single-sex schools and a $3-million appropriation for single-sex classrooms and schools. As a result of this provision and the active support of politicians, the DoE issued rules in 2006 that reinterpreted Title IX to allow for the creation of single-sex classes, programs, and schools. These guidelines required voluntary student enrollment and the availability of "substantially equal" coeducational classes for students not participating in single-gender classes. Many states interpret these regulations as legal protection for single-gender education and have permitted the growth of single-sex education in public schools.

Purported Benefits and Critiques of Single-Gender Education

The expansion of same-sex-education education stems from three, at times intersecting, developments: (1) the growing support for greater choice in educational programs, (2) increased hopes and pressure for academic gains, (3) and emerging research that developmental and physiological differences between boys and girls may influence learning styles. In states with a significant number of single-gender classes, like South Carolina, the popularity of expanded choice in education and the drive to boost academic performance, especially on accountability tests, drives the development of this educational approach and organization. While research suggests that low-income children of both sexes might gain from single-gender education, and high school boys could reap the greatest academic benefits, few studies have assessed long-term trends in achievement in this learning environment over a typical coeducational approach. Individual schools report varied success with the single-gender approach. Evidence from one of the earliest single-gender public schools, The Young Women's Leadership School (TYWLS) in Harlem, New York, which has graduated 100% of the school's seniors and helped all these students earn acceptance at a 4-year college, suggests positive results. In the first public middle school to reorganize as a single-gender institution, the Leadership Academies in Long Beach, California, however, evidence of the effectiveness of single-gender education is not as compelling. The school decided in 2007 to return to its previous coeducational format after noticing little improvement on test scores.

Prominent groups, like the American Association of University Women (AAUW) and the American Civil Liberties Union (ACLU), which have fought for equity within the coeducational classroom, have voiced concern over the growing trend of single-gender education. The AAUW argues that the potential loss of attention to equity within single-gender schools could lead to the strengthening of problematic stereotypes, discrimination, and a decrease in educational opportunities for both sexes. Fearing dissolution of Title IX protections, increased segregation within schools, and possibly a violation of the Equal Protection clause of the Constitution, these groups have publicly both criticized the government's support for expanded single-sex education and threatened to bring the issue to court.

Kara D. Brown

See also Catholic Schools; Charter Schools; Coeducation; De Facto Segregation; Differentiated Instruction

Further Readings

Datnow, A., & Hubbard, L. (Eds.). (2002). *Gender in policy and practice: Perspectives on single-sex and coeducational schooling.* New York: RoutledgeFalmer.

The Jossey-Bass reader on gender in education. (2002). San Francisco: Jossey-Bass.

Salomone, R. C. (2003). *Same, different, equal: Rethinking single-sex schooling.* New Haven, CT: Yale University Press.

Speilhagen, F. R. (Ed.). (2008). *Debating single-sex education: Separate and equal?* Lanham, MD: Rowman & Littlefield.

Tyack, D., & Hansot, E. (1991). *Learning together: A history of coeducation in American schools.* New Haven, CT: Yale University Press.

SITE-BASED MANAGEMENT

Site-based management, or school-based decision making (SBDM), as it is more commonly known, is an innovative reform that swept the nation during the 1990s in an attempt to allow building level decision making for curricular and other educational issues. SBDM was designed to improve student learning by reducing districtwide bureaucracies while creating opportunities for shared decision making by educators, parents, and community members. This entry focuses on key legal dimensions of SBDM.

SBDM is a novel governance structure, with various permutations, that has been adopted in at least 40 states, whether jurisdiction-wide as in Kentucky, home to the most extensive statute, or on the local level as in Chicago, Illinois.

The move to local control, a precursor to what is now known as SBDM, began in New York City and Detroit in the mid-1960s. Although other school boards, most notably in Chicago, Los Angeles, and Philadelphia, considered similar initiatives, their efforts failed to get beyond the planning stage.

In New York City and Detroit, the then-largest and fifth-largest school systems in the United States, educational and political leaders turned to local control due to growing dissatisfaction with desegregation efforts more than a decade after *Brown v. Board of Education* (1954). Beginning in 1969, New York City's decentralization experiment afforded local school boards power over budgets, curricula, and personnel in elementary and junior high schools; high schools remained under the control of the central board. This reform, which remains in place, has long had mixed success but was able to break the city's massive centralized educational bureaucracy into 31, now 32, local community school districts.

Detroit decentralized into eight regional districts in 1971, granting local boards power over curricula, financing, staffing, and students. The central office retained power to coordinate personnel and other services.

About 20 years after New York City and Detroit decentralized their schools, proponents of educational change turned to SBDM, an initiative that began in Australia and England at least a decade earlier. The remainder of this entry focuses on developments in the two most noteworthy initiatives, one that was local in nature, in Chicago, Illinois, and another that was jurisdiction-wide, in Kentucky.

Based on how poorly the city's public schools were performing, the Illinois General Assembly enacted the Chicago School Reform Act of 1988. The statute's goal was to improve student achievement, hoping to make it comparable with national norms within 5 years. The Act called for the creation of Local School Councils (LSCs), consisting of a principal and 10 elected representatives who serve 2-year terms. Two of the 10 representatives must be teachers who perform most of their duties at the same school, six must be parents of children in the school, and two must be residents of the community that the school serves. LSCs at high schools include nonvoting student members on one-year terms.

The most significant governance power of LSCs is to select principals to serve 4-year terms, to fill vacancies, to decide whether to renew principals' contracts, and to develop job-related performance criteria. Among their other duties, LSCs can approve school improvement plans; make recommendations or offer advice to principals over textbook selection, curricular issues, staff, and policies such as discipline. The results in Chicago are mixed on improving student achievement.

Kentucky enacted the most comprehensive systemwide plan for SBDM as part of the much larger Kentucky Education Reform Act (KERA) of 1990. KERA was designed to improve the poor academic performance of students in public schools. Under KERA's SBDM provisions, with limited exceptions for schools that exceeded their threshold levels of accountability, all schools in the commonwealth must create councils.

SBDM councils in Kentucky consist of a school's principal, three teachers, and two parents; teachers and parents are elected by their peers. Schools with enrollments of 8% or more minority students must select a minority member, with principals authorized to call special elections in order to ensure such representation. Parents who are school board members, married to board members or their employees, or who are board employees are ineligible to serve on councils.

Once SBDM councils are in place, they are free to set the length of the terms for later councils except that terms cannot exceed 2 years or be consecutive. Councils can allow elected members to serve 1- or 2-year terms and may permit 1-year terms to which individuals can be reelected.

As important as SBDM councils in Kentucky are, it is also important to note two significant limitations under which they work. First, school boards retain such traditional functions as establishing and operating schools, setting tax rates, creating budgets, providing student transportation, and planning for the construction of new facilities. Second, councils are statutorily limited in five other overlapping areas: Councils may not violate federal or Kentucky law; cannot unreasonably place the health or safety of employees or students at risk; cannot unreasonably risk liability for litigation; cannot exceed their available financial resources; and cannot breach contracts with outside service providers.

SBDM councils in Kentucky have, or share in, 16 statutory governance functions, at least 8 of which they exercise independent of school boards. Rather than review each of these items, this entry highlights the major responsibilities of councils. Perhaps the most significant duties of councils are that they can fill (but not create) vacancies on school staffs, including hiring (but not dismissing) principals and selecting textbooks and instructional materials. Other key council duties include devising policies in such important areas as curricular and instructional practices, staff and student assignments, school space and schedules, discipline, classroom management, and extracurricular activities.

As with initiatives elsewhere, the Kentucky reforms have yet to yield significant improvements in student outcomes. Even so, to the extent that SBDM is beginning to take root in many school systems throughout the country, it may just take time to determine whether it has achieved the success that its proponents seek.

Charles J. Russo

See also Accountability Era; Boards of Education; Business and Educational Reform; Collective Bargaining; District Schools; Small-School Movement

Further Readings

Boyd, W. L. (1992). The power of paradigms: Reconceptualizing educational policy and management. *Educational Administration Quarterly,* 28(4), 504–528.

Brown v. Board of Education of Topeka, 347 U.S. 483 (1954).

Illinois Compiled Statutes, Chapter 105, 5/34–2.1 et seq. (2000).

Kentucky Revised Statutes § 160.345 (2008).

Raisch, C. D. (2008). School-based decision making. In C. J. Russo (Ed.), *Encyclopedia of education law* (pp. 729–732). Thousand Oaks, CA: Sage.

Russo, C. J. (1994–1995). School-based decision making in Kentucky: Dawn of a new era or nothing new under the sun? *Kentucky Law Journal, 83*(1), 123–156.

Russo, C. J. (1995). School-based decision making councils and school boards in Kentucky: Trusted allies or irreconcilable foes? *Education Law Reporter, 97*(2), 603–617.

SIZER, THEODORE R. (1932–)

Theodore R. (Ted) Sizer has significantly influenced the way in which educators have thought about schooling in general, and the structure of schools in particular. His work led to educational reforms in secondary education that have caused policymakers and classroom practitioners to rethink how schools should be programmatically designed and how teachers should engage students in the learning process.

Sizer was born on June 23, 1932, in New Haven, Connecticut. His father was a faculty member at Yale University. Sizer earned his B.A. degree at Yale and his doctorate from Harvard University. He was recruited into the Army as a training officer and teacher. By the age of 31, he was a full-time faculty member at Harvard, had written two books, and had become the dean of the Graduate School of Education at Harvard. After resigning from Harvard, he became the headmaster of Phillips Academy in Andover, Massachusetts, from 1972 to 1981. In 1983, he accepted a teaching position at Brown University and remained there until 1997. After retiring from Brown, he designed the Francis W. Parker Essential School and took a 1-year position as co-principal with his wife, Nancy Sizer. Ted Sizer is a University Professor Emeritus at Brown University and was awarded Brown University's highest award in 1996, the President's Award.

A leader in the high school educational reform movement in the United States, Sizer founded the Coalition of Essential Schools in 1984 and is currently serving as chair emeritus. Three of his books, *Horace's Compromise* (1985), *Horace's School* (1992), and *Horace's Hope* (1996), explore the fundamental components of the Essential School reform effort. Sizer's latest book is *The Red Pencil,* published in 2004. Sizer's mission has always been to put his research work into real-world application. In 1993, he became the Founding Director of the Annenberg Institute for School Reform.

Although he has been engaged in numerous reform efforts, Sizer's work with the Coalition of Essential Schools (CES) has been a hallmark of his career. Starting with a dozen schools in 1984, the Coalition now has almost 600 formal members. In the beginning, CES was headquartered at Brown University. As the movement gained momentum, regional centers were created to coordinate the reforms, coach teachers and administrators, and evaluate schools for membership. The activities of these decentralized centers are now coordinated from Oakland, California. Through a grant from the Gates Foundation, the Coalition is now engaged in a 5-year initiative to document the work of the organization and create a "Mentor Schools Guide." The Coalition's work has had a widespread impact on the school improvement movement in the past 20 years. Such reform phrases as "critical friends," "school coaches," "student exhibitioner learning," and "teacher as coach" have become key components of school reform efforts throughout the country.

Ted Sizer has always opposed the top-down reform model. His work with the Coalition and other reform initiatives was founded on his belief that schools must be active partners in any reform effort. He rejected the new-and-improved-model approach and embraced the concept that key ideas/principles needed to be employed within schools in ways that made sense to the local community. Like John Dewey, Sizer has insisted on the give-and-take dialogue between teachers and students, rather than the traditional lecture. He saw teaching as coaching. He particularly wanted the bureaucratized, comprehensive high schools replaced by smaller institutions where personalization, student as worker, and demonstration of mastery were common principles within the schools. Not all of Sizer's recommendations have been universally accepted by educators. His skepticism of sports and extracurricular activities within the high school structure and his objection to numerous elective courses within the high school curriculum did not endear him to many educators and parents.

In addition to the school reform movement, Ted Sizer has had a profound impact on curriculum. His emphasis on the connections between subjects and disciplines, his call for longer class periods, his concern for depth over coverage, and his desire for more student-driven curriculum have forced educators to frame the discussion of curriculum in completely different ways. Interdisciplinary studies, in-depth projects, and collaboration between students and teachers are all commonplace features of curriculum and instruction frameworks.

Sizer has been one of the leading voices of educational reform in the United States. He remains an important figure through the work of the Coalition of Essential Schools and the Annenberg Institute for School Reform.

Timothy Ilg

See also Coalition of Essential Schools; Curriculum Controversies; Dewey, John; Foundations in the Local School District; Project Learning; Secondary Curricular Reform; Standards Movement

Further Readings

Goldberg, M. F. (1993). A portrait of Ted Sizer [Electronic version]. *Educational Leadership, 51*(1), 53–56.

O'Neil, J. (1995). On lasting school reform: A conversation with Ted Sizer [Electronic version]. *Educational Leadership, 52*(5), 4–9.

Sizer, T. R. (1984). *Horace's hope: What works for the American high school.* Boston: Houghton Mifflin.

Sizer, T. R. (1985). *Horace's compromise: The dilemma of the American high school.* Boston: Houghton Mifflin.

Sizer, T. R. (1992). *Horace's school: Redesigning the American high school.* Boston: Houghton Mifflin.

SKINNER, B. F. (1904–1990)

Born on March 20, 1904, in Susquehanna, Pennsylvania, Burrhus Frederic Skinner initially wanted to become a writer. After graduating from Hamilton College, he spent a year writing fiction in Greenwich Village, New York City. He then turned to psychology, completed a PhD at Harvard University in 1930, and introduced his analysis of behavioral change in 1938. The ensuing 50+ years of research included verbal behavior, applied behavioral analysis (also known as behavior modification and contingency management), programmed instruction, and the teaching machine. Skinner's books, *Beyond Behaviorism,* and particularly *Walden Two* and *Beyond Freedom and Dignity,* reflected his belief that the physical and biological sciences cannot solve social problems such as the population explosion, environmental pollution, and nuclear war without an understanding of human behavior. Skinner's approach to designing individually paced stand-alone instruction (known as programmed instruction) was a part of the curriculum reform precipitated by the launch of the capsule *Sputnik,* the first earth-orbiting artificial satellite, by the USSR in 1957.

Misunderstandings about Skinner's ideas led to controversy on three issues. They are his exclusion of mental processes from learning, the teaching machine, and the concept of behavioral control.

Basic Concepts

Skinner maintained that the goal of any science is to discover the lawful relationships among natural events in the environment. For psychology, this meant studying behavior and the events that change behavior. Skinner's experiments indicated that the immediate consequences of behavior are responsible for behavioral change. For example, an infant accidentally shakes a rattle, the action produces a sound (consequence), and the infant repeats the action again and again. The outcome, the sound, has changed the infant. It responds in the future as a changed being, shaking the rattle whenever the opportunity arises.

Outcomes that lead to an increased frequency of a behavior are *reinforcers.* In the laboratory, Skinner demonstrated the role of reinforcement in learning when, for example, he taught pigeons to play Ping-Pong and rats to hoard marbles. These sets of behaviors are the result of a schedule of intermittent reinforcement such that the responses more and more approximate the final complex behavior. This process is referred to as *shaping*.

In human beings, complex behaviors such as reading result from varied schedules of any of myriad reinforcers that shape behavior. Among them are, initially, the teacher's commendations for the child's correct reading of individual words to, eventually, the child making sense of the sentences. In other words, behavior is not determined from within but is shaped by its consequences. Skinner named his behavioral principles *operant conditioning* because an operant is a behavior that operates on the environment to produce reinforcing consequences. The two key processes in operant conditioning are *variation* (of behavior) and *selection by consequence*. Different behaviors are executed, but only some are strengthened (increase in frequency) by the outcomes.

Applications of Skinner's principles include programs for behavioral management, often referred to as behavior modification. Implemented in a variety of clinical, institutional, and educational settings in the 1960s and 1970s, they continue to be used by researchers and clinicians. Behavioral management was one aspect of the curriculum reform in public education in the 1960s.

Controversies About the Theory

Skinner's writings precipitated extensive criticism. The linguist Noam Chomsky, who believed that language structures are innate, harshly criticized Skinner's *Verbal Behavior*. Skinner, however, had not addressed the origins of language. Instead, he described verbal communication—a speaker's verbalizations that develop according to consequences provided by other people.

Other critics maintained that Skinner had ignored the role of internal processes in learning. But, Skinner noted, describing mental states or feelings as "causing" human behavior means that (a) the states themselves remain to be explained, (b) an emphasis on states treats behavior as simply a symptom of some inner activity and a second-class variable, and (c) a focus on inner states diverts attention away from research that may identify both the sources of problems and their solutions. Also, cognitive processes are behavior and can be analyzed. For example, we perceive objects and events, process information, and manipulate relevant variables in making a decision because these behaviors have reinforcing consequences.

In the mid-1950s, Skinner developed the teaching machine, which used self-instructional materials known as programmed instruction. The purpose was to teach basic skills and free the teacher to listen to and talk with students about their writing and other topics. Poorly designed imitations of programmed instruction and teachers' fear that the machine would replace them contributed to its demise. Nevertheless, programmed instruction was the forerunner of instructional design, and Skinner is often identified as the father of educational technology.

Skinner's application of his concepts to the ways that society functions also drew strong reactions. He described cultures and political systems as controlling behavior through coercion. Individuals obey laws primarily to avoid censure, fines, imprisonment, and other aversive consequences. Skinner's goal was to change the environment from punitive to positive consequences so that cultural practices would guarantee a livable future for all. In other words, by scientifically reshaping institutional controls, the future could be better. Critics maintained, however, that, although Skinner argued for social good, behavioral science seemed to be asking people to give up individual freedom. Skinner responded that control is always present, in such forms as peer pressure, fear of punishment, seeking approval, and so on. He sought to replace such aversive conditions with positive consequences so as to reinforce the kinds of behavior that benefit everyone.

Skinner's later work included an analysis of aging; problems of daily life in the Western world; and a comparison of evolution, cultural practices, and operant conditioning. Skinner is the only post–World War II psychologist to be featured on the cover of *Time* magazine, and his many awards include the National Medal of Science (1968), and the Joseph P. Kennedy Jr. Foundation Award (1970). In August 1990, 8 days before his death from leukemia, Skinner received the Lifetime Achievement Award from the American Psychological Association.

Margaret E. Gredler

See also Behaviorism; Educational Technology; Programmed Instruction

Further Readings

Bjork, D. W. (1997). *B. F. Skinner: A life.* Washington, DC: American Psychological Association.

Skinner, B. F. (1953). *Science and human behavior.* New York: Macmillan.

Skinner, B. F. (1968). *The technology of teaching.* New York: Appleton-Century-Crofts.

Skinner, B. F. (1987). *Upon further reflection.* Englewood Cliffs, NJ: Prentice Hall.

Skinner, B. F. (1989). *Recent issues in the analysis of behavior.* Upper Saddle River, NJ: Prentice Hall.

SLAVIN, ROBERT

See Success For All

SMALL-SCHOOL MOVEMENT

No Child Left Behind (NCLB) requires that schools must be restructured if they do not make adequate yearly progress (AYP) as measured by meeting test score targets for a period of 6 consecutive years. In order to meet this mandate, school districts have attempted several models in an effort to restructure. In some cases, schools have been "taken over by the state," closed completely and then reopened as a charter school, have fired all current administrators and staff and started all over with new staff, or have had the management of the school taken over by private management firms. Recent studies have shown that all of these efforts at restructuring have met with limited success.

It appears that NCLB will be a driving force in school districts and communities for some time to come. If this is the case, then it is important to discover a successful approach to school restructuring. Closing schools, state takeover, and firing all staff members are draconian approaches to restructuring schools that have met with limited success and are extremely disruptive to the school and the community. Under consideration are other approaches to restructuring schools in order to increase the potential of academic improvement and attaining AYP.

One approach that bears consideration is the small-school model. Although the number of students within the school can vary as far as what qualifies as a "small school," many experts consider a number of approximately 350 to 500 students as constituting a small school. Although there are many schools that already have a student population in that range, many schools are considerably larger. What is to be done with a high school, for example, that has a student population of more than 1,500 students, or a large elementary school with over 600 students? The answer may lie in the concept of a school within a school. A school within a school is exactly what the name implies. The larger school is subdivided into smaller organizational units, each of which functions as an independent and yet coordinated instructional unit. By way of example, the units could be organized by grade level, location in the facility, or by discipline. This arrangement provides the potential to promote student achievement, raise the graduation rate, improve student attendance, cultivate a sense of a learning community within the school, reduce the feeling of anonymity that is so prevalent among students in larger schools, and increase teacher–student and teacher–parent contact.

There is considerable evidence supporting the belief that students in smaller schools do better regarding academic achievement than do students in larger schools. There is some evidence to suggest that students in smaller schools have about the same level of academic achievement as their peers in larger schools. However, there is little or no support for the notion that students in larger schools outperform students in smaller schools in terms of academic achievement.

Second, it appears that students who attend smaller schools have a significantly improved graduation rate at the high school level. This may be because students have an increased sense of belonging to the school because of more personal attention by teachers afforded by fewer numbers. Increased teacher-to-student interaction seems to have a positive impact on student life in the school. Another factor that could influence increased graduation rates might be that parents tend to remain more involved in their child's school life in smaller schools. Smaller classes make it easier for teachers and parents to discuss student-related issues. This appears to have numerous positive outcomes. Regardless of the reason, smaller schools historically tend to have better student graduation rates than larger schools.

A third benefit of smaller schools appears to be that students who attend such schools have a much better attendance rate than those who attend larger schools. Once again, this may stem from a sense by students of feeling more attached to the school due to an increased amount of interaction with teachers. Further, students who have had poor patterns of attendance in the past at large schools sometimes have been known to improve their attendance pattern after changing to a smaller school setting.

A fourth potential benefit of smaller schools is their capacity to promote a strong sense of community within the school among staff and students. From an academic perspective, larger schools may have the ability to provide a wider range of curricular offerings. As noted earlier, however, smaller schools tend to promote increased interaction between staff and students that leads to a sense of belonging and togetherness that is often absent in larger, more impersonal school settings. The sense of being connected to the school seems to promote improvement not only in academics, but also in social behavior on the part of students. The synergy that is created by the sense of belonging promotes the idea of a learning community, along with positive social behavior on the part of students.

A fifth advantage of smaller schools is that students have increased opportunities to participate in extracurricular activities. Increased participation seems to be another factor that promotes student connectedness to the school. In addition, there are numerous positive outcomes for students who are involved in extracurricular activities in school. Intellectual, social, and physical gains are often credited to student participation in extracurricular activities. Although it is true that larger schools often have the resources to provide more in the way of extracurricular activities, the number of students who actually participate in relation to the student population is much less than in smaller schools.

In summary, it appears that smaller schools have the potential to offer numerous advantages to students. Increased academic performance, higher student attendance rates, an enhanced sense of a learning community among staff and students, a feeling of being a part of the school, and a better chance to participate in extracurricular activities all are positive aspects of smaller schools. Although many school districts have

buildings that are larger than those recommended for maximum student academic and social development, the concept of forming schools within schools may bear consideration as a way of restructuring.

David Alan Dolph

See also Accelerated Schools; Accountability Era; Community Control; Dual Enrollment; Early College High Schools; Effective Schools Movement; High Schools That Work; Local Control; Magnet Schools; No Child Left Behind Act (NCLB); School Size; What Works Clearinghouse

Further Readings

Allen, L., & Steinberg, A. (2004). *Big buildings, small schools: Using a small schools strategy for high school reform.* Boston: Jobs for the Future.

Chicago Public Schools. (2003). *Small schools: Research.* Retrieved May 9, 2009, from http://smallschools.cps .k12.il.us/research.html

Hammack, F. M. (2008). Off the record—something old, something new, something borrowed, something blue: Observations on the small schools movement. *Teachers College Record, 110*(9), 2067–2072.

Kafka, J. (2008). Thinking big and getting small: An ideological genealogy of small-school reform. *Teachers College Record, 110*(9), 1802–1836.

Semel, S. F., & Sadovnik, A. R. (2008). The contemporary small-school movement: Lessons from the history of progressive education. *Teachers College Record, 110*(9), 1744–1771.

SMITH-HUGHES ACT

Passed by the U.S. Congress in 1917, the Smith-Hughes Act provided federal aid to states for the purpose of promoting and reforming precollegiate vocational education in agricultural, industrial, and home economics subjects at a moment when reformers were rapidly expanding secondary education and broadening its curriculum to prepare youths for modern life. Spearheaded by the National Society for the Promotion of Industrial Education (NSPIE), the effort for federal aid encompassed an array of interest groups with different reasons for supporting the bill. While the law helped expand vocational courses and enrollment, it often did not live up to the lofty aspirations of its supporters. Historians have also pointed to its unintended effects in differentiating and stratifying curriculum in ways that often reinforced existing inequities.

Historical Background

Beginning in the late 19th century, a variety of groups began to advocate the addition of new manual training courses like woodworking and cooking in schools, on the basis of a societal belief in the moral, educative, and practical value of work. Many supporters, like businessmen and labor unions, saw it as an answer to labor problems in a rapidly industrializing society. Employers hoped it would weaken the power of labor unions in training and supplying positions in industry while workers saw in it an opportunity for individual advancement and for dignifying labor itself. Many philanthropists and moral reformers, on the other hand, viewed manual training as an opportunity to inculcate the moral values of work that they feared were being eroded by modern society. In contrast, many educators and pedagogical reformers saw work as a way to put into practice new teaching methods and philosophies that emphasized cultivating children's interest through active learning and to vitalize the curriculum.

While hundreds of cities experimented with manual training classes in the late 19th century, in the early 20th century supporters began to advocate more systematic programs of work education and to emphasize its economic and utilitarian values more forcefully. Business groups, for example, began to argue that American economic progress and global competitiveness required public funding of trade instruction as found in Europe. In 1905, the Massachusetts state legislature appointed the Massachusetts Commission on Industrial and Technical Education, known as the Douglas Commission, to investigate the need for state-aided vocational training. Its oft-cited final report urged state aid, arguing higher levels of technical training and industrial intelligence was a pressing individual and state interest. It left ambiguous whether this industrial education should take place in the existing public schools or whether new vocational schools should be established. In the next decade, dozens of cities and states, including Massachusetts,

experimented with vocational education, trying both separate technical and trade schools as well as vocational programs within the existing public school system.

The findings of the Douglas Commission were embraced by a diverse group of reformers who came together to support vocational education at local, state, and national levels. In 1906, they formed the National Society for the Promotion of Industrial Education (NSPIE) to organize publicity and lobbying efforts on behalf of vocational education and draw together the supporting groups, including the American Federation of Labor, National Association of Manufacturers, National Education Association, and social welfare reformers. As a result of their efforts, Congress appointed the Commission on National Aid to Vocational Education in 1914 to investigate the possibility of federal aid. Staffed by four pro-vocational-aid congressmen and five members of NSPIE, the Commission's final report declared that vocational education was an urgent national interest that necessitated federal action. Vocational training, it argued, would vitalize general education and democratize schooling by adapting it to the real needs of children, promote industrial efficiency and national prosperity, decrease labor and social unrest, and promote a higher standard of living for workers. It recommended federal grants to the states to promote vocational education, with particular focus on supporting the training and salary of vocational teachers. The Commission proposed legislation that was introduced by two of its members, Senator Hoke Smith (Georgia) and Representative D. M. Hughes (Georgia), and was passed by Congress in 1917, with minor modifications, as the Smith-Hughes Act.

Provisions and Effects

The Smith-Hughes Act was one of the first federal grant-in-aid programs, meaning it provided federal aid on a matching basis to states for support of vocational teachers and laid out requirements for how this money was to be used. It created the Federal Board of Vocational Education to oversee the distribution of money, approve state plans, and disseminate informational bulletins and materials. The Act required every participating state to designate or create a state-level body that would be the liaison between the Federal Vocational Board and local districts and therefore augmented the power of state governments at a time when they were beginning to expand their oversight over local schools in new ways. While much of the advocacy had centered on industrial education, Congress included agriculture and home economics subjects within its definition of vocational subjects but excluded from aid popular commercial and business courses that would later be given federal support. In framing the Act, one source of controversy had been how to provide for the vocational education of girls: Should this training prepare girls to work in industry, the home, or both? The final bill reached a compromise of sorts, providing aid for industrial classes in female-dominated trades like millinery and garment making but ultimately emphasizing and expanding domestic instruction for women's work in the home. The Act left it up to states and localities to decide whether vocational education should be given in special schools or within the existing public schools, but they tended to the latter as a growing consensus emerged on the ideal of a comprehensive high school offering differentiated instruction and programs to all under the same roof.

The Smith-Hughes Act succeeded in dramatically expanding funding and enrollments in vocational subjects, and encouraging states and localities to support vocational education. Subsequent federal laws extended and expanded aid for vocational education as national interest in manpower, economic development, and youth training intensified in the Great Depression, World War II, and beyond. While enrollments in the programs grew, the percentage of young people enrolled in the classes leveled off and remained far lower than supporters had hoped, rarely reaching 20%. Assessments of vocational aid were mixed as studies showed that vocational training did not necessarily produce economic benefits for the individual. While supporters continued to emphasize the value for the individual and nation, critics questioned whether the tremendous resources dedicated to the programs were justified based on the results and whether the programs diverted important resources from the rest of the educational program. Critics argued that the job training provided in these programs often lagged behind actual needs and demands in industry.

Historians have also pointed to the unintended consequences of vocational education programs on the school, noting that they intensified the process of differentiating and sorting in the school, once dominated by an ideal of a single common education for all. Vocational education not only separated students by gender, but sorted them into tracks within the high school that often reinforced existing differences based on class and race. African American students, for example, were often steered in vocational education programs toward preparation for lower-paying, less-desirable jobs because with widespread employment discrimination those were the only ones open to Black youths. Historians have also pointed to the programs as producing an ideology of "vocationalism" in the schools, by which they mean the increasing dominance of economic motivations, aims, and values in education.

Tracy L. Steffes

See also Comprehensive High Schools; Federal Educational Reform; Manual Training; Progressive Education; Vocational Education

Further Readings

Grubb, W. N., & Lazerson, M. (2004). *The education gospel: The economic power of schooling.* Cambridge, MA: Harvard University Press.

Kantor, H. (1988). *Learning to earn: School, work, and vocational reform in California.* Madison: University of Wisconsin Press.

Kliebard, H. M. (1999). *Schooled to work: Vocationalism and the American curriculum, 1876–1946.* New York: Teachers College Press.

Wirth, A. G. (1972). *Education in the technological society: The vocational–liberal studies controversy in the early twentieth century.* Scranton, PA: Intext Educational Publishers.

SOCIAL EFFICIENCY

Social efficiency, the idea that education is a whole framework that involves the school, the community, and the learner, is most often associated with William Chandler Bagley, an American educator and professed essentialist whose progressive educational values were known in the early 1900s.

Bagley suggested social efficiency be incorporated into public schools through teaching and lessons in character education. He suggested that incorporating lessons and activities planned for students in the school and applied in the community would benefit the community as a whole. Students would be performing civic responsibilities from an application of concepts learned in school and thus would apply the values of character education in their daily lives. The result would be valuable for the community and society as a direct result of students' learning in school. It was Bagley's strong belief that students should contribute to and aid in the advancement of society as a whole.

Several years later, Franklin Bobbitt and David Snedden refined Bagley's theories and added new parameters to the concept of social efficiency. They developed a deeper understanding of and application for the development of character education. They advocated classifying and training students for specific occupations for future endeavors. Bobbitt believed that education is a lifetime commitment, and that life and education are united into a whole unit and should never be viewed individually. Education is more than an experience; it is a part of a process. Students, for example, should view education as information and knowledge that can be transferred as a learning tool into society. In Bobbitt's vision, education would uncover the inherent abilities of an individual, cultivate growth and development, and productively transfer the newly learned information into society.

The Work of Franklin Bobbitt

The Curriculum (1918) and *How to Make a Curriculum* (1924) were Bobbitt's most widely known publications. Using Frederick Winslow Taylor's principles of scientific management, Bobbitt developed a curriculum that outlined specific goals and objectives that were clear and concise. His approach was not unlike those Taylor articulated earlier in the century to make American industry more efficient. The key principle in Taylor's theory was task analysis to develop roles and responsibilities for each worker. Each worker was given a narrowly defined production assignment to be performed at a specific rate, using certain predefined procedures. The precise steps would be developed by the manager. Bobbitt applied this

concept of job analysis to curriculum development. It was evident that Taylor's work was successful and that the notion of defining specific activities could be transferred to various occupational, citizenship, family, and societal roles. With this in mind, Bobbitt applied these factors, objectives, and goals to education.

Bobbitt knew that vision and knowledge were two factors that would prove influential in the application of his theories. Vision, according to Bobbitt, is the underlying mental activity that influences a person's interpretation of the world. For example, enjoying music, developing art appreciation, reading literature, and applying math and reading skills all require learned educational concepts. In addition, knowledge helps the student become skilled and provides the basis for upward mobility and advancement. He felt it was important to keep members in society stratified or on equal ground within the stratification. Therefore, knowledge was for skill development within the prescribed occupation or vocation, not for self-advancement.

As a result, Bobbitt promoted the student's vision, knowledge, and mastery of subject matter important for lifelong skills, societal challenges, and basic character education values so that they could all be applied in the future. Additionally, those involved with curriculum development would assign children to specialized curricular tracks, based upon assessments of their intellectual ability. Therefore, when developing the school's curriculum, educators would establish objectives in line with the constructs of the social efficiency model. They noted the importance of integrating individuals into society, but only within the various classes of society. As Bobbitt's theory expanded, he became famous for developing the modern concept of "objective analysis." This became the starting point for curriculum making. His pseudoscientific approach to curriculum making served as a precedent for numerous educators in developing the procedures for designing a course of study. This concept of objective analysis became the driving force behind his curriculum design model. Even today, objectives are an integral part of a teacher's lesson design in the PreK–12 classroom context. His model was valuable as it presented a clear understanding of the connection between outcomes and instruction. Bobbitt noted that to achieve a desirable outcome, objectives would be necessary in order for the instructional experience to be complete.

Bobbitt's work contributed to four areas of curriculum development. The first, previously mentioned, is the identification of objectives as the starting point in lesson design. Second is the use of the scientific approach to curriculum making by delineating the procedures for designing a course of study. Third are the different programs for academic and vocational study. And, finally, the fourth is the definition of curriculum as an instrument of social control or regulation for addressing the problems of modern society. True to the ideals of social efficiency, he saw the task of the schools as that of instilling the skills, knowledge, and beliefs that youth require to function in urban, industrial, and heterogeneous societies in America. Bobbitt also theorized that some objectives are general in nature and, as a result, represent the knowledge that all children require to become valuable citizens and adults. Such an education, he maintained, would provide students with the values in character education that are necessary for them to unite for the common good. The construction of the curriculum that Bobbitt advocated included elements of general education for all youth, which were differentiated into a number of very specialized vocational tracks. Influenced by the mental testing movement, Bobbitt believed that schools should assign children to these specialized curricular tracks on the basis of assessments of their intellectual abilities, and that these abilities would be directly related to their ultimate destinies in life. Teachers were expected to develop a curriculum based upon real-life experiences. They were also expected to teach the associated skills needed to perform based upon those experiences. As teachers taught using his structured curriculum, the social efficiency model centered on social control. In schools, students were taught to be good workers, a reflection of Taylor's industrial theory. Students were not encouraged to become free thinkers. Students did not have choices in Bobbitt's curriculum construction philosophy. Their intellectual abilities determined what contribution to society they could make.

Current Developments

Bobbitt did contribute a useful means of curriculum writing still used today. As noted, his theory of curriculum development was content specific. The process involved identifying needed skills, then separating these skills into specific units, organizing them into experiences, and teaching these experiences to children. Bobbitt's five-step process in curriculum writing is useful in today's teaching process. The first step is the analysis of human experience as a whole. The second step is job analysis, which breaks the human experience down into specific activities. Third is deriving objectives. The fourth step, selecting objectives, is the process of identifying which objectives are best able to meet the goal. The objectives are determined and serve as the driving point in the planning stage. Therefore, the fifth and final step of planning is the detail stage. Here the educator uses the activities to create the lesson or curricula.

The original concept of social efficiency can be seen in today's educational system, particularly in the practice of differentiated instruction. Additionally, guidance counselors, whose function is to develop the most beneficial program for each student, analyze the results of standardized tests; student participation in extracurricular activities; intellectual, personal, and physical goals; and aid the student in determining a possible vocation. In order to further the philosophy of social efficiency, curriculum specialists were hired to address concerns outside the classroom. This process allowed the teacher to focus on the needs of the students within the classroom. Issues such as scheduling, discipline, health, and supplies were resolved without disrupting the classroom. This aspect of school life is observable today.

In Bobbitt's final work, *Curriculum of Modern Education*, his opinions about curriculum and its place in society reflect a change in judgment. Bobbitt recognized that neither he nor any other educator could predict the lives of their students by examining the outcomes of an intelligence test. Today we see testing employed as only one method for determining a student's placement. There are multiple criteria used when referring a student for college or vocational placement. The idea of students focusing their attention during school hours on only their future careers was abandoned as broader criteria began being used. Bobbitt in his later thinking favored general education for the masses. No longer would students be separated into specific vocational tracks, but instead the learning would be broadened and more worldly. This broadening of the student's educational offerings would also include an appreciation and respect for the work done by the authors of great literary works. Bobbitt also proposed that the school's curriculum develop each student's intellect. Instead of guiding students to a predetermined vocation, students were encouraged to become free thinkers and were motivated to learn on their own. In addition, their career path was not selected for them. The new goal was to make them lifelong learners.

Our current educational system provides students the opportunity to learn through an enriched curriculum that offers varied subjects. These general education offerings provide students with the information, background, and exposure to many vocational and academic areas. This method emulates Bobbitt's beliefs that students should continue on a general education track until they are 18 years of age. By the age of 18, students will have been exposed to various subjects and will have the ability to make informed decisions regarding their future. This reform in his thinking was the beginning of a new approach for social efficiency and its role in determining students' roles in the future of society.

Curriculum is no longer vocationally driven once schools are reorganized. Instead, teachers are the facilitators of education. They encourage students to test, evaluate, and think abstractly when making the most appropriate learning decisions. Teachers are an integral part of the lesson design today, as conceived by Bobbitt. They now engage in curriculum mapping in order to provide a holistic approach to curriculum construction. Bobbitt's beliefs are evident in the role teachers have in writing curriculum construction and courses of study for their classes. Their opinions are being heard, and they are being empowered to shape and mold curriculum based on the needs of the learner and state core curriculum content standards. Linking the subject matter to the interest of the students is seen today in teachers' specific daily lesson plan construction and design. Students' learning styles are being used in curriculum construction and in lesson planning. A vast amount of knowledge has been uncovered while researching the human brain as it relates to how the learner learns and therefore how educational goals are developed. Knowing how the learner learns enables teachers to plan more effectively.

Bobbitt's philosophy, thoughts, and objectives are seen in today's models for curriculum development. His initial thoughts evolved, and with his change of heart came the involvement and motivation of students in the learning process for the improvement of society. Although not widely known, the prevalence of Bobbitt's social efficiency theory still impacts education. Bobbitt may be remembered as one of the great reform thinkers whose constructs are still applicable in educational policy and practice.

Mario C. Barbiere

See also Curriculum Controversies; Dewey, John; Essentialism; Experiential Learning; Herbartian Movement; Progressive Education

Further Readings

Bagley, W. C. (1905). *The education process*. New York: Macmillan.
Bobbitt, J. F. (1941). *Curriculum of modern education.* York, PA: Maple Press.
Drost, W. H. (1977). Social efficiency reexamined: The Dewey-Snedden controversy. *Curriculum Inquiry, 7*(1), 19–32.
Kliebard, H. (1995). *The struggle for the American curriculum, 1893–1958* (2nd ed.). New York: Routledge.

SOCIAL RECONSTRUCTIONISM

The 1920s brought a resurgence of concern for the individual among many American intellectuals and a decline in their desire to continue the social reform of the Progressive era. This attitude led most progressive educators to emphasize fostering the natural and creative impulses of the child as the primary role of the school. Throughout the decade and into the 1930s, these child-centered progressives dominated the Progressive Education Association, founded in 1919. By the 1930s, however, the Great Depression was again leading American intellectuals to see the individual as shaped by society. They believed that improving American society by solving the dire problems of the Depression would in turn benefit the individual. Among these intellectuals were progressive educational theorists who saw the school as one institution that could promote social reform. Led by George S. Counts, William H. Kilpatrick, Harold Rugg, and others affiliated primarily with Teachers College, Columbia University, they rejected the traditional idea that the role of the school was simply to transmit the culture, arguing instead that schools should lead in the reconstruction of society by promoting a collectivist economy that would cure the ills of capitalism. They even went so far as to advocate the use of indoctrination to achieve that goal. Their educational theory, called social reconstructionism, generated considerable debate among educators and other intellectuals during the 1930s. The debate eventually spilled over into the larger society when some of their ideas appeared in the American Historical Association's proposal to reform the social studies curriculum and in a controversial series of social studies textbooks written by Harold Rugg. For more than a decade, social reconstructionism faced growing criticism, and by the mid-1950s, the conservative mood of the country and calls for a return to traditional schooling led to the demise of this reform effort along with the larger progressive education movement.

Beginning in 1927, a small group of progressives, including Counts, Kilpatrick, and Rugg, gathered with America's leading philosopher, John Dewey, to discuss the role of the school in a changing industrial society. Early in the Depression, their discussions expanded into a raging debate with the child-centered progressive educators. At the annual meeting of the Progressive Education Association in 1932, George Counts asked the membership, "Dare Progressive Education be Progressive?" He criticized progressive education for not having a theory of social welfare beyond individualism and argued for ridding the economy of the evils of capitalism through a planned, collective economy. His speech soon generated considerable discussion for the remainder of the meeting. Counts later expanded his argument in a pamphlet titled *Dare the School Build a New Social Order?* Answering this question, he opined that truly progressive education required investigating social issues, developing a theory of social welfare, overcoming the fear of imposition and indoctrination in the classroom, and creating a collective economy to save democracy.

By 1933, Counts and his colleagues sought to develop and disseminate social reconstructionism. In addition to Counts's pamphlet, these scholars participated in a symposium titled The Educational Frontier, whose published proceedings were edited by Kilpatrick and created a journal called *The Social Frontier*. Counts edited the journal, Kilpatrick, Rugg, and others joined the enterprise, and John Dewey agreed to write a monthly article.

Contributors to *The Social Frontier* generally agreed with Counts on the conflict between the individualism of the old agrarian society and the values of the new corporate industrial society. They also thought teachers ought to be leaders in planning the social and economic reconstruction of America, and schools should be part of that transformation. They disagreed with Counts, however, on the use of indoctrination in the classroom, and some of them were not optimistic about the power of the school to foster the reconstruction until it had been appropriately reformed.

The Social Frontier first appeared in October 1934, and throughout its life, the role of education in the social and economic crisis of the 1930s was its central theme. Editorials reflected the perspective of social reconstructionism, asserting that the age of individualism in America was being superseded by an age of collectivism. Counts and some contributors contended that the success of such a transformation depended on the degree to which organized education became identified with social reconstruction. They saw schools and teachers as potentially powerful forces in the effort to reform the society. In an early issue devoted to the topic of indoctrination, all but one contributor argued that indoctrination was necessary for inculcating the ideas of social reconstruction into the minds of students. The lone dissenter, philosopher Boyd H. Bode, objected to indoctrination, except, ironically, to convince others it was wrong.

As radicalism in America diminished after 1935, so did social reconstructionism. The radical rhetoric of *The Social Frontier* brought a decrease in subscriptions by 1937. Editorials by Kilpatrick, the new editor, emphasized the principles of democracy and the need for changes in the economy. The softening of social reconstructionism also became evident as contributors began criticizing the New Deal and its apparent failure to alleviate the problems of the Depression. In 1939, the Progressive Education Association agreed to support the journal and changed its title to *Frontiers of Democracy,* but even discussions about World War II failed to keep the journal alive after 1943.

Before the decline of radicalism, however, social reconstructionism had spread beyond a group of radical progressive educators to the larger intellectual community and the schools. In 1934, the report of the American Historical Association's Commission on the Social Studies, authored by eminent historian Charles A. Beard and others, showed Counts's influence in its support of social reconstruction and a movement toward collectivism. This politically charged report elicited immediate condemnation from some progressive educators and criticism of its threat to freedom of thought from Boyd Bode, who, like John Dewey, was generally sympathetic to the concerns of the social reconstructionists.

The impact of social reconstructionism in the schools resulted from the work of Harold Rugg. In the 1920s, Rugg had sought to introduce social problems into the school curriculum. By 1929, he had developed a series of pioneering social studies textbooks titled *Man and His Changing Society.* Between 1929 and 1939, the series sold nearly 1.4 million copies, a considerable achievement amid a shrinking economy. These textbooks became the most significant achievement of the effort to reform the schools along the lines of social reconstruction. Yet, like *The Social Frontier* and the report of the American Historical Association Commission, *Man and His Changing Society* felt the effects of declining radicalism in the late 1930s and the stinging criticism of journalists, school districts, and the American Legion. Despite a defense from some of the "frontier thinkers," by 1940 interest in Rugg's textbooks had declined sufficiently that he never revised them.

The post–World War II period brought renewed emphasis on patriotism in American society and a return to the traditional role of the school as transmitter of culture. In the face of growing criticism of the schools by the mid-1950s, social reconstructionism and the idea the school should lead in social reform died along with the progressive education movement. Nevertheless, the question of the role of the school in society at the heart of this educational theory continues to foster discussion and debate

among intellectuals, educational policymakers, and the public.

Dalton B. Curtis, Jr.

See also Counts, George S.; Dewey, John; Educational Reform During the Great Depression; Eight-Year Study; Progressive Education; Progressive Education Association (PEA); Rugg, Harold

Further Readings

Bowers, C. A. (1969). *The progressive educator and the Depression: The radical years.* New York: Random House.
Cremin, L. A. (1961). *The transformation of the school: Progressivism in American education, 1876–1957.* New York: Knopf.
Graham, P. A. (1967). *Progressive education: From Arcady to academe: A history of the Progressive Education Association, 1919–1955.* New York: Teachers College Press.
Kliebard, H. M. (1995). *The struggle for the American curriculum, 1893–1958* (2nd ed.). New York: Routledge.

SOCIAL STUDIES, NEW

The New Social Studies refers to the movement that attempted to revise, update, and improve social studies instruction by creating innovative, inquiry-based curricula, and curriculum materials for K–12 social studies classrooms founded upon the structures and modes of exploration of each of the academic disciplines that comprise the social studies. Between 1962 and the early 1970s, the U.S. Office of Education (USOE), the National Science Foundation (NSF), and the Ford Foundation funded more than 50 projects that sought to reform how social studies was taught.

Background

When the Soviet Union launched *Sputnik,* the world's first artificial satellite, in 1957, the general public perception was that the Russians had pulled ahead of the United States in terms of scientific advance. American military and political leaders began to examine areas in K–12 education that were said to account for the supposed deficiency. The National Science Foundation, created in 1950 in order to improve science education and research, and the 1958 passage of the National Defense Education Act provided the impetus and the funding to reform curriculum and instruction in K–12 science and mathematics, and in foreign languages.

The federally funded movement led to the development of curriculum materials that were labeled "the new math" or "the new science." In September 1959 the Education Committee of the National Academy of Sciences sponsored a conference at the Woods Hole Oceanographic Institute on Cape Cod in order to examine the fundamental processes involved in imparting the substance and method of science to young learners. The report summarizing the proceedings of the conference was written by Jerome Bruner and published in 1960 as *The Process of Education*. It set out the themes for the entire curriculum reform movement in all academic subject areas, including that which would be called the New Social Studies.

The Process of Education has four basic themes that would establish the agenda for the New Social Studies. The first was that the structures that make up academic disciplines should form the basis for curriculum; the second was readiness, or, as Bruner wrote, the notion that "any subject can be taught effectively in some intellectually honest form to any child at any stage of development," which reflected Piaget's influence on Bruner. The third theme was intuition, particularly as a learned skill, and finally, motivation, including those factors that support or that threaten a child's motivation to learn.

There had been little call for reform of social studies in the decade of the 1950s, and as a result, the field was slow in responding to the general trend following Woods Hole. In 1961, Charles R. Keller, a historian and former director of the Advanced Placement program, wrote an article for the *Saturday Review* chastising the social studies for lagging behind other content areas. He challenged social studies educators to undertake the type of curriculum reform characteristic of the new math and the new science. Keller urged a revamping of the entire social studies construct, acknowledging the artificial nature of the subject and replacing the term *social studies* with "history and the social sciences."

Prior to the appearance of Keller's piece, some university faculty were already beginning to engage in the types of inquiry-based curriculum development that would be characteristic of the New Social Studies. Economist Lawrence Senesh of Purdue University was working on an economics program and a textbook series aimed at elementary aged students. Edward Fenton was a historian at Carnegie Institute of Technology in Pittsburgh whose teaching load included the social studies methods course. In his history courses, and in work that he was doing with Pittsburgh-area high schools, Fenton began to introduce primary source documents as a way to introduce high school students, undergraduates, and pre-service teachers to the actual work of the historian. As a result of his experiences, Fenton produced a social studies methods text and a series of inquiry-based K–12 history texts that elevated him to a leadership role in the curriculum reform movement. Similar to Fenton's work was that of the Amherst (Massachusetts) History Project, which used primary sources and secondary historical accounts in order to provide secondary students with opportunities to develop and test their own hypotheses about historical causation.

Inquiry-Based Instruction: Rationale and Key Projects

University faculty from the Arts and Sciences were vital to the success of the New Social Studies. The underlying belief behind inquiry-based instruction was that students would be exposed to the structures that lay beneath each of the social sciences. The content taught in the classroom should be derived from the structure, concepts, and methodology of each academic discipline. Teachers would teach students how historians and social scientists create new knowledge in their disciplines, thereby allowing students to "do" the work of a sociologist or anthropologist, an economist, a political scientist, or a historian.

In the October 1962 issue of *Social Education* there appeared a small notice announcing USOE funding for Project Social Studies. Funds were to be made available for research, curriculum study centers, academic conferences, and seminars. By July of 1963, the USOE reported that 7 curriculum centers, 11 research projects, and 2 developmental activities had been approved for funding. Four more were funded in 1964, and by 1965 there were over two dozen projects and curriculum centers funded by the NSF, the USOE, or private foundations.

These included funding for the work of Fenton, Senesh, and the Amherst consortium. New projects tended to follow a similar design; the Anthropology Curriculum Study Project, the High School Geography Project, and The Sociological Resources for Secondary Schools all were headed by university faculty and were sponsored by professional academic associations within each respective field. Each project sought to develop curriculum materials that would explore principles specific to the field, using the inquiry approaches distinctive to each discipline.

The Harvard Social Studies Project, headed by Donald Oliver and his protégé, James P. Shaver, was unique among the funded projects in that it alone attempted to integrate skills and concepts from virtually all of the social studies disciplines. Designed to teach students to analyze controversial issues through discussion and written argument, the project produced a series of individual units that covered a wide array of historical and contemporary social studies issues ranging from economic interpretations of the American Revolution to the tension between communalism and individual identity in communist China.

The most controversial of the projects was an anthropologically and sociologically based project named *Man: A Course of Study,* or MACOS. Funded by the NSF, MACOS was developed by Harvard University and Massachusetts Institute of Technology faculty working with the Educational Development Center, Inc., in Cambridge, Massachusetts. Aimed at Grades 4 through 9, MACOS used nontraditional teaching exercises. Students wrote "field notes" as they watched documentary films without narration about animal studies and then about the Netsilik Eskimos. They also wrote journals and poems as they explored recurring themes about human collective behavior in an effort to promote an appreciation for the common humanity all persons share.

How Well Did the New Social Studies Succeed?

By 1975, MACOS was under attack from parents, school administrators, and politicians who claimed

that the curriculum exposed children to animal cruelty as well as to Netsilik cannibalism, adultery, female infanticide, and the killing of the old and infirm. The MACOS debate highlighted a general criticism of schools by the 1970s, in that the social and behavioral scientists who designed the curriculum were looked upon as agents of social change determined to influence children against the beliefs or wishes of their parents.

While the New Social Studies produced quality instructional materials, the movement ultimately failed to meet its own targets. Largely designed by university faculty in colleges of arts and sciences with minimal input from curriculum designers in schools of education, few of the projects were designed to meet the reality of K–12 classrooms. Many of the projects required teachers to make radical changes to their styles of teaching in order to make the materials work. In addition, teachers with minimal training in economics, anthropology, and sociology were expected to be able to teach children how to do the work of an economist, anthropologist, or sociologist. Although the federal government provided funds for summer teacher training institutes aligned with several of the projects, most teachers were ill prepared for teaching with curriculum materials designed by college faculty with little sense of precollegiate needs.

The New Social Studies also failed because of the traditional role of the social studies in American schools. The social studies have always played a civic function in preparing students for specific civic roles. The New Social Studies, with its emphasis on the structures of the social sciences, stood somewhat aloof and above the mundane world of preparing young people to understand issues of voting, taxation, and the Constitution. With a few exceptions, the college professors who designed New Social Studies projects were interested in initiating young people into the particular skills they used in conducting research—their goal was not citizenship education.

The distance between general American society and the world that the academicians sought to bring to the classroom was highlighted by the social upheaval of the late 1960s and 1970s. The model of the high school student as a young historian or sociologist seemed far removed from the drama that was playing itself out on America's streets, and was quickly replaced with the model of the student as a young activist, which, although still a departure from the earlier civic model of the social studies, still connected students to the realities of American life in a vivid and immediate manner. As funding ended after the election of Richard Nixon in 1968, the production of new material slowed and eventually ended.

The New Social Studies did help to stimulate the development of entire curricula rather than simply textbooks, and while the textbook was never eliminated as the primary instructional material, the work of Edwin Fenton and the Amherst History Project, in particular, established student engagement with primary source materials as one of the hallmarks of good history instruction. By increasing the use of inquiry-based strategies, the New Social Studies also served as a harbinger of later constructivist arguments concerning the need for active student engagement in the classroom.

John J. White

See also Critical Literacy; National Council for History Education; National Endowment for the Humanities; Teacher Education

Further Readings

Evans, R. W. (2004). *The social studies wars: What should we teach the children?* New York: Teachers College Press.

Fenton, E. (1967). *The new social studies.* New York: Holt, Rinehart & Winston.

Haas, J. D. (1977). *The era of the new social studies.* Boulder, CO: Social Science Education Consortium.

Krug, M. M., Poster, J. B., & Gillies, W. B. (1970). *The new social studies: Analysis of theory and materials.* Itasca, IL: F. E. Peacock.

Society of Friends Schools

The Society of Friends (Quakers) originated in the 1650s in the context of the English Revolution. Like the Puritans, Quakers were viewed as dissenters and were not allowed access to many schools. Quakers viewed most schools as teaching false understandings of religion and therefore in need of reform. George Fox, founder of the Society of Friends, established schools for both boys and girls as early as 1668. Quaker schools emphasized a religiously guarded education, creating a context for each student to experience the leadings of the Inner Light, especially as those are manifested in community. The schools practiced and taught Quaker testimonies, especially equality, simplicity, honesty, and peace, with the aim of helping students develop knowledge, skills, and moral understanding to live in the world, not simply as it is, but as it ought to be. These religious commitments and practices led to reforms in education, including the adoption of the Lancasterian (also Lancastrian) method, a commitment to the education of women, a stress on equality in education, and dissent from common practices of corporal punishment and competition. Quakers in England and the United States eventually developed schools at all levels from elementary through college and adult education. Many of these schools retain their Quaker affiliation and commitments.

The primary teaching of the Society of Friends is that each person can experience the Inner Light, that of God within. This presence of God within has the power to guide each person, but there is a discipline required to experience the leading of that Light. Friends' schools were established to provide a religiously guarded education, one that protects children from influences that might lead them astray. In the early period of Quakerism, this meant guarding children from the influence of certain books and teachers. They were also kept from activities such as music, drama, and visual arts. School, however, was not a place of religious indoctrination, but rather an environment in which students were more likely to be able to have direct experience of the Inner Light. Over time, Friends have become more accepting of music and art, seeing the spiritual merits of these forms of experience.

The Society of Friends is made up of small groups that meet regularly for worship and business. Consensus decision making guides the meetings for business. The community must be united in the leading of the Spirit before any action is taken. Social testimonies arise out of the worship and business practices. Testimonies take the form of queries, questions for reflection and meditation that guide the lives and practices of Quakers. The focus and structure of Friends' schools are guided by testimonies, especially the aforementioned.

The early schools in Philadelphia illustrate the importance of community. William Penn envisioned a society with universal public education and founded Friends Public School in Philadelphia in 1689. Schools provided Quaker and non-Quaker children with opportunities to grow and develop their own inner conscience as well as practical skills. Competition, prizes, and awards were discouraged. Early Quaker schools in Philadelphia were modeled on the monitorial system developed in England by Joseph Lancaster (1778–1839). Students were grouped according to ability and were taught by means of simultaneous instruction rather than individual recitation. Students were promoted to more advanced groups as they developed individually. The entire system was guided by a set of rules that set out behavioral expectations for students, monitors, and managers. These schools continued until a general public school system was established in the 1800s.

The testimony on equality may have had the most important impact on educational reform. Friends were committed to the equality of the sexes in worship and business from the beginning. This greatly influenced Quaker schools. Girls were given the same education as boys. Friends founded boarding schools, initially for their own children. These were coeducational schools. All Quaker colleges were founded as coeducational schools except for Haverford College, for men, and its counterpart on an immediately adjacent campus, Bryn Mawr College, for women. Today, Haverford is coeducational. In addition, Quakers were early to employ women as teachers, and as early as 1702 a woman was appointed mistress of a Philadelphia school. Friends have also always been committed to education for all races and classes. As early as 1671, George Fox asked Friends to educate Indians and Negroes. The Philadelphia schools as well as Friends schools in other colonies educated poor children and supported the work of teachers to educate Black children, usually in separate settings. After the Civil War, the Friends Freedman's Association was active in maintaining schools. In 1870 there were 46 such schools in Philadelphia alone.

The testimony of simplicity influenced Friends to develop an emphasis on practical subjects as well as classical courses of study. This resulted in Friends schools introducing the serious study of science before many other schools. Swarthmore College was one of the first to place an emphasis on science, and John Griscom, a Quaker educator, was the first to teach chemistry in the United States. Quaker educators did not see a contradiction between science and religion, but rather saw the practical and experimental nature of science as an extension of the experiential relationship to the world of the spirit. The testimonies on honesty and peace led Quakers to be some of the first to abandon corporal punishment in schools. Honesty requires a person to live in the truth at all times. Moral education should be structured to make external rules and coercion unnecessary as students learn to be guided by the presence within. Abandoning corporal punishment also demonstrates the power of peace-building. Sarah Grubb (1756–1790) was instrumental in emphasizing the importance of the workability of love in the education of children. Peace education continues to be an important aspect of Friends schools.

Contemporary Friends schools are diverse, supported by a variety of Quaker traditions. They span all educational levels including institutions such as Pendle Hill that focus on adult education. Quaker schools continue to emphasize educational programs that are in keeping with Friends practices and testimonies and so continue to be committed to reforms that emphasize diversity, equality, and peace-building. The Friends Council on Education maintains information on all current schools.

Patricia Altenbernd Johnson

See also Coeducation; Peace Education; Women in Educational Leadership

Further Readings

Barbour, H., & Frost, J. W. (1988). *The Quakers.* Westport, CT: Greenwood.

Brinton, H. H. (1940). *Quaker education in theory and practice* (Pendle Hill Pamphlet No. 9). Wellington, PA: Pendle Hill.

Kashatus, W. C. (1997). *A virtuous education: Penn's vision for Philadelphia schools.* Wellington, PA: Pendle Hill.

Oliver, J. W., Cherry, C. L., & Cherry, C. L. (2007). *Founded by Friends: The Quaker heritage of fifteen American colleges and universities.* Lanham, MD: Scarecrow.

SOUTHERN EDUCATION BOARD

The southern education reform movement of the late 19th and early 20th centuries was a multifaceted effort that included a number of philanthropic funds and a lobbying arm, the Southern Education Board (SEB). The SEB's advocacy led to an increase in appropriations for education in all of the southern states between 1900 and 1930. Even as educational opportunities widened for White children, however, a system of separate and unequal schools for Black children became firmly established in southern U.S. culture, enthusiastically supported by the philanthropists who governed the SEB.

The policies and programs of the SEB grew out of northern reformers' support for Hampton and Tuskegee institutes. New Yorker Robert C. Ogden was one of the founders of Hampton Institute and served on its board from 1874 until his death in 1913. Ogden believed that industrial education for Blacks would promote economic recovery and political stability in the postwar South by creating a skilled labor force. As Ogden solicited support for Hampton and its offshoot, Tuskegee Institute, among his wealthy acquaintances, he spread the idea of industrial education in northern philanthropic circles and was regarded as an authority on the topic. At the same time, he gained the respect of progressive White southerners for his understanding of southern society and White supremacist values. Ogden found an ally in Wall Street banker George Foster Peabody, who joined him on the Hampton board in 1884. Peabody's investment expertise helped place Hampton and Tuskegee on a solid financial footing and bankrolled both the SEB and the General Education Board. The third member of the triumvirate was William H. Baldwin, Jr. As general manager of the Southern Railway Company, Baldwin employed thousands of Black laborers and thus had a vested interest in a stable, skilled Black workforce.

The southern education movement began in 1901 when Ogden took a group of northern industrialists on a train journey to North Carolina where they met with members of the Conference for Education in the South. Their alliance was founded on a combination of disfranchisement and Jim Crow laws with a two-tiered educational system. The northerners would furnish technical assistance and limited funding while the southerners provided local leadership and political will. The arrangement was formalized in 1901 as the Southern Education Board at the annual meeting of the Conference for Education in the South. Its mission was to promote free education for all southerners by providing information to newspapers and magazines, speaking at educational meetings, supporting lobbying efforts, and maintaining networks of correspondence. The Board was funded first by individual contributions, then by grants from the General Education Board.

The 11 northern and 15 southern members of the SEB worked for 13 years to advance their reform agenda, with mixed results. In some states the SEB was able to build on existing efforts to create school systems; in others its success was limited by special interests that feared widespread public education as destabilizing and intrusive. The Virginia Constitution of 1902 contained provisions for a modernized and professionalized school system and the legislature subsequently organized a Cooperative Education Association specifically to coordinate with the SEB. In North Carolina, Governor Aycock worked with the SEB to stimulate local efforts to improve public education. Kentucky and Tennessee both enacted pro-education legislation for primary, secondary, and postsecondary levels of schooling. In South Carolina, however, opposition by mill owners and railroads led to the defeat of progressive education legislation. In Georgia, a constitutional amendment permitting county levies to fund schools was adopted, but localities were reluctant to actually impose the taxes.

There was a racial subtext to all discussions of public education in the South. While there was little disagreement that improving access to education for White children was desirable, extending educational benefits to Black children was far more controversial. Much of the resistance to universal education was rooted in a conviction that African Americans should not be educated at all. Other opponents resented northern interference in what was regarded as a local prerogative. The consortium of northern and southern interests that the SEB represented was convinced that education for Blacks would contribute to the prosperity of the New South and benefit all of its citizens. Many southern industrialists, however, saw universal education as threatening to the status quo. They feared that educated Blacks would become discontented with their place in the southern economy, claim their Fourteenth Amendment right to vote, and be vulnerable to calls for unionization.

Elizabeth P. Harper

See also General Education Board; Peabody Fund; Progressive Education

Further Readings

Anderson, J. A. (1988). *The education of Blacks in the South, 1860–1935*. Chapel Hill: University of North Carolina.

Cremin, L. A. (1988). *American education: The metropolitan experience, 1876–1980*. New York: Harper & Row.

Harlan, L. R. (1957). The Southern Education Board and the race issue in public education. *Journal of Southern History, 23*, 189–202.

SOUTHERN STUDY

The Southern Study (1938–1945), sponsored by the Southern Association of Colleges and Secondary Schools and funded by the General Education Board, was established to assist 33 high schools in the 11 southern states to experiment with their academic programs. Similar to the efforts of other projects of the 1930s and 1940s—the Progressive Education Association's Eight-Year Study, the American Council on Education's Cooperative Study, the Association of Colleges and Secondary Schools for Negroes' Secondary School Study, the Carnegie Foundation's Pennsylvania Study—the Southern Association's Commission on Curricular Problems and Research attempted to articulate the relationship between high school and college curriculum. As a way to encourage substantive reform and "radical departures from conventional procedures," accrediting regulations were waived for those participating schools so that the secondary school programs could be adapted as forms of true experimentation in the areas of curriculum and instruction. It should be noted that while no Southern Association schools elected to take part in the Eight-Year Study, begun in 1930, the Southern Study must be seen as a direct outgrowth of the Progressive Education Association's project. While focusing the curriculum around the needs of students, Southern Study teachers participated in Progressive Education Association-like summer workshops, local and state conferences, and in-school visits with Southern Association administrators and Southern Study and Eight-Year Study staff members.

Of the 33 participating Southern Study secondary schools, 14 were urban, 4 rural, and 15 suburban; 31 schools were coeducational and 6 were demonstration schools and represented a much broader school population than the Eight-Year Study. The following schools were included in the study:

Holtville High School, Deatsville (AL)

Montevallo High School, Montevallo (AL)

Tuscaloosa High School, Tuscaloosa (AL)

Dixie County High School, Cross City (FL)

Miami Beach High School, Miami Beach (FL)

St. Petersburg High School, St. Petersburg (FL)

Moultrie High School, Moultrie (GA)

Peabody Training School, Milledgeville (GA)

University Demonstration School, Athens (GA)

Benham High School, Benham (KY)

Frankfort High School, Frankfort (KY)

Lafayette High School, Lexington (KY)

Campti High School, Campti (LA)

E. E. Lyon High School, Covington (LA)

Minden High School, Minden (LA)

Canton High School, Canton (MS)

Meridian High School and Junior College, Meridian (MS)

Okolona High School, Okolona (MS)

Lee H. Edwards High School, Asheville (NC)

Goldsboro High School, Goldsboro (NC)

Greenville High School, Greenville (NC)

Dreher High School, Columbia (SC)

Parker High School, Greenville (SC)

Sumter High School, Sumter (SC)

Collierville High School, Collierville (TN)

Norris High School, Norris (TN)

Peabody Demonstration School (TN)

Edinburg High School, Edinburg (TX)

Highland Park High School, Dallas (TX)

Thomas Jefferson High School, Port Arthur (TX)

Cradock High School, Portsmouth (VA)

Radford High School, Radford (VA)

Waynesboro High School, Waynesboro (VA)

Directly linked to the "implementative research" and experimental reform efforts of other 1930s and 1940s General Education Board–funded projects, the Southern Study, also called the Cooperative Study for the Improvement of Education, organized its practices around the then-popular method of "cooperation"—a distinguishable research method where individuals from different areas (regions) discussed differing viewpoints and cooperated to address a research problem and/or to determine a method of investigation. Project consultants—a network of resource staff and workshop instructors—collaborated with participants to examine common problems and innovative practices in what proved to be a distinguishing factor for this type of method, as teachers came together to "work" in meaningful ways toward school reform. "Cooperation" became emblematic of the entire Southern Study project as member schools were placed together in settings where they could begin to formulate purposes and plans for educational reform. Cooperative planning represented a tangible practice that served to address the Southern Study's one central problem: What curricular reforms will better meet the needs of the youth in our community?

With more than $200,000 in grant support from the General Education Board, Southern Study staff compared schools' standardized test results with academic performance from a control group, and a follow-up study of student success at the college level was also conducted. The Southern Study maintained that high school students' academic success was greater at participating schools and their graduates were more successful at the post-secondary level than those from the control group of students. In addition, Southern Study staff found that the personal–social outcomes of schooling were greater and more positive for students from participating schools.

While the Study refrained from presenting a "best practices" approach to educational reform

and secondary school success (for students in the South), the final report implicitly identified successful practices to include a curriculum focused on student needs, school procedures conceived with complexity rather than simplicity, the acceptance of unconventional school activities, school faculty comfortable with continual educational change, and communities engaged in a continuous effort to define the function of school in society (guided by a conception of democracy as a way of life). In many respects, the Southern Study (and Secondary School Study) extended the practices of the Eight-Year Study, set in different contexts and implemented in different ways, and embracing a basic approach to educational reform to represent an academically oriented form of progressive education at the secondary school level.

Craig Kridel

See also Eight-Year Study; General Education Board; Laboratory Schools; Progressive Education

Further Readings

Aikin, W. (1942). *The story of the Eight-Year Study.* New York: Harper & Brothers.

Jenkins, F. C., Kent, D. C., Sims, V. M., & Waters, E. A. (1947). *The Southern Study: Cooperative study for the improvement of education.* Durham, NC: Duke University Press.

Kridel, C., & Bullough, R. V., Jr., (2007). *Stories of the Eight-Year Study: Reexamining secondary education in America.* Albany: State University of New York Press.

SPECIAL NEEDS EDUCATION

Special education has historically evolved from dissent and reform movements, and continues to do so. Such efforts emerged early in American history and continued with limited success until the latter part of the 20th century, when organized reform movements, largely fueled by parents of children with disabilities, succeeded in ushering in sweeping changes in the American educational system. This entry discusses reform and dissent from the early period of American history through the 1990s. During this portion of American educational history, students with disabilities progressed from largely being excluded from public school programs to being included in general education classrooms and the general education curriculum. However, for much of the 20th century, physical integration into schools was more common than integration into the general education curriculum.

Early Reform Efforts

In Europe during the 1600s and 1700s, advances were made in educating individuals with disabilities (the term *individuals* refers to both students and adults with disabilities), including those who were deaf or blind or had intellectual disabilities such as mental retardation. These advances came to America during the 1800s and primarily in the provision of services to individuals with disabilities in institutional settings expressly designed for them. Even into the early 20th century, some educational and medical professionals continued to believe that intellectual disabilities in particular were the result of divine punishment for violating natural laws. These beliefs were based on studies (albeit scientifically flawed studies) indicating higher rates of poverty, alcoholism, criminality, and promiscuity among people with intellectual disabilities.

Ronald L. Taylor, Lydia R. Smiley, and Stephen B. Richards summarized historical trends in reform and dissent in special education pointing out that, fortunately, there were reform-minded professionals in early American history who sought to improve the quality of life of individuals with disabilities. Thomas Hopkins Gallaudet cofounded the American School for the Deaf in 1816. His son, Edwin Miner Gallaudet, would become the first president of Gallaudet College (now Gallaudet University), the premier higher education institution in the United States that includes sign language in its curriculum and culture. Horace Mann was also instrumental in developing services for deaf individuals. Samuel Gridley Howe founded the

New England Asylum for the Blind in 1832, which later became the Perkins School for the Blind, which is still in existence today. The Perkins School was also where Helen Keller received a portion of her education and where the Perkins Brailler was developed, still an important tool in reading and writing braille. Howe also was involved in the development of the Massachusetts School for Idiotic and Feebleminded Children in the mid-1850s. Similarly, Edouard Seguin worked at Howe's institution and developed methods of education focusing on the individual's intelligence, activity, and will. Seguin was also important in forming an association that would eventually evolve into today's American Association on Intellectual and Developmental Disabilities, a professional and advocacy organization that is at the forefront of efforts to better understand and assist individuals with disabilities in obtaining a high quality of life in the mainstream of society.

While this discussion is by no means exhaustive, it illustrates that there were currents of reform in American society and culture led by professionals who believed that individuals with disabilities could and should be educated. Such educational efforts were intended to benefit both the individual and society in general.

Early-Twentieth-Century Reform and Dissent

Richard Scheerenberger describes in detail reform and dissent in relation to individuals with mental retardation or intellectual disabilities. In the very early 20th century, negative beliefs about the origins of such disabilities persisted. The Eugenics movement was very much alive in America at the turn of the 20th century. Eugenicists were concerned that individuals who were "feebleminded" represented a threat to society due to their immoral behavior and rate of birth of illegitimate children. Eugenicists believed intellectual disabilities were largely hereditary and, therefore, separation from the mainstream of society and even sterilization of such individuals were necessary for the greater good. In turn, these beliefs increased the institutionalization of individuals with intellectual and other disabilities. Eugenics lost favor, however, as the century progressed and professionals recognized studies supporting these views were scientifically unsound.

Other professionals continued efforts to improve educational services. For example, in 1922, the Council for Exceptional Children was formed and is now the largest organization in the United States dedicated to enhancing the education of students with disabilities.

Of considerable importance in the early to mid-20th century was the overall political and social climate. Two world wars led to large numbers of Americans suffering both physical and psychological disabilities. The rehabilitation movement, designed to address the needs of injured war veterans, became more prominent and eventually would include individuals with all types of disabilities. Politically, presidents Franklin D. Roosevelt, who had contracted polio, and John F. Kennedy, who had a sister with an intellectual disability, helped to create a climate of reform with movement toward inclusion of children and adults with disabilities in schools and society. Additionally, the post–World War II era ushered in the civil rights movement, which in turn affected special education reform movements. *Brown v. Board of Education* established that a separate education based on race was inherently unequal. By the early 1950s, advocacy movements were in full swing and dissent regarding the lack of universal and integrated educational services for students with disabilities led to the most prominent era of dissent and reform in American schools.

Challenging the System

During the 1950s, the National Association for Retarded Children (now known as *the ARC*) evolved from efforts of parents to obtain better services and quality of life for their children. The Pennsylvania chapter challenged the lack of educational services provision in their state. *Pennsylvania Association for Retarded Children (PARC) v. Commonwealth of Pennsylvania* (1971) was a landmark case. In this class action suit, the district court ruled in favor of the PARC and for the first time used the terms "free, public education" as a right in Pennsylvania for children with mental retardation. In a similar case in 1972, the courts established in *Mills v. the Board of Education of the District of Columbia* that *all* children with disabilities were entitled to a free public education.

With the establishment of the right to an education for all children with disabilities, a major hurdle in the reform efforts of parents and professionals to obtain services had been cleared. Other court cases established additional precedents that would eventually impact legislation concerning special education in American schools. *Hobson v. Hansen* (1967), *Larry P. v. Riles* (1972), and *Diana v. California Board of Education* (1973) were all class action suits that established that assessment of students for eligibility for special education services should be nondiscriminatory and consider ethnic, cultural, and linguistic diversity. These cases were based on a trend that arguably is still evident today, that there is overrepresentation of students from some diverse backgrounds, particularly African American and Latino backgrounds, in special education classes.

Major Legislative Reform

The 1970s included the passage of the two major federal laws that reformed special education in the United States. The Rehabilitation Act of 1973 established that no individual, by reason of disability alone, could be excluded from a program receiving federal funding. Also, this act included a rather broad perspective of what a disability was, including conditions that had a significant impact on major life activities such as learning, ambulation, and communicating, among others. This act was important in breaking down architectural barriers in government buildings, including schools. Because its provisions were so broad, it also included service provision in school programs as nearly all schools (even many private ones) receive some type of federal funding. This Act clearly established that exclusion of individuals with disabilities based on their disability alone was a violation of U.S. law.

The Education for All Handicapped Children Act of 1975 (Public Law 94-142) (subsequently and retroactively now known as the Individuals with Disabilities Education Act [IDEA]) outlined specific provisions for educating students with disabilities. The major provisions of IDEA today still include the following:

- Provision of a free, appropriate public education for all children with disabilities from ages 6–21 years (subsequent reauthorizations have extended these ages to birth–21 years)
- Nondiscriminatory testing and evaluation in establishing eligibility for special education services

- Individualized education programs (IEPs) for all students receiving special education (gifted and talented students receive IEPs in some states but not all as they are not necessarily individuals with disabilities)
- Education in the least restrictive environment (LRE)
- Due process protection in all phases of identification and implementation of services
- The right of parental participation (and student participation as appropriate)

While Public Law 94-142 did establish the right of students with disabilities to a free, appropriate, public education in the least restrictive environment, what was appropriate education and where the least restrictive environment was were *not* clearly established. From the passage of the IDEA through the 1990s, these two provisions would frequently be central in dissent and reform efforts that have molded special education in American schools.

Least Restrictive Environment: What Is Appropriate?

Even in the 21st century, there lingers the interchangeable use of the terms *mainstreaming* and *inclusion*. Although mainstreaming may have as many definitions as there are professionals and advocates, it is the case that mainstreaming was governed by two major principles that were applied in the years following passage of IDEA in 1975. Once a student was identified as needing special education, that student most likely received services in a special education classroom. Second, if a student was capable of working in the general education curriculum without support, then she or he could remain in the general education classroom working on the same activities and assignments, and be assessed largely in the same way as students without disabilities. In other words, mainstreaming focused on the LRE as being the special education classroom unless the student could learn in the general education classroom without benefit of significant support and accommodations. The mainstreaming approach led to what many would term "categorical" service delivery. That is, many students with the same disability label (learning disability, mental retardation,

deafness, blindness, etc.) would be educated together by a special education teacher who was specifically licensed/certificated to meet the needs of that population. Unfortunately, this led to segregation of students with disabilities into separate classrooms and often ineffective curricula that ill prepared them for life as adults. Eugene Edgar summarized this dilemma, eloquently noting that this trend also tended to sustain the overrepresentation of students from some diverse backgrounds in separate special education programs.

The Regular Education Initiative (REI) emerged in the 1980s in response to these trends. This initiative emphasized the LRE should be determined based on learning needs rather than on a disability label such as learning disability, mental retardation, or serious emotional disturbance. The LRE could be any of a variety of settings, but should be where the student would learn best, and adapting general education learning environments to meet those needs were important in the REI. Margaret Wang and Jack Birch described the adapted learning environments model that focused on meeting diverse needs in general education settings. Although the REI did not become a groundswell movement that immediately altered the landscape of education in American schools, it clearly had an impact on how LRE should be viewed and addressed. This, in turn, affected what could be considered the "inclusion" movement.

At the Turn of the 21st Century

Dissent and reform movements are alive and well among those concerned with special education. Subsequent reauthorizations of IDEA have ushered in changes such as:

- Establishing procedures for disciplining students with disabilities
- Expansion of the categories of disabilities included under IDEA (e.g., traumatic brain injury and autism)
- Accountability for district- and statewide testing results for students with disabilities

Arguably, IDEA has been among the most influential laws impacting the American educational system. IDEA has affected public education in significant ways. Just a few of these effects include:

- About 9% (sometimes a larger percentage in any given district) of the school population receives special education
- Schools, districts, and states are held accountable for the learning progress of students with disabilities
- Funding to cover the "excess costs" of educating these students must be appropriated through federal, state, or local resources
- Special education teachers must be highly qualified in content areas to teach that content to students with disabilities
- General education teachers must be adequately trained to accommodate diverse learning needs
- There are extensive paperwork requirements to document implementation of special education services within the due process protections of the law
- Schools, districts, and states must address the transition of students with disabilities to postsecondary life to promote desirable adult outcomes

Dissent and reform have been significant forces in special needs education. Dissenters and reformers have served to remind us that it is the *individual* in IDEA that matters most—not the teachers, not the district, not the experts or even the reformers themselves. The student, the citizen, is entitled to the same protections and opportunities that all of us wish to enjoy.

Stephen B. Richards

See also Accountability Era; Alternative Assessment; Council for Exceptional Children

Further Readings

Braddock, D., & Parish, S. (2002). An institutional history of disability. In D. Braddock (Ed.), *Disability at the dawn of the 21st century and the state of the states* (pp. 3–43). Washington, DC: American Association on Mental Retardation.

Edgar, E. (1987). Secondary programs in special education: Are many of them justifiable? *Exceptional Children, 53,* 555–561.

Marschark, M., Lang, H. G., & Albertini, J. A. (2002). *Educating deaf students: Research into practice.* New York: Oxford University Press.

Scheerenberger, R. (1983). *A history of mental retardation.* Baltimore: Brookes.

Taylor, R. L., Richards, S. B., & Brady, M. P. (2005). *Mental retardation: Historical perspectives, current practices, and future directions.* Boston: Allyn & Bacon.

Taylor, R. L., Smiley, L. R., & Richards, S. B. (2009). *Exceptional students: Preparing teachers for the 21st century.* Boston: McGraw-Hill.

Wang, M., & Birch, J. (1984). Comparison of a full-time mainstreaming program and a resource room approach. *Exceptional Children, 51,* 33–40.

STANDARDIZED TESTS

Standardized tests have been an integral part of the American education system since the mid-19th century. Current examples of standardized tests include the Stanford Achievement Test, which is used to assess students in K–12; the ACT college entrance examination; and the United States Medical Licensing Examination, which is used to license physicians. These tests are characterized by the uniformity of the content, administration conditions, and scoring. Though this form of assessment has been subject to changes, one aspect of educational standardized testing that has remained constant throughout the course of its history is its ability to remain at the center of controversy and debate. The role, effectiveness, and intent of standardized testing have always been questioned—whether an instrument attempts to assess student competency or potential or to measure effectiveness of instruction and administration, especially when connected to a reform effort.

Beginnings of Standardized Testing in the United States

In the mid- to late 1800s, cities in the United States grew at a rapid pace. Contributing to this growth was a large influx of immigrants. To educate and assimilate the growing populace, states established universal schooling. As the costs of this public education increased, the pressure to show that the money was a wise investment also increased. The desire for accountability contributed to the growth of standardized testing in America. In Massachusetts, for example, rapid growth meant that school supervisors could no longer administer oral examinations to students. Horace Mann, then secretary of the Board of Education of Massachusetts, replaced oral examinations with a standardized, written examination. From the very beginning, the written test faced criticism in that the content tested was narrow and covered the basic subject areas, whereas the objective of the schools was to provide a comprehensive education. In addition, the results of the written examination were designed to measure student achievement but were also used to make comparisons among schools and to drive reform.

Initial testing in schools measured student achievement in subject areas. During the late 19th and early 20th centuries, however, testing development focused on measuring mental capacity, that is, examinees' potential for learning. The trend toward intelligence testing and departure from achievement testing during this period might be in part due to the lack of any effect of educational reforms on the improvement of achievement test scores. Administrators looked to the innate ability of the students (i.e., intelligence) for answers to low student achievement.

In France at the turn of the 20th century, Alfred Binet, working with Theodore Simon, developed psychological methods to measure the mental ability of students. Their work resulted in the Binet-Simon test, which formed the basis of mental testing in America. Binet and Simon created the test for the specific purpose of identification of students with mental challenges who might benefit from special training. The test required the student to complete a set of short tasks related to everyday life. Though the test assigned a single, age-based score, Binet refrained from interpreting this score for purposes other than identification of students who might benefit from intervention. He warned people against reading the results too narrowly and reiterated that the test was not designed to measure the construct of intelligence.

Binet's words of caution did not deter Henry H. Goddard from transforming the instrument to an intelligence measure when Goddard brought the Binet-Simon test to America. In *The Mismeasure of Man,* Stephen J. Gould indicated that Goddard regarded the score derived from the Binet-Simon test as an accurate measurement of a person's innate intelligence. Goddard's association with eugenics, a philosophy that strives to direct evolution

toward a superior race through selective breeding, likely contributed to his transformation of the test's purpose. Goddard changed the purpose from one of identification of students with mental challenges to that of classification and segregation of people. He extended the scale by administering the test to adults and people who were "normal," and subsequently used the scale to label people, coining the term *moron* and attaching this label to some of the immigrants in Ellis Island.

Lewis M. Terman, a researcher at Stanford University, also contributed to the use of mental testing in America. He added items to the Binet-Simon scale and extended the scale to include "superior adults." Subsequently, the test was known as the Stanford-Binet scale; it allowed testing of examinees along the full continuum of mental abilities. For example, in the early 1900s, the Stanford-Binet was administered to students in Oakland, California, to group them into different classrooms based on their scores, a practice favored by some progressive reformers.

Also contributing to the expansion of intelligence testing was Robert M. Yerkes's persuading the army to test all its recruits in World War I. The purpose of the testing was to classify recruits efficiently into jobs for which they were most suited. The literate recruits were given the written examination called the "Army Alpha" test, and others were given the pictorial exam called the "Army Beta" test. After the war, this system was used in schools to provide students with instruction based on their "innate" abilities.

More than a century has passed since the initial burgeoning of standardized testing in the United States. Considerable progress has been made in the art and science of the development of standardized tests. Such tests continue to serve a variety of purposes.

Purposes of Testing

In education, the goal of standardized testing is to provide accurate information about students in order to make well-informed decisions. Results from tests have served multiple purposes, such as guiding instruction, meeting accountability demands, promoting equity, and increasing efficiency. Interwoven with these purposes is the use of standardized tests as instruments of reform.

Guiding Instruction

A major purpose of testing in education is the improvement of student knowledge and achievement. To achieve this purpose, states often develop standardized tests to measure student achievement of subject-area learning goals, typically referred to as curriculum standards. States develop curriculum standards to serve as frameworks to guide teachers in planning classroom instruction. These standards then guide the design of the state tests. In turn, the state tests provide information about student achievement of the curriculum standards and the need for instructional reform.

Accountability

Taxpayer expenditures for public education contribute to a demand for accountability. Often legislators and state and district educational agencies rely on standardized testing for gauging school success. Test data contribute to policy-making decisions that target reform, such as retention/promotion of students, pay raises for teachers, and the reassignment of administrators.

Equity

Historically, both egalitarians and eugenicists, whose philosophies are polar opposites, have looked to standardized tests as instruments of reform. Advocates of eugenics hoped to use standardized tests as a means to classify people with lower intelligence and to use selective breeding to gradually eliminate those with mental challenges. On the other hand, egalitarians hoped that standardized tests, such as the SAT, would level the playing field in admissions to higher education and open the gates to all students regardless of family legacy or the quality of a student's high school. By gauging the aptitude (i.e., learning potential) of a student, the intent was for standardized tests to promote fairness in the admission process. Others claimed, however, that standardized tests preserved elitism by admitting only a select few based on their aptitude scores.

Classification for Efficiency and Intervention

Standardized tests also have been used for the purpose of classification to increase efficiency. The intent of the use of the Army's Alpha and the Beta tests was to increase efficiency by assigning the right job to a person with the right capabilities for the position. Public schools attempted to classify students based on intelligence tests in order to group students with similar abilities to make instruction more efficient. Currently, classifications on the basis of scores on standardized tests continue in public schools in the form of "pullout" programs for academically gifted students and special-needs students.

Designing Standardized Tests

Designing a standardized test is a demanding, systematic process. A well-designed standardized test attempts to capture the differences in examinees' abilities in a subject area (e.g., social studies) that is tested while minimizing errors in scores. Procedures followed in test development contribute to the quality of test scores and the minimization of error. Test quality is supported by involvement of subject-area experts (e.g., teachers and university faculty) and other stakeholders in the test development. The work is guided by experts in test design. Subject-matter experts write test items to measure student achievement in an area, such as reading, mathematics, or science. The items in standardized tests take different forms, including multiple-choice items, short-answer items, essay prompts, and performance tasks. Prior to operational use, the test items are reviewed for adherence to item-writing guidelines, and a field test is conducted to examine the statistical qualities of the items.

The scores derived from standardized tests can be converted into two common types: percentages and percentile ranks. For example, the number-correct score for a driver's license test typically is converted into a percentage and is used for criterion-referenced interpretations, such as examinees who answer 85% of the items correctly meet the criterion for passing. In criterion-referenced interpretations, an examinee's item-correct score is compared to a cut score to determine if an examinee passes or fails the test or whether a student's score reflects a basic, proficient, or advanced performance level.

Percentiles provide norm-referenced interpretations—a score at the 75th percentile on the Stanford Achievement Test means that an examinee scored better than 75% of the students who completed this examination. Thus, norm-referenced scores allow the comparison of an examinee's performance to a group of peers. To achieve this, a test company recruits a group of examinees to take the newly developed test. These examinees are referred to as a norm group. The standardized test is administered and scored, and the item-correct scores of the members of the norm group are converted to percentiles. Thereafter, when an examinee takes the test, his or her item-correct score is compared to the scores of the norm group to determine the percentage of the norm group who scored below the examinee's score.

Advances in technology have also played a major role in standardized tests. For example, technology has helped shape a new type of test called the computer adaptive test. An adaptive test adjusts the difficulty of the questions according to student ability. By monitoring when a student gets an item correct, and when a student gets an item incorrect, the computer adjusts the difficulty of the subsequent items presented to the examinee and efficiently determines the student's achievement level.

Diversity in language and culture of students pose test–design challenges. For example, the needs of diverse learners, such as students with special needs, must be addressed while writing and reviewing items for a test. Thus, the reading level of the test and directions must be appropriate for the level of the examinees. In addition, accommodations (e.g., large print, voice recognition programs) must be developed for students with special needs.

Impact of Standardized Tests

Standardized tests shape educational policies as well as influence the content that is taught and the instructional practices of teachers. Standardized tests have been accused of narrowing the curriculum, consuming a large part of the education budget, decreasing teacher morale, limiting instructional time, and stressing school administrators. On the other hand, they have been considered invaluable for diagnosing learning problems, selecting and assigning examinees to appropriate programs, equalizing opportunity, evaluating effectiveness of programs and institutions, focusing instruction on

curriculum standards, and, importantly, informing decision making in educational reform.

Robert L. Johnson and Vasanthi Rao

See also Ability Grouping; ACT and SAT Tests; High-Stakes Testing; Progressive Education; Terman, Lewis M.; Testing Students

Further Readings

Gould, S. (1981). *The mismeasure of man.* New York: Norton.

Office of Technology Assessment. (1992). *Testing in American schools: Asking the right questions* (OTA-SET-519). Washington, DC: Government Printing Office.

Phelps, R. (2005). *Defending standardized testing.* Mahwah, NJ: Erlbaum.

STANDARDS MOVEMENT

As in past decades, "What should I teach?" and "What do my students need to know and be able to do to become productive citizens?" are the questions being asked by the current generation of teachers and by policy reformers focused on enhancing the competitiveness of U.S. schools. Other questions include how all children can be educated to their full potential, and how schools should use higher standards to help students prepare for college and for a competitive global job market.

Early Development

Arguably, the 1983 report *A Nation at Risk* was the initial, federal call to develop educational standards. While suggested as a means to obtain the ideal learning society, the report mentions educational standards in terms of expectations for student learning. Though specific content standards were not provided in this document, it did form the impetus for the current standards movement.

The first entities to develop educational standards were national curriculum organizations led by the National Council of Teachers of Mathematics in 1989. Other professional organizations quickly followed with their own subject-area standards.

Following the work of national organizations, states began to develop content standards. For those states without standards, the federal government made it a requirement. That is, as part of the 1994 reauthorization of the Elementary and Secondary Education Act (ESEA) of 1965, Congress mandated that every state adopt content standards in reading and mathematics by the 1997–1998 school year and establish science standards by the 2005–2006 school year. To date, all states have adopted state-level standards in these content areas, with the exception of Iowa, which has district-level content standards.

The state-level content standards adopted so far have come under criticism regarding their quality and quantity. External forces have functionally reduced what is actually taught in today's schools. As an example, some teachers prepare their students for the tests by teaching them how to answer the general form of the questions on a typical standards-based test. There is also increased attention being given to the need for national standards. Rather than allowing each state to set its own standards, policy reformers are calling for more uniform national standards.

Quality and Quantity of Standards Developed

While the federal government required states to develop standards in reading, mathematics, and science, little guidance was provided as to what constituted an educationally sound content standard. Specifically, no parameters were established for the breadth of the content to be covered or the depth of the learning to be achieved by the students following the curriculum developed using the state-developed content standards. Thus, while the actual number of state-developed content standards was minimal, supporting skills required to attain those standards were not. Further, not all content standards, and their component parts, were of equal value.

The quality of the standards developed varied, and continues to vary, from state to state. At various intervals, the Fordham Foundation (a conservative education policy think tank) has examined the quality of state-developed content standards and released reports (e.g., *The State of Standards 2006*). Such reports assess state-developed content

standards and gauge progress made by the individual states. The Fordham Foundation asked content-area experts to review each state's current content standards; the content standards that were clear, rigorous, and "right-headed" about content were judged as superior. Three states—California, Indiana, and Massachusetts—have content standards ranked all equally high with a rating of "1." Those states that were judged at the lower end of the spectrum were Alaska (ranked 47th), Hawai'i (ranked 48th), Montana (ranked 49th), and Wyoming (ranked 50th).

The Fordham Foundation report provided four reasons why states fell short when it came to their content standards. First, states used *consensus instead of vision* in developing their content standards. In simplest terms, the content standards developed read as if they were written by a committee. Second, standards were developed in the *absence of real expertise*. This translates into what is described as a state belief that K–12 educators can develop content standards without the assistance of content experts (e.g., mathematics professors). Third, standards developed by national organizations may have tainted state education agency content standard development processes with an *antiknowledge orientation*. Last, *rampant exceptionalism* drives many states. This may be viewed as educational isolationism— only those standards developed in a given state are good enough for their students. Many states did not look to the good work of their neighbors or others across the continent when developing content standards.

Further, in an attempt to be all encompassing, states included more fine-grained components of standards than students can theoretically and legitimately be expected to master in the course of a public school education. For example, Ohio has more than 1,200 "indicators" in the area of mathematics. Critics of Ohio's content standards argue that the method used in Ohio to develop its standards created a set of learning expectations that were "a mile wide and an inch deep."

While the prospect of teaching every part of every content standard in a state would be a daunting task, external forces have been at work to reduce the number of components inherent in today's content standards. An unwitting ally in this effort has been the No Child Left Behind Act.

External Forces Influence Content Standards

The next authorization of ESEA was signed into law in January of 2002. Known as No Child Left Behind (NCLB), this statute mandated that all states comply with all of the provisions of the 1994 law. This mandate included both the implementation of standards in reading and mathematics, with annual assessments in Grades 3 through 8 (and once during Grades 9 through 12) to gauge the extent to which students in a given state successfully attain the content standards established by the state. In essence, the standards movement met the accountability movement.

As part of NCLB, schools, districts, and states had to meet performance targets in reading and mathematics or suffer consequences. These targets also apply to groupings of students (e.g., racial/ethnic categories, students with disabilities, etc.) and increase periodically until 100% of all students are proficient with regard to state content standards. The target date for *all* students mastering content standards is 2013–2014.

Schools, districts, and states could meet these targets, otherwise known as achieving adequate yearly progress (AYP), by meeting the target in a given year, meeting the target with a 2-year average of student performance, or through safe harbor. Safe harbor is a 10% reduction in the percentage of students not achieving proficiency of the state's content standards. New developments add a fourth way to achieve AYP—the growth model. It is the requirement to attain AYP that has restricted instruction in some states' content standards.

When a state assesses student knowledge of content standards, there are a limited number of questions that can be asked of students using an assessment instrument. In some states, the amount of time to be used to assess students is also determined by statute. Given the vast number of *parts* of content standards to be taught, only a relatively small sample of these *parts* can be built into any assessment instrument. This leaves some *parts* of standards tested repeatedly and others infrequently, or never, assessed. The *parts* most likely to be assessed are illustrated in some states by the release of an "assessment instrument blueprint" and/or the release of test items. An analysis of released information could then be used to guide the construction of curricula to be taught in a given school or school district. If a component of a standard is not assessed often, it is unlikely to receive time in the instructional calendar. Therefore, a state assessment—a requirement of NCLB—restricts instruction to only those components of standards that will be assessed and be part of a school and school district's AYP attainment. Given that the stakes are high for schools and school districts to make AYP, there is a real advantage to pursuing the strategy of teaching to the test. So, where does that leave the standards movement?

Current Status

Many states are now reexamining their content standards to determine the extent to which each component is still meaningful in today's instructional world. Textbook publishers have aligned their basal series to various state content standards and many have tailored their respective products to specific state markets. Textbook publishers have produced and marketed assessment systems purported to increase student performance on state tests if the product is implemented with integrity and followed religiously. Most of the items used in these assessment systems are derived from existing item banks developed over many years and then aligned to a given state's content standards.

School districts have developed pacing guides to assist teachers in managing instruction so that all of the various parts of all the content standards are covered by the time of state testing. Further, school districts are developing assessment instruments to gauge the extent to which students have learned and teachers have taught the content specified in the school district's pacing guide. These efforts further reduce the quantity of content standards receiving instructional time.

With the faults listed here, has the standards movement as an educational reform effort been successful? It has been used to frame discussions around what students in public education should know and be able to do. In addition, it has focused instruction so that no one area of a subject area dominates instruction. For example, there is more to American history than the Civil War. In at least these ways, the movement has been a positive force in education.

Conversely, the standards movement, as some critics of standards assert, has changed over time and in conjunction with the accountability movement the emphasis on standards has restricted teacher creativity in responding to changes in knowledge and requisite skills needed by today's student. In some ways, it has restricted access to a wide range of topics to be taught, especially if a school or school district is at risk of receiving the sanctions specified in a state's NCLB implementation plan. In at least these areas, the standards movement has been less successful. History will be the ultimate judge of the effectiveness of the standards movement as an educational reform effort.

Fred Dawson

See also Accountability Era; High-Stakes Testing; Minimum Competencies; Neoconservatives; Testing Students

Further Readings

Hirsch, E. D., Jr. (1996). *The schools we need and why we don't have them.* New York: Doubleday.

Ravitch, D. (2000). *Left back: A century of failed school reforms.* New York: Simon & Schuster.

Zimmelman, S., Daniels, H., & Hyde, A. (1998). *Best practice: New standards for teaching and learning in America's schools.* Portsmouth, NH: Heinemann.

STATE DEPARTMENTS OF EDUCATION

Education in the United States is and has been established as primarily a state function. Under the Tenth Amendment to the U.S. Constitution, education is a commission of the state rather than the national administration. Each state department of education functions completely or in part through a state agency. There are varying degrees of control and authority from state to state, but generally each state has a controlling board or state board of education and a state superintendent or commissioner of education. In Ohio, for example, both the offices of the state superintendent and the state board of education are mandated by the Ohio Constitution. In addition, Ohio's department of education was created by the General Assembly as the administrative unit for oversight of Ohio's schools. The state board of education in Ohio and other states exercises policymaking and supervisory authority over elementary and secondary education in the state through the Superintendent of Public Instruction and the state department of education. The superintendent is the chief executive officer of the department of education and secretary to the state board of education.

While much influence is exerted by a state board and department of education, the primary operations of local schools are controlled by local boards of education and local superintendents. Many of the growth and specific functions of a state department of education have resulted from court decisions and the increased level of support and control from the federal government. State departments of education have grown over time to provide the leadership needed to maintain the states' interests and to support the local districts' needs. Today those primary functions include supporting school reform efforts, providing technical assistance, defining and controlling educational content, and assessing the outcomes of education.

It was not until the mid- to late 1800s, however, that state departments of education emerged in a leadership capacity. The functions of early education departments were to be consultative, to gather statistics, and to offer encouragement. However, depending on the strength of the state superintendent, some state departments of education exerted broad influence on areas of schooling, including teacher training, curriculum development, and funding. As state legislatures increased their role in support and control of local schools, so too did the role and control of state departments of education increase. State departments of education had significant influence on the development of state minimum standards for local districts, teacher training and licensure, education of handicapped individuals, increased vocational training, and increased control of school funding. Today most state departments of education are responsible for the following:

- Determining whether local districts are in administrative compliance with federal, state, and local statutes
- Ensuring that federal and state finances are used appropriately
- Ensuring that health and safety regulations are enforced

- Ensuring that facilities are safe
- Monitoring licensure qualifications and compliance of educators
- Enforcing compulsory attendance and child labor regulations
- Developing and regulating state educational standards and student performance expectations
- Ensuring that all schools are organized and operating in accordance with applicable standards, regulations, and statutes
- Providing school districts and legislatures information regarding the status of education, statistics regarding student success, and recommendations for continuous improvement of schools

In addition to numerous operational responsibilities, state departments of education have a responsibility to provide vision and reform for local districts. State departments of education are charged with promoting whole-school unit-reform efforts. They are responsible for assisting local schools in planning and implementing building and district level change, especially in underperforming and low-performing districts. Researchers such as Heather Hill and others show conclusively that the outcome of comprehensive school reform implementation in terms of both sustainability and impact is directly coupled to the alignment of school reform models with school district and state department of education policy.

In case studies conducted in Maine and Puerto Rico as described by Edmund Hamann and Brett Lane, state departments of education had a positive impact on the educational reform efforts in both cases. The comprehensive school reform, supported by the state departments of education in both Maine and Puerto Rico, enabled the school change process to be more broadly and deeply implemented within their systems.

In addition to creating and supporting local school districts, state departments of education, through state legislatures, have the authority to create and fund innovative and alternative forms of schooling. One such innovative or alternative approach to education is the charter school. There are numerous other creative and innovative forms of education that state departments of education are involved in including vouchers, consolidation of school districts, alternative forms of funding,

alternative educator licensure standards, and control of school boundaries.

State departments of education are not without their critics. Critics such as Jonathan Kozol, Michael Kirst, and others conclude that while public education in the United States promises quality education for all children, the fact remains that many children do not have equal opportunities to learn and are often not likely to attend a quality school. Critics suggest that the education structure is in part responsible for poverty and inadequacy, supporting wealthy and deprived schools with complete contrasts in learning situations and material surroundings. Five issues surface in the public's perception of public schools, which are: (1) inequality of opportunity, (2) burdensome bureaucracy, (3) achievement-based outcomes, (4) school choice, and (5) general reform of public education.

The relationship between the federal, state, and local boards of education is often questioned, but it is certain that providing quality education for America's children is of utmost importance to our citizens. Because of the desire to provide quality education, the relationship is constantly adjusted in an attempt to meet the needs of the local communities.

C. Daniel Raisch

See also Accreditation; Boards of Education; District Schools; Educational Policies Commission; Education Commission of the States (ECS); Federal Educational Reform; National School Boards Association

Further Readings

Criticism of public education—Inequality of opportunity, highly bureaucratic systems, achievement-based outcomes, school choice, reform after reform. (2009). Retrieved May 25, 2009, from http://education.stateuniversity.com/pages/2341/Public-Education-Criticism.html

Datnow, A., Hubbard, L., & Mehan, H. (2002). *Extending education reform: From one school to many.* London: Routledge Farmer.

Hamann, E., & Lane, B. (2004). The role of state departments of education in comprehensive school reform. *Benchmark: The Quarterly Newsletter of the National Clearinghouse for Comprehensive School Reform, 5*(2), 1–11.

Herndon, F. (1965). State supervision through leadership and services. *National Business Education Quarterly, 33*(4), 20–25.

Hill, H. (2001). Policy is not enough: Language and the interpretation of state standards. *American Educational Research Journal, 38*(2), 289–318.

Kozol, J. (1992). *Savage inequalities: Children in America's schools.* New York: Perennial.

Lusi, S. F. (1997). *The role of state departments of education in complex school reform.* New York: Teachers College Press.

Spillane, J. (1998). State policy and non-monolithic nature of the local school district: Organization and professional practice considerations. *American Educational Research Journal, 35*(1), 33–63.

STUDENT ASSESSMENT AND SCHOOL ACCOUNTABILITY

Educating children in public schools in the United States has been influenced by economic and fiscal policies, by political movements and systems, and by social systems and patterns. Prominently, today's competitive global economy calls for American education systems to prepare students to be successful in work, in life, and in the swiftly evolving, globalized world. Demographic, technological, social, and political changes have transformed the world into a diverse and multifaceted technology-driven place. Being successful in the global economy requires mastering knowledge and competencies, including basic academic skills such as mathematics and literacy, science skills, foreign language fluency, and critical thinking skills. This means that in order to survive in the world economy and the new information age, students must be equipped and empowered with the ability to access, interpret, analyze, and use information for making decisions.

This global status has called for evaluating how well American schools are preparing students to succeed in the international marketplace of today's information-based society. Fundamentally, schools must ensure that all students have equal access to a quality education that will prepare them for success in the 21st century. This focus on student achievement has called for educational reform efforts based on defined learning outcomes and on linking assessment and accountability known as *standards-based accountability*. The requirement is that students of all racial and socioeconomic groups should graduate possessing the knowledge, motivation, and opportunity to participate fully in an expanding global and economic society. The challenge is to help all students learn at higher levels; accountability reform focuses on making judgments that until recently were difficult to make because academic standards were not clearly articulated and performance (proficiency) expectations were not defined.

Standards-Based Accountability

Standards-based accountability requires collecting student data and reporting information based on clear and defined standards for what students must know and be able to do. Student mastery of the academic content is derived from state-mandated standards. There are two types of standards: content and performance. Content standards identify what students should know and be able to do. Performance standards define how or how well students perform on the content standards. Decisions regarding student learning and achievement, professional development, curriculum and instruction, and resource allocation should be based on both content and performance standards. The standards represent the foundation for determining student achievement.

Standards are the means specifying what students need to know and be able to do at various grade levels; they are also the foundation for state and local curriculum and instructional alignment and assessment efforts. The purpose of an accountability system is to document and improve student learning relative to defined standards. Each component of the system should align with and support student learning and achievement; that is, standards should be aligned with assessments. A systematic approach to accountability allows for an alignment among all the critical instructional elements: student performance, content goals, instructional strategies, curriculum materials, and assessment protocols. An accountability system should define how outcomes should be measured; who is responsible for assessing performance outcomes; to whom results should be reported; and what constitutes satisfactory progress and advanced progress. A recent example of a national standards–based policy is found in the No Child Left Behind Act (NCLB) of 2001 that was designed to improve schools by developing content as well as achievement standards to measure student academic progress. Accountability system designs include the articulated academic goals and the curricula and instructional elements that one needs to meet academic goals. Assessment procedures are used to measure student performance, and the entire professional learning community is involved in gathering and interpreting the assessment data. Progress and outcomes relative to defined state academic proficiency goals are reported to the public; the academic progress information is used to plan and inform further instructional decision making.

Educational Accountability

In order to transform schools and meet challenging learner outcomes, there must be a focus on performance, which requires a means of measuring whether or not students are succeeding in meeting school improvement goals. Accountability is the obligation to or responsibility for demonstrating effectiveness along four components: standards that define academic outcomes, an evaluation system to assess student progress, data that can be analyzed, and rewards or sanctions based on student performance. This definition offers an outline of the relationship among student assessment, accountability, and student learning outcomes as measured in today's schools. Accountability, then, refers to the systematic collection, analysis, and use of data to hold schools, educators, and others responsible for student performance.

The Foundation for School and District Success

The primary purpose of education is to provide students with the knowledge, skills, and tools they need to be successful in life. Since standards are the basis for measuring how well students have learned what they need to know and be able to do at various grade levels and academic growth, they are the foundation for state and local curriculum and instructional alignment and assessment. NCLB was designed to improve American schools by requiring states to measure student progress in defined academic areas (e.g., reading and mathematics). Low student-achievement scores and the growing disparity in educational opportunities (or achievement gap) for students in some schools and districts require that accountability systems hold schools, districts, and individuals responsible for student learning.

Educational accountability calls for holding key individuals and groups responsible for measuring and improving student academic progress. There are a variety of ways by which stakeholders are responsible for student performance. Students are responsible for achieving mastery on individual and classroom assessments correlated with state-mandated academic content standards; schools are accountable for providing students with a curriculum that is aligned with state standards and for assessing student progress relative to those standards; and classroom teachers are responsible for aligning instruction, curriculum materials, the content standards, and then teaching to mastery.

Schools are accountable for administering a standards-based curriculum and providing staff development to staff. School districts are responsible for strategic planning related to school improvement and overall district oversight. Schools and school districts create assessment systems to evaluate student performance. These systems use performance data to monitor and identify student performance and learning activities and to assist teachers in meeting students' diverse needs. Inherent in such systems is ongoing professional development and team building among staff. States create systems of accountability. Data are used to evaluate grade-level performance and student academic progress. Strong accountability systems use performance data to identify under- and high-performing schools and school districts. Importantly, parents are provided information about their children's learning and the quality of their children's schools.

States are held responsible for providing guidelines and assistance to schools and school districts by stipulating growth targets that are measured in terms of adequate yearly progress (AYP). AYP goals assist schools in helping students achieve proficiency over time. These AYP targets are set to help schools ensure that all students reach a certain level of proficiency over a predetermined number of years. Fundamentally, states should be prominent in providing significant training around curriculum alignment, assessment, writing skills, data collection, and the professional development process.

Educational Assessment

Assessment and *accountability* are often used interchangeably when discussing standards-based learning and high academic achievement. They are, in fact, different. Accountability is defined as the systematic collection, analysis, and use of information to hold schools, educators, and others responsible for student performance. Accountability is an end, assessment is a means. Essentially, assessment systems offer information that is useful in determining student mastery of learning content and for providing information that teachers can use to "modify" instruction.

Test results offer data that drive curriculum, instruction, and educational planning. These learning outcomes are usually measured through one of the following means: criterion-referenced tests, norm-referenced tests, teacher-made tests, portfolio assessment, Web-based assessment, writing assessments, or any of the alternative forms of assessments. The outcomes data are analyzed and disseminated to provide valuable information that may be useful in overall school and school-district planning of classroom instruction. All of those factors offer reliable, fair, and valid measures of assessment and are useful for formative feedback, monitoring of student progress, program analysis, and information gathering.

Assessments in the form of achievement tests have been used as regulatory devices in some states since the beginning of the 1970s. Many states began mandating minimum competency examinations (MCEs) in the 1970s to hold students accountable for learning. States are now replacing those MCEs with standards-based examinations (SBEs) and end-of-course (EOC) examinations.

The MCEs and EOCs have been and are being used to make decisions regarding graduation, promotion, retention, remediation, and tracking of students. Additionally, federal support for low-achieving students was based on mandatory large-scale testing of children who did not meet grade-level achievement under Title I of the Elementary and Secondary Education Act of 1965. This practice has been in effect since the 1980s. Currently, NCLB requires annual testing of students in reading and mathematics in Grades 3 through 8 and once in high schools. This is a national assessment that provides an index for testing, with the emphasis on strengthening academic and curriculum planning

used in all 50 states. Assessments in the form of tests are given to students in selected grades to access content mastery. The assessments are aligned with academic content standards. As in all forms of assessment, the purpose of the policy inherent in NCLB is linked to improving student learning. Precise and carefully planned technical standards for assessment are developed and adapted to ensure high-quality assessments and to observe and oversee the consequences of the use of standardized assessment tools in schools and districts. Fundamentally, the significance of this educational process is that it conveys high expectations and provides a stimulus for the teaching and learning process. NCLB placed accountability as a central feature of the educational process.

Assessments of student learning are not new to educators; they have been present since the early days of formal schooling. The real reform is the emphasis on accountability and requiring that teachers, schools, and school districts measure and improve to defined levels of student proficiency and to make public their progress toward state-mandated academic proficiency.

Assessing Student Learning

The improvement of instruction in schools in America in the changing global economy necessitates that educational leaders and policymakers understand learning environments and recognize their responsibility to meet the needs of diverse student populations. If schools are to prepare students adequately for college and 21st-century jobs, they must raise expectations and enhance student achievement. Setting high academic standards, or statements defining what students are expected to know and be able to do at various levels of academic growth, is foundational to the improvement of student achievement and central to the design and implementation of student learning goals.

States have been authorized by NCLB to oversee school districts and hold them accountable for AYP in relation to state-defined academic standards. Each state must include scores of all students enrolled in school for at least a full academic year, even if they have attended several different schools. Significantly, state assessment programs must be developed to provide schools with a systematic way of determining student achievement.

Education is changing as accountability measures in the new global economy are forcing districts and schools to better address the measure of "proficient" performance for all children. Once academic content standards are defined (by each state) and school and student progress are measured against those standards, performance can be measured and evaluated. This standards-based movement has allowed accountability systems to become performance-based. As a result, state leaders are gauging performance on a state level, which allows them to change and improve the way education policy and practice decisions are made. Unfortunately, it also means that student proficiency is defined differently across all 50 states, a circumstance that has caused neoconservative reformers to call for national rather than just state academic content standards. In the ideal, assessment practices within schools, school districts, and states are positively driving the teaching and learning process in American schools. That is, goals are set and performance goals are defined to foster whole school improvement. Those focused on equity issues argue that holding all districts, schools, teachers, and students accountable for high academic achievement will provide equitable and adequate education for all children and make our education system more aligned with the needs of the 21st-century workforce.

Accountability and assessment practices instituted in schools today are transforming instruction in schools in America. High-quality teaching and learning environments rest on strong educational policy and systems of responsibility. Assessment systems in education constantly evolve and improve as they adapt to increased knowledge and changes in the social, political, and economic environments. If education in America is to continue to play a positive role in meeting the needs of all students, educational leaders and policymakers must rely on the following principles of educational accountability:

- Design curriculum for proficiency in the core subject areas of language arts and mathematics.
- Integrate present-day (21st-century) skills into core content-area teaching.
- Provide a vision for learning that takes into account diverse stakeholder needs.

- Provide schools and teachers clear curriculum and assessment goals.
- Provide balanced assessment, with a combination of assessment strategies (norm-referenced tests, criterion-referenced tests, teacher-made tests, portfolio assessment, writing samples, etc.).
- Inform parents of what their children need to achieve in order to be successful (which increasingly means being "college ready").
- Take into account specific critical thinking skills and performance criteria for subgroups (minorities and English language learners).
- Align professional development, assessment, and curricular tools with state and district needs.

States and districts must work to create learning environments that will empower students to successfully compete in the 21st century. Standards-based school reform and accountability measures are ensuring that students are empowered with the skills and tools needed for success.

Brenda F. Graham

See also Achievement Gap; No Child Left Behind Act (NCLB); Standards Movement

Further Readings

American Association for Higher Education. (1996). *9 principles of good practice for assessing student learning.* Retrieved June 12, 2008, from http://ultibase .rmit.edu.au/Articles/june97/ameri1.htm#About

Armstrong, J. (2002). *What is an accountability model?* Denver, CO: Education Commission of the States.

Frye, R. (n.d.). *Assessment, accountability, and student learning outcomes.* Retrieved May 4, 2008, from http://www.ac.wwu.edu/~dialogue/issue2.html

Hamilton, L. S., Stecher, B. M., Marsh, J. A., McCombs, J. S., Robyn, A., Russell, J. L., et al. (2008). *Standards based accountability under No Child Left Behind: Experiences of teachers and administrators in three states.* Santa Monica, CA: RAND.

Hershberg, T. (2005). Value-added assessment and systemic reform: A response to the challenge of human capital development. *Phi Delta Kappan, 87,* 276–283.

Raham, H. (1998). *Linking evaluation and school success: Building school success through accountability.* Retrieved June 25, 2008, from http:// www.sqep.ca/archives/presentations/Rahamh_ colsqep98.pdf

STUDENT-CENTERED CLASSROOM

See Constructivism

SUCCESS FOR ALL

Success For All (SFA) is a curriculum reform effort initially targeted at students in kindergarten through the third grade who are falling behind in reading. Its core focus is on literacy (i.e., reading, writing, and language arts). The program is not a theory but a compilation of strategies that work to improve student achievement. The program focuses on prevention and intensive intervention designed both to detect and to resolve reading difficulties as early as possible. This entry examines Success For All, beginning with a brief history, followed by a description of the SFA model, and concluding with comments about the impact of model implementation.

History

Success For All is a schoolwide curricular program that organizes resources in an attempt to ensure that each student acquires adequate basic skills in reading, writing, and language arts. SFA was created by Robert Slavin, his wife Nancy Madden, and colleagues at Johns Hopkins University and was based on existing principles of reading instruction that were shown to be effective in teaching children to read. These principles favored an approach in which phonics skills were explicitly taught. SFA was launched in 1987 with a pilot program in one elementary school in Baltimore, Maryland. That year, Slavin found that SFA students had better reading scores than students not participating in the program. The program expanded to five other schools in Baltimore the next year. Since its inception, SFA has grown to include students in PreK–6 and to address other curricular areas (e.g., math).

The Success For All Model

Success For All is one of the most widely implemented, widely researched, and widely critiqued curriculum reform models in the United States. At the heart of the SFA program is 90 minutes of uninterrupted, daily reading instruction. This instruction is scripted so that regardless of teacher, classroom makeup, or geographic location of the school, the instruction is the same. Students are generally grouped across classes and grades by reading level. The program is purchased as a comprehensive package that includes materials, training, ongoing professional development, and a prescribed plan for delivering and sustaining the model. Salient features of the model include: prescribed reading sessions, regular assessments, one-to-one tutoring, establishment of a solutions team, and appointment of a full-time facilitator.

Prescribed reading sessions include various strategies that focus on development of language skills for students in primary grades and development of comprehension skills for students in the upper grades. Specifically, the reading program in kindergarten and first grade emphasizes language and comprehension skills, phonics, sound blending, and decoding of shared stories. In Grades 2–6, students use novels or basal readers and focus on comprehension skills of summarization and clarification, and development of writing skills. Teaching strategies most often used, regardless of grade level, include: reading by the teacher to the students, choral reading, phonics and word-attack strategies, vocabulary lessons, writing, and direct instruction. Each 90-minute session is strictly choreographed. That is to say, at any given time during the lesson an observer might see and hear virtually the same thing from both teachers and students in each class of the same grade.

Regular assessments (every 8 weeks, or quarterly) are used to monitor student progress in reading. The assessments generate data for each child that are used to design appropriate interventions (e.g., tutoring), suggest alternate teaching strategies and guide instruction, and move students into appropriate reading groups. In some states, these assessments are state aligned. All assessments are predictive and diagnostic in nature.

One-to-one tutoring to students who are failing to keep up with their classmates in reading is provided by teachers and paraprofessionals who are specially trained. Tutorial sessions are designed to parallel and reinforce regular classroom instruction. Students' daily tutorials are 20 minutes in length and scheduled during times other than their

90-minute reading periods. Instead of being placed in special classes or retained in grade, most students who need additional help receive tutoring.

Each SFA school is expected to establish a Solutions Team or Support Team that links students, families, educators, and community resources together. The Solutions Team helps families support the learning of their children by focusing on areas like the importance of school attendance, positive student behavior, and parent involvement in student learning. According to model developers, these combined energies support children's academic achievement by providing immediate intervention and support when necessary.

Finally, a full-time, certified teacher is designated as facilitator to help the school personnel implement the SFA program. The facilitator works closely with lead SFA trainers, organizes several professional development days, monitors the assessment data, and provides support and coaching to teachers.

Impact of Model Implementation

Like all reform models, comprehensive or curricular, implementation is the key to the success of the reform. The Success For All model brings together many effective instructional strategies in phonemic awareness, phonics, vocabulary, fluency, and comprehension. Because of this, teachers have tools at their disposal that assist in improving student achievement in reading. Consistent commitment to these strategies is essential by all teachers and at every leadership level; otherwise, implementation of the model is compromised. The model is used in more than 1,200 schools in 46 states.

As mentioned previously, the Success For All program is one of the most debated school improvement models in the country. More than 40 studies, many conducted by Slavin and his colleagues, have looked at the program's impact. Because Slavin is often involved in the program effectiveness research, critics suggest there may be potential bias in the reported results. To counter such criticism, Slavin notes that skeptics of the program might legitimately question whether the results are worth the schools' hefty financial investment (i.e., at least $130,000 over a 3-year period), but not whether or not his program works.

Julie K. Biddle

See also Assessment; Phonics

Further Readings

Borman, G. D., Hewes, G. M., Overman, L. T., & Brown, S. (2003). Comprehensive school reform and achievement: A meta-analysis. *Review of Educational Research, 73*(2), 125–230.

Borman, G. D., Slavin, R. E., Cheung, A., Chamberlain, A., Madden, N., & Chambers, B. (2005). The National Randomized field Trial of Success For All: Second-year outcomes. *American Educational Research Journal, 42*(4), 673–696.

Slavin, R. E., & Madden, N. A. (2006). *Success For All/ roots & wings: 2006 summary of research on achievement outcomes.* Baltimore: Johns Hopkins University, Center for Research and Reform in Education.

Viadero, D. (2005, May 11). Long-awaited study shows Success For All gains. *Education Week.*

SWANN V. CHARLOTTE-MECKLENBURG

The U.S. Supreme Court's decision in *Swann v. Charlotte-Mecklenburg Board of Education* (1971) stands out as one of its most important school desegregation cases for two reasons. First, *Swann* was the Supreme Court's last unanimous judgment in a major school desegregation case. Second, *Swann* is the first case in which the justices examined, and ultimately upheld, the use of busing to achieve school desegregation in systems that operated under de jure, as a matter of law, racial segregation. *Swann* thus helped reform public school systems in the American South by allowing educators to employ busing as a means of transforming their student bodies in a manner consistent with allowing schools to provide equal educational opportunities for all children.

Swann began when a federal trial court in North Carolina approved a desegregation plan that the Fourth Circuit subsequently modified. Included in the desegregation plan's extensive provisions were calls for what turned out to be its most noteworthy feature in creating restructured attendance zones in the Charlotte-Mecklenburg district, which relied on busing to bring about greater racial balances in public schools. After the Fourth Circuit upheld the desegregation plan, including busing for secondary schools, but vacated and remanded the plan to the trial court for additional consideration as it applied to students who attended elementary schools, both sides sought further review.

As *Swann* was progressing through the federal courts, it did so in the context of increasing judicial calls to speed up the slow pace of desegregation in public school systems that, more than a decade after the original *Brown v. Board of Education* (1954), continued to operate dual, or segregated, schools. In fact, the Supreme Court made its sense of urgency to take dramatic steps to end segregation clear in its 1969 declaration in *Alexander v. Holmes County Board of Education*. In *Alexander,* frustrated with the slow pace of desegregation, the Court unequivocally ended its reliance of the "all deliberate speed" standard that it had announced in *Brown v. Board of Education II* (1955). Instead, the *Alexander* Court thus declared that "the obligation of every school district [is] to terminate dual school systems at once and to operate now and hereafter only unitary schools."

The immediate impact of the Supreme Court's judgment in *Alexander* resulted in a plethora of lower federal court orders demanding that educational officials desegregate their dual school systems. Insofar as the lower federal courts implemented a wide variety of arrangements, however, inconsistencies emerged over the constitutional dimensions of what the plans needed to accomplish and how they could direct officials to achieve their desegregative goals. Against this background, the *Swann* Court addressed the responsibilities of school officials in desegregating a dual school system.

In *Swann v. Charlotte-Mecklenburg Board of Education* the Supreme Court affirmed the trial court's order in whole while upholding those parts of the Fourth Circuit's judgment that supported the trial court's remedy. More specifically, the Court began by acknowledging that since public school officials in the district had intentionally maintained segregated, or dual, schools, the federal trial court had the authority to develop equitable remedies to dismantle the formerly dual system, thereby rendering it unitary or desegregated. As such, the Court reasoned that even though it would not establish rigid mathematical guidelines or ratios for busing students, if assigning children to

neighborhood schools did not effectively dismantle segregated schools, then the federal trial court could rely on busing as a means of implementing an equitable solution.

As part of its analysis in *Swann,* the Supreme Court discussed issues that it had not reviewed in any detail previously. In addressing school construction, the justices pointed out that in developing remedies for de jure segregation, educational officials and the courts had to ensure that future construction and abandonment is not used to perpetuate or reestablish dual systems. As to one-race schools, the Court found that where proposed plans for conversions from dual to unitary systems considered the continued existence of some schools that were all or predominately of one race, in order for the plans to survive judicial scrutiny, officials had to have proven that these assignments were truly nondiscriminatory. Moreover, the Court was of the view that while it was unnecessary for every school in a district to reflect a system's racial composition as a whole, a federal trial court may apply a racial ratio or quota as a starting point in shaping a remedy since so-called racially neutral assignment plans are insufficient to counteract the continuing effects of past segregation. At the same time, at the end of its opinion, the Court looked to the future, indicating that school boards did not have to make annual adjustments in the racial compositions of student bodies once they ended segregation.

In 2001 the Fourth Circuit terminated judicial oversight in Charlotte-Mecklenburg, 30 years after *Swann* reached the Supreme Court. The Fourth Circuit determined that the district achieved unitary status because its officials met the judicially created tests for doing so (*Belk v. Charlotte-Mecklenburg Bd. of Education,* 2001, 2002). In other words, the Fourth Circuit agreed that the district was desegregated because it had achieved the benchmarks that the Supreme Court set when it addressed freedom of choice plans in a case from Virginia, *Green v. County School Board of New Kent County* (1964). The Fourth Circuit ruled that the board could be released from its desegregation order because it met the six *Green* factors that the judiciary continues to apply in considering whether school systems have become desegregated. Once the court determined that the board properly balanced the composition of a student body, faculty, staff, transportation, extracurricular activities, and facilities, it released the school district from its long-running desegregation order. Insofar as *Swann* was the first case in which educational officials could use busing to broaden the composition of student bodies in formerly segregated schools, it is a noteworthy opinion because it contributed to the transformation of schools first in the South and then beyond when other courts applied its precedent in seeking to reform other school systems that were in need of change.

Charles J. Russo

See also Brown v. Board of Education; Desegregation/ Integration

Further Readings

Alexander v. Holmes County Board of Education, 396 U.S. 19 (1969).

Belk v. Charlotte-Mecklenburg Board of Education, 269 F.3d 305 (4th Cir. 2001), cert. denied sub nom.

Brown v. Board of Education, 347 U.S. 483 (Brown I, 1954); 349 U.S. 294 (Brown II 1955).

Capacchione v. Charlotte-Mecklenburg Board of Educ., 535 U.S. 986 (2002).

Green v. County School Board of New Kent County, 391 U.S. 430 (1968).

Swann v. Charlotte-Mecklenburg Board of Education, 402 U.S. 1 (1971).

Taba, Hilda (1902–1967)

Born in a small village in southeastern Estonia, Hilda Taba (1902–1967) is known as one of the most significant contributors to the fields of intergroup education and curriculum theory. Taba's academic career climaxed with the publication of the monograph *Curriculum Development: Theory and Practice* (1962), published just 5 years before her early death. This entry reviews her educational biography, her work with the intergroup and social studies curricula, and her philosophy of curriculum design. Taba's theoretical insights and direct work with teachers led to significant curricular reforms, including an expanded understanding of the value of a multicultural curriculum and attention to critical thinking in learning for democratic participation.

Taba's educational path began in Estonia, then a province of the Russian Empire, at her father's elementary school. After completing her undergraduate studies at University of Tartu (B.A. 1926), where she majored in history and education, Taba began postgraduate studies at Bryn Mawr College (M.A. 1927), supported by a Rockefeller Foundation grant. She completed her doctoral degree at Columbia University (Ph.D. 1932) under the guidance of William H. Kilpatrick. Unable to secure a job in Estonia in 1933, Taba became a German teacher at the Dalton School, which was involved in the Eight-Year Study. Taba's participation in this study brought her together with Ralph Tyler, who hired her as part of his research team. In 1939, she became the director of the curriculum laboratory at the University of Chicago, which she headed until 1945. In the following years, Taba initiated, designed, and directed several research projects aimed at intergroup education (1945–1951). Next she undertook her most influential curriculum project, in Contra Costa County, California, and became a full professor of education at San Francisco State University. Taba died unexpectedly on July 6, 1967.

Intergroup Education and Social Studies Curricula

Interest in intergroup education, which was seen as an antidote to tension in people's interpersonal relationships, surged in the period following World War II. Taba's Intergroup Education Project, launched in New York City in 1945, explored how to increase the level of tolerance between pupils from different ethnic and cultural backgrounds. The success of the project led to the establishment of the Center of Intergroup Education at the University of Chicago (1948–1951). Taba's approach focused on combating stereotypes and prejudices and drew extensively on concepts from cognitive and social psychology. The ideas of intergroup education and the experience of cooperating schools contributed to efforts to desegregate American society and to the strengthening of democracy.

In 1951, Taba accepted a proposal to reorganize and develop the social studies curricula in Contra Costa County, California. Initially, the study focused on the identification and analysis of students' learning capabilities and teachers' problems in the field of social studies. Many ideas underlying her curriculum model were born in the framework of this research, including the spiral curriculum; inductive teaching strategies for the development of concepts, generalizations, and applications in students; the organization of the learning content on the three levels—key ideas, organizational ideas, and facts; and her general strategy for developing thinking through the social studies classes. These curricular developments gained worldwide recognition in the 1960s and early 1970s. Taba and her Intergroup colleagues' attention in the 1950s to the value of a multicultural and meaningful curriculum in cultivating a strong relationship between the community and school foreshadowed similarly significant intercultural and multicultural reforms in the 1990s.

Philosophy of Curriculum Design

Many of Taba's ideas about the curriculum evolved gradually throughout her career. The most central of them, already clearly present in her doctoral dissertation, *The Dynamic of Education: Theory and Practice* (1932/1980), is her understanding that social processes are not linear and cannot be modeled through linear planning. Therefore, in curriculum design, it is unrealistic to set up rigid general goals of education from which more specified learning objectives are derived. The general goals (e.g., parents' expectations for their children's future achievements and career) are also subject to modification by the real circumstances of instruction. A second principle Taba develops is the bottom-up approach to curricular development as the most convenient way to help individuals and social organizations to accept and to adapt to new ideas. Her initiatives of curriculum design always started from the grassroots level, from consulting with practicing teachers. The third principle expressed her beliefs in the supremacy of democracy—the development of new curricula is more effective when based on the principles of democratic guidance and on the well-funded distribution of work. The fourth principle admits that transforming the school curricula, if not limited to formal and superficial changes, is a long process, lasting for years.

Taba's scientific heritage in the field of educational philosophy, intergroup education, and curriculum development undeniably provided educational theory with many important ideas of lasting value. Her work in the field of curriculum studies helped to challenge and reform understandings of the ways schools help to prepare children to live in a multicultural democracy.

Kara D. Brown and Edgar Krull

See also Eight-Year Study; Multicultural Education; Progressive Education; Tyler, Ralph

Further Readings

Bernard-Powers, J. (1999). Composing her life: Hilda Taba and social studies history. In M. S. Crocco & O. L. Davis, Jr. (Eds.), *"Bending the future to their will": Civic women, social education, and democracy* (pp. 185–206). Boulder, CO: Rowman & Littlefield.

Costa, A. L., & Loveall, R. A. (2002). The legacy of Hilda Taba. *Journal of Curriculum and Supervision, 18,* 56–62.

Fraenkel, J. R. (1994). The evolution of the Taba Curriculum Development Project. *Social Studies, 85,* 149–159.

Krull, E. (2003). Hilda Taba (1902–1967). *Prospects, 33,* 481–491.

Middaugh, E., & Perlstein, D. (2005). Thinking and teaching in a democratic way: Hilda Taba and the ethos of *Brown. Journal of Curriculum and Supervision, 20,* 234–256.

TAX CREDITS

During the latter half of the 20th century, legislators in a number of states began to propose statutes designed to provide public relief, via adjustments to state tax codes, to those constituencies choosing private, religious, K–12 schools for their children's education in place of public schools. These initiatives, in effect, were intended to divert some public funds to those parents. Politically, such initiatives tended to be supported by Republicans, who favor lesser involvement of government and greater tax breaks for individuals, and opposed by Democrats, who tend to support increased governmental services.

The philosophical justification for such legislation was that a significant portion of the essential function of even the most religious of such schools was largely identical to the secular function of the public schools: prepare students for successful citizenship, further education, and eventual employment to enable them to become self-sufficient participants and taxpayers in the economy of the United States. Since parents choosing private education already supported the public schools through their income and property taxes, those supporting tax credit legislation reasoned that those parents were entitled to tax relief because of the additional expenses incurred in paying the costs of private education.

Among the state statutes proposed in that time period were those that allowed parents to reduce their state tax burdens through either tax credits or tax deductions for private school expenses. An understanding of the difference between tax credits and tax deductions is more important for an understanding of economic impact than for constitutionally justifiable status. Tax credits provide for a direct dollar reduction of actual tax liability: a credit toward taxes due. Tax deductions allow for a reduction of gross income, the basis on which most state and federal income taxes are calculated. Generally, tax credits have a more dramatic effect on an individual's tax situation.

As is the case with many contentious political actions, constitutional questions arose making state and federal courts the scene of final resolution. Into the 1970s, federal courts consistently ruled that direct provision of resources to religious schools was in violation of the Establishment Clause of the First Amendment to the U.S. Constitution. The often-cited Lemon test (*Lemon v. Kurtzman*, 1971) specified that statutes would not be in conflict with the Establishment Clause of the First Amendment if such laws proposed action that was secular in purpose, neither advanced nor inhibited the free exercise of religion, and did not involve "excessive entanglement" of the state with religious agencies or groups. State statutes granting tax relief to parents raised constitutional questions, although the aid certainly was not flowing directly to religious schools. The resolution of two cases by the U.S. Supreme Court provided direction.

In *Committee for Public Education and Religious Liberty v. Nyquist* (1973), the Court declared a New York law designed to provide tuition reimbursement or tax relief (credits) only to parents of students attending nonpublic schools

unconstitutional in violation of the First Amendment's Establishment Clause. By contrast, 10 years later in *Mueller v. Allen*, the Court upheld a Minnesota law allowing all parents tax deductions for their dependent children's educational expenses for tuition, materials, and transportation even though private school parents were much more likely to benefit from the law than public school parents (LaMorte, 2008). The Court's conclusions suggest that portions of state tax codes made applicable to broad classifications of citizens are much less likely to be successfully challenged under either the Establishment Clause or as "suspect classifications" under the Fourteenth Amendment's Equal Protection Clause.

More recently, state courts (Minnesota, Pennsylvania, Florida) have upheld laws allowing business tax credits for contributions to private schools, and the Arizona Supreme Court has upheld tax credits for individuals making direct contributions to private schools (Alexander & Alexander, 2005). Clearly, creative legislative initiatives to provide public tax relief for participation in private education have not been exhausted.

William Patrick Durow

See also Accountability Era; Achievement Gap; Alliance for School Choice; Alliance for the Separation of School & State; Alternative Schools; Charter Schools; National Association of Independent Schools

Further Readings

Alexander, K., & Alexander, M. D. (2005). *American public school law* (6th ed.). Belmont, CA: Thompson West.

Brimley, V., Jr., & Garfield, R. R. (2005). *Financing education in a climate of change* (9th ed.). Boston: Pearson, Allyn & Bacon.

LaMorte, M. W. (2008). *School law: Cases and concepts* (9th ed.). Boston: Pearson, Allyn & Bacon.

Russo, C. J. (Ed.). (2008). *Encyclopedia of education law*. Thousand Oaks, CA: Sage.

TEACHER EDUCATION

The evolving history of the role of teacher education in the United States reflects the changing purposes and characteristics of schools and schooling. Schools in the United States from colonial times to the middle of the 19th century were primarily focused on the basics of reading, writing, and skills in arithmetic. Values important to the emerging nation were clearly evident in daily lessons often conducted as group and individual recitations. During those years, most teachers in both rural and urban areas had no training for their position, and teachers often had little more than an eighth-grade education. Schoolmasters in the Latin grammar schools in major population centers, however, were often graduates of liberal arts study at universities founded in the early days of the new nation. Teaching was often a temporary position taken by men on their way to other callings or by women until marriage.

By the mid-1800s, common schools, or publicly supported schools that enrolled all children, began to take hold in communities, particularly in the northern United States. The primary goal of these schools was to strengthen the foundations of the United States by transmitting the cultural heritage and by creating a literate citizenry who could participate in the democratic processes. As industrialization and immigration dramatically increased in the mid- to late 19th century, the pressures on the common schools, and on finding teachers to teach in the common schools, also increased. In response, the first state-sponsored normal schools were created for the purpose of preparing teachers to meet the needs of the growing numbers of common schools. Many students were admitted to the first normal schools after completing the equivalent of an elementary education, and the curriculum was considered to be at the secondary level rather than at the collegiate level. By the beginning of the 20th century, most universities and colleges had established departments for teacher preparation. It is important to note, however, that by the 1930s, most teachers at the secondary level had university training, but fewer than 10% of elementary teachers held a bachelor's degree.

The 20th century brought global upheaval, with two world wars bridged by economic crisis. During that time teacher education, within both normal schools and universities, expanded curricula by enhancing professional, disciplinary, and general education studies. The final decades of the 20th century and the early years of the 21st century have been marked by increasing criticism of teacher

education programs. Documentation of program fragmentation, weak standards for admission and graduation, and poor connection to the real world of practice have supported the complaints targeted at schools and departments of education. The profession has responded through a broadly constructed reform agenda for improving teacher education that has been in motion from the 1980s to the present time.

Reform Agenda for Teacher Education

The reform agenda for teacher education in the United States has evolved in conjunction with calls for reform in schools and schooling. As John I. Goodlad noted, good schools and good teacher education programs must come together. Many scholars of education have noted that reform efforts in teacher education and schooling have occurred in repeating cycles with predictable patterns. The conversations about reform are complicated by debates around the purposes of schooling that continue into the 21st century, which is emerging into a knowledge-based economy. Preparing graduates to meet demands of a postindustrial economy and to participate as an informed citizenry in a democratic society are complex and often contradictory. When one considers that educational policy and practice are implemented by teachers who, for the most part, are prepared in teacher education programs, it becomes clear that the reform agenda in teacher preparation programs is as complex and contradictory as the reform agenda for public education.

Responses to the call for reform in teacher preparation have been based on multiple perspectives. These perspectives have included, among others, radically restructuring teacher education programs; recognizing teaching as a profession guided by clear standards and related program accreditation policy and practice, and establishing a clear research agenda that continues to inform a comprehensive knowledge base.

Restructuring Teacher Education

The decades encompassing the 1980s to the present time have seen multiple reform initiatives in teacher education. This section addresses three of the most widely known, which have in common the goal of radically restructuring how teacher education is organized.

In 1983, a group of deans at research universities convened to discuss concerns about the quality of teacher preparation at their institutions. With funding from several private foundations and the U.S. Department of Education, several meetings were held for the purpose of articulating a reform agenda for teacher education. *Tomorrow's Teachers: The Report of the Holmes Group,* was published in 1986 and a second report, *Tomorrow's Schools: Principles for the Design of Professional Development Schools,* was published in 1990. Three key features characterize the changes recommended by the Holmes Group, which was named for Henry Wyman Holmes, the dean of the Harvard Graduate School of Education in the 1920s. First, the group proposed a three-tier system of teacher licensing that reflected rigorous standards of practice, ongoing professional development, and educational accomplishments. A second design feature is the creation of professional development schools where university faculty and school faculty engage in the joint enterprise of educational research and teacher preparation. A third structural aspect is that teacher preparation occurs postbaccalaureate. The Holmes Partnership, a consortium of universities, school districts, teacher associations, and national organizations, is based on the principles articulated by the Holmes Group.

In 1985, the Center for Educational Renewal, a research center located at the University of Washington, and the National Network of Educational Renewal, a network of universities and schools, were founded to study and engage in simultaneous renewal of schools and educator preparation programs. Foundational to the work of the Center and the Network is defining a mission of schools and teacher education that incorporates enculturating the young in a social and political democracy, providing access to knowledge for all children, practicing pedagogical nurturing, and ensuring the responsible stewardship of schools. The cornerstone design feature to achieve this mission for teacher education is a center of pedagogy that brings together departments of arts and sciences; school, college, or department of education; and school districts.

In 2001, the Carnegie Corporation of New York launched an initiative inviting institutions to participate in reforming teacher education at their institutions. Eleven institutions participated in this effort, and 30 additional institutions became part of the Learning Network. Three design principles frame the efforts to redesign teacher education. First, teacher education programs should be designed and evaluated based on research evidence, including pupil learning. Second, university faculty in the arts and sciences must be fully engaged in the education of prospective teachers. Third, teaching must be viewed as an academically taught clinical practice profession. Each of the institutions receiving awards from Teachers for a New Era have reported how they designed their teacher education programs around these principles.

The reform initiatives described here, as well as the many that were not included, have resulted in some restructuring of teacher education. Many teacher preparation programs are offered only as graduate professional programs. Professional development schools do function in partnership with departments of teacher education. Faculty in the arts and sciences do participate in preparing teachers. Evidence is becoming increasingly more important in design and evaluation of teacher preparation programs. Presentations at national conferences and publications attest to the changes that have occurred in teacher preparation since the 1990s.

What is less clear, however, is the extent to which substantive changes in teacher preparation have occurred across the teacher preparation landscape, and many critics would suggest that most programs suffer from the same shortcomings that have been identified since the 1980s, and that teacher education is still a weak intervention in teacher development. It is also unclear the extent to which any changes have translated to broad changes in classroom practice. More research is needed to support the claim that simultaneous renewal is taking place.

Standards and Accreditation for Teacher Education

A second lever for reform in teacher education that has commanded attention is the concerted effort to establish clear national standards of professional practice for teachers, reframing accreditation processes from input to performance models, and integrating licensing policy and practice with standards of performance. Professional standards are statements that describe what teachers should know and be able to do. They are performance based, and are therefore observable and provide a context for assessment. Standards developed for a national audience include those developed by the Interstate New Teacher Assessment and Support Consortium appropriate for initial licensing and those developed by the National Board for Professional Teaching Standards appropriate for professional certification. States have also developed standards, and the extent to which state standards play a role in licensing, mentoring, and induction varies.

Standards for developing and evaluating teacher preparation programs also exist. The National Council for Accreditation of Teacher Education conducts reviews of schools, colleges, and departments of education based on six standards. The standards and required evidence for review for program accreditation are also performance based. This shift from relying on completing required coursework to documentation of outcomes has been one of the major shifts in reform of teacher education. Some would argue that accreditation processes are weak, and that poor preparation programs are as likely to be accredited as strong programs. Furthermore, many strong programs have chosen to follow another accreditation process developed by the Teacher Education Advisory Council that follows a self-study format rather than one that is standards-based, and some programs are not accredited at all. Many argue that teacher preparation, like public schools, should be open to alternative providers and not encumbered by the constraints of traditional programs operating in higher education.

A Research Agenda for Teacher Education

Current research has strongly supported, and public policy is reflective of, the assertion that teachers are an important, and perhaps the most important, factor in student learning. The consequences of that reality in relation to the quality of teacher preparation programs are immense. Important emerging questions include: What are the characteristics and classroom practices of teachers who contribute positively to student learning? What are the most critical aspects of teacher preparation that contribute to teacher quality?

People are turning to the research base in teacher education to address these questions, and many agree it is lacking. Interestingly, research on teacher preparation is relatively new, and much of the research that has been conducted is small scale and inadequate to address complex questions. Defining a research agenda for teacher education in the current policy, political, and practice environment is a challenge, but progress is evident. Educators are responding to questions about what is most important to study and what methodologies are appropriate for inquiry, and there are indications that more attention to systematic inquiry around teacher education will have more priority in the decades to come.

Kathryn Kinnucan-Welsch

See also American Association of Colleges for Teacher Education; Carnegie Foundation for the Advancement of Teaching; Holmes Group; Interstate New Teacher Assessment and Support Consortium (INTASC); National Assessment of Educational Progress (NAEP); National Commission on Teaching and America's Future (NCTAF); Professional Development Schools; Teacher Education Accreditation Council (TEAC)

Further Readings

Cochran-Smith, M., & Zeichner, K. (2005). *Studying teacher education: The report of the AERA Panel on Research and Teacher Education*. Mahwah, NJ: Erlbaum.

Darling-Hammond, L., Wise, A. E., & Klein, S. P. (1999). *A license to teach: Raising standards for teaching*. San Francisco: Jossey-Bass.

Goodlad, J. I. (1990). *Teachers for our nation's schools*. San Francisco: Jossey-Bass.

Goodlad, J. I. (1994). *Educational renewal: Better teachers, better schools*. San Francisco: Jossey-Bass.

Goodlad, J. I., Soder, R., & Sirotnik, K. A. (Eds.). (1990). *Places where teachers are taught*. San Francisco: Jossey-Bass.

Holmes Group. (1986). *Tomorrow's teachers: A report of the Holmes Group*. East Lansing, MI: Author.

Holmes Group. (1991). *Tomorrow's schools: Principles for the design of professional development schools*. East Lansing, MI: Author.

Levine, A. (2006). *Educating school teachers*. Washington, DC: Education Schools Project.

Schwartz, H. (1996). The changing nature of teacher education. In J. Sikula, T. J. Buttery, & E. Guyton (Eds.), *Handbook of research on teacher education* (2nd ed., pp. 3–13). New York: Simon & Schuster Macmillan.

TEACHER EDUCATION ACCREDITATION COUNCIL (TEAC)

Teacher education accreditation provides an incentive for program improvement, holds institutions accountable for the quality of their programs, and offers assurance that the programs produce knowledgeable, skilled, caring, and effective educators eligible for state certification. The Teacher Education Accreditation Council (TEAC) was founded in 1997 to improve professional preparation programs for those who work in schools by reframing accreditation in terms of inquiry, evidence, experimentation, and improvement. The TEAC system shifts the focus of accreditation away from conforming to a set of externally prescribed standards and toward developing a framework within which faculty use evidence of candidate learning to demonstrate how well the program prepares classroom teachers and school and district leaders.

A New System for Accreditation

TEAC accreditation centers around a system of faculty inquiry into the quality of their education programs. The focus is on questions such as: What do we (as teacher education institutions) claim about our graduates? What is the evidence we use to determine whether we meet these claims? Why do we rely on this evidence? Is the evidence sufficient to convince others? While questions like these drive accreditation generally, TEAC encourages faculty to start their inquiry with the mission, goals, and claims of the program and the institution rather than to measure their effectiveness against standards set by others. The program's self-study results in an *Inquiry Brief* that documents the evidence it relies upon that graduates know the subject(s) they will teach, know a variety of ways to teach students with differing skills and backgrounds, and are caring and effective teachers whose students learn. Additionally, faculty include evidence that graduates have mastered the content and skills of a liberal arts education. Finally, faculty describe how they examine the quality control system to determine whether it yields reliable and valid evidence about the program's practices and results. This inquiry-driven, evidence-based accreditation model lends itself to an ongoing and continuous improvement process that integrates routine program review and self-analysis with accreditation.

TEAC accreditation differs from other accreditors in three important ways. First, TEAC initiated an accreditation-by-audit process by which, as part of the self-study, faculty conduct an internal academic audit to examine how the program manages quality, testing each policy and practice to determine if the system functions as designed. In its site visit, the TEAC audit team checks the program's claims and evidence and reports on whether the cited evidence is accurate and trustworthy and whether the program is able to ensure quality. Second, it focuses on evidence of candidate learning as the sine qua non of program evaluation. The quality of the evidence and the quality of the system that produced it are the two key factors in the TEAC accreditation decision. Third, TEAC promotes the development of an evidentiary base for teacher education. Although teaching has many of the elements of a profession (professional degrees, licenses, certificates, national examinations, accreditation, state program approval, tenure reviews, recertification, professional development requirements, professional associations, etc.), none of these elements seems to provide much confidence. In times of teacher shortages, state and district leaders willingly ignore or waive any of the above; many education reformers even recommend terminating one or more of these elements as a means to improve teacher quality; and teacher education programs themselves do not embrace accreditation as a vehicle for quality assurance. Of the approximately 1,500 colleges, schools, and departments of education that produce teachers and school administrators, only 43% are nationally accredited.

TEAC offers a way for teacher education to respond to its critics by turning the tools of scholarship on itself. Accreditation self-reports become scholarly contributions to the field because they make a convincing case that advance knowledge about what works and what does not can be debated, and can stimulate the next round of experimentation and success.

History of the Teacher Education Accreditation Council

TEAC was formed in 1997 to recognize and promote high-quality teacher education programs in colleges and universities. In addition to its 2001 recognition by the Council of Higher Education (CHEA), TEAC was accepted into membership in the Association of Specialized and Professional Accreditors (ASPA) and its petition for federal recognition was endorsed by the Council of Independent Colleges (CIC), the American Association of Universities (AAU), the American Council on Education (ACE) (of which TEAC is a member), the National Association of Independent Colleges and Universities (NAICU), the National Association of State Universities and Land-Grant Colleges (NASULGC), the American Association of State Colleges and Universities (AASCU), and the Consortium for Excellence in Teacher Education (CETE). In December 2004, the National Advisory Committee on Institutional Quality and Integrity (NACIQI) unanimously recommended that TEAC be recognized as having met the accreditation standards of the U.S. Department of Education. As of January 2009, TEAC has accredited 79 programs at 65 institutions of higher education and has 93 candidate institutions in the process of obtaining accreditation. TEAC is fully accepted in the accrediting community as representative of a promising and an increasingly imitated approach to accreditation.

Diana Wyllie Rigden and Frank B. Murray

See also Accreditation; National Council for Accreditation of Teacher Education (NCATE); Schools of Education; U.S. Department of Education

Further Readings

Dill, D. (2000). Is there an academic audit in your future? Reforming quality assurance in U.S. higher education. *Change Magazine, 32*(4), 35–41.

Dill, D., Massy, W., Williams, P., & Cook, C. (1996). Accreditation & academic quality assurance: Can we get there from here? *Change Magazine, 28*(5), 17–24.

Ewell, P. T. (2008). *U.S. accreditation and the future of quality assurance.* Washington, DC: Council for Higher Education Accreditation.

Murray, F. B. (2001, Spring). From consensus standards to evidence of claims: Assessment and accreditation in the case of teacher education. *New Directions for Higher Education, 113,* 49–65.

Murray, F. B. (2005). On building a unified system of accreditation in teacher education. *Journal of Teacher Education, 56*(4), 301–317.

TEACHER EVALUATION

As noted by numerous critics and scholars, the practice of teacher evaluation in many U.S. schools is antiquated, ineffective, and in dire need of reform. Although some school districts have brought classroom teachers, school administrators, and other stakeholders together to study and rebuild old and poorly conceptualized models, others continue to employ practices that are outdated given current knowledge of teaching and learning. If the school reform movement is to fulfill its promise, improving methods of teacher evaluation will play a critical role. The past decade has seen the development of new tools, methods, and metrics that are now part of the public discourse about teacher evaluation and, in some cases, are already driving significant change.

Historical Context

The process of evaluating classroom teachers has historically pursued two distinct goals: monitoring teacher performance for the purpose of making personnel decisions, and supporting teachers in their efforts to improve their classroom practice. Unfortunately, there is considerable evidence that in many schools neither of these goals has been achieved. For many teachers and school administrators, teacher evaluation remains a process they are mandated to participate in, but one that makes little or no significant difference in their respective professional lives.

Teacher evaluation in the United States occurs in a constellation of contexts that vary not only by state, but by local school district as well. This contextual diversity includes a variety of factors including, but not limited to, the frequency of evaluations for teachers on limited or continuing contracts; the tools and methods employed to conduct the evaluations; the training, or lack thereof, of administrators to effectively facilitate the evaluation process; and the criteria used to define good teaching itself.

With regard to this last factor, the foci of teacher evaluation have evolved over time. For example, in the 1950s many school administrators were largely concerned with *teacher traits* such as enthusiasm and interpersonal warmth, among others. The 1960s and 1970s, influenced by an emerging emphasis on the *teacher effects* research, were characterized by a new focus on a teacher's classroom behaviors and their correlations with student performance as measured on standardized tests. In the early 1980s, the work of Madeline Hunter at the University of California, Los Angeles, focused on the identification of a specific planning and teaching model that included seven steps of instructional design. The findings of the teacher effects research of the 1960s and 1970s, along with practices from the Hunter model, made their way into many teacher evaluation systems appearing on teacher performance checklists and classroom observation forms. In other districts, however, teacher evaluation protocols remained unchanged and continued to focus on criteria such as personal appearance, professional preparation, and effective communication.

School Reform and Teacher Evaluation

Beginning with the modern school reform movement that found its birth in the publication of a *Nation at Risk* in 1983, education reformers began to pay increasing attention to teacher evaluation as a tool for improving America's schools. In the late 1980s and continuing into the 21st century, views of teaching and learning began to shift toward placing greater focus on student learning and understanding. Influenced by research from the cognitive sciences and a deeper understanding of how people learn, opinions regarding quality teaching began to embrace a *constructivist* view of learning. In the 1990s, other events transpired that had a significant influence on discussions of how to improve teacher evaluation. Two events that played such a role were the Tennessee Value Added studies led by William Sanders and the publication of *Enhancing Professional Practice: A Framework for Teaching* by Charlotte Danielson.

The disparate work of Sanders and Danielson raised critical questions about the purposes and processes of teacher evaluation and led to a number of new debates and reform initiatives.

Compelled by Sanders's value-added assessment model and its capacity to link student learning gains over time to specific classroom teachers, some reformers issued the call for tying teacher assessment to value-added data in lieu of traditional approaches that relied on the observation of teachers by school administrators. Some of these reformers called for dismantling the system of teacher compensation known as the single-salary schedule that is widely employed throughout the United States and that pays teachers based on years of experience and college credits earned across their career. At the same time, others pushed for new models of teacher evaluation that did not rely solely on value-added data, but that employed a variety of new practices and processes designed to focus on student learning.

For example, many school districts adopted the Danielson framework, which consists of 22 standards for thinking about teaching and learning. The 22 standards are organized in a four-domain framework: (1) Planning and Preparation, (2) The Classroom Environment, (3) Instruction, and (4) Professional Responsibilities. Each standard is described in a set of rubrics articulated across four levels of professional performance ranging from *Unsatisfactory* to *Distinguished*. The Danielson framework and similar systems are designed to increase the probability of increased student learning by focusing attention on the array of research-based standards that have been linked to student learning. Teachers and school administrators employing the Danielson framework often speak to how it provides a common language to foster professional dialogue and enhances the consistency and objectivity of the evaluation process by placing greater emphasis on evidence-based judgments of teacher performance. A number of districts employing the Danielson model have not only adopted the framework as their public definition of good teaching, but have revamped their teacher evaluation programs by creating *differentiated* evaluation *tracks* designed to meet the needs of teachers at different phases of their careers.

Historically, the only difference between the evaluation of novice and veteran teachers has been the frequency of the evaluations conducted. Many district teacher evaluation programs are negotiated between the local board of education and the professional teachers association. Such agreements typically call for school administrators to conduct two to four classroom observations of teachers in the first 3 to 4 years of practice, a time period when they are typically working under a limited contract. In contrast, the evaluation of tenured teachers varies widely, with such teachers being evaluated on a negotiated evaluation cycle that in many cases ranges from 3 to 5 years. Despite the influential work on *clinical supervision* pioneered by Professors Robert Anderson, Morris Cogan, and Robert Goldhammer at Harvard University in the 1960s, many classroom observations are conducted without a preobservation or postobservation conference. These "drive-by" evaluations, often conducted by principals using a rating sheet or checklist that includes outdated or irrelevant performance criteria, do little to foster any meaningful dialogue about teaching and learning.

The practice of conducting summative evaluations of tenured teachers on a multiyear cycle, such as every 4 years, was first advanced by Thomas Sergiovanni and Robert Starratt, who argued for multiple forms of formative assessment that would occur in the years when a teacher was not being formally evaluated for summative purposes. Peer coaching, self-assessment, involvement in school improvement initiatives, and other professional growth activities were all advanced as job-embedded ways of promoting teacher development and formative assessment. Unfortunately, in many districts, such practices were never realized. Or, if implemented, they were abandoned over time leaving veteran teachers on a multiyear evaluation cycle consisting of one drive-by assessment every 3 to 5 years.

Promising Practices

As education stakeholders search for ways to improve teacher evaluation, returning to historical practices that failed to realize their potential while simultaneously embracing new tools such as value-added assessments and researched-based frameworks, may provide a promising pathway to reform. The most promising new programs for teacher evaluation are likely to be *differentiated* models that respect the differences between novice and veteran practitioners without employing frequency of evaluation as the differentiating factor. Instead, they will endeavor to create a culture of continuous improvement that

involves *every teacher, every year,* in an evaluation process that is just as much a process of professional development. Teachers in the early years of practice, for example, may be observed multiple times by a principal trained to employ the clinical model of supervision and the Danielson framework. In contrast, veteran teachers, working together or alone, may work to achieve classroom or school-based goals. Such goals would be negotiated with, supported by, and monitored by building principals who meet with teachers in annual planning and reflection conferences. In doing this work, teachers might employ the array of job-embedded professional growth experiences envisioned by Sergiovanni and others. Tenured teachers working in such a model may not be formally observed by their principal or other evaluator unless the visit is requested by the teacher or initiated by the principal based on an interest in or concern about the teacher's daily classroom performance.

Models such as the ones described above will place high value on evidence of student learning as provided by the careful and collaborative analysis of value-added assessments or other data on student learning. Such data, whether provided by an external agency or generated at the classroom level, will facilitate teachers and administrators in the process of engaging in meaningful and informed conversations about teaching and learning that places student understanding at the heart of the dialogue.

James B. Rowley

See also Academic Freedom; Alternative Licensure; Association for Supervision and Curriculum Development; Carnegie Foundation for the Advancement of Teaching; Differentiated Staffing; Interstate New Teacher Assessment and Support Consortium (INTASC); National Council for Accreditation of Teacher Education (NCATE); Test of Teaching Knowledge (TTK)

Further Readings

Danielson, C. (1996). *Enhancing professional practice: A framework for teaching.* Alexandria, VA: Association for Supervision and Curriculum Development.

Danielson, C., & McGreal, T. L. (2000). *Teacher evaluation to enhance professional practice.* Alexandria, VA: Association for Supervision and Curriculum Development.

Peterson, K. (2000). *Teacher evaluation: A comprehensive guide to new directions and practices.* Thousand Oaks, CA: Corwin.

Rothman, R., & Toch, T. (2008, January 29). Rush to judgment: Teacher evaluation in public education. *Education Sector Reports.* Retrieved January 3, 2009, from http://www.educationsector.org/research/research_show.htm?doc_id=656300

Sanders, W. (1998). Value-added assessment. *School Administrator, 11*(3), 24–27.

Tucker, P. D., & Stronge, J. H. (2005). *Linking teacher evaluation and student learning.* Alexandria, VA: Association for Supervision and Curriculum Development.

TEACHER INSTITUTES

Henry Barnard is generally credited with originating teacher institutes when he assembled 26 young men and taught them for a period of 6 weeks in the late 1830s in Hartford, Connecticut. The curriculum consisted of extending their knowledge of the subjects taught in schools and the best methods of school arrangements, instruction, and government. Observational visits to Hartford schools were part of Barnard's program.

Institutes were especially helpful in their early days in the preparation and improvement of teachers in rural areas. Lessons consisted of lectures and discussions, often including general lectures by leading figures in the evenings that were open to the general public.

Horace Mann supported the creation of institutes in Massachusetts in the mid-1840s, in addition to preferring normal schools for teacher preparation. In 1845 Mann reported the existence of teacher institutes in one half of the counties of New York, Ohio, Pennsylvania, New Hampshire, and Rhode Island, as well as his own Massachusetts. By 1847 teacher institutes existed in Connecticut, Massachusetts, New York, New Hampshire, Rhode Island, Pennsylvania, Michigan, Ohio, and Illinois. They existed alongside normal schools, being most prevalent in rural areas where there were no normal schools.

Although regarded as inferior to normal schools in the preparation of teachers, the curriculum of teacher institutes was very similar; namely, content

knowledge and pedagogical skills. Like normal schools, the institutes were public, not private; were controlled by the state or district; and were not operated by teachers. Institutes went on record favoring supervision, the creation of state normal schools, higher salaries for teachers, and state aid for public education. On occasion their students—teachers—were active on behalf of schools, approaching state legislatures in an organized way. Unlike normal schools, institutes often functioned on behalf of individuals who were teaching, emphasizing improvement for the individuals. Often conducted by teachers of acknowledged reputation, they were held at various times and for various lengths, and were ultimately replaced by summer schools. Enrollees often had to pay for their instruction, although in 1846 the Massachusetts legislature earmarked $2,500 for institutes in that state.

Moral character occupied a primary role in teacher institutes' conduct, as it did in the textbooks used and in normal school preparation. Protestant clergy played a critical role in their operation, as they did in public schools' leadership positions. Often the sessions opened with a devotional exercise, and harmony was expected between the institutes' focus on moral character, or "awakening" for the students, and the Protestant faith. Indeed, the institutes often took on the nature of a religious revival, and were frequently conducted in churches. Women attended, but did not take part in these activities.

Barnard, while superintendent of schools in Rhode Island described to the county superintendents what the institutes should include in their operation in that state: (a) a review of studies taught in the public schools with examples of the best methods to teach them; (b) lectures and discussions among members on the organization of schools, classification of pupils, and the theory and practice of teaching; and (c) public lectures and discussions in the evenings on topics calculated to interest parents and the community on the subject of education and the organization, administration, and improvement of public schools. This remained, James Fraser asserts, the basic curriculum of teacher institutes for 80 years.

Institutes were conducted for varying lengths of time and at various times of the year. As state governments became more involved, they often mandated how institutes operated, for example, one per year in each county. Institutes grew in popularity in accord with student enrollment and the growing activity of state governments in schools. For instance, in Michigan, 8 institutes held for 1,251 teachers in 1860; in 1870 there were 12 for 2,005 teachers; and in 1889 there were 65 for 4,482 teachers. Other states experienced similar growth. In 1886–1887, the U.S. Commissioner of Education reported 2,003 institutes for 138,046 teachers, a sum that was almost one-half of the number of teachers the U.S. Office of Education reported for the nation in 1890.

Teacher institutes affected the lives of more teachers than any other educational institution in the 1840s, and they continued to have an impact, especially in the certification of teachers, until 1920. As late as 1919, county institutes existed in 35 of the 48 states. In 1922, 44 states employed some form of institute; 30 maintained them by law. Twenty-six of the 48 states held them on school time in 1933. As time went on, they had become a means of continuing education, predating summer school, but not for entry into the profession of teaching; this became the role of normal schools, and later of teachers colleges and education departments in universities.

Thomas C. Hunt

See also Normal Schools; Rural Education; Schools of
Education

Further Readings

Elsbree, W. (1939). *The American teacher: Evolution of a profession in a democracy.* New York: American Book Company.

Fraser, J. (2007). *Preparing America's teachers: A history.* New York: Teachers College Press.

Mattingly, P. (1975). *The classless profession: American schoolmen in the nineteenth century.* New York: New York University Press.

Wittrock, M. (Ed.). (1986). *Handbook of research on teaching* (3rd ed.). New York: Macmillan.

TEACH FOR AMERICA (TFA)

Teach For America (TFA) is a nonprofit organization founded by Wendy Kopp. Kopp proposed the radical reform related to recruiting teachers to high-needs school districts in 1990, utilizing her undergraduate thesis at Princeton. The Teach For America program places some of the nation's top recent college graduates in 26 of the nation's poorest urban and rural public school systems for 2-year teaching commitments. In its first year, Teach For America started with 500 young men and women teaching in six low-income communities across the country. In 2008, approximately 4,400 TFA teachers reached about 375,000 students.

Background, History, and Mission

Teach For America selects and places graduates from the most competitive colleges as teachers in the lowest-performing schools in the country. TFA exists to address educational inequity and it does so by enlisting academically talented young people and placing them in economically disadvantaged contexts.

Teach For America reports that the TFA corps members are a very diverse and talented group. They have been recruited from all disciplines of study and have no prior teaching experience, training, or formal education degree. They demonstrate strong leadership ability and evidence an ability to work with young people in a way that motivates them to learn. TFA tries to identify young people who have the skills and personal presence to enter high-needs classrooms in ways that will be both academically and culturally transformative.

Teach For America officials are quick to point out that their corps members possess the leadership skills needed to make a real impact over the short- and long-term. While TFA does not seek any single personal profile, corps members have an average GPA of 3.6, and 95% have held leadership positions on their college campuses. Their average SAT score approximates 1,300, which is considerably higher than the average SAT for students matriculating through traditional teacher education programs.

Some studies suggest that TFA teachers are more effective than other, "experienced" classroom colleagues. According to one study, high school students taught by TFA corps members performed significantly better on state-required end-of-course exams, especially in math and science, than peers taught by far more experienced instructors. Results from that same research suggest that the TFA teachers' effect on student achievement in core classroom subjects was nearly three times the effect of teachers with 3 or more years of experience. In essence, researchers were able to document an academic performance advantage for students who had TFA teachers. Neoconservatives have used this type of research to argue for significant policy changes relative to the education of teachers for classrooms in the United States.

Making a Difference? The Effects of Teach For America in High Schools

Teach For America recruits and selects from some of the most elite colleges and universities across the country to teach in the nation's most challenging K–12 schools. Some would suggest that TFA is helping to address the crucial need to staff the nation's schools, particularly the acute need in high-poverty schools. Advocates for TFA graduates would suggest that TFA attracts higher quality candidates and such that they can have a more profound impact on student achievement. Many of the neoconservative think tanks have released policy papers arguing for ending the education monopoly relative to the preparation and licensure of teachers. However, TFA also has its critics. Criticisms of the TFA approach fall in two categories. The first is that most TFA teachers have not received traditional teacher training and therefore are not as prepared for the demands of the classroom as traditionally trained teachers. As a result, the students with the highest needs (i.e., students in high-poverty environments) are placed in classrooms with teachers with the least amount of formal preparation (i.e., TFA graduates). TFA corps members participate in an intensive 5-week summer national institute and a 2-week local orientation/ induction program prior to their first teaching assignment, but this limited intensive preparation is viewed by many as too superficial to really prepare TFA teachers for the demands of a high-needs classroom. The second criticism is that TFA requires only a 2-year teaching commitment, and the majority of corps members leave at the end of that commitment. The short tenure of TFA teachers is troubling because research shows that new teachers are generally less effective than more experienced teachers. Those in TFA often point out that the tenure for traditionally prepared teachers is not

especially long, with almost 50% dropping out of teaching by their fifth year.

As noted earlier, advocates of the TFA approach often cite research documenting that TFA teachers are more effective, as measured by student exam performance, than traditional teachers. They suggest that the "TFA effect," at least in grades and subjects investigated, exceeds the impact of additional years of experience, implying that TFA teachers are more effective than experienced secondary school teachers. The positive TFA results are robust across subject areas, but are particularly strong for math and science classes.

Reformers and traditionalists often use research to support the ideas that promote their particular ideological perspectives. Just as there is research to support the efficacy of TFA teachers in classrooms, there is also research suggesting that students in TFA classrooms perform less well. For example, some studies have found that the students of TFA teachers perform at a lower level in reading than those of newly certified teachers, with the negative effects most pronounced in elementary grades. In math, three recent studies report significantly lower scores for beginning TFA teachers' students than for prepared teachers. When TFA teachers obtain additional training and certification, their students generally do as well as those of other teachers and sometimes better in mathematics. However, most TFA teachers leave after 2 or 3 years (more than 80% are gone after 3 years), so the benefits of their training are lost.

Clearly, many urban school districts may be forced to use TFA graduates to improve the educational opportunities that are available in their highest need classrooms. Neoconservatives would argue that such reforms are both warranted and necessary in order to meet the needs of the young people who come from cultures of poverty. They would assert that traditional programs have not been able to populate traditional classrooms with a sufficient number of appropriately prepared teachers and that reforms are needed that attract more intellectually capable young people to the challenges evidenced in urban environments.

Teach For America is maturing and is becoming more embedded within the educational world as an acceptable way to prepare teachers for urban environments. It is a reform idea with sufficient success that it will likely emerge as a permanent solution to the highly problematic issue of staffing high-need urban classrooms. Even though there are criticisms of the program, there are clearly enough indicators of success to suggest that for the foreseeable future TFA teachers will be part of the landscape of urban schools.

Janet E. Kearney

See also Finn, Chester E., Jr.; Neoconservatives; School Choice; Schools of Education

Further Readings

Boyd, D., Grossman, P., Lankford, H., Loeb, S., & Wyckoff, J. (2006). How changes in entry requirements alter the teacher workforce and affect student achievement. *Education Finance and Policy, 1*(2), 176–216.

Darling-Hammond, L., Holtzman, D., Gatlin, S. J., & Heilig, J. V. (2005). Does teacher preparation matter? Evidence about teacher certification, Teach For America, and teacher effectiveness. *Education Policy Analysis Archives, 13*(42). Retrieved August 14, 2009, from http://epaa.asu.edu/epaa/v13n42/v13n42.pdf

Graves, L. (2008). What is Teach for America really like? *U.S. News and World Report.* Retrieved August 14, 2009 http://www.usnews.com/articles/education/k-12/2008/03/05/what-is-teach-for-america-really-like.html

Katz, S. (2007). *Teach For America, hope for the future.* Retrieved August 14, 2009, from http://www.aibs.org/eye-on-education/eye_on_education_2007_10.html

Teach For America: http://www.teachforamerica.org

TECH PREP EDUCATION

Should public schools provide training to fit students into specific businesses or careers, or does such career selection and sorting lead to a type of caste system with students tracked into industry or career training at an early age? By the beginning of the 20th century, business leaders began to challenge the purpose of the common schools in each of the states. Led by groups like Chambers of Commerce and the National Association of Manufacturers, policymakers and public school leaders were urged to create schools and curriculum that would address the needs of industry and commerce. In many

cases, the business bosses and managers demanded that schools focus more on teaching obedience to authority and loyalty to employers, and inculcating desirable work habits and workplace efficiency. As the scientific management theory began to dominate business and political economics, this tracking and training for business efficiency became even more prominent in the public schools. This vocational education movement has been known by many terms, including industrial or trade education, vocational training, tech prep, and more recently, career and technology education (CTE or CATE).

Critics of the tech prep approach emerged from a variety of interests. Classical scholars sought to establish common schools, especially secondary schools, focusing on studying the classics of Western civilization, even creating a curriculum called Great Books. Progressive educators challenged the scientific management approach and helped to form professional associations, like the National Education Association and the American Federation of Teachers, to emphasize public schools as institutions promoting democracy and civic education. The American Federation of Teachers adopted the slogan "education for democracy, democracy for education." Some business leaders attacked such associations as promoting a one-sided focus on workers. They saw such associations as unions and as enemies of the business interests of vocational education. Many school administrators followed the powerful interests of the business community and endorsed the vocational education movement as a central role for public schools. Some educational historians, like Professor Raymond Callahan, suggested that this emphasis led to a narrow focus, with public school missions mirroring the business world and molding students to fit neatly into business and industry.

An outcome of these competing interests was the growth of the comprehensive secondary schools that used a variety of assessments and initiatives to track students into vocational education or college preparatory programs. Generally, vocational education students did not pursue postsecondary education. Instead they were sorted and selected into a variety of more traditional trades, such as auto mechanics, wood shop or carpentry, metal shop or welding, and other building trades. Often students identified as slow or problem students were tracked into tech prep programs. Guidance counselors played a significant role in directing students into these competing pathways—tech prep or college prep.

Critics of such tracking challenged these programs as being narrowly focused; limiting students' well-rounded development in the arts and sciences, as well as failing to promote citizenship education. As technology advanced, information exploded via the Internet, globalization increased and the industrial base began to shrink, and educators and policymakers began to recognize the need to revise vocational education away from the traditional tracking of tech prep and toward college prep programs. Led by Governor Bill Clinton of Arkansas and the National Governors Association, state leaders began in the latter stages of the 20th century to respond to this shift from an industrial economic base to high-tech information businesses and consumer services. By the early 1990s, President George H. W. Bush established the Secretary's Commission on Achieving Necessary Skills (SCANS). SCANS was also supported in Goals 2000: Educate America Act. Subsequently, President Clinton moved this high-tech prep initiative into the School-to-Work Opportunities Act. Federal funding of such career tech prep initiatives has been provided by the Carl D. Perkins Vocational & Technical Education Act of 1998, and recently reauthorized and revised in 2006 to ensure that public schools provide all students with an education that will help them succeed in the workplace and throughout life. Tech prep programs were now seen as lifelong learning initiatives preparing citizens with the knowledge and skills necessary to meet emerging economies.

By the beginning of the 21st century, business, community, and government leaders joined with school leaders to develop the PreK–16 initiatives, trying to assist professionals to guide students into career pathways requiring some postsecondary training. The narrowly focused tech prep programs failed to prepare students for 21st-century work. Thus the tech prep programs became CTE programs aimed at developing advanced information and technology skills, along with creative and critical thinking skills, and interpersonal and team building skills. Leaders recognized that students needed skills that could be applied to jobs that have not even been created.

The debate continues between more traditional high schools based on Carnegie Units requiring more English Language Arts, Social Studies, Math,

and Science courses with a spattering of some electives in Fine Arts, Physical Education, and Foreign Language on the one hand, and more comprehensive tech prep competency and traditional skill-based education on the other. The career and technology educational leaders are influenced by business and government leaders like the National Center on Education and the Economy, and groups like Achieve, Inc. These groups are pushing for higher standards in public schools to better prepare all students for postsecondary education and work. This CTE initiative no longer sees an either/or world of tech prep for work and college prep for 4-year colleges and universities. Led by Achieve, Inc., National Center on Education and the Economy, and other business and government leaders, and the Association for Career and Technical Education, they recognize that tech prep or CTE must address all students and close any academic achievement and skills gaps by focusing on higher level skill-based education for all that includes career exploration as mandatory for all public school students. Such exploration is distinctly different from the old tech prep tracking system. Twenty-first-century students will learn how to think creatively and critically as preparation for emerging careers and changing economies. How to achieve this integration of tech prep and lifelong learning, including formal postsecondary education, will be a challenge for current educational leaders.

Steve Jenkins

See also Business and Educational Reform; Cardinal Principles Report; Career Education; Comprehensive High Schools; School-to-Work; Smith-Hughes Act; Social Efficiency

Further Readings

Callahan, R. (1962). *Education and the cult of efficiency: A study of the social forces that have shaped the administration of the public schools.* Chicago: University of Chicago Press.

Cuban, L. (2007). *The blackboard and the bottom line: Why schools cannot be businesses.* Boston: Harvard University Press.

Gelberg, D. (1997). *The "business" of reforming American schools.* Albany: State University of New York Press.

National Center on Education and the Economy. (2007). *Tough choices or tough times: The report of the New Commission on the Skills of the American Workforce.* San Francisco: Jossey-Bass.

Wagner, T. (2008). *The global achievement gap: Why even our best schools don't teach the new survival skills our children need—and what we can do about it.* New York: Basic Books.

TERMAN, LEWIS M. (1877–1956)

Lewis Terman stands as both a pioneer and a controversial figure in the field of intelligence testing in the United States. Terman's work on the second version of the Binet-Simon scale, which had been introduced in the United States in 1916 by the French psychologist Alfred Binet, led to a revised scale known as the Stanford-Binet Intelligence Scale. The latter was considered to be the most successful among various versions available at the time, leading to Terman's reputation as one of the leaders in the American intelligence testing movement. Terman's work, along with that of others interested in intelligence testing, began to reform the way in which educators thought about students' academic abilities and especially about what it meant to be gifted.

Terman's contributions to the science of intelligence testing, including his attention to rigorous procedures for test development, norming, administration, and scoring, hold as true today as they did in the early 20th century. His support of hereditarian theories of intelligence and the related uses of intelligence testing in schools and society have, however, been the subject of much debate.

Terman's interest in the study of intelligence is often traced to the story of an itinerant book peddler and phrenologist who visited his family's farm in the late 1890s. Terman, the 12th of 14 children, was proclaimed by the visitor to possess a skull formation indicating strong mental powers and the likelihood of great success in life. At the age of 15, Terman left the family farm (he was born in central Indiana) to attend Central Normal College in Danville, Indiana. From there, he served as a teacher and principal, obtained a master's degree from Indiana University, and was eventually encouraged to enter Clark University. At Clark, Terman received a fellowship and studied under the psychologist G. Stanley Hall, whose beliefs about social evolution theory were purported to have an enormous influence on Terman's emerging views on the relationship between heredity and intelligence. Although Hall was not a proponent of the measurement of intellect, Terman became captivated with the potential use of such tests and began to work with his thesis advisor, Edmund C. Sanford, to develop tests designed to discriminate between "bright" and "dull" students.

Following his studies at Clark, Terman moved to California where, in 1910, he received a faculty appointment in education at Stanford University. He remained at Stanford, where he served as head of the Psychology Department, until his retirement in 1942. It was at Stanford that Terman came into his own as a researcher and leader in testing reform in the fields of education and psychology, primarily through his successful revision of the Binet-Simon scales that had been introduced to the United States in 1908 by Henry H. Goddard. Goddard and other researchers worked on various translations of the scale, but it was Terman's 1916 revision that came to be considered the most comprehensive and well-known among the measures of intelligence available at that time.

Terman conducted extensive renorming of the original scales and added a number of new tests, with the result that the Stanford-Binet consisted of 90 tests and 16 alternatives, as compared to the 54 tests of the original Binet-Simon scale. The 1916 revision was published with an accompanying manual designed to ensure that test administration, scoring, and interpretation occurred under standardized conditions that resulted in the highest possible levels of objectivity. It also introduced a numerical index of intelligence that calculated intelligence on the basis of the ratio between an individual's mental age and chronological age. The resulting "intelligence quotient" (IQ) had been devised by the German psychologist William Stern in 1912, but it was not until Terman's introduction of IQ that the concept became widely known in both academic and public circles in the United States.

Terman's views on intelligence have been the subject of much debate among both supporters and critics. He believed that innate intelligence could be accurately measured, that social class was a function of native intelligence rather than environmental factors, and that universal intelligence testing held promise as an efficient and objective approach for "tracking" children into homogeneously grouped educational and vocational programs. According to Terman, students considered to be of "superior intellect" should be educated separately in accelerated classrooms and programs. He saw this as a necessary condition for advancement in a democratic society. Indeed, Terman suggested that one of the most significant problems for democracy was how to adjust for the radically different IQ variances within and between races and nationality groups. From Terman's perspective, the leaders needed to come from the top quartile and especially the top 5% in order to ensure the advance of social, academic, and governmental entities.

In contrast, Terman described persons scoring in the lowest 15th or 20th percentiles on intelligence tests as "democracy's ballast." Again, his proposal was to use intelligence testing as a means to classify and to provide separate educational and vocational systems for this group of children and adults, thereby avoiding increases in crime, poverty, and industrial inefficiency that he believed would likely result if these individuals were not identified and served accordingly.

Terman's views came under increasing scrutiny following his later work with Robert M. Yerkes on large-scale intelligence testing of the armed forces during World War I. Discussions of intelligence that had been largely confined to psychologists and educators came into the public purview as both the technical and philosophical underpinnings of intelligence testing were questioned. The emerging "nature versus nurture" argument continued when potential flaws in intelligence tests were implicated in debates about the degree to which patterns and variations in intelligence could be ascribed to specific racial and ethnic groups. Terman, who had advocated for the use of intelligence testing as a way to strengthen a democratic society, now faced critics such as William C. Bagley of Teachers College, Columbia University, who argued that testing was being used unfairly to increase the opportunities of some social classes at the expense of others, thereby perpetuating an already unjust social order.

In considering Terman's contributions to testing reform in education, it seems important to view him within his particular historical context: a time marked by the rise of industrialism, optimism about the potential for advancements in psychology and science, and a belief in the power of objective and rational thinking to lead to a more efficient and orderly society. There is little doubt that the reform advancements he made with respect to the technical aspects of the measurement of intelligence have been, in many respects, positive and enduring. In the end, it may be most important to revisit his assumptions to carefully evaluate contemporary notions of intelligence and intelligence testing. It would seem wise to examine the ways in which current beliefs and practices—including homogeneous grouping in schools, large-scale group achievement testing, and commonly held beliefs about the "innateness" of intelligence—may be reminiscent of aspects of his work.

Katharine Shepherd and Susan Hasazi

See also Achieve, Inc.; ACT and SAT Tests; Educational Testing Service (ETS); Intelligence Testing; Standardized Tests; Testing Students

Further Readings

Evans, B., & Waites, B. (1981). *IQ and mental testing: An unnatural science and its history.* Atlantic Highlands, NJ: Humanities Press.

Gould, S. J. (1981). *The mismeasure of man.* New York: W. W. Norton.

Hilgard, E. R. (1989). The early years of intelligence measurement. In R. L. Linn (Ed.), *Intelligence measurement, theory, and public policy.* Chicago: University of Illinois Press.

Minton, H. (1987). Lewis Terman and mental testing: In search of the democratic ideal. In M. M. Sokal (Ed.), *Psychological testing and American society, 1890–1930.* New Brunswick, NJ: Rutgers University Press.

Minton, H. (1998). Introduction to: "The uses of intelligence tests" Lewis Terman (1916). *Classics in the history of psychology.* Retrieved September 11, 2008, from http://psychclassics.yorku.ca/Terman/intro.htm

Terman, L. M., & Merrill, M. A. (1916). *Measuring intelligence: A guide to the administration of the new revised Stanford-Binet tests of intelligence.* Boston: Houghton Mifflin.

Terman, L. M., & Merrill, M. A. (1973). *Stanford-Binet intelligence scale: Manual for the third revision.* Boston: Houghton Mifflin.

TESTING STUDENTS

Testing, also called assessment, is the procedures used to measure students on the education variables we are interested in. The purpose of a test is to assess students' aptitudes, achievements, knowledge, or skills. The result of testing is called the measurement. Generally, there are two separate testing strategies: criterion-referenced measurement and norm-referenced measurement.

In norm-referenced tests, a student's performance is compared to the scores of a well-defined norm group of students who have previously taken the same test. The norm group has the same characteristics as the students in the study, such as age and grade level. Therefore, this kind of test is called norm-referenced because educators interpret a student's test score to the performance of the norm-group; emphasis is not on the absolute amount of performance, but on the relative position (called percentile rank) of the student compared to the norm group. Thus, students with a percentile rank of 50 on a norm-referenced test score higher than or equal to 50% of the group with which they are compared.

In contrast, a criterion-referenced test is an absolute measurement because the score is interpreted by comparison to a standard or criterion. The student's test performance can be interpreted according to the degree to which the domain has been mastered. The purpose is to show how an individual student compares to some established level of performance. Rather than interpreting that a student has "scored better than 50% of the students in the norm group," a criterion-referenced test is interpreted as a student having "mastered 50% of the test's content."

The scores from a norm-referenced test can be used to decide whether a student should enroll in remedial courses. But the information from criterion-referenced tests does not give information about students' actual knowledge. The inference from the test scores relies on whether or not the expected knowledge in a particular school district matches the content of the norm-referenced test.

On the other hand, criterion-referenced tests specify, on each test content included in that test, how well students have mastered the content. Therefore it is easier to match the knowledge and

skills expected by the school district with a criterion-referenced test. If the content of the criterion-referenced test matches the content that is expected by the school district, the criterion-referenced test gives more information about the extent to which students have mastered the content than a norm-referenced test.

Reliability and Validity

Generally, there are two criteria to evaluate whether or not a test is of high quality: reliability and validity. Reliability, also called consistency, represents the degree to which a test consistently measures what it intends to measure. Reliability in education assessment appears in three forms: stability reliability, alternate form reliability, and internal reliability. A stability estimate of reliability is also called test-retest reliability. A stability estimate of reliability is obtained by administering one test to one group of students, waiting a week or two, then retesting them with the same test. To measure alternate-form reliability, we administer two equivalent forms of the test to one group of students and then correlate the scores from the two administrations. For example, if a pretest and a posttest are administered to the same group of students in an educational research study, the researcher usually administers alternate but equivalent tests instead of giving the same test twice. Internal reliability deals with the extent to which questions in an educational test are working in a consistent fashion. For this type of reliability, only one form of an instrument is given only once to a group of students; the estimate of reliability is calculated by studying the correlations between the items in the instrument.

Most commercially published standardized tests have reliability coefficients that are greater than .80, and often greater than .90. How high the reliability should be depends on the purpose of the test.

If the test is a high-stakes test, such as the test used for high school graduation requirement, the reliability coefficients have to be very high, at least .90. The high coefficient will lower the chance of misclassification.

On the other hand, classroom assessments do not need to have high internal consistency reliabilities. Because more and more students will know the content, the internal consistency reliability will go down. Also, the teacher can gather the information about students' mastery of the content from multiple sources. If a classroom assessment developed by the teacher has a low reliability coefficient, the teacher should be able to recognize the inaccuracy by her or his knowledge of the student.

Also, reliability depends not only on the test, but also on the student group. Therefore, caution should be used when evaluating test reliability. For example, a test with a reliability of .95 with 9th- and 10th-grade students tested together might not have such a high coefficient if only 9th graders take the test.

Until recently, validity has been defined as the extent to which a test measures what it is supposed to measure. In the more contemporary definition, validity is the degree to which the test scores provide information that is relevant to the inferences that are to be made from them. Therefore, evidence that test scores are appropriate for one purpose does not necessarily mean that the scores are appropriate for another. In other words, validity is a judgment of the appropriateness of a test for the specific decisions that result from the test scores. The same test can be valid in one circumstance or for one use and invalid for another.

There are generally three forms of validity: (1) content-related evidence of validity, (2) criterion-related evidence of validity, and (3) construct-related evidence of validity. Content-related evidence of validity displays the degree to which the items in the test are representative of the appropriate domain of content it was intended to measure. Content-related evidence of validity is determined by having content experts review the contents of the instrument and indicate the degree to which they measure the intended contents. Construct-related evidence of validity indicates the extent to which scores from a given test relate to similar tests of the same construct. For example, when the scores from one test are highly correlated with scores from another test of the same construct, there is high construct-related evidence of validity. The third form of validity is called criterion-related evidence of validity, which deals with the extent to which a test accurately predicts a student's future performance. For example, in a test to measure students' teaching skills, the test scores would be correlated with future teaching behavior. If students with low test scores turned out to be poor teachers and students with high scores became good teachers, this test showed high criterion-related evidence of validity.

In today's high-stakes testing, two sources of invalidity should be emphasized.

One source of invalidity is content underrepresentation. Content underrepresentation occurs when the test fails to include some important dimensions of the content that the test claims to have included. Therefore, the test scores will underrepresent students' true knowledge or abilities because the test content is incomplete.

Another source of invalidity is called content irrelevance, which means that the test measures many dimensions that are irrelevant to the content that the test is intended to measure. Content-irrelevant invalidity has two forms: content-irrelevant easiness and content-irrelevant difficulty. The content-irrelevant easiness happens when the irrelevant content dimensions give extra clues to help students answer the test items correctly. The content-irrelevant difficulty happens when the irrelevant content dimensions make answering the test items more difficult. Thus, content-irrelevant easiness will cause students to score higher than they normally would, and content-irrelevant difficulty will cause students to score lower than they normally would.

Broad Categories of Tests

There are several broad categories of tests:

- A performance test is a test procedure that approximates a real-life situation. In the test, students create responses to an assigned task by demonstrating their knowledge of how to do the real-life task.

- A standardized test is a test that is administered and scored in a consistent way. The majority of the commercial tests are standardized. A standardized test with significant consequences for the students is also called a high-stakes test. One example of educational high-stakes tests would be a statewide graduation exam that must be passed before a student graduates.

- A standardized test is characterized by a uniform procedure for administration and scoring. Generally there are directions specifying the test procedures, including qualification of the person administering the test, time allowed for the test, materials that students can use, and other conditions. There are also instructions on how to score the student responses objectively. The majority of the standardized tests are norm referenced so that the results can be compared against the norm group. Standardized tests are produced commercially by testing companies that have experts in assessment and measurement. Commercially available standardized tests have been reviewed on issues such as validity, reliability, and item analysis.

- A standardized achievement test is a test that measures students' knowledge of a domain of related content. The tests are produced commercially, and careful attention has been given to their reliability and validity. These achievement tests put emphasis on what has been learned by the students, and students are scored as either proficient or not proficient in the content area. Standardized achievement tests have several categories: Some measure a single subject, for example, reading. Others, such as survey batteries, are tests that survey various subjects; for example, reading, writing, and mathematics.
- If available achievement tests do not meet the needs of teachers, a test can be developed locally to examine classroom learning. This test is usually called a locally developed test.
- The purpose of a standardized aptitude test is to measure knowledge or skill that are predictive of future performance. The test is produced to measure knowledge or skills that are predictive of future performance. Although their test items might be very similar, achievement and aptitude tests have different applications. Achievement tests measure a specific type of knowledge defined by the content of the test. Aptitude tests usually measure a student's ability to comprehend and apply knowledge in solving a problem.

Controversies About Testing

An example of a standardized aptitude test is the SAT test, which is used as a basis for entrance into higher education institutions. Although some experts may argue that SAT tests may actually measure the practice effects rather than the accumulated knowledge of students, this argument is not well based because SAT is used to predict future performance, not current knowledge.

However, other experts argue that college entrance exams such as SAT are not accurate predictors of freshmen performance in college. This argument is also not correct, because SAT scores are designed to be used in combination with other measures to predict freshman GPA; it is not used as the only predictor of the GPA. Colleges and universities can also take into consideration a student's high school GPA and extracurricular activities.

Another criticism of standardized tests is that they are not used in accordance with their intended purposes. However, the validity of a test lies in the interpretation of the test scores. If a teacher uses a test for other than the intended purposes, the teacher has to justify the validity of the interpretation.

Another confounding factor for test performance is stress. Students have different stress levels. Some have low stress levels and can easily perform well in a test, while others may become nervous and perform badly in a test. To counter this stress factor, teachers may also use portfolio assessment—not giving grades based only on test scores, but also placing considerable weight on attendance record and homework.

Teaching to the Test

Nowadays, the public thinks that making teachers accountable for their students' achievement will result in better student achievement, and that the best evidence of teachers' efforts is students' performance in the standardized achievement tests. Yet students' scores in the standardized achievement tests have their limitations. Because test scores are closely linked to public perception of teachers' performance, teachers may cross the line and teach directly to the test. While the practice of teaching to the test has existed for many years, it is becoming more frequent now because of the current emphasis placed on test scores.

Teaching to the test can be done in either a positive or a negative way, depending how teachers carry out the practice. In this sense, it is very important to distinguish between the ethical and unethical practices of teaching to the tests. Williams Mehrens and John Kaminski (1989) proposed a continuum of teaching to the test, which consists of seven points:

1. Introducing the school district's objectives for the achievement test, but not mentioning the objectives of the standardized achievement test;

2. Introducing general test-taking techniques;

3. Studying the test objectives of several standardized achievement tests, and teaching the test objectives to the students;

4. Studying the specific test objectives (skills and subskills) of the standardized achievement test that is going to be administered, and teaching students those specific objectives;

5. Teaching the specifically matched test objectives (skills and subskills) of the standardized achievement test in the same format as the test questions;

6. Providing instruction on a parallel form of the same test;

7. Providing instruction on the test itself.

Mehrens and Kaminski (1989) indicated that points 6 and 7 on the continuum are never ethical, and point 1 is always ethical. Mehrens and Kaminski suggest that the line between ethical and unethical test preparation practices should be drawn between point 4 and point 5.

Glynn Ligon and Phil Jones (1982) suggest that an ethical test preparation practice is one that enhances students' ability to perform on the test near their true ability level, one that contributes more to their test performance than spending an equal amount of time on regular classroom instruction.

Therefore, the ethical practice of preparing students for the test should focus on teaching students test-taking skills. If students have mastered the knowledge, these test-taking skills will help students perform close to their true ability level.

Generally, a test score is used to draw inference from students' performance on test items to measure students' knowledge about a broader domain. But teaching to the test provides instruction on the specific content sampled in the test, thus it will be invalid to use test scores to draw inference about students' knowledge or skills.

Another misinterpretation of test scores is that some people use the test scores to draw inference about why students perform in a certain way in the test. For example, some people may claim that students perform well in a test because of a specific remedial program. Indirect inference of the test scores will lead to incorrect conclusions about school programs.

Xiaogeng Sun

See also Achievement Gap; ACT and SAT Tests; Alternative Assessment; Guidance and School Counseling; Student Assessment and School Accountability

Further Readings

Ligon, G. D., & Jones, P. (1982). *Preparing students for standardized testing: One district's perspective.* Paper presented at the annual meeting of the American Educational Research Association, New York.

McMillan, J. H. (2001). *Essential assessment concepts for teachers and administrators.* Thousand Oaks, CA: Corwin.

Mehrens, W. A., & Kaminski, J. (1989). Methods for improving standardized test scores: Fruitful, fruitless or fraudulent? *Educational Measurement: Issues and Practices, 8*(1), 12–22.

Thorndike, R. M. (1997). *Measurement and evaluation in psychology and education.* Upper Saddle River, NJ: Prentice Hall.

TEST OF TEACHING KNOWLEDGE (TTK)

Tests of teaching knowledge (TTKs) are used by various stakeholders to assess teachers' knowledge before, during, and after teacher preparation programs. TTKs identify individuals with formal teacher preparation, predict teaching success, or both. This entry reviews and discusses types of TTKs, associated knowledge, relevant criticisms, and provides examples of existing TTKs.

Three types of tests are used to measure teacher knowledge, namely tests of basic skills, tests of content knowledge, and tests of professional knowledge. Tests of basic skills are typically used for selection into teacher preparation programs. While these tests are often criticized for their low cutoff scores, many educators hold that increasing the passing rate may result in a less diverse teaching force. Examples of basic skills tests include the Educational Testing Service's (ETS) Praxis I:

Academic Skills Assessment and the Pre-Professional Skills Test (PPST).

Even though educators today may disagree about the relative value of pedagogical and academic content knowledge as the ultimate goal for licensing, tests of content knowledge and professional knowledge are required for credentialing and are typically completed as candidates near graduation. Candidates may take one to several content knowledge tests, depending on their licensure area. ETS offers several Praxis II tests on subject matter. Similarly, ETS offers a variety of tests of professional knowledge that are purported to target academic and functional professional knowledge. Examples include the Praxis II: Principles of Learning and Teaching (PLT). Critics of the professional knowledge tests target their effectiveness as requirements for teacher licensing, claiming that it is nearly impossible to represent the profession of teaching with such exams, or capture the complexity of informed decision making in context. Critics claim that professional knowledge tests measure general and academic knowledge rather than provide effective measures of functional pedagogical knowledge and skills. These critics question the validity of professional knowledge tests as predictors of future teaching competence.

In some states, candidates are required to satisfactorily complete an additional test at the end of their first or second year of teaching. Results of this performance assessment provide the final evidence required to issue ongoing or permanent licensure. Examples of these performance assessments include Praxis III: Classroom Performance Assessment for Beginning Teachers and the Interstate New Teacher Assessment and Support Consortium's (INTASC) Test of Teaching Knowledge (under construction).

The National Council for Accreditation of Teacher Education (NCATE) and the federal government require teacher education institutions to report pass rates of their graduates on content and professional knowledge tests. A further requirement is alignment of the TTKs with adopted state standards for teacher education, such as the Interstate New Teacher Assessment and Support Consortium standards and principles.

Danielle E. Dani

See also Accountability Era; Alternative Licensure; College Board; Interstate New Teacher Assessment

and Support Consortium (INTASC); Licensure and Certification; National Council for Accreditation of Teacher Education (NCATE); Teacher Education; Teacher Evaluation

Further Readings

Brandt, R. (1992). On making sense: A conversation with Magdalene Lampert. *Educational Leadership, 51*(5), 26–30.

D'Agostino, J. V., & VanWinkle, W. H. (2007). Identifying prepared and competent teachers with professional knowledge tests. *Journal of Personnel Evaluation in Education, 20*(1), 65–84.

Jones, J. (1992). *Praxis III teacher assessment criteria research base.* Princeton, NJ: Educational Testing Service.

THORNDIKE, EDWARD L. (1874–1949)

Edward Lee Thorndike is best known as America's quintessential scientific educational theorist. His theories and empirical and quantitative research conducted in understanding animal intelligence would ultimately become foundational to the development of human educational psychology, philosophy, and policy. Of special significance in terms of reforming the way in which educators thought about human behavior was Thorndike's work on operant conditioning. His research interests varied from adult learning to intelligence tests for the U.S. military.

Born August 31, 1874, in Williamsburg, Massachusetts, Thorndike received his master's degree from Harvard University in 1897 and his doctorate of philosophy from Columbia University in 1898. Thorndike's 40-year career in the professorship was spent at Columbia University Teachers College. During that time his comprehensive contributions in understanding, measuring, and quantifying human learning and intellectual potentials helped solidify Teachers College as one of the most prestigious training institutions for educational leaders in the United States. It is believed that Thorndike did not fully receive the recognition and appreciation worthy of a scholar of his magnitude, despite his indisputable intellectual contributions.

His detractors, primarily Progressives, viewed his scientific educational approaches (including Law and Exercise), along with other concepts in learning, as being resoundingly positivist and deterministic. Thorndike argued that heredity (race) had much to do with differentiations and limitations in learning, which further aroused harsh criticism.

Thorndike's theory of connectionism or belonging was at the core of his assertions about how individuals learn through forming connections and associations among situations, conditions, or responses in either short- or long-term sequences involving changes in connections either pleasant or unpleasant. His research revealed that individuals possess a broad range of connected intellectual capacities, which led him to conclude that testing measured only a narrow range of human intelligence. Darwinism, experimentalism, and the work of William James were substantive influences on his scholarship. Thorndike's research of, and knowledge in, the field of scientific educational psychology was encyclopedic. Therefore, only three of his notable theories are highlighted and especially because they have impacted educational activities and reform within schools throughout the United States. They include the halo effect, law of effect, and principles of learning.

The Halo Effect

The *halo effect* is much like its name suggests, in that when individuals tend to view and judge others predominately by one specific desirable attribute, or characteristic, they render those persons as virtually consisting of that perceived favorable attribute—*angelic*. For example, one person may view another as being primarily good, and therefore judge that individual as being inherently good in most, if not all, aspects of his or her nature. These judgments are subjective and predicated on cognitive bias due to denial or lack of recognition of less desirable attributes. Thorndike had concerns as to how the halo effect influenced psychological ratings and experiments. This theory has been appropriated recently by human resources and technology industries.

Law of Effect

The precursor to the (S–R) theory or stimuli/response began with Thorndike's experimentation

with the puzzle box and a cat, wherein several solutions were given for the same situation. The outcome was that certain stimulus/teaching, enforcements, consequences, and connections within an environment produced satisfactory responses while other stimuli/teaching and changes in environment demonstrated student dissatisfaction with the exercise. Information gained from the puzzle box study was extrapolated and applied to understanding human learning behavior. For example, in learning, individuals will wish to repeat and adapt to the learning exercise due to increased learning, satisfaction, and habit within a given environment. Connections in human behavior can be changed or modified; consequently, all effective learning ranges along a continuum of connectivity or connection-forming with different or situation-specific responses. Without connections, learning appears to be only a dissatisfactory series of repetitious actions not conducive to substantive long-term learning. Thorndike's *law of exercise* figures prominently in this theory: Specifically, rigorous repetition of identical elements in an environment, exercise, and duration of connection increase remembrance and learning.

Principles of Learning

In an effort to understand human principles of learning or *laws*, Thorndike distinguished several key elements that predisposed human learning; these were later added to by educational psychologists. *Readiness* is just that, a state of readiness on multiple levels to engage in learning. *Exercise* is necessary to grasp simple to complex learning tasks. *Effect,* as stated above under law of effect, occurs for most students within environments they find satisfying versus those that are deemed unsatisfactory. With regard to *primacy,* ideally, early or primary learning should be positive, effective, and the basis for all future learning. As for *recency,* human memory is indeed fallible; consequently, those things learned more recently can be recalled more readily and effectively than earlier learning. The importance of *intensity* is that, comparable to experiential learning, students tend to learn when involved firsthand in the learning experience, and particularly when the learning is accompanied by vibrant and intense teaching pedagogy and praxis.

At the close of the 20th century, educators at all levels from K–12 and in higher education began advocating for more interactive, transactional, realistic, and meaningful student learning. Of the three theories addressed here, along with connectionism, it appears that Thorndike worked from a position of relationship among these theories rather than having each stand on its own. While Thorndike's models in educational psychology may appear to be outdated, especially to those with progressivist views, his perspectives on the need for student satisfaction in the learning process remain constant, highly contemporary, and clearly a part of the dialogue evidenced by more conservative educational policymakers who continue to argue for reform in schools throughout the United States.

B. Lara Lee

See also Behaviorism; Direct Instruction; Finn, Chester E., Jr.; Neoconservatives; Skinner, B. F.

Further Readings

Elliott, S., Kratochwill, T., Cook, J., & Travers, J. (2000). *Educational psychology* (3rd ed.). Boston: McGraw-Hill.

Joncich, G. (Ed.). (1962). *Psychology and the science of education.* New York: Columbia University, Teachers College, Bureau of Publications.

Slavin, R. (2000). *Educational psychology theory and practice* (6th ed.). Boston: Allyn & Bacon.

Thorndike, E. L. (1916). *Theory of mental and social measurements.* New York: Columbia University, Teachers College.

Thorndike, E. L. (1921). *Educational psychology: Vol. 2. The psychology of learning.* New York: Columbia University, Teachers College.

Thorndike, E. L. (1935). *The psychology of wants, interests and attitudes.* New York: D. Appleton-Century.

Thorndike, E. L. (1966). *Human learning.* Cambridge: MIT Press.

Thorndike, E. L. (1977). *The fundamentals of learning.* New York: Columbia University, Teachers College.

TIME ON TASK

Researchers and experts on student learning in the United States seem to agree that, currently, school time is insufficient to accomplish all the learning goals set for K–12 education and at the same time provide a well-rounded education for students. Some reformers say we need a longer school year. Dissenters say no, what we must do is create longer school days. Other reformers insist that the only way we will see consistent, long-term learning improvements is to spend more time on math skills and basic reading. Dissenters believe it is essential that teachers and learners spend considerable more time on problem solving, reasoning, science, and even social studies. Most reformers agree that whatever method we use to increase learning time in schools, it is not nearly as important as the fact that somehow we must find more time. A more recent dissenting analysis raises the issue that our more pressing problem may well be making better use of the time we have now.

Support for longer school days seems to be the most popular suggestion for reforming instruction time in K–12 schools found in the literature today. A recent Brookings Institution study concluded that even adding just 10 minutes to eighth graders' math instruction each day translated into increased scores. The researchers in the Brookings' study concluded it was smarter to add more time to each day than to extend the year. Ten more minutes of math instruction was associated with a 19-point gain, on an 800-point scale, whereas adding 40 days of 45-minute classes yielded only an 8.5-point gain. Dissenters are quick to point out, however, that using the same Brookings' data, even adding 450 minutes of math instruction in the United States would shrink the gap between U.S. and Singapore math scores by only 5%.

A statewide middle school steering committee in Maryland recently recommended a longer school day and a longer school year as a part of the state's recognition of a significant problem. Middle school students who are having trouble learning are at a much higher risk of dropping out of high school. Besides increased instruction time, the panel also recommended more planning time and collaboration time for teachers and other support staff, declaring that this would result in more individualization of learning and behavioral plans for students in need of additional help. A common dissenting thought from administrators is that, although they would love to see a longer day and longer year in their districts, and although they agree that it would eventually lessen the high school dropout problem, extending the school day by even 30 minutes would cost millions. Unless the state is willing to fund this reform, it cannot be implemented because the local districts cannot fund it. Most reformers believe students in other nations are working harder and longer and learning more than students in the United States. Based on the information from the Trends in International Mathematics and Science Study (TIMMS), on average students in other nations spend 193 days in school each year compared to 180 in the United States. Over a dozen years this difference translates into a gap of nearly one full year. Dissenters point to examples where the combination of more time in the school day and the school year or giving districts the option of how the extra time will be generated might be better solutions.

In 2006, a Massachusetts state grant program allowed schools to add 300 hours to the school schedule, in any way they chose, to provide more time for academics, enrichment, and personalized attention. Sixth-grade math scores at Clarence R. Edwards Middle School in Boston jumped to the 68th percentile compared to the previous year's scores at the 48th percentile. Seventh-grade math scores went from 46% in the previous year to 67%, and eighth-grade scores increased from 45% to 53%. Dissenters are quick to point out the cost of this program is $1,300 per student, a sum many states and maybe even Massachusetts will not be able to afford if the concept is expanded to many other districts.

One of the more popular and well-known charter school programs in the United States is the Knowledge Is Power Program (KIPP), which is a charter school network. Students begin each day at 7:30 a.m. and end at 5 p.m. Half-day classes are held on Saturdays, and students attend a summer school session ranging in length from 2 to 4 weeks. In total, KIPP students get about 60% more class time than their peers in other schools. In general, KIPP schools are recognized for their high student performance. Dissenters ask this question: Can this school organization and instruction concept be adopted in a broad way in the United States, knowing the resistance to changing the old agrarian school calendar, the family vacation traditions, and the other summer, nonschool activities that have become a major part of U.S. culture?

The newly created National Center on Time and Learning is involved in a reform effort related to time and learning different from previous reform efforts. Cochair of the Center, Paul Reville, who is also chairman of the Massachusetts State Board of Education, agreed to serve as cochair because of his belief that what we all expect from schools today far exceeds what can realistically be accomplished. Dissenting from the most common school reform efforts like longer school days and longer school years, the Center plans to sponsor and/or conduct research into how time is used now in schools. Another major impetus for the Center will be to review the scholarly literature describing the most effective uses of expanded learning time. A third part of the Center's mission will be to study how other countries structure their school day and school year, and what effect the different strategies identified have on student learning. A key objective of the Center's efforts is to let schools see from the evidence that it is not just adding time that will make the difference, but that rethinking how the school day is structured—for example, how many minutes are allotted for each subject and when is the best time to teach the basic academic subjects—may also provide significant learning growth for students.

Dissenters from the strong reform efforts that involve primarily longer school days and longer school years, and even from those who feel the real opportunity for learning improvements come from making better use of the time each day, feel these reform efforts ignore the biggest problem that exists in failing schools. It is not the quantity of time that really matters; it is the quality. They believe the time and energy and money going into the typical reform efforts involving time should be devoted to efforts to improve the quality of the underperforming teachers in failing schools. Most experts agree that it is the quality of the teacher in the classroom that has the biggest impact on student learning. Things like significant bonuses for teachers agreeing to work in underperforming schools and much larger school budgets for professional development would go much farther toward improving school performance than just adding more time. After all, do we really want to extend the amount of time an underperforming teacher has with his or her students?

The pressures on K–12 schools to add time to their school calendars and to find more efficient and effective ways to use the current and added time are increasing. Be it the negative comparisons on international tests of achievement, the fact that university systems like that in California now enroll a higher percentage of first-year students in remedial courses than ever before, or the 50% failing rate on the entrance exam to join the International Brotherhood of Electrical Workers, schools are not able to accomplish everything expected of them using the current school day structure and current school year calendar. Changes will be made. Time on task has taken on new meanings. No longer will students just need to pay close attention to the teacher and abide by the classroom rules to be considered "on task," but they can also expect to spend more time each day in class or more days in school each year, and probably live with a daily schedule that uses the allotted time quite differently from what they find in their school today.

Larry D. Cook

See also Accountability Era; Class Size; Trends in
    International Mathematics and Science Study (TIMSS)

Further Readings

Fagan, A. (2007). *Center to help extend school days, calendar.* Retrieved August 15, 2009 from http://www.renniecenter.org/news_docs/0710CentertoExtend SchoolDay.html

Hernandez, N. (2008). *Experts urge longer day to raise scores.* Retrieved August 15, 2009, http://www .washingtonpost.com/wp-dyn/content/article/ 2008/06/24/AR2008062400952.html?nav=emailpage

Manzo, K. (2007). *New center to study use of time in school and to aid enrichment.* Retrieved December 13, 2007, from http://www.edweek.org/ew/articles/2007/ 10/10/07time h27.html?tmp=1372487549

Treviño, M. (2008). *Longer school days aren't a panacea.* Retrieved June 20, 2008, from http://blogs.usatoday .com/oped/2007/04/post_43.html

TITLE IX

Advocates for full rights for girls and women in publicly funded schools achieved that goal in 1972. In that year Title IX of the Educational Amendments passed and simply stated that "no person in the United States shall, on the basis of sex, be excluded from participation in, be denied the benefits of, or be subjected to discrimination under any education program or activity receiving federal financial assistance." This act is codified as Title 20, United States Code, Chapter 38, Sections 1681–1688. The Act was also amended by the Civil Rights Restoration Act of 1988. While prohibiting discrimination based on sex, it was the evidence of bias against girls and women that motivated feminists to push for this legal protection during the 1960s women's movement. A brief history of Title IX is presented along with stories of reformers who were important to its passage and eventual impact on public education within both the K–12 and higher education communities over the past 35 years. Legal challenges to the law have continued through these 3 decades and selected ones are highlighted here.

Presidential Executive Order 11246 that had, since 1965, prohibited job discrimination on racial, color, national origin, or religious bases was amended by President Lyndon Johnson in 1968 to include sex. Several reformers on the scene succeeded, unknowingly at the time, in building the link that ensured that Johnson's amendment would grow into a stronger protection against sex-based discrimination in schools—ultimately in the form of Title IX.

First, in 1969, Bernice R. Sandler, a part-time lecturer at the University of Maryland, knew the university had contracts with the federal government and was the first to point out the connection to employment of women; that is, that the university could not discriminate by sex in university employment. Following Sandler's move, for the first time a congressperson addressed the House of Representatives about discrimination against women in education. On March 9, 1970, Representative Martha Griffiths (D–Michigan) delivered such an address. Motivated by discrimination she had faced in completing her university degree, Representative Patsy T. Mink (D–Hawai'i) drafted the legislation. And, finally, in the summer of 1970, Edith Green (D–Ohio) held the first hearings in the U.S. Congress to address women and education. In addition, Senators Birch Bayh (D–Indiana) and George McGovern (D–South Dakota) navigated the successful passage of the emergent legislation from

Representative Green's efforts, legislation that ultimately became Title IX, signed into law on June 23, 1972, by President Richard Nixon.

The Department of Health, Education and Welfare (HEW) published regulations guiding enforcement of Title IX in 1975. They prohibited restricting any educational activity (in a school receiving federal financial support) to only one sex except under circumstances of classes in human sexuality, contact sports, and activities that were designed to remedy sex discrimination. High schools and universities were given a 3-year compliance window and elementary schools a 1-year timeline. Title IX covered all dimensions of education including facilities, career guidance, financial aid, residence halls, extracurricular activities, academic courses, and athletics. The regulations required institutional recipients of federal funds to designate a Title IX coordinator to monitor enforcement of the law.

Subsequent to the published regulations, numerous complaints originated from compliance officers attempting to ensure equal treatment of young men and young women in college athletics. HEW suspended its response to these complaints until 1979 when they provided the "three-pronged test" of compliance: evidence that the numbers of men and women athletes were equivalent to their proportion of enrolled students, evidence of continuing to add women's sports, and evidence of accommodating women's interests in sports. The three-pronged test has been controversial ever since, frequently facing challenges from schools and colleges.

In 1980, the U.S. Office for Civil Rights within the newly established Department of Education assumed responsibility for Title IX enforcement. Within a few years, in 1984, a landmark U.S. Supreme Court decision (*Grove City v. Bell*) had the effect of removing Title IX enforcement. The Court ruled that only programs that specifically and directly received federal funds must comply with Title IX regulations. This decision effectively removed enforcement from college athletics. However, in 1988, the Civil Rights Restoration Act passed and reinstituted Title IX compliance for all programs and activities across the institution. Athletics once again was under mandate to comply. Enforcement was strengthened when monetary damages were allowed to be awarded to successful plaintiffs in Title IX legal challenges, a Supreme Court ruling in 1992 (*Franklin v. Gwinnett County*

Public Schools). Since the passage of Title IX 35 years ago, other challenges have been brought to the Department of Education by those seeking revised or additional regulations in Title IX. For example, sexual harassment and employment were eventually added to Title IX oversight.

A dramatic reinterpretation of Title IX in 2006 addressed single-sex schools and classrooms. A body of research literature had been accumulating, attesting to the success of Title IX: narrowing of differences in academic achievement between males and females, increasing numbers of women participants in athletics, and increasing access by women to educational programs across the full spectrum of the academy. Separating students by sex for educational purposes had been considered not only illegal under Title IX but was also believed to unfairly impede effective learning and equal access to opportunity for both girls and boys. Nevertheless, in 2006 the language of Title IX was rewritten to allow public schools to structure single-sex schools (and single-sex classes) as an alternative model to coeducational schools and coeducational classes. The genesis of Title IX was to remove differences in school treatment by sex; in 2006, the political move seemed to be at least a partial return to differential treatment.

A new accountability movement helped motivate this change. The federal No Child Left Behind Act (2002) mandated standardized test scores as a measure of school effectiveness. Sex discrimination concerns had become subordinate to student test scores by the late 1990s. Furthermore, many pointed to evidence of the vast educational successes of girls and women over the past 3 decades to assert that discrimination against women had waned. In fact, in the mid-1990s, growing evidence showed educators' concerns shifting to boys, their school failures, and their overrepresentation in special education. In this new push for accountability from schools, policymakers sought school reform models that promised to increase student test scores, especially in low-performing urban communities. Some claimed new neurological research suggested potential sex-based differences in cognition, while others objected to drawing pedagogical implications from an initial body of few studies. Although few public single-sex schools had heretofore existed, successful girls' schools and boys' schools in the private and religious sector were considered possible effective alternative school models.

Federal regulations in Title IX were rewritten by the U.S. Department of Education to specify conditions under which public schools could legally allow single-sex schools or classrooms. The conditions included those where school officials could (a) provide a rationale for offering a single-sex class in a subject; for example, if few girls or boys had enrolled in a specific class in the past, the school could offer a class for one gender or the other; (b) provide a coeducational class in the same subject in accessible ways for students who chose not to enroll in the single-sex class; and (c) conduct an analysis of the single-sex schools or single-sex classes every 2 years to determine whether or not they were still needed to remedy the circumstances that prompted the school district to offer single-sex options. Single-sex schools and classrooms began to open in 2007.

According to the 2006 guidelines, participation of students in single-sex options was to be completely voluntary. Two years after these new regulations were implemented, controversy surrounds single-sex schools. On one hand, feminists as well as others oppose this Title IX reversal and warn of a return to narrow gender stereotypes after 35 years of progress for girls and women. Lawsuits challenging the 2006 regulations have been filed. On the other hand, some educators agree with the new direction. They point to promising pedagogical practices tailor-made for girls and boys in separate settings, practices that may serve to improve the academic performance of struggling students in urban schools.

Carolyn S. Ridenour

See also Civil Rights Act of 1964; Concerned Women for America (CWA); Elementary and Secondary Education Act; Equal Education Opportunity; Equity; Federal Educational Reform; Feminist Perspectives; National Organization for Women (NOW); Single-Sex Schools

Further Readings

Title IX at 35: Executive summary: A report of the National Coalition for Women and Girls in Education. (2008). Retrieved June 30, 2008, from http://www.ncwge.org/PDF/TitleIXat35-summary.pdf

Valentin, I. (1997). *Title IX: A brief history.* Newton, MA: Women's Educational Equity Act (WEEA) Resource Center.

Trends in International Mathematics and Science Study (TIMSS)

Since 1995 and in 4-year cycles afterward, the Trends in International Mathematics and Science Study (TIMSS) has provided the United States and other nations with achievement data related to mathematics and science learning at different levels of schooling. The data from the carefully constructed assessments and implemented sampling methods provide participating nations with objective information on teaching and learning in mathematics and science. Interest in reforming education in these two subject areas has been a priority in the United States since the launching of the Soviet satellite *Sputnik* in 1957. TIMSS data have been used extensively to compare student achievement and instructional practices within and across participating countries. Information about U.S. performance has influenced numerous curriculum initiatives and reform policies and galvanized efforts to improve American competitiveness.

TIMSS is currently a project of the International Study Center housed at the Lynch School of Education at Boston College, but an outgrowth of and sponsored by the International Association for the Evaluation of Educational Achievement (IEA). IEA began in the late 1950s as a result of scholars seeking evidence across national education systems that might be informative to all.

TIMSS in 1995 was known as the Third International Mathematics and Science Study. With IEA's ongoing commitment to international comparisons, a 1999 mathematics and science study was published under the title *Repeat of the Third International Mathematics and Science Study* (TIMSS-R), and then beginning in 2003 the title *Trends in International Mathematics and Science Study* has been used.

International Studies Leading to TIMSS

FIMS, the First International Mathematics Study, was conducted in the 1960s and involved 13-year-olds and students in their last year of secondary school from 10 countries. The First International Science Study (FISS) was conducted between 1966 and 1973 and involved 10-year-olds from 16 countries as well as 14-year-olds and students in their last year of secondary school from 18 countries. These first studies identified the predictive quality of the construct "opportunity to learn" (how mathematics or science are actually taught vs. the intention of printed curricula) and provided evidence of differences in achievement. Based on the success of the first studies, IEA launched the second mathematics and science studies, known by acronyms SIMS and SISS. SIMS was conducted in 1980–1981, addressing the same age groups as FIMS across 20 countries, and SISS focused on the same age groups as FISS across 24 countries during 1983–1984. The second round of studies included a classroom environment study to gain information related to teaching behaviors and the effects of schools.

TIMSS Methodology

The first TIMSS focused on three populations of students based on age: Population 1 consisting of students 9 years of age and in the equivalent of Grades 3 and 4 in the United States; population 2 consisting of students 13 years of age and in the equivalent of Grades 7 and 8; and population 3 consisting of those in the final year of study in secondary education. Performance of students in populations 1 and 2 seems to draw the most attention. Weak performances by U.S. students in population 3 have been attributed to a lack of motivation of these older students to participate seriously in the testing. Random sampling techniques ensure that all students of a nation are eligible to participate in testing, thereby avoiding problems inherent to past international comparisons in which sampling for some nations included only those children privileged to attend school. Where sampling protocols are compromised, data reports clearly make note of concerns. Test content is based on curriculum studies that identify topics common across international systems. Data from TIMSS not only provide a reference regarding student achievement, but also allow for comparison of curriculum and expectations, classroom instruction, teacher work environment, and student motivation and attitudes.

TIMSS data are compiled using a variety of assessment techniques. Achievement data are gathered using tests that include multiple-choice and free-response items. The data provide evidence of the evaluated curriculum. Questionnaires are administered to students, teachers, and school administrators to gather data about attitudes and beliefs, teaching practices, and education policies, thereby gathering data about the implied curriculum. Textbook and curriculum documents are studied to draw conclusions about mathematics and science content and sequencing as well as intended outcomes.

TIMSS-R provided the first round of longitudinal evidence using aligned curriculum frameworks and methods comparable to the 1995 implementation. TIMSS 2003 provided new data, and the results of TIMSS are available on the TIMSS Web site (http://nces.ed.gov/timss).

Mathematics

In mathematics, TIMSS data from 1995 indicated that the Grade 4 sample of U.S. students ranked 12th among the 26 participating nations, performing above the international average. For the Grade 8 sample, U.S. students ranked 28th among the 41 participating nations, performing at the international average. For the sample of students in their final year of secondary education addressing mathematics literacy, the U.S. students ranked 19th among the 21 participating nations, performing significantly below the international average. While the performance of younger U.S. students was encouraging, attention was given to the middle-grade students' performance and concerns were expressed for a U.S. mathematics curriculum that was characterized as "a mile wide and an inch deep." Attention was also given to the performance of Asian students from Singapore, Japan, South Korea, and Hong Kong, the highest scoring nations at all levels.

Data from TIMSS-R in 1999 and from TIMSS 2003 provided longitudinal information. For Grade 4 mathematics, U.S. students performed at the same level in 2003 as students did in 1995. Grade 8 students experienced gains with a significantly higher performance in 2003 compared with 1995, in contrast to significant decreases in scores for nations such as Japan and Sweden.

Videotapes, compiled to be representative of how mathematics was taught in German, Japanese, and U.S. classrooms, were released to help inform how instructional methods might have influenced performance. The lessons on the tapes revealed very different instructional strategies and patterns of interaction between teachers and students across the three nations. Japanese lessons were focused sharply on the day's objective and included evidence of careful crafting to elicit students' reasoning. German lessons were not as sharply focused, and the U.S. lessons were characterized as having low expectations with little evidence of student thinking beyond reproducing examples demonstrated by the teacher.

Science

In science, TIMSS 1995 data indicated that the Grade 4 sample of U.S. students ranked third among the 26 participating nations, performing well above the international average. For the Grade 8 sample, U.S. students ranked 17 among the 41 participating nations, performing slightly above the international average. For the sample of students in their final year of secondary education addressing science literacy, the U.S. ranked 16th among the 21 participating nations and performed significantly below the international average.

Retesting in 2003 indicated that U.S. Grade 4 students' performance in science dropped, but not significantly, from 1995. While not negative, this trend is in sharp contrast to significant increases by 9 of the 15 participating nations. In Grade 8 science, U.S. students scored significantly higher in 2003 (compared to 1995), demonstrating the fifth greatest increase among the 34 participating nations.

As in mathematics, a video study was also conducted for science teaching in 1999. Classes in high achieving countries from the 1995 testing (Australia, the Czech Republic, Japan, and the Netherlands) and the United States were videotaped and compiled into representative samples of science teaching in each country's Grade 8 classes. Lessons revealed that in the United States, science learning involved a variety of activities that engaged students in doing science work, but with less focus on connecting the activities to science content. In contrast, lessons from countries like the Czech Republic and the Netherlands focused more heavily on science content, either through whole-class or independent learning activities.

Conclusion

TIMSS achievement data, curriculum analyses, and video studies have greatly influenced mathematics and science reform efforts in the United States. The first IEA comparisons raised concerns about competitiveness that contributed to the initial standards movement. The National Council of Teachers of Mathematics *Principles and Standards of School Mathematics* referenced TIMSS specifically and cited data as well as curriculum frameworks in its Preface that describes how the document was created. Similarly, many National Science Foundation–funded curriculum reform initiatives drew heavily from TIMSS curriculum and video studies.

Data and reports from TIMSS continue to be cited by groups recommending changes and improvement to the teaching and learning of mathematics and science. Using data from the 1995, 1999, and 2003 assessments, weaknesses in U.S. performance are most often cited and programs from high-scoring nations are held up as exemplary and worthy of emulation. Strong performances of U.S. students, as in the case of Grade 4 science, or the significant improvements in mathematics between 1995 and 2003 often receive little or no attention. TIMSS remains the most rigorous and respected source of data comparing educational systems across national borders.

Edwin M. Dickey

See also Assessment; National Assessment of Educational Progress (NAEP); Singapore Math; Standardized Tests; Standards Movement; Testing Students

Further Readings

Beatty, A. (Ed.). (1997). *Learning from TIMSS: Results from the Third International Mathematics and Science Study.* Washington, DC: National Academy Press.

Bracey, G. W. (1996). International comparisons and the condition of American education. *Educational Researcher, 25*(1), 5–11.

Brief history of IEA. (n.d.). Retrieved June 10, 2008, from http://www.iea.nl/brief_history_of_iea.html

Dossey, J. A. (2003). Large-scale assessments: National and international. In G. M. A. Stanic & J. Kilpatrick (Eds.), *A history of school mathematics* (pp. 1435–1491). Reston, VA: National Council of Teachers of Mathematics.

Trends in International Mathematics and Science Study (TIMSS): http://nces.ed.gov/timss

TYLER, RALPH (1902–1994)

The educator Ralph W. Tyler is perhaps best known for his theory that what needs to be measured in the classroom is student learning. As a high school science teacher in Pierre, South Dakota, in 1923, it occurred to him that the tests that students were being given were measuring only a low level of science mastery and not necessarily what students had learned. Throughout his 70-year career, Tyler continued to pursue the question of how to effectively measure student learning and develop curriculum that would meet the unique student learning needs in American classrooms. The challenge of how best to measure and assess student learning still occupies educators today.

Tyler had two areas of focus throughout his professional life: curriculum development and evaluation. He worked with many notable educators who shaped some of his views on education, including his mentors Charles Judd and W. W. Charters, with whom he first connected as a doctoral student at the University of Chicago. Afterward he followed his mentor W. W. Charters to Ohio State University. There he worked in the area of testing and evaluation as the director of accomplishment testing. In this position he continued to find ways to link the objectives to be taught with the measurement that was used to determine the students' mastery of the subject. He was looking for a variety of measurements that would demonstrate student mastery beyond the use of a paper-and-pencil test. He wanted to collect artifacts of students' work that demonstrated their mastery of the topic. This was a radical change from the thinking of the time, where paper-and-pencil testing constituted the norm. In addition, he felt that successful teaching and learning techniques could be determined through the use of a more scientific approach.

In 1931, Tyler brought the scientific approach to evaluating educational practice in the Eight-Year Study, the purpose of which was to evaluate high school programs. Tyler had a major role in the evaluation portion of the study. From this work, Eugene R. Smith, Ralph W. Tyler, and the Evaluation Staff authored *Appraising and Recording Student Progress Evaluation, Records and Reports in the Thirty Schools.*

An exponent of the progressive thought of his time, Tyler believed that schools needed to present subject matter in a way that would meet the needs of both the learner and society. Following his work on the Eight-Year Study, he authored *Basic Principles of Curriculum and Instruction,* published in 1949. This brief book has had a lasting impact in the field of curriculum development. According to Tyler, curriculum development should define appropriate learning objectives, establish useful learning experiences, organize learning experiences to have a maximum cumulative effect, and evaluate the curriculum and revise those aspects that did not prove to be effective. These remain the major considerations of curricular planning today.

Later, Tyler was one of the primary architects of the National Assessment of Educational Progress (NAEP). In 1963, President Kennedy's commissioner of education was interested in producing a national test to measure the progress of students across the United States. The hope was to establish national standards for education and to report student progress state by state and district by district. Francis Keppel, the commissioner of education, approached John Gardner, president of the Carnegie Corporation, to fund the project. Tyler was approached to undertake the task of developing the test. From his background in testing and measurement, he viewed this project as a way to "take the pulse" of the educational system. He developed a test that sampled students and gave an overall view of their progress. This idea of a national test might have met with great opposition, but with the selection of Tyler, widely considered the leader in educational testing, the educational community decided to trust the new testing process.

In 1953, Tyler moved to Stanford University, where he became the founding director of the Center for Advanced Study in Behavioral Sciences. He held this position until his retirement in 1967. When the institute was first conceived, it was expected to last for perhaps 5 years, but it is still active today and recruits researchers from a wide variety of fields to do research in the field of education.

Tyler was well liked and held an optimistic view of the world. He was known for his ability to chair groups with divergent points of view and to forge consensus. This ability enabled him to contribute to many organizations, such as American Association for the Advancement of Science, National Science Board, Research and Development Panel of the U.S. Office of Education, Social Science Research Foundation National Council on Disadvantaged Children, and Armed Forces Institute. He was the founder and first president of the National Academy of Education. In 1969, Tyler became president of the Systems Development Foundation.

Tyler was advisor to six U.S. presidents and was instrumental in writing the Elementary and Secondary Education Act of 1965. He received 22 honorary doctorate degrees. After his retirement, he continued as a lecturer and consultant in the United States and abroad. He worked until his death in 1994, just shy of his 92nd birthday. Teachers continue to use the four principles he set forth in his *Basic Principles of Curriculum and Instruction* to structure curriculum delivery in their classrooms.

Donna Elder

See also Bloom's Taxonomy; Curriculum Controversies; Curriculum Reconceptualists; Direct Instruction

Further Readings

Aikin, W. (1942). *The story of the Eight Year Study.* New York: Harper & Bros.

Chall, M. (n.d.). *Excerpts from an interview with Ralph Tyler.* Retrieved October 10, 2008, from http://wredu .com/~wriles/Tyler.html

Epstein, J. (2005). The National Assessment of Educational Progress: The story of a national test in the making. *American Educational History Journal, 32*(1), 10–20.

Finder, M. (2004). *Educating America: How Ralph W. Tyler taught America to teach.* Westport, CT: Praeger.

Nowakowski, J. R. (1981). *Interview with Ralph W. Tyler* (Occasional Paper Series No. 13). Education Center, College of Education. Kalamazoo: Western Michigan University, College of Education, Education Center.

Ralph Tyler, one of the century's foremost educators dies at 91. (1994). Retrieved November 1, 2008, from http://news.stanford.edu/pr/94/940228Arc4425.html

Rubin, L. (1994). Ralph W. Tyler: A remembrance. *Phi Delta Kappan, 75*(10), 784–787.

Schugurensky, D. (Ed.). (n.d.). *History of education: Selected moments of the 20th century: 1949: Ralph W. Tyler publishes* Basic principles of curriculum and instruction. Retrieved March 1, 2009, from http:// www.oise.utoronto.ca/research/edu20/moments/1949 tyler.html

Tyler, R. (May, 1969). National assessment: Some valuable by-products for schools. *National Elementary Principal, 48*(6), 42–48.

University of Chicago Library. (2008). *Guide to the Ralph W. Tyler papers 1932–1988.* Retrieved August 15, 2009, from http://ead.lib.uchicago.edu

TYLER RATIONALE

See Tyler, Ralph

Unionization of Teachers

The unionization of teachers is a phenomenon that began haltingly in the 1890s and continued throughout the 20th century, to the point that a large majority of public school teachers are now members of a teachers' union and are employed according to a collective bargaining contract negotiated by their union. The unionization of teachers was not accompanied by collective bargaining regarding their working conditions until the post–World War II period when, initially in large cities in the North and Midwest, teachers joined unions that won bargaining agreements from their respective school boards.

Prior to the development of bargaining, however, teacher unions were embraced by some teachers, mainly in larger cities where numbers of teachers employed meant a certain impersonality in their employment. In order to ameliorate employment problems, whether an unsatisfactory salary situation, a lack of employment protection, or insufficient financial support for their schools, teachers began to join unions in the hope that those unions could win concessions from school boards, school administrators, and/or state legislatures that legally were responsible for public schools in their states. Most notably, in Chicago in the late 1890s, elementary teachers joined the Chicago Teachers' Federation, led by its noted leaders Margaret Haley and Catherine Goggin, initially to protect their pension rights and status, as well as to enhance their meager salaries. Haley and Goggin became famous

for their investigations into the tax situations of Chicago's major utility corporations, which had managed to avoid payment of their franchise fees and tax levies. They sued the city and the corporations and, in 1904, won a legal victory that made the leaders and their federation nationally famous as a reform-minded group that refused to allow tax evasion by their city's major corporations.

Chicago, New York, and other major cities, even some in the anti-union South such as Atlanta, all had teacher unions as a part of their educational landscape in the early 20th century. While these groups varied in their orientation from a near radical socialism in New York to an almost rigid defense of a traditional agenda of protection of salaries and benefits in Atlanta, all the groups had a variety of social, political, and educational positions represented within their membership, whatever position was taken by the individual union. Teacher unions prospered in the immediate post–World War I years, benefiting from prolabor policies of wartime governments, which feared employment disruption. They languished in the probusiness environment of the 1920s, characterized by the rise of American capitalism and the rise in power of employers buoyed by political fears of radicalism and suspicion of organized labor as incipient, if not avowed, proponents of that radicalism.

The Great Depression of the 1930s changed the situation of the previous decade, and the crisis of capitalism in the Depression resulted in a resurgence of teacher unionism, again concentrated in the nation's largest cities. Teacher unions became the target of communists before the Depression in New York City, and elsewhere during the Depression. Communists sought to join and to influence teacher unions toward social and political activism at the same time that their members also often sought democratic political reforms and progressive educational improvements in public schools. The noted national union, the American Federation of Teachers (AFT), fought communists in their New York local in the 1930s and expelled them from the AFT in the early 1940s under the leadership of the noted educational scholar and activist George S. Counts.

World War II was a time of quiescence for teacher unions, but the immediate postwar years saw the unions try to react to a situation in which city teachers engaged in a series of teacher strikes in places such as Buffalo, New York; Norwalk, Connecticut; and St. Paul, Minnesota. The unions were faced with a situation where striking teachers were acting in violation of their union's own formally stated "no strike" policy. While the strike activity gradually diminished, the economic causes of the strikes continued to plague teachers, who faced an increasingly deteriorating set of employment conditions characterized by stagnant or declining salaries, poor working conditions, and class sizes increasing because of the postwar baby boom. That set of conditions became increasingly acute in the 1950s and, late in that decade, teachers began to unionize in increasing numbers, to demand that their unions help them improve their job situations, and to take actions such as strikes to enforce those demands. While New York City was the most visible location for teacher militancy and mass unionization in this period, teachers in most other cities and many other school districts resorted to unionization to address their occupational plight.

Noted teacher unionists emerged in this period, such as Albert Shanker of the United Federation of Teachers (UFT), the American Federation of Teachers local organization in New York City. The National Education Association (NEA) joined the teacher union movement late in the 1960s and, by the early 1970s, emerged as a formidable organizational rival for the allegiance of teachers in their fight for occupational improvement. As they embraced militancy and the collective bargaining process to improve their job situations, teachers and teacher unions could, and did, identify their cause with the larger causes of social, political, and even educational reform. That identification began to come under attack, however, in the late 1960s when African Americans, frustrated by the lack of success of school desegregation, sought community control of their schools as an alternative, a political reform that put teachers and their unions concerned with occupational protection on the defensive. Teachers and teacher unions remained on the defensive in subsequent decades as various school change policies, such as a series of accountability movements, the rise of standards-based educational reform campaigns, and various privatization initiatives such as school vouchers, all threatened the hard-won occupational gains of teachers and their unions and depicted both the leaders and members of those unions as opponents of reform.

Teacher unions both nationally and in their locals began to try to counteract the antireform image, particularly in the 1990s. A new unionism emerged as a vital force in the AFT and the NEA in that decade, a movement that sought to put teachers clearly on the side of school reforms and allied with school reformers. That movement had enough success to at least encourage teachers themselves not to abandon their unions but to try to use them as levers for change.

The most interesting recent historical scholarship on teacher unions, like the unions themselves, stresses the local context as the place where the essential character and qualities of teacher unionism are illustrated. Recent studies of Chicago teachers in the middle of the 20th century, and of Newark, New Jersey, teachers amidst the racial turmoil of the 1960s are exemplars of this scholarship. In Chicago, a consciously reform unionism of the 1940s eventuated in a quite protectionist and antireform body 2 decades later, largely with the same leadership. Reform unionists became locked into their positions of power and influence and eventually used that power and their positions to thwart the designs of Chicago's African Americans for the educational changes necessary to improve the life chances of their children. In contrast, Newark, New Jersey, saw conflict within the teachers' union over the issues of school reform for the increasingly African American city, with unionists at least in part attuned to the needs of their constituents and intent on meeting them. The situations in Chicago and Newark were not unique, nor was their resolution, or lack of resolution. Teacher unionists throughout the nation struggled with the issues of desegregation and school improvement for their districts' minority populations, with different outcomes in different districts. The net result, however, was a decline in the image, and the reality, of teacher unions as reform advocates in American education, a decline that the unions themselves are now trying to reverse in the interest of both their own revival and the educational improvement of their school populations.

Wayne J. Urban

See also American Federation of Teachers (AFT); Collective Bargaining; Community Control; Counts, George S.; Haley, Margaret; National Education Association (NEA)

Further Readings

Golin, S. (2002). *The Newark teacher strikes: Hopes on the line.* New Brunswick, NJ: Rutgers University Press.

Henderson R., Urban, W. J., & Wolman, P. (Eds.). (2004). *Teacher unions and educational policy: Retrenchment or reform?* Boston: Elsevier.

Kerchner, C., Koppich, J., & Weeres, J. (1997). *United mind workers: Unions and teaching in the knowledge society.* San Francisco: Jossey-Bass.

Lyons, J. (2008). *Teachers and reform: Chicago public education, 1929–1970.* Urbana: University of Illinois Press.

UNIVERSITY CONSORTIUM FOR CATHOLIC EDUCATION

The University Consortium for Catholic Education (UCCE) is an alliance of institutions of higher education that has implemented graduate-level teaching service programs to serve the Catholic and private schools in the United States.

Beginning with the University of Notre Dame in 1993, the UCCE now includes 15 universities that have committed to training teachers with a distinct educational philosophy, expressed in three pillars: academic preparation, community, and spirituality. The UCCE acts strongly upon its belief that Catholic education is at the heart of the church's evangelical mission. These programs are intended to help renew and reform Catholic schools by creatively and effectively responding to the need for highly qualified teachers for Catholic schools.

In 1998, the University of Notre Dame offered invitations and financial support to fellow institutions of higher learning to adopt its successful teacher formation model, popularly known as ACE, the Alliance for Catholic Education. The acceptance of this invitation began the initial partnership between Boston College, the University of Portland (Oregon), and Notre Dame in their action toward serving Catholic schools. This original partnership entailed meeting twice a year to exchange information and practices that were successful in their own programs. As more schools became affiliated, the group decided to organize and formed the official University Consortium for Catholic Education, approving the bylaws in spring 2005. Today there are over 400 teachers serving Catholic schools through the 15 Consortium programs across the country.

History

Consortium programs subscribe to the conviction that Catholic school education is an essential component of the church's mission and utilize a holistic approach to preparing teachers to serve in under-resourced schools in areas across the United States. Catholic schools face many challenges, including financial instabilities and declining staff and enrollment numbers. In the past, Catholic schools were staffed by vowed women religious who received formation as educators from their communities. Recognizing the impact that these vowed religious made in the classroom, the Consortium's method of training is based very much on the mission of the women religious. In the past, the vowed religious women, commonly known as Sisters, were assigned mentors who guided them through their years of teaching and provided them with support. Most important, however, the Sisters' prayer and community life centered upon service to their students as they prepared for classes with up to 100 students. Clearly, the women religious saw their teaching placements as a way to fulfill their vocation and serve God through serving their school communities. While the participants in Consortium programs are not members of a religious community, nor is acceptance limited specifically to Catholic applicants, they are historically linked to this original mission. Consortium programs assert that students serve the church through serving school communities. In the Consortium programs' three-pillar teacher formation model, new teachers view their work through the lens of service.

Model for Teacher Preparation

Each of the Consortium programs is committed to using the Notre Dame model of teacher formation. The educational philosophy is contained in the three-pillar approach: academic preparation, community, and spirituality.

Academic Preparation

This pillar is twofold in that students are educating while being educated. Consortium programs are primarily education programs that respond enthusiastically to the needs in Catholic education. Along with their teaching responsibilities, teachers are also engaged in a professional development program. During their years of service they are required to complete graduate-level work in order to earn a graduate degree and initial teaching licensure from their respective universities.

Community

Participants are assigned to live in communities of four to seven members. In this community, the novice teachers partake in regular community meals, the common managing of the household, community prayer, and service. Living in a community also makes possible ease of access to professional and personal support, structuring daily life and work so that the demands of teaching can be shared in a faith-based community context. The community thus becomes a place where developing teachers can share the joys and struggles of their common work in schools.

Spirituality

While participants are asked to participate in community prayer, they are also encouraged to nourish their personal spiritual lives. This is accomplished through regular participation in church services, but it is also fostered with reading materials

and professional support from colleagues who encourage them to view their work as a service to God as well as the church.

The focus on the integration of these three aspects of life is the foundation of Consortium programs. Intentionally forming new teachers in these three areas is a unique element that Consortium programs offer to their participants and is in part why they are so successful and popular.

Current UCCE programs include the following:

- *Alliance for Catholic Education* (ACE), The University of Notre Dame: http://ace.nd.edu
- *Urban Catholic Teachers Corps* (UCTC), Boston College: www.bc.edu/schools/lsoe/cce/prek-12/uctc.html
- *Providence Alliance for Catholic Teachers* (PACT), Providence College: www.providence.edu/pact
- *Pacific Alliance for Catholic Education* (PACE), University of Portland: http://education.up.edu/default.aspx?cid=4322&pid=278
- *Lalanne Program,* University of Dayton: http://campus.udayton.edu/~lalanne
- *Educational Partners in Catholic Schools* (EPICS), Seton Hall University: http://education.shu.edu/epics/flash.html
- *Lutheran Educational Alliance in Parochial Schools* (LEAPS), Valparaiso University: http://www.valpo.edu/education/programs/leaps
- *Teachers Enlisted to Advance Catholic Heritage* (TEACH), College of Notre Dame of Maryland: www.ndm.edu/Academics/CertificatePrograms/Teachingcertificates/operationteach.cfm
- *Partners in Los Angeles Catholic Education* (PLACE), Loyola Marymount University: www.lmu.edu/Page25802.aspx
- *Mentoring Academic Gifts in Service* (MAGIS), Creighton University: www2.creighton.edu/magis
- *Loyola-University Chicago Opportunities in Catholic Education* (LU–CHOICE), Loyola University: www.luc.edu/education/luchoice.shtml
- *LaSallian Association for New Catholic Educators* (LANCE), Christian Brothers University: www.cbu.edu/lance
- *Learning Through Understanding by Mentoring and Engaging New Teachers* (LUMEN), University of Great Falls, Montana: www.ugf.edu/Academics/Graduate/LUMEN/tabid/1143/Default.aspx

- *Gulf Region Academy for Catholic Educators* (GRACE), University of St. Thomas: www .stthom.edu/Public/index.asp?page_ID=4381
- *Remick Fellowship Program,* St. Mary's University Winona, MN: www.smumn.edu

Ronald J. Nuzzi

See also Catholic Schools; Cristo Rey Schools

Further Readings

Notre Dame Task Force on Catholic Education. (2006). *Making God known, loved and served: The future of Catholic primary and secondary schools in the United States: Final report.* Notre Dame, IN: University of Notre Dame.

Smith, P. A. (2007). The University Consortium for Catholic Education (UCCE): A response to sustain and strengthen Catholic education. *Catholic Education: A Journal of Inquiry and Practice, 10*(3), 321–342.

Smith, P. A., & Nuzzi, R. J. (2007). Beyond religious congregations: Responding to new challenges in Catholic education In G. Grace & J. O'Keefe (Eds.), *International handbook of Catholic education* (pp. 103–124). New York: Springer.

University Council for Educational Administration (UCEA)

The University Council for Educational Administration (UCEA) is devoted to improving the practice of school leadership and the preparation of educational administrators. UCEA is a nationwide voluntary association of colleges and universities that have programs in educational leadership and administration. The organization seeks to fulfill its mission by

- Supporting research on topics relevant to leadership preparation and practice
- Increasing the dissemination and accessibility of research on educational administration
- Improving the professional development available to pre-service administrators, educational practitioners, and preparation program faculty

- Encouraging and facilitating the distribution of new methods (reform) for both preparation and practice, and
- Advancing policy issues that affect educational administration at all levels of government

From a founding membership of 15 institutions, UCEA now has 80 university members located in 34 states as well the United Kingdom and China.

History and Structure

The initial idea for the Council came from the Middle Atlantic Region of the Cooperative Program in Educational Administration (CPEA), which in 1947 identified the need to create an organization to focus on the preparation and practice of educational administration. The organization now known as UCEA officially began in 1959 with financial support from the W. K. Kellogg Foundation and technical assistance from staff members at Teachers College at Columbia University. It was housed at Ohio State University after its initial founding; since then Arizona State University, Pennsylvania State University, the University of Missouri–Columbia, and the University of Texas at Austin have also served as host institutions for the Council.

Structurally, UCEA has two main official governing bodies—the Executive Committee and the Plenum. Modeled after a state legislature, the Plenum includes a representative of each UCEA member institution. The duties of the Plenum include electing nine members to serve on the Executive Committee; addressing finance, governance, and membership issues for the Council; and encouraging students and faculty from member institutions to participate in UCEA programs by serving as liaisons at their home institutions. Members of the Executive Committee also serve as leaders and organizers for the UCEA Convention, which is held annually. Led by the UCEA president, the Executive Committee is responsible for approving appointments, establishing compensation for Council personnel, and helping to set the agenda and activities for the Plenum.

Outside of the two main governing bodies, UCEA also establishes task forces as needed to devote attention to special projects and issues. In

2001, the Council created the Taskforce on Evaluating Leadership Preparation Programs (ELPP). The objectives of this task force are to compare and evaluate school leadership preparation programs according the reflections and feedback of their graduates and the graduates' impact on the schools that they lead, foster the development of instruments and methodologies that focus on evaluating and sharing knowledge related to effective practices in preparation programs, and encourage the entire field of educational preparation to increase efforts at evaluating the impact and effectiveness of these programs.

Similarly, UCEA also serves as a member and contributor to the Joint Research Taskforce on Leadership Preparation sponsored by the American Educational Research Association (AERA). Like the ELPP task force, this joint task force also focuses on improving educational preparation by fostering research on these programs, distributing related research data, and encouraging junior faculty members to complete research projects in this area. UCEA serves as a key member of this task force by using its journals and other publications to help make research materials on educational preparation programs available to a wide range of faculty members and institutions.

Initiatives and Services

UCEA promotes a variety of initiatives and programs. Each fall, UCEA holds its annual convention, in which faculty from both member and nonmember institutions converge to share research data and discuss reform issues related to the preparation and practice of educational administration. The Council also maintains program centers that serve as clearinghouses for research and professional development information on specific topics. Housed at member institutions, program center foci include urban schools, school leadership, academic leadership, technology leadership in education, and ethics in school leadership. In addition to creating the program centers, UCEA has also been instrumental in helping to establish other organizations, such as the Commonwealth Council for Educational Administration, the Inter-American Society for Educational Administration, and the National Policy Board for Education Administration.

The Council also participates in the development and analysis of educational policies. One policy strategy used by the Council is UCEA "Day on the Hill," which brings faculty members who research educational administration into contact with policymakers who make decisions that affect the teaching and practice of school leadership. Other services in this area include drafting policy briefs, sharing resources with policymakers, and providing tips for faculty members and institutions on how to contact policymakers and influence educational policy decisions.

Research and Publications

UCEA sponsors a range of publications covering research and issues in educational leadership. In the area of preparation, the Council helps to develop instructional materials such as simulations that allow pre-service administrators to gain experience in what it is like to actually function in a school leadership position.

Moreover, UCEA also assists in the dissemination of educational research data and information through the publication of three journals: Established in 1965, *Educational Administration Quarterly* is one of the leading journals on research related to school leadership and management. The *Journal of Cases in Educational Leadership* provides examples of actual problems that occur in a variety of school settings. *The Journal of Research on Leadership Education* is a multidisciplinary publication that covers a broad range of areas that influence school leadership.

In addition to the journals, the Council also maintains the *UCEA Review* as a newsletter to help member institutions stay up to date with activities and initiatives within the organization. UCEA also publishes and distributes research findings through books, monographs, and research reports.

Awards and Honors

Beyond its publications, UCEA also offers various awards to acknowledge valuable contributions from researchers and faculty members in the field of educational administration. In addition, the Council also provides development opportunities for graduate students studying school leadership through the David L. Clark Graduate Student

Research Seminar and the Barbara L. Jackson Scholars Network.

Saran Donahoo

See also American Association of School Administrators (AASA); National Council of Professors of Educational Administration (NCPEA); Professional Development; Professional Development Schools; Schools of Education

Further Readings

Lumby, J. (2008). *International handbook on the preparation and development of school leaders.* New York: Routledge.

Mulkeen, T. A., Cambron-McCabe, N. H., & Anderson, B. J. (1994). *Democratic leadership: The changing context of administrative preparation.* New York: Ablex.

Murphy, J. F. (1992). *The landscape of leadership preparation: Reframing the education of school administrators.* Thousand Oaks, CA: Corwin.

University Council for Educational Administration. (2008, January 24). *History.* Retrieved September 21, 2008, from http://www.ucea.org/history

U.S. DEPARTMENT OF EDUCATION

The role of the U.S. Department of Education seems clear to most educators today: carry out congressional mandates, fund research, support the use of scientific evidence-based research strategies, "regulate" preschool through postgraduate education, vocational education, and special education; and collect and disseminate national performance data. The U.S. Constitution did not specifically identify public education as a federal responsibility. The Tenth Amendment to the Constitution placed education on the list of states' rights and responsibilities. As America grew, so did the need to govern all aspects of citizenship. In 1789, George Washington's cabinet of advisors—the Secretaries of State, Treasury, and War—and the Attorney General's offices were created. Over time, additional cabinet posts such as the Secretary of the Interior and the Postmaster General followed. Proponents of public education soon began the call for the creation of a Department of Education.

Historical Background

The debate temporarily ended in 1867 when, through the legislative creation of a Department of Education, the federal role in education became formalized. The commitment wavered when in 1868 the department was reduced to a bureau level within the Department of Interior (post–Civil War). Funds were cut and more than 30 separate entities were responsible for public education. None of these had a unified direction, common leadership, or working relationships.

The first official review on the effectiveness of America's educational system was found in the Commission on the National Emergency in Education. This post–World War I taskforce was charged with finding the "principal defects of the national educational system as revealed by the war." It is pertinent to list the identified concerns put before the 1918 Commission because of the similarity they have with issues facing today's U.S. educational system. The 1918 Commission on the National Emergency in Education believed the issues to be as follows:

- The failure of the schools to reach non–English-speaking aliens and native illiterates
- The failure of the schools to provide an effective program of health education
- The great inequalities of public schools and particularly the inferiority of many rural schools
- The lack of a sufficient supply of trained teachers

As is also the case today, external factors began influencing educators' decision making regarding educational programming for America's children. The return of thousands of military personnel after the end of Word War II required new job skills and job training to meet the national need for engineers, computer scientists, and mathematicians. The baby boom that followed their return necessitated the nationwide building and development of new schools as well as housing. Later, in 1957, the launch of the Soviet Union's satellite *Sputnik* left Americans worried about the country's ability to compete in a more scientifically and technically sophisticated world.

The then-Department of Health, Education and Welfare responded to the academic needs and began financing graduate programs in counseling and guidance. These newly trained high school guidance counselors were charged with the responsibility of identifying America's future talented and gifted mathematicians and scientists. Schools were built in new subdivisions. Institutes of higher education were encouraged to create or strengthen their teacher preparation programs in addition to their graduate and postgraduate degrees in math and sciences.

During the same decade, the 1954 U.S. Supreme Court ruled on *Brown v. Board of Education*. The Court found that discrimination through racial segregation was unconstitutional. The impact of the ruling left many states in turmoil. Districts restructured their schools to accommodate the influx of new students. Public schools were mandated to open their doors, if not their minds, to working with all children, regardless of race.

In 1964, President Lyndon B. Johnson's administration declared its intent to eradicate poverty in the United States. Part of the artillery in this War on Poverty was the funding of Title I of the Elementary and Secondary Education Act of 1965. Title I was charged with the responsibility of assisting low-income and low-performing students in math and reading. In 1972, Title IX was signed into law. This required that any public educational entity receiving any federal dollars or support would not discriminate on the basis of sex, and that students would not be excluded from participation in, be denied the benefits of, or be subjected to discrimination under, any education program or activity receiving federal financial assistance. Prior to Title IX, K–12 public schools and higher education had focused on financial support for male sports. Title IX has been credited with the equalization of funding for American girls' athletic programs. Because the U.S. Constitution did not give the federal government authority over public schools, they did not have to adhere to Title IX. Although the federal government could not mandate participation, it could legally withhold financial support from those educational institutions that failed to comply—assistance that spanned the spectrum from the federal School Lunch Program to Title programs to student scholarships. Institutions generally chose to comply.

In 1975, Public Law 94-142 was passed and special education became a responsibility of every public school in the nation. This aligned with the growing recognition of individual rights and a national obsession with testing. Public Law 94-142 required individualized intelligence testing, aptitude testing, and achievement testing. Colleges and universities required standardized college entrance exams (ACT and SAT). In 1976, the military wanted schools to start administering the Armed Services Vocational Aptitude Battery to all juniors in high school.

The many attempts to elevate education to cabinet level in the national government had met with decades of resistance. Yet, without a cabinet-level position, the management of these nationally legislated mandates and U.S. Supreme Court rulings became increasingly more difficult. Supporters of public education pushed again for the creation of a cabinet-level department of education. Helena Howe, in her testimony before the Committee on Governmental Affairs of the U.S. Senate stated,

> Quality education, free or at most reasonably priced and readily available to all who may want it and who may benefit from it, is necessary for the survival of any nation. It is critical for a democracy. Perhaps the time has come to stop the scare headlines about American education and to do something about improving American education and reaffirming our commitment to provide for the national welfare. Education is too valuable a national resource for it to continue to be treated in the manner of benign neglect. (Howe, 1978)

The following year, in 1979, the Department of Education was created during the administration of President Jimmy Carter. Two years later, presidential candidate Ronald Reagan promised to eliminate the cabinet position of the Department of Education. His subsequent attempts to do so, however, were thwarted.

The 1980s and 1990s brought the Internet, fiber optic and wireless infrastructures, outcomes-based education and then standards-based education, and an emphasis on accountability. In 2002, No Child Left Behind became law and all public schools and states receiving federal funding were mandated to focus on continuous improvement of their reading, math, and science scores for all learners. Here the Department of Education's role was approval of state implementation plans and, to a small degree, funding. Results of how effectively schools and districts performed on state testing and graduation and attendance rates were published for parents and communities to view. Schools and districts that did not achieve standards were placed under state determined sanctions.

Impact and Critique

Since the U.S. Department of Education was created in 1979, observers have continued to question how much impact it has had on America's educational system. Others have asked whether it is feasible for one agency to preside effectively over the education of more than 49 million K–12 students, citing not just the immense numbers of students but also the complexities that the numbers represent. Between 1979 and 2006, the number of school-age children (ages 5–17) who spoke a language other than English at home increased from 3.8 to 10.8 million, or from 9% to 20% of the population in this age range. In 1976–1977, about 3.7 million children and youth in this age group were served under IDEA (5%); by 2006–2007, about 6.7 million received services (about 9%). National data for the 2005–2006 school year found as many as 40.9% of students to be from low-income families.

Historically, the American educational system has experienced a succession of reform movements. In the 20th century and up to the present day some states and many districts have tried outcomes-based education, value-free education, constructivist math, whole language, whole classroom instruction, small-group instruction, new math, alternative education, alternative certifications, block scheduling, integrated lessons, same-sex classes, heterogeneous and homogeneous classes, open-classrooms, and nongraded classrooms, and more.

The general public has always ranked the nation's schools lower than its own local neighborhood school, which usually receives a grade of B or better. For 90 years the force of criticism, professional and lay, of the system, has not abated, and this applies to the U.S. Department of Education as well. The 1918 Commission on the National Emergency in Education report to Congress identified the issues as follows:

- The failure of the schools to reach the non–English-speaking aliens and native illiterates. (In 2009, English language learners continue to score lower on the standardized testing than traditional students. There has been a failure to recruit and train bilingual teachers to work with these students and families.)
- The failure of the schools to provide an effective program of health education. (In 2009, America is the most obese country in the world. Diabetes and heart conditions have reached an alert status of more than 30% of America's children.)
- The great inequalities of public schools and particularly the inferiority of many rural schools. (In 2009, due to declining enrollments and increasing costs, rural schools struggle to provide a quality education for all learners.)
- The lack of a sufficient supply of trained teachers. (In 2009, teacher recruitment and teacher training continue to be a national issue. This is especially evident in teacher shortages in math, science, and technology.)

Conclusion

Today, when indicators that American public education is improving coexist alongside other indicators that it is not, the U.S. Department of Education must respond to the perennial issues and problems affecting the nation's schools. In so doing, it confronts a spectrum of policy choices that are being shaped by powerful social forces, rapid technological change, and a citizenry more culturally diverse than ever before.

Donna Sue McCaw

See also Accountability Era; Achievement Gap; Educational Policies Commission; Education Commission of the States (ECS); National Governors Association; *Nation at Risk, A*; State Departments of Education

Further Readings

Congress day by day: A daily record of proceedings on the floor of the Senate and Senate for the period April 1 to 30, 1926. (1926). *Congressional Digest, 5*(5), 149–150, 173–175.

Doss, D. A. (1998). The missing piece in the school improvement puzzle. *Phi Delta Kappan, 79*(8), 592–595.

Elam, S. (1993). *The state of the nation's public schools: A conference report.* Bloomington, IN: Phi Delta Kappa. (ERIC Document Reproduction Service No. ED376567)

Finn, C. E., & Rebarber, T. (1992). *Education reform in the '90s.* New York: Macmillan.

Friedman, T. L. (2005). *The world is flat: A brief history of the twenty-first century.* New York: Farrar, Straus, & Giroux.

Howe, H. (1978). Should Congress establish a separate cabinet-level U.S. Department of Education? PRO. *The Congressional Digest, 57*(11), 284–286.

Kirst, M. W. (1993). Strengths and weaknesses of American education. *Phi Delta Kappan, 74*(8), 613–616, 618.

Nock, A. J. (1932). *The theory of education in the United States: The Page-Barbour lectures from 1931 at the University of Virginia.* New York: Harcourt, Brace.

Planty, M., Hussar, W., Snyder, T., Provasnik, S., Kena, G., Dinkes, R., et al. (2008). *The condition of education 2008* (NCES 2008-031). Washington, DC: U.S. Department of Education, National Center for Education Statistics, Institute of Education Sciences.

Radin, B. A., & Hawley, W. D. (1988). *The politics of federal reorganization: Creating the U.S. Department of Education.* New York: Pergamon.

UTOPIAN REFORMERS

Early in the 19th century the new American nation seemed, to European visionaries, to offer endless possibilities for experiments in the fundamental reordering of human relations in society. Many of these experiments were communitarian, reacting against the social disruption of revolutions and industrialization through seeking to reproduce on a secular basis the cooperative spirit of religiously based communities. Education—notably the ideas associated with Swiss educator Heinrich Pestalozzi—played a key role in most of these schemes, offering the promise of remaking humanity, an ambition as old as Plato's *Republic.*

Among the Britons who tried, in various ways, to carry out such plans in the United States were William Maclure (1763–1840), Robert Owen (1771–1858), his son Robert Dale Owen (1801–1877), and Frances Wright (1795–1852). Bronson Alcott (1799–1888), an American educator, became for a time a favorite of British enthusiasts for this utopian program of a "New Moral World."

Maclure was a successful businessman who became an American citizen, retiring early to devote himself to the first extensive geological survey of the United States. Interested in social reform, he became convinced that only an appropriate education of young children could produce fundamental change: "I have so far lost the little confidence I had in adults or parents that I believe no good system of education can have a fair trial but with orphans" (Bestor, 1948, p. 351). Concluding that the new methods of Pestalozzi could have the most powerful effect, he financed the move of several Pestalozzian educators to Philadelphia, where he had become president of the Academy of Natural Sciences. One of them, Joseph Neef, published in 1809 *Sketch of a Plan and Method of Education,* the first book on pedagogical method published in America.

Like Maclure, Robert Owen was a successful businessman who turned to social and educational reform. Owen managed for more than 20 years a cotton mill that his father-in-law had built in a sparsely populated area of Scotland, housing a labor force gathered from the Highlands and urban orphanages. New Lanark was thus an early "company town," and Owen took advantage of his complete control to experiment in a variety of ways with improving the attitudes and habits of his workers. Widely admired by contemporary reformers was the significantly named Institution Established for the Formation of Character, in which children were enrolled as soon as they could walk since, "in ninety-nine cases out of a hundred, parents are altogether ignorant of the right method of treating children" (Gilman, 1899, p. 52). Children under 10 were "trained collectively," while those older and employed in the factory had an evening school. Owen insisted that "the children were not to be annoyed with books, but were to be taught the uses and nature or qualities of the common things around them" (Silver, 1969, pp. 55, 65). This was the crowning element of the "total institution" that Owen had created, in which all the residents were directly dependent on him and in which he sought to direct their lives both on and off the job.

Intoxicated with the celebrity of New Lanark, Owen distributed widely "A New View of Society"

(1816). "The fundamental principle," he wrote, "on which all these Essays proceed is, that 'Children collectively may be taught any sentiments and habits'; or, in other words, 'trained to acquire any character'" (Silver, 1969, p. 130). Through state-controlled schooling, "the governing powers of any country may easily and economically give its subjects just sentiments, and the best habits" (p. 144). This would be the basis for a new social and economic order and for universal peace and progress; through the right sort of education, man would come to understand "that his individual happiness can be increased and extended only in proportion as he actively endeavours to increase and extend the happiness of all around him" (p. 73). The villages of Unity and Mutual Cooperation would create a surplus of production that would make all prosperous.

Disappointed by the reluctance of British policymakers to restructure society according to his prescription, and convinced of the greater openness of America (in part by reading about Shaker and other flourishing religious communities), Owen purchased property in Indiana from one such community. In a series of lectures, including several to members of the U.S. Congress and President Adams, he announced that he was ready to institute his New System in Indiana, and predicted that its benefits would be so obvious that it would soon be emulated nationwide.

Owen persuaded Maclure to join him in the venture, transferring the scientific and educational work Maclure had been sponsoring in Philadelphia. So was born, in 1825, the short-lived New Harmony community. Nothing, Owen told the colonists, had ever produced so much evil as individualism, and the residents of New Harmony would show by their example how the human race could be transformed. Almost immediately, however, the New Harmony residents broke into squabbling factions, with a succession of short-lived arrangements for governance and economic affairs that collapsed entirely after 2 difficult years.

Owen and Maclure disagreed profoundly, as well: Owen was convinced that the cooperative life would reshape its participants, while Maclure argued that only a long process of education would make men and women fit to live in such a community. They differed also about education, with Owen

contending that anyone could teach effectively by using the right methods, while Maclure sought to gather leading scientists and experienced teachers for his schools.

Despite the failure of New Harmony as a utopian community, the educational institutions sponsored by Maclure, including free schools for girls as well as boys, the first "infant school" in America, a school for teens that combined study with productive work, all strongly Pestalozzian in inspiration, and (after his death) the Working Man's Institute and Library, made this for decades a center of research and education on the frontier.

A visitor to New Harmony during its brief "Owenite" phase was Frances "Fanny" Wright, a Scottish heiress who shared Owen's enthusiasm for communities as a means of social reform. Wright founded, in 1825, the Nashoba Community in Tennessee, intended to allow slaves to purchase their freedom through cooperative work while living together with White and free Black fellow workers. This effort, despite an international board chaired by General Lafayette, soon collapsed like other communities without a religious basis of unity.

Owen's oldest son, Robert Dale Owen, published in 1824 a highly Pestalozzian account of the education provided in New Lanark, and in New Harmony became one of the primary leaders in the frequent absence of his father. After the failure of plans for communal living, he and Frances Wright moved to New York City in 1829, where they published the *Free Enquirer*. This newspaper promised to expose the tyranny of organized religion and described what they called State Guardianship Education. All children 2 years of age and older would be enrolled in government boarding schools, wear the same clothes, eat the same food, receive the same education; this, they predicted, would eliminate the influence of family wealth and culture in giving some children advantages over others. This idea was not original with them; it had been a cornerstone of the Jacobin program of education during the radical phase of the French Revolution, and Maclure had also argued for boarding schools because pupils were confused by the contrast between harmony in school and the social contradictions experienced at home.

In that same year, influenced by a slightly earlier development in Philadelphia, an organization was formed in New York by discontented working men; Robert Dale Owen was chosen as one of the secretaries of the new political party, and Wright became a fiery orator for the movement, which was able to elect two of their candidates to the state assembly.

Wright and Owen's proposal for government boarding schools was incorporated into the platform of the Mechanics and Working Men. This association with Fanny Wright—called by the mainstream press the "great Red Harlot of Infidelity"—and an educational proposal that lay "siege to the very foundation of society" proved fatal to the new party, and the majority of its members, opposed to state assumption of the family's role, abandoned it; by the 1830 election the party had lost its drive. One newspaper called the idea of government boarding schools "one of the wildest fancies that ever entered into the brain of the most visionary fanatics"—a system designed "to sever those strong ties of affection that keep families together" (Eckhardt, 1984, p. 218).

While Robert Owen and Frances Wright had no significant role in later developments in the United States, and William Maclure retired to Mexico for his health, Robert Dale Owen was later elected to Congress from Indiana and had a major role in the creation of the Smithsonian Institution. As a framer of the Indiana Constitution of 1850, he incorporated language for a uniform system of common schools with state and local tax support, and after the Civil War he had a role in drafting the Fourteenth Amendment to the U.S. Constitution. Like his father and other militant 19th-century secularists, he became a convert to Spiritualism, publishing several books on communication with the spirits of the dead.

Amos Bronson Alcott established, in 1834, the Temple School in Boston, which enjoyed a brief vogue among the Unitarian elite before it closed. Alcott (the "Papa" of *Little Women*), who sought to elicit the "spiritual existence" of each pupil by having the pupils maintain each their own journal to record their most intimate thoughts, was convinced that education was not so much a matter of pouring knowledge into the children as of drawing out the divine wisdom that each possessed. An 1835 account by his assistant Elizabeth

Peabody (one of whose sisters married Horace Mann, the other Nathaniel Hawthorne) of the instructional method used made Alcott internationally known. Alcott's own *Conversations With Children on the Gospels* (1836) caused such a scandal, however, that the school closed, and Alcott went to England, where some saw him as "the American Pestalozzi."

Returning to Massachusetts in 1842 with two English admirers, Alcott started a communitarian experiment called Fruitlands, intended as a model of education and society, that attracted many visitors but fell apart because of internal disagreements after 7 months.

Although the efforts of Owens, Wright, and Alcott to implement new models of community all ended quickly in failure, their widely publicized optimism about the transformative power of education on individuals and, through them, on society as a whole, helped to create the climate of ideas that fostered the rapid spread of the common school movement. The success of the latter, in contrast with their own failures, can be attributed in part to its respect for the role of families, expressed through local control of schools.

They, together with Maclure, popularized for an American audience the idea that education should focus on the child's interests rather than on the skills and knowledge to be taught, a theme recurring more persistently in educationist circles here than in other countries.

Charles L. Glenn

See also Common School Movement; Infant Schools; Kindergarten; Montessori, Maria; Montessori Schools; Peabody, Elizabeth Palmer; Peabody Fund; Pestalozzianism

Further Readings

Bernard, P. R. (1988). Irreconcilable opinions: The social and educational theories of Robert Owen and William Maclure. *Journal of the Early Republic, 8*(1), 21–44.

Bestor, A. E., Jr. (Ed.). (1948). *Education and reform at New Harmony: Correspondence of William Maclure and Marie Duclos Fretageot, 1820–1833.* Indianapolis: Indiana Historical Society.

Bestor, A. E., Jr. (1950). *Backwoods utopias: The sectarian and Owenite Phases of communitarian socialism in America: 1663–1829*. Philadelphia: University of Pennsylvania Press.

Burgess, C. (1963). William Maclure and education for a good society. *History of Education Quarterly, 3*(2), 58–76.

Carlton, F. T. (1907). The Workingmen's Party of New York City: 1829–1831. *Political Science Quarterly, 22*(3), 401–415.

Eckhardt, C. M. (1984). *Fanny Wright: Rebel in America*. Cambridge, MA: Harvard University Press.

Gilman, N. P. (1899). *Dividend to labor: A study of employers' welfare intuitions*. Boston: Houghton Mifflin.

Harrison, J. F. C. (Ed.). (1968). *Utopianism and education: Robert Owen and the Owenites*. New York: Teachers College Press.

Pawa, J. M. (1971). Workingmen and free schools in the nineteenth century: A comment on the labor-education thesis. *History of Education Quarterly, 11*(3), 287–302.

Silver, H. (Ed.). (1969). *Robert Owen on education*. Cambridge, UK: Cambridge University Press.

VALUE-ADDED EDUCATION

In education, value-added methodologies represent a collection of statistical models that endeavor to account for the contribution of schools and teachers to growth in student achievement. Interest in value-added measures is rooted in the standards and accountability movement that began in the 1980s. This entry begins with a description of value-added measures and contrasts them with static achievement indicators. Next, the history of value-added methodology is outlined. The entry ends with a discussion of the variety of value-added methodologies.

Value-Added Measures

Educational policy circles borrowed the term *value-added* from the economics lexicon during the 1980s. In the field of economics, "value-added" refers to the additional value of a commodity beyond the value of the inputs required to create it, such as materials and energy. In education, value-added methodologies attempt to ascertain the gains in student achievement that can be attributed to educators separate from other influences on achievement. These adjusted student achievement gains are the "value" a district, school, or teacher "adds" to student achievement over and above what students' families and neighborhoods contribute. Some students experience less academic growth than would otherwise be expected because they are assigned to a less-effective teacher and

school while other students experience greater than expected growth, reflecting the effectiveness of their teacher and school.

Studies using value-added methodology have contributed to establishing the importance of teacher quality, contradicting the findings of the 1966 *Coleman Report*. For example, the Dallas Independent School District compared a group of elementary students with 3 consecutive years of highly effective reading teachers with a similar group with 3 consecutive years of very ineffective teachers. By the end of the third year, a substantial gap of 34 percentage points separated the groups' average reading achievement scores while their average mathematics achievement scores diverged by 50 percentage points. Using data from Tennessee, William Sanders and June Rivers discovered that the effects of teachers are long lived as well as cumulative. Even 2 years later, a significant gap remained between students with ineffective third-grade teachers and those with excellent third-grade teachers. While family income is strongly predictive of student achievement test scores, Sanders and his colleagues demonstrated that teacher quality is the single most important influence on student academic growth.

Comparison With Static Achievement Measures

Value-added measures represent a shift from the static achievement indicators that have dominated education accountability practices. Static achievement indicators offer a snapshot of average student achievement scores at a single point in time. Comparisons of static indicators are based on cross-sectional, not longitudinal student data. In other words, conclusions drawn from static achievement indicators are based on comparisons of different groups of students. For example, the achievement of economically disadvantaged students on an end-of-year test can be compared with that of noneconomically disadvantaged students. Static achievement indicators are also used to illustrate trends over time in average scores for students at a given grade level. For example, the current year's eighth graders can be compared with the previous year's eighth graders. Static achievement measures do not provide information about the same group of students' growth over time.

Instead of a snapshot of achievement at a point in time, value-added measures report a cohort of students' academic growth from one grade to the next. Proponents of value-added measures argue value-added measures offer educational accountability systems a needed complement to static measures of achievement. Alone, static indicators can mask the contribution of educators to student achievement because they do not document student progress. However, high achievement does not necessarily correlate with high growth during a school year. Schools whose students who enter an academic year with a high level of achievement may appear to be highly effective on end-of-year tests even when their students make little progress during the year. Conversely, schools with students entering well below grade level may appear ineffective on end-of-year tests despite great gains during the academic year. Value-added methodologies have the potential to illustrate progress in student achievement and disentangle the independent contributions of educators from student factors, including socioeconomic status.

Historical Context

On both sides of the Atlantic, interest in value-added measures arose from discontent with static achievement test scores as the centerpiece of educational accountability policies. In the United Kingdom, large-scale educational assessments of student performance on the National Curriculum were in place by the 1990s. The resulting static achievement data were reported by schools on

so-called league tables. Critics asserted that the league tables' raw examination scores revealed more about the students' previous educational attainment and family background than the efficacy of a given school. By the mid-1990s, calls for value-added measures as a fairer and more accurate indicator of school effectiveness were widespread.

In the United States, momentum for value-added measures has evolved more slowly. The 1990s saw scattered forays into applying value-added models in the United States, beginning with the Dallas, Texas, school district and the state of Tennessee. The Dallas Independent School District collected longitudinal student achievement data from Grades 3 through 8 to measure absolute performance and schools' contribution to improvement. School improvement indices combined regression models and hierarchical linear models to account for student characteristics (including race, free lunch status, prior achievement, and attendance) and school factors (such as mobility and crowdedness). School faculties became eligible for financial awards based on both performance and contributions to improvement.

The most widely known value-added model, the Tennessee value-added assessment system (TVAAS), was pioneered by statistician William Sanders. During the 1980s Sanders pioneered a mixed-model, multivariate, longitudinal methodology to estimate the impact of schools and individual teachers on student academic progress. In 1992, prompted by a court order to make Tennessee's school finance system more equitable, Tennessee legislators adopted Sanders's approach. In Sanders's model each student acts as his or her own control for background characteristics such as prior achievement and socioeconomic status. Versions of TVAAS are in place in Pennsylvania, Ohio, and several other states.

The watershed No Child Left Behind Act of 2001 (NCLB) required states to establish learning standards and measure schools' progress toward having all students meet those standards. With NCLB came requirements for schools to make "adequate yearly progress" toward meeting benchmark goals for the percentage of students in each school that are expected to demonstrate proficiency on state end-of-year tests. Adequate yearly progress was originally defined only in terms of static achievement measures. Paralleling the English experience, critics in the United States voiced concerns about the fairness of calculating adequate yearly progress without taking progress into account, and several states had independently incorporated value-added results into their school accountability system. In 2005, U.S. Secretary of Education Margaret Spelling announced a pilot program in which states could include growth models as part of adequate yearly progress calculations. By 2007, nine states' growth-model proposals had been approved and the secretary invited all eligible states to submit proposals.

Creating a value-added accountability system has four key data requirements, only one of which is required by NCLB. First, in order to calculate value-added measures students must be tested at least annually with a reliable and valid achievement test. Second, the test used must have a sufficiently wide range of items to avoid "ceiling" and "floor" effects. Third, students must be assigned a unique identification code so their scores can be linked across tests and years. Fourth, to compare scores from one year to the next, test scores must be reported on a common scale. NCLB precipitated the establishment of large-scale student achievement data sets by legislating the testing of at least 95% of all regular education students in language arts/reading and mathematics each year in Grades 3 through 8. However, states were not compelled by NCLB to adopt tests with a common scale or a wide range of items. In addition, by 2003 only 16 states had the ability to link student records from one grade to the next.

Variation in Value-Added Methodologies

Value-added measures include a range of statistical models. The simplest of these rely on the average of unadjusted differences between previous and later student scores. More sophisticated value-added models incorporate multiple levels of factors into their analysis, including both student and school level influences on student achievement. These models build on key advances in statistical methodology, software, and hardware that were necessary precursors to the development of this multilevel modeling. Harvey Goldstein developed software for multilevel analyses used widely in the United Kingdom and Europe, while Anthony Bryk and Steven Raudenbush's hierarchical linear modeling software dominates in the United States.

The choice of a statistical model appears to have a significant impact on resulting estimates of teacher and school effectiveness. Several contributors to bias and unreliability of teacher estimated effects have been identified, including missing and incomplete data; potential sampling errors; confounding variables such as school composition and the effect of prior teachers; issues with the timing, content, and conditions of the achievement tests the data are based on; and the accuracy of linking students to the correct teacher. Because of the above issues, concerns have been raised about using value-added measures for high-stakes decisions, especially with respect to evaluations of individual teachers.

Value-added models also vary in the depth of the data investigation they support. The most basic use of value-added measures is to determine whether students in a classroom, school, or district made an expected year's worth of growth in a year's time. However, some value-added models also allow educators to dig deeper into the data for patterns of student growth. Student progress might be disaggregated by several categories including grade, subject area, race or ethnicity, English language status, economic disadvantage, and disability status. Some diagnostic reports also allow exploration of distinctive patterns of growth for students with low, average, or high previous levels of achievement.

Regardless of the value-added model employed, value-added measures do not by themselves promote educational improvement. Intensive professional development in interpreting value-added results and using them for decision making appears to be required. Studies of Pennsylvania, Ohio, and the United Kingdom's initial adoption of value-added measures suggested limited use of value-added data for decision making by educators. In addition, while value-added measures in combination with other data sources may indicate where improvement is needed, they do not illuminate why one school or teacher is more or less effective than another. Next, value-added methodology is based on standardized test scores, which in themselves are controversial. Finally, value-added measures, like static achievement measures, do not tell educators how to go about improving education.

Rachel M. B. Collopy

See also Accountability Era; Achievement Gap; Assessment; Coleman, James S.; Differentiated

Instruction; High-Stakes Testing; No Child Left Behind Act (NCLB); Professional Development; Standardized Tests; Standards Movement; Testing Students

Further Readings

McCaffrey, D., Korentz, D., Lockwood, J. R., & Hamilton, L. S. (2003). *Evaluating value-added models for teacher accountability.* Santa Monica, CA: RAND Corporation.

Rivers, J. C., & Sanders, W. L. (2002). Teacher quality and equity in educational opportunity: Findings and policy implications. In L. T. Izumi & W. M. Evers (Eds.), *Teacher quality* (pp. 13–23). San Francisco: Hoover Institution Press.

Value-added assessment [Special issue]. (2004). *Journal of Educational and Behavioral Statistics, 29*(1).

Value-added assessment [Special issue]. (2004). *Journal of Educational and Behavioral Statistics, 29*(2).

Zurawsky, C. (2004). Teachers matter: Evidence from value-added assessments. *Research Points: Essential Information for Education Policy, 2*(2). Retrieved October 1, 2008, from http://www.aera.net

VALUES CLARIFICATION

Since the middle of the 20th century, moral education in the public schools has involved efforts to inculcate in students a given set of moral values or to encourage students to discover their own values. In an attempt to avoid "indoctrination," several educators in the mid-1960s, such as Louis Raths, Sidney B. Simon, Leland Howe, and Howard Kirschenbaum, advocated a reform in moral education known as values clarification. These proponents asserted that students needed a system that would assist in decision making, critical thinking, and a conscious examination of their values. Simon, Howe, and Kirschenbaum sought to arm teachers with lessons that would lead to values clarification. No longer would the student live an "unexamined life." Students as critical thinkers would focus on questions and issues such as race relations, love, sex, and material possessions. Educators of the 1960s and 1970s were prepared for a reform movement and found ways to incorporate values clarification into several different content

areas. School districts sponsored in-service education programs on values clarification. And the question, "What is values clarification?" was asked by teachers, parents, religion, and other organized groups.

Values clarification is a process approach to assist students and others to develop a system of values. This process enables a person to learn about the values he or she holds, and to become aware of beliefs, attitudes, feelings, and ultimately to determine that which he or she values. Values clarification does not provide or prescribe a set of values, but rather allows a person to explore and discover his or her values.

Values clarification involves a process wherein students are encouraged to critically examine their own moral decisions by clarifying their own values. This process was adopted in many schools, but by the late 1970s critics frequently charged that it was not a "neutral" process but rather rested on a relativistic foundation. In the 21st century, values clarification remains as one of several approaches to moral education in the public schools; other approaches include character education and cognitive moral development.

Values clarification proponents such as Raths, Simon, Howe, and Kirschenbaum set forth the following criteria for holding a value:

- *Choosing:* freely from alternatives after thoughtful consideration of the consequences of each alternative.
- *Prizing:* cherishing, being happy with the choice; willing to affirm the choice publicly.
- *Acting:* doing something with the choice; doing something repeatedly, in a consistent manner.

Proponents of values clarification have designed exercises, case studies, and lessons that may be used by classroom teachers either in the context of a teaching unit or as an exercise in values clarification. *Values Clarification: A Handbook of Practical Strategies for Teachers and Students* is one text that offers numerous examples of value activities for the classroom. One of the most popular classic activities that provide an "X-rated version" as well as a "PG version" is Alligator River. The Alligator River (either version) presents a very short story with a cast of characters. After reading the stories, students (of various ages) are asked to rank order the characters from the one they liked the best to the one they liked the least. The Bomb Shelter is another classic example of values clarification. In The Bomb Shelter, students are asked which persons described in a case study might be admitted to the "bomb shelter" and which persons will be denied entry. Other values clarification lessons might ask students to do "values voting" on a list of 5 to 10 questions. "Values voting" is a process in which the student signals strong agreement to strong disagreement. Another lesson in values clarification is "rank order." Students are given a list of 5 to 10 questions with 3 possible answers. Students are asked to rank order the answers from 1 to 3. Popular songs, poetry, political cartoons, and other media were often selected as springboards to values clarification activities. Teachers selected a song or other media item and designed a set of value questions to explore with the students.

Various life experiences may result in value change. Comprehending value changes and recognizing the affect on actions and behaviors is the goal of the values clarification process. The values clarification process is not intended to prescribe "correct values," but rather is a cognitive method to provide the process to discover one's own values. It is important to note that the values clarification approach assumes no right or wrong answers. These exercises are designed to assist individual students to identify their values and the relative importance of these values in their personal lives. The overriding goal of values clarification is that each person (student) will be able to independently define his or her own value structure. Several educators concur that this is the most important function of the general curriculum.

Educators who have studied values clarification theory maintain that students hold beliefs that have not been fully examined. Echoing Socrates, these educators assert that "the unexamined life is not worth living." While Raths, Simon, Howe, and Kirschenbaum are cited for their work with values clarification in education, John Dewey is often credited with the conceptual development of the fundamentals of values clarification. The values clarification lessons are in line with Dewey's experience-based education approach.

Proponents of values clarification maintain that the educational curriculum should provide a cognitive method that enables students to examine their beliefs. Student beliefs should be challenged, examined, accepted, rejected, or modified in order for the belief to become a value. Moreover, a process of values clarification may result in a new or different belief system. The values clarification process may be a slow process, and the process may or may not become a "habit" of critical thinking.

If teacher preparation is amenable to the values clarification approach, then the content methods course will present teacher education candidates with a few lessons from texts similar to those of Raths, Simon, Howe, and Kirschenbaum. During the course of a semester, teacher education candidates will develop specific content exercises that employ values clarification lessons. For example, social studies teacher education candidates will develop lessons that may be used in a history or sociology class during the student teaching phase. It is difficult to know how many teacher preparation institutions include values clarification as part of the curriculum.

Opponents of values clarification have criticized the approach as a form of indoctrination operating under the guise of "neutrality," as a usurpation of parental authority, and as devoid of moral content. Such criticisms took their toll on the approach in the 1980s. Since then, values clarification has clearly taken a back seat to the No Child Left Behind Act, to various back-to-basics movements, and to high-stakes state education assessment programs.

Today values clarification may exist in certain sex education classes, in multicultural education courses, in higher-level thinking courses, and in courses that focus on critical thinking and controversy. It is difficult to quantify the number of teachers and schools that employ values clarification techniques. It is clear, however, that values clarification education is much less robust today than in the 1960s and 1970s. Educators can still find current values clarification materials from groups like Advocates for Youth, an education organization based in Washington, D.C.

Ronald G. Helms

See also Character Education; Civic Education; Dewey, John; Moral Development; Moral Education

Further Readings

Dewey, J. (1916). *Democracy and education*. New York: Macmillan.

Goodlad, J. (1994). *Educational renewal: Better teachers, better schools*. San Francisco: Jossey-Bass.

Huitt, W. (2004). *Values. Educational psychology interactive*. Valdosta, GA: Valdosta State University. Retrieved October 10, 2008, from http://chiron .valdosta.edu/whuitt/col/affsys/values.html

Kirschenbaum, H. (1976). *Clarifying values clarification: Some theoretical issues and a review of research.* Retrieved April 25, 2008, from http://gom.sagepub .com/cgi/content/abstract/1/1/99

Mensing, S. (n.d.). *Tips on value clarification*. Retrieved August 9, 2009, from http://www.emoclear.com/ valuesclarification.htm

Raths, L., & Simon, S. (1978). *Values and teaching: Working with values in the classroom*. Columbus, OH: Charles E. Merrill.

Simon, S., & Howe, L. (1999). *The values clarification approach*. Retrieved May 2, 2008, from http://www .sntp.net/education/values_clar.htm

Simon, S., Howe, L., & Kirschenbaum, H. (1972). *Values clarification: A handbook of practical strategies for teachers and students*. New York: Hart.

Sizer, T. (1992). *Horace's school: Redesigning the American high school*. New York: Houghton Mifflin.

Values clarification. (n.d.). Retrieved October 11, 2008, from http://www.usd.edu/med/som/genetics/ curriculum/4ICLARI9.htm

VOCATIONAL EDUCATION

Although vocational education has ancient roots, the impetus for the development of vocational schools was not evident until the 1800s. Vocational education is typically defined as education that prepares individuals with the necessary skills to be successful at work. Now commonly referred to as career and technical education, vocational education has undergone many transformations since the 19th century as a result of the efforts of reformers, supporters, and dissenters. Because of various movements, legislation, and the addition of dynamic programs in career and technical education, the definition has evolved as educational systems change. At this point there is an advocacy to define career and technical education as education for both work and higher education.

Early Beginnings

In 1762, Jean-Jacques Rousseau wrote a novel about an orphan boy who learned from interacting with his environment, as opposed to book learning. Rousseau believed that individuals did not necessarily have to be formally educated to obtain the skills for a successful life socially, morally, physically, and vocationally. This philosophy lent support to the idea that manual training was important for the development of cognitive advancement.

Nineteenth-century educational systems supported a social class differential in that the wealthy were deemed worthy of education while the working or lower classes were more suited to skilled or manual training. Pestalozzi, in the early 1800s, was one of the few advocates of the notion that individuals should not only learn manual skills but should also be taught to think. This was not a widespread viewpoint; however, this dissension was important in building the career and technical educational system that exists today.

Early American Vocational Schools

Apprenticeship programs in Europe (especially in Germany) had been established for centuries and were one of the first vocational educational designs implemented in the United States. An apprenticeship is an agreement with an employer for a specified time period in which the employer agrees to train a person in exchange for that person's labor. There were voluntary apprenticeships that were entered into freely and imposed apprenticeships whose purpose was to take care of the poor or orphaned. Apprenticeship agreements were formalized in writing, setting out the time frame and what would be exchanged: food, shelter, additional education, and so forth, from the teacher, and labor from the apprentice. Both girls and boys participated in apprenticeships, customarily from early adolescence to early adulthood, albeit the number of years of service did vary. This type of educational agreement was an important avenue for many citizens to obtain shelter and the skills for living and training in a specific trade.

Apprenticeships gradually declined in number because of the various industrial innovations that took place in the United States. With centralized manufacturing and division of labor, it was no longer necessary for an individual (master) to have all the skills necessary in terms of knowledge, experience, and attitudes to engage in a craft. Not until 1937 with the passage of the Fitzgerald Act was there a concerted effort to provide renewed standards and working relationships with business and industry. Many states passed laws and created councils to support the apprenticeship movement.

Today's apprenticeships are no longer agreements between employer and employee that offer basic living accommodations, such as food, shelter, and clothing, in return for labor. A modern apprenticeship program is more of a credentialing agency at the postsecondary level where individuals attend the program during the day but have a separate living arrangement.

Apprenticeships vary in length and can cover such disciplines as public administration, medicine, manufacturing, construction, and electronics, among others. Apprentices attend classes for core knowledge skills and are supervised in on-the-job experiences, for which they are paid wages.

In addition to decreasing the need for apprenticeships, the Industrial Revolution in the 1800s also spurred the manual training movement. This philosophy advocated that there is dignity in all work, and work is a necessary component to build appreciation and a sense of worth. These schools (often called polytechnic institutes) offered theory-based curriculum along with the opportunity to work in exchange for the payment of tuition. The popularity of the manual training programs led to their being offered at the high school level in public institutions' shop system. Manual training courses helped students realize the connection between knowing and doing. Despite the many advocates for this system, some opposed it, claiming that these programs were just replacements for the apprenticeship programs and would hinder students' moral and intellectual development, and that public education should be based on general academic education subjects as opposed to developing manual skills.

In the mid-1800s, the mission of the colleges included preparing individuals for professions and the ministry, which resulted in the colleges serving a select few. The Morrill Act of 1862 paved the way for U.S. land grant colleges in each state. This legislation allocated each state 30,000 acres of land per congressperson. The state could sell the land to create agricultural and mechanical arts colleges. This helped to support the vocational education movement by establishing colleges for selected vocations.

The Second Morrill Act, in 1890, stipulated that land grant colleges in the Southern states had to be open to both White and Black students, or a separate college of equal stature had to be built to accommodate the Black population. Supplemental funds were also allocated to maintain the land grant institutions.

Despite philosophical opposition, many high schools at the turn of the 20th century did offer shop classes. Near the end of the 1800s and the beginning of the 1900s, Booker T. Washington was a strong advocate of education beyond book learning. He believed that a scholar was an individual, regardless of class or race, who not only had cognitive skills and morals, but also had respect for a day's work. W. E. B. Du Bois, on the other hand, was a strong advocate for African Americans concentrating on those cognitive skills that are associated with attaining a liberal academic education. Du Bois believed that developing decision-making skills would help encourage individuals to improve their socioeconomic status. This academic versus vocational controversy has waxed and waned throughout our educational history, and continues today to some degree.

Support for Vocational Schools

Although there were advocates of vocational education, at the turn of the century the secondary schools were not serving the majority of school-aged citizens because of their emphasis on academic subjects. David Snedden and his student Charles Prosser were strong advocates of preparing individuals for an occupation through not only cognitive practice, but also vocational experience. Prosser is noted for his 16 theorems associated with designing successful vocational education experiences. These theorems pertain to setting an effective environmental stage and delivering instruction in such a manner that students will obtain necessary vocational skills effectively and efficiently.

Snedden and Prosser, being strong advocates of vocational education, were also supporters of promoting a dual educational system in which general education schools would be separated from vocational schools. They wanted the governance and faculty of vocational schools to be separated so that they could follow the vocational education philosophy. John Dewey, on the other hand, opposed the dual system, warning that a separation would make both types of schools narrower in scope, and students in both systems would lose out on valuable interaction and knowledge. Also, he advised that there would be duplication of efforts with two parallel systems in terms of buildings, teachers, equipment, and related issues. Dewey believed in the exploration of vocational subjects, but cautioned that industry should not control the curriculum in schools. He believed that students should develop an appreciation for vocational blue-collar occupations; the cognitive skills associated with vocational occupations were important in developing students' knowledge. He believed students should not just be trained in a specific limited set of manual skills as this would limit a student's higher-level thinking potential and support a system in which industry was the benefactor of a narrowly skilled workforce.

Passed just before World War I, the Smith-Hughes Act provided federal funds to high schools in the areas of industry, trades, home economics, agriculture, and teacher training. World War I made it clear that there was a need for individuals with specific skills to aid in the war efforts. This aided in the support for vocational education programs.

In the 1920s, several pieces of legislation provided support through federal funds and facilitated the expansion of vocational education. One such act, the Vocational Rehabilitation Act, expanded services to the handicapped. The American Vocational Association (AVA) professional organization was also formed, which gave support, leadership, and decision-making strength to the vocational education movement. AVA was renamed the Association for Career and Technical Education in 1998.

The 1930s brought forth several pieces of legislation that supported vocational education, and with the advent of World War II in the 1940s, the U.S. government passed training acts to prepare industrial workers at home and to reintegrate veterans on their return. The 1950s and 1960s brought about legislative support when the economy warranted the need for training programs. The Vocational Education Act and The Economic Opportunity Act were instrumental in providing monies and paid training for unemployed youth so they could continue in school.

Current Trends in Vocational Education

Among the several pieces of federal funding in the 1970s and 1980s, the Comprehensive Employment and Training Act (CETA), the Job Training Partnership Act (JTPA), and the Carl D. Perkins Vocational Education Act were instrumental in providing programs that contributed to the economy by offering training to maintain a viable workforce.

Two of the several acts in the 1990s included the Job Training Reform Amendments, which were important in individualizing training programs, and the School-to-Work Opportunities Act (STWOA, 1994), which promoted partnerships with business and industry, emphasizing the need to ease the transition of students from high school to work and/or higher education. The STWOA emphasized providing schooling that integrated the knowledge, skills, and attitudes taught in classes with authentic learning experiences to promote the skills students would need later in the workforce or in continuing their education.

The STWOA was a result of several research studies that indicated our youth were not prepared to enter the workforce or to pursue continuing education. *A Nation at Risk* indicated that students were graduating without the necessary skills to be successful after high school. *America's Choice: High Skills or Low Wages* warned against sending high school graduates to low-paying dead-end jobs. The report called for a better educated workforce to compete in the worldwide market. The SCANS (Secretary's Commission on Achieving Necessary Skills), in 1991, indicated that employers were not satisfied with the skills of the entry-level employees they were receiving. It was determined that employees need more than technical skills; they also need more cognitive skills, such as problem solving, decision making, and communication and affective skills, including self-esteem, integrity, and sociability, to be successful in the workforce.

These sources were the impetus for the call for educational reform in the 1990s that would result in a more qualified workforce. The purpose of the

STWOA was to provide federal funding to states to seed educational reform across the nation. States were given flexibility in the structure of the programs.

The funding was intended to start programs whose purpose was the integration of academic and technical skills through the delivery of instruction employing authentic on-the-job learning experiences. It was determined that rote memorization and traditional learning techniques were not very successful in building pertinent knowledge, skills, and attitudes. Better were hands-on real-life experiences that applied the subject matter immediately.

A major component of the School-to-Work design was the integration of school-based learning (e.g., math) and work-based learning (e.g., converting different temperature scales on the job). It was determined that providing learning experiences that applied academic subject matter to a real situation not only assisted students in understanding the importance and usefulness of the topic, but also aided in retention of the information.

Initially, there was controversy associated with the School-to-Work movement from traditionally oriented liberal arts philosophers. The word *work* in the title was a major concern to some, who saw it as limiting students' scope to preparation for low-level wage jobs, leaving out long-term career goals and attendance in higher education. Some programs and states, therefore, replaced *work* in the title with *career*. Some individuals and states thought the School-to-Career title was still too limiting, and thus it was necessary to emphasize that the programs were designed to aid students in their transition from school not only to work but also to higher education. The important aspect of the School-to-Work movement is that the philosophy behind the programs is sound. Many educational systems have integrated authentic experiences into their curriculum, even though the curriculum might not have an explicit title.

The year 2001 brought the No Child Left Behind philosophy, which focused on setting standards and offering curriculum so that all students would succeed. The Individuals with Disabilities Education Act (IDEA) was implemented to sustain support for individuals with disabilities to ensure they received a free public education.

Other legislation that is worthy of note includes the Carl D. Perkins Acts of 1990, 1998, and 2006

that promoted the integration of academic and vocational education and supported the notion that technological skills were an important part of a global economy. Tech prep was an important product of these pieces of legislation. Tech prep programs offer curriculum that links academic and technical subject matter through authentic learning experiences. In 2006, the New Commission on the Skills of the American Workforce published its report, *Tough Choices or Tough Times*, delineating 10 steps for revising the current educational system to meet the demanding requirements needed to compete in the global economy.

Throughout its history, vocational education has been notably supported by government legislation and funding. Career and technical education has been the prominent educational system that has provided our society with a competitive workforce.

Vocational education has also supported a wide variety of populations to help them to be successful. Women during wartime were trained to take part in business and industry, which filled a significant need in the U.S. economy. The Smith-Hughes Act provided programs for not only agriculture, industrial education, and the trade fields, but also for home economics.

Starting in the 1960s, more attention was paid to supporting women and pushing sex equity across careers and industries through legislation and training. During the 1960s and 1970s, more attention was also paid to providing equal access for all races and for individuals with special needs. Federal vocational funding and mandates through legislation assisted the educational and training systems by providing equal access to populations that previously might have been screened out.

The first support for youth organizations began in the 1950s and has continued; there are 10 career and technical student organizations to date, one associated with each of the 10 major vocational areas. These include: Future Farmers of America; Future Business Leaders of America; Distributive Education Clubs of America; Family, Career and Community Leaders of America; SkillsUSA; Health Occupations Students of America; Technology Students Association; National Postsecondary Agricultural Student Organization; National Young Farmer Educational Association; and Business Professionals of America. In addition,

4-H is a youth organization that is supported by the Department of Agriculture Cooperative Extension Service and is widespread across the nation. These groups are important as they build unity and leadership, and provide experiences that aid in the future support of vocational education not only at the secondary level, but also at the postsecondary level.

Future Vocational Programs

Vocational education was reformed, restructured, and enhanced throughout the 20th century. Starting with agriculture and mechanics as the major areas of concentration, it has grown to 10 major areas. Vocational education has traditionally supported a system that provides authentic learning experiences to prepare students for success in the workforce. As times have changed in the nation, vocational education funding and support have met these changes with expanding services to a wider population base. Although initially slated to offer education only for those occupations that do not require an advanced degree, there is a push not to limit the scope, but to broaden it to a greater range of careers. Vocational education is now called career and technical education, supporting the point of view that academic and vocational fields should integrate their efforts to provide education that prepares individuals for both the workforce and for attendance in higher education if desired.

Qetler Jensrud

See also Ability Grouping; Age Grading; Business and Educational Reform; Individuals with Disabilities Education Act (IDEA); Manual Training; National Society for the Promotion of Industrial Education; School-to-Work; Smith-Hughes Act; Tech Prep Education

Further Readings

Bernhardt, A., Morris, M., Handcock, M., & Scott, M. (1998). *Work and opportunity in the post-industrial labor market: Summary of findings* (IEE Working Paper No. 6). New York: Rockefeller Foundation. (ERIC Document Reproduction Service No. ED 422 475)

Berryman, S. (1995). Apprenticeship as a paradigm of learning. In W. N. Grubb (Ed.), *Education through occupations in American high schools* (Vol. 1, pp. 192–213). New York: Teachers College Press.

Boesel, D., Hudson, L., Deich, S., & Masten, C. (1994). *National assessment of vocational education: Final report to Congress: Vol. 2—Participation in and quality of vocational education.* Washington, DC: Government Printing Office.

Burghardt, J., & Gordon, A. (1990). *More jobs and higher pay: How an integrated program compares with traditional programs.* New York: Rockefeller Foundation.

Commission on the Skills of the American Workforce. (1990). *America's choice: High skills or low wages.* Washington, DC: National Center on Education and the Economy.

Evans, R. (1971). *Foundations of vocational education.* Columbus, OH: Charles E. Merrill.

Gordon, H. (2008). *The history and growth of career and technical education in America.* Long Grove, IL: Waveland Press.

Gray, K. C., & Herr, E. L. (1998). *Workforce education: The basics.* Needham Heights, MA: Allyn & Bacon.

Grubb, W. N., Brown, C., Kaufman, P., & Lederer, J. (1989). *Innovation versus turf: Coordination between vocational education and job training partnership act programs.* Berkeley, CA: National Center for Research in Vocational Education.

Grubb, W. N., & McDonnell, L. M. (1991). *Local systems of vocational education and job training: Diversity, interdependence, and effectiveness.* Santa Monica, CA: RAND Corporation and the National Center for Research in Vocational Education.

Keller, F. (1948). *Principles of vocational education.* Boston: D. C. Heath.

National Commission on Excellence in Education. (1983). *A nation at risk.* Washington, DC: Author.

The New Commission on the Skills of the American Workforce. (2006). *Tough choices or tough times.* Washington, DC: National Center on Education and the Economy.

Packer, A., & Pines, M. (1996). *School-to-work.* Princeton, NJ: Eye On Education.

Scott, J. L., & Sarkees-Wirenski, M. (2001). *Overview of career and technical education* (2nd ed.). Homewood, IL: American Technical Publishers.

The Secretary's Commission of Achieving Necessary Skills. (1991). *What work requires of schools.* Washington, DC: Author.

Watts, R., & Greenberg, J. (1990). *Post-secondary education: Preparation for the world of work: 5th Canada/UK Colloquium.* Halifax, Nova Scotia, Canada: Institute for Research on Public Policy.

VOUCHERS

At the end of World War II, the United States provided government payment or vouchers to returning veterans to support their college costs at the institution of their choice. Vouchers have also been used in the form of food stamps and supplemental rent payments. More recently, vouchers have been linked to school choice and therefore have been discussed and implemented in terms of payments to schools for tuition expenses by parents who favor a wider school choice for their children. In the education choice environment, a voucher is a certificate issued by a state government to enable parents to pay for a portion of their children's education at a school of their choice rather than at a public school. Vouchers constitute one of the most significant reforms to be instituted in the late 20th century, though the idea of vouchers emerged much earlier in the writings of economists and education policymakers.

Origins and Development of Vouchers in School Choice

One of the earliest advocates for school choice was the economist Milton Friedman, who introduced the idea in the mid-1950s. Friedman postulated that vouchers would promote competition and thereby improve schools. Many looked favorably upon his concept, but political support was lacking despite the fact that some of the most significant think tanks in the United States (e.g., the Brookings Institution) focused on the expansion of choice options for students in underperforming school districts.

Since Friedman's suggestion in 1955, there have been many attempts to define and apply vouchers as an educational possibility or as a way to permit school choice. As a result, multiple interpretations exist. The concept of vouchers can be difficult to grasp due to varying philosophical orientations and diverse political/social/economic ramifications. For example, Terry Moe and John Chubb connect politics and markets to school choice. Milton and Rose Friedman believe and posit that schooling, even in the inner cities, does not have to be the way it is (i.e., far too many failing schools and ineffective teachers). They argued that it was not that

way when parents had greater control of the children's education. Voucher advocates often assert that nonpublic schools are generally superior to public schools.

The idea of school choice has been around for some time, although it had been often described in earlier usages in terms of school vouchers or a voucher plan. In this sense, the basic ideas behind vouchers and school choice are quite similar. Both plans seek to allow parents to apply their individual share of public school funds to the cost of any school, private or public, for their children; that is, the parent or student chooses the school to attend. In effect, this equates to a redistribution scheme of some tax money assigned to a public education entity within a state to students in private schools.

Supporters of school choice offer both economic and educational rationales for vouchers. Following the notions advanced earlier by Milton and Rose Friedman, school choice plans institutionalize the essentials of a free market system in education. Similar to business endeavors, this policy permits supply and demand forces to determine both successful and unsuccessful schools. Public education, when viewed as a monopoly and not truly subject to the laws of supply and demand, permits poor schools to continue operating even if and when they fail their students.

At the national level and beginning in the 1980s, presidents Reagan and Bush endorsed a movement for school choice that had the support of some influential academics such as Milton Friedman. James S. Coleman conducted a study during that decade that found private schools superior to public schools; Coleman's findings gave support to the school choice or voucher concept. The movement gained additional support in the early 1990s when John Chubb and Terry Moe, political scientists with the Brookings Institution, authored *Politics, Markets, and America's Schools*. Arguing that public schools were too bureaucratic, they advanced the idea that a school choice program was the only viable alternative to the public schools.

Although school choice was a major plank in the campaign to reform schools in the 1990s, surprisingly the school choice concept received little endorsement at state and local levels during the early years of the decade. A major factor instrumental in fostering opposition to the concept was the influence of the two major teacher organizations in the United States: the American Federation of Teachers and the National Education Association. Both groups and their state and local affiliates encouraged strong opposition to the concept.

Over time a variety of serious approaches to school choice were introduced: school vouchers, charter schools, and privatization. Of these approaches, vouchers are the option that was most intensely debated, including whether or not vouchers could be used at private religious schools. Frequently, supporters of vouchers hoped that competition would do what previous regulation had failed to do. In 1996, at the national level, both major political parties (Republicans and Democrats) accepted the concept of vouchers, but Democrats opposed their use at private (religious) schools, based on the constitutional provision of separation of church and state.

Noting the possibility of no action at the national level, several states then considered voucher proposals. Only two states, Wisconsin and Ohio, adopted voucher proposals, with programs initiated in Milwaukee in 1990 and Cleveland in 1995.

Milwaukee's plan began in 1990 and today has over 15,000 students using vouchers resulting in more than $100 million paid in vouchers. One-fourth of Milwaukee students receive public funding to attend schools outside the Milwaukee public school system. Although the Milwaukee program initially did not include the use of vouchers at religious schools, in 1995 the plan was expanded to include these schools, due to the Cleveland plan.

The Cleveland plan began in 1995 when the state of Ohio undertook to provide tuition assistance in the form of vouchers for Cleveland grade school students. These vouchers could be used by students at private schools or at different public schools outside the Cleveland system rather than at a failing public school within the system. Although this plan did not specify a preference for the private school option, a dominant majority (96%) of students and their parents involved in the program chose and attended parochial or religious (here Catholic) schools.

The *Zelman* Decision and Its Aftermath

Both plans were challenged in the courts in the late 1990s. Conflicting lower court decisions regarding whether the use of vouchers at religious schools was an unconstitutional support of religion—that is, a violation of the separation of church and state—paved the way for appeals to the U.S. Supreme Court. In 1998 the U.S. Supreme Court chose not to review the Wisconsin Supreme Court decision that upheld the program. In 2002, the U.S. Supreme Court ruled in *Zelman v. Simmons-Harris* that the Cleveland program, which was aimed at providing scholarships of up to $2,250 for students to attend the school of their parents' choice, was not unconstitutional (i.e., the plan did not violate the Establishment Clause of the First Amendment to the U.S. Constitution) as long as parents had a choice among a range of public and nonpublic schools. In this landmark case, the U.S. Supreme Court rendered a 5 to 4 vote or decision that dealt with school choice and with the use of vouchers by focusing on both the Milwaukee and the Cleveland plans. Both cities had established viable school choice programs wherein children from failing public schools could enroll, with a substantial subsidy, in private schools, including religious schools.

According to Carey in his *Anderson's Ohio School Law Manual,* in 2002 the U.S. Supreme Court declared it constitutional to use public dollars for tuition at nonpublic schools. The Court's decision, *Zelman v. Simmons-Harris,* is significant because it demarcates the elimination of "traditional notions of church–state separation in the realm of public education."

Emboldened by the U.S. Supreme Court's ruling in *Zelman,* the Ohio General Assembly enacted legislation in 2003 to allow tuition payments of up to $2,700 and to extend the voucher program to Grades 9 and 10. In 2005, the maximum tuition payment was increased to $3,105 and the voucher program was extended to Grades 11 and 12.

Subsequent to the *Zelman* decision, voucher supporters anticipated a widespread adoption of vouchers. However, this did not occur, due to declining state budgets and the availability of other school choice options. Indeed, some other states have enacted voucher laws. Five states—Texas, Louisiana, Colorado, Florida, and Utah—have considered statewide programs. In Colorado the proposal was adopted and then was limited to students in Denver who scored poorly on state exams. In 2006, Florida's highest court struck down legislation known as the "Opportunity Scholarship Program," which would have implemented a school voucher program in that state. The court stated that the law violated Florida's Constitution. In Utah, a statewide universal school voucher system that provided a maximum tuition subsidy of $3,000 was passed in 2007, but voters repealed it in a referendum before the law took effect.

On the national level, vouchers were given some federal support in early 2004 when the U.S. Congress passed legislation to provide vouchers to nearly 2,000 students in Washington, D.C. Also, as a result of Hurricane Katrina in 2006, the federal government currently operates the largest voucher program for evacuees from the region affected.

Conclusion

Although public support for vouchers has not increased since the mid-1990s, support for vouchers continues to be in evidence across the political spectrum. The belief that introducing the forces of the marketplace into the provision of education will drive or force improvement in the public school remains strong among school choice advocates and especially for those who embrace a broader school reform agenda.

Thomas A. Kessinger

See also Alliance for the Separation of School & State; Alternative Schools; American Federation of Teachers (AFT); Brookings Institution; Catholic Schools; Charter Schools; Coleman, James S.; Council for American Private Education (CAPE); Friedman, Milton; National Education Association (NEA); Presidents and Educational Reform; School Choice; *Zelman v. Simmons-Harris*

Further Readings

Carey, K. H. (2006). *Anderson's Ohio school law manual* (2nd ed., Rev.). Newark, NJ: Matthew Bender.

Chubb, J., & Moe, T. M. (1990). *Politics, markets, and America's schools*. Washington, DC: Brookings Institution.

Friedman, M., & Friedman, R. (1980). *Free to choose: A personal statement*. New York: Harcourt, Brace, Jovanovich.

Hoxby, C. M. (Ed.). (2003). *Economics of school choice*. Chicago: University of Chicago Press.

Peterson, P. E., & Campbell, D. E. (2001). *Charters, vouchers, & public education*. Washington, DC: Brookings Institution.

VYGOTSKY, LEV (1896–1934)

Lev Semenovich Vygotsky (1896–1934) was born of middle-class parents in the Jewish enclave of Orsha, a town in western Russia near Minsk. From childhood, he excelled in multiple educational pursuits, earning a gold medal for the highest grades in all of his subjects, organizing his adolescent friends to debate such ideas as Hegel's philosophy of history, and completing studies at two Moscow universities in 1917. In 1924, a presentation on psychology at a national conference by Vygotsky, then a teacher in Gomel province, led to his appointment at the Moscow Institute of Experimental Psychology.

Vygotsky's goal was to formulate psychology as part of a unified social science. For him, this task required explaining the qualitative cognitive changes involved in the development of higher forms of thinking. His major writings include identification of the higher mental processes, the role of cultural symbols and subject-matter concepts in cognitive development, the relationship of thinking to speech, and the sequence of critical and stable periods in development. He also defined the role of culture in cognitive development as providing (a) the symbols (e.g., mathematical and verbal) that are used for thinking and (b) the culture's methods of reasoning.

Dissatisfaction with some perceived concepts of Piagetian theory led to a search for alternatives in the 1980s. Vygotsky, as portrayed in a small 1978 book, seemed to be the answer. This sketchy discussion absent Vygotsky's thinking popularized his name in the 1980s. English translations of most of Vygotsky's writings were not available until the late 1990s, however, and they present a different view of his work.

Vygotsky defined the higher mental processes, which are not fully developed until the end of adolescence, as self-organized attention, categorical perception, conceptual thinking (verbal and mathematical), and logical memory. For example, categorical perception is a synthesis of concrete images and word (concept) meanings, and logical memory is the recall of subject-matter concepts that directly reflect one's analysis and systematic organization of ideas.

These processes undergo four developmental stages, two of which are premastery stages. Stage three involves mastery of one's thinking through external symbols, such as identifying concrete examples of concepts. Stage four is completed when external symbols that facilitate thinking are transformed into new internal connections and ways of thinking. For example, in true conceptual thinking, the concept becomes an element in a network of concepts that are linked through a system of acts of thinking.

Each aspect of cognitive development appears first as a relation between two people (interpsychological) and then within the child (intrapsychological). This general law of genetic development refers to interactions between the ideal form of behavior (the adult) and the present form (the child), beginning with the child learning speech. Then the child must imitate, invent, and practice the same forms of behavior that adults practiced with him or her. Also, the key collaborations in the classroom are the interactions between teacher and child because only these interactions advance cognitive development.

Vygotsky maintained that teachers should determine the child's higher mental processes as they are beginning to mature. The assessment consists of identifying the problems the child can solve in cooperation with either the teacher or a more advanced peer. This area of maturing intellectual processes is the zone of proximal development (zpd). In other words, the zpd refers to a diagnostic assessment of cognitive development by the teacher that allows instruction to address the emerging capabilities.

Vygotsky disagreed with Piaget's perspective that (a) the young child moves from complete self-centeredness (solipsism) to understanding a social reality that includes others, and (b) the preschool child's egocentric speech, which accompanies his or her activity, gradually disappears. For Vygotsky, (a) the child is a social being from birth who gradually moves from social interaction to independent thinking; (b) egocentric speech, which first guides the preschool child's activity, subsequently becomes internal speech; and (c) speech also undergoes several stages of development from preintellectual to inner speech.

Like other academics in the Bolshevik USSR, Vygotsky's several responsibilities included a heavy teaching load, clinical diagnoses, supervising research, and traveling (often over poor roads) and lecturing. He also translated and edited manuscripts for publishers. In 1934, he died from a severe bout of tuberculosis, 2 years before a Communist decree banned psychological testing and writings on individual cognitive differences. The decree effectively suppressed Vygotsky's work in the USSR for more than 20 years. In the United States, however, beliefs about his concepts have been used since the 1980s to legitimize peer group learning in the classroom.

Margaret E. Gredler

See also Piaget, Jean

Further Readings

Gredler, M., & Shields, C. (2009). *Vygotsky's legacy: A foundation for research and practice*. New York: Guilford Press.

Van der Veer, R., & Valsiner, J. (1991). *Understanding Vygotsky: A quest for synthesis*. Cambridge, MA: Blackwell.

Vygotsky, L. S. (1997). *Collected works of L. S. Vygotsky: Vol. 4. The history of the development of higher mental functions* (R. W. Rieber, Trans.). New York: Plenum. (Original work published 1982–1984)

Vygotsky, L. S. (1998). *Collected works of L. S. Vygotsky: Vol. 5. Child development* (R. W. Rieber, Trans.). New York: Plenum. (Original work published 1982–1984)

Waldorf Schools

Waldorf schools are based on the educational philosophy of Rudolf Steiner (1861–1925), an Austrian educator and founder of Anthroposophy. Steiner's first school opened in 1919 in Stuttgart, Germany, for the children of the Waldorf-Astoria Company's employees, giving the name "Waldorf" to schools associated with Steiner's educational philosophy. Steiner's school flourished, and by 1938 schools based on his philosophy had opened their doors in Austria, Germany, Great Britain, Hungary, the Netherlands, Norway, and the United States. Political interference by the Nazi regime forced closure of most Waldorf schools in Europe until after the end of World War II. Today, Waldorf schools make up one of the most swiftly growing independent educational movements in the world and have expanded to over 900 schools in 83 countries with 253 PreK–12 schools in the United States.

Steiner's philosophy of education countered the conventional German educational philosophy of the early 20th century and challenged common European educational practices. He disagreed with existing curricular structures that were teacher centered and focused on basic literacy, mathematics, German history, and religion; he opposed a schooling system that was exclusive, with few students continuing schooling past *Volksschulen*, the 8-year elementary school. In contrast, Steiner's mandate for educational reform featured development of the whole child without sole emphasis on the intellect, and a pedagogy that included trust and confidence in the child as part of the learning process. He wanted his schools to be open to all children, coeducational, and designed as a 12-year school. Additionally, he believed in education that was teacher-directed yet emphasized collaboration among students, service to the community, interdisciplinary approaches, and the development of students' imaginations. This blend of educational elements merged progressive beliefs about the social nature of learning in authentic learning situations with more traditional teacher-centered pedagogical methods. Steiner also proposed that teachers maintain primary governance of the schools, a tradition upheld from the first school in 1919 to the present.

Steiner was particularly concerned with the development of school-age children and suggested that they evolved through three pedagogical stages, each stage shaped by children's developmental proclivities. These beliefs continue to influence curricula and pedagogy in today's Waldorf schools.

Steiner suggested that during the first stage, from birth to age 6 or 7, children learn by imitation, empathy, and experience, and early childhood curricula engage children in traditional life activities (e.g., baking, cleaning, gardening), cultivating feelings through the arts, and stimulating creativity and fantasy through imaginative play. Retaining this focus, modern Waldorf schools take a position against television and the use of computers for students at this age.

The second stage of development, between ages 7 and 12 or 13, is marked by the child's need to learn through rhythm and images. Teachers remain with their students during the second stage as they study visual and dramatic arts, movement, music, foreign languages, and what Steiner referred to as meaningful literacy. Although Waldorf schools' literacy curriculum has been challenged by some mainstream educators because reading instruction does not begin until age 7, Steiner adopted a wide definition of literacy that included not only reading and writing but experiences that allow students to derive meaning from music, the visual arts, and dance.

During the third stage, from puberty through young adulthood, curricula are designed to develop students' capacities for abstract thought, conceptual judgment, ethical thinking, and social responsibility. This stage focuses on academics, with teachers who specialize in academic subject areas.

Steiner's educational beliefs were based on Anthroposophy, a philosophy rooted in the concept that individuals, through meditation and study, have the potential to become more highly conscious of their complete humanity. Steiner believed that just as the mind and body were inseparable, the visible and spiritual worlds were intertwined. He posited that human beings had the potential to perceive and enter into the spiritual world through imagination, inspiration, and intuition, proposing that the purpose of investigating the spiritual world was to gain the same kind of precision and clarity that he ascribed to natural science's investigations of the physical world.

Issues related to Anthroposophy, however, have been at the center of most of the critique of Waldorf schools. In particular, Steiner's writings about the racial organization of culture and the evolution of consciousness have led to charges that racism is inherent in Anthroposophy and prevalent among those who believe in its tenets. Such charges have been strongly refuted in responses by Waldorf educators and the Association of Waldorf Schools, who point out that today's Waldorf schools are proudly and conspicuously multicultural. Other critics have contended that although the spiritual foundation of Waldorf education may not be explicitly integrated into material taught in the classroom—Waldorf schools identify themselves as nondenominational and nonsectarian—this occurs implicitly, and students are consistently exposed to Anthroposophical values and concepts of spirituality.

Pamela Carol Jewett

See also Montessori Schools; Progressive Education

Further Readings

Clouder, C., & Rawson, M. (1998). *Waldorf education.* Great Barrington, MA: Anthroposophic Press.

Steiner, R. (2003). *What is Waldorf education? Three lectures by Rudolf Steiner.* Great Barrington, MA: Steiner Books.

Uhrmacher, P. (1995). Uncommon schooling: A historical look at Rudolf Steiner, Anthroposophy, and Waldorf education. *Curriculum Inquiry, 25*(4), 381–406.

WAR ON POVERTY

President Lyndon B. Johnson's legacy is one of the most conflicted in American presidential history. His escalation of the war in Vietnam is juxtaposed with his unrelenting desire to make the United States fulfill a vision of The Great Society in which equality was promoted in all spheres of public life. The War on Poverty, as it came to be called, was a dramatic challenge that Johnson presented to the country. The War on Poverty and its associated reforms became a lightning rod for conservative criticism as well as an idealistic touchstone for liberals for generations.

After the assassination of President John F. Kennedy in November 1963 and the appointment of Vice President Lyndon Johnson as president, Johnson's State of the Union Speech of 1964 announced an "unconditional war on poverty in America." Johnson did not stop there; he continued to treat poverty with a message that did not state that the poor were to get an unearned handout. Instead, Johnson's notion was that of opportunity. His desire was to address the national disgrace of poverty (of nearly 20% at the time), which he felt merited a national response. Further, he identified the cause of systemic poverty not as personal moral weakness of the poor but as a societal failure. Johnson, in his 1964 State of the Union address, said, "The cause may lie deeper in our failure to give our fellow citizens a fair chance to develop their own capacities, in a lack of education and training." Johnson made clear that the opportunities he sought to extend were to those who were most disenfranchised, including all Americans regardless of race, ethnicity, and gender. The speech was historic in its idealism for the creation of a more just society. Several months later, Johnson proposed an even broader dream for America in a speech at the University of Michigan. He hoped The Great Society would emerge from a broad range of efforts such as the War on Poverty, as well as White House task forces on civil rights promotion and strengthening education.

The rhetoric of the War on Poverty quickly found its way into law and the creation of new administrative organizations. The Economic Opportunity Act of 1964 (Public Law 88-452, 78 Stat. 508, 42 U.S.C. § 2701) was passed by Congress and became law on August 20, 1964. The Act created the Office of Economic Opportunity (OEO), which administered various programs that were directed at the poor, including Job Corps, Youth Corps, Head Start, VISTA, and legal representation. In 1966, a program to improve the nutrition of children of the poor was also implemented.

However, this great explosion of programs was short lived. From the outset, Johnson encountered resistance from almost all quarters (the South on issues of race, conservatives who thought federal money should not be spent, and liberals who thought his reforms did not go far enough) to his call for an appropriate response to what he saw as a significant crisis. Johnson's War on Poverty was soon eclipsed by a backlash against his policies and, eventually, the human and economic costs of the Vietnam War. As opposition to the Vietnam War mounted and American society became deeply divided over issues of national policy, Johnson's administration was crippled, and he felt he could not muster enough popular support to be a viable candidate for reelection in 1968.

In the decades since Johnson called for the War on Poverty, many of its central programs have continued, although the OEO was eliminated by President Richard Nixon in 1974. However, the overall legacy of the War on Poverty remains controversial. Some scholars and economists maintain that Johnson's efforts did not achieve a substantial reduction in the poverty rate; others have gone farther and claim that his programs locked poor people into lives of government dependency. However, these conclusions are more often than not ideologically based and may say more about the critics than about the policies. In the end, the War on Poverty marked a turning point in America's political discourse, as it was the high-water mark of idealistic liberalism.

Aaron Cooley

See also Civil Rights Act of 1964; Elementary and Secondary Education Act; Northwest Ordinance; Presidents and Educational Reform

Further Readings

Clark, R. F. (2002). *The war on poverty: History, selected programs, and ongoing impact.* Lanham, MD: University Press of America.
Gillette, M. (1996). *Launching the war on poverty: An oral history.* New York: Twayne.
Johnson, L. (1964). *Annual message to the Congress on the state of the union.* Retrieved September 5, 2008, from http://www.lbjlib.utexas.edu/johnson/archives.hom/speeches.hom/640108.asp
Stricker, F. (2007). *Why America lost the war on poverty—and how to win it.* Chapel Hill: University of North Carolina Press.

WARREN, EARL (1891–1974)

Earl Warren was the 14th Chief Justice of the U.S. Supreme Court and served in office from 1953 to 1969. In 1954, he wrote the opinion for the unanimous ruling in *Brown v. Board of Education*, outlawing segregation by race in public schools. The ruling declared that mandatory or permissive segregation was unconstitutional. Although there was significant public dissent over the issue, school districts would be required to reform their policies and practices in order to comply with the Court's decision, thus beginning the desegregation of public schools in the United States.

Earl Warren was born March 19, 1891, in Los Angeles, California. His father was of Norwegian descent, and his mother was a Swedish immigrant. Warren went to school in Bakersfield, California, and attended the University of California at

Berkeley. At Berkeley, he earned an undergraduate degree in Legal Studies and his Juris Doctor in 1914. He was admitted to the California bar that same year. He worked for a private law firm and enlisted in the U.S. Army in 1917 for service in World War I. He was a first lieutenant and was honorably discharged in 1918. He served as a clerk of the judicial committee of the California State Assembly, deputy city attorney for Oakland, and deputy district attorney of Alameda County in California. As his reputation spread for being tough on crime and sensitive to the rights of the accused, he was appointed district attorney for Alameda County, where he served three 4-year terms from 1925 through 1939. Warren married Nina P. Meyers, a Swedish widow, in 1925 and they had six children.

In 1938, Earl Warren was elected Attorney General of the State of California. He led anticrime efforts and cracked down on illegal offshore gambling. Following the United States' entry into World War II, Warren supported the internment of American citizens of Japanese descent to relocation camps, a move for which he would later express regret in his memoirs. In 1942, Warren was elected governor of California. He was a popular governor, and was reelected twice.

Warren ran on the Republican national ticket as the vice presidential candidate for Thomas Dewey in 1948, and in 1952 lost the Republican presidential nomination to the eventual winner, Dwight D. Eisenhower. In 1953, President Eisenhower appointed Earl Warren Chief Justice of the U.S. Supreme Court. Eisenhower wanted a conservative justice, but instead got a liberal justice: The Warren-led court was to make decisions directly affecting social progress in the United States. During Warren's term as Chief Justice, his Court ruled on controversial issues such as civil rights cases, separation of church and state, and protection of individual rights.

Earl Warren took over a Court whose members were divided between a more active role for the Court and those who supported judicial restraint. In 1954, one of the first cases for the Warren Court was *Brown v. Board of Education,* which turned out to be a landmark case dealing with banning segregation in public schools. In the 1950s racial segregation in schools was common, and most schools attended by Black students were inferior to

those attended by Whites. The existing *Plessy v. Ferguson* ruling allowed "separate but equal" school systems for Blacks and Whites.

The *Brown v. Board of Education* case involved a Black third-grade girl from Topeka, Kansas, who had to walk one mile through a railroad switchyard to get to school, even though a White elementary school was only seven blocks away. Her father tried to enroll her in the White school but was denied. Neighboring Black parents and the National Association for the Advancement of Colored People (NAACP) challenged the segregation of Topeka's public schools. They argued that the schools were inherently unequal.

Chief Justice Warren was a proponent of individual rights and he believed the U.S. Constitution prohibited the government from acting unfairly against the individual. He believed that civil rights and civil liberties should be protected by the Court. Warren, knowing that this would be a controversial case, acquired strength from the Court members to reach a unanimous decision. The previous "separate but equal" doctrine would not survive. The Court ruled that segregation should not take place in public schools, because children would be denied the equal protection of the laws guaranteed under the Fourteenth Amendment. The Court concluded that in the field of public education the doctrine of "separate but equal" has no place. The Court's action, through unanimous agreement, reformed educational policies and practices and paved the way for desegregation. At the time, the *Brown v. Board of Education* decision did not abolish segregation in other public facilities, such as restaurants and restrooms, but it was an important step toward the eventual complete desegregation of public schools.

During his term on the Supreme Court, Earl Warren dealt with controversial issues of civil rights, civil liberties, and politics. The Warren Court became noted for its use of judicial powers to effect social progress in the United States. Warren served as Chief Justice for 16 years and retired in 1969. He is widely regarded as one of the most influential and powerful Supreme Court Justices in the history of the United States.

After leaving public office, Warren was selected by President Lyndon B. Johnson to be chief investigator of the assassination of President John F. Kennedy. The distinguished group of investigators he led became known as the Warren Commission; its exhaustive investigation culminated in the publication of a voluminous report whose findings are still controversial.

Earl Warren died on July 9, 1974, and is buried in Arlington National Cemetery in Washington, D.C.

Eugene Paul Cordonnier

See also *Board of Education v. Rowley; Brown v. Board of Education;* Busing; Civil Rights Act of 1964; Desegregation/Integration; National Association for the Advancement of Colored People (NAACP)

Further Readings

Newton, J. (2007). *Justice for all: Earl Warren and the nation he made.* New York. Penguin Group.

Scheiber, H. (2007). *Earl Warren and the Warren court: The legacy in American and foreign law.* Lanham, MD: Lexington Books.

Supreme Court Historical Society: History of the Court. Retrieved March 19, 2008, from http://www.supreme courthistory.org

Warren, E. (1977). *The memoirs of Earl Warren.* Garden City, NY: Doubleday.

WASHINGTON, BOOKER T. (1856–1915)

Booker Taliaferro Washington (1856–1915), born into slavery in southwestern Virginia, became the most widely known African American leader and educator of the late 19th and early 20th centuries. The founder and president of Tuskegee Institute in Alabama, he advocated racial uplift through material improvement rooted in practical skills and individual industry. His ideology clashed with that of many African Americans—notably W. E. B. Du Bois—who favored a path to racial advancement shaped by political and cultural progress and charged that Washington's emphasis on vocational means would hinder racial equality. These divergent ideologies sparked enduring debates about the objectives and methods of education, with Washington and the Tuskegee curriculum firmly committed to industrial training or economic betterment in the work areas immediately available to African Americans. Radical proponents of racial uplift viewed this position as simply accommodating views of Whites who preferred a Black menial labor force to Black citizens schooled in humanistic and liberal traditions.

Washington was born to a slave, Jane, and an unidentified White father on a farm owned by the James Burroughs family in Hale's Ford, Virginia. The exact date of his birth has never been fully verified, but for practical purposes he took it as April 5, 1856, making him about 4 years younger than his half brother, John, and 4 years older than his half sister, Amanda. His home was a one-room cabin within a community of aunts and uncles who served in various work capacities in the fields and farmhouse. With no shoes, one shirt, and no opportunity to learn reading or writing, young Washington ran errands and performed farm chores while his mother slaved as the farm cook. Several years after Booker was born, Jane married Washington Ferguson, a slave on a nearby farm, who escaped to West Virginia during the Civil War. Jane, with her two sons and daughter, joined him in Malden, West Virginia, soon after the Confederate surrender at Appomattox. Booker Washington and his brother were sent to work, first packing salt from the saline springs in the area; they later switched to mining coal. In his early teens, Washington worked as a houseboy for the wife of General Lewis Ruffner, the owner of the area's salt and coal mines.

Self-taught in basic literacy, Washington was able to attend a local school several months each year by working early mornings and late afternoons. He long maintained, however, that his most valuable lessons came from his work for Viola Ruffner, a Vermont native who demanded perfection, honesty, and systematic organization. To continue his schooling, Washington managed to get to Hampton (Virginia) Normal and Industrial Institute by scraping together just enough money for transportation and then working at the school to support his room, board, books, and clothes. He thrived on Hampton's system of classroom instruction, industrial training, and manual labor; and he graduated in 1875. After a brief stint as a teacher back in West Virginia, he studied for a year at a small Baptist institution, Wayland Seminary, in Washington, D.C. There he discovered the striking contrast between a classical curriculum that included Greek and Latin and Hampton's pragmatic emphasis on basic life skills and employment training. By the spring of 1879, he was back at Hampton as director of the institute's night school and resident superintendent at the dormitory for the school's large contingent of American Indian male students.

When Hampton Institute president Samuel C. Armstrong suggested Washington as the first principal of a new normal school being founded in 1881 in Tuskegee, Alabama, the school as envisioned was limited to modest goals, supported by some promised state funding. Noting the extreme poverty of the Black citizens in and around Tuskegee, Washington quickly committed to the manual labor system he had experienced at Hampton Institute as the premise for education and racial uplift at Tuskegee Normal and Industrial Institute. He identified a location, made Black and White friends in the town, raised some funds, and started the school first in a local church and soon on donated acreage. Early students, male and female, provided much of the labor for building the growing school with work that paid their tuition and provided experience in trades such as carpentry, masonry, and bricklaying. At the end of the school's first year, Washington married Fannie N. Smith, whom he had courted in Malden, West Virginia. Their daughter, Portia M. Washington, was born in 1883. Fannie died the following year. Washington would later marry Olivia A. Davidson, who bore him two sons, Booker T. Washington, Jr., and Ernest D. Washington. Four years after Olivia's death in 1889, Washington married Margaret J. Murray, who would outlive him.

Washington eventually added a night school that allowed the neediest students to work full-time during the day and attend Tuskegee at night. As Tuskegee Institute grew, so did Washington's reputation. He traveled to raise funds in the Northeast and Midwest and discovered a talent and passion for oratory. Predictably, his public speeches soon moved beyond promoting Tuskegee and its industrial training program to include issues of race relations. His approving audiences appreciated the notion of Black citizens becoming responsible for their own uplift through manual labor in fields and factories. Southern Whites typically found the idea of racial progress through economic means far more palatable than progress through political means such as voting or serving in elected office.

At the Atlanta Cotton Exposition of 1895, the opportunity to address a national audience catapulted Washington toward his status as the most powerful African American leader of his era. His theme of a route to Black material progress that was not dependent on acquiring social or political equality met great approval from his largely White audience and from conservative African Americans. It created a schism, however, with those African Americans, especially in the Northeast, who viewed him as accommodating White power and prejudices responsible for the injustices of the age of Jim Crow. Washington's most eloquent Black critic, the Harvard University–educated W. E. B. Du Bois, telegrammed his congratulations after the Atlanta speech. But Du Bois later recoiled from Washington's conservative educational concepts and insisted that racial justice required educating Blacks for political and intellectual leadership in the same manner and subjects that dominated White higher education.

Controversy surrounding Washington also concerned his use of presidential power on campus at Tuskegee at the expense of academic freedom and his use of political power in furthering his leadership of African American causes. Nevertheless, his image as a successful educator, reformer, and the leader of Black Americans in the early 20th century was secure. It was symbolized by a 1901 invitation from President Theodore Roosevelt that made him the first African American to dine at the White House; and it was narrated in his autobiographies, *The Story of My Life and Work* and *Up From Slavery*. Washington died in 1915 at age 59 of heart failure following long-term high blood pressure.

Katherine Chaddock

See also Du Bois, W. E. B.; Southern Education Board

Further Readings

Harlan, L. R. (1972). *Booker T. Washington: The making of a Black leader*. London: Oxford University Press.
Washington, B. T. (1900). *Up from slavery*. New York: Doubleday.

WEB-BASED TEACHING

Web-based teaching (WBT) is broadly defined as any systematic instruction delivered via the Internet. The nearly instantaneous transmission of information in a wide array of formats that characterizes use of the World Wide Web presents a variety of options for applying Web-based tools to instruction. Further, the decentralized nature of the Internet allows individuals to rapidly sort and select available tools and information or develop and disseminate their own. In combination, these characteristics generate the tremendous spectrum of learning activities that constitute WBT. Instruction can be formal or informal, synchronous or asynchronous, and either self-contained or dependent on interactions with others in virtual or physical settings. The technologies and media used may include text, video, audio, animations, simulations, games, chat rooms, asynchronous threaded discussions, and video-conferencing or lectures via video streaming.

Heralding WBT as a transformative technology for education, advocates claimed that in addition to bringing an international range of content and learning materials into the classroom, it would fundamentally change pedagogy to adhere more closely to constructivist ideals. As with other technologies expected to transform education at previous points in history (e.g., radio, television, and microcomputers), however, examinations of WBT practices and impacts have reflected little to no substantive change in pedagogy or effectiveness since the World Wide Web made its educational debut, despite 98% of public K–12 classrooms having access to the Internet.

The advent of WBT was heralded in the early 1990s as a revolutionary force in education with the power to shift the focus of learning activities from the teacher to the student, adapt instruction to the strengths and weaknesses of individual learners, and foster lifelong learning available at any time and place with an Internet connection. Three major factors, however, have limited the success of WBT to engender such educational reform. First, the effectiveness of WBT is dependent solely on adherence to principles of instructional design that operate independently of the medium in which the instruction is delivered. In other words, the technology itself does not impact students' academic success. When learning experiences on the World Wide Web are designed using effective pedagogical practices, they are likely to be as effective as experiences of similar design and content delivered via more conventional media. Second, the preparation of education professionals at the K–12 and postsecondary levels does not typically entail the necessary training to maximally utilize Web-based technologies. Third, the traditional culture of formal education and the high demands on professionals' time tend to lead them to develop Web-based facsimiles of their existing course models.

Web-Based Applications of Theories of Learning

Many of the technologies used by educators are inspired by ideas about effective student learning. For example, social theories of learning suggest that students learn best when they are able to collaborate and communicate with peers during learning projects. To this end, virtual worlds have been constructed that allow students to interact in simulated environments to assume specific roles related to the learning of curricular content. *Quest Atlantis, River City,* and *Whyville* are Web-based environments that allow students to act as scientists who are able to investigate various phenomena as scientists and members of concerned communities of computer users. Although teachers and students are frequently enthusiastic about such activities, the results of empirical studies of learning gains have been mixed and have not demonstrated advantages over traditional forms of instruction.

Cognitive learning theories that lend more emphasis to individual student efforts have attempted to leverage Web-based instruction's ability to respond to specific user actions and correct or incorrect responses to assessment items. One approach has been to utilize Web-based agents—animated figures that offer suggestions and provide feedback as learners attempt to solve problems online. As with other Web-based technologies, the design and specific application of this approach make a significant difference when its impact on learners is assessed. Another Web-based technology with greater demonstrated efficacy is the use of adaptive tutors and testing technology. Based on analysis of learners' knowledge and misconceptions, adaptive technologies make targeted decisions about which instructional content or test items should be presented next in a sequence to optimally facilitate students' learning.

Utilization of Web-Based Teaching

Although WBT has not often embodied the reformatory aspirations of its advocates in terms of changing the relationship between teacher and learner, it has succeeded greatly in improving access to educational resources for students in K–12 schools with limited offerings. Public secondary schools in many states have adopted WBT to offer courses to students that faculty members located on site are not qualified to teach. Twenty-two states have extended their use of WBT to offer high school degrees exclusively through online coursework. The U.S. Department of Education estimates that more than 300,000 students nationwide take online courses for high school credit.

WBT has also had a major impact on postsecondary and adult education. In 2005, approximately 7% (1.2 million) of all students in higher education were enrolled in WBT-only certificate and degree programs. Figures from 2006 indicate that an additional 3.5 million students (20% of American higher education students) were enrolled in at least one online course as part of traditional degree programs. Available projections suggest that these numbers will continue to grow at a rate of between 10% and 25%.

David F. Feldon and Catherine Flynn

See also Educational Technology

Further Readings

Allen, I. E., & Seaman, J. (2007). *Online nation: Five years of growth in online learning*. Needham, MA: Sloan Consortium.

O'Neil, H. F., Jr., & Perez, R. S. (Eds.). (2006). *Web-based learning: Theory, research and practice*. Mahwah, NJ: Erlbaum.

Spector, J. M., Merrill, M. D., van Merriënboer, J. J. G., & Driscoll, M. P. (Eds.). (2008). *Handbook of research on educational communications and technology* (3rd ed.). New York: Routledge.

WEBSTER, NOAH (1758–1843)

Noah Webster was an energetic educator whose strong belief in American nationalism, individual self-sufficiency, and popular government was reflected in his distinctive approach to crafting early spelling books, grammar guides, writing and speaking texts, and eventually his 70,000-entry *An American Dictionary of the English Language*. By 1790, Webster had authored six instructional books that were used regularly by parents, tutors, students, and schoolteachers as educational texts and reference guides. He had also successfully tackled the widespread problem of plagiarism by traveling to the 13 states to convince legislators to pass copyright laws; he extended his lobbying to the First U.S. Congress, which passed the Copyright Act of 1790. In the area of educational reform, he can be credited with bringing the practice of a particularly American version of the English language to citizens and schools.

Born in West Hartford, Connecticut, to a middle-class farming family, at age 16 Webster entered Yale College, a campus heady with student activists consumed with revolutionary zeal. After graduating in 1778, Webster taught school and studied law; and, although admitted to the bar at Hartford, he found no suitable employment in that crowded profession. He initiated several failed schools in Connecticut, always emphasizing literature and the proper uses of grammar and pronunciation, areas he found sorely lacking in American education. One of his schools was a unique progressive venture in Hartford with tuition based on economic status. One by one the schools failed. At the same time, his essays appeared in various New England and New York periodicals, mostly aimed at promoting strict American nationalism and supporting the break with all vestiges of British rule.

Webster's career as an instructional writer aiming to improve education and correctness in the English language began when he moved to Goshen, New York, in 1782. He produced a uniquely American spelling book that served his patriotic commitment by replacing the available British spellers, *The Grammatical Institute of the English Language*. Webster's spelling choices began new and enduring traditions by veering from British examples. *Honour, gaol, publick,* and *musick* became *honor, jail, public,* and *music.* His innovations generally favored simplification; and he also peppered the book with stories and advice on the goodness of books, study, hard work, and general American citizenship. Unique to Webster's book was a pronunciation guide, which Webster felt necessary to promote national unity and end the habits of localism that highlighted regional differences. Although he had difficulties finding a publisher and managed to obtain one only by taking nearly no royalties, Webster established himself as an educator with the *Blue Back Speller,* as the book became known. Almost immediately, it sold 20,000 copies a year and went into continual new editions. By 1829, an estimated 20 million copies of Webster's spellers had been purchased.

Webster quickly produced the grammar and the reader he had planned for the series that began with the speller. He vigorously marketed his volumes throughout the 13 states and then used his platform as a notable to embark on a wide variety of publishing projects, such as: *Sketches of American Policy* (1785), *The New England Primer* (1798), *A Brief History of Epidemic and Pestilential Diseases* (1799), and *The Little Reader's Assistant* (1790). Typical of Webster's nationalistic philosophy and moralistic determination was his title for the 1797 edition of his reader: *An American Selection of Lessons in Reading and Speaking, Calculated to Improve Minds and Refine the Taste of Youth.* Webster believed that American citizens should not wait to come to patriotism; they should be taught patriotism while being taught to read and write. Selections in that edition emphasized the founding of the nation, the Revolutionary War, the Declaration of Independence, and his vision of a nation of distinct manners and language. Interestingly for a savvy salesman with a national market, but appropriate for his own abolitionist commitment, he included a selection unfavorable to slavery. For Webster, young minds were meant to be shaped in the direction of correct thought and behavior, rather than instructed toward informed choices.

Webster's enthusiasm and avid writing of essays promoting national unity unmarred by differences in spelling, pronunciation, or politics suffered a blow when the election of Thomas Jefferson (1800) increased awareness of the reality of sectional interests—especially North and South. Webster,

now married to his wife Rebecca Greenleaf Webster and living in New Haven with a family that would eventually include eight children, responded by initiating the work that would establish his lasting fame, lexicography. He completed his first complete book on language, *Compendious Dictionary,* in 1806. In it, American words from "dime" to "tomahawk" began to gain scholarly approval. Critics, while for the most part admitting his breadth of knowledge, complained about the inclusion of utilitarian spoken words, considered colloquialisms, such as "congressional." Webster simply continued to promote an American spoken language, moving his family to Amherst, Massachusetts, where he served as president of the board of trustees of Amherst Academy and was instrumental in its development into a college in 1821. Two new editions of his first dictionary appeared, abridged for school use; and, in 1828, his great and enduring work was published, *An American Dictionary of the English Language.* The 2,000-page, two-volume dictionary was well received, particularly for its nuanced definitions that often described differences in American and British meanings. The U.S. Congress, as well as many courts and educational institutions, adopted it as a standard reference. Between age 70 and his death at age 84, Webster produced seven more American language books for schools, including new editions of his original speller and such volumes as *The Elementary Primer, The Teacher: A Supplement to the Elementary Spelling Book; Biography, for the Use of Schools;* and the widely adopted *History of the United States.*

Katherine Chaddock

See also Jefferson, Thomas; Rush, Benjamin

Further Readings

Babbidge, H. D. (1967). *Noah Webster: On being American, selected writings, 1783–1823.* New York: Praeger.

Rollins, R. M. (Ed.). (1989). *The autobiographies of Noah Webster: From the letters and essays, memoir, and diary.* Columbia: University of South Carolina Press.

Unger, H. G. (1998). *Noah Webster: The life and times of an American patriot.* New York: Wiley.

WHAT WORKS CLEARINGHOUSE

In 2002 an act of Congress created the Institute of Education Sciences (IES) to provide for improvement of federal education research. The act stipulated that the IES provide to the public a database for dissemination of statistics, evaluation, and information. To meet this goal, the Institute established the What Works Clearinghouse (WWC) to provide policymakers, educators, and researchers with scientific evidence of what works in educational interventions. The intent of the Clearinghouse was to provide an independent evaluation by analyzing and summarizing research on the effectiveness of instructional interventions in order for educators to know what and how to teach. The very act of establishing the WWC had a larger impact than just providing a public database as it also reformed the nature and opinion of educational research. Research would now have to be evaluated according to certain criteria in order to be considered effective.

Establishing "what works" by using scientifically based research in education is not without controversy. Initial controversy stemmed from the definition of scientifically based research, qualifications and bias of the evaluators, and ability to obtain all research on a given topic. When it was first established, the way to determine "what works" was to determine cause and effect through experimental studies. These studies had to develop evidence based on designs for intervention that randomly assigned treatment and control groups. The WWC has since developed and published a well-defined and systematic process to review studies of educational interventions. Current study designs that are considered to provide the strongest evidence for effects include randomized controlled trials and also regression discontinuity designs, quasi-experimental designs, and single-subject designs. Studies are also reviewed on the topic area definition, the time period set for the topic, the relevant outcome, adequate outcome measure, relevant sample for the topic, and adequate reporting. For each topic area, a principal investigator who is a well-known expert in the field oversees this process. Finally, topic areas can be nominated by the public through e-mail or are identified in meetings with leaders in various areas and educational organizations. Nominated topics are then reviewed for their potential to improve student outcomes, ability to apply to broad groups of students, importance to education, and availability of research-based studies.

The WWC reviewers evaluate all research, and based on the methodology and results establish whether the research "Meets Evidence Standards," "Meets Evidence Standards with Reservations," or "Does Not Meet Evidence Screens." In order to evaluate all the research in the topic area, WWC trained staff conduct hand searches of journals for the past 20 years, review electronic and Web databases, incorporate independent submissions, search conference proceedings, and contact topic experts and organizations for relevant studies. Throughout the review process the original researchers are provided an opportunity to review coding, and the intervention developers are allowed to review the reports. Finally, all reports undergo extensive review, including external peer review.

To date the clearinghouse has conducted comprehensive research reviews of seven topical interventions. *Beginning Reading* included reading interventions for students in Grades K–3. Targeted interventions focused on skills in alphabetic, reading fluency, comprehension, or general reading achievement. *English Language Learners* in Grades K–6 concentrated on interventions to increase English language skills, development, reading achievement, or math achievement. *Early Childhood Education* was defined as curricula and practices for 3- to 5-year-olds designed to develop school readiness skills. *Elementary School Math* and *Middle School Math* focused on math curricula that increased achievement for students in Grades K–5 and Grades 6–9, respectively. *Dropout Prevention* featured both secondary school and community interventions designed to assist students to remain in school. The *Character Education* topic included any K–12 program designed to increase outcomes relative to social behavior and academic performance.

For each topic area, the WWC provides information in the form of two publications. Intervention reports include those that have one or more studies that meet WWC Evidence Standards and include key findings from each of the studies pertaining to the particular intervention. In contrast, Topic reports include only interventions that passed

WWC standards, and they briefly describe the topic and provide an overview of ratings of effectiveness, improvement indexes, and effect size.

The WWC also provides two other types of publications: *Quick Reviews* and *Practice Guides*. The quick reviews focus on studies recently featured in the media to determine if they meet WWC evidence standards. Practice guides, on the other hand, contain practical recommendations for educators regarding current challenges in their classrooms and schools. The WWC updates these publications frequently in order to keep educators and the public up to date on interventions and practice. The WWC disseminates all publications and research reviews through its Web site. Additional information on definition of research terminology, effect sizes, and research designs can be found at the Web site. The WWC continues to reform and shape education as new research is evaluated and disseminated as "what works."

Cheryl A. Wissick

See also Institute of Education Sciences; No Child Left Behind Act (NCLB); Reading First

Further Readings

Doing What Works: http://dww.ed.gov/index.cfm
Education Sciences Reform Act, H. R. 3801, 107th Cong. (2002).
Institute of Educational Sciences: http://ies.ed.gov
What Works Clearinghouse: http://ies.ed.gov/ncee/wwc

WHITENESS

Race is a lens through which many individuals see and are seen—sometimes consciously or intentionally and sometimes not. The dominant race and standard within U.S. society, historically, is White. In U.S. society the color of one's skin impacts one's daily experiences, although numerous White educators do not acknowledge White as a race nor Whiteness as a set of cultural beliefs and practices. Yet these beliefs and practices permeate and are reinforced in American schools as well as in other institutions and avenues of life on a daily basis.

The consideration of Whiteness, the opposite of non-White, and its organizing effect on teaching and learning for school-age children, both White students and students of color, is indeed an issue of educational reform. Following is a brief discussion of some of the relevant factors and existing tensions surrounding Whiteness that are present as a result of practices, as well as a body of knowledge that is grounded in the history of the United States.

On the surface, Whiteness and its related privileges are indications of the benefits of having white skin versus skin that is not white. The darker the pigmentation of the individual's skin, the fewer the racial privileges. In many educational institutions, the higher expectations that some educators have for White students, versus lower expectations for students of color, exist from the moment a child enters school. The advantages, encouragement, and opportunities afforded White students as a result of skin color often translate into additional challenges and pressures for students of color, who must learn not only expected content but also the rules of Whiteness and related correct behaviors in order to survive; non-White students, lacking such benefits, are viewed negatively when set expectations are not met.

The notion of color blindness is also worthy of mention. Some White individuals attempt to sidestep issues of race by denying or ignoring racism, racial differences, and White privilege and by rejecting the notions of uneven power and privilege that are enjoyed by some, but not all, Americans. Some persons of color are not comfortable addressing issues of race, and may therefore further complicate situations that involve students of color who may be in search of an ally, or at least someone who has some relevant racial understanding as a result of prior experiences. A colorblind lens can be harmful to students of color as well as White students through the diminishing of experiences and realities of minority students while permitting White students to ignore their own benefits and societal advantages along with potential damages of Whiteness to their minority peer students.

Scholars of race and race relations have noted the importance for educators to recognize and begin to consciously assess and understand the profound effects of the accepted White culture, the basis of the educational system that identifies the standards as well as measurements of student achievement. If we look at the perspective from which history is taught in schools, for example, it is not the complete story for all Americans.

The implications of the foregoing discussion are many and varied, given that the majority of American educators currently are White while students in increasing numbers are non-White. In the same way that it is beneficial for each individual to acknowledge and further explore who he or she is racially as a result of personal experiences, both in-service and pre-service White educators and their counterparts of color need opportunities to explore, discuss, and understand Whiteness and its impact on their students of color and their White students, with a focus on improving student achievement and the goal of a positive school experience for all students.

There are many benefits to discussing race from diverse perspectives—everyone can win, as each individual's experience is valued within the discussion. Perhaps, then, the place to start is to consciously acknowledge Whiteness as one element of such discussions about race and its relationship to success in the classroom. The expected results include improvements in both teaching and learning, which may lead to individual transformation as well as the transformation of many through innovative and differentiated instruction. In order to reach that goal and achieve positive results, individuals must acknowledge the gaps between current beliefs, practices, and reality.

Consider ongoing conversations regarding the 2008 presidential race that resulted in a victory for Barack Obama. The issue of race was most often downplayed or sidestepped. Since White skin is viewed positively and darker skin is not, White voters, who were an essential component of the victory, had to become comfortable with the racial uniqueness of Obama. Or consider in the aftermath of Hurricane Katrina in 2005, the resulting devastation and delay of services provided to the affected persons of color in New Orleans. Efforts were not handled effectively at the time and are not discussed much now, although much extensive work remains to be done.

In conclusion, the color of one's skin and related beliefs and practices within American society shape one's experiences as well as reality. Currently, the playing field is not level and the classroom does not offer equal success opportunities for all students. Gaps remain when actual behaviors are examined from the viewpoint of those not in power and control.

Pamela Cross Young

See also Ability Grouping; Achievement Gap; Affirmative Action; Black Alliance for Educational Options; Comer, James P.; Desegregation/Integration; Diversity; *Hobson v. Hansen;* Kozol, Jonathan; Racism

Further Readings

Calderon, D. (2006). One-dimensionality and Whiteness. *Policy Futures in Education, 4*(1), 73–82.

Singleton, G. E., & Linton, C. (2006). *Courageous conversations about race.* Thousand Oaks, CA: Corwin.

Sue, D. W. (2004, November). Whiteness and ethnocentric monoculturalism: Making the "invisible" visible. *American Psychologist, 59*(8), 761–769.

WHOLE LANGUAGE

The history of whole language is rich in dissent and reform and in fact may be considered one of the most controversial topics in the history of reading. The roots of whole language begin with the progressive education movement of the 1920s and 1930s and can be particularly found in the work of John Dewey. However, it was not until the 1980s that whole language practices became popular across the United States and began what have often been referred to as the Reading Wars. This entry examines the dissent around the definition of whole language, the pubic backlash against whole language teaching, and the whole language practices that have reformed today's classrooms.

Dissent exists even in the attempt to define whole language. Previous reviews of whole language have found that there is no common agreement as to what whole language is or is not. Though there is no single definition of whole language, three themes emerge when examining classrooms taught from a whole language perspective. First, students are the center of the curriculum and respected as a central component of the learning process. This manifests in classrooms by students choosing their reading material and studies. Second, the role of the teacher is that of a guide or co-learner. In this way the teacher serves as a facilitator of the student's learning process rather than as a director. Third, learning is viewed as a social event through authentic experiences and use of authentic literature. Whole language classrooms nurture and encourage social engagement as all members discuss their learning together. The basal texts that had previously been the dominant text in primary classrooms were replaced with trade book literature.

The use of trade book literature, rather than structured basal readers, became one of the most controversial pieces behind the whole language approach to teaching. The underlying philosophy of whole language resides in the belief that reading should be taught in an integrated manner and never as an isolated, separate subject. Thus the meaning of a text takes priority over the sounds of letters, and phonics is taught through the trade book literature that is selected by the teacher, rather than through workbook pages.

This method of teaching is often referred to as a top-down approach. It requires the reader to construct personal meaning from the text and to utilize prior knowledge as he or she is reading rather than to rely solely on letter–sound understandings. Top-down models are also referred to as "whole to part," because reading is seen as a process through which readers first understand the meaning of a text, then break words down into smaller parts when difficulty occurs.

Though often misrepresented and misunderstood, whole language incorporates phonics instruction. This instruction occurs through literature-based reading and writing activities and not through a more direct instruction approach. Students are taught phonics skills through the literature that they read together and in the context of the readings that they engage in individually. This critical foundation to the whole language teaching approach is often the focus of dissent among researchers, parents, and the media. Critics argue that this approach provides ample opportunity for skills to be missed, leaving students with potentially weaker phonetic skills.

This dissent may derive from the direct implication that follows from the whole language approach

to teaching: A heavy burden is placed upon the teacher. The teacher holds the primary responsibility for developing and directing the curriculum, rather than relying on the direction provided by the previously used basal reader. The teacher is the primary individual responsible for identifying needed phonetic skills and developing instruction as needed. As a result of complete teacher autonomy, critics have argued that some teachers miss teaching critical phonetic skills, and that leads to weaker reading abilities.

In an attempt to find an answer to the now very public debate regarding whole language and phonics, Congress commissioned Marilyn Jager Adams to research and disseminate her findings. Her consequential book, *Beginning to Read: Thinking and Learning About Print,* did not definitively select an approach. Rather she reported that though phonics instruction is critical, many elements of a whole language approach are supportive of students learning phonics.

Under intense media pressure, most teachers abandoned using the whole language approach in their classrooms. Two large-scale reports, by the National Research Council's Commission on Preventing Reading Difficulties in Young Children (1996) and the National Reading Panel (2000), added to the demise of whole language instruction with their common finding that varying approaches of phonetic instruction (particularly analytic and synthetic) contributed positively to a student's ability to read successfully.

Yet, as many argued throughout the years of the Reading Wars, the use of authentic literature and the systematic approach for the teaching of phonetic skills do not have to be mutually exclusive. From this growing understanding, balanced literacy has developed as a new approach to teaching literacy skills. Teachers utilizing a balanced literacy approach incorporate literature as the core of their program, but teach skills and strategies (including phonics skills) both directly and indirectly. This reformed model of whole language incorporates strengths from both the whole language and explicit phonics approaches to teaching.

Jackie Marshall Arnold

See also Phonics; Reading First; Reading Recovery; Reading Reform

Further Readings

Adams, M.J. (1990). *Beginning to read: Thinking and learning about print.* Cambridge: MIT Press.

Goodman, K. S. (1986). *What's whole in whole language? A parent/teacher guide to children's learning.* Portsmouth, NH: Heinemann Educational.

Newman, J. M. (1985). *Whole language: Theory in use.* Portsmouth, NH: Heinemann Educational.

WILLARD, EMMA HART (1787–1870)

Born in Berlin, Connecticut, Emma Hart Willard (1787–1870) was one of the pioneer advocates for female education. Tutored by her father and educated at a local seminary, she began her teaching career in 1805 by opening a dame school, and in 1807 she became preceptress of a female school in Middlebury, Vermont. Upon marrying John Willard in 1809, she left teaching, but returned when her family fell into economic hardship. Willard was determined to provide women a higher education denied to her, one comparable to that of men, although she remarked that its purpose would uniquely serve female character and duties. Her role as an educational leader is exemplified by her contributions to common school reform; she provided respectability in the struggle for equal education for females in arguing for equal funding, in developing the Troy Female Academy, and in her development of textbooks and experiential methods.

In 1819, Willard wrote *Plan for the Improvement of Female Education* to persuade New York legislators to give financial support to a female seminary, the counterpart to men's colleges. Female seminaries provided opportunities for a liberal arts education across the North, rooted in the desire to foster female intellectual capacity. She appealed for state funding so that female seminaries would not be dependent on students for income and contended that the state is compelled to ensure an accountable and appropriate education for women. She defended women's right to intellectual and curricular equality with men, although she did not promote careers outside the home. Her rationale for educational equality was based on the idea of "republican motherhood": Future mothers would require character and intelligence to raise virtuous citizens and ensure social stability. Although this ideology identified gender as the primary determinant of women's lives, it is nonetheless viewed as an early expression of feminism. Willard and others were able to justify higher education for women without threatening traditional gender roles. Her Plan found supporters in John Adams and Thomas Jefferson, as well as many others from around the world.

Although the New York legislature rejected Willard's Plan, in 1821 the city of Troy, New York, offered Willard a subsidy to open the Troy Female Academy. Within 10 years it became one of the most profitable female institutions, accepting affluent students from across the country and graduating multitudes of future teachers well versed in mathematics, science, history, logic, and domestic and finishing school studies such as art and music. The Troy Female Academy thus allowed Willard to actualize her Plan and cultivate the intellectual, moral, and physical nature of her students. Rooted in her dissatisfaction with the learning materials available, she wrote a number of geography and history textbooks, focusing on innovative experimental methods that became standards at the time. Widowed in 1825, Willard remarried in 1838. After divorcing in 1843, she retired to Troy, spending her days traveling and writing about her views on common schools and female education until her death in 1870.

Sylvia L. M. Martinez

See also Academies; Curriculum Controversies; Experiential Learning; Women in Educational Leadership

Further Readings

Beadie, N. (1993). Emma Willard's idea put to the test: The consequences of state support of female education in New York, 1819–1867. *History of Education Quarterly, 33,* 543–562.

Goodsell, W. (Ed.). (1931). *Pioneers in women's education in the United States.* New York: AMS Press.

Woody, T. (1929). *A history of women's education in the United States* (Vol. 1). New York: Octagon Books.

WINNETKA PLAN

The Winnetka Plan was an innovative curriculum developed by Carlton W. Washburne and implemented in the Winnetka Public School District in 1919. The Winnetka Plan was a curriculum that featured common essentials (e.g., spelling) and creative group activities (e.g., art) as a means of dividing subjects. Students were required to demonstrate mastery in order to advance in the common essential subjects. Students were not required to demonstrate mastery of the creative group activities. The Winnetka Plan emphasized the well-rounded development of the child through the creative activities.

The Plan took its name from Winnetka, Illinois, where Carleton W. Washburne (1889–1968) was superintendent of schools from 1919 to 1943. He served as president of the Progressive Education Association from 1939 to 1943.

The Winnetka Plan was influenced by John Dewey's work. Dewey encouraged innovative pedagogy, and the Winnetka Plan reflected the innovative spirit. The curriculum and school day, according to this Plan, had two parts: common essentials (common knowledge and skills) and creative activities (group activities and self-expression subjects).

Common essentials, or common knowledge and skills, included: spelling, reading, writing, and counting. One-half of the school day was given to the common essentials. Students progressed at their own pace in these subjects. Mastery was at the 100% level, and no student failed according to this Plan. The work was divided into units and each pupil self-checked progress on a worksheet, and when 100% perfect, moved to further work. An advantage of the Winnetka Plan was the absence of a time element for the achievement of goals.

Creative activities included: art, music, drama, crafts, and physical activities. These were social or creative activities that featured projects, reports, and hands-on activities. One-third or more of the school day was given to the creative group activities. Unlike the common essentials, there were no tests of mastery or defined standards for the creative activities. The creative activities of the Winnetka Plan were viewed as a positive feature of the curriculum because they balanced the common essentials and their more traditional format.

According to Ellwood Cubberley, the Winnetka Plan represented a reorganization and a redirection of the school that called for new teaching materials, methods of work, and new testing procedures. Washburne is often credited with the development of workbooks. The self-instruction booklets used

by students as part of the Winnetka Plan were early "workbooks." Students proceeded through the booklets at their own pace and corrected the self-instruction booklets themselves. The students took placement tests to determine the work they needed to master. A recordkeeping system was used to track the progress of individual students. After mastery was demonstrated through completion of a test, the student moved to new material. Mastery learning was an essential feature of the Winnetka Plan.

Marilyn L. Grady

See also Dewey, John; Mastery Learning; Progressive Education; Progressive Education Association (PEA)

Further Readings

Cubberley, E. P. (1929). *Public school administration.* Boston: Houghton Mifflin.

Washburne, C. W. (1953). *What is progressive education?* New York: Day.

Washburne, C. W., & Marland, S. P., Jr. (1963). *Winnetka: The history and significance of an educational experiment.* Englewood Cliffs, NJ: Prentice Hall.

WISCONSIN V. YODER

The 1972 Supreme Court decision in the case of *Wisconsin v. Yoder* is the definitive Court case involving Amish and Mennonite education. The case answered two fundamental questions: Should the Amish be permitted to have their own schools, and may they limit school-based education to the completion of eighth grade? Key individuals involved in the case included William Ball, attorney for the Amish; Rev. William Lindholm of the National Committee for Amish Religious Freedom (NCARF); John Hostetler, witness for the defense; Jonas Yoder, defendant; and Chief Justice Warren Burger.

The Amish

The Amish and the Old Order Mennonites (OOM) are Christian groups with common roots in the Anabaptists of 16th-century Europe. They believe in plain dress, pacifism, and close-knit communities. They reject many aspects of the modern materialistic world and value manual trades such as baking, quilting, farming, and carpentry. The Amish refrain from hiring lawyers to settle arguments. They are resolute in their belief that formal school-based education (book learning) should be completed by the eighth grade. During adolescence, Amish youth will be engaged in learning by doing and will work alongside their parents to learn all of the skills required to support a family and become contributing members of Amish society.

The Case

Amish families from Iowa (seeking to escape the ongoing school controversy in Hazleton—requiring children to attend public schools) and Ohio arrived in New Glarus, Wisconsin, in the 1960s. The Amish enrolled their children in public school but eventually became concerned about several aspects of the school, including attire required in physical education classes. As a result, Amish parents started their own school. Public school officials hoped to convince the Amish to send their children to public school for at least several days at the beginning of the school term so that the school district would receive state funds based on their attendance. The Amish refused to go along with this scheme; therefore public officials decided to pursue truancy charges. Three Amish and Mennonite farmers were cited for violating Wisconsin's compulsory school attendance laws because the children (eighth-grade graduates) in question were under the age of 16 and not attending a public school. Rev. Lindholm and NCARF came to the aid of these men and hired attorneys to defend them.

The initial trial in this case took place on April 2, 1969. The key witness for the Amish was John Hostetler, Ph.D., professor at Temple University and noted authority on the Amish faith. During cross-examination, the prosecuting attorney attempted to refute Hostetler's testimony. Because this tactic was unsuccessful, the attorney used a series of questions to corner Hostetler. Hostetler, aware of the approach, testified that there is a great deal of difference in definitions of education. The attorney replied that education is designed so students can take their place in the world. After a pause, Hostetler stated, "It depends on which

world." Amish education was to prepare students for a life in Amish society and eventually heaven. Hostetler had made an important distinction. The Amish fathers were found guilty, but the testimony of Hostetler recounting Amish beliefs was fundamental and would serve as a key element of the defense in future trials. The case was appealed at the Wisconsin district court level where the lower court ruling was affirmed.

Attorney Ball, with support from NCARF, appealed the case to the Wisconsin Supreme Court. This time the ruling was in favor of the Amish; however, the state of Wisconsin appealed the decision to the U.S. Supreme Court. Oral arguments were heard by the high Court on December 8, 1971.

In May of 1972, the Supreme Court voted 7–0 (two Justices did not participate) that the First and Fourteenth amendments prevented states from compelling Amish children to attend public school through age 16. Chief Justice Warren Burger stated that the Amish objection to formal education beyond eighth grade is grounded in central religious beliefs. The Amish object to high school because of its emphasis on individual achievement, as well as many of the values in the written and unwritten curriculum; all of which are in distinct divergence from Amish principles.

Though voting for the Amish, Justice Douglas wrote a dissent because he was concerned about Amish children. He believed that not requiring children to attend high school would limit their career aspirations. Chief Justice Burger disagreed and wrote that there is no evidence that individuals who leave Amish life are a burden to society, nor are there data indicating that the Amish values of patience, reliability, self-reliance, and hard work vary from the skills needed and valued by employers. Further, there is no evidence to suggest that making Amish youth attend public school until age 16 would improve any of these values. Finally, Justice Burger noted that while one might be concerned for the children, it was the parents who faced incarceration.

This decisive verdict gave the Amish and the Old Order Mennonites freedom to maintain their own schools while limiting school-based formal education to eight grades. As a result, there are now more than 1,400 Amish and 300 OOM schools scattered throughout the countryside of 28 states.

Mark W. Dewalt

See also Alliance for the Separation of School & State; Amish and Mennonite Schools; *Pierce v. Society of Sisters;* Separation of Church and State

Further Readings

Hostetler, J. (1963). *Amish society.* Baltimore: Johns Hopkins University Press.

Kraybill, D. (1993). *The Amish and the state.* Baltimore: Johns Hopkins University Press.

Peters, S. (2003). *The* Yoder *case: Religious freedom, education and parental rights.* Lawrence: University Press of Kansas.

WOMEN IN EDUCATIONAL LEADERSHIP

As professions, school teaching and school administration have evolved over the history of schools in the United States as two separate and distinct roles with separate professional foundations and doorways to access. On the surface they seem to have a common goal—children's academic achievement. Classroom teaching, however, has been women's work and school administration men's work, with only minor deviations throughout U.S. history. One exception is the fact that teachers in the earliest schools were all men because only men were employed in public roles outside the home. A second exception, which did not last long, occurred when women dominated some administrative categories for a short period in the early 20th century. These were White women—as will be described throughout this entry. The lives of Black and other minority women educators have been neglected by most education historians, and data on their lives are sparse.

Understanding when, why, and how some women successfully crossed the boundary and entered the traditional male world of school administration may contribute to a wider understanding of how dissent has contributed to the transformation of schooling over time. Women have dominated the demographic profile of the teaching profession. Superintendents come from the teaching profession, but women have not been represented in the superintendency in any way close to their share of the teaching profession.

Historical Perspective

The social history of the two sexes plays a role in this trend. Scholars in western Europe in the 18th century characterized men as essentially rational, logical, and authoritative, with an underlying sexuality that was in need of control. Women, on the other hand, were considered to be essentially nurturing figures, emotional, caring, and a necessary complement to men. The "cult of true womanhood" limited women to the domestic realm and ascribed to them the virtues of piety, purity, and submissiveness. Their "angelic" natures could be called on to control the brutishness of men. Man's world was the cold world of business, politics, and science. Men were rough, tough, and less controlled than were women. These strong assumptions ruled what it meant to be male and female during the 18th and early 19th centuries in what is now the United States; and, the same assumptions were manifest in the roles men and women played throughout school history.

Until almost the close of the 18th century, all classroom teachers were men. Teaching was an occupation, a public role, outside the home. Schooling was only informal and locally governed. As the colonial period came to a close, some women began to teach a few children at a time in their homes, expanding their domestic roles into those of "teacher homemakers" in "dame schools." They supervised children, in a hierarchy of power, the only group with less power than the women themselves.

The Nineteenth Century

As business and industry grew in the 1820s and beyond, men who might have been teachers chose other occupations. School boards began to face shortages of teachers. Women could be moved into the schools; they were a relatively cheap labor source, and they retained their "natural" role as caring and nurturing mothers.

Catharine Beecher was a strong proponent of women as teachers although she was not among those who would now be looked back on as a feminist. She believed women's true sphere of life was in the role of nurturer and caregiver. Beecher opposed women working in factories and mills; but classroom teaching, to her, was acceptable. Ironically, Beecher's own advocacy might have been a violation of "women's sphere" to some extent, although she avoided public speeches—instead seeking out men to deliver the words she had written.

Without alternatives for financial self-support, some women chose teaching as preferable to depending on their families. (During the early 20th century, only unmarried women were employed as teachers; the legal prohibition against married women in the classroom was consistent with the domestic stereotype of women's "natural place" in the home.)

Ella Flagg Young: A Transitional Figure

Until 1866, women were not openly and freely admitted to the National Education Association (NEA), the national organization of teachers. It was a men's organization and women were admitted as members only if sponsored by male mentors. Over time, however, men's control over teaching and administration was diminished—caused by economic need—and a shortage of male educators ensued as men's options expanded. By 1910, women had become sufficiently accepted into the profession that Ella Flagg Young became president of NEA. Her accomplishment along with the influx of women into the educational profession raised fears among some men that the NEA would be dominated by women teachers. The old stereotypes based on what were believed to be biological sex differences were not easily thrown aside.

Young also was hired as the first superintendent of a large urban school district by the city of Chicago that same year, 1910. This same year approximately 9% of superintendents in the country were female. Jackie Blount documents the dramatic gains women had made in a relatively short period, since the 1850s—from being relegated solely to the home to holding 70% of all teaching positions. In 1905, 61.7% of elementary principalships were held by women. On the other hand, it was not until 70 years after Flagg was hired that Chicago hired a second woman as superintendent.

David Tyack and Elizabeth Hansot linked the bureaucratization of teaching in large urban schools after 1830 to strengthening the gendered division of labor. Male managers were seen as "natural" in

that role, informed by science and reason. Female teachers were also "natural" in their roles as nurturers of children. As leaders, men had the authority to supervise women in what men intended to be highly controlled institutions. Women experienced both stress and relief as a result. Not only did they feel pressure to become increasingly more scientific in their nurturing, child rearing, and housekeeping, but also the increased layers of bureaucratic administrative structure gave women additional options for administrative jobs.

The Twentieth Century

As women made gains in teaching and administration in the early 1900s, fears that schools would become too "feminized" influenced hiring practices. Female teachers were a majority in both elementary and secondary schools. The majority of high school graduates were women. A movement of male educators in the NEA sought unity with boards of education. They attempted to ensure that boards would continue to hire women only at lower-level positions. They pressured employers to favor men as both teachers and administrators on the grounds that young boys needed men as their role models.

In the early 1920s, U.S. society was focused on the growth of business; Americans began to believe in the business model as a way to run the schools. Corporate values drove the organization of businesses as well as of schools, and men were at the helm of both. Hierarchical bureaucratic structures grew out of the earlier writings of Max Weber—an attempt to explain how society might work most efficiently. A specialized division of labor became the way to obtain effective outcomes and increase productivity.

Industrial organizations thrived, and schools adopted the same philosophy in their attempts to become "modern" and "scientific." Organizations that were impersonal and offered managers greater control were valued as rationalist, legitimate, and authoritative. The corporate model valued those qualities assumed to be inherent among men and missing among women—rationality, logic, toughness, and physical strength.

The period between 1900 and 1930 is sometimes called a golden age for women in school administration. Women dominated some educational leadership roles. By 1928, White women held 55% of elementary principalships, 25% of county superintendencies, 8% of secondary principalships, and 1.6% of district superintendencies. These gains were not sustained after 1930. The persistent pattern of male dominance reinforced beliefs about women that both women and men accepted. Women were not as strong as men, could not make "tough" decisions, and were unreliable as employees because they could leave their jobs to marry or have children. For men, sponsorship, not competition, became a common pathway into administrative jobs, a practice that lowered the probability of women and minorities being hired for leadership positions.

From the 1930s on, a human relations model of organizations grew and gained credibility. As a consequence, the heavy dominance of logic, science, and objectivity began to weaken. Organizational theorists increasingly recognized that informal dynamics play an important role in social organizations. Personal relationships (in addition to hierarchical structure) were recognized as part of what makes organizations work. These new insights paralleled those qualities assumed to be women's natural traits. In the 1950s a psychotherapeutic ideology continued this trend, replacing the pre–World War II stress on efficiency and bureaucratic control.

Jobs for women had been more available during the 1940s as men went off to war. The end of World War II and the G.I. Bill moved men into school administration. The rise of the "organizational man" in the 1950s signaled a more organized set of mechanisms for regulating business, industry, private institutions, and then school organizations. The "man in the gray flannel suit" image emerged as a symbol of the conformity and narrowness of a rigidly structured business world.

The 1950s brought other concerns. To these unhealthy consequences of the "organizational man" bureaucracies were added concerns about student achievement. The "race to space" between the United States and the Soviet Union highlighted what were perceived as weaknesses in U.S. students' preparation in math and science after *Sputnik,* the world's first artificial satellite, was launched. Policymakers found themselves in a world of growing global competition and threat. Schools were forced to react.

On top of those dual concerns, the dawn of the 1960s was about to bring in a new era of gendered social changes that hinted at newly expanded opportunities for women—the heart of the teaching force. Ultimately, however, few opportunities would materialize in school administration at the highest levels of school leadership, the superintendency.

The burgeoning women's movement in the 1960s challenged the stereotypical expectations for women. Job opportunities expanded beyond the home and the fields of nursing, teaching, and jobs as secretaries or librarians. Women entered medicine and law in greater and greater numbers. Policy changes in the form of pay guaranteed to be equal with men's, equal educational opportunities, and access to reproductive rights and more effective means of birth control—all changed the landscape of women's lives. Many were drawn away from teaching. Many aspired to leadership roles in education as well as to other male-dominated professions.

The new humanistic organizational structures of the 1960s and beyond might have been a foundation on which the number of women in school leadership ranks could grow, if, in fact, it is logical to assume some "female" parallel to such an organizational style. Such was not the case. The same trends that showed men dominating at the highest organizational levels early in educational history persisted in the 1960s, 1970s, and beyond. In the principalship, for example, this trend was clear. Women held 55% of elementary principalships in 1928, 41% in 1948, 38% in 1958, 22.4% in 1968, and 19.6% in 1973. In the 1970s and 1980s, the greatest proportion of women "administrators" were in central office positions, not "line" positions. In the early 2000s, approximately 12% of women were in district superintendent positions.

Conclusion

According to educational feminists, a more "female" organizational style seemed to be only a specific leadership strategy, not a belief embedded throughout the system that valued women's experiences and their ways of knowing and leading sufficiently to convince employers to hire women for the highest levels of school leadership. On the other hand, perhaps it is unfair to ascribe a gender dimension to any organizational milieu. A less bureaucratic and more relational organization might be as much male as it is female, if one moves beyond the gendered social history of the United States.

Women earn more than half the Ph.D.s awarded in school administration programs, but still lag far behind men in gaining the superintendent license and gaining the superintendent position. The socialization, recruitment, hiring, and mentoring of men into top school leadership positions continue in the 21st century. The deeply embedded cultural barriers to placing large numbers of women into superintendency positions seem, so far, to be insurmountable.

Carolyn S. Ridenour

See also American Association of School Administrators (AASA); Council of the Great City Schools; Equal Education Opportunity; National Council of Professors of Educational Administration (NCPEA); National Organization for Women (NOW); Title IX

Further Readings

Blount, J. M. (1998). *Destined to rule the schools: Women and the superintendency, 1873–1995.* Albany: State University of New York Press.

Ortiz, F. I., & Marshall, C. (1988) Women in educational administration. In N. J. Boyan (Ed.), *Handbook of research on educational administration* (pp. 123–141). New York: Longman.

Reiger, K. (1993). The gender dynamics of organizations: A historical account. In J. Blackmore & J. Kenway (Eds.), *Gender matters in educational administration and policy: A feminist introduction* (pp. 17–26). London: Falmer.

Shakeshaft, C. (1989). *Women in educational administration.* Newbury Park, CA: Sage.

Shakeshaft, C. (1999). The struggle to create a more gender-inclusive profession. In J. Murphy & K. S. Louis (Eds.), *Handbook of research on educational administration* (2nd ed., pp. 99–118). San Francisco: Jossey-Bass.

Tyack, D., & Hansot, E. (1982). *Managers of virtue: Public school leadership in America, 1820–1980.* New York: Basic Books.

YEAR-ROUND SCHOOLS

Year-round schooling is an educational reform effort that has made inroads into the traditional agrarian calendar but has not had the widespread implementation its advocates claim it deserves. Opponents argue that it is important to maintain 3 months in the summer free of schooling, to allow children and youths some respite from highly structured activities, to allow older students opportunities for summer employment, and in order to make sure family vacation schedules are not disrupted. At the same time, representatives of the vacation industry, including theme parks and other venues, actively lobby to ensure that their interests are not disadvantaged. A casual Internet search will disclose that year-round schooling is a significant topic of interest; among the many references available may be found arguments both pro and con.

Background

According to the National Association for Year-Round Education (NAYRE), the movement for year-round schooling is growing. Information provided by NAYRE indicates that nearly 3,000 schools had year-round education programs in 2006, with an enrollment of over 2 million students. This represents only about 4% of all schools, but it is nearly four times the number of students in year-round schools just a decade or so ago.

Many schools are successfully increasing student learning by restructuring the school year and by lengthening the school day and/or school year. It is important to consider restructuring the school day and year as national expectations increase and as academic standards continue to rise. This is particularly true in our lowest performing schools where many students will never catch up unless they spend more time on learning and are given substantial individual support and intervention.

Contrary to widespread belief, year-round school does not inevitably mean less break time. The conventional school-year calendar, with a September start date and a June ending that allows for a 2- to 3- month summer break, was planned when countless American families were earning a living in agriculture or managing a family business. At that time, school calendars were developed around students working in the family, especially so that children could be home to help during the busy summer months. Schools remained in sync with the agrarian calendar even after family farms declined, in part because teaching and learning during the sweltering summer days without air conditioning were practically impossible.

Although year-round schooling exists in many diverse forms, the process, in effect, involves restructuring the conventional school calendar so that the extended summer vacation is replaced by numerous smaller breaks evenly spaced throughout the year. As early as the 1900s, American schools began experimenting with a switch to year-round schedules. But the idea did not begin to catch on until the 1970s and 1980s, when studies began to show that U.S. students were scoring poorly on national and international examinations.

The term *year-round schooling* can be misleading; it causes students to imagine that they would have to say goodbye forever to summer traditions, such as summer camp or seaside vacations. In reality, students in most American year-round school districts spend a similar amount of days in class as do students in traditional calendar schools—the days are just arranged differently, with smaller, more frequent breaks throughout the year.

Advantages

Over the years many school districts adopted year-round calendars, but a significant number of them have switched back. One of the reasons was that school officials were unable to determine whether academic performance improved, and they were unable to gain the support of the school community; in the end it was simply too complicated to overcome past practice. By contrast, however, a few districts have had successful year-round schooling experiences.

For some districts, student learning is not the sole rationale for adoption of the year-round calendar. Switching to a year-round schedule on a multitrack system (groups of students stagger start dates and/or times) allows overcrowded districts to avoid the expense of new construction. Some critics challenge the idea that year-round schedules improve student learning and have raised other concerns as well, especially for districts on both the standard and year-round schedule. For example, a family with children in a district that had both calendars may have a difficult time arranging for family activities, because the children may not be on the same schedule.

In addition, extracurricular activities in competing districts might have different schedules, resulting in certain activities being scheduled during breaks for other districts. Students who participate in extracurricular activities on a year-round schedule may find it difficult to coordinate practices and game times.

Many school districts have adopted year-round schooling only in the elementary schools, since most students' schedules become more complicated as they advance through the grades. Also, older students have a harder time adjusting to such a radical change, since they are accustomed to long summer breaks. Many high school students worry that they would not be able to take a summer job to earn the income to help make family expenses or to save for college education.

Studies have addressed the issue of the quality of time as it relates to student learning. Research on time on task and academic learning time has focused on the relationship between the amount of time students spend engaged in academic activities and academic growth. Studies in this area have demonstrated that simply exposing students to more classroom time may not be sufficient to affect learning. Several literature reviews on year-round education have been conducted, however, with the consensus that outcomes of year-round education are at least as positive as (or better than) those achieved under the traditional school calendar.

Future Challenges

Although researchers have not adequately addressed the reasons why achievement may be slightly higher in year-round schools, one possibility is that year-round schools can use intercessions to provide remediation and/or enrichment activities, thereby increasing students' exposure to the curriculum. One researcher found that students, on average, lose 1 month of learning over a long summer break. Students in year-round schools tend to lose only about half that much. But researchers caution that proponents of year-round schooling should not be too extravagant in their claims.

Movement toward adopting year-round schools is generally credited to three recognized advantages of a year-round schedule: improved student-learner success; greater agreement among parents, educators, and students; and less capital outlay. Improved learning and greater agreement among stakeholders are frequently mentioned in combination with all year-round schools, while savings in capital outlay are usually linked only with multitrack year-round schools, as the multitrack process can help delay the need to build new facilities in districts experiencing increases in student enrollment. Although currently there is limited public pressure for changes in the PreK–12 academic calendar, year-round schooling may be a superior model for the contemporary American lifestyle.

C. Daniel Raisch

See also Accountability Era; Co-Curricular Activities; Equity; Extracurricular Activities; High-Stakes Testing; School Choice; School Climate; Transportation

Further Readings

Alcorn, R. D. (1992). Test scores: Can year-round schools raise them? *Thrust for Educational Leadership, 21*(6), 12–15.

Ballinger, C., & Kneese, C. (2006). *School calendar reform: Learning in all seasons.* Lanham, MD: Rowman & Littlefield Education.

Glass, G. V. (2002). Time for school: Its duration and allocation. In A. Molnar (Ed.), *School reform proposals: The research evidence* (pp. 79–93). Greenwich, CT: Information Age Publishing.

McMillen, B. J. (2006). *Academic achievement in year-round schools.* Raleigh: North Carolina Department of Instruction, Division of Accountability Services.

National Association for Year-Round Education. (2009). Statistical summaries of year-round education programs: 2006–2007. Retrieved July 31, 2008, from http://nayre.org

Wintre, M. G. (1986). Challenging the assumptions of generalized academic loss over summer. *Journal of Educational Research, 79*(5), 308–312.

YOUNG, ELLA FLAGG (1845–1918)

The first woman to become superintendent of a major city school system, Ella Flagg Young was an advocate for teachers throughout her long career. A reform-oriented leader in the Progressive movement, Young worked closely with John Dewey at the University of Chicago, earning her Ph.D. when she was 55 years old. She led the Chicago schools during a tumultuous period when progressivism warred with industrialization as a model for education. Her tenure as superintendent was marked by a number of reforms, but also by conflict with the conservative Board of Education.

Ella Flagg Young graduated from the Chicago Normal School and began teaching in Chicago in 1862, when she was 18 years old. Her career in administration began 3 years later when she was appointed director of practice-teaching classrooms. During the next 14 years she served as a high school

math teacher and as principal of two Chicago schools. Young's reputation as a democratic leader grew as she encouraged her teachers to develop their own teaching methods and established faculty study groups to enrich the curriculum.

In 1887 Young was promoted to assistant district superintendent, a new position in the rapidly growing Chicago system. In this position she continued her democratic education practices, including popular teacher institutes on a variety of topics. Young herself often led the institutes, but she also invited faculty from the pedagogy and philosophy departments at the University of Chicago to speak. She used the institutes to advance her ideas about democracy in education and encouraged teachers to take an active role in shaping curriculum. The Chicago Teachers' Federation, organized in 1897 and the first teacher advocacy organization in the United States, was started by teachers who had been influenced by Young's ideas.

Her tenure as assistant district superintendent ended in 1899 when she resigned after a conservative and autocratic superintendent was appointed. She left the school system and went to the University of Chicago to study with John Dewey in the new Department of Education. Within a year she had completed her Ph.D. and joined the faculty. Young's dissertation, published in 1900 as *Isolation in the Schools,* laid out the stark contrast between the industrial model of education, with its clock-driven mechanization and rigid bureaucracy, and the humanistic and democratic Progressive model. Dewey later said that during Young's time at the University, she acquired a theoretical base for the ideas she had developed earlier through practical experience. In return, Dewey learned how the theories he was developing at the University actually translated into educational practice. Young remained at the University as a professor of education for 5 years, administering Dewey's Laboratory School, editing a journal for teachers, and developing new courses. She left the University in 1904 when John Dewey's philosophical conflicts with University President William R. Harper led to his resignation. Dewey went to Columbia University and Young went abroad for a year.

In 1905 she returned to Chicago as principal of the Chicago Normal School, where she put into practice the reforms and scientific approach to education espoused by Dewey. Young restructured the Normal School and improved relations among the faculty, students, and community. Her pragmatic approach to education stressed content as well as pedagogy, and she cautioned her teachers to be concerned with both *what* students learned and *how* they learned it.

In 1909 the Chicago school system was in turmoil. Conflict between the Chicago Teachers' Federation (CTF) and the Board of Education had intensified until Superintendent Edwin G. Cooley resigned in 1909. After 5 months of debate, the Board of Education voted unanimously to appoint Young as his replacement. Young announced that democracy would be the hallmark of her tenure as superintendent and added that she would resign if the board tried to prevent the open, collaborative style of leadership that she espoused.

True to her commitment, Young moved swiftly to eliminate the secret evaluations that governed promotions, recommended salary increases, and began working with teachers to revise the curriculum. Over the next 2-1/2 years she expanded the manual arts curriculum, started a technical high school for girls, introduced programs in ethics and morality (including sex education), and modeled the elementary curriculum after Dewey's lab school. Her reforms were so well received that teachers, principals, and board members united to support her election as the first woman president of the National Education Association in 1910.

The following year a new board, less sympathetic to Young's reforms, was appointed. The board began to chip away at her authority and she became increasingly frustrated. At the same time, she found herself in conflict with the CTF over the administration of the pension plan. Finally, in 1913, Young submitted her resignation. She was persuaded to withdraw it, but a few months later was forced out of office in what can only be described as a coup by her enemies on the board. Public outrage erupted and pro-Young rallies were held all over Chicago. The board was forced to reinstate her, and she continued as superintendent until her retirement in 1915, but her effectiveness was diminished. She continued to work with the NEA as an advocate for progressive education until her death in 1918.

Elizabeth P. Harper

See also Dewey, John; Haley, Margaret; Progressive Education; Unionization of Teachers

Further Readings

Blount, J. M. (2008). Ella Flagg Young (1845–1918). *Education encyclopedia.* Retrieved August 31, 2008, from http://education.stateuniversity.com/pages/2555/Young-Ella-Flagg-1845-1918.html

Schugurensky, D. (Ed.). (2002). Ella Flagg Young, first female superintendent of a major city school system. *History of Education: Selected moments of the 20th century.* Retrieved August 31, 2008, from http://www.oise.utoronto.ca/research/edu20/moments/1909ella.html

Smith, J. K. (1979). *Ella Flagg Young: Portrait of a leader.* Ames, IA: Educational Studies Press.

Smith, J. K. (1980, Spring). Progressive school administration: Ella Flagg Young and the Chicago schools, 1905–1915. *Journal of the Illinois State Historical Society.* Retrieved August 31, 2008, from http://dig.lib.niu.edu/ISHS/ishs-1980spring/ishs-1980spring27.pdf

University of Chicago Library. (1991). The university and the city: A centennial view of the University of Chicago. *University of Chicago centennial catalogs.* Retrieved August 31, 2008, from http://www.lib.uchicago.edu/e/spcl/centcat/city/citych3_10.html

ZELMAN V. SIMMONS-HARRIS

In *Zelman v. Simmons-Harris* (2002), a bitterly divided U.S. Supreme Court upheld the voucher part of the Ohio Pilot Project Scholarship Program (OPPSP) under which qualified poor students can attend private schools, including ones that are religiously affiliated, at public expense. In so doing, the Court granted poor inner-city parents the opportunity to send their children to the schools of their choice.

Zelman traces its origins to 1992 when Governor George Voinovich asked a panel of experts to investigate whether a voucher program could be implemented in Ohio. In March 1995 the Ohio General Assembly adopted the OPPSP in response to a federal trial court order requiring judicial supervision and management of the Cleveland school district by the state superintendent of public instruction.

The primary goal of the statute was "to provide for a number of students...to receive scholarships to attend alternative schools, and for an equal number of students to receive tutorial assistance grants while attending public school" (Ohio Rev. Code Ann. § 3313.975(A)).

Under the law, students could use vouchers to attend nonpublic schools in Cleveland or public schools in contiguous public school districts.

At its heart, the OPPSP created publicly funded scholarships for students from poor families. In order to avoid First Amendment concerns, the voucher checks were made out to parents or guardians who were to endorse them before the schools could use the funds. Other parts of the law were designed to provide greater choices to parents and children via the creation of community and magnet schools; the law also contains antidiscrimination provisions. Since its implementation, only private schools participated in the OPPSP because public schools in suburban Cleveland chose not to participate in the program.

The voucher program survived an initial challenge in state court when a trial judge granted the state's motion for summary judgment on the basis that since the aid to private schools participating in the OPPSP was indirect, the statute did not violate the Establishment Clause (*Gatton v. Goff*, 1996). On further review, an intermediate appellate court reversed in determining that the statute had the impermissible effect of advancing religion (*Simmons-Harris v. Goff*, 1997). Then, the Supreme Court of Ohio decided that although the OPPSP passed analysis under *Lemon v. Kurtzman* (1971), it violated the state constitutional provision that requires every statute to have only one subject; the court therefore invalidated the law (*Simmons-Harris v. Goff*, 1999). The court stayed enforcement of its order until June 30, 1999, to avoid disrupting the then current school year. The General Assembly of Ohio addressed the court's concerns and reenacted the statute on June 29, 1999.

When opponents again filed suit, a federal trial court in Ohio, relying largely on the U.S. Supreme Court's judgment in *Committee for Public Education and Religious Liberty v. Nyquist* (1973). In *Nyquist* the Court invalidated a program from

New York that, in part, provided tuition for low-income children whose parents wished to send them to religious schools, enjoined the operation of the revised statute in maintaining that it violated the Establishment Clause (*Simmons-Harris v. Zelman,* 1999). A divided Sixth Circuit, also applying *Nyquist,* affirmed that the OPPSP had the impermissible effect of advancing religion (*Simmons-Harris v. Zelman,* 2000).

On further review, the Supreme Court reversed the judgment of the Sixth Circuit and upheld the constitutionality of the OPPSP. The Court began by considering "whether the government acted with the purpose of advancing or inhibiting religions [and] whether the aid has the 'effect' of advancing or inhibiting religion" (p. 649). Recognizing the lack of a dispute over the program's valid secular purpose in providing programming for poor children in a failing school system, the Court addressed whether the program had the forbidden "effect" of advancing or inhibiting religion. The Court reasoned that the voucher program was constitutional because, as part of the state's far-reaching attempt to provide greater educational opportunities in a failing school system, it allocated aid pursuant to neutral secular criteria that neither favored nor disfavored religion, was made available to both religious and secular beneficiaries on a nondiscriminatory basis, and offered assistance directly to a broad class of citizens who directed the aid to religious schools based entirely on their own genuine and independent private choices.

The Supreme Court was untroubled by the dissent's fear that most of the participating schools were religiously affiliated insofar as this situation arose because surrounding public schools refused to take part in the program. The Court also ruled that since the OPPSP differed significantly from the program in *Nyquist,* the lower courts misplaced their reliance on that case. The Court concluded that since it was following an unbroken line of its own cases supporting true private choice that provided benefits directly to a wide range of needy private individuals, its only choice was to uphold the constitutionality of the voucher program.

As significant as *Zelman* was, it is important to keep in mind that its impact is probably very limited. Put another way, insofar as post-*Zelman* litigation challenging vouchers has focused largely on state constitutional grounds since they are typically more stringent than under the federal constitution, it is unlikely that vouchers will spread to other school systems.

Charles J. Russo

See also Alliance for School Choice; Alliance for the Separation of School & State; Charter Schools; *Lemon v. Kurtzman;* No Child Left Behind Act (NCLB); Vouchers

Further Readings

Committee for Public Education and Religious Liberty v. Nyquist, 413 U.S. 756 (1973).
Gatton v. Goff, 1996 WL 466499 (Ohio Common Pleas July 31, 1996).
Lemon v. Kurtzman, 403 U.S. 602 (1971).
Ohio Revised Code Annotated, as cited.
Simmons-Harris v. Goff, 1997 WL 217583 (Ohio Ct. App. Ct. 1997), aff'd in part, rev'd in part, *Simmons-Harris v. Goff,* 711 N.E.2d 203 (Ohio 1999).
Simmons-Harris v. Zelman, 7 F. Supp.2d 834 (N.D. Ohio 1999), 234 F.3d 945 (6th Cir. 2000).
Zelman v. Simmons-Harris, 536 U.S. 639 (2002).

Index

Entry titles and entry page numbers are in **bold**.

Ivar Lovass's work in, **1**:81
mental retardation mislabeling of, **1**:81
research-based practices regarding, **1**:81–82

Babbitt, Irving, **2**:740
BAEO. *See* **Black Alliance for Educational Options** (BAEO)
Bagley, William C., **1**:352, **2**:740, **2**:885
See also **Social efficiency**
Bailey and Sullivan Leadership Institute (BSLI), **1**:102
Bakke, Regents of the University of California v., **2**:548
Bakke v. Regents of the University of California, **1**:320
Baldwin, William H., **2**:846
Ball, William B., 1:83–84
   Amish parents exempted from compulsory attendance supported by, **1**:83–84
   Bob Jones University v. U.S. and, **1**:83
   constitutional religious liberty expertise of, **1**:83
   Employment Division v. Smith and, **1**:84
   freedom of religion and religious expression issue and, **1**:83
   Lemon v. Kurtzman and, **1**:83, **1**:84
   parental right to choose religious education issue and, **1**:83
   Roman Catholic religious views of, **1**:83–84
   tax credits, vouchers, nonintrusive state issues supported by, **1**:83
   tax credits for students in religious schools issue and, **1**:84
   Wisconsin v. Yoder and, **1**:83
   works published by, **1**:84
   Zobrest v. Catalina Foothills School District and, **1**:83
Bandura, Albert, **1**:268
Banking method of education, **1**:225, **1**:392
Banks, James Albert, **1**:19, **1**:250, **2**:581
Barnard, Henry, **1**:87, **1**:191, **2**:879
   See also **Teacher institutes**
Barnard, James, **1**:259
Barnett, West Virginia v., **1**:162
Beard, Charles, **1**:233, **2**:841
Becker, Wesley, **1**:276–277
Beckner, William M., 1:84–86
   Beckner Amendment (Kentucky constitution) and, **1**:84, **1**:85
   Bill of Rights of Kentucky Constitution and, **1**:84
   Catholic *vs.* Protestant conflict and, **1**:85
   common-school reform supported by, **1**:85
   early years and education of, **1**:84–85
   Edwards Law and, **1**:85
   parents' rights supported by, **1**:85–86
   Roman Catholic rights supported by, **1**:85
   state mandated public school attendance issue and, **1**:84
   state's rights, slavery views of, **1**:85
Beecher, Catharine, 1:86–87
   Lyman Beecher (father) and, **1**:86
   books written by, **1**:86–87
   college-level education for women supported by, **1**:86–87
   "difference feminism" concept supported by, **1**:86
   domestic sciences as woman's profession and, **1**:368
   Essay on the Education of Female Teachers written by, **1**:86

Hartford Female Seminary founded by, **1**:6, **1**:86
A Treatise on Domesticity written by, **1**:368
women as common school teachers supported by, **1**:86–87, **1**:368, **2**:945–946
Behaviorism, 1:87–91
   A-B-C concept (antecedent stimulus, behavior, consequence) and, **1**:88–89
   applied behavior analysis application of, **1**:90–91
   behavior as a process *vs.* "thing" and, **1**:90
   cause and effect relationships focus of, **1**:90
   classical conditioning and, **1**:88
   constructivism *vs.*, **1**:215–216
   definition of, **1**:87
   determinism element of, **1**:90
   direct instruction methods, student achievement and, **1**:89, **1**:276
   education of visually impaired and, **1**:328–329
   empiricism element of, **1**:90
   experimental analysis of behavior research area and, **1**:90
   extinction consequence and, **1**:88–89
   functional relations element of, **1**:90
   history of, **1**:87–90
   individualized instruction, self-paced learning and, **2**:513
   introspection process and, **1**:87
   Journal of Applied Behavior Analysis (JABA) and, **1**:91
   Journal of the Experimental Analysis of Behavior and, **1**:90
   Abraham Maslow's criticism of, **2**:549
   methodological behaviorists and, **1**:91
   operant behavior and, **1**:88
   Ivan Pavlov's methodology and, **1**:88
   philosophic doubt element of, **1**:90
   punishment consequence and, **1**:88
   purpose and structure of, **1**:90–91
   radical behaviorists and, **1**:91
   rate of response as dependent variable and, **1**:88
   reinforcement consequence and, **1**:88
   scientific manipulation element of, **1**:90
   B. F. Skinner's work in, **1**:xlvi, **1**:88
   special education and, **1**:89–90
   stimulus-response relationship focus of, **1**:88, **1**:90
   student learning and teaching application of, **1**:87
   three-way contingency, voluntary behavior and environment relationship and, **1**:88–89, **1**:90–91
   John B. Watson's work in, **1**:87–88
   See also **Assertive discipline; Autism; Direct instruction; Skinner, B. F.; Thorndike, Edward L.**
Belk v. Charlotte-Mecklenburg Board of Education, **1**:267, **2**:866
Bell, Alexander Graham, **1**:64, **1**:396
Bell, Derrick, **1**:116
Bell, Grove City v., **2**:895
Bellevue Hospital, first nursing school, **1**:xlv
Belton, Gebhardt v., **1**:24
Bender, William N., **1**:273
Bennett, William, **1**:239, **2**:579
Bennett Law, 1:91–93
   compulsory attendance issue and, **1**:91–92
   Desmond Law replacement of, **1**:93

English *vs.* German language instruction issue and, **1**:92, **2**:532–533

Protestant support of, **1**:92

Wisconsin Catholic-Lutheran alliance opposition to, **1**:92, **2**:532–533

Wisconsin 1890 gubernatorial election and, **1**:92–93

See also **Catholic schools; Lutheran schools**

Berkeley plan, **1**:93–95

ability grouping system element of, **1**:94, **1**:95

Brown v. Board of Education of Topeka, Kansas and, **1**:93

busing element of, **1**:94–95

Congress of Racial Equality proposal and, **1**:94

de facto segregation of Berkeley schools and, **1**:94

desegregation issue and, **1**:93–95

John Hadsell, Hadsell Report and, **1**:94

NAACP and, **1**:93

Princeton Plan and, **1**:94

redistricting changes element of, **1**:94–95

C. H. Wennerberg and, **1**:93–94

Bestor, Arthur, **1**:352, **2**:740

Bethune, Mary McLeod, 1:95–96

awards and honors received by, **1**:96

Bethune-Cookman Collegiate Institute and, **1**:96

Daytona Normal Industrial School for Negro Girls founded by, **1**:95–96

early years and education of, **1**:95

education, business, and social change accomplishments of, **1**:96

National Council of Negro Women's work of, **1**:96

Bilingual education, 1:96–100

benefits *vs.* disadvantages of, **1**:99–100

Bilingual Education Act (1968) and, **1**:284–285, **1**:338, **2**:654

bilingual teachers requirement of, **1**:97

compensatory education programs and, **1**:195

definition of, **1**:96–97

desegregation and mainstreaming issues and, **1**:97–98

ESEA and, **1**:284

Lau v. Nichols ruling regarding, **1**:97

minority languages maintenance and, **1**:98–99

National Research Council study of, **1**:100

policy implications of, **1**:99–100

rationales in support of, **1**:97

remedial purpose of, **1**:97

George Sánchez's work in, **1**:98

segregated education settings, negative effects of, **1**:98

"separate but equal" issue and, **1**:98

transitional bilingual education (TBE) term and, **1**:97

two-way bilingual programs *vs.*, **1**:97

See also **Civil Rights Act of 1964; Cristo Rey** (Network) **schools; Education of the Deaf; English as a second language (ESL); Hispanic/Latino education;** *Lau v. Nichols;* **Lutheran schools; National Council of La Raza (NCLR); Native American education**

Bill and Melinda Gates Foundation. *See* **Gates Foundation**

Binet, Alfred, **1**:319, **1**:407, **2**:853, **2**:884

Black, Hugo

Central School District v. Allen dissenting opinion written by, **1**:144

Engel v. Vitale court's opinion written by, **1**:344

Everson v. Board of Education of Ewing Township majority opinion written by, **1**:356, **2**:788

Black Alliance for Educational Options (BAEO), **1:100–102**

activities of, **1**:101

Bailey and Sullivan Leadership Institute (BSLI) established by, **1**:102

Kaleem Claire's leadership of, **1**:101

conservativism of, **1**:100, **1**:102

criticism of, **1**:101–102

educational options supported by, **1**:101, **1**:102

Howard Fuller's leadership of, **1**:100–101

Bill and Melinda Gates Foundation grants to, **1**:102

grassroots organizational methods of, **1**:102

history and mission of, **1**:100–101

Institute for the Transformation of Learning (ITL), Marquette University and, **1**:100, **1**:102

media campaigns of, **1**:102

mission statement of, **1**:101

origins of, **1**:100–101

parental choice focus of, **1**:101

project-based high schools founded by, **1**:102

Project Clarion public information campaign of, **1**:102

school vouchers work of, **1**:100, **1**:101

U.S. Department of Education grants to, **1**:102

See also **Cristo Rey** (Network) **schools; School choice**

Black High School Study, 1:102–104

cooperation focus of, **1**:103

"cooperative study" represented by, **1**:103

curriculum and staff development elements in, **1**:103

democratic school policy and practices element in, **1**:102–103

General Education Board-funded projects affiliated with, **1**:103

"implementation research" represented by, **1**:103

issues addressed by, **1**:102–103

participating schools in, **1**:102–103

project consultants in, **1**:103

school-community relations element in, **1**:102

sponsorship and funding of, **1**:102

See also **Minorities in educational leadership**

Blake, R. L., **2**:725

Block scheduling, 1:104–106

alternate-day block schedule and, **1**:104, **1**:105 (table)

Carnegie-unit schedule limitations and, **1**:104

change management element in, **1**:106

creative pedagogy methods and, **1**:105–106

4/4 block schedule and, **1**:105, **1**:105 (table)

impetus for, **1**:104

implementation challenges in, **1**:106

models for, **1**:104–105

school calendar variations and, **1**:105

subject-specific teaching methods advantages and, **1**:105

teacher preparation and student number benefits of, **1**:104

training and support requirements in, **1**:104, **1**:106

conflict following decision in, **1:**115–116

controversy regarding, **1:**116

de factor *vs.* de jure segregation issue and, **2:**752

de jure segregation ruling of, **1:**xlvi, **1:**230, **1:**260, **1:**262, **1:**264–265

equity in education focus (adequacy issue) of, **1:**26, **1:**280

Fourteenth Amendment, Equal Protection clause and, **1:**115, **1:**121–122, **1:**163, **1:**262, **1:**263–264

importance and impact of, **1:**115, **1:**263–266

integration not ordered by, **1:**265

Little Rock school desegregation and, **1:**xlvi, **1:**265, **2:**547

NAACP and, **1:**116

Rosa Parks, Montgomery Bus-Boycott and, **2:**500, **2:**547

Plessy v. Ferguson decision overturned by, **1:**262, **2:**547

psychological effects of segregation element in, **1:**264, **2:**547

school rezoning and, **1:**260

school segregation as unconstitutional element of, **1:**115, **1:**163, **1:**262, **2:**751, **2:**931–932

"separate but equal" focus of, **1:**115, **1:**116, **1:**121–122, **1:**263–264, **1:**350, **2:**791, **2:**805

site-based management systems and, **2:**828

White Resistance Council to prevent integration and, **2:**547

See also **Busing; Civil Rights Act of 1964; Desegregation/ integration; Marshall, Thurgood;** *Milliken v. Bradley;* **National Association for the Advancement of Colored People (NAACP); Warren, Earl**

Bruner, Jerome S., 1:117–118

Center for Cognitive Studies, Harvard University established by, **1:**117

child development work of, **1:**117

cognitive psychology work of, **1:**xlvii, **1:**117–118

curriculum reform movement and, **1:**117–118

Head Start and, **1:**117

human perception research of, **1:**117

infant cognition, preschool education work of, **1:**117

Kennedy and Johnson administrations and, **1:**117

learning theory of, **1:**117–118

Man: A Course of Study social studies curriculum project and, **1:**117, **2:**617, **2:**643, **2:**843

New Look methodology and, **1:**117

The Process of Education written by, **1:**117, **2:**843

A Study in Thinking written by, **1:**117

Toward a Theory of Instruction written by, **1:**xlvii

Bryk, Anthony, 1:138

Burger, Warren

Lemon v. Kurtzman court's opinion written by, **2:**515–516

Milliken v. Bradley majority opinion written by, **2:**562

Wisconsin v. Yoder court's opinion written by, **2:**944

Burke, Abbott v. (NJ), 1:166

Burke, Edmund, 1:160

Burton, Harold

Everson v. Board of Education of Ewing Township dissenting opinion written by, **1:**356

Bush, George H. W.

America 2000: An Education Strategy and, **1:**11, **1:**409

Charlottesville education summit convened by, **1:**231, **2:**636

governors' education and economic policy summit of, **1:**119, **2:**722, **2:**883

NAACP and, **2:**594

school choice and excellence standards supported by, **2:**722

Secretary's Commission on Achieving Necessary Skills (SCANS) and, **2:**883, **2:**922

Bush, George W.

American Enterprise Institute (AEI) for Public Policy Research and, **1:**56

Education Sciences Reform (ESR) Act (2002) and, **1:**357, **1:**468

IDEA reauthorized by, **1:**348

NAACP and, **2:**594

NCLB signed into law by, **1:**xlviii, **1:**56, **1:**409, **2:**723

White House Office of National Service, Points of Light Foundation and, **2:**814

See also **Individuals with Disabilities Education Act (IDEA); No Child Left Behind Act (NCLB)**

Business and educational reform, 1:118–121

accelerated complexity in global markets and local education and, **1:**119

accountability "fixes" issues and, **1:**120

bottom line regarding, **1:**118–119

business and education learning from each other and, **1:**120–121

business-education reform organizations and, **1:**119

business remedial education of employees and, **1:**119

commercialization of school day issue and, **1:**120

Conference Board and, **1:**119

education as "work preparation" concept and, **1:**118

efficiency principles and, **1:**120

globalization issues and, **1:**118

A Nation at Risk and, **1:**119

private good from public education and, **1:**119–120

proponents *vs.* opponents regarding relationship between, **1:**118

school privatization issue and, **1:**120

specific entities and partnerships in, **1:**119

Sputnik launch significance and, **1:**119

The War Against America's Public Schools (Bracey) and, **1:**120

See also **Carnegie Foundation for the Advancement of Teaching (CFAT); Cristo Rey (Network) schools; National Society for the Promotion of Industrial Education (NSPIE); Tech prep education; Vocational education**

Busing, 1:121–125

background regarding, **1:**121–122

Berkeley Plan and, **1:**94–95

in Boston, MA, **1:**xlvii, **1:**123

in Charlotte, NC, **1:**122–123, **1:**262

definition of, **1:**121

implementation of, **1:**122–124

in Los Angeles, CA, **1:**124

magnet schools and, **1:**122

in Nashville, TN, **1:**123

neoconservative evaluation of, **2:**658

opposition and dissent regarding, **1:**122, **1:**124

Index

970   Index

literature review regarding, 1:166
in middle school, 1:166–167
Project STAR and Beyond 13-year database and, 1:167
pupil-teacher ratio (PTR) term and, 1:167–168
Reduce Class Size Now Web site, 1:167
in secondary school, 1:166
STAR (Student Teacher Achievement Ratio) database and, 1:165–167
studies and initiatives regarding, 1:168 (table)
web sites regarding, 1:169
See also Age grading; Time on task
Clausen, Zorach v., 1:356
Clay, Marie, 2:758–759
Clinton, Bill
Achieve, Inc. and, 1:17
Educational Excellence for All Children Act (not enacted), 2:722
Education Flexibility Partnership Act: Ed-Flex, 2:722
ESEA amendments and, 1:338, 2:722
Goals 2000: Educate America Act, Public Law 103-227 and, 1:11, 1:409, 2:722, 2:883
National and Community Service Trust Act (1993) and, 2:722, 2:814
Progressive Policy Institute (PPI) and, 2:744
race issue in U.S. and, 2:752
School-to-Work Opportunities Act (1994) and, 2:722, 2:800, 2:883
Telecommunications Act (1996) and, 1:315
See also Goals 2000 Educate America Act (1994); Improving America's Schools Act (IASA, 1994)
Coalition for Evidence-Based Policy, 2:664
Coalition of Essential Schools (CES), 1:170–172
Annenberg Institute for School Reform and, 1:170, 2:830
CES benchmarks tool, classroom and organizational practices of, 1:171
CES ChangeLab Web site of, 1:171
CES Small Schools Project of, 1:171
common principles of, 1:170
current organizational direction of, 1:171
essential schools' characteristics and, 1:170
Gates Foundation and, 2:830
history of, 1:170–171
journal and DVD series of, 1:171
mission of, 1:170, 1:171
Theodore R. Sizer and, 1:170, 2:741, 2:830
standards-aligned interdisciplinary studies of, 1:170
underserved student populations focus of, 1:170
Coalition on Urban Renewal, 1:38
Cobb, Sanwood, 2:743
Cochran-Smith, Marilyn, 1:19
Cochran v. Louisiana State Board of Education, 1:143
Co-curricular activities, 1:172–174
academic performance enhanced by, 1:173
cost effectiveness of, 1:173
curricular activities balanced with, 1:172
definition and explanation of, 1:172
educational benefits of, 1:172–173
elimination necessity and, 1:172
financial issues regarding, 1:174

high-stakes testing issue and, 1:173, 1:174
music programs example of, 1:173
National Federation of State High School Associations support of, 1:173
social development facilitated by, 1:172–173
threats to, 1:173–174
time requirement of, 1:173
See also Extracurricular activities; Family and consumer sciences (FCS) of secondary education
Coeducation, 1:174–175
definition of, 1:174
early feminist focus on, 1:174–175
early women's colleges and, 1:174–175
economic and moral pressures and, 1:175
gender inequality and, 1:175
Oberlin College, Ohio and, 1:175
statistical data regarding, 1:175
subordination of women in, 1:175
See also Hall, G. Stanley; Single-sex schools
Cognitive assessment. See Intelligence testing
Cognitive moral development, in education, 1:146
Cohen, Michael, 1:17
Coleman, James S., 1:175–178
The Adolescent Society written by, 1:176
aggregate socioeconomic background of students studied by, 1:176
Brown v. Board of Education of Topeka, Kansas outcome work of, 1:176
busing to achieve racial balance work of, 1:176–177
childhood years of, 1:176
"composition effects" research of, 1:176
conclusions regarding, 1:178
Equality of Educational Opportunity Survey of 1996 and, 1:xlvii, 1:10
equal opportunity and desegregation work of, 1:176–177, 1:248, 1:320
High School Achievement: Public, Catholic, and Private Schools Compared written by, 1:177
peer culture work of, 1:176
public availability of research data work of, 1:177–178
public vs. Catholic vs. private schools research of, 1:177
resource inequities studied by, 1:176
social capital concept of, 1:177
teacher quality studied by, 1:176
voucher research of, 1:177, 2:925
See also Busing
Collective bargaining, 1:178–180
American Federation of Teachers union and, 1:178–179
controversy regarding, 1:178
educational reform process and, 1:179
Education Sector's work regarding, 1:330
interest bargaining and, 1:179
Myron Lieberman's analysis of, 1:179
National Education Association teachers union and, 1:178–179
A Nation at Risk, standards-based school reform movement and, 1:179
NCTQ database on, 2:626
new teacher unionism and, 1:179

student safety and, **1:**208
terms related to, **1:**205
timeline of: New England colony laws, **1:**205
timeline of: early Massachusetts colony, **1:**206
timeline of: pre-Civil War movement, **1:**206
timeline of: Reconstruction, **1:**206
timeline of: Progressive Era, **1:**207–208
time spent in school factor and, **1:**209
unintended consequences of, **1:**208–209
universal education goal of, **1:**205
"vocationalizing" of schooling and, **1:**208–209
Wisconsin v. Yoder and, **1:**209
See also **Beckner, William M.;** *Meyer v. Nebraska;*
Pierce v. Society of Sisters; Wisconsin v. Yoder
Conant, James Bryant, 1:210–211
The American High School Today work of, **1:**210, **2:**794
comprehensive high schools supported by, **1:**201, **1:**202,
1:210, **1:**211, **2:**794, **2:**804
Educational Policies Commission work of, **1:**308
education as preparation for democratic citizenship views
of, **1:**210–211, **1:**352
Education Commission of the States (ECS) created by,
1:211, **1:**322
The Education of American Teachers written by, **1:**210
essentialism supported by, **1:**352
general education curriculum views of, **1:**210, **2:**740
gifted students scholarship program and, **1:**210
as Harvard University president, **1:**210
life-adjustment education criticized by, **2:**526
Manhattan Project work of, **1:**210
National Defense Research Committee work of, **1:**210
SAT as admissions criteria views of, **1:**210, **1:**319, **2:**804
Shaping Educational Policy written by, **1:**322
Slums and Suburbs written by, **1:**210
teacher preparation work of, **1:**210
See also **Comprehensive high schools**
Concerned Women for America (CWA), 1:211–212
Biblical values focus of, **1:**211
conservative Christian groups and, **1:**xlviii, **1:**211
core issues of, **1:**211–212
grassroots activism of, **1:**212
Beverly LaHaye's work and, **1:**211
Mozart v. Hawkins County Board of Education
(Tennessee) and, **1:**212
parent choice supported by, **1:**212
People for the American Way (PAW) *vs.*, **2:**692
"secular humanism" opposed by, **1:**212
See also **Exodus Mandate Project; Family Research
Council (FRC)**
Condliffe, Ellen, **1:**132
Conflict management, 1:212–214
anti-bullying programs and, **1:**213
character education programs and, **1:**213
conflict resolution term and, **1:**212
definition of, **1:**212–213
effectiveness of, **1:**213
interpersonal and communication skills focus of, **1:**213
peer mediation program, direct skills instruction
and, **1:**213

schoolwide behavior programs and, **1:**213
See also **Peace education**
Congress of Industrial Organizations (CIO), **1:**56
Connecticut, Cantwell v., **2:**788
Consolidation of school districts, 1:214–215
collegiate achievement research regarding, **1:**214
economic costs issue and, **1:**214
local community debate issue and, **1:**214
National Rural Education Association research
regarding, **1:**215
quality of education for tax dollars issue and, **1:**214
teachers with special content training issue
and, **1:**214
See also **District schools; Rural education**
Constructivism, 1:215–218
accelerated schools and, **1:**9
active construction of knowledge element of, **1:**xlviii
behaviorism *vs.* maturationism learning theories and,
1:215–216
cognitive and sociocultural perspectives regarding,
1:215–216
cooperative sociomoral atmosphere with mutual respect
and, **2:**709
direct instruction *vs.*, **1:**89, **1:**276
external control minimization and, **2:**709
inquiry-based learning and, **1:**xlviii, **1:**467
learning in a social setting element of, **1:**215–216
mathematics knowledge construction, mathematizing
and, **1:**217
meaning construction in social settings using language
and, **1:**216
meaning making of learner and, **1:**216
physical knowledge activities and, **2:**710
Jean Piaget and, **2:**708, **2:**709
preconceptions and, **1:**216
quality teacher evaluation and, **2:**877
scientific knowledge construction and, **1:**216
*In Search of Understanding: The Case for Constructivist
Classrooms* (Brooks and Brooks) and, **1:**xlviii
teacher education influenced by, **1:**217
teacher facilitator role in, **1:**216
teacher respect of children and, **2:**709–710
as theory of knowledge, **1:**215
voicing ideas, language use and, **1:**216–217
See also **Differentiated instruction; Elementary
curricular reform; Experiential learning; Piaget,
Jean,** Piaget learning theory; **Process-product
research; Project learning**
Continuation schools, 1:218–219
conclusions regarding, **1:**219
delivery methods and applications of, **1:**219
drop-out intervention program and, **1:**218–219
European origins of, **1:**218
gifted students and, **1:**219
National Society for the Promotion of Industrial
Education and, **1:**218
Smith-Hughes Act (1917) and, **1:**218
student apprenticeship work and, **1:**218
in the United States, **1:**218

structure emphasized by, **1:**89

teacher presentation techniques of, **1:**276

See also **Behaviorism; Experiential learning; Thorndike, Edward L.**

Discipline-based art education (DBAE), **1:**68–69

Dispositions

controversy regarding, **1:**277, **1:**278

culturally responsive characteristic and, **1:**278

measurement controversy regarding, **1:**278

National Council for the Accreditation of Teacher Education standards and, **1:**278

NCLB highly qualified teacher requirement and, **1:**278

performance-based assessment systems to measure, **1:**277–278

of pre-service teachers, **1:**277

social justice disposition and, **1:**278

teacher characteristics and, **1:**278

teacher education value-added professional skills and, **1:**277

District schools, 1:279–283

board of education role in, **1:**279

common school movement and, **1:**279

districts in receivership and, **1:**282

district superintendent responsibilities and, **1:**280–281

evolution of, **1:**279–280

future trends of, **1:**282

governance issues regarding, **1:**280–281

local *vs.* state control conflict and, **1:**279, **1:**281, **1:**282

number and size data regarding, **1:**280

one-room school house and, **1:**279

public sector agencies and, **1:**281

state fiscal support and, **1:**279–280

state governance and, **1:**281, **1:**282

urban governance issues and, **1:**281

See also **District schools: court cases; Educational management organizations** (EMOs); **Local control; National School Boards Association** (NSBA); **Site-based management**

District schools: court cases

Brown vs. Board of Education of Topeka, Kansas, **1:**280

San Antonio Independent School District v. Rodriguez, **1:**280

Serrano v. Priest, **1:**xlvii, **1:**280

Diversity, 1:283–286

additive approach to, **1:**29

affirmative action *vs.,* **1:**29–30

age and age group issues and, **1:**285

at-risk term and, **1:**283

bilingual-bicultural deaf education approach and, **1:**65

Bilingual Education Act (1968) and, **1:**284–285, **1:**338

characteristics of, **1:**30

conclusions regarding, **1:**285

culturally deprived and culturally disadvantaged terms and, **1:**283

culture, race, and class and, **1:**283–284

culture definition and, **1:**29, **1:**283

decision-making and social action approach to, **1:**29

demographic trends projections and, **1:**283

diversity term and, **1:**283

in Episcopal schools, **1:**348

ESEA and, **1:**284

ethnic groups element of, **1:**283

exceptional students and, **1:**285

gender issues and, **1:**284

institutional *vs.* personal racism and, **1:**283

linguistic diversity and, **1:**284–285

multiculturalism and, **1:**29–30

as philosophy, goal, and process and, **1:**29

religious issues and, **1:**285

social class element of, **1:**283–284

teacher diversity, alternative licensure programs and, **1:**44

teaching approach to, **1:**29

transformation approach to, **1:**29

See also **Affirmative action; Afrocentric schools; Culturally relevant teaching; Ebonics; Hispanic/Latino education; Lesbian, gay, bisexual, and transgender (LGBT) issues; Minorities in educational leadership; Multicultural education; Race- and ethnic-based schooling; Whiteness**

Dobson, James, **1:**449

Doe, *Puyler v.,* **1:**455

Doe, *Santa Fe Independent School District v.,* **2:**812

Donnelly, John, **1:**221

Douglas, William O.

Central School District v. Allen dissenting opinion written by, **1:**144

Lau v. Nichols court's opinion written by, **2:**511

Milliken v. Bradley dissenting opinion written by, **1:**122

Wisconsin v. Yoder dissenting opinion written by, **2:**944

Douglass, Frederick, 1:286–287

abolitionist movement and, **1:**286

Civil War and, **1:**286–287

The Liberator, William Lloyd Garrison and, **1:**286

The North Star newspaper created by, **1:**286

post-Civil War statesman activities of, **1:**287

power of the written word and education views of, **1:**286

slave narratives written by, **1:**287

women's suffrage movement and, **1:**286

Dover Area School District, *Kitmiller v.,* **1:**474–475

Dovey, Steven, **1:**120

Dowell, *Board of Education of Oklahoma City Public Schools v.,* **1:**263, **1:**267

Dred Scott v. Sanford, **1:**163

Drexel, Katharine, 1:287–289

Catholic education reform impact of, **1:**287–288

new religious congregation and, **1:**287–288

racial justice and educational reform work of, **1:**288

Sisters of the Blessed Sacrament for Indians and Colored People founded by, **1:**288

Xavier College, Black Catholic college and, **1:**288

See also **Seton, Elizabeth Anne**

Dropout Prevention Act, **1:**339

Drop-outs

achievement gap and, **1:**351

African American student drop-out rates and, **1:**218–219

continuation schools intervention and, **1:**218–219

Hispanic/Latino(a) drop-out rates and, **1:**351

international and political importance of, **1**:345

second-language acquisition theory and, **1**:346

sheltered instruction method and, **1**:346–347

specially designed academic instruction in English (SDAIE) methods and, **1**:346–347

Title III, Language Instruction for Limited Education Proficient and Immigrant Students (NCLB) and, **1**:195

See also **Bilingual education;** *Lau v. Nichols;* **Multicultural education**

EPC. *See* **Educational Policies Commission** (EPC)

Episcopal schools, 1:347–348

British loyalist stigma and, **1**:347

current extant schools of, **1**:347

for ethnic minorities, **1**:347

parish day schools and, **1**:347, **1**:348

secondary boarding schools and, **1**:347–348

vocational and industrial education at, **1**:348

"White flight academies" issue and, **1**:348

Epperson v. Arkansas, **1**:356

Epstein, Joyce, **1**:251

Equal Education Opportunities Act of 1974, **1**:195

Equal education opportunity, 1:348–350

Education for All Handicapped Children Act (EACHA, 1975) and, **1**:xlvii, **1**:348

ESEA, **1**:349

free and appropriate public education (FAPE) concept and, **1**:348, **1**:349

Individuals with Disabilities Education Act (IDEA) and, **1**:348–350

Individuals with Disabilities Education Improvement Act (IDEIA, 2004) and, **1**:348–349

learning disabilities classification and, **1**:349

"overidentification" issue and, **1**:349

See also **Adequacy; Coeducation;** Education for All Handicapped Children Act (EAHCA, 1975); **Elementary and Secondary Education Act (ESEA); Equity; Extracurricular activities;** *Hobson v. Hansen;* **Individualized Education Program (IEP); Individuals with Disabilities Education Act (IDEA);** *Lau v. Nichols;* **National Organization for Women (NOW); No Child Left Behind Act (NCLB); Title IX** of Educational Amendments

Equality of Educational Opportunity Survey (Coleman), **1**:xlvii, **1**:10

Equal Protection Clause, of Fourteenth Amendment, **1**:115, **1**:121–122, **1**:163

See also **Brown v. Board of Education** of Topeka, Kansas; *San Antonio Independent School District v. Rodriguez; Serrano v. Priest*

Equal Rights Amendment (ERA), **1**:378, **2**:640

Equity, 1:350–352

achievement gap, drop-out rates and, **1**:351

Brown v. Board of Education of Topeka, Kansas, "separate is not equal" ruling and, **1**:350

Civil Rights Act of 1964 and, **1**:350–351

defining equity as equal issue and, **1**:350

horizontal *vs.* vertical equity and, **1**:350, **1**:351

identifying what should be equitable issue and, **1**:350

measurement of inputs *vs.* outcomes and, **1**:350

NCLB and, **1**:351

school choice and, **1**:351

school finance, property tax issue and, **1**:350, **1**:351

Title IX and, **1**:351

See also **Adequacy; Culturally relevant teaching; Elementary and Secondary Education Act (ESEA); Equal education opportunity; Individualized Education Program (IEP); No Child Left Behind Act (NCLB);** *Paideia Proposal: An Educational Manifesto* (Adler); **Title IX** of Educational Amendments

Erikson, Erik, **2**:549

ESEA. *See* **Elementary and Secondary Education Act (ESEA)**

ESL. *See* **English as a Second Language (ESL)**

Essentialism, 1:352–353

accountability and, **1**:10

antiprogressive sentiments and, **1**:352

basic skills of reading, writing, mathematics, science, and history focus of, **1**:352

Council for Basic Education (1950s) and, **1**:352

Educational Wastelands: The Retreat From Learning in our Public Schools (Bestor) and, **1**:352

idealism and realism philosophical orientations of, **1**:352

life-adjustment and child-centered education criticized by, **1**:352

A Nation at Risk report and, **1**:352–353

NCLB and, **1**:353

proponents of, **1**:352

Sputnik launch and, **1**:352

teacher as primary authority in classroom element of, **1**:352

testing to determine mastery element of, **1**:352

Establishment Clause of First Amendment

Agostini v. Felton and, **1**:35–36

Child Benefit Test and, **1**:144

dual enrollment controversy and, **1**:290

Epperson v. Arkansas and, **1**:356

intelligent design *vs.* evolution and, **1**:475

McCollum v. Board of Education and, **1**:356

Title I, Elementary and Secondary Education Act and, **1**:35

Zobrest v. Catalina Foothills School District and, **1**:83

Zorach v. Clausen and, **1**:356

See also ***Agostini v. Felton;** Aguilar v. Felton;* **Ball, William B.;** *Central School District v. Allen; Engel v. Vitale; Everson v. Board of Education* of Ewing Township; **Intelligent design;** *Lemon v. Kurtzman; School District of Abington Township v. Schempp;* **Tax credits**

Ethical theories, 1:353–355

application of, **1**:354–355

John Dewey and, **1**:354

ethical decision-making in schools and, **1**:354–355

ethic of care and, **1**:354

ethic of critique and, **1**:353–354

ethic of justice and, **1**:354

"integrity of human relationships" (Noddings) concept and, **1**:354

Title IV educational act, sex bias elimination in schools and, 1:369

A Treatise on Domesticity (Beecher, 1841) and, 1:368

women's education at land-grant schools and, 1:368–369

Family Educational Rights and Privacy Act (1974), 1:338

Family Research Council (FRC)

James Dobson and, 1:370

Focus on the Family and, 1:370

issues focused on by, 1:370

social policy organization of, 1:369–370

traditional family and anti-homosexuality issues of, 1:370

See also **Concerned Women for America (CWA)**

Faribault-Stillwater Plan, 1:371–372

James Gibbons and, 1:371–372

John Ireland and, 1:371

liberal *vs.* conservative perspectives on Catholic education and, 1:371–372

public and parochial schools relationship issue and, 1:371

Third Plenary Council of Baltimore (1884) and, 1:371–372, 1:405–406

Vatican acceptance to, 1:371–372, 1:405–406

See also **Gibbons, James Cardinal; Ireland, John; Lowell Plan; Poughkeepsie Plan**

FCS. *See* **Family and consumer sciences (FCS)**

Federal educational reform, 1:372–375

academic content and pedagogical classroom practices focus of, 1:374

"complexity of joint action" concept and, 1:373

discipline-based professional organization models of, 1:374

ESEA and, 1:373

"high standards for all students" goal and, 1:374

local, state, and federal layers of decision making and, 1:373

loose coupling concept of educational change and, 1:373–374

A Nation at Risk report and, 1:373

policy and practice relationship and, 1:372

standards-based reform and, 1:372, 1:374–375

state standardized testing programs and, 1:373

state standards-based reform policy drivers and, 1:374

student performance data focus of, 1:372, 1:373

See also **American Legislative Exchange Council (ALEC); Comprehensive school reform (CSR); Elementary and Secondary Education Act (ESEA); Individuals with Disabilities Education Act (IDEA); National Science Foundation (NSF);** *Nation at Risk, A;* **No Child Left Behind Act (NCLB); Office of Economic Opportunity (OEO); Smith-Hughes Act; Title IX** of Educational Amendments; *specific act, law, and presidential administration*

Federal Office of Gifted Education, 1:196

Felton, Agostini v., 1:36

See also **Agostini v. Felton**

The Feminine Mystique (Friedan), 1:377, 2:639

Feminist perspectives, 1:375–379

anti-abortion laws constitutionality and, 1:378

capitalist structure criticism and, 1:378

civil rights movement and, 1:377

"consciousness raising" of women's shared experiences and, 1:377

Declaration of Sentiments, Seneca Falls Convention and, 1:376

In a Different Voice: Psychological Theory and Women's Development (Gilligan) and, 1:378

Equal Rights Amendment (ERA) and, 1:378, 2:640

The Feminine Mystique (Friedan) and, 1:377, 2:639

feminism criticism and, 1:378

feminism definitions and, 1:375

feminism perspectives and, 1:375

feminist revolution and, 1:377–378

gendered power structures focus of, 1:375

gender equality through critique of power differences and, 1:375

middle-class White cultural values and, 1:376

National Organization for Women (NOW) and, 1:377

oral contraceptive methods and, 1:377

race, class, and sexual orientation discrimination and, 1:378–379

relevance to education of, 1:376

school gender constructs and, 1:376

sexual oppression and sex discrimination and, 1:375

social justice movements and, 1:376

timeline of: first wave, 1848-1920, women's suffrage, 1:375, 1:376–377

timeline of: second wave, 1960s and 1970s, women's liberation movement, discrimination policies resistance, 1:375, 1:377–378

timeline of: third wave, 1990s through early 2000s, postcolonial and poststructuralism, race and class focus, 1:375, 1:378–379

Title VIII, ESEA amendment, prohibition of sex discrimination in federally funded programs and, 1:338

Title IX of Educational Amendments and, 1:378

Vindication of the Rights of Woman (Wollstonecraft) and, 1:376

women in the labor force and, 1:378

women's studies programs and, 1:378

See also **Beecher, Catharine; Coeducation; Feminist perspectives:** notable individuals; **National Organization for Women (NOW); Title IX** of Educational Amendments

Feminist perspectives: notable individuals

Susan Brownell Anthony, 1:377

Betty Friedan, 1:377, 2:639

Carol Gilligan, 1:378

Martha Griffiths, 1:378

Lucretia Coffin Mott, 1:376–377

Margaret Sanger, 1:377

Elizabeth Cady Stanton, 1:376

Mary Wollstonecraft, 1:376

Fenton, Edward, 2:842, 2:843, 2:844

Ferguson, Plessy v., 1:115

Financial Assistance to Meet Special Educational Needs of Children, 1:338

race and achievement negative correlation and, **1:**442

school identity *vs.* street identity development and, **1:**440

segregated education settings, negative effects of, **1:**98

student body language and response etiquette elements in, **1:**441

"subtractive schooling" concept and, **1:**440, **1:**442

teacher development programs and, **1:**441

teacher-family "alliances" element in, **1:**441

traditional classroom discourse alterations and, **1:**441

See also **Bilingual education; Cristo Rey (Network) schools; Diversity; Immigration and education reform; Minorities in educational leadership; Multicultural education; National Council of La Raza (NCLR); Race- and ethnic-based schooling**

Hobbes, Thomas, **1:**354

Hobson v. Hansen, **1:**442–443

college preparatory track criteria and, **1:**443

discriminatory practice of tracking focus of, **1:**442

equal educational opportunity focus of, **1:**442, **1:**443

optional attendance zones ruling of, **1:**443

special education legislation and, **2:**850

Washington D.C., Division I *vs.* Division II schools structure and, **1:**442–443

Washington D.C., race-based teacher assignment system in, **1:**443

Hodge, Charles, **1:**443–445

Bible as textbook views of, **1:**444

Catholic schools and, **1:**444–445

Christian schools supported by, **1:**444–445

common schools criticized by, **1:**444

Robert Dabney influenced by, **1:**257–258

early years and education of, **1:**444

Horace Mann's "natural religion" supported by, **1:**444

religious instruction in school supported by, **1:**444

state-sponsored education criticized by, **1:**84, **1:**444

tax credits issue supported by, **1:**444–445

Hodgkinson, Harold, **1:**249

Hoffer, Thomas, **1:**177

Hollingworth, Leta Stetter, **1:**408

Holmes County Board of Education, Alexander v., **1:**265, **2:**548, **2:**866

Holmes Group, **1:**445–447

diversity of students focus of, **1:**446

effective teaching and teacher preparation recommendations of, **1:**446, **2:**799–800, **2:**872

goals of, **1:**445, **1:**446

Henry Wyman Holmes and, **1:**445

Holmes Partnership and, **1:**446

Holmes Partnership-Teachers Network Leadership Institute and, **1:**446

Holmes Scholars initiative, minorities in teaching profession and university professors and, **1:**446

Holmes Scholars program and, **1:**447

National Association of Holmes Scholars Alumni (NAHSA) and, **1:**447

A Nation at Risk report and, **1:**445

organizational collaboration of, **1:**446

research universities consortium and, **1:**445

school-university collaboration tenet of, **1:**445, **1:**446, **2:**732

teacher professional development focus of, **1:**446, **2:**872

Tomorrow's Schools of Education published by, **1:**446

Tomorrow's Schools published by, **1:**446

Tomorrow's Teachers (Holmes trilogy) published by, **1:**446, **2:**872

Urban Network to Improve Teacher Education (UNITE) and, **1:**447

See also **Teacher education**

Holt, John, **1:**447–448

early years and education of, **1:**447

Free School Movement and, **1:**390

Growing Without Schooling (GWS) homeschooling newspaper published by, **1:**448, **1:**449

homeschooling advocated by, **1:**xlviii, **1:**447, **1:**448

How Children Fail and *How Children Learn* written by, **1:**447

Ivan Illich and, **1:**447

A. S. Neill's Summerhill School and, **2:**656

radical educational views of, **1:**448, **2:**676

Home economics. *See* **Family and consumer sciences (FCS) of secondary education**

Homelessness

NCLB Title X, McKinney-Vento Homeless Education Assistance Improvements Act (2001) and, **1:**339

Home Mortgage Disclosure Act (1975), **1:**262

Homeschooling and the Home School Legal Defense Association (HSLDA), 1:448–450

Christian day schools and, **1:**156, **1:**450

Concerned Women for America and, **1:**212

James Dobson's advocacy of, **1:**449

evangelical Protestantism and, **1:**156

John Holt's *Growing Without Schooling* and, **1:**448, **1:**449

Home School Burnout (Moore) and, **1:**449

HSLDA and, **1:**449–450

increase in, **1:**xlviii

learning packages used in, **2:**515

McGuffey Readers and, **2:**553

Raymond Moore and, **1:**449

Mozart v. Hawkins County Board of Education (Tennessee) and, **1:**212

National Household Education Surveys Program data and, **1:**46

parental reasons for, **1:**46–47

prohomeschool legislation and legal actions and, **1:**448

religious conservative groups and, **1:**449–450

Rousas Rushdoony and, **2:**778–779

Singapore Math curriculum and, **2:**826

Deborah Stevenson and, **1:**450

virtual charter schools and, **1:**450

See also **Alternative schools; Holt, John**

Hoover, Herbert, **2:**720

Horan, Carolyn, **1:**275

Horkheimer, Max, **1:**241

Hornbooks, **1:**259

Houston, Charles, **1:**116, **2:**547–548, **2:**593

Howard, Gary, **1:**248

HSLDA. *See* **Homeschooling and the Home School Legal Defense Association (HSLDA)**
HSTW. *See* **High Schools That Work (HSTW)**
Huebner, Dwayne, **1:**253, **2:**764
Hughes, John, 1:450–452
 Catholic education for every Catholic child goal of, **1:**451
 Catholic education movement in mid 1800s and, **1:**450, **1:**484
 educational equity campaign of, **1:**451
 nonsectarian public schools and, **1:**451
 parochial schools system developed by, **1:**xliv, **1:**451
 Public School Society and, **1:**451
 state funds for Catholic schools in New York City and, **1:**xliv, **1:**451
 See also **Gibbons, James Cardinal; Ireland, John**
Hull House. *See* **Addams, Jane**
Hunt, Charles W., **1:**49
Hunter, Madeline, **1:**xlviii
Hurston, Zora Neale, **1:**301
Hutchins, Robert Maynard, **2:**740

IBO. *See* **International Baccalaureate Organization (IBO)**
IEP. *See* **Individualized Education Program (IEP)**
IES. *See* **Institute of Education Sciences (IES)**
Illegal Immigration Reform and Immigration Responsibility Act (1996), **1:**456
Illich, Ivan, 1:453–454
 corrupting impact of learning institutions on education of children views of, **1:**453
 deinstitutionalizing of school and society views of, **2:**521
 Deschooling Society written by, **1:**xlvii, **1:**453
 early years and education of, **1:**453
 Paul Goodman and, **1:**413
 hierarchical educational models rejected by, **1:**454
 John Holt and, **1:**447
 nontraditional learning views of, **1:**454
 peer learning webs proposed by, **1:**454
 schools as tool to institutionalize society views of, **1:**xlvii, **1:**453–454, **2:**521
Imig, David, **1:**50
Immigrants, immigration. *See* **Cardinal Principles Report (CPR); Immigration and education reform**
Immigration and education reform, 1:454–457
 Adult Education Act and, **1:**455
 anti-immigration sentiment and, **1:**454–455
 California's public education exclusion of Hispanic students and, **1:**455
 civic education and, **1:**161–162
 conclusions regarding, **1:**457
 curriculum reforms and, **1:**457
 ESL programs and, **1:**455
 historical overview of, **1:**454–455
 Hull House, settlement movement and, **1:**24–25
 Illegal Immigration Reform and Immigrant Responsibility Act (1996, CA) and, **1:**455
 immigration demographic changes and, **1:**455
 immigration population statistics and, **1:**455
 Immigration Reform and Control Act (IRCA, 1986) amnesty program and, **1:**454–455

 industry labor demands and, **1:**455
 Lau v. Nichols and, **1:**455–456
 legislation in support of, **1:**454
 No Child Left Behind (NCLB) and, **1:**456–457
 physical health and welfare issues and, **1:**456
 policy shifts and legislation regarding, **1:**456
 poverty level of immigrant children factor and, **1:**456
 Puyler v. Doe and, **1:**455
 State Legislation Impact Assistance Grants (SLIAG) and, **1:**455
 teacher preparation programs and, **1:**456
 See also **Americanization; Bilingual education; Cardinal Principles Report (CPR); English as a second language (ESL);** Greek Orthodox schools; **Hispanic/Latino education;** *Lau v. Nichols;* **Lutheran schools; Multicultural education; No Child Left Behind Act (NCLB)**
Improving America's Schools Act (IASA, 1994), **1:**196, **1:**338, **1:**454, **2:**722
Improving America's Schools Act (IASA, 2000), **1:**11, **1:**196
Inclusion, 1:457–460
 conclusions regarding, **1:**459–460
 continuum of services opponents to, **1:**458–459
 developmentally appropriate practice issue and, **1:**269
 Education for All Handicapped Children Act (1975) and, **1:**xlvii, **1:**458
 equality promoted through, **1:**458
 ESEA reauthorization and, **1:**459
 full inclusion as a civil right issue and, **1:**458
 general education classroom placement and, **1:**459
 Goals 2000: Educate America Act (1994) and, **1:**459
 IDEA and, **1:**459, **1:**460
 mainstreaming efforts and, **1:**458, **2:**851
 regular education initiative (REI) and, **1:**458
 research results regarding, **1:**459
 timeline of: 1970s-1980s, early efforts, **1:**458
 timeline of: 1990s-2000s, change in philosophy regarding, **1:**458–459
 of the visually impaired, **1:**328
 See also **Culturally relevant teaching; Differentiated instruction; Individualized Education Program (IEP); Mainstreaming**
Individualized Education Program (IEP), 1:460–463
 assistive technology issue and, **1:**462
 behavioral intervention plan element of, **1:**461–462
 collaborative IEP team element of, **1:**461, **1:**463
 Council for Exceptional Children support of, **1:**227
 definition of, **1:**460–461
 general education alignment issue and, **1:**462
 general education curriculum access plan element of, **1:**461–462
 IDEIA's FAPE mandate and, **1:**461
 least restrictive environment (LRE) element of, **1:**461, **2:**539
 mandated components of, **1:**461–462
 measuring quality of implementation issue of, **1:**462
 quality of education element in, **1:**461
 role of disability label issue and, **1:**463
 state or district wide assessments element of, **1:**462

financial support for, **2**:546
William Torrey Harris views regarding, **2**:546
industrial economy skilled workforce needs and, **2**:544
Manual Training School for boys, St. Louis and, **2**:545
Massachusetts Institute of Technology, engineer
    preparation and, **2**:545
moral rehabilitation for marginalized groups and,
    2:545–546
practical skill building *vs.* trade preparation and, **2**:545
promises of, **2**:545
support for, **2**:545–546
vocational training transition from, **2**:546
See also **Life adjustment education; Smith-Hughes Act;**
    Vocational education
Marcuse, Herbert, **1**:241
Marland, Sidney P. Jr., **1**:131
Marshall, Thurgood, 2:546–548
affirmative action cases and, **2**:548
graduate and professional school admission discrimination
    and, **2**:547
Charles Hamilton Houston and, **2**:546–547, **2**:593
Kennedy and Johnson administration legislation
    and, **2**:548
liberal record of, **2**:545
NAACP and, **1**:116, **1**:264, **2**:546–547, **2**:593
psychological doll studies and, **1**:116, **2**:547
Public Education Initiative, equal pay for White and Black
    teachers and, **2**:547
See also **Marshall, Thurgood:** court cases; **National**
    Association for the Advancement of Colored
    People (NAACP)
Marshall, Thurgood: court cases
Browder v. Gale, **2**:547
Brown v. Board of Education of Topeka, Kansas, **1**:116,
    1:264, **2**:546–548
Cooper v. Aaron, **2**:547–548
Milliken v. Bradley dissenting opinion, **2**:548
Murray v. Pearson, **2**:547
Regents of the University of California v. Bakke, **2**:548
Sipuel v. University of Oklahoma, **2**:547
Sweatt v. Painter, **2**:547
Wygant v. Jackson Board of Education dissenting
    opinion, **2**:548
Maslow, Abraham, 2:548–550
Association of Humanistic Psychology co-created
    by, **2**:548
basic physiological needs and, **2**:549
esteem need and, **2**:549
Freud's theory and, **2**:548–549
hierarchy of needs and information work of, **2**:549
humanistic movement in psychology founded by, **2**:548
human potential development views of, **2**:549
human sexuality studies of, **2**:549
love and sense of belongingness need and, **2**:549
self-actualization views of, **2**:549
Skinner's theory and, **2**:549
Mastery learning, **2**:550–551
assessments used in, **2**:551
Benjamin Bloom's learning for mastery model and, **2**:550

classroom characteristics in, **2**:550
computer advances and, **2**:550
criterion-references tests used in, **2**:550
criticism of, **2**:551
individualized instruction, one-to-one tutoring and, **2**:550
individual learning rate element in, **2**:550
Fred Simons Keller's personalized system of instruction
    and, **2**:550
outcome-based education and, **2**:550
process *vs.* content focus of, **2**:551
self-instruction, self-paced learning and, **2**:550
time issue in, **2**:551
Carleton Washburn's work and, **2**:550
Winnetka Plan element of, **2**:943
See also **Bloom's taxonomy; Learning packages**
Maxwell, William H., **1**:185
McAuliffe, Christa, **1**:xlviii
McCollum v. Board of Education, **1**:356
McDonald, James, **2**:764
McDonald, Kevin, **1**:4
McGreevy, John, **1**:139
McGuffey Readers, 2:551–554
as basal reader forerunner, **2**:553
Calvinistic ethic characteristic of, **2**:553
character education and, **1**:xliv, **1**:145
common school movement and, **1**:190
content and moral tone of, **2**:553
copyright issue and, **2**:552
criticism of, **2**:553
English language standardized by, **2**:553
illustrations element of, **2**:552, **2**:553
language arts curriculum element of, **2**:552
Horace Mann's criticism of, **2**:553
William H. McGuffey and, **2**:552
The New England Primer vs., **2**:553
origins and early editions of, **2**:552
Rhetorical Guide of, **2**:553
Winthrop B. Smith publishers of, **2**:552
McLaren, Peter, **1**:242, **1**:249
McLaurin v. Oklahoma State Regents for Higher Education,
    1:265, **2**:593
Meek v. Pittenger, **1**:144
Mehrens, William, **2**:888–889
Meier, Deborah, **2**:741
Meier, Kenneth J., **1**:98
Mennonite schools. *See* **Amish and Mennonite schools;**
    Wisconsin v. Yoder
Mercer, Charles F., 2:554–555
abolitionist and social reform activities of, **2**:554
Thomas Jefferson, University of Virginia and, **2**:554
Literacy Fund of Virginia general Assembly and, **2**:554
Virginia public school system recommendations of, **2**:554
Meredith, James, **1**:xlvi
Mergens, Westside Community Board of Education v., **2**:812
Meriam, Lewis (Meriam Report), 2:555–556
boarding school termination recommended by, **2**:556
full-day study recommended by, **2**:556
Indian school teacher standards and, **2**:555–556
Native American education reform work of, **2**:554–555

war sanctioned as problem resolution tactic and, 2:689
See also **Society of Friends schools**
Pearson, Murray v., 2:547
Pedagogy of the Oppressed (Freire), 1:391–392
Pederson, Paul B., 1:29
Pennsylvania Academy of Fine Arts, 1:xliv
Pennsylvania Association for Retarded Children (PARC) v. Commonwealth of Pennsylvania, 2:850
Pennsylvania Study, The, 2:690–691
   Carnegie Foundation for the Advancement of Teaching and, 2:690, 2:691
   Carnegie Unit *vs.*, 2:690
   college admissions process and, 2:690–691
   Cooperative Test Service and, 2:691
   Eight-Year Study and, 2:691
   multiple-choice, true-false, and matching items format of, 2:691
   standardized testing measurement and, 2:690–691
People for the American Way (PFAW), 2:691–693
   Alliance for the Separation of School and State supported by, 1:40
   anti-school vouchers sentiment of, 1:102
   BAEO criticized by, 1:102
   Bible curriculum issues and, 2:692, 2:693
   Concerned Women for Education and, 1:212
   initiatives and ideals promoted by, 1:xlviii, 2:692
   Norman Lear and, 2:691–692
   National Council on Bible Curriculum in Public Schools and, 2:693
   privatization of education opposed by, 2:692
   right-wing extremist groups opposed by, 1:xlviii, 2:692
   Supreme Court justices issue and, 2:692
   Texas religious literacy elective law and, 2:693
   vouchers opposed by, 2:692
Performance-based assessment, 2:693–695
   alternative terms for, 2:693–694
   elements of, 2:694
   process and product emphasis of, 2:694
   scoring guide development importance and, 2:694
   selected-response tests and, 2:693
   special needs students and, 2:694
   student involvement in evaluation and grading in, 2:694
   teacher education programs and, 2:694–695
   time requirements of, 2:694
   Toward Performance-Based Federal Education Funding (Rotherham) and, 2:745
   See also **Assessment; Evidence-Based Education (EBE); High Schools That Work (HSTW); Management by objectives; National Assessment of Educational Progress (NAEP); Problem-based learning (PBL)**
Performance contracting, 2:695–697
   Arkansas School District use of, 2:696
   benefits and shortcomings of, 2:696–697
   contract period and, 2:695
   education and, 2:695–696
   efficiency *vs.* educational performance contracting and, 2:695
   federal, state, and local accountability and, 2:695
   process elements of, 2:697
   teacher unions and, 2:695, 2:697

Texarkana Dropout Prevention Program and, 2:696
See also **Differentiated staffing**
Perkins Applied Technology and Vocational Education Act, 2:801
Perkins School for the Blind, 1:xliv, 1:326
Perkins Vocational and Technical Education Act (1998), 2:801, 2:883, 2:922, 2:923
Perry, Arthur C., 2:786
Personal Responsibility and Work Opportunity Reconciliation Act (1996), 1:456
Peshkin, Alan, 1:157
Pestalozzianism, 2:697–699
   child-centered reform work and, 2:736
   common school movement and, 1:191
   criticism of, 2:699
   effective teacher characteristics and, 2:699
   Free School Movement and, 1:390
   impact of, 2:699
   inherent goodness of children concept and, 2:698
   intellectual, moral, and physical development instruction elements in, 2:699
   knowledge acquisition through sense perception premise of, 2:697
   Horace Mann influenced by, 2:543
   object lesson format of, 2:697, 2:698–699
   Oswego Normal School, New York and, 2:669, 2:680
   Robert Owen's infant schools and, 1:465
   Johann H. Pestalozzi and, 1:189, 2:697–698
   social activism, education of the poor and, 2:697, 2:698
   student attentiveness, carefulness, and reliability elements in, 2:698
   teacher licensure movement and, 2:698
   See also **Infant schools; Oswego movement**
Peterson, Bob, 2:741
PFAW. *See* **People for the American Way** (PFAW)
Phelps Stokes Fund, 1:404–405
Phenix, Philip, 2:764
Philanthropy in education, 2:699–703
   charitable giving *vs.*, 2:699
   to colleges and universities, 2:701
   in colonial America and 1800s, 2:699–700
   corporate foundation and, 2:701, 2:702
   development of modern philanthropy and, 2:699–700
   in early childhood education, 2:701
   in elementary and secondary education, 2:701–702
   foundations, endowments and, 2:700–701
   future trends regarding, 2:702–703
   great wealth of industrialists and, 2:700
   high-profile business wealth and, 2:700
   improving understanding of, 2:703
   National Center for Education Statistics data on, 2:701
   national directories of foundations and, 2:703
   national school site data collection and, 2:701
   private *vs.* community foundations and, 2:700–701
   supporters and critics of, 2:702–703
   in teacher preparation, 2:702
   See also **Carnegie Foundation for the Advancement of Teaching (CFAT); Gates Foundation; Peabody Fund; Philanthropy in education:** notable individuals

School size, 2:794–796
James Bryant Conant's views on, 2:794
consolidation and, 2:794
rural schools and, 2:794
small-school conversions and, 2:794–795
student outcomes measurement and, 2:794
See also Class size; Consolidation of school districts;
District schools; Rural education; Small-school
movement
School social services, 2:796–798
attendance or truant officers, 2:797
child abuse and sexual abuse prevention, 2:797
childhood psychosocial problems and, 2:796
collaboration importance and, 2:796–797
community mental health counselors, 2:797
conclusions regarding, 2:798
crisis counseling services, 2:797
DARE drug prevention program and, 2:797
elementary level services, 2:797
family services, 2:797
high school level services, 2:798
homeless family services, 2:797
middle school level services, 2:797
nursing services, 2:797
probation services, 2:798
substance abuse prevention, 2:797
teen pregnancy services, 2:798
vocational guidance, 2:797
Schools of education, 2:798–800
Elwood Cubberley's work regarding, 1:244–245
educating for teacher quality issue and, 2:800
elementary vs. secondary training differences
and, 2:799
historical perspectives on, 2:798–800
Holmes Group initiative and, 2:799–800
junior high school development and, 2:799
licensure exams and, 2:800
mandatory attendance laws and, 2:799
NCLB and, 2:800
normal schools and, 2:798–799
professionalizing teaching and, 2:799–800
schools or colleges of education at undergraduate level
and, 2:799
state teacher colleges and, 2:799
teacher testing and, 2:800
See also National Network for Educational Renewal
(NNER); Normal schools; Teacher education;
Teacher Education Accreditation Council (TEAC);
Teacher institutes; Teach For America (TFA)
Schools Uniting Neighborhoods (SUN), 1:382
School-to-Work, 2:800–802
apprenticeship and on-the-job training concepts and,
2:801
career education predecessor of, 1:132
career exploration and career decision-making and, 2:801,
2:922
collegiate internships model and, 2:801
lifelong learning encouraged by, 2:801
NCLB termination of, 2:801

school-based and work-based learning integration and,
2:923
School-to-Work Opportunities Act (1994) and, 1:411,
2:722, 2:800–801, 2:883, 2:922
state boards of vocational education and, 2:801, 2:923
Tech Prep 2-year postsecondary institution and, 2:801,
2:883
U.S. employment/wage statistics, education level and,
2:800–801
work vs. career word use and, 2:923
See also Job Corps; Tech prep education; Vocational
education
School vouchers. See Vouchers
Schwartz, Robert B., 1:17
Science and Behavior (Skinner), 1:xlvi, 1:89
Science technology engineering and math (STEM)
schools, 1:47
Science technology engineering math and medicine
(STEMM) schools, 1:47
Scientifically based research, 2:802–803
Best Evidence Encyclopedia (BEE) and, 2:803
causal relationship research and, 2:803
Center for Data-Driven Reform in Education (CDDRE,
Johns Hopkins) and, 2:803
characteristics of, 2:802
critics of, 2:802–803
NCLB definition and, 2:802
qualitative research vs., 2:803
randomization of trials and, 2:802–803
single-subject research and, 2:803
What Works Clearinghouse and, 2:803
See also Evidence-Based Education (EBE); Institute of
Education Sciences (IES); No Child Left Behind Act
(NCLB)
Scopes "Monkey Trial," 1:155, 1:234, 1:474–475
See also Creationism; Intelligent design
Scott-Clayton, Judith, 1:114–115
Seattle School District No. 1, Parents Involved in
Community Schools v., 1:261, 1:263, 1:267–268, 2:714
Secondary curricular reform, 2:803–806
Boston English Classical School and, 2:805
Carnegie Units as graduation condition and, 2:805
compulsory attendance and, 2:805
conclusions regarding, 2:806
educated workforce demands and, 2:804
funding secondary schools with taxes collected to support
public schools and, 2:804
industrialization and urbanization and, 2:804
Kalamazoo Court Case (1874, Michigan) and, 1:293,
2:790, 2:805
plurality and diversity of American society issue
and, 2:805
"separate but equal," Brown decision and, 2:805
small-school movement and, 2:805–806
state minimum competency exams and, 2:805
timeline of: beginnings, 2:804
timeline of: Conant, the SAT, and the Committee of Ten,
2:804
timeline of: Cardinal Principles Report, 2:804–805

Shumaker, Ann, **2:**737
Sikkink, David, **1:**157
Simmons-Harris, Zelman v. *See Zelman v. Simmons-Harris*
Simmons-Harris v. Goff, **2:**953
Simmons-Harris v. Zelman, **2:**954
Simulation computer programs, **1:**316
Singapore math, **2:**825–826
    "bar modeling" as a problem-solving tool in, **2:**826
    concrete, pictorial, and abstract levels of understanding
        of, **2:**825
    Curriculum Planning Development Institute of Singapore
        and, **2:**825
    homeschooling and, **2:**826
    international recognition of, **2:**826
    primary grades mathematics program and, **2:**825
    teacher professional development requirements and, **2:**826
    textbook series used in, **2:**825
    Trends in International Mathematics and Science Study
        (TIMSS) results and, **2:**826
    U.S. curriculum testing of, **2:**826
Single-sex schools, **2:**826–828
    academic gains issue and, **2:**827–828
    American Association of University Women opposition
        to, **2:**827
    American Civil Liberties Union opposition to, **2:**827
    bias against girls and, **2:**827
    feminist movement and, **2:**827
    greater choice in educational programs and, **2:**827
    increase in, **2:**827
    learning styles differences between boys and girls issue
        and, **2:**827–828
    NCLB and, **2:**827
    policy context of, **2:**827
    Progressive era reform regarding, **2:**827
    purported benefits and critiques of, **2:**827–828
    Title IX law, discrimination by sex in schools receiving
        federal funds and, **2:**827, **2:**895–896
    See also **Coeducation**
Singleton, Glenn, **2:**752
Sipuel v. Oklahoma State Board of Regents, **2:**593
Sipuel v. University of Oklahoma, **2:**547
Site-based management, **2:**828–829
    in Chicago and Kentucky, **2:**829
    Chicago School Reform Act (1988) and, **2:**829
    decentralization in New York and Detroit and, **2:**828
    Kentucky Education Reform Act (KERA, 1990)
        and, **2:**829
    limitations of, **2:**829
    local control precursor to, **2:**828
    Local School Councils (LSCs) element in, **2:**829
    origins of, **2:**828–829
    school-based decision making (SBDM) term and, **2:**828
    shared decision making by educators, parents, and
        community members element in, **2:**828
    See also **Local control; School finance**
Sizer, Theodore R., **2:**830–831
    "age of the academies" concept of, **1:**6
    Annenberg Institute for School Reform and, **1:**170, **2:**830
    books written by, **2:**830

Coalition of Essential Schools (CES) founded by,
        1:170–171, **2:**741, **2:**830
    curriculum reform views of, **2:**831
    early years and education of, **2:**830
    *Horace's Compromise: The Dilemma of the American
        High School* written by, **1:**170
    sports and extracurricular activities views of, **2:**831
    teacher-student give-and-take dialogue model supported
        by, **2:**830
Skinner, B. F., **2:**831–833
    aging analysis research of, **2:**831
    awards and recognitions of, **2:**832
    basic concepts of, **2:**831–832
    behavioral control issue and, **2:**831, **2:**832
    behavior modification implementations and, **2:**832
    The Behavior of Organisms: An Experimental Analysis
        written by, **1:**88
    Beyond Freedom and Dignity written by, **1:**89
    Noam Chomsky criticism of, **2:**832
    controversies regarding, **2:**831, **2:**832
    determinism and free will views of, **1:**89
    direct instruction methods of, **1:**89
    early years and education of, **1:**88
    Abraham Maslow's criticism of, **2:**549
    mental processes role in learning views of, **2:**831, **2:**832
    operant behavior (operant conditioning) work of, **1:**xlvi,
        1:88, **2:**832
    reflexes studied by, **1:**88
    reinforcement role in learning and, **2:**831–832
    response centered programs and, **2:**734
    school challenges identified by, **1:**89
    Science and Behavior written by, **1:**xlvi, **1:**89
    shaping process and, **2:**832
    teaching machine and programmed instruction developed
        by, **2:**733, **2:**734, **2:**831, **2:**832
    variation (of behavior) and selection by consequence
        concepts of, **2:**832
    Verbal Behavior written by, **1:**89, **2:**832
    Walden Two written by, **1:**89
    See also **Behaviorism; Programmed instruction**
Slavin, Robert E., **1:**2, **2:**864, **2:**865
    See also **Success For All (SFA)**
Small-school movement, **2:**833–834
    academic performance enhancement and, **2:**833
    attendance rate factor and, **2:**834
    Bill & Melinda Gates Foundation support of,
        2:795, **2:**805
    early college high schools and, **1:**298
    extracurricular activities participation factor in, **2:**834
    healthier relationships and, **2:**794
    improved graduation rates and, **2:**833
    NCLB school failure restructuring and, **2:**833
    parent involvement factor and, **2:**833
    practices and features required in, **2:**795
    school within a school option and, **2:**833
    strong sense of community factor and, **2:**834
    supporting evidence for, **2:**833
    valued outcomes research and, **2:**794
    See also **Rural education; Site-based management**